한 권으로 끝내는

IELTS MASTER

시원스쿨어학연구소 지음

시원스쿨 LAB

한 권으로 끝내는

IELTS MASTER

초판 1쇄 발행 2019년 11월 8일
개정 1쇄 발행 2024년 12월 3일

지은이 시원스쿨어학연구소
펴낸곳 (주)에스제이더블유인터내셔널
펴낸이 양홍걸 이시원

홈페이지 www.siwonschool.com
주소 서울시 영등포구 영신로 166 시원스쿨
교재 구입 문의 02)2014-8151
고객센터 02)6409-0878

ISBN 979-11-6150-917-4 13740
Number 1-110505-18180400-08

머리말

수많은 영어 능력 시험 중 세계에서 가장 많은 응시인원과 인지도를 자랑하는 IELTS(아이엘츠)는, 국내에서도 수험생 수가 증가하는 추세입니다. 유학과 이민, 그리고 해외 취업의 관문인 아이엘츠 시험은 난이도가 높은 시험으로도 유명합니다.

보통 아이엘츠 수험생들은 시험을 준비할 때, 비싼 영문 원서나 과목별(Listening, Reading, Writing, Speaking), 그리고 모듈별(Academic, General Training)로 나눠진 교재들을 각각 구매하여 학습해야 합니다. 이러한 교재 구입에 대한 수험생들의 부담을 없애고, 한 권으로 아이엘츠에 대한 모든 것을 깔끔하게 정리하여 수험생들의 혼란을 없애자는 취지로 본 교재가 집필되었습니다.

이 책은 프리미엄 시험영어 인강 브랜드 시원스쿨랩에서, 호주와 영국의 석사 이상을 공부한 원어민급 아이엘츠 전문 연구진과 강사진, 그리고 원어민 시험 전문가들이 연구한 결과물입니다. 책에서 소개되는 정보는 아이엘츠 공식 사이트와 시험 주관업체의 답변들을 정리한 것으로, 가장 객관적이고 정확함을 자신합니다. 또한 수록된 문제들은 실제 아이엘츠 시험을 보며 축적한 빅데이터를 바탕으로 만들었기에 기출 문제와 가장 유사함을 자부합니다. 특히 2019년부터 2024년까지, 최근 5년 간 시험 기출 문제에 비중을 두어 반영함으로 수험생들에게 최신 시험 트렌드를 가장 정확하게 소개하려고 노력하였습니다.

이 책은 영어 실력은 어느 정도 있지만, 아이엘츠를 처음 접하는 수험생들에게 아이엘츠 시험에 대한 명확한 이해를 제공하는 기본서입니다. 또한 단기간에 아이엘츠를 완벽하게 정리하고자 하는, 시험이 얼마 남지 않은 수험생 모두에게 필독서입니다.

본 교재로 아이엘츠를 준비하는 모든 수험생이 아이엘츠라는 중요한 관문을 성공적으로 통과하여, 유학과 이민, 그리고 해외 취업의 꿈을 이룰 수 있기를 진심으로 바랍니다.

시원스쿨어학연구소

목차

SPEAKING MASTER

ACTUAL TEST

부록

별책: 정답 및 해설

온라인 학습 자료

- Speaking & Writing 최신 기출 문제집
- 스피킹 빈출 표현 200
- IELTS Test – Answer Sheets
- IELTS MASTER 기출 단어장

책의 구성과 특징

❶ 과목별/모듈별 완벽 정리

Listening, Reading, Writing, Speaking의 각 파트에 대한 자세한 설명

+

이론으로 공부한 각 파트를 곧바로 실전 연습 문제(Practice Test)로 복습

- 각 영역에서 반드시 알아야 되는 모든 사항들을 꼼꼼하게 정리
- 최근 10년 이상 실제 IELTS 시험을 보면서 축적한 기출 빅데이터를 통해 문제 유형과 빈출 토픽 분석
- Academic의 전 영역은 물론 General Training의 Reading Section 1 & 2, 그리고 Writing Task 1의 편지 쓰기 내용까지 완벽 정리
- 일반 페이퍼 시험과 컴퓨터 기반 시험의 답안 작성 및 시험 진행 관련하여 완벽한 가이드 제공
- 출제 기관의 답변을 근거로 아이엘츠에 대한 모든 논란 종결

❷ 빅데이터 기반 족집게 실전 문제

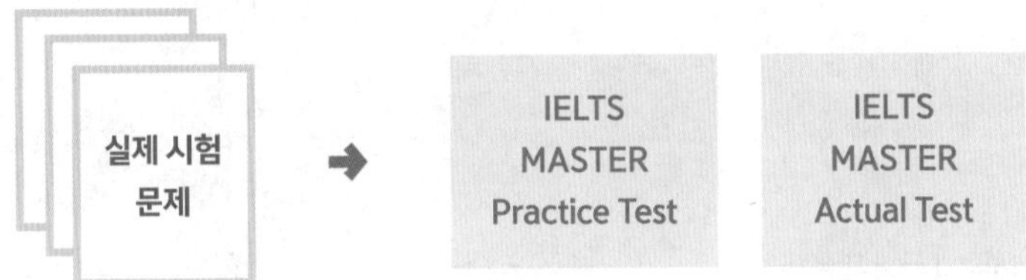

- 실제 시험과 동일한 형태와 구성의 실전 연습 문제(Practice Test) 및 모의고사(Actual Test) 제공
- 2001년부터 분석된 기출 문제 중 특히 최근 10년(2015년~2024년)의 시험 문제에 가중치를 두어 문제 제작
- Academic과 General Training 모듈 각각 두 개의 실전 모의고사 세트를 통해 충분한 실전 연습 가능
- 첫 번째 모의고사(Actual Test 1)는 일반 페이퍼 시험 형태로, 두 번째 모의고사(Actual Test 2)는 컴퓨터 시험 스타일로 제공

❸ 아이엘츠 점수와 영어 실력 동반 상승을 위한 다양한 팁 제공

- 문어체(Writing), 구어체(Speaking) 영어 표현 차이 정리
- 미국식과 영국식 스펠링 비교
- Formal과 Semi-formal 톤 완벽 정리
- IELTS에 꼭 필요한 필수 영문법 정리

❹ 별책으로 구성된 해설집

- 교재의 모든 문제에 대한 지문 해석, 문제 해설, 어휘 정리 등을 친절하게 정리한 해설집 제공
- 해설집을 분권으로 구성하여 보다 편하게 해설 및 해석을 대조하며 학습할 수 있도록 함

❺ 다양한 학습 자료들

- 영국, 호주, 미국 원어민 성우 MP 3 제공(Listening&Reading: 영국/호주 성우, Speaking: 영국/미국 성우)
- Reading 지문 녹음 파일 제공(영국 원어민 성우)
- Writing, Speaking 공식 채점기준표 수록
- Listening, Reading, Writing 실제 시험 답안지(온라인 제공)
- Speaking & Writing 최신 기출 문제집(온라인 제공)
- Expressions for IELTS Speaking: 스피킹 빈출 표현 200(온라인 제공)
- IELTS MASTER 기출 단어장(온라인 제공)
- IELTS 스타 강사진의 친절한 온라인 강의(유료)

학습 자료 다운로드

lab.siwonschool.com > 교재/MP3 > 교재/MP3 페이지의 과목명 탭에서 「아이엘츠」 클릭 후 「IELTS MASTER」 찾기

아이엘츠(IELTS) 소개

IELTS(International English Language Testing System)는 호주 IDP 산하기관인 IELTS Australia와 영국 문화원(British Council), 그리고 영국 Cambridge English Language Assessment의 주관으로 학업과 이민 및 취업을 위한 영어능력을 평가하기 위해 만들어진 국제공인 영어능력 평가시험입니다. 현재 영국, 호주, 뉴질랜드, 미국, 캐나다, EU, 싱가포르, 홍콩, 인도, 중국 등 세계 대부분의 대학에서 일정 수준 이상의 IELTS 점수를 입학 자격으로 인정하고 있습니다. 또한 이민 자격 요건으로 영국, 호주, 뉴질랜드, 캐나다 정부에서 IELTS 점수를 요구하고 있습니다.

시험 영역과 평가 방식

유학을 하려는 사람들은 아카데믹(Academic Module), 이민 및 취업을 위한 사람들은 제너럴 트레이닝(General Training Module)에 응시해야 합니다.

<table>
<tr><th>시험 영역</th><th>Academic (유학용)</th><th>General Training (이민/취업용)</th></tr>
<tr><td>LISTENING
30분, 40문제</td><td colspan="2">대화 혹은 1인 발화 내용에 대한 문제 풀기
Part 1 일상 대화 (2인 대화)
Part 2 안내 및 공지 (1인 위주 발화)
Part 3 연구 과제 (2~4인의 대화)
Part 4 전문 강좌 (1인 발화)</td></tr>
<tr><td>READING
60분, 40문제</td><td>총 3개의 지문에 대한 문제 풀기
저널, 신문, 잡지, 서적 등의 글 - 인간의 신체와 정신, 환경, 역사, 경제, 생물, 공학 등 학문적인 내용</td><td>총 5개의 지문에 대한 문제 풀기
짧은 광고 및 공지 등 생활 관련(2개 지문), 계약서 규정 및 사내 규칙 등 직장 관련(2개의 지문), 학문적인 내용(1개의 지문)</td></tr>
<tr><td rowspan="2">WRITING
60분,
2개의 글쓰기</td><td>Task 1 - 150 단어 이상의 분석 글쓰기
도표나 도해 분석</td><td>Task 1 - 150 단어 이상의 편지 글쓰기
정보 요청이나 상황 설명</td></tr>
<tr><td colspan="2">Task 2 - 250 단어 이상의 에세이 글쓰기
특정 주제에 대한 논리적인 주장 전개</td></tr>
<tr><td>SPEAKING
11~14분</td><td colspan="2">시험관과의 1:1 대화 방식
Part 1 자기 소개 등 친근한 주제로 질의응답
Part 2 특정 주제에 대해 2분 정도로 설명하기
Part 3 Part 2 주제에 대해 시험관과 토론</td></tr>
</table>

2020년 시험 변경 내용 정리

컴퓨터용 시험(IELTS on computer)으로의 IELTS 일원화 추세에 따라 2020년 1월부터 다음과 같이 종이 시험(IELTS on paper)이 변경되었습니다.

LISTENING	1. Section 대신 Part란 용어로 통일 2. Part 1이 예제(Example) 없이 바로 1번부터 시작 3. 문제에 페이지 번호가 더 이상 나오지 않음

* Listening 외에 다른 영역은 변경사항이 없습니다.

시험 응시

IELTS 응시료, 접수 및 진행 방법은 국가마다 조금씩 차이가 있습니다. 따라서 정확하고 자세한 정보는 시험을 접수하기 전에 IELTS 공식 홈페이지에서 확인해야 합니다. 다음은 국내 기준 일반적인 시험 응시 사항입니다.

공식 접수처	영국문화원 또는 IDP 홈페이지에서 온라인 접수
시험 접수 준비물	여권(성적발표일까지 유효기간이 남은 여권) 시험 접수할 때 사용한 여권을 시험 당일에 지참해야 함
성적표 수령	우편 수령(성적발표일에 발송), 방문 수령(성적발표일부터 1주일간)
재채점 요청	시험 응시일부터 6주 이내에 재채점 신청 가능(신청 후 8주 전후 소요)

자세한 사항은 다음 공식페이지에서 확인:
영국문화원 https://www.britishcouncil.kr/exam/ielts, IDP http://www.ieltskorea.org

IELTS on paper와 IELTS on computer

컴퓨터로 시험을 보는 형태인 IELTS on computer가 2018년 9월부터 도입되었습니다. 종전의 형태와 차이점은 다음과 같으니 본인에게 유리한 형태로 응시하도록 합니다.

	종이	**컴퓨터**
답안작성방법	손글씨로 작성	컴퓨터로 작성
응시료	299,000원 (2024년 11월 기준)	299,000원 (2024년 11월 기준)
성적 발표	응시일로부터 13일 후	응시일로부터 3~5일 후
시험 일정	월 4회	월 50회 이상
시험 순서	Writing - Reading -Listening - 휴식 - Speaking * 2019년 4월부터 Listening과 Writing 시험 순서가 바뀜 * 일부 국가는 Listening - Reading - Writing - 휴식 - Speaking 순서임	Listening - Reading - Writing - 휴식 - Speaking 또는 Speaking - 휴식- Listening- Reading - Writing
스피킹 시험 시간	무작위 배정	사전에 선택 가능

One Skill Retake

아이엘츠 시험을 응시 후 처음에 목표로 한 점수를 얻지 못했을 경우, One Skill Retake를 통해 4가지 영역의 읽기, 듣기, 말하기, 쓰기 중 하나를 선택하여 재시험을 치를 수 있습니다.

One Skill Retake는 영국, 뉴질랜드 호주 이민성 및 호주 정부기관, 여러 대학교와 교육기관 등에서 인정받고 있는데, One Skill Retake 시험 결과를 인정하는 기관 리스트들은 계속해서 바뀌고 있기에 자신이 지원하려는 대학 또는 기관에서 자신이 지원하는 학기에 인정하는지 반드시 직접 확인해야 합니다.

접수 조건	1. 시험 시행일 기준 60일 이내에, 컴퓨터로 일반 시험을 완료한 응시자 (UKVI 불가) 2. 원시험 당 하나의 과목만 다시 응시할 수 있음 3. 원시험과 동일한, 유효 기간 내에 있는 여권만 사용 가능 (여권 만료 시, 응시 불가)
접수 방법	응시자 포털 에 로그인하면 IELTS 결과를 확인할 수 있는데, 다시 응시하고 싶은 과목의 'Retake' 버튼을 클릭
성적표	응시자는 새로운 성적표를 받게 되는데, 새로 받은 IELTS One Skill Retake 점수와 원시험의 나머지 세 과목 결과가 표시됨 (원시험의 성적표와 새로운 성적표 중 선택하여 사용 가능)
비용	약 20만원

2024년 4월 영국문화원 기준
https://www.britishcouncil.kr/exam/ielts/one-skill-retake

IELTS Online

아이엘츠 온라인은 집에서 노트북 또는 데스크탑 컴퓨터에 인터넷 연결을 통해 시험을 보는 방식입니다. 컴퓨터 시험과 동일한 문제, 형식, 시간으로 진행되며, 스피킹 테스트도 온라인 인터뷰로 진행됩니다.

유의할 점은 정부 기관에서 IELTS Online을 인정하지 않고, 인정하는 대학 역시 한정되어 있기에, 자신이 지원하는 곳에서 IELTS Online을 인정하는지 먼저 확인해야 합니다.

접수 조건	1. 만 18세 이상 2. Academic 응시만 가능 3. IDP 공식 사이트에서만 접수(영어로만 나와 있음)
성적 발표	응시일로부터 6~8일 후
성적표	인터넷으로 확인 가능하지만 종이 성적표는 발급 불가
비용	약 30만원 (224.30 USD로 환율에 따라 금액 변동 있음)

2024년 4월 IELTS 공식 홈페이지 기준
https://ielts.org/take-a-test/test-types/ielts-academic-test/ielts-online

일반 IELTS와 IELTS for UKVI

IELTS for UKVI는 영국 비자 Tier 1, Tier 2, Tier 4의 발급 조건에 해당하는 시험으로 2015년부터 도입되었습니다. UKVI는 UK Visas and Immigration(영국 비자와 이민)을 칭합니다.

일반 아이엘츠와 IELTS for UKVI를 모두 인정하는 학교도 있지만, IELTS for UKVI 점수만 인정하는 학교도 있으므로 반드시 자신이 목표로 하는 학교가 요구하는 시험이 무엇인지 정확히 파악해야 합니다.

IELTS for UKVI도 Academic과 General Training 시험이 있고, 시험 과목 및 문제도 일반 IELTS와 동일합니다. 다만 응시료의 차이가 있으며(IELTS for UKVI 응시료: 333,000원), 시험 장소도 영국 정부가 인정한 소수의 장소로 한정되어 있습니다.

시험 점수 계산

IELTS 점수는 성적표에 Overall Band Score로 표시되는 것으로, 각 영역(Listening, Reading, Writing, Speaking) 밴드 값의 합을 4로 나눈 평균에서 반올림한 값입니다.

하지만 최종 점수와 함께 '과목별' 최저 점수를 요구하는 경우가 대부분입니다. 따라서 자신이 가려는 곳의 요구 점수를 정확히 숙지하여 전략적으로 공부하는 것이 필요합니다.

예를 들어 'Overall score of 6.5 or above, with at least 5.5 in each component'가 요구되는 점수라면, 최종 점수 6.5 이상에 각 과목별 점수는 5.5 이상을 받아야 한다는 뜻입니다. 이 기준에서 아래 표의 A 학생은 최종 점수 6.5에 모든 과목의 점수가 5.5 이상이므로 조건을 충족시키지만, B 학생은 최종 점수가 6.5로 나왔더라도 Speaking 점수가 5.5 미만인 5.0을 받았기 때문에 자격 조건에 미치지 못하게 됩니다.

	Listening	Reading	Writing	Speaking	평균 점수	최종 아이엘츠 점수
A 학생	6.5	7.0	5.5	6.0	6.25	6.5
B 학생	8.0	7.0	5.5	5.0	6.375	6.5

시험 점수

아이엘츠 점수는 밴드(Band) 단위로 산정되는데, 범위는 0~9이고 0.5 단위로 구분합니다. 각 점수가 의미하는 바는 아래의 표와 같습니다. 대다수 수험생들의 목표 점수는 5.5 ~ 7.0이지만, 각자 자신의 유학 또는 이민에 필요한 구체적인 점수를 목표로 설정해 공부하는 것이 중요합니다.

밴드	레벨	설명
9.0	Expert User	완벽한 영어를 구사함. 적절하고 정확하며 유창한 영어를 구사하며 완벽한 이해력을 보임
8.0	Very good user	익숙하지 못한 상황에서 간혹 부정확하거나 부적절한 표현을 갖고 있지만 거의 완벽한 영어를 구사. 복잡한 토론을 이어 나감
7.0	Good user	때때로 부정확하거나 부적절한 경우도 있지만 거의 완벽한 영어 구사. 일반적으로 복잡한 언어를 다루고, 상세한 추론을 이해함
6.0	Competent user	약간 부적절하거나 부정확한, 그리고 잘못 이해하는 경우에도 불구하고 효과적인 영어를 구사함. 익숙한 상황에서는 상대적으로 복잡한 표현을 이해하고 사용함
5.0	Modest user	많은 실수를 하는 경향이 있지만, 대부분 상황에서 영어를 부분적으로 구사하며 전반적인 이해 가능. 자신의 분야에서 기본적인 의사소통 가능
4.0	Limited user	친숙한 상황에서만 기본적인 소통 가능함. 이해하고 표현하는데 있어서 자주 문제점을 드러냄. 복잡한 언어소통은 어려움
3.0	Extremely limited user	아주 친숙한 상황에서만 기본적인 의미를 이해함. 의사 소통에 있어서 자주 문제가 발생함
2.0	Intermittent user	말하기와 쓰는데 있어서 상당히 어려움
1.0	Non-user	아주 제한적인 어휘를 제외하곤 언어 사용 능력이 없음
0	Did not attempt the test	시험을 보지 않음

Academic 1개월 완성 (기본 플랜)

한 달 동안 학습플랜을 밀리지 않으려면 매일 규칙적으로 공부할 시간을 정하여 학습해야 됩니다. 끝까지 포기하지 말고 꾸준히 공부하세요.

• 1개월

Day 1	Day 2	Day 3	Day 4	Day 5	Day 6
Unit 1 완료 □	Unit 2 완료 □	Unit 3 완료 □	Unit 4 완료 □	Unit 5 완료 □	Unit 6 완료 □
Day 7	**Day 8**	**Day 9**	**Day 10**	**Day 11**	**Day 12**
Unit 7 완료 □	Unit 8 완료 □	Unit 9 완료 □	Unit 10 완료 □	Unit 13 복습 완료 □	Unit 14 완료 □
Day 13	**Day 14**	**Day 15**	**Day 16**	**Day 17**	**Day 18**
Unit 15 완료 □	Unit 17 완료 □	Unit 18 완료 □	Unit 19 완료 □	Unit 20 (1) 완료 □	Unit 20 (2) 완료 □
Day 19	**Day 20**	**Day 21**	**Day 22**	**Day 23**	**Day 24**
Unit 21 완료 □	Unit 22 완료 □	Unit 23 완료 □	Unit 24 완료 □	Unit 25 완료 □	Unit 26 완료 □
Day 25	**Day 26**	**Day 27**	**Day 28**	**Day 29**	**Day 30**
Unit 27 완료 □	Unit 28 완료 □	Unit 29 완료 □	Unit 30 완료 □	Actual Test 1 완료 □	Actual Test 2 완료 □

General Training 1개월 완성 (기본 플랜)

한 달 동안 학습플랜을 밀리지 않으려면 매일 규칙적으로 공부할 시간을 정하여 학습해야 됩니다. 끝까지 포기하지 말고 꾸준히 공부하세요.

- **1개월**

Day 1	Day 2	Day 3	Day 4	Day 5	Day 6
Unit 1 완료 □	Unit 2 완료 □	Unit 3 완료 □	Unit 4 완료 □	Unit 5 완료 □	Unit 6 완료 □
Day 7	**Day 8**	**Day 9**	**Day 10**	**Day 11**	**Day 12**
Unit 7 완료 □	Unit 8 완료 □	Unit 9 완료 □	Unit 10 완료 □	Unit 11 완료 □	Unit 12 완료 □
Day 13	**Day 14**	**Day 15**	**Day 16**	**Day 17**	**Day 18**
Unit 13 완료 □	Unit 16 완료 □	Unit 17 완료 □	Unit 18 완료 □	Unit 19 완료 □	Unit 20 완료 □
Day 19	**Day 20**	**Day 21**	**Day 22**	**Day 23**	**Day 24**
Unit 21 완료 □	Unit 22 완료 □	Unit 23 완료 □	Unit 24 완료 □	Unit 25 완료 □	Unit 26 완료 □
Day 25	**Day 26**	**Day 27**	**Day 28**	**Day 29**	**Day 30**
Unit 27 완료 □	Unit 28 완료 □	Unit 29 완료 □	Unit 30 완료 □	Actual Test 1 완료 □	Actual Test 2 완료 □

Academic 10일 완성 (시험이 얼마 남지 않은 수험생)

모든 영역을 매일 공부하면서 정리합니다.

- **10일**

Day 1	Day 2	Day 3	Day 4	Day 5
Unit 1, 6, 13, 21 완료 □	Unit 2, 7, 14, 22 완료 □	Unit 3, 8, 15, 23 완료 □	Unit 4, 9, 17, 24 완료 □	Unit 5, 10, 18, 25 완료 □
Day 6	**Day 7**	**Day 8**	**Day 9**	**Day 10**
Unit 1-5 복습 Unit 19, 26, 27 완료 □	Unit 6-10 복습 Unit 20, 28 완료 □	Unit 13-20 복습 Unit 29, 30 완료 □	Actual Test 1 완료 □	Actual Test 2 완료 □

General Training 10일 완성 (시험이 얼마 남지 않은 수험생)

모든 영역을 매일 공부하면서 정리합니다.

- **10일**

Day 1	Day 2	Day 3	Day 4	Day 5
Unit 1, 6, 13, 21 완료 □	Unit 2, 7, 16(1), 22 완료 □	Unit 3, 8, 16(2), 23 완료 □	Unit 4, 9, 17, 24 완료 □	Unit 5, 10, 18, 25 완료 □
Day 6	**Day 7**	**Day 8**	**Day 9**	**Day 10**
Unit 1-5 복습 Unit 11, 19, 26, 27 완료 □	Unit 6-10 복습 Unit 12, 20, 28 완료 □	Unit 13-20 복습 Unit 29, 30 완료 □	Actual Test 1 완료 □	Actual Test 2 완료 □

LISTENING MASTER

IELTS LISTENING에 대한 모든 것

오늘의 학습 목표

1 IELTS LISTENING의 시험 방식과 진행 과정을 이해하고, 각 파트별 특징(화자, 빈출 주제, 문제 유형)을 구분하여 파악한다.
2 IELTS LISTENING의 올바른 정답 기입 방법을 익힌다.
3 쉐도잉(Shadowing)을 통해 자신의 Listening 실력을 업그레이드한다.

IELTS LISTENING 기본 정보

시험 방식	• Academic 모듈과 General Training 모듈의 문제가 동일함 • 방송을 한 번만 들려줌 • 방송은 중앙 방송이 아닌, 시험장 교실에서 CD플레이어를 틀어 진행 (단, 컴퓨터 시험은 개별 헤드폰을 사용) • 답안지에 연필로 작성 (단, 컴퓨터 시험은 정답을 키보드와 마우스를 사용하여 작성)
시험 시간	• 4개 Part, 총 40문제를 약 30분 동안 테스트 • 방송 종료 후 10분간 답안지 작성 시간이 주어짐 (단, 컴퓨터 시험은 답안 작성 시간이 따로 주어지지 않고 2분 정도의 추가 시간만 주어짐)
진행 과정	오리엔테이션 (10여분 동안 영어로 진행) ⬇ 음원이 제대로 나오는지 방송 테스트 진행 ⬇ 리스닝 시험지와 답안지 배포 ⬇ 리스닝 시험 시작 ⬇ 시험 종료 ※ 감독관이 연필을 내려 놓으라고 하는데 이를 무시하고 계속 답안을 작성하면 부정행위로 간주되어 감점 혹은 해당 시험 무효 처리됨

각 Part별 특징

파트 당 10문제씩 출제되고, 한 파트가 끝나면 정답을 숙고할 수 있도록 약 30초 정도 시간을 줌

Part 1 (1~10번) 일상생활 질의응답	화자	• 두 사람 간 질의 응답 ➡ 한 사람은 묻고 다른 한 사람은 대답하기에 대부분의 정답은 답변하는 사람의 말에서 등장
	빈출 주제	• 시설: 주민회관, 도서관, 헬스클럽, 극장 등 시설이나 프로그램의 등록과 예약, 대여 문의 • 주거: 숙박, 임대, 이사, 수리 문의 • 여행/지역: 여행/지역 예약 및 프로그램 문의 • 기타 문의: 배송, 길거리 설문 조사, 인터뷰 등 • 구직/자원봉사: 파트타임/자원봉사 지원 문의 • 불편 접수: 서비스 불만족, 분실물 신고
	문제 유형	• 노트(note), 표(table), 양식(form)의 빈칸에 들어갈 말을 채우는 주관식 문제 유형이 90% 이상 출제 • 전화번호, 우편번호, 이름, 생일, 주소 등의 철자(letter)와 숫자(number)를 받아쓰는 문제 유형(dictation)이 한 문제 정도 출제
Part 2 (11~20번) 일상생활 설명/소개	화자	• 한 사람의 투어 가이드나 안내원, 발표자 등이 특정 관광지나 시설, 정책 등을 안내 • 간혹 두 사람이 나오기도 하지만, 이때 한 사람은 단순히 주요 화자를 소개하는 역할만 함 ➡ 뒤이어 나오는 주요 화자가 말하는 내용에서 모든 정답이 등장하므로 한 사람의 화자라고 봐도 무방
	빈출 주제	• 관광: 관광지, 시설 소개 • 직장: 일터, 업무, 규정 설명 • 동네: 동네의 변화, 새로운 시설 설명 • 기타: 기관, 단체, 정책 등의 안내 및 소개
	문제 유형	• 선다형 문제(multiple choice)가 33% 이상으로 출제되고 정보 연결 문제(matching)도 25% 이상 출제 • 지도(map)/평면도(plan)/도해(diagram) 안에 있는 명칭 표시 문제(labelling)도 출제되는데, 본 문제 유형은 Part 2에서만 출제
Part 3 (21~30번) 대학 과제 논의	화자	• 주로 두 사람이 등장하고 많게는 네 사람까지도 등장 • 동료 학생 간, 또는 학생과 교수, 선후배 간 수업 및 과제 등과 관련한 토론
	빈출 주제	• 대학 수업, 과제, 프로젝트 등과 관련한 학생 간의 대화가 주로 출제
	문제 유형	• 선다형 문제가 절반 정도 출제되고 난이도가 높은 편이며, 순서도(flowchart), 노트/표 완성 문제, 정보 연결(matching) 문제 유형도 출제

Part 4 (31~40번) 대학 강의 또는 발표	**화자**	• 한 명의 화자가 대학 전공 수업 강의 혹은 연구 발표 • 화자는 교수, 강사, 학생이 주로 등장
	빈출 주제	• 도시 및 자연환경: 건축, 도시계획, 지구과학, 환경공학 등 • 동식물 생태: 생물, 동물학, 식물학 등 • 판매, 조직 관리 및 리더쉽: 경영, 심리학 등 • 특정 지역의 문화나 인종, 특정 사물이나 기술의 역사: 문화인류학, 역사 등
	문제 유형	• 노트 완성하기(note completion) 문제 유형이 70% 이상 출제 • 문장 완성하기(sentence completion), 요약문 완성하기(summary completion) 문제 유형도 출제

IELTS LISTENING 채점표

Listening은 아래의 채점표를 통해 자신의 점수를 예상할 수 있다.

밴드	1.0 ~1.5	2.0 ~2.5	3.0 ~3.5	4.0 ~4.5	5.0 ~5.5	6.0 ~6.5	7.0 ~7.5	8.0 ~8.5	9.0
맞은 개수	1	2~3	4~9	10~16	17~24	25~32	33~37	38~39	40

IELTS LISTENING 답안 작성법 논란 정리!

IELTS LISTENING의 답안을 작성할 때 가장 논란이 되는 부분인 단 · 복수, 대 · 소문자, 숫자, 철자 관련 내용을 시험 주관기관의 답변을 바탕으로 다음과 같이 정리한다.

LISTENING

1 단 • 복수 문법에 맞게 쓰자.

시험 주관기관 British Council에 따르면, 답안을 쓸 때 방송에 나온 그대로 단수와 복수를 정확히 가려 쓰지 않으면 오답 처리 된다. 하지만 경우에 따라 단수와 복수를 구분하지 않아도 정답이 되는 경우가 있는데, 바로 문법상 크게 영향이 없는 경우이다.

예문 The (window / windows) must be washed every day. 문법상 둘 다 맞기에 둘 다 정답 처리
창문은 매일 세척되어야 한다.

2 대 • 소문자 구분에 스트레스 받지 말자.

시험 주관기관 British Council과 IDP Education에 따르면, 대문자/소문자를 구분하지 않고 써도 정답이 된다. 예를 들어, London을, london, London, LONDON, 심지어 LonDoN이라고 써도 정답으로 처리된다. 비록 대문자/소문자를 구분하지 않아도 정답이 되지만, 구분해서 쓰는 것은 영어의 기본이므로, 될 수 있으면 대문자/소문자를 구분하여 정답 작성하도록 하자.

3 숫자는 철자로 써도 한 글자(one word)로 간주한다.

시험 주관기관 Cambridge Assessment English에 따르면, 숫자 정답은 무조건 한 글자로 간주한다. 예를 들어, 숫자 200을 two hundred로 써도 글자 수는 하나인 것이다. 즉, 숫자를 아라비아 숫자로 쓰든 영어 철자로 쓰든 하나의 글자로 본다. 그러나 숫자를 철자로 쓰다가 스펠링이 틀리면 오답 처리가 되므로, 아라비아 숫자로 쓰는 것이 안전하다.

4 철자는 틀리면 오답 처리된다.

정답이 무엇인지 확실히 들었지만 철자가 헷갈리는 경우가 있는데, 철자가 틀리면 무조건 오답 처리된다. 또한 영국식/미국식 철자 모두 정답 처리된다. 단 일관되게 영국식 또는 미국식으로 쓴다. 참고로 본 Unit의 Practice Test에서는, 실제 시험에서 자주 틀리는 철자의 단어들을 소개하고 있다.

5 단어 개수를 지시문에 맞게 쓴다.

문제 지시문에서 단어 또는 숫자 수를 정해주는 문제 유형이 있는데, 반드시 정해진 단어 또는 숫자 수에 맞게 정답을 써야 한다. 정해진 단어 수를 초과하여 작성시 오답 처리된다. 관사(a, an, the)도 단어의 개수에 포함된다. 또한 audio-recording과 같이 하이픈(-)으로 단어가 연결되면 한 글자로 간주된다.

6 방송에 나온 단어 그대로 정답을 쓴다.

Cambridge Assessment English의 IELTS 시험 공식 가이드 도서에 따르면, IELTS LISTENING 정답은 방송에서 나온 단어 그대로를 정답으로 옮겨 적는 것이 원칙이다. 따라서 방송에서 나온 단어가 아닌, 유사어를 적으면 오답 처리된다.

IELTS LISTENING 정복 비법

1 핵심어(Keywords) 노려 듣기

IELTS LISTENING은 단순히 듣기 실력만을 요구하는 것이 아니다. 짧은 시간에 문제의 핵심을 파악해서 읽을 수 있는 독해 실력도 요구된다. 방송 시작 전 최대한 빨리 문제들을 읽으면서 keywords(핵심어)에 동그라미를 친 후, 정답이 나올 부분을 노려 들어야 된다. 또한 Part가 바뀔 때에도 빨리 다음 문제들을 읽어서 핵심어에 동그라미를 친 후 그 단어들을 노려 들어야 된다. 아무리 듣기를 잘해도 핵심어를 노려 듣지 못하면 IELTS LISTENING에서 고득점을 맞기 어렵다.

예문 What **TWO** activities are described as useful by teachers?
어떤 두 개의 활동이 유용하다고 선생님들이 기술하였는가?

문제에서는 두 개의 활동을 묻기에, 두 개를 선택해야 된다. 따라서 two activities를 핵심어로 잡는다. 또한 선생님들이 유용하다고 말한 것이므로, 학생들이 유용하다고 말하거나 선생님들이 유용하지 않다고 말하는 것들은 제외해야 한다. 따라서 useful과 teachers에도 핵심어 동그라미를 친다.

2 패러프레이징(Paraphrasing) 정리

IELTS LISTENING에서 핵심어 및 핵심어와 관련된 부분은 방송에서 그대로 들리지 않고, 같은 의미를 가진 다른 말로 바꿔 표현되는 경우가 대부분이다.

예문 It is not permanent hair dye. (문제지 표현)
그것은 영구적인 머리 염색은 아니다.

➡ That colour will wash out after about one month. (방송에서 정답이 패러프레이징된 표현)
그 색은 한 달 후에 씻겨질 것이다.

이를 패러프레이징(paraphrasing)이라고 하는데, 이때 지면에 나온 문제가 방송에서는 어떻게 패러프레이징 되는지를 빠르게 파악할 수 있어야 정답을 맞출 수 있다. 따라서 IELTS 문제를 풀면서 정답 부분이 어떻게 paraphrasing되는지 정리하고 익혀 둘 필요가 있다.

3 쉐도잉(Shadowing) 반복 연습

아무리 핵심어를 노려 듣는 스킬이 좋고 패러프레이징을 많이 알아도, 영어 듣기 실력 자체가 안 좋다면 IELTS LISTENING에서 고득점을 받을 수는 없다. 그럼 어떻게 하면 듣기 실력이 좋아질까? 많은 학생들이 무작정 영어 MP3를 반복해서 듣는다. "이렇게 강제로 많이 듣다 보면, 귀가 뚫리겠지"란 생각에 무작정 듣는다. 하지만 자신이 이해 못하는 단어는 들리지 않기에 이러한 학습방법은 효과가 거의 없다. 이해가 안 되는 영어 단어는 처음 들어보는 언어와 다를 바가 없다.

영어를 들었는데 귀에서 영어가 소음처럼 웅웅거리며 들리거나 너무 빨리 들려서 대충 감으로 문제를 풀어왔던 수험생들은 이제부터 '따라 말하기'를 하기 바란다. 쉐도잉(shadowing), 즉 그림자처럼 따라 말하기란 영어 MP3를 들으면서 발음, 속도, 호흡을 MP3와 똑같이 하는 것이다. 이때, 내가 따라 말하는 내용을 먼저 알아들어야 한다. 무슨 내용인지도 모르면서 따라하면 여러분은 앵무새가 되고 그러한 쉐도잉은 도움이 되지 않는다. 정확하게 이해한 내용을 그대로 따라 말하는 것, 그것이 바로 쉐도잉이다.

"발음할 수 없으면 들을 수 없다"는 원칙을 꼭 명심하자!

TIP

쉐도잉(Shadowing) 방법

❶ MP3를 듣고 바로 쉐도잉을 할 수 있으면 좋지만 그렇게 하기 어렵다면, 먼저 해당 스크립트를 보면서 어려운 단어와 표현, 잘 안 들리는 부분을 읽으며 외운다.

❷ MP3를 들으며 스크립트를 따라 읽는다.

❸ MP3를 들으며 스크립트를 보지 않고 쉐도잉을 한다.

❹ 쉐도잉이 제대로 되면 성공이고, 안되면 1, 2, 3번을 반복한다.

※ 쉐도잉에 걸리는 시간: 자신의 레벨에 따라 다른데, 하나의 파트 지문을 완벽하게 쉐도잉 하는데 10분 이내에 끝낼 수도 있고, 반대로 반나절이 걸려도 하나의 지문을 완벽히 쉐도잉하기 어려울 수도 있다. 하지만 꾸준히 연습하다 보면 누구나 쉐도잉 시간은 줄어들고 영어 듣기 실력도 향상된다.

TIP

딕테이션(Dictation) 방법

딕테이션(dictation), 즉 받아쓰기는, 쉐도잉과 함께 가장 효과적인 리스닝 학습 방법 중 하나이다. 특히 IELTS LISTENING 문제의 절반 정도가 음원에서 등장하는 단어를 받아쓰는 것이기에 받아쓰기는 점수 향상에 직접적인 도움이 된다.

하지만 음원에서 들리는 전체 문장이나 구절을 다 받아쓰려고 하면 너무 힘들고 시간도 지나치게 많이 소비하게 된다. 따라서 음원을 들어 보면서 자신에게 생소한 단어들 또는 쉬운 단어지만 막상 받아쓰기가 어려운 단어만을 선별하여 받아쓰기 연습을 해본다.

만일 받아쓰기 하려는 단어를 바로 영어 철자로 쓰기 어려우면, 우선 들리는 대로 한글로 적어본 다음에 한글 발음을 영어 철자로 옮겨 적는 방법으로도 연습 가능하다.

받아쓰기 틀린 단어는 반드시 자신만의 오답노트나 메모장에 적고 수시로 보면서 철자를 완벽하게 외우도록 반복 학습하도록 한다.

PRACTICE TEST

Spelling 시험에 정답으로 출제되었던 철자가 어려운 단어들을 받아써 보자. MP3 Unit1_1

1 ....

2 ....

3 ....

4 ....

5 ....

6 ....

7 ....

8 ....

9 ....

10 ....

11 ....

12 ....

13 ....

14 ....

15 ....

정답 및 해설 p.004

Grammar 문법을 고려하여, 빈칸에 알맞은 형태의 단어를 선택하자.

1 The consumption of .... in China increased in 2015.

A tea
B teas
C a tea

2 Do not wear ....

A jean
B jeans
C a jean

3 The Industrial Revolution had a significant impact on social and .... parts.

A politic
B politics
C political

Shadowing 다음 스크립트를 쉐도잉(Shadowing) 해보자.

MP3 Unit1_2

It's my pleasure to welcome you all to Lilydale. I'm sure you'll all enjoy your stay here in our beautiful town. I know that most of you are here to go kayaking on our local lakes and rivers. I'll tell you more about the kayak routes in a moment. First, I'll briefly describe how to get around town, and where to find some local amenities you might need.

UNIT 02

Part 1 - 두 사람 간 시설, 주거, 여행 관련 질의 응답

오늘의 학습 목표

1. Part 1의 빈출 주제를 이해한다.
2. Part 1에서 자주 등장하는 문제 유형인 노트 완성하기(note completion)와 표 완성하기(table completion) 문제 유형에 대해 숙지한다.
3. Part 1에서 나오는 딕테이션(dictation) 문제는 반드시 맞춘다.

Part 1 빈출 주제

Part 1은 보통 남자 한 명과 여자 한 명, 총 두 명이 등장하는데, 한 사람은 질문을 하는 사람, 또 한 사람은 그 질문에 답하는 사람이다. 따라서 대부분의 정답은 질문에 답하는 사람의 말에서 나온다.

Part 1은 보통 다음과 같은 내용이 출제된다.

- 주민회관(community centre) 직원과 주민 간 시설 사용 문의 또는 프로그램이나 강좌 등록 등에 대한 질의 응답
- 도서관(library) 직원과 주민 간 시설이나 사용 규정 문의 및 프로그램 등록 등에 대한 질의 응답
- 지역 여행 안내소(information desk) 직원과 방문객 간 지역, 행사, 축제, 프로그램 등에 대한 질의 응답
- 여행사 직원(travel agent)과 손님 간 여행 이동, 숙박, 가격, 일정, 자동차 렌트 등에 대한 질의 응답
- 부동산 중개인(real estate agent)과 이사 가려는 사람 간 이사, 임대, 수리 등에 대한 질의 응답
- 파트타임이나 자원봉사를 지원하는 사람과 해당 기관 직원 간 업무 및 일정 관련 대화
- 상기 내용(시설, 프로그램, 여행, 주거, 일자리 등)을 해당 기관 사람이 아닌 친구 또는 지인 간 질의 응답

※ IELTS 시험 초창기부터 2010년대 초반까지 빈번하게 출제되던 대학 기숙사 및 학교 생활 관련 토픽은 2015년 이후 부터 거의 등장하지 않고 있다.

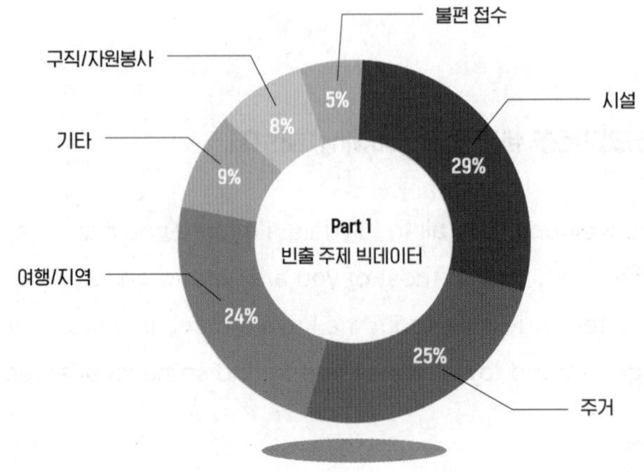

Part 1 빈출 문제 유형

Part 1에서는 노트(Note), 표(Table), 양식(Form)의 빈칸에 들어갈 말을 주관식으로 채우는 문제, 즉 노트 완성하기(note completion), 표 완성하기(table completion), 양식 완성하기(form completion) 문제 유형이 90% 이상 출제된다.

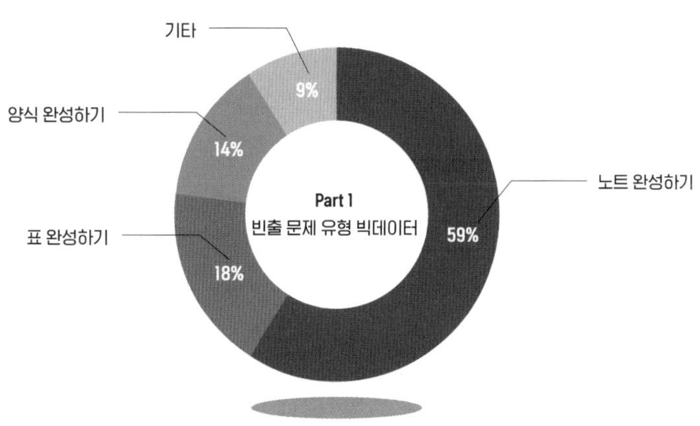

1 노트 완성하기(Note Completion)

Complete the notes below.
*Write **NO MORE THAN TWO WORDS** for each answer.*

Laverton Public Library

The library now has
- a new section of books for **1** ....
- an expanded section for magazines on **2** ....
- a **3** .... room for meetings

Other information
- weekends: free **4** .... is available

방송 대화의 중요 내용을 하나의 큰 제목과 여러 개의 소제목으로 구분하여 정보를 요약한 노트가 제시되는데, 이 노트의 빈칸을 채워 완성시키는 문제 유형이다.

2 표 완성하기(Table Completion)

Complete the table below.
*Write **ONE WORD AND/OR A NUMBER** for each answer.*

Event	Cost	Venue	Notes
Rock Concert	£20	**1** .... Hall	Appearing: Terry Hartnett, Super Sonics, Kools
Jazz Dance	Free	Community Centre	Need to contact **2** .... in advance
Circus Show	£10	Public Park	Tickets can be bought in the **3** ....

노트 완성하기와 마찬가지로 대화의 중요 내용이 요약된 표에 있는 빈칸을 채우는 문제 유형이다. 비록 규칙적으로 일정한 칸에 내용이 요약되어 있지만, 노트와 다르게 표는 가로와 세로로 문제가 흩어져 있어서 시각적인 혼란을 준다.

3 양식 완성하기(Form Completion)

Complete the form below.
*Write **NO MORE THAN TWO WORDS AND/OR A NUMBER** for each answer.*

Childcare Centre Enrolment Form	
Name	Christine Hutchison
Address	**1** .... Avenue, Lakewood
Phone	5327 8825
Fees	**2** .... per month

노트 완성하기와 유사한 문제 유형으로 이름이나 주소, 시간과 날짜 등의 개인정보가 포함된 신청서가 주로 출제된다.

철자 또는 숫자 딕테이션(Dictation) 만점 팁 정리

Part 1에서 노트, 표, 양식의 빈칸에, 전화번호, 우편번호, 이름, 생일, 주소 등의 철자(letter)와 숫자(number)를 받아쓰는 문제(dictation)가 한 문제 정도 나온다. IELTS 시험에 익숙하지 않은 많은 수험생들이 의외로 어려워하는 문제인데, 충분히 연습을 하면 누구나 딕테이션은 다 맞출 수 있다. 아래에 정리한 딕테이션 만점 팁으로 자신감을 갖도록 하자.

철자 r	영국식 r 발음은 [아-]라고 발음한다. 미국식 r 발음인 [알]에만 익숙하면 놓치기 쉽다.
철자 m vs. 철자 n	얼핏 들으면 m[엠]과 n[엔]이 헷갈릴 수 있다. 따라서 m과 n 발음이 헷갈리게 들릴 수 있음을 명심하고 각별히 유의해서 'ㅁ' 발음의 유무를 듣도록 한다.
숫자 0	zero[지로]라고 읽기도 하지만 O[오]로 더 많이 출제된다. 이 때, 숫자 5(five)와 헷갈리지 않도록 한다.
연 이은 같은 철자 또는 숫자	IELTS 시험에서 같은 철자 또는 숫자가 겹칠 때는 그 철자를 두 번 읽어 주는 것이 아니라, double [더블]이라고 한 후 철자를 한 번만 말한다. 예 allow [에이 – 더블엘 – 오 – 더블유] 007 [더블오 쎄븐]
70 vs. 17	70와 17 발음이 헷갈릴 수 있는데, 70는 앞에 강세가 있어서 [세븐티]로 발음하고, 17은 뒤에 강세가 있어서 [세븐틴]으로 발음한다. 뒤에 강세가 있다 보니 n 발음이 명확히 들린다.

TIP

도로명 주소

Part 1 문제 중에 도로명 주소가 자주 등장하는데, 이때 접하게 되는 도로의 종류는 다음과 같다.

Avenue (Ave.)	(가로수가 있는) 큰 도로
Boulevard (Blvd.)	(가로수가 있는) 큰 도로
Street (St.)	길, 도로
Road (Rd.)	(차가 다닐 수 있는) 도로
Lane (Ln.)	(차가 다닐 수 있는 좁은) 도로
Drive (Dr.)	(주택의) 진입로
Court (Ct.)	(주로 아파트 등의 공동주택에 사용되는) 도로

참고로, 우편번호를 영국은 postcode, 미국은 ZIP code라고 한다.

Part 1 다음 실전 문제(Questions 1-10)를 연습해 보자.

MP3 Unit2_1

Questions 1-6

Complete the notes below.

*Write **ONE WORD ONLY** for each answer.*

MOTORBIKE TOURS OF SCOTLAND

Name: Maria Smith

Address: 38 **1** .... Street, London

Postcode: E1 6AN

Phone: (mobile) 07215 667883

How did the customer find out about our company? 2 ....

Recommended motorbike tours

Tour A:

- Dunblane area: the customer wants to visit some **3** .... where TV shows were filmed
- Morar: the customer wants to spend time on a **4** ....

Tour B:

- The customer wants to see the **5** .... in downtown Edinburgh
- At Ullapool: the customer would prefer not to take a cruise
- At Inverness: her husband probably is interested in visiting **6** ....

정답 및 해설 p.005

Questions 7-10

Complete the table below.

Write ***ONE WORD AND/OR A NUMBER*** *for each answer.*

	Duration	Distance travelled	Price (per person)	Price Covers (per person)
Tour A	9 days	**7** ………………… miles	£2,000	• accommodation • motorbike • **8** …………………
Tour B	10 days	1,000 miles	**9** £ …………………	• accommodation • motorbike • meals • two **10** …………………

Part 2 - 한 사람의 시설, 장소, 정책 관련 설명

오늘의 학습 목표

1. Part 2의 빈출 주제를 이해한다.
2. Part 2에서 자주 등장하는 문제 유형인 선다형(multiple choice)과 정보 연결(matching) 문제 유형에 대해 숙지한다.
3. Part 2에서만 출제되는 지도(map)/평면도(plan)/도해(diagram)의 명칭 표시(labelling) 유형에 대해 이해한다.

Part 2 빈출 주제

Part 2는 한 사람이 등장하는데, 등장 인물은 보통 투어 가이드나 안내원, 발표자이며 특정 관광지나 시설, 정책 등을 설명한다. 간혹 두 사람이 나오기도 하지만, 이때 한 사람은 단순히 뒤에 나오는 주요 화자를 소개하는 역할만 하고, 뒤이어 나오는 주요 화자가 스토리를 이끌며 정답도 주요 화자의 내용에서만 나온다.

Part 2는 보통 다음과 같은 내용이 출제된다.

- 관광(관광지/시설) 소개
- 직장(일터/업무/규정) 설명
- 동네의 변화 및 새로운 시설 설명

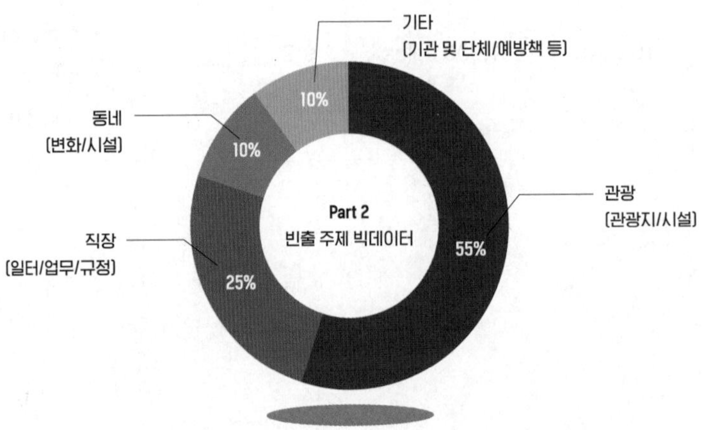

Part 2 빈출 문제 유형

우리가 일반적으로 생각하는 객관식 문제, 즉 선다형(multiple choice) 유형이 33% 이상으로 가장 많이 출제되고, 박스 안에 정보를 정답과 연결하는 정보 연결(matching) 유형도 25% 이상으로 출제된다. 지도(map)/평면도(plan)/도해(diagram) 명칭 표시(labelling) 유형도 출제되는데, 본 문제 유형은 Part 2에서만 출제된다.

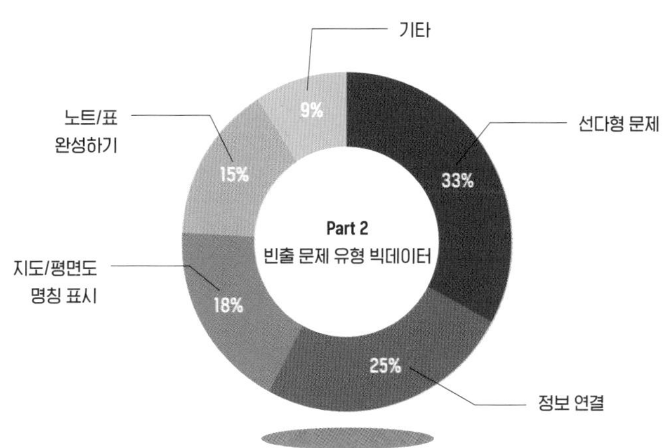

보통 Part 2에서는 총 10문제가 다음의 두 가지 유형으로 분배되어 출제된다.

- 선다형 유형 세트 + 정보 연결 유형 세트
- 선다형 유형 세트 + 명칭 표시 유형 세트
- 명칭 표시 유형 세트 + 정보 연결 유형 세트

1 선다형(Multiple Choice)

보기 중 질문에 알맞은 답을 찾는 객관식 문제 유형이다. 대부분 정답이 패러프레이징(paraphrasing) 되고, 정답이 아닌 보기들은 오답을 유도하는 함정이 있기에, IELTS LISTENING에서 난이도가 가장 높은 문제 유형이다. 선다형 문제는 크게 두 가지 유형으로 구분되는데, 보기에서 정답을 하나 고르는 유형(한 개의 문제)과 또는 두 개 고르는 유형(두 개의 문제)이 있다.

Question 11

*Choose the correct letter, **A**, **B** or **C**.*

보기 A, B, C 중 옳은 것을 고르시오.

11번, 한 개의 문제로 A-C 중 하나의 정답을 선택하면 됨

11 Students seeking accommodation in the halls of residence have to
대학 기숙사에서 숙박을 구하는 학생들은 ~해야 한다

A meet with a student advisor.
학생 상담사와 만나야 한다.

B fill out an application form.
신청서를 작성해야 한다.

C register for a building tour.
건물 투어에 등록해야 한다.

Questions 12 and 13
*Choose **TWO** letters, **A-E**.*
A-E 중 두 개를 고르시오.

12번과 13번, 두 개의 문제로 A-E 중 두 개의 정답을 선택하여 각각 12번과 13번 답안지에 기입함

Which **TWO** immediate benefits can the university get from Michael's advertising campaign?
마이클의 광고 회사로부터 대학은 어떠한 **두 가지** 즉각적인 이득을 얻을 수 있는가?

A increased enrolment
증가한 등록생 수
B extra funding
추가적인 자금조달
C media coverage
언론 보도
D higher ticket sales
더 높은 티켓 매출
E more job opportunities
더 많은 취업 기회

상기 12-13번과 같은 선다형 문제에서 정답 순서는 무관하다. 즉, A와 C가 정답이라면, 12번에 A, 13번에 C, 또는 12번에 C, 13번에 A라고 써도 정답 처리된다. 단, 12번에 A, C 두개를 함께 적으면 오답처리 된다. 참고로 이러한 다수의 보기를 정답으로 고르는 선다형 문제는 Part 2 보다는 Part 3에서 주로 출제된다.

이 문제 유형 중에서 두 번째 문제처럼 두 개 정답을 고르는 유형은 문제지에서 제시된 보기의 순서가 방송에서 나오는 순서와 다른 경우가 대부분임을 염두에 둔다.

선다형 문제 풀이 방법

선다형 문제는 철자를 틀릴 염려도 없고 이미 나와 있는 선택지(보기) 중에 답을 선택하는 것이기에 쉬워 보이지만, 사실은 IELTS 리스닝에서 가장 어려운 문제 유형이다. 선다형 문제에서 고득점을 올리기 위해서는 다음의 방법을 활용해 본다.

❶ 문제와 선택지 먼저 읽기
음원 내용이 나오기 전에 먼저 시험지 또는 화면에 나타난 문제와 선택지를 읽어서 내용을 이해해야 한다. 그렇지 않으면 방송을 들으면서 동시에 선택지를 해석해야 하는데, 이는 영어를 아주 잘하는 사람들도 하기 어렵다. 따라서 문제와 선택지는 지문이 나오기 전에 미리 읽고 내용을 파악해 두는 것이 좋다. 이때, 읽으면서 키워드 중심으로 표시를 해두면, 방송 내용이 나올 때 문제 및 보기와 방송 내용을 확인하기가 수월하다.

❷ 오답 피하기
보통 선택지에 나온 단어들이 그대로 방송에 들리는 경우가 많은데, 선다형 문제에서는 이런 경우의 선택지는 오답인 경우가 많다. 따라서 같은 단어가 나왔다고 손쉽게 정답을 고르는 것은 금물이다.

2 정보 연결(Matching)

보기가 들어있는 박스 안에 정보를 정답으로 선택하는 정보 연결(Matching) 유형은 선다형 문제와 유사하다.

Questions 11-13

Which career advisor should you meet with?
어떤 직업 상담사를 만나야 하는가?

박스 안 보기 A-C 중에서 각 문제에 맞는 하나를 선택하여 11-13번 답안지에 각각 기입

Write the correct letter, **A**, **B** or **C**, next to Questions 11-13.
11-13번 문제 옆에 A, B, C 중 옳은 것을 쓰시오.

A Colin Stanton
B Simon Johnson
C Elaine Brewster

11 if you are expected to graduate this year .... 올해 졸업 예정이라면
12 if you are interested in working overseas .... 해외 근무에 관심이 있다면
13 if you made an appointment through the website ....
웹사이트를 통해 예약을 했다면

3 지도/평면도/도해 명칭 표시(Labelling Map/Plan/Diagram)

지도(map)나 평면도(plan), 도해(diagram)의 빈칸에 들어갈 명칭을 정보 연결(Matching) 유형처럼 박스 안에 주어진 보기 중에 고르거나 방송에서 들은 내용을 바로 적는 유형으로 Part 2에서만 출제된다.

Questions 11-13
Label the map below.
다음 지도에 표기하시오.

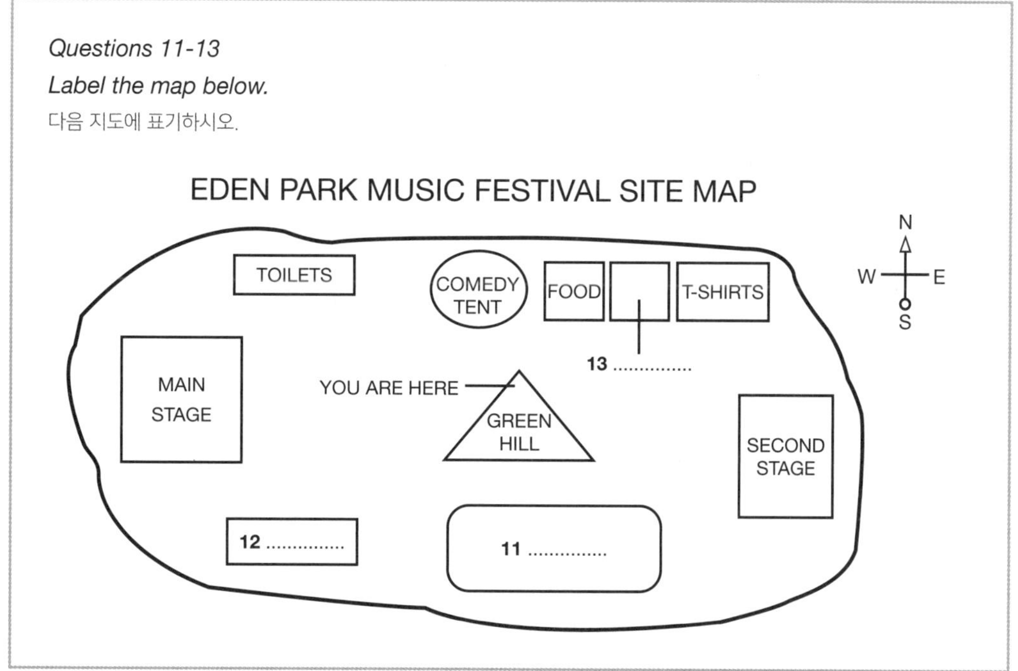

유의 한번 흐름을 놓치면 그 이후로 다 틀리기 쉬운 유형으로 문제 풀 때 흐름을 놓치지 않도록 집중한다.

Part 2 다음 실전 문제(Questions 11-20)를 연습해 보자.

MP3 Unit3_1

Questions 11-13

*Choose the correct letter **A**, **B** or **C**.*

Cycling Changes in Waterfield

11 Why were changes to cycling amenities proposed in Waterfield?

A To reduce the number of road accidents
B To attract a greater number of tourists
C To make the city more environmentally-friendly

12 At a recent public forum, local residents strongly demanded

A safer city roads.
B wider cycle paths.
C access to free bicycles.

13 According to the speaker, one problem with the new amenities will be

A securing funding for annual maintenance.
B making them accessible to all age groups.
C finding a way to prevent bicycle theft.

정답 및 해설 p.010

Questions 14-20

Label the map below.

*Write the correct letter, **A-I**, next to Questions 14-20.*

Proposed Changes to Cycling Amenities in Waterfield

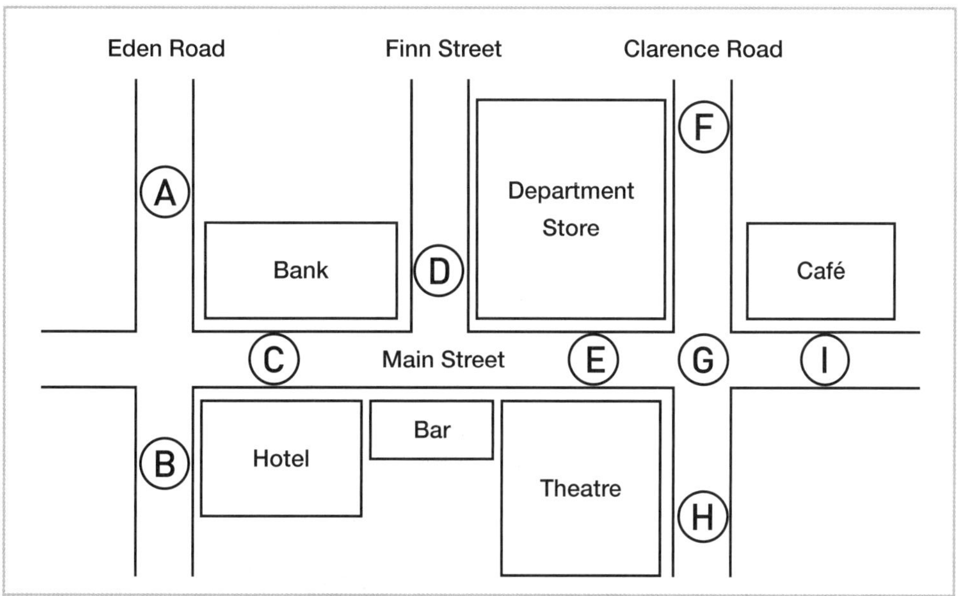

14 New bike rental station ....

15 Pedestrian/cyclist underpass ....

16 Designated bicycle lanes ....

17 Bicycle storage rails ....

18 Resurfaced road ....

19 Bicycle repair booth ....

20 Pedestrian/cyclist bridge ....

UNIT 04

Part 3 - 두 사람 이상의 학업 관련 대화

오늘의 학습 목표

1 Part 3의 빈출 주제를 이해한다.
2 Part 3에서 자주 등장하는 문제 유형에 대해 숙지한다.
3 Part 3에서 자주 사용되는 어휘를 익힌다.

Part 3 빈출 주제

Part 1과 2가 일상 생활에서 접할 수 있는 주제의 내용이라면 Part 3와 4는 대학에서 학문적(academic) 주제를 다루는 내용이다. 특히 Part 3는 수업이나 과제에 대한 대화 내용이 주를 이루는데, 보통 같은 수업을 듣는 학생 간 또는 학생과 교수 간 대화가 이루어 진다.

최근 추세와 관련해서, IELTS LISTENING의 파트 중 가장 난이도가 높아지고 있는 파트가 바로 Part 3이다. 또한 예전에는 3인 이상, 4인까지도 등장하여 대화를 나눴지만, 최근에는 두 사람만 등장하는 경향을 보이고 있다. 주제 역시 대학 과제나 프로젝트 내용 위주로 한정되는 추세이다.

Part 3는 보통 다음과 같은 내용이 출제된다.

- 학생 간 수업이나 과제에 대한 대화
- 선배와 후배 간 수업이나 과제에 대한 대화
- 학생과 교수 간 수업이나 과제에 대한 대화

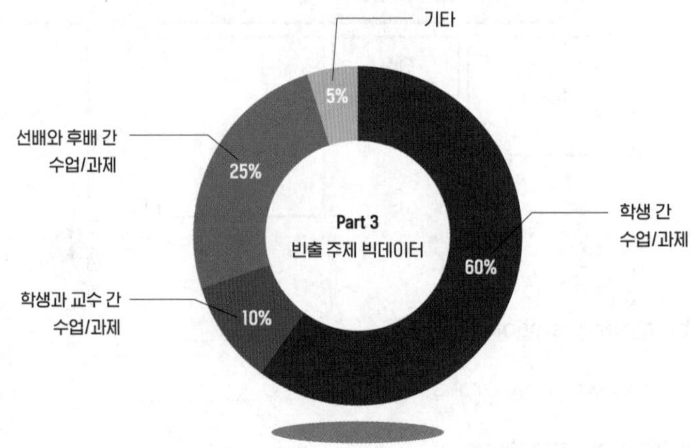

Part 3 빈출 문제 유형

Part 3에서 고난도 문제인 선다형 문제(multiple choice)가 50% 이상 출제된다. 선다형 문제에 대한 자세한 설명은 Unit 3를 참고한다.

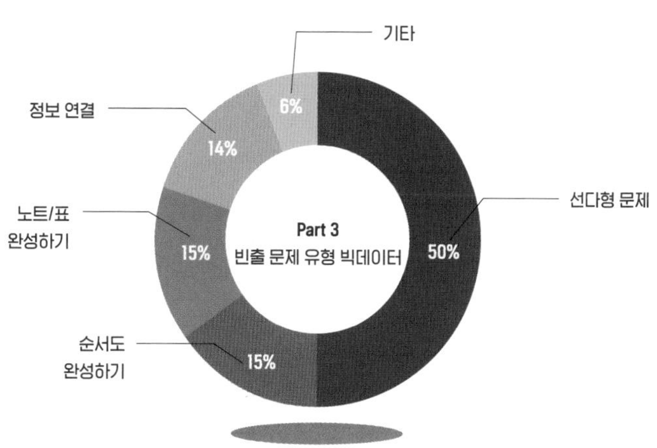

이외에 순서도 완성하기(flowchart completion) 유형이 출제되기도 하는데, 본 문제 유형은 주로 Part 3에서만 다뤄지는 추세이다.

Questions 28-30

Complete the flowchart below.

아래 순서도를 완성하시오.

순서도의 빈칸을 채우는 유형으로, 대화에서 정답이 순서대로 나옴

*Write **ONE WORD ONLY** for each answer.*

각 정답에 한 단어만을 적으시오.

Grant Application Process

장학금 신청 절차

Submit an application form along with a **28** .... outline.
신청서를 28 ....과 함께 온라인으로 제출하시오.

⬇

Committee members will contact shortlisted applicants by **29** ....
장학금 위원회 사람이 최종 리스트에 오른 신청자들에게 29 .... 까지 연락할 것이다.

⬇

Candidates will attend a panel interview in the **30** .... department.
후보자는 30 .... 부서에 패널 인터뷰에 참가할 것이다.

Part 3 빈출 어휘 정리

Part 3는 대학에서 수업, 연구, 과제, 프로젝트 등과 관련된 대학 생활 용어들이 많이 등장한다. 따라서 이러한 어휘들을 많이 알면, Part 3 방송을 듣거나 문제를 읽을 때 많은 도움이 된다.

lecture	강의	project	프로젝트, 과제, 연구
lecturer	강사	assignment	과제
tutorial	개별(소그룹) 지도 시간	task	과제
tutor	개별(소그룹) 지도 교사	findings	연구 결과
course leader	강좌 책임자	bibliography	참고문헌
professor	교수	reference	참조, 참고문헌
dean	학과장	literature review	문헌 조사
peer	동료	work on	작업하다
scholar	학자	revise	수정하다
scholarship	장학금	review	검토하다, 복습하다
grant	보조금, 장학금	modify	수정하다, 변경하다
fellowship	유대, 연구비, 장학금	specify	(구체적으로) 명시하다
curriculum	교육과정	turn in	돌려주다, 반납하다
syllabus	(강의) 개요, 요강	plagiarise	표절하다
semester	학기	plagiarism	표절
hall of residence	기숙사	paraphrase	다른 말로 바꿔 표현하다
undergraduate	대학 학부생	deadline	마감기한
graduate	대학원생, 졸업생	submit	제출하다
graduation	졸업	hand in	제출하다
faculty	(대학) 교수단, 학부	hand out	나눠주다
bachelor	학사	handout	유인물
master	석사	outline	개요, 요약문
PhD	박사	abstract	개요, 초록
postdoctoral training	박사 학위 취득 이후의 연수	draft	초안
hypothesis	가설	material	자료
thesis	학위 논문	periodical	정기 간행물

dissertation	학위 논문	statistic	통계
research paper	연구 논문	figure	수치, ~라고 생각하다
case study	사례 연구	struggle	애쓰다
presentation	발표	procedure	절차
competition	대회, 공모전	initiative	계획
survey	설문조사	objective	목적, 목표
questionnaire	설문지	feedback	의견
discipline	학문, 분야, 학과	sort out	정리하다, 분류하다
interdisciplinary	학계 간	contradictory	모순적인
focus group	포커스 그룹(각 계층을 대표하는 소수의 사람들로 이뤄진 그룹)	social science	사회 과학
drawback	문제점, 결점	rationale	이론적 근거, 원리
literacy	읽고 쓰는 능력	socio-economic	사회 경제적
investigate	조사하다	leave out	배제하다
carry out	수행하다	tailor	조정하다, 맞추다
laboratory	실험실	distract	(주의를) 산만하게 하다
analysis	분석	fascination	매료, 관심분야
optional module	선택 모듈(교과목)	assume	가정하다
grade	성적	additive	첨가물
theoretical	이론적인	complicated	복잡한
practical	실용적인, 실질적인	comprehensive	포괄적인
article	글, 기사, 논문	subtle	은은한, 미묘한
chronological order	연대순	sensible	합리적인
go into	검토하다	implication	영향, 결과
exhibition	전시(회)	plausible	그럴듯한
audience	청중	term	학기
attendee	참석자	classification	분류
translation	번역(물)	diary	일지, 일기
physical book	종이형태의 책	visual	시각 자료

Part 3 다음 실전 문제(Questions 21-30)를 연습해 보자.

MP3 Unit4_1

Questions 21 and 22

*Choose **TWO** letters, **A-E**.*

Which **TWO** characteristics were shared by the athletes involved in Matthew's sport research?

A They had all won important sports competitions.
B They had all taken nutrition supplements.
C They were all under 20 years old.
D They had all played sports professionally.
E They all played for the same sports team.

Questions 23 and 24

*Choose **TWO** letters, **A-E**.*

Which **TWO** points does Matthew make about his use of questionnaires?

A It resulted in comprehensive responses.
B It meant that he could not ask follow-up questions.
C It enabled him to easily compare various data.
D It had been successful in previous studies.
E It allowed him to save some research time.

Questions 25 and 26

*Choose **TWO** letters, **A-E**.*

Which **TWO** topics did Matthew focus on in his research?

A the side effects of nutritional supplements
B the effects of dehydration on athletes
C the relationship between diet and performance
D the benefits of high-calorie foods in sports
E the availability of nutritional information

정답 및 해설 p.014

Questions 27-30

Choose the correct letter, ***A, B*** *or* ***C****.*

27 Matthew included both male and female subjects in his study because

A he wanted to focus primarily on sports that are played by both sexes.
B he predicted there would be a large data discrepancy between the two sexes.
C he thought his research would be of interest to both men and women.

28 Frank Allen's research paper suggests that in professional sport, an athlete's performance is significantly influenced by

A their pre-match exercise regimen.
B their consumption of fluid.
C their intake of nutrient supplements.

29 What did Matthew note about the diet plans of his subjects?

A They were created by qualified dietitians.
B They were highly personalised.
C They included regular light meals.

30 According to the speakers, athletes are still not given enough information on

A the importance of post-exercise recovery techniques.
B the negative impact of carbohydrates on fitness.
C the benefits of a balanced daily diet.

UNIT 05 Part 4 - 한 사람의 강의 또는 발표

오늘의 학습 목표

1 Part 4의 빈출 주제를 이해한다.
2 Part 4에서 자주 등장하는 문제 유형에 대해 숙지한다.
3 Part 4에서 자주 사용되는 어휘를 익힌다.

Part 4 빈출 주제

Part 4는 Part 3와 마찬가지로 학문적 주제를 다루는데, 주로 대학의 전공 수업 강의 또는 연구 발표가 출제된다. 이에 따라 화자는 교수, 강사, 또는 연구 조사한 내용을 발표하는 학생이 주로 등장한다. Part 4에서는 한 사람만 등장하며, 주로 경영, 환경(도시 및 자연), 생물, 문화인류학 관련 주제가 출제된다. 특히 요즘 이슈가 되는 환경 문제가 다른 주제에 비해 자주 출제되는 편이다.

Part 4는 보통 다음과 같은 내용이 출제된다.

- 도시 및 자연환경(건축, 도시계획, 지구과학, 환경공학 전공)
- 동식물 생태(의학, 동물학, 식물학 전공)
- 판매, 조직 관리 및 리더쉽(경영, 심리학 전공)
- 특정 지역의 문화나 인종(문화인류학, 역사 전공)
- 특정 사물이나 기술의 역사(기술/공학 전공)

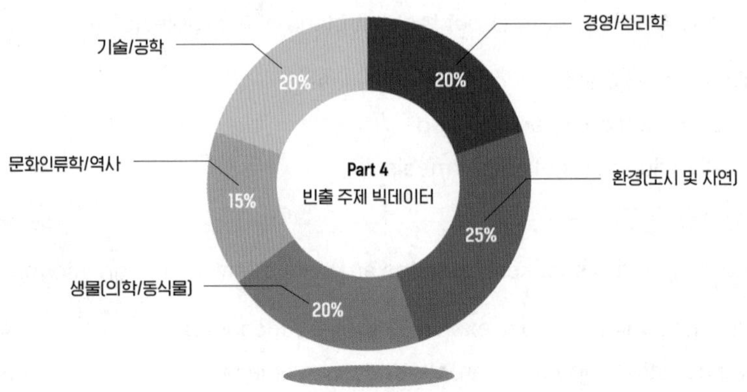

Part 4 빈출 문제 유형

Part 4는 강의를 듣고 노트에 요약하는 노트 완성하기(note completion) 유형으로 대부분 출제된다. 간혹, 강의 내용 중 일부 내용의 빈칸을 채우는 문장 완성하기(sentence completion) 유형이나 강의 요약문의 빈칸을 채우는 요약문 완성하기(summary completion) 유형도 출제되기도 한다. 또한 선다형이나 주관식 단답형 문제 유형이 노트 완성하기 유형 뒤에 몇 문제 나오기도 한다. 노트 완성하기 유형에 관한 설명은 Unit 2를 참고하기 바란다.

LISTENING

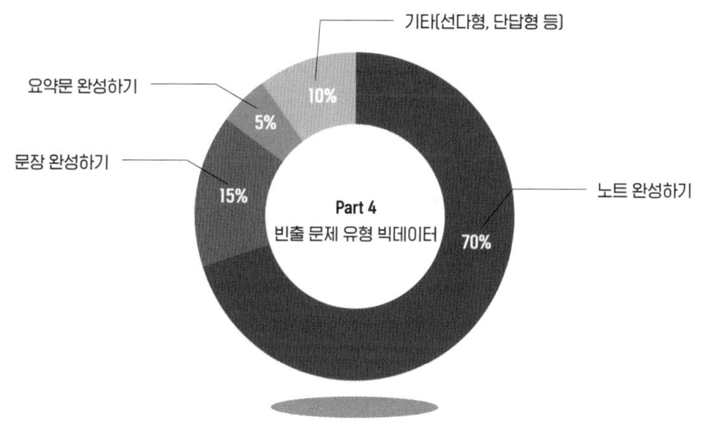

Listening 방송 자투리 시간 활용법

Listening 방송을 듣기 전에, 먼저 문제를 읽고 핵심어(keywords)를 파악한 상태에서 방송을 들으며 문제를 푸는 것이 시험의 기본 접근법이다. 하지만 짧은 자투리 시간동안 10개의 문제를 모두 읽기는 어렵다. 다행히 각 Part마다 문제 유형이 바뀌는 구간에, 약 20~30초 정도 방송 중간 쉬는 시간이 있다. 보통 뒤에 남아있는 문제 당 5초 정도 추가 시간을 주는 방식으로 계산되기에, 남아 있는 문제가 많을수록 더 많은 자투리 시간이 주어진다. 따라서 이러한 자투리 시간에 남아있는 문제들을 읽고 내용을 파악한 상태에서 이어지는 방송을 들으면 된다.

하지만 Part 4는 다른 파트들과 달리, 방송 중간 쉬는 시간이 5초 이내만 주어진다. 대신 Part 4는 처음에 주어지는 시간이 다른 파트들(약 30초 이내) 보다 더 긴(1분 정도) 시간이 주어지기에, Part 3가 끝나고 이 시간까지 최대한 활용하여 Part 4의 10 문제를 모두 미리 읽도록 한다.

Part 4 빈출 어휘 정리

Part 4는 대학 전공 강의 또는 수업 발표 내용에서 발췌되기에, 전문적이고 어려운 단어들이 등장하여 많은 수험생들이 어려워하는 파트이다. 따라서 빈출단어들을 미리 익혀 두면 Part 4 내용을 이해하고 문제 푸는데 많은 도움이 된다.

climate change	기후 변화	strategy	전략
carbon dioxide	이산화탄소	wage	임금, 급료
fuel	연료	taxation	조세
global warming	지구 온난화	occupation	직업
ecosystem	생태계	shift	교대근무
contamination	오염	collaboration	협동
toxic	독성의	hierarchy	계급, 계층
waste	폐기물	deficit	적자, 부족액
emission	(빛·열·가스) 배출	output	생산량, 산출량
drought	가뭄	gross	총, 통틀어
sustainable	(환경 파괴 없이) 지속 가능한	facilitate	용이하게 하다
urban environment	도시 환경	manipulate	조종하다, 조작하다
deforestation	삼림 벌채	consolidation	강화
habitat	서식지	distribution	배급, 유통, 분배
infection	감염, 전염	fishery	어장, 어업
biodiversity	생물의 다양성	expert	전문가
migration	이주, 이동	expertise	전문 지식, 전문 기술
cultivation	경작, 지배	adverse	부정적인, 불리한
predator	포식 동물	property	소유물, 재산, 부동산
prey	먹이, 사냥감	release	내보내다, 출시하다
extinction	멸종	trade	거래, 교역
evolve	진화하다, 발달하다	colonisation	식민지화
evolutionary term	진화적인 측면	plantation	농장
stranding	좌초, 오도가도 못함	pioneer	선구자, 개척자
mammal	포유류	fertiliser	비료
reptile	파충류	autocratic	독재의

rodent	설치류	mediator	중재인, 조정관
mating	짝짓기	assimilate	동화하다
biologist	생물학자	folklore	민속, 전통 문화
ecological	생태계의, 생태학의	relic	유물, 유적
germination	발아, 싹이 틈	artefact	인공물, 유물
feature	특징	rite	의식, 의례
autism	자폐증	excavation	발굴
conscious	의식 있는	civilisation	문명
diseases and conditions	질병 및 질환	nomadic	유목의, 방랑의
neurological	신경의	archaeology	고고학
doze	졸다	chronological	연대순의
gene	유전자	fossil	화석
psychological	정신의, 심리적인	fragile	부서지기 쉬운, 취약한
physician	의사, 내과의사	erosion	침식, 부식
physics	물리학	architect	건축가
experimenter	실험자	migrating	이주하는, 이동하는
ingest	섭취하다	digest	소화하다
be excreted	배설되다	atmosphere	대기
variable	변수	variation	변화, 차이
thermometer	온도계	substance	물질
reproduction	생식, 번식	composition	구성, 구성 요소
incompatible	양립할 수 없는	optimistic	낙관적인
term (= terminology)	전문 용어	pessimistic	비관적인
coordinates	좌표	cargo	화물
aboriginal	토착의, 원주민의	hand-over	이양, 양도
altitude	고도	authority	권위(자)
rectify	바로잡다	catastrophe	참사, 재앙
sediment	침전물	impairment	손상

Part 4 다음 실전 문제(Questions 31-40)를 연습해 보자. MP3 Unit5_1

Questions 31-36

Complete the notes below.

*Write **ONE WORD ONLY** for each answer.*

African Art

An overview of African art

- Diverse art forms are common in Africa
- The term generally exclude the art of **31** .... Africa and Ethiopia

African mask art and sculpture

- Masks are often used in **32** .... ceremonies but rarely resemble gods
- Bronze was used to decorate **33** .... in some countries
- Akan goldweights were used to measure the weight of goods and **34** ....

African figurine art

- The **35** .... of West African figurines are distinctively cylindrical
- South African figurines mixed human and animal features and are made from **36** ....

정답 및 해설 p.019

Questions 37-40

Answer the questions below.

*Write **ONE WORD ONLY** for each answer.*

What are the three main thematic elements of African art?

- **37** ....
- human figure
- **38** ....

What two materials are mentioned as being in plentiful supply?

- **39** ....
- **40** ....

READING
MASTER

Unit 6 IELTS READING에 대한 모든 것

Unit 7 READING Skills 1 - T/F/NG, Matching Features, Summary/Note/Table Completion

Unit 8 READING Skills 2 - Sentence Completion, Matching Information

Unit 9 READING Skills 3 - Matching Headings, Y/N/NG

Unit 10 READING Skills 4 - Short-answer Questions, Diagram Label Completion, Multiple Choice

Unit 11 READING Skills 5 - General Training Section 1

Unit 12 READING Skills 6 - General Training Section 2

UNIT 06 IELTS READING에 대한 모든 것

오늘의 학습 목표

1 IELTS READING의 시험 방식과 진행 과정을 이해한다.
2 자신의 모듈(Academic 또는 General Training) 특징을 파악하고 그에 맞게 공부한다.
3 Skimming과 Scanning 연습을 한다.

IELTS READING 기본 정보

시험 방식	• Academic 모듈과 General Training 모듈의 문제가 다름 • 종이 기반 일반 시험의 경우, 시험지에 메모 가능함 (컴퓨터 시험의 경우, 메모지와 연필이 지급되어 여기에 메모해도 되고, 컴퓨터에서 본문이나 질문 문장을 드래그 한 후 마우스 오른쪽 클릭하면 하이라이트 기능과 메모 기능 중 하나가 팝업으로 떠서 취사선택 가능함)
시험 시간	• 총 40문제를 한 시간 동안 테스트 • 한 지문(passage) 또는 한 섹션(section) 당 20분을 넘기지 않고 풀어야 한 시간 동안 세 개의 지문 또는 세 개의 섹션을 다 풀 수 있음 • Listening과 달리, 답안지 작성 시간이 따로 주어지지 않음
진행 과정	Listening 시험 이후 쉬는 시간없이 바로 Reading 답안지 및 시험지 배포 후 시험 진행 ⬇ 한 시간 동안 문제 풀며 답안지 작성 ⬇ 시험 종료 ※ 감독관이 연필을 내려 놓으라고 하는데 이를 무시하고 계속 답안을 작성하면 부정행위로 간주되어 감점 혹은 해당 시험 무효 처리됨

각 모듈별 특징

<table>
<tr><th>모듈</th><th>Academic</th><th>General Training</th></tr>
<tr><td>문제 유형</td><td colspan="2">• 아래의 문제 유형들이 Academic과 General Training에 동일하게 출제됨
- T/F/NG 또는 Y/N/NG (정보 일치 또는 견해 일치 여부)
- Matching features (관련 정보 고르기)
- Matching information (정보가 포함된 문단 고르기)
- Matching headings (문단 제목 고르기)
- Summary/Note/Table completion (요약문/노트/표 빈칸 채우기)
- Sentence completion (문장 완성하기)
- Short-answer questions (단답형 문제)
- Multiple choice (선다형 문제)
- Diagram label/Flowchart completion (도해/순서도 빈칸 채우기)</td></tr>
<tr><td>시험 구성</td><td>• 총 3개의 Passage(지문)로 구성
• 보통 Passage 1(첫 번째 지문)에서 13문제, Passage 2에서 13문제, Passage 3에서 14문제 출제</td><td>• Section 1(두 개의 지문으로 구성되어 있고 각 지문에서 7문제씩 출제)에서 14문제
• Section 2(두 개의 지문으로 구성되어 있고 각각 6, 7문제씩 출제)에서 13문제
• Section 3(Academic과 유사한 하나의 지문)에서 13문제 출제</td></tr>
<tr><td>지문 내용</td><td>• 각 Passage에, 논문, 잡지, 책, 신문 등에서 발췌된 아카데믹(학술적) 내용의 글이 출제
• 대학 전공서의 입문 단계
• 인간의 신체와 심리, 역사, 기술 공학, 생물, 자연 환경, 교육/언어, 경영/경제 주제 등이 주로 출제</td><td>• Section 1: Social survival 능력을 평가하기 위해 일상 생활에서 만날 수 있는, 여행 또는 관광지 안내, 상품 목록 또는 안내서, 광고지, 지역 정책, 시설 이용 안내문 등이 출제
• Section 2: Workplace survival 능력을 평가하기 위해 직장 생활에서 만날 수 있는, 업무 사항 메모, 구인 광고, 업무 증진 방안, 직장 규정 또는 계약서, 비즈니스 관련 글들이 출제
※ Section 1과 2의 각 Section에는 두 개의 글이 출제되는데, 두 글 간에는 연관성이 없는 독립된 글과 문제임
• Section 3: Academic과 유사</td></tr>
<tr><td>지문 난이도</td><td>• 보통 뒤에 나오는 Passage가 더 어려운 경향이 있지만 꼭 그런 것은 아님</td><td>• Section 1과 2에 나오는 지문들은 Academic이나 Section 3의 지문보다 쉬움
• Section 3의 경우 Academic 모듈의 Passage와 거의 동일한 난이도임</td></tr>
</table>

IELTS READING 채점표

Reading은 아래의 채점표를 통해 자신의 점수를 예상할 수 있다.

밴드 / 맞은 개수	1.0 ~1.5	2.0 ~2.5	3.0 ~3.5	4.0 ~4.5	5.0 ~5.5	6.0 ~6.5	7.0 ~7.5	8.0 ~8.5	9.0
Academic	1	2~3	4~9	10~16	17~24	25~32	33~37	38~39	40
General Training	1	2~4	5~11	12~17	18~25	26~34	35~37	38~39	40

IELTS READING 답안 작성법 논란 정리!

Reading 답안 작성법과 Listening 답안 작성법은 같다(Unit 1 참조). 단, 방송으로 들은 단어를 그대로 적는 Listening보다, 지문에 있는 정답 단어를 찾아서 그대로 옮겨 적는 Reading이 단/복수에서는 보다 엄격하게 채점이 적용된다. 즉, 지문에 복수(books)로 나온 단어를 정답에 단수(book)로 적지 않도록 한다.

또한 TRUE / FALSE / NOT GIVEN, YES / NO / NOT GIVEN 문제 유형에서, 정답을 T / F / NG처럼 축약해서 써도 정답 처리된다. 이때, NOT GIVEN을 NO GIVEN이라고 쓰면 오답 처리됨에 유의한다.

문제 먼저 읽고 지문 읽기

독해 시험에서 제일 먼저 고민하는 부분은 문제를 먼저 읽을지 아니면 지문을 먼저 읽을지 선택하는 것이다. IELTS 시험은 반드시 문제 먼저 읽고 접근해야 한다. 지문 내용이 방대하기 때문에 지문을 읽고 문제를 풀려고 하면 지문 내용에 대한 기억이 잘 나지 않아 문제를 풀 때 다시 지문을 읽어야 한다. 따라서 먼저 문제를 읽고, 문제를 풀기 위해 필요한 부분을 지문에서 찾아(스캐닝) 그 부분을 중점적으로 읽으며 문제를 풀어야 한다.

IELTS READING 정복 비법

1 영단어 최대한 많이 알기

"영어 실력은 단어 실력에 비례한다"는 사실을 명심하고 본 교재 또는 Cambridge IELTS 시리즈 교재를 보면서 모르는 단어가 나오면, 바로바로 암기 및 반복 학습하도록 한다. 단어를 많이 알면 문법 실력이 떨어져서 문장을 제대로 해석하지 못해도 어떤 의미인지를 알 수 있다.

2 문장 정확히 해석하는 능력 기르기

단어를 아무리 많이 알아도 문장을 정확히 해석하는 능력이 없으면, 문장과 문맥을 명확히 이해하지 못하고 두루뭉술하게 감으로 이해하는 경우가 빈번하게 발생한다. 따라서 본 교재 또는 Cambridge IELTS 시리즈 교재를 공부하면서, 한 문장 한 문장을 정확하게 해석하는 연습을 통해 독해 능력을 기르도록 한다.

참고로 영어 실력이 부족한 수험생의 경우, IELTS READING 지문의 한 문장을 제대로 해석하는데 30분이 걸리기도 한다. 하지만 끈기를 갖고 한 달 두 달 그렇게 해석 연습을 하다 보면, 어느새 빠르게 문장을 읽고 이해하는 자신을 발견하게 될 것이다.

3 스키밍(Skimming) & 스캐닝(Scanning) 스킬 기르기

시간 제약으로 인해, 실제 IELTS READING 시험에서 모든 문장을 다 읽고 이해하여 문제를 푸는 사람은 거의 없다. 충분한 단어와 문장 해석 능력을 길렀다면, 이제 스키밍과 스캐닝 기술을 습득하여, 실전 IELTS READING 문제 푸는 연습을 해야한다.

대부분의 Reading 고득점자들은 글을 완전히 다 읽지 않고, 글 어디에 무슨 정보가 있고 글 흐름이 어떻게 흘러간다 정도만 파악하고는 문제에서 물어보는 부분만 집중적으로 읽는다. 여기서 전체 글 흐름을 이해하는 읽기를 스키밍(skimming)이라고 한다. 스치며 나가듯이, 문장의 주어, 동사 부분들 위주로 빠르게 흐름만 이해하면서 읽는 방법이다. 스키밍을 하는 이유는 자신이 읽고 있는 문단이 어떠한 내용인지를 빠른 시간에 파악하기 위함이다. 이렇게 스키밍을 하면, Matching information (정보가 포함된 문단 고르기), Matching headings (문단 제목 고르기) 문제를 보다 빠르게 풀 수 있다. 또한 스키밍을 통해 전체적 맥락과 흐름을 이해하고 있으면, 세부 내용을 찾는 스캐닝도 보다 빠르게 할 수 있다.

문제에서 물어보는 특정 부분이 지문 어디에 있는지 빠르게 찾아가며 읽는 스킬을 스캐닝(scanning)이라고 한다. 마치 공항 검색대에서 반입 불가 물품을 찾아 내듯이 어떤 특정 정보를 찾기 위해 지문에서 문제의 핵심어 또는 이 핵심어의 유의어를 찾는 스킬이다. IELTS READING 문제의 80% 이상은 세부 내용을 묻는 문제 유형이기에 반드시 핵심어 또는 유의어를 스캐닝해야된다.

여기서 유의할 점은 대부분 문제 또는 보기의 정답이 되는 핵심어는 지문에서 패러프레이징(paraphrasing)되어 표현이 된다는 것이다. Listening 시험에서 방송 내용이 문제 또는 보기에서 패러프레이징되는 것과 같다. 따라서 스캐닝을 할 때는 똑같은 단어만 찾으면 안되고 찾는 단어와 의미가 같은 부분도 찾아야 한다.

4 틀린 문제 정리하기

수험생들은 반드시 Listening과 마찬가지로, Reading의 틀린 문제를 다시 한번 검토하면서 정답이 왜 그렇게 되는지 이해해야 한다. 특히 정답이 지문에서는 어떻게 패러프레이징이 되는지 정리하고 외워둔다. 시험에 등장하는 패러프레이징을 많이 알수록 그만큼 점수도 상승하게 된다.

미국식/영국식 영어

❶ IELTS READING 지문은 대부분 논문이나 잡지 내용이 변형되어 출제되는데, 미국식 영어로 작성된 글이 영국식보다 더 많기에, Reading에서는 미국식 철자가 많이 등장한다.

❷ IELTS 시험은 영국 Cambridge University에서 출제되기에, Reading 이외 Listening, Writing, Speaking은 기본적으로 영국식 영어가 사용된다.

❸ 수험생들은 Reading에서 미국식이든 영국식이든 관계없이 지문 또는 문제에 나온 대로 단어를 옮겨 쓰면 된다. Reading 이외 다른 영역은, 미국식이 편하면 미국식, 영국식이 편하면 영국식으로 쓰되, 한 가지 방식으로 일관되게 쓰는 것을 권장한다.

❹ 아래는 IELTS 시험에 등장하는 미국식/영국식 철자가 다른 대표적인 단어들이다.

	미국식	영국식
행동	behavior	behaviour
이웃	neighbor	neighbour
색	color	colour
노동	labor	labour
항구	harbor	harbour
명예, 존경	honor	honour
프로그램	program	programme
아날로그	analog	analogue
디스크	disk	disc
퍼센트 %	percent	per cent
회색	gray	grey
면허, 자격	license	licence
방어	defense	defence
중심	center	centre
극장	theater	theatre
인공 유물	artifact	artefact
여행, 이동	traveling	travelling
취소했다	canceled	cancelled
(고무) 타이어	tire	tyre
수표	check	cheque
도끼	ax	axe
~중에	among	among/amongst
깨닫다	realize	realize/realise
인정하다	recognize	recognize/recognise
문명	civilization	civilization/civilisation
조직, 기관	organization	organization/organisation

❺ 다음은 미국과 영국에서 표현이 다르게 쓰이는 단어이다.

	미국식	영국식
휴대폰	cell phone	mobile phone
이력서	résumé	curriculum vitae (CV)
영화 극장	(movie) theater	cinema
승강기	elevator	lift
1층	first floor	ground floor
2층	second floor	first floor
아파트	apartment	flat
축구	soccer	football
대학 기숙사	dormitory	hall of residence
자동차 뒤 트렁크	trunk	boot
자동차 번호판	license plate	number plate
주차장	parking lot	car park
교통 수단, 교통 체계	transportation	transport
지하철	subway	underground
고속도로	expressway, highway	motorway
기름	gas, gasoline	petrol
보도, 인도	sidewalk	pavement
초등학교	elementary school	primary school
고급 사립 학교	private school	public school
무료 국공립 학교	public school	state school
운동화	sneakers	trainers
바지	pants	trousers
스웨터	sweater	jumper
옷장	closet	wardrobe
기저귀	diaper	nappy
비스킷(과자)	cookie, cracker	biscuit
스콘(빵)	biscuit	scone
감자칩	chips	crisps
감자튀김	French fries	chips
사탕	candy	sweet
쓰레기통	garbage can	dustbin
우체통	mailbox	postbox
우편번호	ZIP code	postcode
약국(편의점 유사)	drugstore	chemist

Sustainable Development

A The beginnings of sustainable development can be traced back to 17th and 18th century England, where the country's depleting timber resources led to new forest management practices. The idea became more prominent throughout 19th century Europe in response to the environmental concerns brought on by industrialization. From here, sustainable development continued to evolve, influencing both economic development and social progress while also highlighting the importance of safeguarding the environment for future generations.

B The modern concept of sustainable development was defined within the report *Our Common Future*, commonly called the Brundtland Report, which was released by the United Nations World Commission on Environment and Development in 1987. The Brundtland Report defines sustainable development as development that meets the needs of the present without compromising the ability of future generations to meet their own needs. This is the most frequently cited definition of the concept to date. Since the Brundtland Report, the concept of sustainable development has developed beyond this initial intergenerational framework to also focus on the goal of socially inclusive and environmentally sustainable economic growth.

C In 2015, the United Nations General Assembly adopted the 2030 Agenda for Sustainable Development and its 17 Sustainable Development Goals (SDGs). The SDGs are a call to action by all countries – poor, rich and middle-income – to promote prosperity while protecting the planet. These long-term goals recognize that ending poverty, encouraging economic growth, and improving social conditions must go hand-in-hand with those of curbing and adapting to climate change and ensuring environmental protection.

정답 및 해설 p.024

Skimming **다음 i-vi 중 각 문단의 제목으로 알맞은 것을 선택하자.** [Matching headings 유형]

> **제목 목록**
>
> **i** The methods of sustainable forest management
>
> **ii** The importance of protecting natural systems
>
> **iii** The United Nations' plans for sustainable development
>
> **iv** The technology behind sustainable development
>
> **v** The birth of the concept of sustainable development
>
> **vi** The report defining sustainable development

1 A 문단

2 B 문단

3 C 문단

Scanning **지문 내용과 아래 문장의 의미가 일치하면 T, 다르면 F, 이에 대한 판단 정보가 지문에 없으면 NG라고 적자.** [T/F/NG 유형]

4 In the 19th century, environmental protection was a higher priority than economic development.

5 Before the Brundtland Report, social aspects were not considered in the concept of sustainable development.

6 Addressing the issue of climate change is one of the Sustainable Development Goals.

READING Skills 1 - T/F/NG, Matching Features, Summary/Note/Table Completion

오늘의 학습 목표

1 T/F/NG, Matching features, Summary/Note/Table/Sentence completion 문제 유형을 파악한다.
2 20분이란 시간 내에 Practice Test(Passage 하나)를 풀어본 후, IELTS READING 정복 비법(Unit 6)대로 철저한 복습을 한다.

T/F/NG 문제 유형

T/F/NG(정보 일치 여부) 문제는 IELTS 시험에서 Completion(빈칸 채우기) 유형 다음으로 가장 많이 나오는 문제 유형으로, 항상 다음과 같은 지시문으로 시작한다. 지금 여기서 확실히 공부해 두면, 실제 시험 때 이러한 지시문을 읽지 않아도 되어 다른 부분을 읽는 데 시간을 더 투자할 수 있다.

Questions 1-3 ▶ 해당 문제 유형 범위: 1번부터 3번까지
Do the following statements agree with the information given in Reading Passage 1?
In boxes 1-3 on your answer sheet, write
▶ 문제(1-3번) 진술과 독해 지문 1에 주어진 정보가 일치하는가?
답안지 1-3번 칸에, 다음을 적어라.

TRUE	*if the statement agrees with the information*
FALSE	*if the statement contradicts the information*
NOT GIVEN	*if there is no information on this*
▶ TRUE	문제 진술이 정보와 일치하면
FALSE	문제 진술이 정보와 다르면
NOT GIVEN	문제 진술에 대한 정보를 독해 지문에서 찾을 수 없으면

1 Galileo witnessed the phases of Saturn.
2 Early astronomers believed that Saturn was surrounded by toxic gases.
3 Halley observed a transit of Venus.

여기서 가장 중요한 것은 TRUE, FALSE, NOT GIVEN의 의미를 제대로 이해하는 것이다. T, F, NG를 결정하는 정보는 독해 지문 안에 있다. 절대 자신의 배경 지식이나 상식으로 문제를 푸는 것이 아니다. 특히 F와 NG가 헷갈리는데, F는 지문 내용과 다른 것이고, NG는 아예 관련 정보를 찾을 수 없어서 T인지 F인지 확인이 불가능한 경우이다.

T/F/NG 정복 비법

많은 IELTS 수험생들, 특히 입문자들이 가장 어려워하는 문제 유형인 T/F/NG는 다음의 사항들에 대한 이해와 스킬이 부족하기 때문이다. T/F/NG 문제에서 틀렸다면, 다음의 3가지 사항 중 하나가 이유이다.

1 관련 정보 찾기

문제 진술이 독해 지문의 어디에 있는지 찾지 못하기에, 정확한 내용 비교가 어려운 경우이다. 이는 스키밍/스캐닝 기술이 부족하여 정보를 찾지 못하기 때문이다. 따라서 문제의 중심 내용과 핵심어를 기준으로, 이와 관련된 내용을 독해 지문에서 찾아야 한다.

2 패러프레이징

문제의 핵심어가 독해 지문에서 똑같이 나오는 것이 아니고 패러프레이징되어 있다. 따라서 패러프레이징에 대해 간과하면 관련 정보를 찾는데 어려울 뿐만 아니라, 내용 해석에도 더 많은 시간이 소요된다.

3 T/F/NG 판단

정확히 지문 어느 부분에 관련 정보가 있는지 찾았어도, T/F/NG 판단이 어려운 경우가 있는데 정리하면 다음과 같다.

복잡한 패러프레이징

어려운 단어 사용 및 문장 구조를 다르게 하여, 지문과 문제가 같은 내용인지 파악하기 어렵게 한 경우이다.

문제 Entrepreneurs tend to be unusually receptive to new experiences. (T/F/NG)
사업가들은 새로운 경험에 비상하게 수용적인 경향이 있다.

지문 Observation of entrepreneurs shows that they embrace novelty while most people avoid things that are different.
사업가들을 관찰해 보면, 대부분 사람들은 다른 것들을 피하는 반면, 사업가들은 새로운 것을 기꺼이 받아들이는 것을 알 수 있다.

해설 정답은 T로, 대부분 T 문장은 지금처럼 단어 및 문장 구조를 바꾸어서 알아보기 어렵게 패러프레이징 하는 경향이 강하다. 따라서 단순히, 얼마나 같은 단어가 많이 쓰였나가 아닌, 정확한 내용 해석을 바탕으로 문장 간 의미 일치 여부를 결정한다. 참고로 T/F/NG 정답 비율은 대부분 비슷하다. 따라서 자신의 정답 중 너무 F나 NG만 있다면 T도 정답이 될 수 있음에 유의하자.

확장된 정보 묻기

지문의 내용과 문제가 거의 똑같은데 단지 추가 정보가 하나 더 있는 경우이다.

문제 Early astronomers believed that Saturn was surrounded by toxic gases. (T/F/NG)
초기 천문학자들은 토성이 독성 가스에 둘러싸여 있다고 믿었다.

지문 At that time, astronomers suspected that the atmosphere of Saturn consisted of a thick layer of gases.
그 당시 천문학자들은 토성의 대기는 두꺼운 가스 층으로 구성되어 있다고 추측했다.

해설 지문에는 '독성 가스'라는 말은 없다. 따라서 정답은 NG이다. 단지 독성(toxic)이라는 한 단어 때문에 정답이 T가 아닌 NG가 된 경우이다. 꼼꼼하고 차분하게 해석하여 함부로 추론하거나 의미를 확대 해석하지 말도록 한다.

always, only, first 등의 수식어

문제에 always, only 또는 first 같은 서수 등의 수식어가 있는 경우이다.

문제 Whales were among the first group of animals to migrate back to the sea. (T/F/NG)
고래는 바다로 되돌아간 첫 번째 그룹의 동물들 중 하나이다.

지문 Whales went back to the sea a very long time ago.
고래는 아주 오래 전 바다로 다시 돌아갔다.

해설 지문에 '첫 번째'라는 말은 없기에 NG이다. 문제에 always, only, first가 등장하는 경우, 이 단어들에 중점을 두어 지문과 문제를 대조하기 바란다. 참고로 이러한 단어들이 등장하면 F 또는 NG가 정답인 경우가 많다.

비교 불가능한 패러프레이징

문제에 진술된 내용이 지문에 나온 내용과 동일한 것처럼 보이지만 사실상 다른 내용이므로 비교가 불가능하기에 NG이다.

문제 Most people are too shy to think and act differently. (T/F/NG)
대부분 사람들은 다르게 생각하고 행동하기에는 너무 수줍음이 많다.

지문 There are many types of fears and among them, the fear of uncertainty and the fear of public ridicule discourage people from thinking differently.
많은 두려움의 종류가 있는데 그 중 불확실에 대한 두려움과 대중의 조롱에 대한 두려움이 우리가 다르게 생각하는 것을 방해한다.

해설 지문에서 '수줍음(shy)'을 언급하지 않았기에, 정답은 NG이다. 많은 수험생들이 '대중의 조롱에 대한 두려움'이 마치 '수줍음'으로 패러프레이징된 것으로 해석하여 틀리기 쉬운 부분이다. 구체적 또는 세부적 내용(shy)이 지문에 없다면 NG이니, 잘못 해석하여 T로 선택하지 않도록 한다.

A가 아닌 A'

문제 주요 핵심어가 전부 지문에 있지만 정답이 NG 또는 F인 경우이다.

문제 Galileo witnessed the phases of Saturn. (T/F/NG)
갈릴레오는 토성의 모양(상) 변화를 목격했다.

지문 In 1610, Galileo Galilei was the first to observe the rings of Saturn using a telescope. He described the rings as being like Saturn's ears. Galileo was also able to observe Venus going through a full set of phases, although he did not reveal his discovery until 1613.
1610년, 갈릴레오 갈릴레이는 망원경을 사용하여 토성의 고리를 관찰한 첫 번째 사람이었다. 그는 그 고리들이 마치 토성에 귀가 있는 것처럼 묘사했다. 갈릴레오는 또한 금성이 완전한 상 변화를 겪는 것을 목격할 수 있었는데, 1613년까지 그의 발견을 공개하지 않았다.

해설 문제 주요 핵심어인 Galileo, witness(=observe), phase, Saturn이 전부 지문에 있지만, 갈릴레오가 토성은 고리, 금성은 모양(상) 변화를 관찰했다고 나와 있다. 즉, 토성의 모양 변화를 관찰했는지는 지문에서 확인할 수 없으므로 정답은 NG이다.

관련 정보가 두 군데 이상 등장

문제 주요 핵심어를 포함한 관련 정보가 지문에 두 군데 이상 등장하는 경우로, 앞에 관련 정보가 나온다고 성급하게 답을 정하지 말고 뒤에 관련 내용이 더 나오는지 확인하고 정답을 정한다.

문제 Halley observed a transit of Venus. (T/F/NG)
핼리는 금성의 (태양면) 통과를 관찰했다.

지문 (C 문단) A transit of Venus is regarded as one of the most interesting events in astronomy. In 1677, Edmund Halley observed a transit of Mercury on an isolated island. ~

금성의 (태양면) 통과는 천문학에서 가장 흥미로운 사건들 중 하나로 간주된다. 1677년에, 에드먼드 핼리는 외딴 섬에서 수성의 통과를 관찰했다. (~ 중략: 수성과 달리 금성의 통과를 보기 어려운 현실)

(D 문단) ~ He did not survive to see transits of Venus.

(~ 중략: 금성의 통과를 보기 위한 핼리의 노력) 그는 금성의 통과를 보지 못하고 죽었다.

해설 C 문단 처음에 금성의 통과가 나오고 이어서 핼리가 수성의 통과를 관찰하였다는 말이 나온다. 여기서 문제 주요 핵심어들이 다 등장하기에 T라고 선택하기 쉽지만, 관련 정보가 D 문단에도 등장하고, 결과적으로 핼리가 금성의 통과는 보지 못했으므로 정답은 F가 된다. 보통 T/F/NG 문제 정답 단서가 지문에 한 군데인 경우가 많지만, 제시된 예제처럼 정답 관련 정보가 두 군데 이상에서 나오는 경우도 출제된다. 이런 경우 관련 정보를 모두 반영하여 T/F/NG를 판단해야 된다. 참고로 이렇게 관련 정보가 지문 여러 곳에 흩어지는 경우, 꼭 그런 것은 아니지만 정답이 F일 확률이 조금 더 높다.

Matching Features 문제 유형

Matching features(관련 정보 고르기)는 리스트에서 보기를 고르는 객관식 문제로 보통 다음과 같은 지시문으로 시작한다.

Questions 1-4 ▶ 해당 문제 유형 범위: 1번부터 4번까지

Look at the following statements (Questions 1-4) and the list of companies below.

Match each statement with the correct company, ***A, B*** *or* ***C.***

Write the correct letter, ***A, B*** *or* ***C,*** *in boxes 1-4 on your answer sheet.*

▶ 문제(1-4번) 진술과 아래의 회사 리스트를 보고 문제 진술에 부합하는 회사 기호(A, B, C)를 연결한 후, 답안지 1-4번 칸에 기호 A, B, C를 적어라.

NB *You may use any letter more than once.*

▶ NB(유의) 같은 기호가 한 번 이상 정답이 될 수 있다.

List of Companies

A Google
B Facebook
C Microsoft

1 Tends to be unusually receptive to new ideas.
2 Has received several awards concerning innovation.
3 Produces customized devices as well as software programs.
4 Was established by two classmates.

보통 리스트에서 관련 이름이나 해당 연도를 골라야 되는 경우가 많은데, 이름이나 연도가 지문에 한 번 이상 나오기에, 나오는 관련 부분을 모두 확인하고 문제를 풀어야 한다.

NB(Nota Bene) 유의

보통 Matching features 문제에서 NB, 즉 유의사항이 함께 나오는데, NB 문구에 따라 같은 기호가 여러 번 정답이 되는 경우가, 반드시는 아니지만, 대부분이다. 따라서 만일 자신의 정답에서 같은 기호가 두 번 이상 사용되지 않았다면, 자신의 답을 한 번 더 의심해보고 검토하기 바란다.

Summary/Note/Table Completion 문제 유형

IELTS READING에서는 Completion(빈칸 채우기) 유형이 가장 많이 출제된다. Summary(요약문), Note(노트 메모), Table(표), Sentence(문장), Flowchart(순서도) 등의 빈칸을 채우는 문제로, 이 중에서도 Summary가 가장 많이 출제되고 있다. Summary의 경우 다른 Completion 유형과 달리 지문 순서와 문제 정답 순서가 뒤바뀌는 경우도 있음에 유의하자.

Completion 유형은 독해 지문에서 해당되는 단어를 찾아 쓰는 주관식 형태와, 주어진 보기에서 선택하는 객관식 형태가 있다.

▸ 주관식 형태 지시문

Questions 1-5 ▶ 해당 문제 유형 범위: 1번부터 5번까지
Complete the notes below.
Choose ***ONE WORD ONLY*** *from the passage for each answer.*
Write your answers in boxes 1-5 on your answer sheet.
▶ 노트 메모를 채워라. 각각의 정답을 독해 지문에서 찾아 한 단어로, 답안지 1-5번 칸에 적어라. (글자 수 유의)

Scot Bike

- Glasgow in an effort to catch up with **1** .... and Amsterdam in terms of green transportation
- 2014: introduced the initiative, which has so far been unsuccessful in reducing **2** ....
- Another problem: that many of the bicycles are being vandalized
- B.K. Ludlow: not provide **3** .... that would be necessary for a proper analysis
  - but maintain that Scot Bike is popular with **4** .... and tourists and that losses as a result of bicycle **5** .... have decreased significantly

▶ **객관식 형태 지시문**

Questions 1-3 ▶ 해당 문제 유형 범위: 1번부터 3번까지

Complete the summary using the list of words, ***A-F****, below.*

Write the correct letter, ***A-F****, in boxes 1-3 on your answer sheet.*

▶ 아래의 A-F 리스트를 이용하여 요약문을 채워라. 답안지 1-3번 칸에 알맞은 기호 A-F를 적어라. (기호 적기)

Problems with birth order research

The effects of birth order are difficult to study due to the wide variety of **1** .... that need to be considered. For example, the **2** .... of families greatly affects the research and results. Third-born children are more likely to come from poorer families, so any **3** .... that is discovered might be a result of socioeconomic factors, and not a result of birth order.

A size	**B** survey	**C** trait
D critics	**E** variables	**F** parents

특히 주관식 형태 지시문에서 정답의 글자 수가 정해져 있기에 반드시 지시문의 글자 수대로 정답을 적어야 한다. 객관식 형태는 기호를 적는 것으로 기호가 아닌 단어를 적으면 오답 처리된다.

READING

Passage 다음 실전 문제(Questions 1-13)를 20분 이내에 풀어 보자.

The Effects of Birth Order on Personality

One of the first theorists to argue that birth order influences personality was the Austrian psychiatrist Alfred Adler (1870 – 1937). Adler, who was a contemporary of Sigmund Freud, firmly believed that birth order can have a significant impact on an individual's personality and emotional responses, including the ways in which they deal with love, friendship, and stress. According to Adler, the introduction of a new baby into a family unit has a profound and lasting influence on the older child or children, who will experience feelings of diminished privilege and value. Adler theorized that the extra parental attention that younger children typically receive greatly affects their personalities later in life. In a three-child family, for example, the youngest child would tend to be pampered, which can result in poorly-developed social skills. The middle child, who would not experience such pampering, was most likely to enjoy a successful and fulfilling life, but would also be most likely to argue with other siblings. Adler believed that the oldest child would be most likely to succumb to substance abuse and experience anxiety due to feelings of excessive responsibility for younger siblings and the lack of parental attentiveness. As a result, he reasoned that this child would be the most likely to end up in jail or suffer from severe mental health conditions.

The effect of birth order has become a controversial issue in psychology in the years since Alfred Adler first presented his theory. In 1996, an American psychologist named Frank Sulloway published a book in which he outlined his theory that birth order had clear effects on the 'Big Five' personality traits: agreeableness, neuroticism, openness, extraversion, and conscientiousness. Sulloway believed that first-borns were less agreeable and less receptive to new ideas than later-borns, but on the other hand, were more socially assertive and conscientious. However, fellow psychologists such as Judith Rich Harris and Toni Falbo published rigorously researched papers that were highly critical of Sulloway's theories and findings. Brian Sutton-Smith, a psychologist who spent most of the career analyzing the cultural and developmental effects of children's playing habits, argued that any perceived effects of birth order would likely be eliminated by experiences that an individual has later in life, as each human being continually adapts to a unique combination of societal and environmental factors.

Researching the possible effects of birth order is a challenge due to the near-impossible task of controlling the vast number of social and demographic variables associated with birth order. Family size, for example, plays a crucial role in any study of the topic. On average, large families are lower on the socioeconomic ladder than small families, which means third-born children involved in a study are more likely to come from poorer families than first-born children. If a researcher identifies a specific trait related to third-born children, it may be a result of family size or other variables rather than birth order. Such problems are virtually unavoidable, which leads to inconclusive studies and findings that are easily disputed by critics.

Swiss researchers Cecile Ernst and Jules Angst evaluated all of the birth order research published between 1946 and 1980 and attempted to control for variables. They concluded that birth order had minimal effects on personality, and even suggested that further research into birth order would be a waste of time and resources. More recently, researchers have analyzed data based on wide-reaching surveys related to the Big Five personality traits, but no evidence was found to support Sulloway's theory that a significant correlation exists between birth order and self-reported personality.

Some smaller studies have partially supported Sulloway's predictions. Delroy Paulhus of the University of British Columbia found that later-borns have a tendency to be rebellious but score higher on agreeableness and openness, while first-borns are more parent-oriented and score higher on conscientiousness and conservatism. Paulhus and his contributors assert that the effect can be seen quite clearly within families, but they concede that results are weak when comparing individuals from different families due to the prevalence of genetic and socioeconomic factors. Paulhus also claims that children who do not have any siblings are not significantly different from those who have siblings. In fact, they share many characteristics with first-borns, particularly the high regard they have for their parents.

Judith Rich Harris concurs that birth order effects may be apparent within a family unit, but she argues that they are not long-lasting personality traits. Harris pointed out that, while first-borns and later-borns behave differently when in the company of their parents and siblings, even in adulthood, the majority of people move out of their childhood home relatively early in their life. Harris' research findings indicate that personality traits adopted in the childhood home have little to no bearing on an individual's behavior outside the home, even during childhood.

Questions 1-4

Do the following statements agree with the information given in the passage?

In boxes 1-4 on your answer sheet, write

TRUE	*if the statement agrees with the information*
FALSE	*if the statement contradicts the information*
NOT GIVEN	*if there is no information on this*

1 Alfred Adler encouraged parents to show more attention to all children in a family unit.

2 Brian Sutton-Smith predicted that birth order effects present in an individual will eventually vanish.

3 The research evaluated by Ernst and Angst showed a clear relationship between birth order and personality.

4 The findings of Judith Rich Harris show that birth order affects personality within the family home.

Questions 5-9

Look at the following statements (Questions 5-9) and the list of researchers below.

Match each statement with the correct researcher, ***A, B*** *or* ***C****.*

Write the correct letter, ***A, B*** *or* ***C****, in boxes 5-9 on your answer sheet.*

NB *You may use any letter more than once.*

List of Researchers

A Alfred Adler

B Frank Sulloway

C Delroy Paulhus

5 Noted that an only child shares personality traits with first-born children.

6 Theorized that middle children are more likely to succeed than their siblings.

7 Argued that birth order affects five distinctive personality traits.

8 Received several criticisms from peers in the psychology field.

9 Believed that the oldest of three siblings is more likely to commit a crime.

Questions 10-13

*Complete the summary using the list of words, **A-F**, below.*

*Write the correct letter, **A-F**, in boxes 10-13 on your answer sheet.*

Problems with birth order research

The effects of birth order are difficult to study due to the wide variety of **10** .... that need to be considered. For example, the **11** .... of families greatly affects the research and results. Third-born children are more likely to come from poorer families, so any **12** .... that is discovered might be a result of socioeconomic factors, and not a result of birth order. Because of this, **13** .... view such studies as being flawed and inconclusive.

A size	**B** survey	**C** trait
D critics	**E** variables	**F** parents

UNIT 08

READING Skills 2 - Sentence Completion, Matching Information

오늘의 학습 목표

1 Sentence completion과 Matching information 문제 유형을 파악한다.
2 20분이란 시간 내에 Practice Test(Passage 하나)를 풀어본 후, IELTS READING 정복 비법(Unit 6)대로 철저한 복습을 한다.

Sentence Completion 문제 유형

Completion(빈칸 채우기) 유형 중 가장 독특한 형태인 Sentence Completion(문장 빈칸 채우기) 유형은, 대체로 문장의 빈칸을 채우는 문제보다는 한 문장의 뒷부분을 완성하는 '문장 완성하기' 형태로 출제된다. 이 때 뒤에 이어질 부분은 보기로 제시되며, 보기 기호로 정답을 기입하면 된다. 아래는 전형적인 Sentence Completion 지시문이다.

Questions 1-4 ▶ 해당 문제 유형 범위: 1번부터 4번까지

*Complete each sentence with the correct ending, **A-F**, below.*

*Write the correct letter, **A-F**, in boxes 1-4 on your answer sheet.*

▶ 아래 A-F 중 알맞은 내용을 선택하여 답안지 1-4번 칸에 알맞은 기호 A-F를 적어라.

1 Jean-Baptiste Bouillaud theorized that
2 Carl Wernicke contributed to the field of language lateralization by
3 Brenda Milner's work showed that
4 Roger Sperry tested for hemisphere dominance by

A devising a test for blocking communication between brain hemispheres.
B lesions on brain hemispheres have little to no effect on language expression.
C designing a map of language processes controlled by the left hemisphere.
D having split-brain patients identify specific objects by hand.
E tasks performed with the right hand are controlled by the left hemisphere.
F a test for hemispherical dominance was an effective technique.

Sentence Completion 유형은 패러프레이징이 많이 되기에 이에 유의하여 정답을 찾도록 한다.

Flowchart Completion

Completion 문제 유형 중에는 순서도 빈칸을 채우는 Flowchart Completion(순서도 빈칸 채우기) 문제도 있다. 문제와 지문 순서가 완전히 같아서 정보 찾기가 수월하기에 난이도가 가장 낮은 유형이다. Academic 모듈에서는 거의 출제가 되지 않지만, General Training 모듈의 Section 2에서 자주 출제되는 편이다.

Matching Information 문제 유형

Matching information(정보가 포함된 문단 고르기) 유형은, 문제에 언급된 정보가 독해 지문의 어떤 문단에 있는지, 그 문단 번호를 고르는 문제이다. 따라서 Matching information이 나오는 독해 지문에는 전부 문단별로 A, B, C, D 등의 기호가 붙어있다.

Questions 1-4 ▶ 해당 문제 유형 범위: 1번부터 4번까지
Reading Passage 1 has eight paragraphs, ***A-H.*** ▶ 독해 지문 1 문단 수: A-H의 8개
Which paragraph contains the following information?
Write the correct letter, ***A-H****, in boxes 1-4 on your answer sheet.*
▶ 어떤 문단이 다음의 정보(문제 진술)를 포함하는가? 답안지 1-4번 칸에 알맞은 기호 A-H를 적어라.

NB *You may use any letter more than once.*
▶ NB(유의) 같은 기호가 한 번 이상 정답이 될 수 있다.

1 a reference to the continuation of an individual's work by a family member
2 the results of a study on hemisphere dominance in relation to handedness
3 a reference to a specific individual whose speech was affected by a brain lesion
4 a conclusion that a previous theory was flawed

Matching information 유형은 스키밍과 스캐닝을 가장 필요로 하는 영역이다. 먼저 문제를 읽으면서 문제의 핵심어와 주요 내용을 파악한 상태에서 지문을 빠르게 읽으면서 해당 정보를 찾도록 한다. 핵심어가 있는 문단을 빠르게 찾은 후, 지문의 핵심어 부분이 문제의 주요 내용과 일치하는지 여부를 확인하면서 핵심어가 있는 문단 중 가장 내용이 일치하는 문단을 정답으로 선택한다.

PRACTICE TEST

Passage 다음 실전 문제(Questions 1-14)를 20분 이내에 풀어 보자.

Lateralization and Language

How hemispheric lateralization of the human brain affects the expression of language

A One of the first theories of hemispheric language lateralization was put forth by the French physician Jean-Baptiste Bouillaud. Bouillaud believed that, because the majority of individuals perform most tasks with their right hand, including writing, the right hand might be controlled by the left hemisphere of the brain. Based on this theory, language, which is fundamental to writing, would also be largely governed by the left hemisphere. Bouillaud's theory was investigated further by his son-in-law Simon Alexandre Ernest Aubertin, who collaborated with the leading French neurologist Paul Broca.

B In 1861, a 51-year-old patient named Leborgne visited Paul Broca. After examining Leborgne, who could understand language but had major difficulties expressing it, Broca determined that a lesion must have formed on the patient's left frontal lobe, a diagnosis that was soon proven to be accurate based on autopsy notes released after Leborgne passed away. Broca studied several other individuals who had lesions or other abnormalities affecting the left frontal lobe and found that all of them had problems articulating themselves through spoken language. Meanwhile, he found that right frontal lesions in other patients had barely any effect on language expression. Subsequently, Broca theorized that language expression is governed only by one hemisphere, predominantly the left.

C Broca's theory of language lateralization was further supported by the findings of the German anatomist Carl Wernicke. In 1874, Wernicke examined a large number of patients whose language capabilities had been severely disrupted. In each of them, he identified lesions in the temporal lobe of the left hemisphere, but in different sections of the lobe from those that Broca had studied, which inhibited the individual's ability to form language. Building on these findings, Wernicke created a map that depicted the organization of language processes in the left hemisphere.

D In 1949, Juhn Wada, a researcher at the Montreal Neurological Institute, devised a test that proved invaluable to early studies of lateralization. The Wada Test involves the injection of an anesthetic into one side of the brain, which will effectively turn off that side for roughly 10 minutes. While one side of the patient's brain is anesthetized, a physician will evaluate the person's language capabilities. In most cases, the left hemisphere is anesthetized. If the left hemisphere is the dominant hemisphere, then the patient will lose his or her ability to express language. Conversely, if the patient's right hemisphere is dominant, then he or she will have no difficulty in continuing to speak with the physician.

정답 및 해설 p.032

E The effectiveness of the Wada Test was documented in a 1977 study conducted by Brenda Milner. By using the process outlined above, Milner found that the left hemisphere is dominant in terms of language expression for 70% of left-handed people and 98% of right-handed people. Her findings also showed that 2% of right-handed people have a dominant right hemisphere. This finding was significant as it correlated with the percentage of individuals whose speech capabilities are disrupted when they develop a lesion on the right hemisphere of their brain. As a result of Milner's research, the Wada Test became accepted by the scientific community, and it began to be implemented as a preliminary procedure in brain surgery, as it allows surgeons to keep the hemisphere associated with speech turned on throughout a surgical procedure.

F Another procedure that has helped to provide crucial information about language lateralization is commissurotomy. During this procedure, the hemispheres of a patient (referred to as a split-brain patient) are disconnected by severing the corpus callosum, a nerve tract which connects both hemispheres. The aim of the procedure is to eliminate communication between hemispheres so that each one carries out processes independently. Roger Sperry conducted some of the most widely publicized split-brain studies throughout the 1970s at the California Institute of Technology, concluding definitively that hemispheric lateralization affects language expression.

G Sperry worked with numerous split-brain patients, asking each of them to identify objects held in each hand without looking at them. Split-brain patients whose left hemisphere remained functional were able to easily describe items placed in their right hand, but could not verbally identify any items placed in their left hand. Meanwhile, patients using their right hemisphere were only able to give a basic description of each object, rather than an accurate identification. For example, some were unable to identify a ruler but could express that the item was long and flat.

H Sperry's research conclusively showed that, in the vast majority of individuals, major language processes are carried out by the left hemisphere of the brain. However, it is wrong to say that the right hemisphere has absolutely zero capacity for language. As shown in Sperry's research, some test subjects were able to provide rudimentary descriptions of objects when using the right hemisphere, showing that the right hemisphere in some individuals is able to express language to a modest degree. As such, Broca's earlier theory that we verbally communicate only with our left brain is not entirely accurate. While it is true that we express language much more effectively with our left hemisphere than with our right, the right hemisphere still plays a role in the emotional shading of our speech.

Questions 1-4

*Complete each sentence with the correct ending, **A-F**, below.*

*Write the correct letter, **A-F**, in boxes 1-4 on your answer sheet.*

1 Jean-Baptiste Bouillaud theorized that

2 Carl Wernicke contributed to the field of language lateralization by

3 Brenda Milner's work showed that

4 Roger Sperry tested for hemisphere dominance by

A	devising a test for blocking communication between brain hemispheres.
B	lesions on brain hemispheres have little to no effect on language expression.
C	designing a map of language processes controlled by the left hemisphere.
D	having split-brain patients identify specific objects by hand.
E	tasks performed with the right hand are controlled by the left hemisphere.
F	a test for hemispherical dominance was an effective technique.

Questions 5-9

Complete the summary below.

*Choose **ONE WORD ONLY** from the passage for each answer.*

Write your answers in boxes 5-9 on your answer sheet.

The Wada Test

The Wada Test was developed by Juhn Wada and requires the injection of an **5** .... into one hemisphere of the brain. Language capabilities are then assessed by a **6** .... for a period of around ten minutes. The test helps to show which hemisphere of an individual's brain is more **7** .... Brenda Milner used the test to show that the left hemisphere is primarily in control of language expression in ninety-eight percent of **8** .... individuals studied. The Wada Test gained widespread acceptance and was eventually used in brain **9** .... so that patients could remain communicative.

Questions 10-14

*The passage has eight paragraphs, **A-H**.*

Which paragraph contains the following information?

*Write the correct letter, **A-H**, in boxes 10-14 on your answer sheet.*

NB *You may use any letter more than once.*

10 a description of a method for disrupting hemispheric communication via nerves

11 a reference to the continuation of an individual's work by a family member

12 the results of a study on hemisphere dominance in relation to handedness

13 a reference to a specific individual whose speech was affected by a brain lesion

14 a conclusion that a previous theory was flawed

READING Skills 3 - Matching Headings, Y/N/NG

오늘의 학습 목표

1. Matching headings, Y/N/NG 문제 유형을 파악한다.
2. 20분이란 시간 내에 Practice Test(Passage 하나)를 풀어본 후, IELTS READING 정복 비법(Unit 6)대로 철저한 복습을 한다.

Matching Headings 문제 유형

Matching headings(문단 제목 고르기) 유형은 문단 제목을 보기에서 고르는 객관식 문제이다. IELTS READING의 구성은 보통 독해 지문이 먼저 나오고 그 뒤에 관련 문제가 출제되는데, Matching headings 유형만 독해 지문 앞에 먼저 문제가 나오는 특징이 있다.

Questions 1-7 ▶ 해당 문제 유형 범위: 1번부터 7번까지

Reading Passage 1 has seven paragraphs, ***A-G.*** ▶ 독해 지문 1 문단 수: A-G의 7개

Choose the correct heading for each paragraph from the list of headings below.

Write the correct number, ***i-x****, in boxes 1-7 on your answer sheet.*

▶ 아래 문단 제목 리스트에서 각각의 문단에 알맞은 제목을 골라, 답안지 1-7번 칸에 알맞은 기호 i-x를 적어라.

List of Headings

i Visual cues to trigger positive emotions
ii Wall color and its effect on psychology
iii Make full use of your display models
iv Speak the language of your consumers
v The appeal of offers and discounts
vi Telling a story to consumers
vii Catching attention through art
viii Visual merchandising and technology
ix Utilizing the checkout to boost sales
x Promoting your products in publications

1 Paragraph **A**
2 Paragraph **B**
3 Paragraph **C**
4 Paragraph **D**

5 Paragraph **E**
6 Paragraph **F**
7 Paragraph **G**

많은 수험생들이 가장 어려워하는 문제 유형 중 하나로 Matching headings를 꼽는다. 이유는 스키밍/스캐닝 스킬만으로 문제를 풀었다가 틀리는 경우가 많기 때문이다. Matching headings에서 고득점을 올리기 위해서는 정독이 필요한데, 독해 지문을 정독하기에는 많은 수험생들에게 IELTS READING 시간은 턱없이 부족하다.

빠른 시간에 정독이 가능한, 최상의 독해 실력을 갖고 있는 수험생들은 Matching headings부터 풀어도 된다. 하지만 대다수 수험생들은 해당 지문의 다른 유형 문제들을 먼저 풀어서 전체적인 지문 내용을 익힌 후에 Matching headings를 풀면 보다 빠르게 글을 읽고 이해하여 시간 절약은 물론 정답을 고를 확률도 높일 수 있다.

Y/N/NG 문제 유형

Y/N/NG(견해 일치 여부 문제)는 T/F/NG와 같은 스타일의 문제이다. 두 유형의 차이는 Y/N/NG가 글쓴이 견해와 문제의 일치 여부를 묻는 것이라면, T/F/NG는 글에 나온 정보와 문제의 일치 여부를 묻는 차이이다. T/F/NG와 같다고 생각하고 문제를 풀다가 정답지에 Y 대신 T를, N 대신 F을 적지 않도록 유의한다.

Questions 1-4 ▶ 해당 문제 유형 범위: 1번부터 4번까지

Do the following statements agree with the views of the writer in Reading Passage 1?
In boxes 1-4 on your answer sheet, write

▶ 문제(1-4번) 진술과 독해 지문 1의 글쓴이 견해와 일치하는가?
답안지 1-4번 칸에, 다음을 적어라.

YES	*if the statement agrees with the views of the writer*
NO	*if the statement contradicts the views of the writer*
NOT GIVEN	*if it is impossible to say what the writer thinks about this*
▶ YES	글쓴이 견해와 일치하면
NO	글쓴이 견해와 다르면
NOT GIVEN	글쓴이가 문제 진술에 대해 어떻게 생각하는지 말하는 것이 불가능하다면

1 Photographs of flowers can have the same level of appeal as fresh flowers.
2 Having an attractive Web site is a key part of visual merchandising.
3 Consumers are increasingly unimpressed with high-tech marketing methods.
4 Displaying multiple products closely together is confusing to consumers.

Y/N/NG는 T/F/NG 유형의 정답 찾는 스킬과 정답 판단 기준이 같다. 다만 한가지 더 유의할 사항으로, 단지 지문에 나와 있다고 일치 여부를 따지는 것이 아니고 문제가 글쓴이의 의견인지, 아니면 글쓴이가 인용한 다른 사람의 의견인지 구분해서 판단해야 된다.

PRACTICE TEST

Passage 다음 실전 문제(Questions 1-13)를 20분 이내에 풀어 보자.

Questions 1-7

Reading Passage 1 has seven paragraphs, ***A-G****.*

Choose the correct heading for each paragraph from the list of headings below.

Write the correct number, ***i-x****, in boxes 1-7 on your answer sheet.*

List of Headings

i	Visual cues to trigger positive emotions
ii	Wall color and its effect on psychology
iii	Make full use of your display models
iv	Speak the language of your consumers
v	The appeal of offers and discounts
vi	Telling a story to consumers
vii	Catching attention through art
viii	Visual merchandising and technology
ix	Utilizing the checkout to boost sales
x	Promoting your products in publications

1 Paragraph **A**

2 Paragraph **B**

3 Paragraph **C**

4 Paragraph **D**

5 Paragraph **E**

6 Paragraph **F**

7 Paragraph **G**

정답 및 해설 p.039

The Art of Visual Merchandising

Visual merchandising is becoming increasingly important in the retail sector. But what are the most crucial psychological elements of this approach?

A In order to promote products and boost sales, owners of retail businesses employ a wide variety of visual merchandising strategies. The overall aim of visual merchandising is to make the shopping experience more engaging and enjoyable for consumers while driving profits for the business itself. One of the first visual marketing techniques, which remains just as effective today, was the notion that the area surrounding a cash register is of utmost importance. While standing in line, customers have a tendency to make last-minute purchases. Business owners began noticing this and setting up displays of low-cost products designed to appeal to 'impulse buyers'. From a psychological perspective, this type of point of sale (POS) visual merchandising must be discreet in order to be effective; if the display is too large or intrusive, it might disrupt the customer's checkout experience.

B A crucial factor in visual merchandising in the retail sector is finding a way to showcase as many products as possible without making the display look cluttered. The most common way to display items in a clothing store is to use mannequins. However, some retailers make the mistake of failing to properly utilize their mannequins. For instance, dressing a mannequin in only one garment is a missed opportunity to present numerous items of clothing that go together well. To make the most of store mannequins, it is recommended to create a theme for each one and dress it in items for sale, from head to toe, even including accessories such as watches, hats, and gloves. Another effective way that apparel retailers can make their merchandise more visible is to have staff members wear in-season garments while working on the shop floor.

C Grouping multiple products together helps customers to envisage how a product will look, function, and feel before they buy it. Stores such as IKEA show how different products complement one another in a home setting. Exemplary real-life bedrooms, kitchens, and living rooms are created on the shop floor, with each one encompassing several products that are available for purchase. This represents a perfect example of the powerful effect of using visual merchandising to paint an appealing picture for shoppers. When grouping products in such a way, it is vital to make sure that displays have a simple and accessible arrangement. If the merchandise is somewhat visually bland, eye-catching items – such as a colorful teddy bear on a bed – are often added to attract the attention of shoppers.

D Aside from merchandise displays, business owners incorporate many other visual elements to appeal to consumers. Flowers are a common addition, as they have been shown to promote relaxation and a sense of calm. This results in shoppers who are happy to linger and peruse the items on display, and more inclined to make a casual purchase. Flowers are commonly given and received as gifts, so the brain connects the image of flowers with feelings of happiness and satisfaction. Studies have shown that even looking at a picture of flowers, or any natural scene, can have the same calming and relaxing effect. Therefore, if a business simply does not have the budget for continually buying fresh flowers, they can strategically place pictures of flowers in the vicinity of product displays.

E On a similar note, unique artwork is known to contribute to a memorable shopping experience. Artwork has been shown to have beneficial effects in a wide variety of different businesses, from boutique hotels to retail stores. In terms of visual merchandising in retail, one-off paintings or sculptures give a sense of exclusivity and distinctiveness to a store. Pieces of art can be commissioned from well-known artists and have a visual connection to your brand and products. In addition, highly visible abstract works of art help to create intrigue and draw potential customers into a store. Some business leaders with a keen eye for visual merchandising take it to the next level, having artworks created from the actual products that a business sells.

F Whatever approach a business owner opts for, they should tailor their displays or store designs to appeal to the age range of their target market. In the case of many clothing retailers, the primary target market is relatively young – generally from 17 to 35 – so it is effective to use common social media language in their visual merchandising strategies. Expressions such as "OMG!" and "Like!" are brief and impactful, and help to attract millennials to merchandise displays. Using Internet-derived language in visual merchandising promotes feelings of familiarity and inclusiveness in younger consumers. They will view the store or brand as being trendy, and might then share images of it with their friends online. Many businesses utilize this strategy in their visual merchandising so that customers make a subconscious connection between the physical store and its online presence, resulting in a higher number of Web site visitors.

G Another way to keep up with the changing times and stay relevant is to incorporate technology into visual merchandising. The majority of customers appreciate innovation and interactivity. Recently, companies such as Bloomingdale's and Ralph Lauren have installed window displays comprised of high-definition touchscreens that allow consumers to customize specific items of clothing, place an order, then pick it up in-store. As technology continues to evolve, an increasing number of retailers are turning to virtual reality as a way to attract customers and improve their retail experience. By donning VR headsets, customers can see how a piece of furniture would look in their home, or explore the interior and exterior of a vehicle that is not physically available for viewing. And with retailers allocating more and more of their marketing budget for high-tech visual merchandising, and demand for such technology increasing, these innovations are just the tip of the iceberg.

Questions 8-13

Do the following statements agree with the views of the writer in Reading Passage 1?

In boxes 8-13 on your answer sheet, write

YES	*if the statement agrees with the views of the writer*
NO	*if the statement contradicts the views of the writer*
NOT GIVEN	*if it is impossible to say what the writer thinks about this*

8 Visual merchandising is an effective way to boost earnings.

9 Mannequin displays should be set up near a store's entrance.

10 Displaying multiple products closely together is confusing to consumers.

11 Photographs of flowers can have the same level of appeal as fresh flowers.

12 Having an attractive Web site is a key part of visual merchandising.

13 Consumers are increasingly unimpressed with high-tech marketing methods.

READING Skills 4 - Short-answer Questions, Diagram Label Completion, Multiple Choice

오늘의 학습 목표

1 Short-answer questions, Diagram label completion, Multiple choice 문제 유형을 파악한다.
2 20분이란 시간 내에 Practice Test(Passage 하나)를 풀어본 후, IELTS READING 정복 비법(Unit 6)대로 철저한 복습을 한다.

Short-answer Questions 문제 유형

Short-answer questions(단답형 문제)는 짧은 질문에 대해 제시된 글자 수에 맞게 주관식으로 정답을 적는 문제 유형으로 다음과 같이 지시문이 나온다.

Questions 1-4 ▶ 해당 문제 유형 범위: 1번부터 4번까지
*Choose **ONE WORD ONLY** from the passage for each answer.*
Write your answers in boxes 1-4 on your answer sheet.
▶ 각각의 정답을 독해 지문에서 찾아 한 단어로, 답안지 1-4번 칸에 적어라. (글자 수 유의)

1 What was known to be a plant commonly eaten by mammoths?
2 Where were mammoths known to be hunted before they were hunted in Alaska?
3 What were found at sites throughout Europe?
4 What did early humans build using parts from mammoths?

독해 지문에서 정답을 그대로 찾아 적는 것이므로, 절대 품사나 시제, 단・복수를 변형시키지 말고 지문에 있는 그대로 정답을 적는다.

답안 작성에 유용한 Ctrl+c, Ctrl+v

컴퓨터로 아이엘츠 시험을 보는 경우, Reading 영역에서 나오는 모든 Completion 문제 유형들과 Short-answer questions 문제 유형은 정답을 직접 쓸 필요없이 지문에 나오는 정답 단어를 복사(Ctrl+c), 붙여넣기(Ctrl+v)의 작업을 통해 빠르고 단・복수 등의 실수 없이 정답을 기입할 수 있다. 따라서 컴퓨터로 시험을 보려는 응시생들은 기본적인 컴퓨터 단축키 사용에 미리 익숙해지도록 한다.

Diagram Label Completion 문제 유형

Diagram Label Completion(도해 빈칸 채우기)은 그림에 빈칸으로 되어 있는 설명 부분을 채우는 문제이다. 주로 기계나 설비, 또는 어떤 흐름이나 과정의 단계를 나타낸 그림이 있고, 이러한 그림에 짧은 설명 라벨(label)이 그림의 해당 부분들에 있는데, 라벨에 빈칸이 있는 경우, 그 빈칸을 채우는 문제이다. 난이도는 높은 편이나 출제 비중이 높지 않고, 최근 들어서는 거의 출제되지 않고 있다.

Questions 1-4 ▶ 해당 문제 유형 범위: 1번부터 4번까지

Label the diagram below.

Choose ***ONE WORD ONLY*** *from the passage for each answer.*

Write your answers in boxes 1-4 on your answer sheet.

▶ 아래 도해의 설명을 달아라. 각각의 정답을 독해 지문에서 찾아 한 단어로, 답안지 1-4번 칸에 적어라. (글자 수 유의)

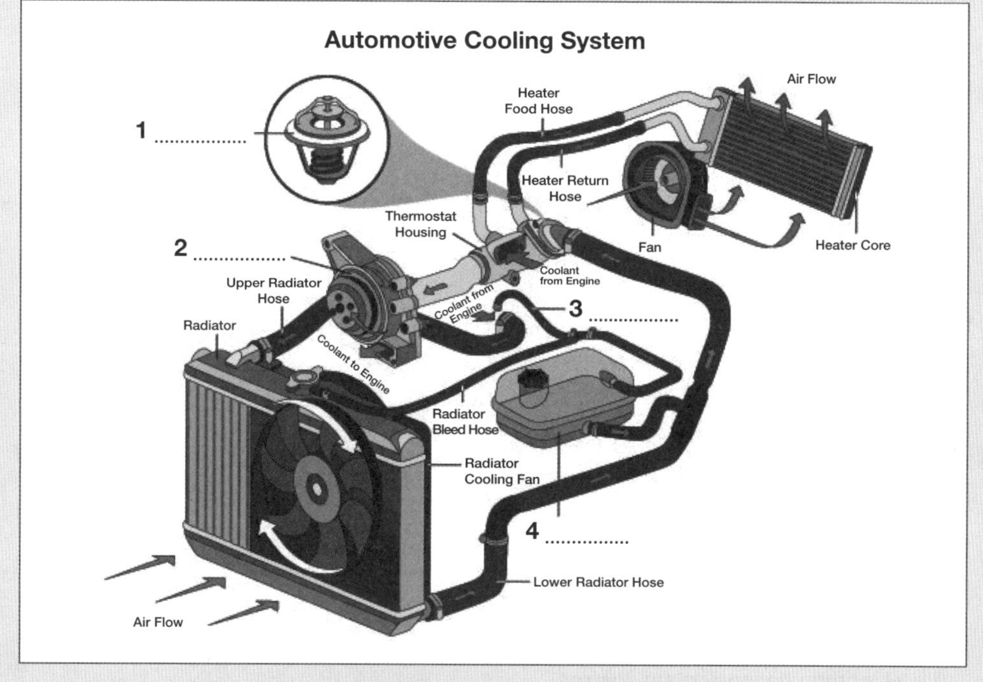

Glossary(용어 설명) 활용법

IELTS READING 지문에는 전문 용어가 나오는 경우가 많다. 이때, IELTS 시험 레벨을 고려할 때 어렵다고 판단되는 단어는 단어 뒤에 *표시를 하고 지문 마지막에 작은 글씨로 설명을 해준다. 이러한 glossary(용어 설명)는 당연히 영어로 풀이되어 있기에, 수험생들은 또다시 용어 설명 부분을 읽고 해석해야 하는 수고가 필요하다.

예 *humus: soil made of decayed leaves and plants

따라서 Reading 시험 시간에 쫓기는 수험생들은 과감히 용어 설명 부분은 읽지 않아도 되는데, 이렇게 용어 설명된 단어가 문제 정답의 핵심어인 경우는 극히 드물기 때문이다. 하지만 시험 시간에 너무 쫓기지 않고 정확한 지문 해석을 원하는 수험생이라면 읽어 보는 것을 추천한다.

Multiple Choice 문제 유형

Listening과 마찬가지로 Reading에서 나오는 multiple choice(선다형 문제)는 난이도가 높으며 한 문제 또는 두 문제로 출제된다.

▸ 한 문제 형태 지시문

Question 1 ▶ 해당 문제 유형 범위: 1번

*Choose the correct letter, **A, B, C** or **D**.* ▶ 보기: A-D (4개)

Write the correct letter in box 1 on your answer sheet.

▶ A-D 중 알맞은 기호를 답안지 1번 칸에 적어라. (한 문제 짜리)

1 What would be the most suitable subtitle for the article?

A How mammoths evolved to adapt to increasingly harsh climates

B The mutually beneficial relationship between humans and mammoths

C Searching for a definitive reason for the disappearance of the mammoth

D New evidence shows that mammoths survived longer than previously thought

참고로 Listening의 multiple choice 문제 유형인 경우, 보기가 3개(A-C) 주어지는데 반해, Reading은 4개(A-D)가 주어진다.

▸ 두 문제 형태 지시문

Questions 1-2 ▶ 해당 문제 유형 범위: 1번부터 2번까지

*Choose **TWO** letters, **A-E**.* ▶ 보기: A-E (5개)

Write the correct letters in boxes 1 and 2 on your answer sheet.

▶ 보기 A-E 중 두 개를 선택하여 답안지 1-2번 칸에 알맞은 기호를 적어라. (두 문제 짜리)

Which **TWO** types of data does the writer mention that scientists have recently used to study the extinction of mammoths in North America?

A ice cores removed from glaciers

B carbon dating of plant species

C changes to mammoth bone structure

D historical data related to changes in climate

E analysis of primitive tools and weapons

Listening과 마찬가지로 정답 순서를 바꿔서 써도 정답이 된다. 즉, B와 E가 정답이라면, 1번에 B, 2번에 E, 또는 1번에 E, 2번에 B라고 써도 정답 처리된다. 단, 1번이나 2번에 B, E 두개를 함께 적으면 오답처리 된다.

참고로 보기(A-E)에 기술된 정보는 독해 지문의 내용 순서와 다르게 섞여 있으므로, 문제와 연관되는 지문 부분을 끝까지 스키밍/스캐닝 할 필요가 있다.

Reading 시험 시간 관리

Academic 모듈의 경우, 일단 각 Passage에 20분씩 동등한 시간 투자를 염두에 둘 필요가 있다. 첫 Passage에서 20분을 훌쩍 넘기고 시간이 모자라 세 번째 Passage는 거의 찍고 나오는 수험생들이 많은데 이러면 7.0 이상의 고득점을 받기가 상당히 어려워진다. 풀다가 시간을 너무 많이 끄는 문제는 과감하게 찍고 넘어가야 내가 풀 수 있는 뒷문제를 놓치지 않게 된다.

또한 자신의 전공과 관련되거나 친숙한 내용의 지문은 가장 먼저 풀도록 한다. 보통 이러한 지문에서 자기 영어 실력보다 더 높은 점수를 획득할 수 있기에, 시간 압박이 적은 초반에 문제를 풀어 확실히 점수를 챙기도록 한다.

General Training 모듈의 경우, Section 1과 Section 2가 상대적으로 쉽게 나오기에 35분 이내에 Section 1과 2를 풀도록 하고, 나머지 25분 이상을 Section 3에 투자한다.

아직 자신의 Reading 점수가 5.5 이하인 수험생들은, 먼저 Section 3 주제가 자신에게 친근한 주제인지를 파악하고 그렇지 않은 경우에는, Section 1과 2에 40분 정도 투자하도록 한다. 이는 Section 3보다 상대적으로 쉬운 Section 1과 2에서 최대한 많은 점수를 챙기기 위함이다.

General Training이 Academic보다 상대적으로 쉽지만, 점수는 생각만큼 잘 나오지 않는다. 그 이유는 General Training은 Academic보다 2~3문제를 더 많이 맞혀야 Academic과 같은 점수가 나오기 때문이다.

IELTS on paper로 시험을 응시할 경우, 시험 시간을 시험장 교실 앞 스크린에 크게 띄운 전자 시계나 벽걸이 시계 등을 통해 시험 중 시간을 확인할 수 있다.

IELTS on computer로 시험을 응시할 경우, 아래와 같이 모니터 상단에서 남은 시간을 알 수 있다: 49 minutes left – 49분 남음.

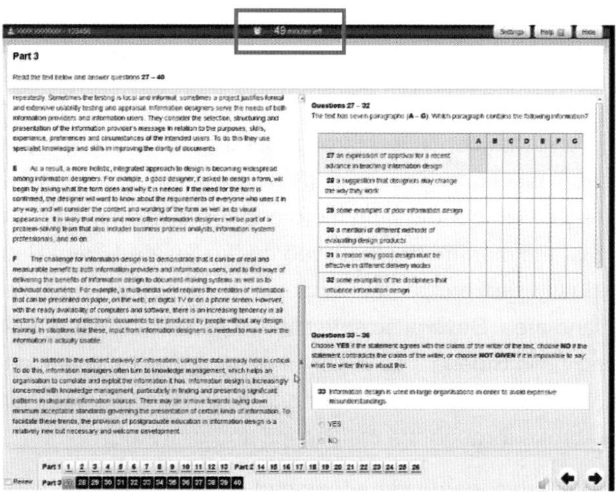

화면 출처: IELTS Official, IELTS on computer, video tutorial – Reading

참고로 컴퓨터용 시험은 초 단위가 나오지 않기에 **1 minute left**라고 나오면 시험을 빨리 마무리 지어야 된다. 뒤에 몇 초가 남았는지 모르는 상황에서 문제를 계속 풀려고 하다가 갑자기 시험이 종료되어 시험 화면이 없어지면 그대로 답안지 제출이 되기 때문이다.

Passage 다음 실전 문제(Questions 1-13)를 20분 이내에 풀어 보자.

The Woolly Mammoth

The definitive factor that caused the extinction of the woolly mammoth has been highly controversial for a long time. When the last glaciation period ended approximately 15,000 years ago, woolly mammoth populations were flourishing. Although the glaciers were melting, temperatures were still low enough to be comfortable for the mammoth, and for the plant life on which it depended. In fact, the conditions were perfect for growing the mammoth's preferred foods, and the cold temperatures prevented the development of terrain that could impede the foraging routes of mammoth populations.

The transition from the Late Pleistocene epoch to the Holocene epoch, around 12,000 years ago, saw a marked reduction in the distribution range of mammoth populations. A steady increase in global temperature brought about significant changes to the mammoth's environment. Grasslands rich in herbs and nutrients were gradually replaced by forested areas, leading to a shortage of viable habitat for several megafaunal species such as the woolly mammoth. The rising temperatures were unsuitable for growth of the mammoth's preferred foods, such as willows, and instead allowed nutrient-deficient conifers to grow and thrive. In addition to impenetrably dense forests, soft marshlands formed, creating geographic barriers that greatly limited the movement and foraging range of mammoths.

The warming trend that continued throughout the Holocene epoch was accompanied by a significant shrinking of glaciers and rising sea levels, and many scientists have argued that these were contributing factors to the extinction of the mammoth. Studies have shown that the mammoths that lived on the isolated Saint Paul Island off the coast of Alaska gradually died out as the rising sea levels caused a decrease of as much as 90% of total land area. Several scientists have proposed that a cause of mammoth population decline in Siberia was largely drowning due to significant changes to glaciers. It is believed that, while traveling to new grazing areas, hundreds of thousands of mammoths broke through the melting ice and drowned.

However, such notable warming periods had occurred several times throughout the previous ice age and had never resulted in any megafaunal extinctions, so it would be shortsighted to say that climate change alone led to the extinction of the mammoth. Another significant contributing factor was the spread of human populations throughout northern Eurasia and the Americas, and the development and refinement of new hunting techniques.

Evidence has been found that indicates that humans learned to adapt themselves to the harsher climates of the regions where mammoths resided. Once humans had figured out how to survive in the cold temperatures, then it was possible for them to hunt mammoths everywhere. Although humans had hunted woolly mammoths in Siberia for thousands of years, it wasn't until the last ice age that hunters crossed the Bering Strait and began killing mammoths in Alaska and the Yukon. As early as 1.8 million years ago, Homo erectus is known to have consumed mammoth meat, although it cannot be proven that this was a result of successful hunting rather than simple scavenging.

More conclusive proof of humans hunting mammoths can be found when studying later human populations. A 50,000-year-old site in England, and various sites dating from 15,000 to 45,000 years old throughout Europe, have yielded mammoth bones whose condition indicates that early man did indeed become adept at hunting and butchering mammoths. Evidence has also been found that primitive dwellings were often constructed by Neanderthals using the bones of mammoths. However, several leading paleontologists have argued that bones of dead mammals that have been trampled by other large mammals may bear the same appearance of those that have come from a butchered animal, and therefore it is impossible to rule out trampling when studying bones from seemingly butchered mammoths.

In the past, theories about the extinction of the woolly mammoth generally focused on one factor as the underlying cause, whether that be climate change, hunting by humans, or something different entirely such as a meteor impact. However, recent paleontological research in North America paints a clearer picture of the demise of woolly mammoths. By creating the most comprehensive maps to date of all the changes that occurred during the mammoth's existence, researchers have shown beyond all doubt that the extinction did not result from any single factor, but from a combination of habitat loss as a result of climate change and overhunting by humans.

Using radiocarbon dating of fossils, scientists have created maps of the changing locations of mammoth herds, human settlements, forests, marshlands, and plant species over several thousand years, and then cross-referenced this data with corresponding data related to climate change. The research takes into account more than one thousand mammoth radiocarbon dates, approximately six hundred peatland dates, and almost five hundred tree and plant species dates, as well as a large number of dates taken from known Paleolithic archaeological sites. After obtaining samples from each site, and radiocarbon dating each of them, scientists were able to create a database that could be used to learn more about thousands of previously dated mammoth samples. This extensive research allowed the researchers to develop a definitive map that unites paleobotanical, paleontological, genetic, archaeological and paleoclimate data to give us an accurate representation of the combined factors leading to the extinction of the woolly mammoth.

Questions 1-4

Choose ***NO MORE THAN TWO WORDS*** *from the passage for each answer.*

Write your answers in boxes 1-4 on your answer sheet.

1 What was known to be a plant commonly eaten by mammoths?

2 Where were mammoths known to be hunted before they were hunted in Alaska?

3 What were found at sites throughout Europe?

4 What did early humans build using parts from mammoths?

Questions 5-8

Label the diagram below.

Choose ***NO MORE THAN TWO WORDS*** *from the passage for each answer.*

Write your answers in boxes 5-8 on your answer sheet.

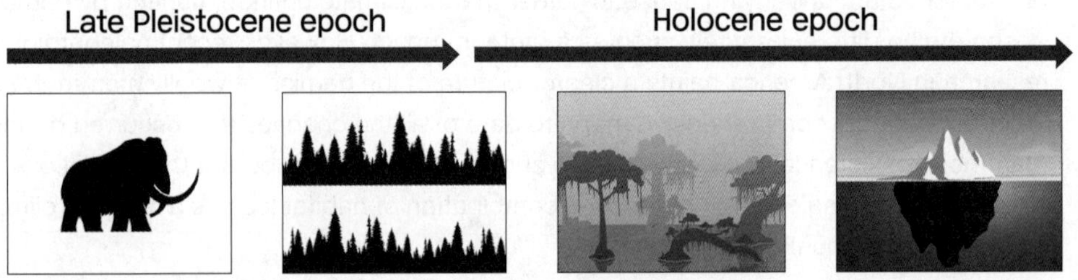

Late Pleistocene epoch

Holocene epoch

Mammoth populations thrive due to an abundance of plant life, and **5** .... is easy due to the absence of difficult terrain.	Rising temperatures result in forested areas taking the place of nutrient-rich **6** .... that contained the mammoth's preferred foods.	**7** .... such as forests and marshlands increasingly restrict the movement of mammoth populations searching for food.	Vast numbers of mammoths perish due to **8** .... as a result of melting ice and rising sea levels.

Questions 9 and 10

Choose ***TWO*** *letters,* ***A-E****.*

Write the correct letters in boxes 9 and 10 on your answer sheet.

According to the information in the passage, which **TWO** factors contributed to mammoth extinction?

A competition between animal species
B strains of new diseases
C a decrease in viable habitat
D periods of low temperatures
E interaction with humans

Questions 11 and 12

Choose ***TWO*** *letters,* ***A-E****.*

Write the correct letters in boxes 11 and 12 on your answer sheet.

Which **TWO** types of data does the writer mention that scientists have recently used to study the extinction of mammoths in North America?

A ice cores removed from glaciers
B carbon dating of plant species
C changes to mammoth bone structure
D historical data related to changes in climate
E analysis of primitive tools and weapons

Question 13

Choose the correct letter, ***A, B, C*** *or* ***D****.*

Write the correct letter in box 13 on your answer sheet.

13 What would be the most suitable subtitle for the article?

A How mammoths evolved to adapt to increasingly harsh climates
B The mutually beneficial relationship between humans and mammoths
C Searching for a definitive reason for the disappearance of the mammoth
D New evidence shows that mammoths survived longer than previously thought

UNIT 11

READING Skills 5 - General Training Section 1

오늘의 학습 목표

1. General Training Section 1의 문제 유형과 글의 종류 및 내용을 파악한다.
2. 20분이란 시간 내에 Practice Test(두 개의 글이 있는 Section 하나)를 풀어본 후, IELTS READING 정복 비법(Unit 6)대로 철저한 복습을 한다.

General Training

General Training은 이민 및 취업용 시험이기에, General Training 지문의 내용 역시 이와 관련된 일상 및 직장 생활에서 접할 수 있는 글이 출제된다. 특히 논문과 전공 서적 등의 긴 글을 읽고 이해하는 Academic과 다르게, General Training은 보다 쉽고 짧은 글들이 출제된다. 즉, Academic 모듈이 3개의 긴 지문이 나왔던 반면, General Training은 총 5개의 지문이 나온다. 이때 처음 두 개 글이 Section 1을, 뒤 이은 두 개의 글이 Section 2를, 마지막 하나의 긴 지문이 Section 3를 구성한다. Section 3의 경우, Academic 모듈처럼 하나의 긴 Passage에 13문제가 출제되며, 문제 유형과 글의 성격 역시 Academic 모듈과 유사하다.

Academic/General Training Reading 본 교재 활용법

Unit 6~10은 Academic과 General Training Section 3 내용이기에 Academic과 General Training 수험생 모두 학습해야 한다. 다만 Unit 11과 12는 General Training Section 1과 2 부분으로 General Training 수험생만 학습하면 된다.

Section 1 특징

Section 1에서는 일상 생활에서 흔히 접할 수 있는 생활 정보, 규정, 광고 등의 글이 두 개 출제된다. 이 때, 두 개의 글에 각각 7문제가 출제되어 한 Section에 총 14문제가 나오게 된다. 두 글 간에는 아무런 연관성이 없기에 각 글에 7문제는 관련 지문 내 정보만 활용해서 풀어야 된다.

Section 1의 두 개 글 중 하나는 보통 한 쪽 분량으로 여러 항목 문단으로 나누어진 광고문 또는 정보지가 출제된다. 이렇게 여러 항목 문단이 등장하는 글은 Matching information(정보가 포함된 문단 고르기) 문제 유형으로 출제된다.

나머지 한 개 글은 통으로 된 생활 정보지 또는 생활과 관련된 공공기관 가이드라인인데, 역시 한 쪽 분량으로 보통 T/F/NG(정보 일치 여부) 문제 유형이 출제된다.

Section 1 빈출 용어 정리

Section 1에 출제되는 내용이 관광, 시설, 제품 소개 관련 용어이기에, 이러한 용어에 친숙하지 않으면 문제를 푸는데 어려움이 많다. 따라서 시험보기 전까지 다음의 빈출 용어를 반드시 숙지한다.

attraction	명소	exhibit	전시하다, 전시물
conservation	보존	venue	장소
itinerary	일정(표)	general practitioner (gp)	일반의, 초진의(영국/호주 등에서는 1차 진료 시 GP 방문을 해야 한다. 심각한 병 등으로 진단되어 2차 진료가 필요하다면 병원을 직접 연계해준다.)
furnished	가구가 비치된	resident	거주자, 거주하는
attendee	참석자	attendance	참석, 출석
catering	음식 제공업	carer	돌보는 사람
symptom	증상	infection	감염
diabetes	당뇨병	flu	독감
sculpture	조각(품)	botanical	식물의
concessionary pass	(학생/노인) 할인권	passenger	승객
pedestrian	보행자	congestion	교통체증
coast	해안	cliff	절벽
instructor	강사	endangered species	멸종 위기에 처한 종
extinction	멸종	enclosure	울타리로 둘러싼 땅
fauna	동물군	flora	식물군
facility	시설	amenity	편의시설
come with	~이 딸려 있다	accompany	동반하다
plaza	광장, 쇼핑센터	concourse	(공항, 역) 중앙 홀
affordable	가격이 알맞은	voucher	상품권, 할인권
terms and conditions	약관, 계약조건	guarantee	품질보증(서)
cuisine	요리, 요리법	culinary	요리의
authentic	진품의	aesthetic	심미적인
complimentary	무료의	manor	대저택
palace	궁전	tomb	무덤
castle	성	ruin	유적
souvenir	기념품	donation	기부

Section 1 다음 실전 문제(Questions 1-14)를 20분 이내에 풀어 보자.

Read the text below and answer Questions 1-7.

Things to See and Do in the Scottish Highlands!

A. Glen Corrie Eco Park

At Glen Corrie Eco Park we not only care for animals that are indigenous to Scotland, but many other birds, mammals, and reptiles from all corners of the planet! Visitors can watch our scheduled feedings and have their picture taken with some of our most impressive creatures for a small fee.

B. Fraser Manor

Fraser Manor was the family home of the renowned Fraser family, whose most notable member was the 18th-century architect James Fraser. Fraser designed the manor himself and it remains unchanged and immaculate to this day. Many of his original blueprints are on display throughout the home.

C. Scottish Heritage Centre

This is a fun, educational attraction for the whole family. You can enjoy more than 150 indoor exhibits that include historical tools and weapons, artwork, and children's games and toys, and then stroll around the recreated 16th-century village in the grounds behind the building.

D. Loch Marr Nature Trails

Visitors can enjoy the stunning views of Loch Marr while walking along the nature trails during any season. Even in winter, appropriate hiking gear can be rented from the visitor center. Picnic areas are available on some of the trails, and you can even stay there overnight for a small fee per tent.

E. Carnegie Castle

This castle is little more than a ruin these days, but it still carries much cultural significance. It played a pivotal role in several historical conflicts, and many of the original structures were destroyed. However, visitors can learn a lot during a guided tour, and the area is known as a popular spot for fishing and birdwatching.

F. Melrose Hall

Melrose Hall is an impressive 19th-century mansion that hosts a wide variety of cultural performance all year round. Check the schedule online and buy tickets for Scottish country dancing performances or the annual Highland Games. It can also be hired out for weddings and large-scale celebrations.

정답 및 해설 p.052

Questions 1-7

Look at the six visitor attractions located in the Scottish Highlands, ***A-F****.*

For which visitor attraction are the following statements true?

Write the correct letter, ***A-F****, in boxes 1-7 on your answer sheet.*

NB *You may use any letter more than once.*

1 People can pay to have their photograph taken here.

2 People can hold a social event at this location.

3 Visitors can see a building that was damaged during a battle here.

4 Camping is available all year round here.

5 Visitors can see animals from various countries here.

6 Building designs are exhibited to the public here.

7 Visitors can see modern replicas of old buildings here.

Read the text below and answer Questions 8-14.

Brisbane Health Clinic, Australia
Making an Appointment with a GP

Please phone or e-mail our clinic as far in advance as possible if you wish to schedule an appointment. When we schedule a doctor's appointment for you, we will automatically schedule a 10-minute appointment. If you are concerned that you will require more time, please let us know and we will do our best to accommodate you. For example, if you are a newly registered family meeting your GP for the first time, 30 minutes is recommended. When making the appointment, please state whether you would prefer to see a health professional of the same gender. Also, if you feel that you may require a translator, this can be arranged for you in advance, for most languages. We understand that emergencies come up and your plans may change. If you cannot keep your appointment, please call us no later than the day before.

How can you prepare for your appointment?
A little preparation can help you to get the most out of your appointment. Think about what outcomes you hope to achieve from your meeting with the doctor. It can be beneficial to bring some written records about specific symptoms you are experiencing. It is very useful to the doctor if you write down when the symptoms occurred, how long they lasted and whether any activities make them worse. Also, make sure that you know the medical history of your family. If you are not sure, then ask your family members. Gather all current or recent prescriptions or medication containers and bring them to show to the doctor, and if you have had any recent medical tests, bring the results of those with you as well. Lastly, allow plenty of time to travel to the clinic so that you do not miss your appointment.

How should you pay for your appointment?
We are pleased to inform you that our clinic uses the Australian bulk billing system, which means that all standard services at our clinic are covered fully by Medicare. In other words, when you come to an appointment, we will bill Medicare directly and will not ask you for anything. However, certain treatments and procedures such as travel vaccinations and mole removal are not covered, nor are prescribed items such as hearing aids, glasses, or contact lenses.

Questions 8-14

Do the following statements agree with the information given in the text?

In boxes 8-14 on your answer sheet, write

TRUE	*if the statement agrees with the information*
FALSE	*if the statement contradicts the information*
NOT GIVEN	*if there is no information on this*

8 Extended appointments are available upon request.

9 Doctors at the clinic can speak a variety of languages.

10 Appointments must be canceled at least two days in advance.

11 Patients are encouraged to bring notes about their condition.

12 Prescriptions can be picked up by a family member.

13 The clinic has opted out of the Australian Medicare program.

14 Patients will need to pay for travel vaccinations themselves.

UNIT 12

READING Skills 6 - General Training Section 2

오늘의 학습 목표

1. General Training Section 2의 문제 유형과 글의 종류 및 내용을 파악한다.
2. 20분이란 시간 내에 Practice Test(두 개의 글이 있는 Section 하나)를 풀어본 후, IELTS READING 정복 비법(Unit 6)대로 철저한 복습을 한다.

Section 2 특징

Section 2에서는 취업, 직장 생활, 업무 규정, 그리고 비즈니스 관련한 글 두 개가 출제되며 각각의 글은 한 쪽 분량으로 총 13문제로 구성되어 있다. Section 1과 마찬가지로 Section 2의 두 글 간에는 아무런 연관성이 없기 때문에 각각의 지문에 딸린 문제는 관련 지문 정보만 활용해서 풀면 된다.

Section 2는 Completion(빈칸 채우기) 문제 유형이 출제되는데, 이 중에서도 Sentence(문장), Note(노트 메모), Summary(요약문), 그리고 Flowchart(순서도)가 제시된다.

Section 2 빈출 용어 정리

Section 2에 출제되는 내용이 직업 관련 용어이기에, 이러한 용어에 친숙하지 않으면 문제를 푸는데 어려움이 많다. 따라서 시험보기 전까지 아래의 빈출 용어를 반드시 숙지한다.

curriculum vitae = CV	이력서	instruction	설명, 지시, 지침
résumé	이력서	manual	설명서, 지침
cover letter	자기소개서, 입사지원서	memorandum	메모, 사내 전언
recruit	모집하다, 신입사원	regulation	규정
employer	고용주	training	연수, 교육, 훈련
employee	피고용인	inspector	조사관, 감독관
representative	대표, 직원	certificate	증서, 자격증
shift	교대 근무	comply with	~을 지키다
customer	고객	compliance	준수, 따름
consumer	소비자	be obliged	의무가 있다
retail	소매	hazard	위험 (요소)
retire	은퇴하다, 퇴직하다	safety	안전
redundancy	정리 해고	security	보안

objective	목적, 목표	assess	평가하다
initiative	계획	enquiry (美 inquiry)	문의
scheme	계획	hospitality	접대
diploma	수료증, (대학 학습) 과정	qualification	자격 요건
job fair	취업 박람회	conference	(대규모) 회의, 학회
tenure	재임 기간	lay off	해고하다
agenda	안건	compensation	보수, 보상
quota	할당(량)	occupation	직업

Section 1 & 2 학습법

많은 IELTS 교재나 강좌들이 General Training Reading에 대해서는 특별한 학습법을 제시하지 않고 있다. 하지만 General Training Reading의 Section 1 & 2는 다른 Reading 영역과 확실히 다른 스타일이기에 이에 대한 특별한 학습법이 필요하다.

❶ 전형적인 문제 반복 학습

Section 1 & 2는 IELTS READING 중 가장 정형화된 내용과 형식으로 출제되기에, 확실하게 문제 스타일과 지문 내용을 파악하고 있으면 보다 쉽게 문제를 풀 수 있다. 따라서 가장 시험에 많이 나오는 전형적인 스타일의 문제를 반복해서 풀어야 한다.

IELTS MASTER의 모든 문제들은 최근 10년 간 시험에서 가장 많이 나오는 주제와 문제 유형을 바탕으로 가장 실제 시험과 유사하게 제작되었다. 따라서 General Training 수험생들은 본 교재의 Practice Test와 Actual Test 문제들만 확실하게 풀면 Section 1 & 2에서 고득점을 얻을 수 있다.

만일 더 많은 문제 풀이 연습이 필요하다면 시험 출제기관 Cambridge의 IELTS 시리즈 문제를 풀어 보기 바란다. 특히 Cambridge IELTS 시리즈의 경우, 번호가 클수록 최신 시험 경향을 반영하고 있기에 큰 번호부터, 17-16-15-14 순으로 풀어보면 된다. 참고로 Cambridge IELTS 시리즈는 11부터 General Training 모듈이 따로 출간되었다.

❷ 점수대에 맞게 스키밍/스캐닝 또는 정독

General Training Reading의 Section 1 & 2는 다행히 Academic 또는 Section 3보다 난이도가 낮은 편이다. 따라서 Section 두 개를 30분대에 풀 수 있어야 하는데, 이를 위해서는 스키밍/스캐닝을 통해 문제를 풀어야 한다. 하지만 Section 1 & 2의 문제는 특정 정보를 묻는 문제들이기에, 너무 빨리 읽다 보면 정보를 놓치거나 잘못 해석하여 틀리는 경우가 많다. 따라서 자신의 실력과 목표 점수에 맞게 접근할 필요가 있다.

만일 자신의 점수대가 아직 5점대 이하라면 Section 1 & 2를 정독하면서, 최대한 많은 점수를 획득하도록 한다. 하지만 현재 6점대로 7점대 이상을 원한다면 스키밍/스캐닝을 통해 보다 빨리 풀어야 한다. 만일 8점에서 9점을 원하는 수험생이라면 Section 3 역시 20분 이내로 풀 수 있는 실력이기에, Section 1 & 2에서 한 문제라도 틀리지 않기 위해 정독을 해야 한다.

Section 2 다음 실전 문제(Questions 15-27)를 20분 이내에 풀어 보자.

Read the text below and answer Questions 15-22.

Tips for Writing an Effective CV

What information should I include?

Although your goal should be to make your CV stand out from others, there is some information that should be always be included. First of all, never forget to include all of your personal details at the top of the page. You might be surprised at the number of people who have missed out on a job because they forgot to include their name, e-mail address, phone number and address on their CV. In fact, your name should be right at the top in large font; there is no need to write Curriculum Vitae! Next, add a short personal statement that clearly describes who you are, what you can offer, and what your professional and personal goals are. Keep it succinct! Limit this to one paragraph, and try to capture the attention of prospective employers.

The next section should detail all of your relevant work experience, including your job titles, the names of the companies you worked for, your dates of employment, and your main job duties. If you have any gaps in employment history, add a brief explanation. Also, always list your academic qualifications, including all relevant details related to courses and institutions. It is not always relevant to mention your hobbies, but if you feel that the information backs up your skills and helps you stand out, by all means, include this.

What vocabulary should I use?

Certain words always look attractive in any CV, such as hard-working, responsible, adaptable, reliable, and confident. On the other hand, there are some words that are seen as clichés by most employers and are best left out. These include multi-tasker, goal driven, self-motivated, detail oriented, and flexible.

How should my CV be presented?

In addition to the information contained on the CV, the way that it is presented is equally important. Limit the length to two sides of A4 paper. Any longer and a potential employer might get bored or irritated. Choose a clear, professional font such as Garamond or Calibri and use size 10.5-12 to ensure that your CV can be easily read. Give the document a well-defined structure, with sufficient spacing between sections and clear headings. Finally, never forget to make sure your spelling is correct before submitting your CV.

정답 및 해설 p.057

Questions 15-22

Complete the sentences below.

Choose ***NO MORE THAN TWO WORDS*** *from the text for each answer.*

Write your answers in boxes 15-22 on your answer sheet.

15 Instead of writing Curriculum Vitae, add your .... to the top of the page.

16 Add a .... below your contact details to explain your strengths and goals.

17 Provide explanations for any noticeable .... in your professional career.

18 While not always necessary, describe your .... if you think they are relevant to the job.

19 Avoid using vocabulary that some employers might consider ....

20 Make sure the information is easy to read by selecting an appropriate .... size.

21 Use clear headings and adequate .... to ensure the CV is structured well.

22 Check the .... on the CV before you send it to a prospective employer.

Read the text below and answer Questions 23-27.

How to Manage Work Stress

Many people arrive at work already stressed due to a hectic morning routine. This might include getting one's children ready for school, enduring rush hour traffic, and skipping breakfast for a quick cup of coffee. If you start off the day with proper planning and good nutrition, your workday will be much more manageable.

With so many people in one workplace, it is inevitable that people will disagree with one another from time to time. Perhaps you have had experiences where conflict has arisen between you and a coworker, resulting in communication problems and stress. One way to avoid this is to refrain from sharing personal opinions with coworkers about subjects like religion and politics, which can be extremely sensitive topics for some people.

One of the key contributors to stress both at home and in a work environment is a lack of organization. Make sure that your workstation is free from unnecessary clutter and you will immediately feel the psychological benefits. A tidy desktop leads to higher productivity, so keep it clear by making use of your drawers for storage.

Another significant stressor at work is physical discomfort. If you work in a job that requires you to remain seated for most of the day, make sure that your employer provides a high-quality, comfortable chair for you. Not only will this boost your mood and limit your stress, but it will reduce your risk of back pain and injury.

Despite your best efforts, you might still have had a stressful morning at work. This is why an increasing number of workers are utilizing their lunch hours for exercise. Burning some calories and working up a sweat can work wonders for people who have work stress building up inside them. Try to organize a regular routine with a group of coworkers, either at a local gym or outside when the weather is nice.

When it is finally time for you to leave work, you might dread your journey home, whether it be in a cramped subway car, or on a congested road. Listening to music has been proven to be an effective way to stay relaxed in chaotic environments, and is a surefire way to rid you of any remaining stress before you get back to your home.

Questions 23-27

Complete the notes below.

Choose ***ONE WORD ONLY*** *from the text for each answer.*

Write your answers in boxes 23-27 on your answer sheet.

Managing Work Stress

- Start your day well with good planning and a healthy breakfast.
- Try to avoid **23** .... at work by keeping your opinions about sensitive issues to yourself.
- Remove **24** .... from your work area to increase your **25** ....
- Ask your boss to give you a suitable **26** .... that will not result in any health issues.
- During your lunch break, enjoy some **27** .... with coworkers, either indoors or outdoors.
- Listen to music on your way home so that you can relax during your commute.

WRITING
MASTER

UNIT 13

IELTS WRITING에 대한 모든 것

오늘의 학습 목표

1 IELTS WRITING 시험(진행 방식, Task별 특징)을 숙지한다.
2 채점기준을 명확히 인지하고 채점기준에 따라 글을 쓰도록 연습한다.
3 구두점, 연결어, 시제 일치 및 수 일치 등에 대해 숙지한다.

IELTS WRITING 기본 정보

시험 방식	• 연필 및 지우개로 작성 • IELTS on computer는 키보드로 타이핑: 영타 250 이상이면 손글씨보다 더 빠르게 작성할 수 있음 또한 ctrl + c(복사하기), ctrl + v(붙여넣기), ctrl + z(되돌리기)의 기능도 사용할 수 있음 • IELTS on computer는 메모할 수 있는 종이와 연필도 나눠 줌 • IELTS on computer는 작성하는 답안이 저절로 저장되므로 따로 저장 버튼 누를 필요 없음
시험 시간	• 총 60분 • Task 1, 2 시간 구분 없이 연속해서 진행 (IELTS on computer는 Task 대신 Part라는 명칭을 사용) • IELTS on computer의 경우, 분 단위로 시간 표시가 되고 초 단위는 나오지 않음 따라서 마지막 1분에 1이라는 숫자가 나오면 최대한 빨리 글을 마무리 지어야 됨

글자 수

IELTS on computer는 글자 수를 자동으로 카운팅한다. 하지만 종이 시험의 경우 자신이 얼마나 적었는지 글자 수를 확인하기 어렵다. 따라서 평소 답안지에 연습할 때 자신이 한 줄에 몇 자 정도 쓰는지 파악해 두고 몇 줄 정도 쓰면 150자, 250자를 넘는지 미리 알아두자. 참고로 글자 수는 Task 1의 경우 150~200 단어, Task 2는 250~300 단어 정도 생각하고 적자.

각 Task별 특징

<table>
<tr>
<td>Task 1
[Academic]</td>
<td>

- 제시된 자료를 바탕으로 객관적으로 분석하여 기술
- 약 20분 동안 150 단어 이상 작성
- Line Graph(선 그래프), Bar Graph(막대 그래프), Pie Chart(파이 차트), Table(표), Map(지도), Diagram(도해) 중 하나 또는 두 개가 자료로 제시됨

Task 1 도표 출제율

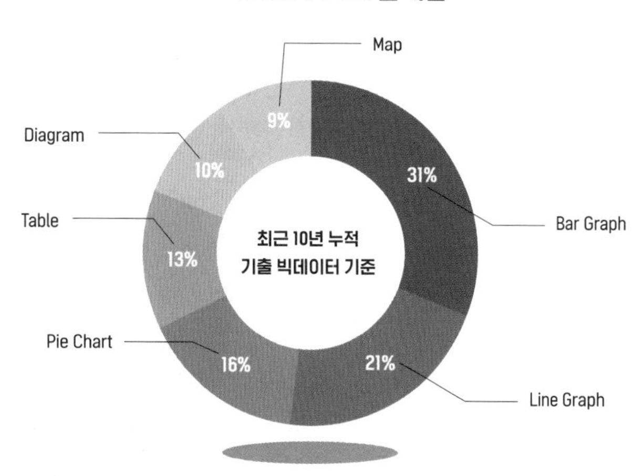

</td>
</tr>
<tr>
<td>Task 1
[General Training]</td>
<td>

- 제시된 상황에 따라 편지글 작성
- 약 20분 동안 150 단어 이상 작성
- 편지 내용과 편지를 받는 상대에 맞게 편지 톤(Formal, Semi-formal 1, Semi-formal 2, Informal) 선택

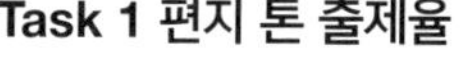

Task 1 편지 톤 출제율

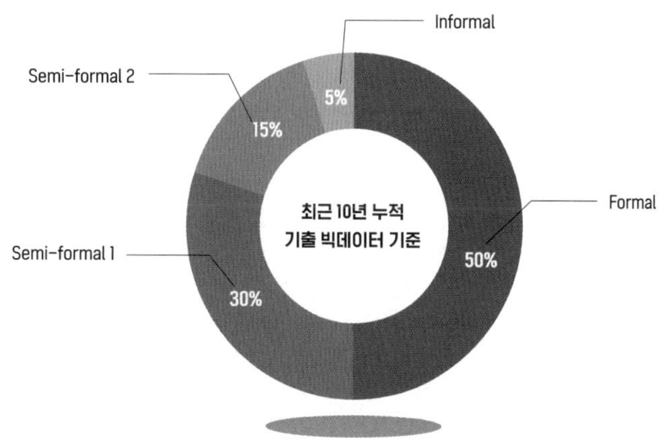

</td>
</tr>
</table>

Task 2 [Academic / General Training]	• 제시된 주제에 대해 자신의 의견을 논리적으로 표현하는 에세이 작성 • 약 40분 동안 250 단어 이상 작성 • 실제 시험에서 Academic과 General Training의 Task 2 시험 문제는 다르지만, 문제 유형은 동일함 • 문제 유형은 Both Views(제시된 두 개의 견해에 대한 생각을 묻는 문제), Agree/Disagree(제시된 견해에 대해 찬반을 묻는 문제), Advantage/Disadvantage(제시된 사항의 장점과 단점을 묻는 문제), Two Questions(두 개의 질문에 대한 답변을 진술하는 문제), Cause[Problem] & Solution(어떤 상황에 대한 원인과 그 해결책을 묻는 문제) 출제 **Task 2 문제 유형 출제율** 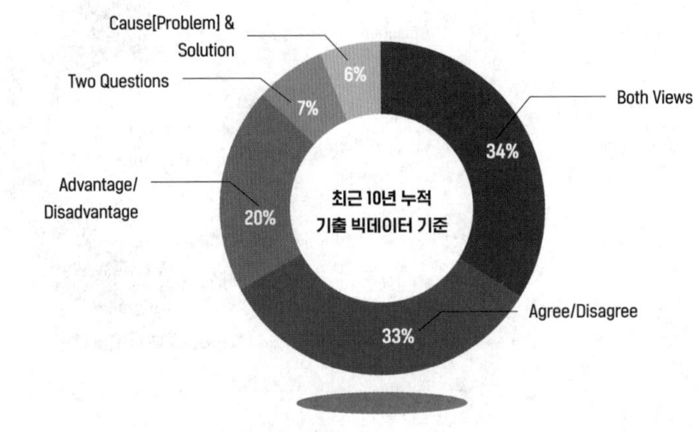

Writing과 Speaking 표현 구분

IELTS 시험에서 Writing은 격식 있는 문어체 표현인 반면에, Speaking은 보다 비격식의 구어체 표현이 사용된다. 따라서 본 교재의 Writing과 Speaking은 이러한 기준이 반영되어 각각의 답변이 다른 톤으로 작성되어 있고 수험생들도 이에 따라 공부하길 바란다.

IELTS WRITING 채점기준

IELTS WRITING은 IELTS 공식 홈페이지에서 공개한 채점기준에 따라 채점이 이루어진다. 수험생들은 아래의 채점기준 세부 내용을 숙지하여 최대한 채점기준에 부합하여 글을 쓸 수 있도록 한다.

채점 영역	채점기준	채점기준에 맞춰 글 쓰는 팁 및 구체적 평가 점수
Task Achievement (≒ Task Response) 과제 달성	• 과제의 모든 요구사항을 다룸 • 완전하게 전개된 자신의 생각 및 입장 또는 문제에 대한 답변을 명확하게 보여줌	• 문제에서 요구하는 사항들에 대해 제대로 답변하지 못하면 과제 달성 영역에서 5점대 넘기기 어려움 • Task 1[A] 그래프의 중요 사항들을 놓치지 말고 반드시 정확하게 설명 • Task 1[A] 주요 추세, 차이점 또는 단계에 대한 명확한 개괄(overview)이 없으면 5점대 넘기기 어려움 • Task 1[A] 중요하지 않은 세부사항에 초점을 맞춰 설명하면 5점대 넘기기 어려움 • Task 1[G] 처음에 편지 쓰는 목적을 분명히 밝히지 못하면 5점대 넘기기 어려움 • Task 1[G] formal, informal의 톤 일치가 안 될 경우 6점대 넘기기 어려움
Coherence and Cohesion 일관성과 응집성	• 자연스럽게 글의 응집성이 있음 • 능숙하게 문단(단락)을 구성함	• 응집 장치(접속사, 부사 등의 연결어, 앞에 단어를 받는 한정사 및 대명사) 사용(완벽한 사용은 8점 이상, 제대로 사용은 했지만 조금 적게 또는 남용하면 7점, 조금 잘못 사용하면 6점, 많이 틀리고 불충분 또는 남용하면 5점 이하) • 서론, 본론, 결론의 문단 구성이 제대로 안되면 아무리 잘 써도 일관성과 응집성 영역에서 고득점 어려움 • 글의 논리성이 떨어지면 7점 이상 고득점 어려움 • 글의 연속성이 떨어지면 6점대 넘기기 어려움
Lexical Resource 어휘력	• 다양한 어휘(같은 단어 반복 사용 안됨)를 자연스럽고 세련된 방식으로 사용함	• 오타 등 약간의 실수가 있어도 글 이해에 전혀 문제가 없으며 폭넓은 어휘를 완벽하게 사용하면 어휘력 영역에서 9점까지 가능 • 제한된 어휘 사용과 오타 등으로 글의 이해가 떨어지면 5점 정도에 머무름 • 구동사 등의 평이한 어휘보다 고급 어휘 사용 예 look into → investigate (조사하다)
Grammatical Range and Accuracy 문법의 다양성과 정확성	• 다양한 문장 형태(형식)를 유창하고 정확하게 사용함	• 다양한 문법 사항(문장의 5형식, to부정사, 동명사, 접속사, 관계대명사, 명사절, 분사구문 등)을 완벽하게 사용 • 문법적 실수가 많으면 문법 영역에서 5점 이하 점수를 받게 됨 • 복문 사용이 불충분하면 문법에서 6점 이하 점수를 받게 됨 • 구두점(punctuation) 사용이 잘못되면 7점 이상 고득점 어려움

문법 정리 1: Punctuation 구두점

IELTS WRITING에 활용할 수 있는 모든 구두점을 정리한다.

1. 마침표 full stop (.) – 북미에서는 period라고 부름

❶ 문장이 완전히 끝날 때

There is no doubt that smartphones can be beneficial for children.

스마트폰이 아이들에게 도움이 될 수 있음은 의심의 여지가 없다.

❷ 축약 또는 약자를 나타낼 때

We arrived in London at 10 am the next morning.

우리는 그 다음날 아침 열 시에 런던에 도착했다.

2. 쉼표 comma (,)

❶ 단어, 구(말 덩어리), 절(주어+동사) 등을 구분할 때

In the long run, it would be better for governments to develop green energy.

장기적으로, 정부는 친환경 에너지를 개발하는 것이 더 좋다.

❷ 나열할 때

The company expanded its operations to Russia, China, India and Korea.

그 회사는 사업을 러시아, 중국, 인도 그리고 한국에 확장했다.

3. 콜론 colon (:)

❶ 대상을 목록(단어 나열)으로 보완 설명할 때

There are three economic factors: labour costs, interest rates and government policies.

세 개의 경제적인 요인이 있다: 노동 비용, 이자율 그리고 정부 정책.

❷ 뒤 문장이 앞 문장을 구체화할 때

There was one clear piece of evidence that the policy ended up as a failure: the country continued suffering from inflation.

그 정책이 실패로 끝났다는 것에 대한 확실한 증거가 있었다: 그 나라는 계속해서 인플레이션으로 고통받았다.

➡ 콜론 뒤에 구체적인 증거가 나옴

❸ 제목을 보완 설명할 때

The title of that movie is *Eagle: The Symbol of America*.

그 영화의 제목은 '독수리: 미국의 상징'이다.

4. 세미콜론 semi-colon (;)

❶ 두 개의 대등한 절을 연결하여 보완 설명할 때(병렬 구조)

New York City is the biggest city in the US; London is the largest in the UK.

뉴욕은 미국에서 가장 큰 도시이다; 런던은 영국에서 가장 큰 도시이다.

➡ but이나 and 등의 접속사 대신 세미콜론을 사용

❷ 접속부사와 함께 쓰여, 역접이나 결과의 절을 연결하여 보완 설명할 때

The oil price increased; however, taxi fares remained unchanged.
유가가 상승했다; 그러나, 택시 요금은 변하지 않았다.

The oil price increased; therefore, taxi fares were also raised.
유가가 상승했다; 그래서, 택시 요금이 또한 인상되었다.

유의 콜론과 세미콜론은 일종의 접속사 역할을 하므로 콜론이나 세미콜론을 사용하였으면 그 다음 오는 절에 접속사가 있으면 안되고, 그 절의 처음도 대문자가 아닌 소문자로 시작해야 한다.

5. 대쉬 dash (—) vs. 하이픈 hyphen (-)

❶ 대쉬는 쉼표나 세미 콜론처럼 절을 연결하여 보완 설명할 때 사용. 다만, 쉼표나 세미 콜론보다 informal하기에 IELTS WRITING에서는 사용을 자제하자.

Thank you for a lovely evening yesterday — I really enjoyed it.
우리는 아름다운 어제 저녁에 대해 고마워 — 나는 정말로 즐거웠거든.

❷ 하이픈은 대쉬보다 짧은 가로줄로 복수의 단어들을 연결하여 하나의 단어처럼 사용할 때

Well-connected lines of trains can encourage people to drive their own cars less.
잘 연결된 철도는 사람들이 자가용을 덜 사용하도록 할 수 있다.

유의 하이픈은 줄이 바뀌어 하나의 긴 단어가 나뉘는 경우 연결되었음을 나타날 때도 사용한다. 하지만 시험에서는 단어가 나뉘어 질 것 같으면 단어를 중간에 끊지 말고 그 다음 줄에 통으로 쓰자. 그래야 가독성이 좋아 채점자가 읽기 편하다.

6. 작은따옴표(single quotation mark) vs. 큰따옴표 (double quotation mark)

❶ 전문 용어 또는 단어를 강조할 때, 또는 단어 의미가 다를 때 작은따옴표 사용

We are very disappointed by her 'apology' since she didn't mean it at all.
우리는 그녀의 '사과'에 매우 실망했는데, 왜냐하면 그녀는 전혀 사과의 의도를 담지 않았기 때문이다.

❷ 인용구 사용

국어에서는 큰따옴표만이 직접 인용에 사용되지만 영어에서는 큰따옴표와 작은따옴표 모두 사용 가능하다. 특히 영국과 호주는 작은따옴표를, 북미는 큰따옴표를 선호한다. 참고로 마침표나 쉼표, 느낌표, 물음표는 따옴표 안에 들어간다.

Socrates said, "To know thyself is the beginning of wisdom."
소크라테스는, "그대 자신을 아는 것이 지혜의 시작이다"고 말했다.

IELTS WRITING 정복 비법

1 문제 분석 및 아웃라인 잡기(Task Achievement/Response)

문제에서 무엇을 묻는지 파악하고, 이에 대한 자신의 답변을 정리하고 각 문단에 답안을 어떻게 배치할지 아웃라인을 잡는다. 각 Task마다 약 1~3분을 이렇게 문제 분석과 아웃라인 잡는데 투자한다. 이때 아웃라인은 한글이 아닌 영어로 잡는다. 컴퓨터 기반 시험의 경우 한글 타자가 불가능하고, 영어로 아웃라인을 잡는 것이 답안 작성을 더 빨리 할 수 있다.

2 영어권 영작 기본 이해(Coherence and Cohesion)

영어권 글쓰기에서, 글의 짜임새는 굉장히 중요하다. 글 도입부인 서론에서 앞으로 어떤 내용을 쓸지에 대해서 언급해야 하고, 본론에서는 구체적 설명이 들어간다. 그리고 결론에서는 한번 더 핵심 내용을 강조하거나 요약해서 글의 결론을 내린다.

글의 가장 큰 비중을 차지하는 본론은, 보통 IELTS Task 2에서는 2~3 문단 정도로 이루어진다. 문단 또는 단락이란, 하나의 생각이 들어있는 생각의 덩어리이다. 즉 한 문단에 여러 생각들을 쏟아내면 안된다. Task 2와 같이 자신의 의견을 표출하는 글에서, 본론 각 문단의 첫 문장은 주제 문장 또는 주장(topic sentence or argument)으로 쓰고, 그 다음 이러한 주제 또는 주장을 뒷받침하는 근거 문장(supporting sentence)을 쓴다. 그리고 나서는 예문이나 부연 설명 문장(supporting details)을 써주고, 마지막 문장으로 이 문단을 마무리 짓는 결론 문장(concluding sentence)을 쓸 수 있다.

이러한 문단 구성은 영어권 학교에서 가르치는 일반적인 글쓰기 형식으로 IELTS 채점자들도 이러한 형식에 익숙하므로, 우리도 이렇게 글을 써야 한다. 한국인들은 미괄식 또는 마지막에 극적 반전으로 자신의 주장을 하려고 하지만, 이러면 IELTS 채점자들이 글을 이해하기 어렵다. 따라서 영어권 글쓰기 형식에 맞게 두괄식으로 글을 쓰고 각 문장 또는 문단을 잇는 응집 장치(접속사, 부사 등의 연결어, 앞에 단어를 받는 한정사 및 대명사)를 사용하여 글을 쓴다면, writing에서 6.0 이상을 받는 것은 결코 어려운 일이 아니다.

3 통으로 암기(Lexical Resource)

자신이 외우고자 하는 단어가 사용된 문장이나 구(말 덩어리)를 통으로 암기하여 통째로 사용하도록 한다. 이렇게 해야 자연스러우면서도 정확하게 단어를 사용할 수 있는데, 단어들이 특정한 문장 구조나 의미 상황에서 맞춤형으로 사용되는 경우가 많기 때문이다.

4 문법 공부를 통해 제대로 된 문장 사용(Grammatical Range and Accuracy)

'표명하였다 안락사에 대한 의견들을 대학교수들이.' 어느 한 외국인이 이렇게 한국어를 썼다면, 우리는 '표명하다'와 '안락사'라는 어려운 한국말을 이 외국인이 아는 것에 놀랄 수도 있지만, 정확히 무슨 말인지 알기 어렵다고 느낄 것이다. 우리가 아무리 어려운 어휘를 많이 알고 있어도 기본 문법이 틀리면, 채점자는 좋은 점수를 주기 어렵다. 따라서 문법 공부는 선택이 아닌 필수이다. 아직도 늦지 않았다. 본 교재 곳곳에서 알려주는 문법 팁들을 차근차근 공부하다 보면 중요한 문법 요소들에 대한 개념이 잡힐 것이다.

5 매일 직접 써 보기

컴퓨터 시험을 준비하는 수험생은 컴퓨터 워드 프로그램에 타자를 치면서, 일반 종이 시험을 준비하는 수험생은 실제 시험지(시원스쿨LAB 교재/MP3에서 다운로드 가능)에 직접 연필로 작성하면서 연습을 한다. 반드시 매일 Writing 최소 한 문제를 풀면서 한 달 이상 공부하고 나서 시험장에 들어간다.

6 교정(Proofreading)

다 쓴 글에 대해서 2~3분 동안 시제 일치, 주어-동사 수 일치를 반드시 확인하며 교정(proofreading)을 하자. 이 두 가지는 영문법의 기본으로 짧은 시간에 쉽게 검토 가능한 영역이다.

① 시제 일치

동사의 시제는 기본적으로 이와 어울리는 부사 및 수식어와 함께 사용한다.

recently 최근에	현재완료 또는 과거시제	예문 정부가 최근에 친환경 에너지 기술을 채택한다. Governments recently adopt green energy technology. (X) ▶ recently는 현재시제에 사용할 수 없다. → Governments have recently adopted green energy technology. (O) Governments recently adopted green energy technology. (O)
since 이래로	since + 과거시점, 주절은 완료시제	예문 2010년 이래로, 20살 이하 인구가 급격하게 줄고 있다. Since 2010, the population of under-20s dramatically decreased. (X) ▶ since가 '~이래로'로 쓰이면, 주절은 과거시제가 아닌 현재완료시제를 쓴다. → Since 2010, the population of under-20s has dramatically decreased. (O)
과거시점 (yesterday, last night, 1988 등)	과거시제	예문 그 수치는 2000년에 최고치에 도달했다. The figure had reached its peak in 2000. (X) ▶ 과거시점에는 과거시제를 사용한다. → The figure reached its peak in 2000. (O)
미래시점 (tomorrow, 2050 등)	미래시제	예문 그 정책은 내년부터 시행될 것이다. The policy is going to take effect from next year. (O) ▶ 예문처럼 be going to를 써서 미래를 표현할 수 있다. 다만 뉘앙스가 조금 다르고 예외가 있는 경우도 있다. IELTS WRITING에서는 will을 사용하면 대부분 논란의 여지없이 미래시제를 표현할 수 있기에, 간단하게 will을 사용하기 바란다. → The policy will take effect from next year. (O)

② 주어-동사 수 일치

현재 시제에서 주어가 단수이면 일반동사에 -s/-es를 붙이거나 be동사 is를 사용하고, 주어가 복수이면 -s/-es를 붙이지 않거나 be동사 are를 사용해야 한다.

예제 아래 문장의 틀린 부분을 고치시오.

There are many things that influences the academic achievements and friendships of school children.

학생들의 학업 성취와 교우 관계에 영향을 주는 많은 것들이 있다.

정답 influences → influence
주격 관계대명사 that은 many things 복수 명사를 받으므로 단수 동사 influences가 아닌 복수 동사인 influence가 되어야 한다.

WRITING

PRACTICE TEST

Proofreading **다음 문장에서 잘못된 부분을 교정해 보자.**

1 임대 주거 가정 비율이 2011년까지 증가했지만, 2012년에는 급격하게 떨어졌다.
The percentage of households in rented accommodation has increased by 2011, but it dropped dramatically in 2012.

* dramatically 급격하게

2 수질 오염이 최근에 전 세계적으로 사망률 상승을 이끈다.
Water pollution recently leads to an increase in mortality rates all over the world.

* mortality rate 사망률

3 유가가 상승했지만, 택시 요금은 변하지 않았다.
The oil price increased, however, taxi fares remained unchanged.

* remain 상태를 유지하다, 남아있다

4 천연 자원 보존 실패의 이유는 만연해 있는 물질 만능 주의이다.
The reason for the failure of preserving natural resources are pervasive materialism.

* pervasive 만연한 materialism 물질 만능 주의

정답 및 해설 p.064

5 그 철로가 건설된 이래로, 클로버대일에 교통 체증이 현저하게 줄었다.
Since the railway was built, traffic jams in Cloverdale decreased remarkably.

* traffic jam 교통 체증 remarkably 현저하게

6 사람들은 예상치 못한 상황에 맞닥뜨리면 취약해지는 경향이 있다.
People tends to become vulnerable when they encounter unexpected situations.

* vulnerable 취약한 encounter 맞닥뜨리다 unexpected 예상치 못한

7 어른들과 비교해 볼 때 아이들은 외부세계와 더 제한된 접촉을 가질 것이다.
Children are more likely to have limited contact with the outside world; compared to adults.

* compared to ~과 비교해 볼 때

8 더 많은 도로를 짓는 것은 도로를 이용한 수송에 대한 더 많은 수요를 유도하고, 결국 교통혼잡을 야기한다.
Building more roads induces more demand for road transport, which result in congestion.

* induce 유도하다, 초래하다 result in 결국 ~을 야기하다, 그 결과 ~가 되다 congestion 체증, 혼잡

Task 1 - 수치 데이터

오늘의 학습 목표

1 Academic Task 1 문제 풀이 방법을 숙지한다.
2 수치 데이터(Bar Graph, Line Graph, Pie Chart, Table)에 자주 사용되는 표현을 익힌다.
3 Academic Task 1 채점기준에 따라 글을 쓰고, 완성된 글을 채점기준에 따라 평가해본다.

Academic Task 1 문제 풀이 방법

기본적인 Task 1 문제 풀이 순서는 '문제 분석 → 아웃라인 잡기 → 글쓰기 → 교정'이다. 가장 빈출되는 Bar Graph(막대 그래프) 유형 예시를 통해 자세한 문제 풀이 방법을 알아보자.

Sample Question

You should spend about 20 minutes on this task.

The chart below shows the numbers of cars rented and privately-owned in New Zealand between 1970 and 2015.

Summarise the information by selecting and reporting the main features, and make comparisons where relevant.

Write at least 150 words.

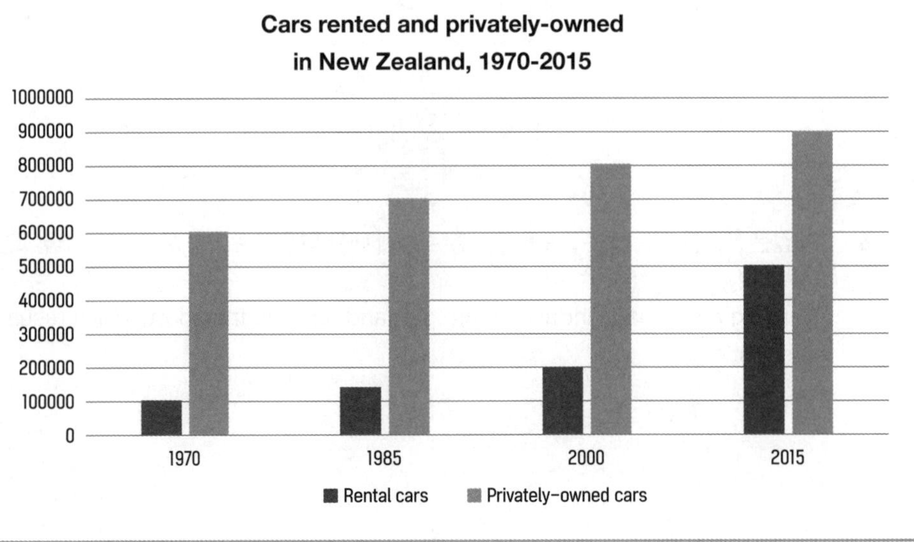

1 문제 분석

You should spend about 20 minutes on this task.

이 문제에 약 20분을 사용한다. ▶ 첫 줄은 모든 Task 1에 항상 똑같이 나오는 문구로 문제 풀이 시간을 언급한다.

The chart below shows the numbers of cars rented and privately-owned in New Zealand between 1970 and 2015.

아래의 차트는 1970년과 2015년 사이에 뉴질랜드에서 자가용과 렌트카 수를 보여준다.

Summarise the information by selecting and reporting the main features, and make comparisons where relevant.

주요 특징들을 선별하여 기술함으로써 정보를 요약하고 관련 정보를 비교하라.

▶ 항상 Task 1 박스 안에 두 문장이 나오는데 첫 문장은 차트 설명, 다음 문장은 항상 같은 내용으로 주요 특징을 요약하여 설명하고, 관련 정보를 비교하기를 요구한다.

→ Task Achievement(과제 달성) 영역으로 반드시 이렇게 답안 작성해야 됨

Write at least 150 words.

최소 150 단어를 적어라. ▶ Task 1에 항상 똑같이 나오는 문구로 150 단어 이상 작성을 요구한다.

유의 Academic Task 1은 객관적으로 자료를 분석하고 글을 쓰는 것이다. 자료에 없는 내용을 쓰면 감점이 된다. 예를 들어, 본 예제에서 전체적으로 자동차 수가 증가하기에 교통 체증과 환경 오염이 예상된다고 글을 쓰면 안된다. 반드시 자료에 있는 내용만 쓰자!

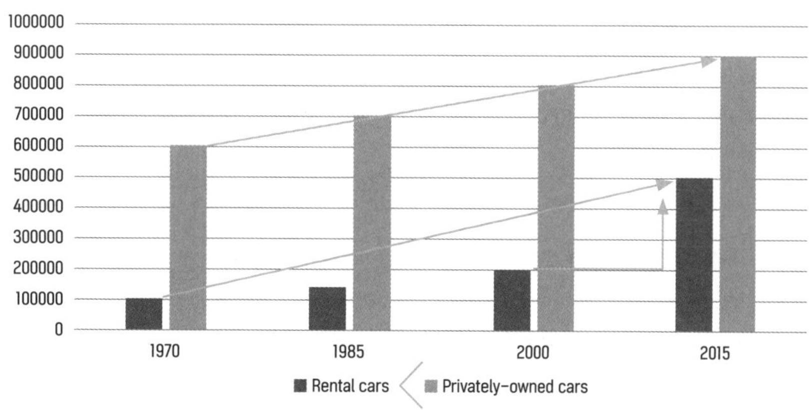

▶ 도표는 항상 박스 안 첫 문장을 읽으면서 함께 검토하며, X축/Y축, 단위(unit)에 유의하고 전체 추세 요약, 주요 특징과 비교 가능 정보 위주로 선별하여 아웃라인을 잡는다.

→ 완벽한 영문이 아니라 영어로 키워드를 나열하기만 하면 됨

WRITING

2 아웃라인 잡기

문제 분석에서 선별한 내용들을 서론 - 본론1 - 본론2에 적는다.

Task 1의 경우, 서론 첫 문장은 문제 박스 안 첫 문장 패러프레이징, 두 번째 문장은 전체적인 특징 요약을 적는다. 이때 전체적인 특징 요약은 트렌드(추세)를 뜻하므로 수치 같은 구체적인 정보는 서론에서 적지 않고 본론에서 적는다.

본론은 두 문단이 적당하며, 두 개의 각 본론은 '주요 특징 문장 + 세부 수치 문장'의 구조로 구성된다. 특히 본론에서 데이터 간 비교가 반드시 기술되어야 한다.

Task 1의 경우 이미 서론 두 번째 문장에서 전체 내용 요약을 하였기에 결론은 특별히 적지 않아도 된다.

서론 문제 박스 안 첫 문장 패러프레이징 + 전체적인 특징 요약	*Paraphrasing* *+ the numbers of both rental and privately-owned cars increase* 렌트카와 자가용 모두 숫자가 상승함
본론 1 선별된 주요 특징과 비교 가능 정보	주요 특징 1 *- during the period, there were always more p-o cars than rental cars* 기간 동안 항상 자가용 수가 렌트카보다 많음
본론 2 선별된 주요 특징과 비교 가능 정보	주요 특징 2 *- both numbers increase steadily until 2015, when the rental car numbers rise significantly* 렌트카, 자가용 모두 꾸준하게 상승하다가 2015년에 렌트카 수가 더 급격하게 상승

3 글쓰기

① 서론 첫 문장: 문제 패러프레이징

The chart below shows **the numbers of** cars rented **and privately-owned in New Zealand between 1970 and 2015.**

→ This graph illustrates **the numbers of** rental **and privately-owned** vehicles **in New Zealand from 1970 to 2015.**
이 그래프는 1970년부터 2015년까지 뉴질랜드에서 렌트 및 자가 차량의 수를 보여준다.

② 서론 두 번째 문장: 전체 추세 요약

For both categories, it is evident that **the total numbers increased over the years, and the total numbers of privately-owned cars remained markedly higher than** those **of rental cars.**
두 영역 모두, 분명하게 그 기간에 걸쳐 전체 수가 증가했고, 전체 자가용 수가 렌트카보다 훨씬 높게 유지되었다.

* 서론 두 번째 문장에 자주 사용되는 템플릿: Overall, it is evident that ~ 전반적으로, 분명히 ~ 하다
We can see immediately that ~ ~임을 쉽게 알 수 있다

* those: the total numbers of 반복 사용을 피하고 coherence and cohesion을 높이기 위해 대명사 사용

③ 본론 1: 주요 특징 중 하나에 대한 문장(본론 1의 주제 문장)

First of all, both categories increased during this time period.
우선, 두 영역 모두 이 기간동안 증가했다.

④ 본론 1: 주제 문장을 뒷받침하는 세부 수치 문장들

In 1970, the total number of privately-owned cars was 600,000. That number grew by 100,000 increments every fifteen years to become 900,000 in 2015. Likewise, the number of rental cars grew over this time period, from only 100,000 in 1970 to 500,000 in 2015.
1970년에, 전체 자가용 수는 60만이었다. 그 수는 매 15년마다 10만 씩 증가해서 2015년에는 90만이 되었다. 마찬가지로, 같은 기간동안 렌트카 수가 1970년에 10만대에서 2015년에 50만대까지 증가했다.

* That: 앞에 600,000를 받으며 문장을 이어줌 ➜ coherence and cohesion을 높이기 위해 대명사 사용

⑤ 본론 2: 주요 특징 중 하나에 대한 문장(본론 2의 주제 문장)

Another intriguing detail on this chart is the drastic increase in the number of rental cars between 2000 and 2015.
이 차트에서 또다른 흥미로운 사항은 2000년과 2015년 사이에 렌트카 수의 급격한 증가이다.

⑥ 본론 2: 주제 문장을 뒷받침하는 세부 수치 문장들

In prior years, the figures for both rental cars and privately-owned cars increased consistently, by 50,000 and 100,000, respectively. However, between 2000 and 2015, the number of rental cars in New Zealand soared from 200,000 to 500,000, while the growth in privately-owned cars remained the same.
이전 연도들에서, 렌트카와 자가용 모두에 대한 수치가 일정하게, 각각 5만, 10만씩 증가했다. 그러나 2000년과 2015년 사이에, 뉴질랜드 렌트카 수가 20만에서 50만으로 치솟았지만, 자가용 증가는 같은 수준을 유지했다.

4 교정

다 쓴 글에 대해서 2~3분 동안 시제 일치, 주어-동사 수 일치를 반드시 확인하며 교정(proofreading)을 하자. 이 두 가지는 영문법의 기본으로 짧은 시간에 쉽게 검토 가능한 영역이다.

> 예문 In 1970, the total number of privately-owned cars was 600,000.
> 과거시제 / 단수명사 주어 / 단수동사/과거시제동사

5 최종답안

This graph illustrates the numbers of rental and privately-owned vehicles in New Zealand from 1970 to 2015. For both categories, it is evident that the total numbers increased over the years, and the numbers of privately-owned cars remained markedly higher than those of rental cars.	이 그래프는 1970년부터 2015년까지 뉴질랜드에서 렌트 및 자가 차량의 수를 보여준다. 두 영역 모두, 분명하게 그 기간에 걸쳐 전체 수가 증가했고, 전체 자가용 수가 렌트카보다 훨씬 높게 유지되었다.

WRITING

First of all, both categories increased during this time period. In 1970, the total number of privately-owned cars was 600,000. That number grew by 100,000 increments every fifteen years to become 900,000 in 2015. Likewise, the number of rental cars grew over this time period, from only 100,000 in 1970 to 500,000 in 2015.	우선, 두 영역 모두 이 기간동안 증가했다. 1970년에, 전체 자가용 수는 60만이었다. 그 수는 매 15년마다 10만씩 증가해서 2015년에는 90만이 되었다. 마찬가지로, 같은 기간동안 렌트카 수가 1970년에 10만대에서 2015년에 50만대까지 증가했다.
Another intriguing detail on this chart is the drastic increase in the number of rental cars between 2000 and 2015. In prior years, the figures for both rental cars and privately-owned cars increased consistently, by 50,000 and 100,000, respectively. However, between 2000 and 2015, the number of rental cars in New Zealand soared from 200,000 to 500,000, while the growth in privately-owned cars remained the same. (165 words)	이 차트에서 또다른 흥미로운 사항은 2000년과 2015년 사이에 렌트카 수의 급격한 증가이다. 이전 연도들에서, 렌트카와 자가용 모두에 대한 수치가 일정하게, 각각 5만, 10만씩 증가했다. 그러나 2000년과 2015년 사이에, 뉴질랜드 렌트카 수가 20만에서 50만으로 치솟았지만, 자가용 증가는 같은 수준을 유지했다.

Paraphrasing(패러프레이징) 방법

패러프레이징을 하지 않고 문제에서 나온 단어, 또는 자신이 쓴 단어를 반복해서 사용하면 좋은 점수를 받을 수 없다. 다음은 Academic Task 1에서 가장 많이 사용되는 패러프레이징 표현들이다.

도표	• graph(x, y축 있는 도표)를 chart(차트)나 data(자료 정보)로 표현 가능 유의 chart가 graph보다 큰 개념으로 x, y축이 있는 도표, 즉 그래프는 차트에 포함된다. 또한 모든 차트와 그래프는 data이다. (data > chart > graph)
보여주다	• show(보여주다) = display(보여주다) = indicate(나타내다) = present(알려주다) = illustrate(자세히 보여주다)
기간	• from 1981 to 2010 (1981년에서 2010년까지) = between 1981 and 2010 • during the period 그 기간 동안(앞에서 명시된 기간을 받을 때) = over the years • during the 30-year period 그 30년 동안(기간을 구체적으로 받을 때) = over the 30 years
수	• number(수) = figure(수치) 유의 셀 수 없는 것은 amount, 셀 수 있는 것은 number 사용
연령 그룹	• older people(노년층) • younger people(젊은 층) • people in their 20s(20대 사람들) = those aged 20-29(20-29살 사람들) • the 20-29 age group(20-29 연령 그룹) = the age group of 20-29 years old

수치 데이터에 자주 사용되는 표현 정리

Bar Graph(막대 그래프), Line Graph(선 그래프), Pie Chart(파이 차트), Table(표)은 모두 수치 데이터를 분석하는 유형으로, 아래와 같은 비교/대조 표현들이 수치를 분석할 때 자주 사용된다.

- ~에 대한 수치 **figure for ~**

  렌트카와 자가용 모두에 대한 수치가 일정하게 증가했다.

  The figures for both rental cars and privately-owned cars increased consistently.

- 그에 반해서/이와 대조적으로 **In contrast(=By contrast), ~**

  그에 반해서, 혼자 사는 사람의 비율이 2011년 20%에서 2017년에 32%로 눈에 띄게 올랐다.

  In contrast, the percentage of people staying single markedly increased from 20 per cent in 2011 to around 32 per cent in 2017.

- 그러나 ~과 달리 **However, unlike ~ ,**

  그러나 2017년과 달리, 2018년에는 수치가 내려가기 시작했다.

  However, unlike in 2017, the figure began to go down in 2018.

- ~과 비교해 볼 때 **compared to ~**

  2015년과 비교해 볼 때, 2025년에는 더 높은 수준의 물부족이 예측된다.

  Compared to 2015, a higher level of water scarcity is expected in 2025.

- ~면에서 나머지로부터 두드러지다 **stand out from the rest in terms of ~**

  그 기간동안 경세 성장 면에서 호주가 가장 두드러졌다.

  Australia stood out from the rest in terms of economic growth during the period.

- 각각 **respectively**

  26-35살 그리고 51-65살 그룹은 각각 35%와 32%를 차지한다.

  The 26-35 and 51-65 age groups account for 35% and 32%, respectively.

- A, B, C를 합친 것보다 **than A, B and C combined**

  2017년에 중국은 베트남, 인도네시아, 말레이시아를 합친 것보다 더 많은 전자 기기를 생산했다.

  China produced more electronic devices than Vietnam, Indonesia and Malaysia combined in 2017.

- 두 배가 되다 **double**

  1960년에서 2000년까지 중국의 인구가 두 배가 되었다.

  The population of China doubled from 1960 to 2000.

- ~의 반 **half the ~**

  도표는 질문을 받은 사람 중 약 반이 행복하다고 대답했음을 보여준다.

  The chart illustrates that approximately half the people questioned answered that they were happy.

• 상승/하락세를 보이다 show an upward/downward trend

아래 선 그래프는 제시된 기간 동안 상승세를 보인다.

The line graph below shows an upward trend during the period.

• ~을 차지하다 account for(=make up=constitute=comprise=represent)

2005년에 그 국가에서 농업이 전체 산업의 27%를 차지했다.

Agriculture accounted for 27% of the total industry in the country in 2005.

Academic Task 1에서 혼동되는 전치사 정리

❶ at ~에 (위치/지점)

2010년에 이민자 수가 약 30만명에 머물렀다.

The number of immigrants stayed at approximately 300,000 in 2010.

❷ in ~에 (연도/국가)

2015년에 뉴질랜드에서 버스 요금이 호주 버스 요금보다 더 비쌌다.

The bus fares in New Zealand were more expensive than those in Australia in 2015.

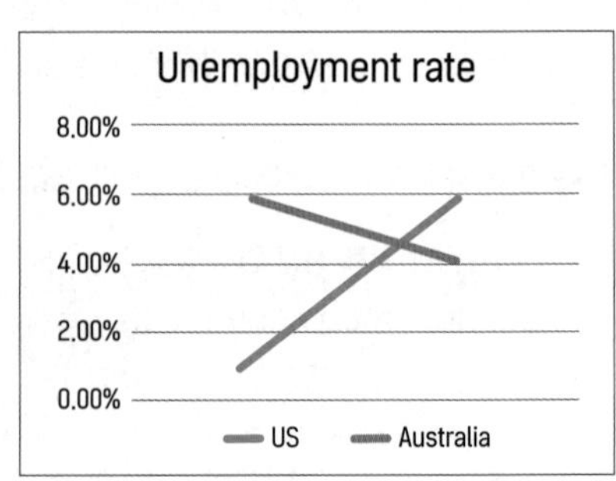

❸ to ~까지(도달 수치)

미국 실업율이 6%까지 급격하게 상승했다.

The US unemployment rate rose drastically to 6%.

❹ by ~만큼(변동량)

호주 실업율이 2%만큼 떨어졌다.

Australia's unemployment rate dropped by 2%.

유의 그래프에서 to와 by 사용이 헷갈리는 경우가 많은데,
상기 그래프처럼 변동량은 by, 도달 수치를 표현할 때는 to를 사용한다.

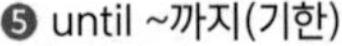

❺ until ~까지(기한)

2015년까지 그 수치는 변함없이 유지되었다.

The figure stayed constant until 2015.

❻ for ~동안(숫자 기간)

채소 가격이 3개월동안 폭등했다.

Vegetable prices soared for three months.

❼ during ~동안(특정 기간)

유제품 가격이 그 3개월동안 폭락했다.

Dairy prices plunged during the three months.

유의 숫자 앞에 the가 붙으면 특정 기간이 되어 for 대신 during이 사용된다.

Table 문제 풀이 연습

You should spend about 20 minutes on this task.

The table below shows data for the largest lakes by area and their depths.

Summarise the information by selecting and reporting the main features, and make comparisons where relevant.

Write at least 150 words.

The Largest Lakes In The World

Ranking	Lake	Area (m^2)	Maximum depth (m)
1	Caspian Sea	371,000	1,025
2	Lake Superior	82,100	406
3	Lake Victoria	69,500	82
4	Lake Huron	59,600	229
5	Lake Michigan	57,800	281
6	Lake Tanganyika	32,600	1,470
7	Lake Baikal	31,500	1,637
8	Great Bear Lake	31,300	446
9	Lake Malawi	28,900	695
10	Great Slave Lake	28,600	614

1 문제 분석

아래의 표는 가장 큰 호수들의 면적과 깊이를 보여준다.
주요 특징들을 선별하여 기술함으로써 정보를 요약하고 관련 정보를 비교하라.

세계에서 가장 큰 호수들

순위	호수	면적·(m^2)	최고 깊이
1	카스피해	371,000	1,025
2	슈피리어호	82,100	406
3	빅토리아호	69,500	82
4	휴런호	59,600	229
5	미시간호	57,800	281
6	탕가니카호	32,600	1,470
7	바이칼호	31,500	1,637
8	그레이트베어호	31,300	446
9	말라위호	28,900	695
10	그레이트슬레이브호	28,600	614

2 아웃라인 잡기

서론 문제 박스 안 첫 문장 패러프레이징 + 전체적인 추세 요약	*Paraphrasing* *+ the largest(Caspian Sea), the deepest(Lake Baikal)*
본론 1 첫 번째 주요 특징과 비교 가능 정보	*<Area>* *- the largest(Caspian Sea, 371,000m^2)* *- the smallest(Lake Malawi, Great Slave Lake)(28,900m^2, 28,600m^2 respectively)*
본론 2 두 번째 주요 특징과 비교 가능 정보	*<Depth>* *- the largest lake's depth(1,025m)* *- the deepest(Lake Baikal 1,637m → Lake Tanganyika 1,470m)* *- the shallowest(Lake Victoria 82m)*

유의 주어진 표는 면적에 따라 가장 큰 호수의 순위가 나오고, 그 호수의 깊이가 추가적으로 주어진 것이다. 세계에서 가장 큰 호수들을 나열한 것이지, 세계에서 가장 깊은 호수들을 나열한 것이 아님에 주의한다.

3 모범답안

The table below lists the largest lakes according to their area and provides information about their maximum depths. It is evident that the Caspian Sea stands out from the rest as the largest in area by far, and Lakes Tanganyika and Baikal are significantly deeper than the rest.	아래 표는 면적에 따라 가장 큰 호수들을 나열하고 그 호수들의 최고 깊이에 대한 정보를 제공한다. 분명하게, 카스피해가 훨씬 면적이 크기에 나머지보다 두드러지고, 탕가니카호와 바이칼호가 나머지보다 현저하게 더 깊다.
The Caspian Sea, with an area of 371,000 m^2, dwarfs the other lakes on the table; in fact, none of the other lakes are even larger than 90,000m^2. Interestingly, the largest lake is also the only one on the table to be referred to as a sea. On the other hand, the smallest lakes on the table, Lake Malawi and Great Slave Lake, are 28,900m^2 and 28,600m^2, respectively.	카스피해는 371,000m^2로 표에 다른 호수들을 작아 보이게 한다; 사실, 다른 그 어떤 호수도 90,000m^2보다도 더 큰 것은 없다. 흥미롭게도 가장 큰 호수는 또한 유일하게 표에서 바다라고 불린다. 한편, 표에서 가장 작은 호수들은 말라위호와 그레이트슬레이브호로 각각 28,900m^2와 28,600m^2이다.
While the Caspian Sea also has an impressive depth of 1,025 metres, it is not the deepest among them; Lake Baikal is with a maximum depth of 1,637 metres. Lake Tanganyika follows it with a depth of 1,470 metres. In stark contrast, Lake Victoria is relatively shallow with a maximum depth of 82 metres. (169 words)	카스피해가 1,025 미터로 깊이도 상당하지만, 그중 가장 깊은 것은 아니다; 바이칼호가 1,637 미터로 최고 깊이이다. 탕가니카호는 1,470 미터 깊이로 그 뒤를 따른다. 아주 대조적으로, 빅토리아호는 82 미터 깊이로 상대적으로 얕다.

I Vocabulary & Expressions I

according to ~에 따라 area 면적 depth 깊이 stand out 두드러지다 significantly 현저하게 dwarf 작아 보이게 만들다 refer to ~로 지칭하다 impressive 인상적인 in stark contrast 아주 대조적으로 shallow 얕은

모범답안 활용법

본 교재 내 모든 Writing & Speaking 모범답안은 영국·미국 원어민 전문가들이 채점표 9.0 기준에 맞게 작성하였다. 따라서 본 모범답안에 나오는 어휘, 표현, 아이디어들 중 자신이 취할 수 있는 것은 취하여 점수를 향상시키도록 하자. 이때 아무리 노력해도 외우기 어려운 표현과 아이디어는 과감히 포기하고 자신에게 익숙한 표현이나 아이디어로 바꿔서 나만의 모범답안을 만들면서 공부하도록 한다.

Line Graph 문제 풀이 연습

You should spend about 20 minutes on this task.

The graph below shows the percentage of the Japanese population by age group from 1940 to 2040.

Summarise the information by selecting and reporting the main features, and make comparisons where relevant.

Write at least 150 words.

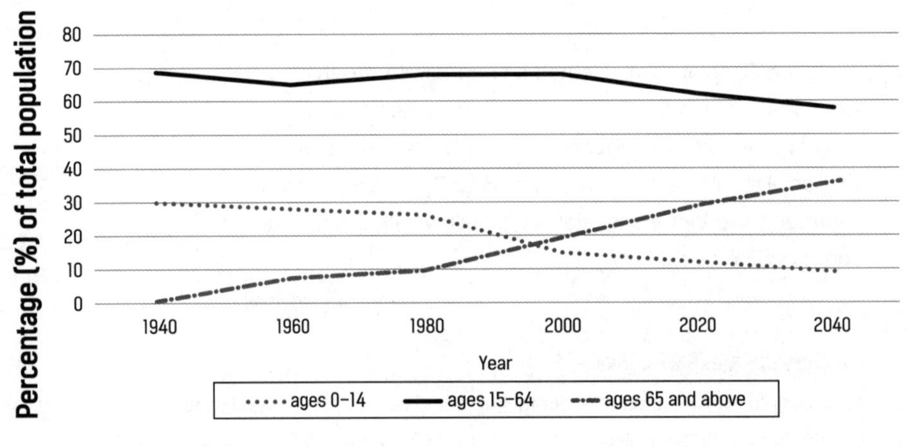

1 문제 분석

아래의 선 그래프는 일본에서 세 연령대의 1940-2040년 간 인구 비율 변동을 보여준다.
인구 비율이 줄어드는 연령대와 반대로 증가하는 연령대의 추세를 비교하여 작성한다.

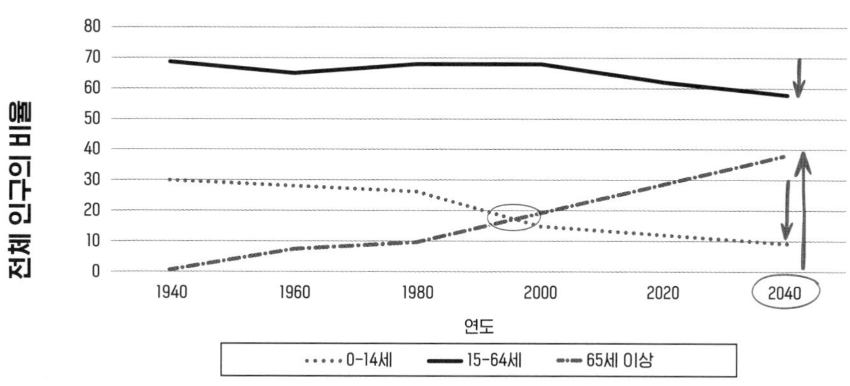

2 아웃라인 잡기

서론 문제 박스 안 첫 문장 패러프레이징 + 전체적인 추세 요약	*Paraphrasing* *+ majority of the Japanese population are between the ages 15 and 64* *+ decrease(ages 0-14, ages 15-64), increase(ages 65 and above)*
본론 1 첫 번째 주요 특징과 비교 가능 정보	*<ages 0-14, ages 15-64>* *- 1940: 0-14 = 30%, 15-64 = 70%* *- 15-64 decrease to 60% in 2020, 55% by 2040* *- 0-14 decrease to 10% by 2040*
본론 2 두 번째 주요 특징과 비교 가능 정보	*<ages 65 and above>* *- 1940 = almost 0%* *- surpass 0-14 age group by 2000*

WRITING

3 모범답안

The line graph displays the proportion of three age groups within the Japanese population since 1940 with projections to 2040. Overall, the majority has consistently been in the 15 to 64 age range, with a decreasing percentage of younger individuals and a growing proportion of older adults. This trend is projected to continue until 2040.	선 그래프는 1940년부터 2040년까지 일본 인구 내 세 연령대의 비율을 보여 준다. 전반적으로, 15~64세 연령대가 지속적으로 다수를 차지하고 있으며, 젊은 층의 비율은 감소하고 고령층의 비율은 증가하고 있다. 이러한 추세는 2040년까지 계속될 것으로 예상된다.
Initially, those between ages 15 and 64 accounted for 70%, making them the dominant group. This proportion remained steady until 2000 but has since declined moderately, constituting 60% in 2020. Although projected to decrease further to 55% by 2040, this age group is still expected to remain the majority. Similarly, the percentage of individuals aged 0 to 14, which was 30% in 1940, has gradually decreased and is predicted to reach 10% by 2040.	먼저, 15세에서 64세 사이의 사람들이 70%를 차지하여, 가장 두드러진 연령대가 되었다. 이 비율은 2000년까지 꾸준히 유지되었지만 이후 완만하게 감소하여 2020년에는 60%를 차지했다. 2040년에는 55%로 더 감소할 것으로 예상되지만, 이 연령대가 여전히 다수로 남아 있을 것으로 예상된다. 마찬가지로, 1940년 30%였던 0세에서 14세의 비율도 점차 감소하여 2040년에는 10%에 이를 것으로 예측된다.
In contrast, there were almost no individuals aged 65 and older in the population in 1940. However, their numbers have increased substantially, eventually surpassing those of the 0 to 14 age group by 2000, making them the second-largest category. This upward trend is likely to persist. (174 words)	반면, 1940년에는 65세 이상의 인구는 거의 없었다. 그러나, 그 수가 크게 증가하여, 2000년에는 0~14세 연령대의 인구를 추월했다. 이러한 증가 추세는 앞으로도 지속될 것으로 보인다.

I Vocabulary & Expressions I

projection 예상, 예측 consistently 지속적으로 be projected ~로 예상되다, 예측되다 initially 처음에, 우선 account for ~을 차지하다 dominant 우세한, 두드러진 remain 남아 있다, 유지하다 steady 꾸준히 age range 연령대 moderately 완만하게 constitute ~을 차지하다 similarly 마찬가지로 gradually 점진적으로 be predicted 예상되다 in contrast 반면, 대조적으로 substantially 상당하게, 크게 eventually 결국, 궁극적으로 surpass ~을 추월하다 upward 증가하는, 위쪽을 향하는 persist 지속되다

Pie Chart 문제 풀이 연습

You should spend about 20 minutes on this task.

The charts below show the percentage of male and female workers in three different sectors in Country A and Country B.

Summarise the information by selecting and reporting the main features, and make comparisons where relevant.

Write at least 150 words.

MALE WORKERS IN COUNTRY A

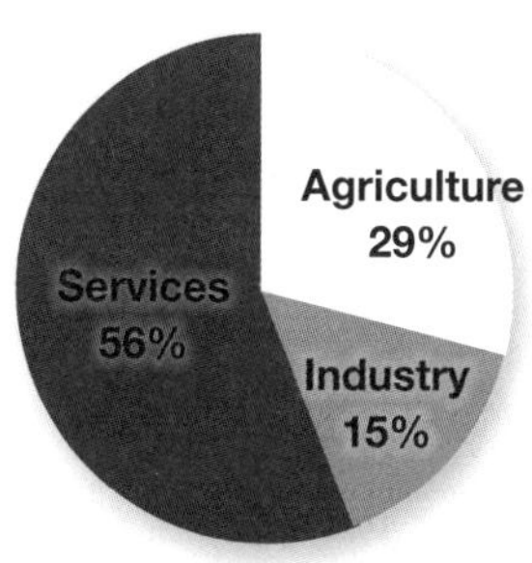

FEMALE WORKERS IN COUNTRY A

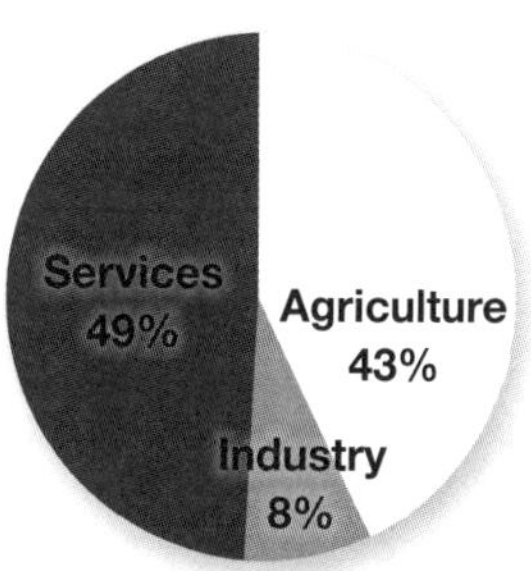

MALE WORKERS IN COUNTRY B

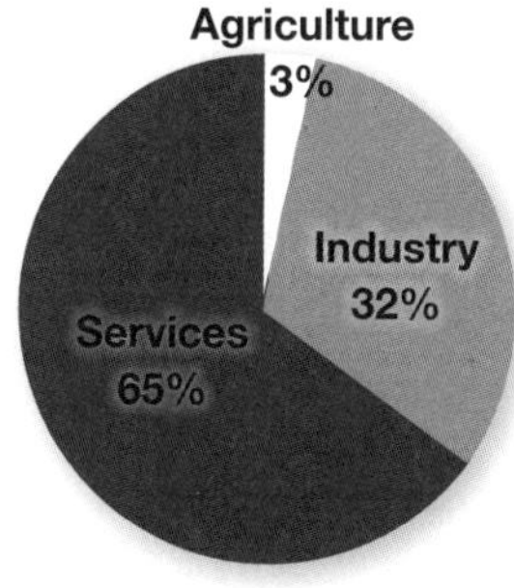

FEMALE WORKERS IN COUNTRY B

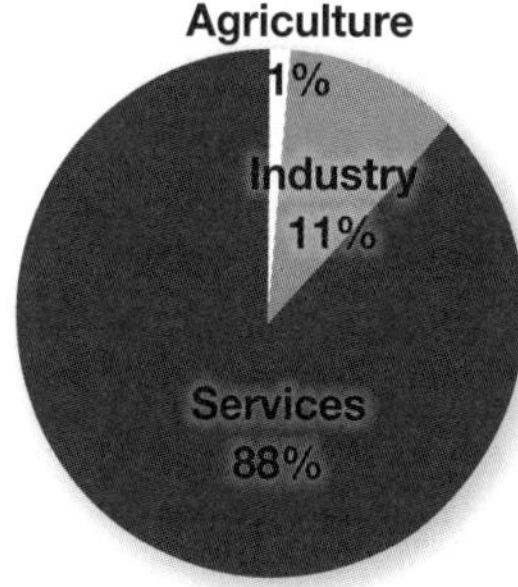

WRITING

1 문제 분석

아래의 파이 차트는 A, B 두 국가에서 남성과 여성 근로자가 각각 어느 업종에 종사하는지 비율을 보여준다. 국가별로 구분하여 주요 특징을 기술하되, 국가 간, 성별 간 차이점을 비교하여 작성한다.

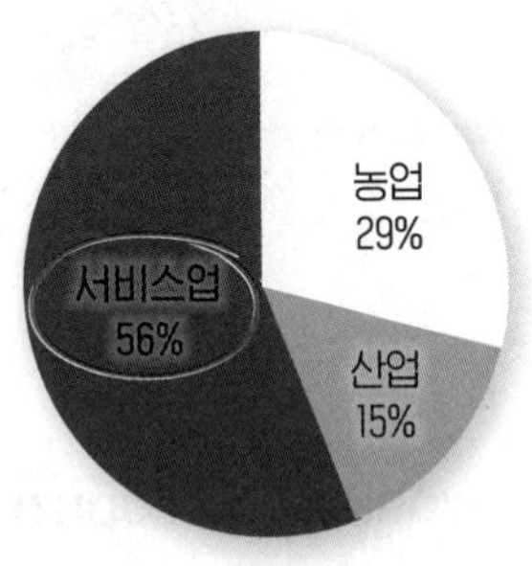

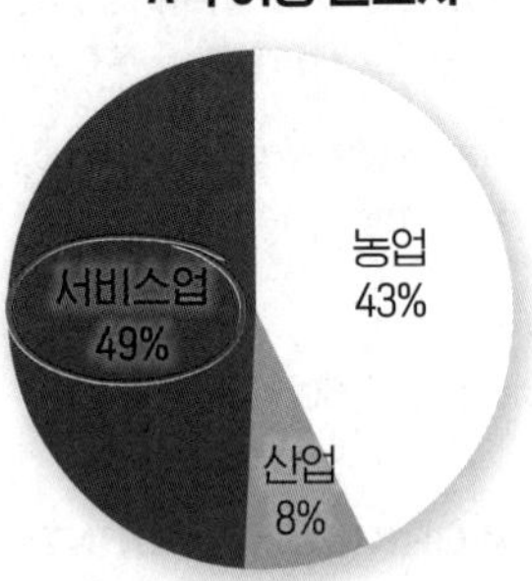

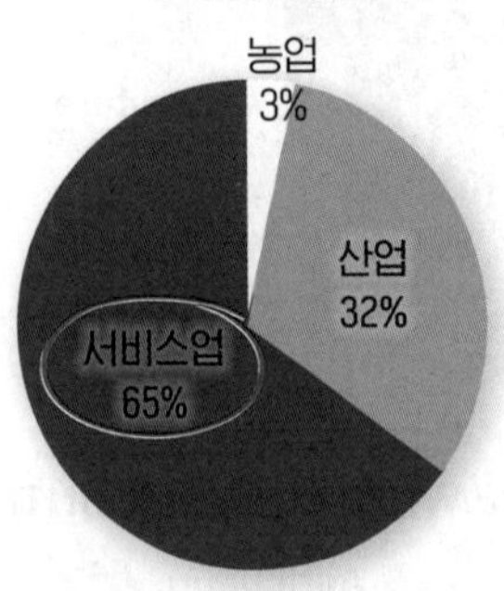

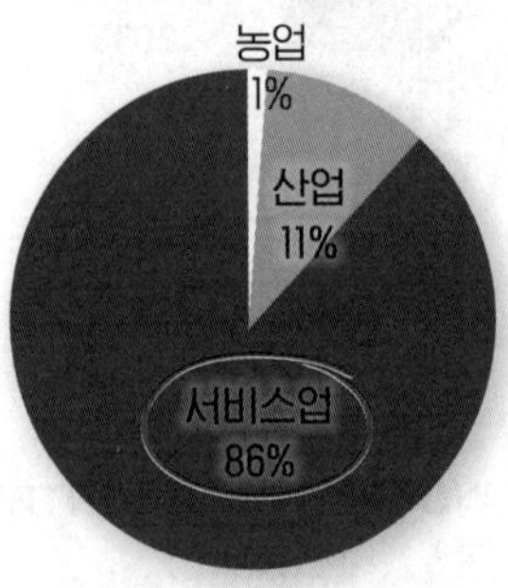

2 아웃라인 잡기

서론 문제 박스 안 첫 문장 패러프레이징 + 전체적인 추세 요약	*Paraphrasing* *+ the largest(services)*
본론 1 첫 번째 주요 특징과 비교 가능 정보	*<Country A>* *- services: male 56%, female 49%* *- agriculture: male 29%, female 43%* *- industry: male 15%, female 8%*
본론 2 두 번째 주요 특징과 비교 가능 정보	*<Country B>* *- services: male 65%, female 88%* *- industry: male 32%, female 11%* *- agriculture: male 3%, female 1%*

3 모범답안

The four pie charts compare the percentage of men and women working in three distinct fields in Country A and Country B. Overall, despite differences in distribution between the two countries, the services sector stands out in both, representing the largest share of employment.	4개의 파이 차트는 A국가와 B국가에서 세 가지 다른 분야에서 일하는 남성과 여성의 비율을 비교한다. 전반적으로, 두 국가 간의 분포에는 차이가 있지만, 두 국가 모두 서비스 부문이 가장 큰 고용 부분을 나타내며 눈에 띈다.
In Country A, a significant proportion of the workforce is employed in services, with 56% of men and 49% of women. In contrast, the industry sector has the lowest representation, with only 15% of men and 8% of women engaged in this area. Interestingly, the agriculture sector shows a markedly higher percentage of female workers than male workers, accounting for 43%, compared to 29% for men.	A 국가에서는, 남성이 56%, 여성이 49%로 상당한 비율의 인력이 서비스업에 고용되어 있다. 반면, 산업 부분은 남성의 15%, 여성의 8%만이 이 분야에 종사하고 있어 가장 낮게 표시되어 있다. 흥미롭게도, 농업 분야에서는 현저히 더 높은 여성 근로자의 비율을 보여주는데, 남성 근로자 29%에 비해, 43%를 차지한다.
In Country B, the services sector is even more dominant, employing the majority of both women and men, at 88% and 65%, respectively. Compared to Country A, a higher percentage of both men and women in Country B work in the industry sector, which has about three times more men (32%) than women (11%). Meanwhile, unlike in Country A, only a small share of the population is involved in agriculture, with men making up 3% and women just 1%.	B 국가에서는, 서비스 부문이 훨씬 더 우세하여 여성과 남성 모두 각각 88%와 65%로 대다수를 고용하고 있다. A 국가에 비해, B 국가에서는 남성과 여성 모두 산업에서 일하는 비율이 더 높으며, 남성(32%)이 여성(11%)보다 약 3배 더 많다. 한편, A 국가와 달리, 인구의 소수만이 농업에 종사하는데, 남성이 3%, 여성은 단지 1%를 이룬다.
(189 words)	

| Vocabulary & Expressions |

distinct 다른, 별개의, 독특한 distribution 분포 stand out 눈에 띄다, 두드러지다 represent ~을 나타내다, ~에 해당하다 share 몫, 부분 significant 상당한 workforce 인력 representation 표시, 표현 account for ~을 차지하다 compared to ~에 비해 dominant 우세한 meanwhile 한편 be involve in ~에 종사하다 make up ~을 이루다

WRITING

Bar Graph 문제 풀이 연습

You should spend about 20 minutes on this task.

The graph below shows greenhouse gas (GHG) emissions by country in 2014 and 2016.

Summarise the information by selecting and reporting the main features, and make comparisons where relevant.

Write at least 150 words.

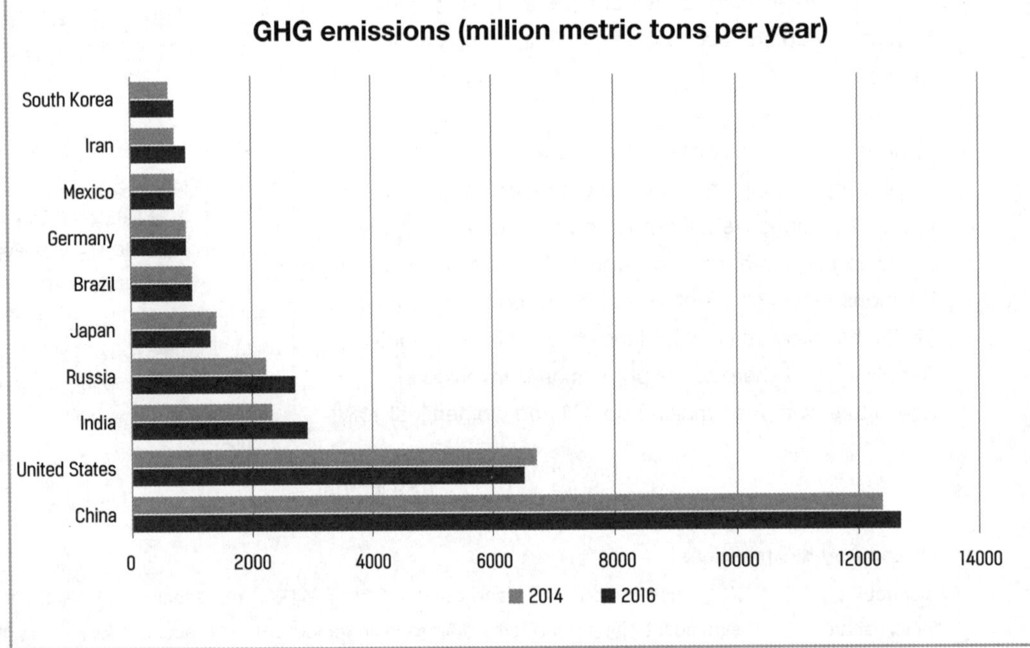

1 문제 분석

아래의 막대 그래프는 국가별 2014년과 2016년 국가별 온실가스 배출량을 보여준다.
배출량이 많은 국가, 배출량이 줄어든 예외적인 국가를 주요 특징으로 선별하여 기술한다.

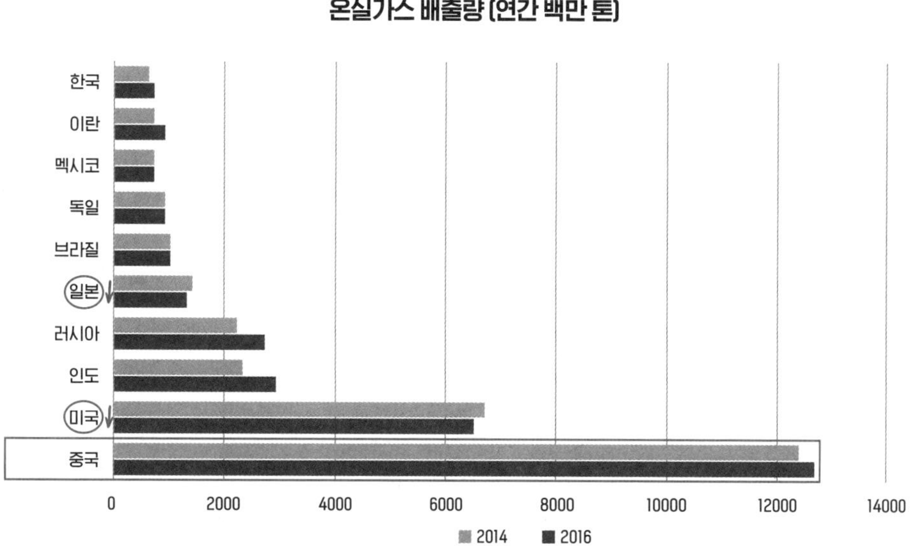

2 아웃라인 잡기

서론 문제 박스 안 첫 문장 패러프레이징 + 전체적인 추세 요약	*Paraphrasing* *+ the leading emitter* *+ countries to reduce GHG emissions*
본론 1 첫 번째 주요 특징과 비교 가능 정보	*<Emissions by country>* *- China: top* *- China vs US* *- China vs 8 countries*
본론 2 두 번째 주요 특징과 비교 가능 정보	*<Changes between 2014 and 2016>* *- reduce: Japan and US* *- no change: Mexico, Germany, Brazil* *- growth: the others*

3 모범답안

This chart displays the amount of greenhouse gas (GHG) emissions in ten countries from 2014 to 2016. It is evident that China was by far the leading emitter of greenhouse gases, while Japan and the United States were the only two countries to reduce their total emissions.	이 도표는 2014년과 2016년에 10개 국가의 온실가스 배출량을 보여준다. 중국이 온실가스 배출국으로 멀찌감치 앞서 있는 반면, 일본과 미국은 전체 배출을 줄인 유이한 국가임이 분명하다.
With more than 12 billion metric tons of GHG emissions in both 2014 and 2016, China stands out as the top contributor of GHG emissions. Most remarkably, China's emission totals were nearly twice those of the US, which followed China as the next top emitter. The other eight countries also emitted around or less than just 2 billion metric tons, further highlighting China's massive amount of GHG emissions.	2014년과 2016년 모두 120억 미터 톤의 배출을 넘으면 서, 중국이 GHG 배출의 일등 원인 제공국으로 두드러진다. 가장 눈에 띄는 것은, 중국의 배출 총액이 미국의 총액에 거의 두 배인데, 미국은 중국 다음의 최고 배출국이다. 다른 8개 국가들은 단지 20억 미터 톤 정도 또는 그 아래에 있음으로, 중국의 엄청난 양의 GHG 배출량을 더욱 강조한다.
Between 2014 and 2016, only two countries managed to reduce their emissions: Japan and the United States. As for the other countries, Mexico, Germany and Brazil showed no change in their emission numbers over the two years. The other five countries included on the chart reported growth in their total GHG emissions. (167 words)	2014년과 2016년에, 단지 두 국가들(일본과 미국)만이 배출을 가까스로 줄였다. 다른 나라들 관련하여, 멕시코, 독일, 그리고 브라질은 두 해 동안 배출 수치 변동이 없음을 보여준다. 도표에 포함된 다른 다섯 국가들은 GHG 총 배출량 증가를 알렸다.

I Vocabulary & Expressions I

greenhouse gas 온실 가스 **emission** 배출, 배출량 **by far** 훨씬 **leading** 선두하는 **reduce** 줄이다 **metric ton** 미터 톤 **stand out** 두드러지다 **contributor** 기여요인, 원인 **remarkably** 눈에 띄게 **nearly** 거의 **follow** 뒤따르다 **further** 더욱 **highlight** 강조하다 **massive** 엄청난 **manage to do** 가까스로 하다, 어떻게든 해내다 **as for** ~에 관련해서 **include** 포함하다 **growth** 성장, 증가

자가 평가

Academic Task 1 문제를 풀고 나서 아래 채점기준에 맞게 자신의 글을 평가하도록 한다. 이때, 자신의 글에 어떠한 부족한 점이 있고, 어떻게 더 발전시켜야 되는지를 고민해 보자,

Academic Task 1 채점기준

채점 영역	채점기준	확인
Task Achievement **과제 달성**	• 과제의 모든 요구사항에 맞게 객관적 도표 분석	Y / N
	• 최소 150자 이상 작성	Y / N
	• 그래프의 중요 사항들을 놓치지 말고 반드시 정확하게 설명	Y / N
	• 주요 추세에 대한 개괄(overview) 작성	Y / N
	• 주요 정보 간에 비교/대조	Y / N
	• 너무 지엽적인 세부정보에 초점을 맞추지 않음	Y / N
Coherence and Cohesion **일관성과 응집성**	• 충분한 응집 장치(접속사, 부사 등의 연결어, 한정사 및 대명사) 사용	Y / N
	• 서론(문제 패러프레이징+개괄) – 본론 1, 2의 문단 구성	Y / N
	• 주제 문장과 뒷받침 문장 간의 논리적 연결	Y / N
	• 문단 간의 연속성	Y / N
Lexical Resource **어휘력**	• 다양한 어휘를 정확하게 사용	Y / N
	• 같은 단어를 반복 사용하는 대신 동의어 및 패러프레이징 사용	Y / N
	• 철자 오류 없음	Y / N
	• 구동사 등의 평이한 어휘보다 고급 어휘 사용	Y / N
Grammatical Range and Accuracy **문법의 다양성과 정확성**	• 다양한 문장 형태(복문, 문장의 5형식)를 완벽하게 사용	Y / N
	• 다양한 문법 사항(접속사, 관계대명사, 명사절, 분사구문 등)을 완벽하게 사용	Y / N
	• 문법 실수가 없음	Y / N
	• 구두점(punctuation) 사용이 완벽함	Y / N

WRITING

PRACTICE TEST

Academic Task 1 다음 기출 변형 문제를 서론 - 본론 형식에 맞게 영작하자.

You should spend about 20 minutes on this task.

The table and chart below show the total number of cruise passengers and their percentage by age group in 1975 and 2003 in the UK.

Summarise the information by selecting and reporting the main features, and make comparisons where relevant.

Write at least 150 words.

Year	Passengers
1975	397,837
2003	1,005,231

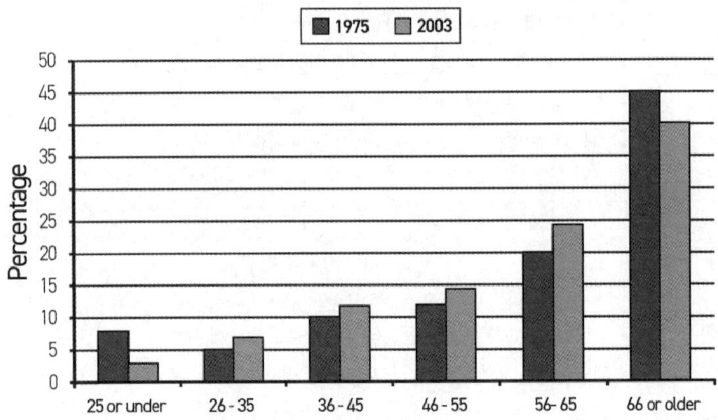

정답 및 해설 p.065

서론

서론 첫 문장(문제 박스 안 첫 문장 패러프레이징)

서론 두 번째 문장(전체적인 추세)

본론 1

본론 2

WRITING

UNIT 15

Task 1 - 도해

오늘의 학습 목표

1 Academic Task 1의 도해(Map, Plan, Diagram)에 자주 사용되는 표현을 익힌다.
2 Map, Plan, Diagram에 사용되는 문장들을 직접 영작해 본다.
3 20분 내에 Practice Test를 풀어본 후, 자신의 글을 채점기준에 따라 분석해 본다.

도해 유형 문제 풀이 방법

기본적인 Task 1 문제 풀이 순서는 '문제 분석 → 아웃라인 잡기 → 글쓰기 → 교정'인 것을 Unit 14에서 배웠다. 그림으로 정보를 전달하는 Map(지도), Plan(평면도), Diagram(다이어그램)의 도해 문제의 경우, 분석 포인트와 아웃라인 관련 단계만 다음 내용으로 알아두자.

1 Map/Plan 유형

문제 분석 포인트	첫 번째 지도와 비교하여 두 번째 지도의 변화에 초점 예 첫 번째 지도에 비해 두 번째 지도에 자동차 도로가 증가했는지
아웃라인	서론: 문제 패러프레이징 + 지도 간의 전체 주요 내용 요약 본론 1: 첫 번째 지도 설명(topic sentence + details) 본론 2: 첫 번째 지도와 비교하며 변화에 초점을 맞춰 두 번째 지도 설명(topic sentence + details) ※ 만일 지도가 세 개 나온다면 본론 3에 세 번째 지도 관련 내용을 두 번째 지도와 비교하면서 작성한다.

참고 문제에서 보통 map이나 plan을 diagram으로 표현한다. 따라서 diagram을 보다 구체적인 map이나 plan으로 패러프레이징하면 된다.

2 Diagram 유형

문제 분석 포인트	단계별 프로세스 묘사와 주요 단계에 초점 예 선후 과정 또는 어떤 과정이 상대적으로 더 빠르고 간편한지 등
아웃라인	서론: 문제 패러프레이징 + 다이어그램의 주요 내용 요약 본론 1: 다이어그램의 처음에서 중간 단계 설명(topic sentence + details) 본론 2: 다이어그램의 중간 단계에서 마지막 단계 설명(topic sentence + details) ※ 처음 단계에서 마지막 단계까지 하나의 본론 문단으로만 작성해도 된다.

참고 문제에서 언급된 diagram을 infographic(시각자료)으로 패러프레이징 할 수 있다.

문법 정리 2: 비교급과 최상급

Academic Task 1에서 반드시 활용해야 하는 비교급과 최상급을 정리한다.

비교급

❶ 형용사/부사 + er

[원급] 여성 사용자 비율은 높았다.

The percentage of female users was high.

[비교급] 여성 사용자 비율이 남성 사용자의 그것보다 훨씬 더 높았다.

The percentage of female users was much higher than that of male users.

※ 비교급을 사용할 때, 비교급 앞에 '훨씬'이라는 의미로 비교급을 강조하는 even, still, far, much, a lot과, 비교급 뒤에 '~보다'라는 의미의 than이 주로 따라옴

❷ more + 긴 형용사/부사

[원급] 2018년에 수치가 급격하게 상승했다.

The figure rose drastically in 2018.

[비교급] 2017년과 비교할 때, 2018년에 수치가 더 급격하게 상승했다.

Compared to 2017, the figure rose more drastically in 2018.

최상급

❶ 형용사/부사 + est

[원급] 인도가 차 생산에 큰 부분을 차지한다.

India accounts for a big proportion of tea production.

[비교급] 인도가 일본보다 차 생산에서 더 큰 부분을 차지한다.

India accounts for a bigger proportion of tea production than Japan.

[최상급] 인도가 차 생산에서 그 나라들 중 가장 큰 부분을 차지한다.

India accounts for the biggest proportion of tea production among the countries.

※ 최상급을 사용할 때, among the countries처럼 비교 범위를 한정하는 말이 반드시 들어가야 된다.

❷ most + 긴 형용사/부사

[최상급] 그 기간 동안에 2018년도 수치가 가장 급격하게 상승했다.

The figure in 2018 rose most drastically during the period.

도해에 자주 사용되는 표현 정리

1 Map/Plan 빈출 표현

• 위치해 있다 be situated = be located = be positioned

놀이터는 도서관 옆에 위치해 있다.
The playground is situated next to the library.

• ~에 둘러싸여 있다 be surrounded(=encircled) by ~

1970년에 그 공원은 나무로 둘러싸여 있었다.
The park was surrounded by trees in 1970.

• 새롭게 지어졌다 be newly constructed(=built)

2000년에 병원이 새로 지어졌다.
A hospital was newly constructed in 2000.

• A에서 B로 이동하다 be moved from A to B

주 출입구가 남쪽 구역에서 동쪽 구역으로 이동했다.
The main entrance was moved from the southern area to the eastern area.

• A가 B로 대체되다 A be replaced with B

상점가가 고층 사무실 건물들로 대체되었다.
The shopping district was replaced with high-rise office buildings.

• 가장 큰 변화 중 하나는 ~이다 one of the biggest changes is ~

두 번째 지도에 따르면, 가장 큰 변화 중 하나는 회사 건물이 주차장까지 확대된 것이다.
According to the second map, one of the biggest changes is that the company building has expanded into the car park.

• ~로부터 맞은편에 있다 be across from ~

극장은 은행 바로 맞은편에 있다.
The cinema is right across from the bank.

• ~의 앞/가운데/뒤에 in the front/middle/back of ~

호수는 마을 가운데에 위치하고 있다.
The lake is positioned in the middle of the town.

• A가 추가되어 with the addition of A

그 극장은 주차장이 추가되어 확장되었다.
The theatre has expanded with the addition of a car park.

2 Diagram 빈출 표현

• 먼저 First of all(=To begin with), ~

먼저, 알이 나비에 의해 생산되어진다.
First of all, eggs are produced by a butterfly.

• 그 다음 Next(=Then=Subsequently), ~

그 다음, 각 알은 나뭇잎을 먹는 유충이 된다.
Then, each egg becomes a larva that feeds on leaves.

• 마지막으로 Finally, ~

마지막으로, 약 10일에서 14일 이후에 나비는 번데기로부터 나오게 된다.
Finally, a butterfly emerges from its chrysalis in about 10 to 14 days.

Map/Plan 문제 풀이 연습

You should spend about 20 minutes on this task.

The diagrams below show the changes that have taken place at a small resort island since 1990.

Summarise the information by selecting and reporting the main features, and make comparisons where relevant.

Write at least 150 words.

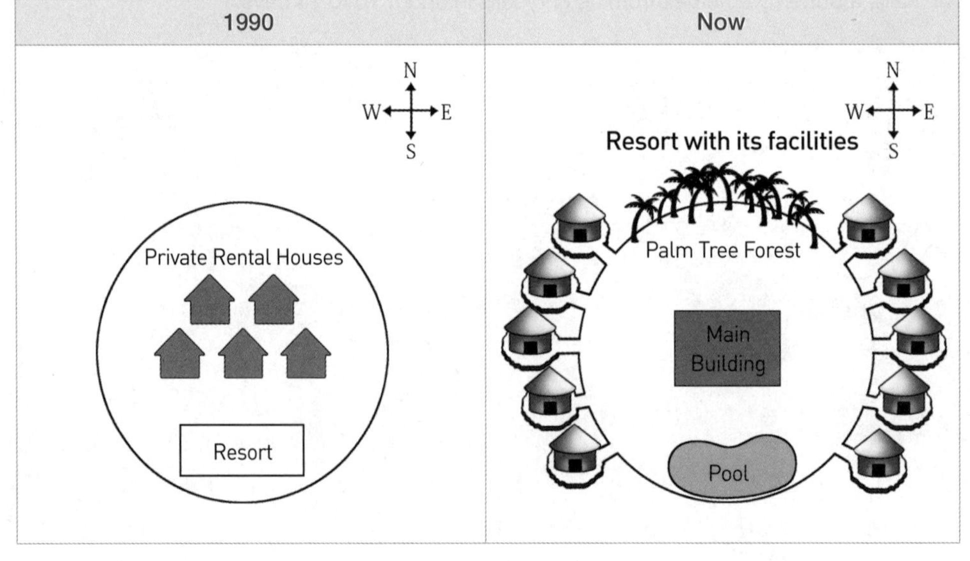

1 문제 분석

아래 도해는 1990년 이래로 작은 휴양섬에서 일어난 변화를 보여준다.
주요 특징들을 선별하여 기술함으로써 정보를 요약하고 관련 정보를 비교하라.

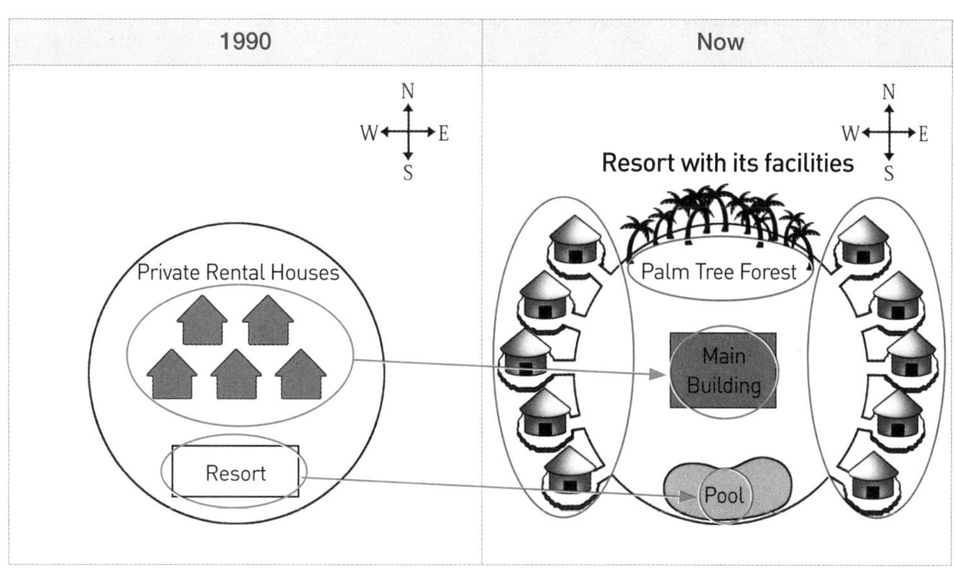

2 아웃라인 잡기

서론 문제 박스 안 첫 문장 패러프레이징 + 지도 간의 전체 주요 내용 요약	*Paraphrasing* *+ added numerous facilities*
본론 1 첫 번째 지도 설명 (topic sentence + details)	*<1990>* *only resort & private rental houses* *- southern end: resort* *- central & north-central: houses* *- eastern, western, northern: empty*
본론 2 첫 번째 지도와 비교하며 변화에 초점을 맞춰 두 번째 지도 설명 (topic sentence + details)	*<Now>* *numerous facilities, renovated* *- old resort → a large pool(southern)* *- rental houses → a main building(centre)* *- new: water bungalows(western, eastern), palm tree forest(north)*

3 모범답안

The maps detail the changes at a small resort island between 1990 and now. Overall, the resort has added numerous facilities over the past several decades.

In 1990, the small resort island only consisted of the resort and a group of private rental houses. The resort was situated in the southern end of the island. Behind it, the houses were constructed in the central and north-central areas of the island. The eastern, western and northern reaches of the island were empty.

Now, the resort features numerous facilities that have been added since 1990, and it has apparently been completely renovated. The old resort has been replaced by a large pool in the southern part of the island. Likewise, the rental houses have been removed, and a new main building has been constructed at the centre of the island. One of the biggest changes is the water bungalows that now line the western and eastern shores of the island. Finally, a palm tree forest has been established in the north.

(169 words)

다음 지도들은 1990년에서 지금까지 작은 휴양섬에서의 변화들을 자세히 보여준다. 전체적으로, 지난 수십년동안 리조트가 많은 시설들을 추가해왔다.

1990년에, 작은 휴양섬은 하나의 리조트와 개인 임대집들로만 이루어졌다. 리조트는 섬 남단에 위치했다. 그 뒤로, 섬 중앙과 중앙 북쪽에 임대집들이 건설되어 있었다. 섬의 동, 서, 북쪽 외곽은 비어 있었다.

이제, 리조트는 1990년 이래로 추가된 다양한 시설들을 특징으로 가지며, 확실하게 완벽히 새로 단장되었다. 섬 남쪽 부분에서 예전 리조트는 커다란 수영장으로 대체되었다. 마찬가지로, 임대집들은 사라지고, 새로운 본관이 섬 중앙에 지어졌다. 가장 큰 변화 중 하나는, 이제는 섬의 서쪽과 동쪽 해안에 나열되어 있는 수상 방갈로들이다. 마지막으로, 야자수 숲이 북쪽에 조성되었다.

I Vocabulary & Expressions I

detail 상세히 나타내다 decade 십년 be situated 위치하다 reach 외곽 apparently 분명히 bungalow 방갈로(목조 단층집) palm tree 야자수 establish 확립하다, 개설하다

유의 연도 및 변화에 맞게, 과거와 현재완료, 현재 시제를 적절히 사용한다.

Diagram 문제 풀이 연습

You should spend about 20 minutes on this task.

The diagram below shows how one type of coal is used to produce electricity.

Summarise the information by selecting and reporting the main features, and make comparisons where relevant.

Write at least 150 words.

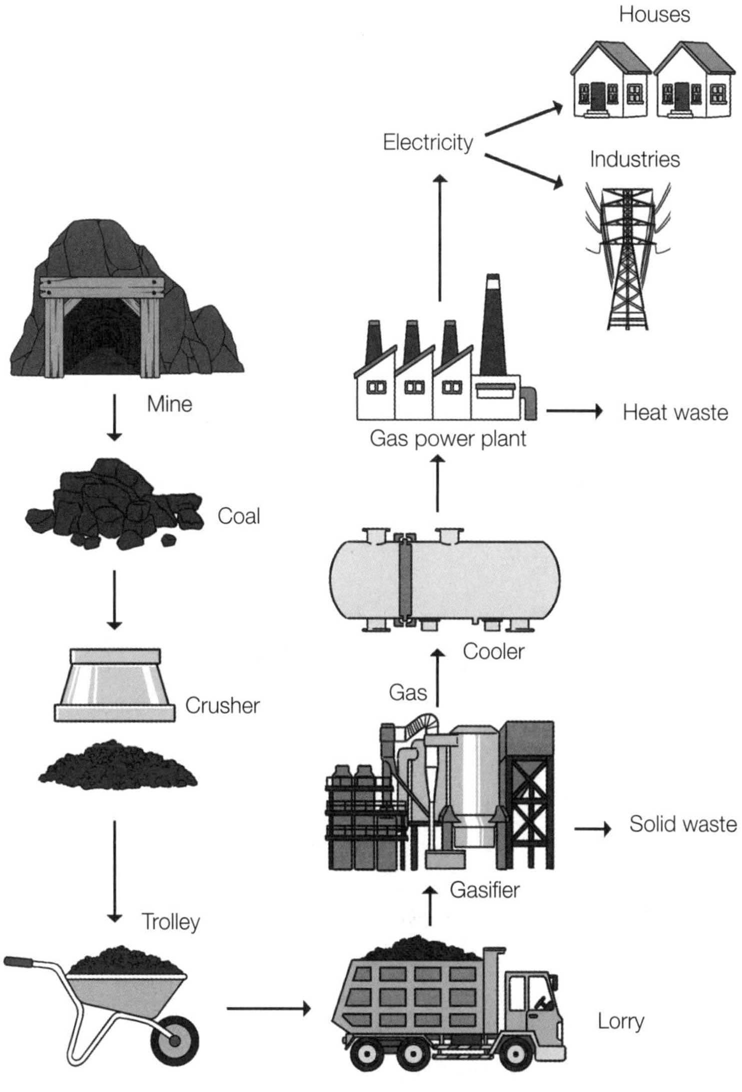

WRITING

1 문제 분석

아래 도해는 석탄의 한 유형이 전기 생산에 어떻게 사용되는지를 보여준다.
주요 특징들을 선별하여 기술함으로써 정보를 요약하고 관련 정보를 비교하라.

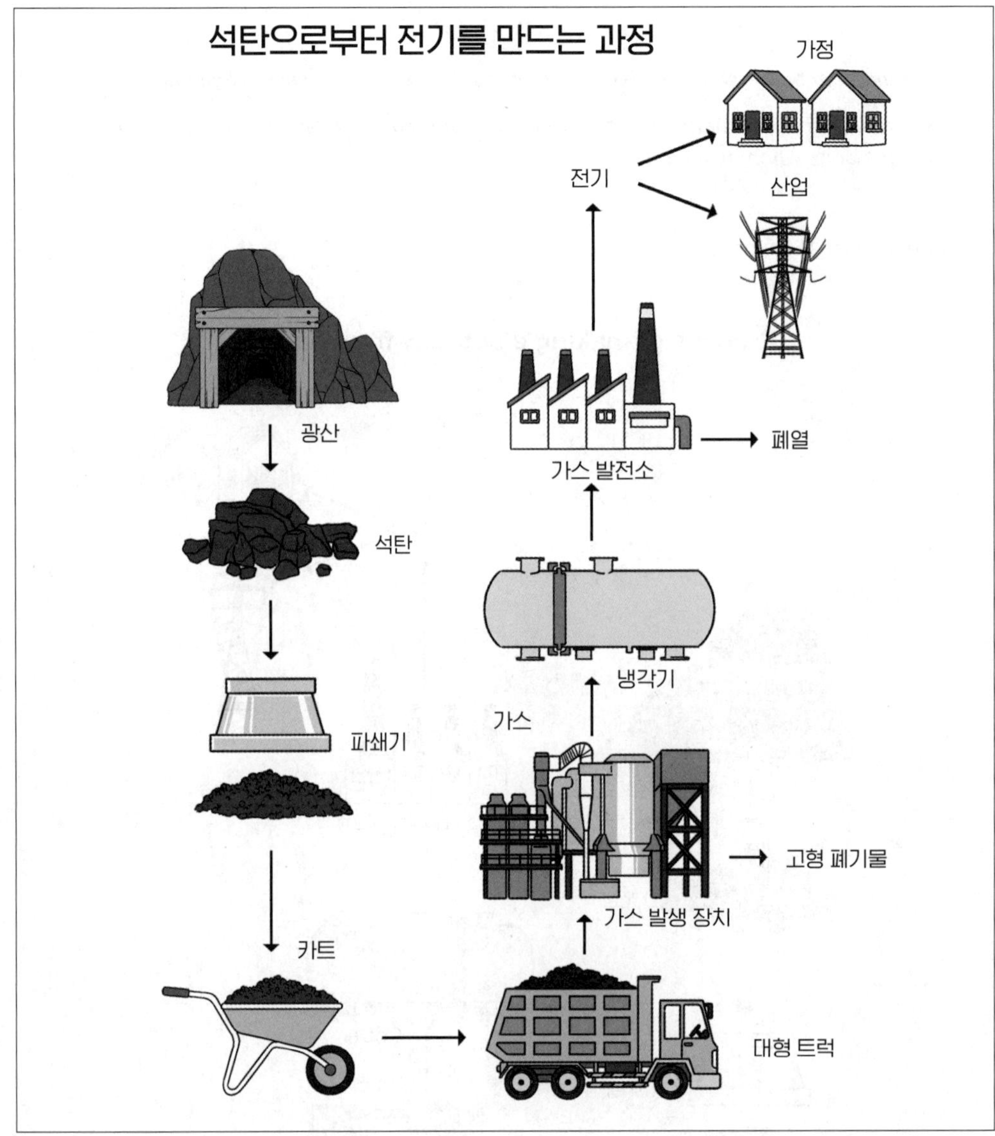

2 아웃라인 잡기

서론 문제 박스 안 첫 문장 패러프레이징 + 전체적인 요약	*Paraphrasing* *+ three steps for electricity generation*
본론 1	*Mine → Coal → Crusher → Trolley → Lorry → Gasifier → Cooler → Gas power plant*

본론 2	*Gas power plant → Electricity → Houses or Industries*

3 모범답안

The diagram illustrates the process of generating electricity from coal. According to the diagram, electricity generation involves three main steps: mining and transporting coal, processing it through dedicated facilities and finally, producing electricity and distributing it to homes and industries.	이 다이어그램은 석탄에서 전기를 생산하는 과정을 보여준다. 이 다이어그램에 따르면, 전기 생산은 석탄 채굴 및 운송, 전용 시설을 통한 처리, 마지막으로 전기를 생산하여 가정과 산업에 분배하는 세 가지 주요 단계를 포함한다.
First, the process begins at a mine, where coal is extracted and sent to be pulverised by a crusher. After that, the crushed coal is transported sequentially by a trolley and then by a lorry. Next, the lorry delivers the coal to a gasifier, which separates it into gas and solid waste. Only the gas proceeds to a cooler and then moves on to a gas power plant.	먼저, 광산에서 석탄을 채굴하여 분쇄기로 분쇄하기 위해 보내는 공정이 시작된다. 그 후, 분쇄된 석탄은 트롤리와 트럭을 통해 순차적으로 운반된다. 그 다음, 트럭은 석탄을 기화 장치로 운반하고, 이 장치는 석탄을 가스와 고형 폐기물로 분리한다. 가스만 냉각기로 이동한 다음 가스 발전소로 이동한다.
In the final stage, electric power is generated at the gas power plant. From there, heat waste is also produced during the electricity generation process although it is not utilised for producing electricity. The created electricity is finally distributed to homes and industries for use. As shown in the diagram, the process of electric energy production from coal mainly occurs in three facilities, during which by-products are discarded. (176 words)	마지막 단계에서, 가스 발전소에서 전력이 생산된다. 이 과정에서, 전기 생산에 활용되지는 않지만 열 폐기물도 생산된다. 이렇게 만들어진 전기는 마침내 가정과 산업에 사용을 위해 분배된다. 다이어그램에서 볼 수 있듯이, 석탄으로부터 전기를 생산하는 과정은 주로 세 가지 시설에서 이루어지는데, 이 과정에서 부산물이 버려진다.

| Vocabulary & Expressions |

generate (열, 전기 등을) 발생시키다, 생성하다 coal 석탄 mine 광산, ~을 채굴하다 transport ~을 수송하다, 운송하다 dedicated 전용의 distribute ~을 분배하다 extract ~을 추출하다, 채굴하다 pulverise ~을 분쇄하다 crush ~을 부수다 sequentially 순차적으로 trolley 카트 lorry 대형 트럭 gasifier 기화 장치 separate ~을 분리하다 solid waste 고형 폐기물 utilise ~을 활용하다 by-product 부산물 discard ~을 버리다

유의 프로세스 설명은 보통 수동태 문장으로 작성한다.

WRITING

PRACTICE TEST

Academic Task 1 다음 기출 변형 문제를 바탕으로 서론 - 본론 영작 연습을 하자.

You should spend about 20 minutes on this task.

The plans below show the layout of a community centre now, and how it will look after development.

Summarise the information by selecting and reporting the main features, and make comparisons where relevant.

Write at least 150 words.

COMMUNITY CENTRE (present)

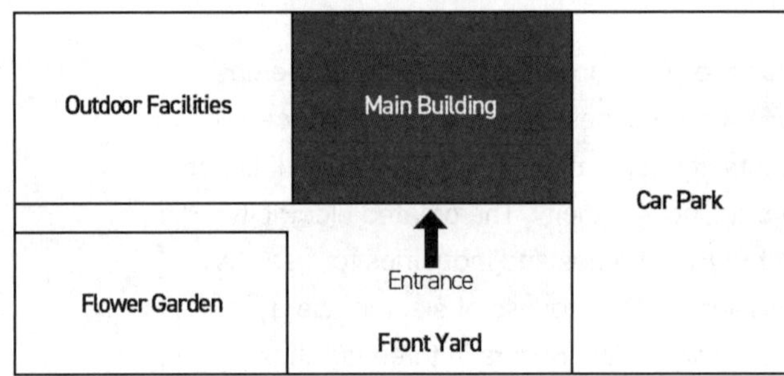

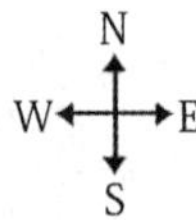

COMMUNITY CENTRE (future)

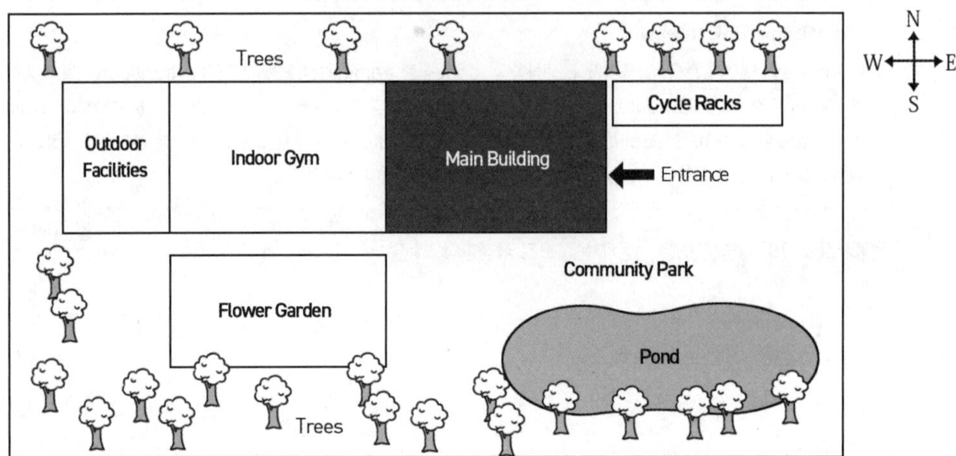

정답 및 해설 p.066

서론

서론 첫 문장(문제 박스 안 첫 문장 패러프레이징)

서론 두 번째 문장(지도 전체 주요 내용 요약)

본론 1

본론 2

UNIT 16

Task 1 - 편지

오늘의 학습 목표

1 General Training Task 1의 문제 분석 방법을 숙지한다.
2 편지의 구성과 빈출 표현을 익힌다.
3 Formal, Semi-formal 톤의 차이점을 파악한다.

General Training Task 1 문제 풀이 방법

General Training Task 1은 편지 쓰기 문제로, 다음과 같이 전형적인 문제 분석 단계를 거친 후 편지 형식에 맞게 글을 구성하여 편지를 작성한다.

Sample Question

You should spend about 20 minutes on this task.

You are unhappy about a plan to expand some roads in your neighbourhood so that large trucks or lorries can access local shopping malls.

Write a letter to the local council. In your letter

- ***give details of your neighbourhood and the road expansion plan***
- ***explain how this plan will affect you and your neighbourhood***
- ***give reasons why you are against this development***

Write at least 150 words.
You do **NOT** need to write any addresses.
Begin your letter as follows:

Dear Sir or Madam,

1 문제 분석

You should spend about 20 minutes on this task.

이 문제에 약 20분을 사용한다. ▶ 첫 줄은 모든 Task 1에 항상 똑같이 나오는 문구로, 권장되는 문제 풀이 시간을 언급한다.

You are unhappy about a plan to expand some roads in your neighbourhood so that large trucks or lorries can access local shopping malls.

당신은 당신 동네에 커다란 트럭과 화물차들이 지역 쇼핑몰에 접근할 수 있도록 도로를 확장하는 계획에 대해 불만이다.

▶ 박스 안 첫 줄은 편지 내용 상황 설명으로, 이 문장을 패러프레이징하여 편지 쓰는 목적을 적는다.

Write a letter to the local council. In your letter 지역 시의회에 편지를 써라. 편지에는

- give details of your neighbourhood and the road expansion plan
  동네와 도로 확장 계획에 대한 구체적 설명을 한다
- explain how this plan will affect you and your neighbourhood
  당신과 당신 동네에 이 계획이 어떻게 영향을 미칠지 설명한다
- give reasons why you are against this development
  왜 당신이 이 개발을 원하지 않는지 이유를 댄다

▶ 박스 안에는 항상 세개의 답변 포인트가 주어지는데, 작성하는 편지 본문에는 반드시 명확하게 이 세개의 답변 포인트를 작성해야 한다.

Write at least 150 words.

최소 150자를 적어라. ▶ Task 1에 항상 똑같이 나오는 문구로, 150자 이상 작성을 요구한다.

You do **NOT** need to write any addresses.

어떠한 주소도 적지 않는다. ▶ Task 1에 항상 똑같이 나오는 문구로, 주소는 적지 않는다.

Begin your letter as follows:

다음과 같이 편지를 시작하라: ▶ Task 1에 항상 똑같이 나오는 문구로, 아래와 같이 편지를 시작한다.

Dear Sir or Madam,

관계자분께 ▶ 글 전체의 톤(Formal, Semi-formal) 결정에 중요한 단서를 제공한다.

2 아웃라인 잡기

아웃라인 잡기 순서

① 편지의 톤 정하기
② 편지 쓰는 목적 파악
③ 세가지 중요 항목(답변포인트) 파악

우선 문제 마지막에 제시되는 Dear Sir or Madam, 또는 Dear ....,로 편지의 톤을 정하고, 문제 박스 안 첫 줄 내용에 따라 편지 쓰는 목적(불만 표현, 요청, 감사 등)을 파악한다. 이후 문제 박스에 나온 세가지 답변 포인트에 대한 내용을 각각 생각해본다. 이 세가지 항목이 편지 본론을 구성하게 된다.

이렇게 편지의 아웃라인을 잡은 후 실제로 편지를 작성하기 위해서는, 편지의 각 구성 부분에 자주 사용되는 필수 표현을 익힐 필요가 있다. 또한 편지에 적용되는 각각의 톤에 대해서도 확실히 이해하도록 한다.

편지의 구성 및 필수 표현

1 인사

글을 받는 사람에 대해 언급하는 부분으로 다음과 같이 쓴다.

- 사람 이름을 알지 못하는 경우 **Dear Sir or Madam,**

  ▶ 글 전체의 톤이 Formal

- 사람 이름을 알고 있는 경우 **Dear 사람 이름,**

  ▶ 글 전체의 톤이 Semi-formal

Dear는 "친애하는"이란 뜻으로 편지 앞부분에 쓰는 인사 표현인데, 문제 마지막에 편지의 시작을 어떻게 할지 알려준다. 예를 들어 'Begin your letter as follows: Dear Sir or Madam,'이라는 문구가 나오면 무조건 'Dear Sir or Madam'으로 시작해야 한다. 그리고 'Begin your letter as follows: Dear ....,'이라는 문구가 나오면 편지를 받을 상대의 이름을 임의로 만들어서 쓰면 된다. (문제에서 상대방의 이름이 따로 제시되지는 않는다.)

2 편지 쓰는 목적

채점기준표에 따르면 편지를 쓰는 목적을 나타내는 것이 필수로, 다음과 같이 첫 문장을 시작한다.

- ~하기 위해 편지를 쓰다 **I am writing to + 동사원형**

  저는 귀사의 웹사이트에서 구입한 물건에 대해 어떻게 환불을 받는지 문의하기 위해 편지를 씁니다.
  I am writing to **enquire about how to get a refund for an item which I bought from your website.**

- ~에 관해 편지를 쓰다 **I am writing concerning(=with regard to) + 명사**

  저는 다음달에 시작하기로 되어 있는 인턴쉽 프로그램에 관해 편지를 씁니다.
  I am writing concerning **the internship programme that I am due to begin next month.**

3 세가지 중요 항목 답변

Task 1의 본론 부분으로 반드시 3가지 중요 항목(three bullet points)에 답변이 되는 근거, 예시 등의 내용을 작성해야 하며, 다음은 이 때 자주 활용할 수 있는 표현들이다.

① 계획/예정 표현

- ~하기로 되어 있다 **be supposed to + 동사원형**

  저는 귀사의 고객 상담 직원 중 한사람에게 연락을 받기로 되어 있었습니다.
  I was supposed to **be contacted by one of your customer service representatives.**

- ~하는 것이 예상되다 **be expected to + 동사원형**

  그것은 어제 도착하는 것으로 예상되었습니다.
  It was expected to **arrive yesterday.**

• ~하는 것이 예정되다 be scheduled to + 동사원형

저는 다음주 월요일에 당신 사무실에 방문할 예정입니다.
I am scheduled to visit your office next Monday.

② 추가설명 부사

• 게다가 Furthermore=In addition=Moreover

게다가 저는 재택근무를 하고 있고, 고객들과 연락하기 위해 인터넷 연결에 의지하고 있습니다.
Furthermore, I work from home and rely on having the Internet so that I can contact my clients.

③ 원인 및 근거 제시 전치사구

• ~ 때문에 Due to(=As a result of) + 명사

열악한 인터넷 연결 때문에, 저는 벌써 이번 주에 두 건의 마감을 놓쳤습니다.
Due to the poor Internet connection, I have already missed two deadlines this week.

WRITING

4 마무리

편지 마지막은 다음의 두 부분으로 세분화된다.

① 마무리 문장

마무리 문장에는 빠른 답변 요구, 감사, 희망 등을 나타내는 다음의 표현이 자주 사용된다.

• 나는 ~하는 것을 기대하다 I look forward to + 동사ing

당신으로부터 들을 수 있기를 기대합니다.
I look forward to hearing from you.

• 나는 당신이 ~하기를 희망한다 I hope (that) you + 동사원형

저는 당신이 당신의 남은 휴가를 즐기길 희망합니다.
I hope (that) you enjoy the rest of your holiday.

• 나는 ~에 대해 고맙게 여기다 I appreciate ~

저는 정말로 그것에 대해 감사하게 생각합니다.
I really appreciate that.

② 끝맺음

편지 마지막에 끝맺음 말(signoff)을 작성하는데, 받는 사람의 특징에 따라 다음과 같이 사용한다.

• 받는 사람의 이름을 모르는 경우 Yours faithfully,

• 이름을 알지만 격식이 필요한 경우 Yours sincerely, Sincerely,

• 격식을 어느 정도 갖추는 경우 Best wishes, Best regards, Kind regards, All the best, 등

• 격식을 갖출 필요가 없는 경우 With love, Cheers, 등

각 편지 톤 특징

Task 1에 출제되는 Letter는, 편지를 받는 대상에 따라 크게 4가지로 구분할 수 있다. 시험에 가장 많이 출제되는 영역은 Formal이고, 그 다음 Semi-formal 1이 자주 나온다. Semi-formal 2는 간혹 출제되고 있고, Informal은 거의 출제된 적이 없다. 특히 최근 5년 동안 한번도 출제되지 않았으며 Informal letter는 Semi-formal 2의 톤으로 작성해도 무방하기에, Formal과 Semi-formal에 집중하여 학습하도록 한다.

종류	Formal 격식	Semi-formal 1 준격식 1	Semi-formal 2 준격식 2	Informal 비격식
대상	모르는 사람이나 사업체	어느 정도 아는 사람 또는 회사 상관	친구나 친한 동료	격식을 갖출 필요 없는 가족 또는 친구
인사 (콤마 포함)	Dear Sir or Madam,	Dear Last Name(성) 예 Dear Mr Kim,	Dear First Name (이름) 예 Dear Chelsea,	Hi나 Hello 뒤에 이름 또는 호칭 예 Hi Mum,
문장 스타일	• 축약 안 됨 • 고급 단어 구사	• 축약 거의 안 됨 • 고급 단어 구사	• 축약 가능 • 너무 격식 있게 쓰면 어색해질 수 있음	• 축약 가능 • 가볍고 친근한 단어
끝맺음	Yours faithfully, (한 칸 띄고) 성명 * Dear Sir or Madam으로 시작할 때, 영국은 Yours faithfully, 미국은 Yours sincerely를 주로 쓴다.	Yours sincerely, (한 칸 띄고) 성명	Best wishes, (한 칸 띄고) 이름	With love, (한 칸 띄고) 이름
출제 빈도	50%	30%	15%	5%(Semi-formal 2로도 쓸 수 있음)

Formal과 Semi-formal 표현 차이

IELTS WRITING 시험에서는 Informal Letter는 출제가 거의 안되기에 아래에 나온 표현들로 Formal Letter나 Semi-formal Letter를 쓰도록 한다.

표현	Formal / Semi-formal 1	Semi-formal 2
원하다	would like	want
요청하다	request	ask for
유감이다	I regret	I am sorry
사과하다	I apologise	I am sorry
~때문에	due to = as a result of	because of
희망하다	look forward to	hope
감사하다	appreciate	thank
제공하다	provide	give
보내다	forward	send
전달하다	forward	pass on
조사하다	investigate	look into
고려하다	consider	think about
탑승하다	board	get on
내리다	alight	get off
들어가다	enter	go in
나오다	exit	go out
돌아보다	reflect	look back

Formal Letter 문제 풀이 연습

General Training Task 1은 편지 쓰기 문제로, 다음과 같이 전형적인 문제 분석 단계를 거친 후 편지 형식에 맞게 글을 구성하여 편지를 작성한다.

You should spend about 20 minutes on this task.

You are unhappy about a plan to expand some roads in your neighbourhood so that large trucks or lorries can access local shopping malls.

Write a letter to the local council. In your letter

- *give details of your neighbourhood and the road expansion plan*
- *explain how this plan will affect you and your neighbourhood*
- *give reasons why you are against this development*

Write at least 150 words.

You do **NOT** need to write any addresses.

Begin your letter as follows:

Dear Sir or Madam,

1 문제 분석

You are unhappy about a plan to expand some roads in your neighbourhood so that large trucks or lorries can access local shopping malls.

당신은 당신 동네에 커다란 트럭이나 화물차들이 지역 쇼핑몰에 접근할 수 있도록 도로를 확장하는 계획에 대해 불만이다.

▶ 편지 작성 목적: 불만에 대한 표출

Write a letter to the local council. In your letter 지역 시의회에 편지를 써라. 편지에는

- give details of your neighbourhood and the road expansion plan
  동네와 도로 확장 계획에 대한 구체적 설명을 한다
- explain how this plan will affect you and your neighbourhood
  당신과 당신 동네에 이 계획이 어떻게 영향을 미칠지 설명한다
- give reasons why you are against this development
  왜 당신이 이 개발을 원하지 않는지 이유를 댄다

2 아웃라인 잡기

톤 선택	Dear Sir or Madam으로 시작: Formal
편지 쓰는 목적	도로 확장 계획에 불만을 표현하기 위해: I am writing to express my displeasure with the city's intent to enlarge roadways
세가지 중요 항목 답변	• 동네와 도로 확장 계획에 대한 구체적 설명 – quiet residential area(조용한 주거지역) • 이 계획이 어떻게 영향을 미칠지 – detrimental effects(해로운 영향들) – polluting the air(공기 오염), noise(소음), children at risk(아이들 위험) • 왜 당신이 이 개발을 원하지 않는지 이유 – not the most effective solution(가장 효과적인 해결책이 아님)

3 모범답안

Dear Sir or Madam,

As a long-time resident of Mapleton, I am writing to express my displeasure with the city's intent to enlarge roadways in my neighbourhood so that lorries can reach the nearby shopping centres.

My neighbourhood is a quiet residential area where children frequently play outside, and my neighbours and I cherish the peaceful atmosphere. However, the city now intends to expand our roads, effectively turning our street into a shortcut for large trucks transporting goods to the new stores.

The detrimental effects this change will have on the neighbourhood are obvious. Delivery lorries are known to be dirty, polluting the air with their exhaust fumes, and since deliveries are made early in the morning and late at night, the noise will be highly disruptive. Most importantly, the local children will be put at grave risk by the increased traffic.

Furthermore, expanding the roads in my neighbourhood is not the most effective solution to this problem. Instead, constructing a new road off the nearby motorway would be better for all involved.

관계자분께,

메이플톤의 오랜 거주자로서, 저는 근처 쇼핑 센터에 화물 트럭들이 도달할 수 있도록 우리 동네에 길들을 확장하려는 시의 의도에 불만을 표현하기 위해 편지를 씁니다.

우리 동네는 조용한 주거 지역으로 아이들이 자주 바깥에서 놀며, 이웃들과 저는 이러한 평화로운 분위기를 소중히 여깁니다. 그러나, 시는 이제 우리 도로를 확장하려고 하는데, 사실상 우리 동네의 길을 새로운 상점들에 상품을 운송할 대형 트럭들을 위한 지름길로 변하게 합니다.

이러한 변화가 동네에 줄 해로운 영향들은 분명합니다. 운송 화물차들은 낙진을 생기게 하는 것으로 알려져 있는데, 배기가스로 공기를 오염시키고, 아침 일찍이나 밤 늦게 배달이 이루어지기에 소음이 매우 지장을 줄 것입니다. 가장 중요하게는, 증가된 교통량으로 인해 지역 아이들이 심각한 위험에 처할 것입니다.

더욱이, 우리 동네에 도로 확장이 이 문제에 가장 효과적인 해결책은 아닙니다. 대신에, 근처 차도 옆에 떨어진 새로운 도로를 건설하는 것이 관련된 모두에게 더 좋을 것입니다.

For these reasons, I humbly request that the local council reconsider its plan. Yours faithfully, Gilbert Hans (190 words)	이러한 이유들로, 저는 시 의회가 본 계획을 재고하기를 겸허히 요청하는 바입니다. 길버트 한스 올림

I Vocabulary & Expressions I

lorry 대형 화물차, 대형 트럭 **intent** 의도 **residential area** 주거 지역 **cherish** 소중히 여기다 **shortcut** 지름길 **detrimental** 해로운 **obvious** 분명한 **dirty** 더러운, 낙진을 생기게 하는 **exhaust fumes** 배기가스 **disruptive** 지장을 주는 **grave** 심각한 **humbly** (예의상 자기를 낮추며) 겸손하게, 겸허하게 **local council** 지역 의회

Semi-formal 1 문제 풀이 연습

You should spend about 20 minutes on this task.

You are an employee at a busy company and would like to take one week off for your sister's wedding, which will be held abroad.

Write a letter to your manager. In your letter

- *say why you need one week off*
- *explain how your work could be covered while you are away*
- *ask for his/her permission*

Write at least 150 words.

You do **NOT** need to write any addresses.
Begin your letter as follows:

Dear ....,

1 문제 분석

You are an employee at a busy company and would like to take one week off for your sister's wedding, which will be held abroad.
당신은 한 바쁜 회사에 직원으로 해외에서 개최될 여자 형제 결혼 기간 동안 일주일을 쉬려고 한다.
▶ 편지 작성 목적: 요청/부탁에 대한 편지

Write a letter to your manager. In your letter 당신의 매니저에게 편지를 써라. 편지에는

- say why you need one week off
  일주일 휴가가 왜 필요한지를 말한다
- explain how your work could be covered while you are away
  당신이 없는 동안 어떻게 당신의 업무가 커버될지 설명한다
- ask for his/her permission
  매니저의 허가를 구한다

2 아웃라인 잡기

톤 선택	*Dear로 시작: Semi-formal, 직장 상사에게 부탁을 하는 편지이므로 Semi-formal 1으로, 보다 격식있게 작성* *(Semi-formal 2로 작성해도 괜찮음)*
편지 쓰는 목적	*누이 결혼식에 참석할 수 있도록 일주일 휴가를 요청하기 위해:* *I am writing to request a week-long holiday next month so that I may attend my sister's wedding.*
세가지 중요 항목 답변	• *일주일 휴가가 왜 필요한지* *- sister's wedding held overseas(해외에서 열리는 누이의 결혼식)* • *당신이 없는 동안 어떻게 당신의 업무가 커버가 될지* *- two of my team members(두 명의 팀원들)* *- leave detailed instructions(세부 지침사항을 남김)* • *매니저의 허가를 구함* *- allow me to take this time off(휴가 허락)*

WRITING

3 모범답안

Dear Mr Hines, Although I fully appreciate how busy our company has been lately, I am writing to request a week-long holiday next month so that I may attend my sister's wedding. Normally, a sibling's wedding would not merit such a long absence from work, but my sister's wedding is unique as it will be held overseas in Ireland, in my grandparents' hometown. Considering the travel time, expenses and significance of this family event, I believe a week off will be necessary. However, I do not intend to leave the company shorthanded during this time. I have already discussed my work responsibilities with two of my team members, Mr Cooper and Ms Lee. Upon reviewing their own project schedules, they have both graciously agreed to help handle my tasks while I am away from the office. In addition, I will leave detailed instructions for my team members that will cover everything they will need to know. I do hope that you will consider my request and allow me to take this time off to attend my sister's wedding. Yours sincerely, Mark Webster (182 words)	하인즈 씨께, 비록 우리 회사가 최근에 얼마나 바빴는지 완전히 알고 있음에도 불구하고, 저는 제 여동생 결혼식 참석을 할 수 있도록 다음달 일주일간의 휴가를 요청하기 위해 편지를 씁니다. 보통, 형제 자매의 결혼이 이렇게 긴 업무 부재 이유에 해당하지 않지만, 제 여동생의 결혼은 해외에서, 제 조부모님 고향인 아일랜드에서 열리기에 특별합니다. 여행 시간과 비용, 그리고 이 가족 행사의 중요성을 고려해 볼 때, 저는 일주일 휴가가 필요하다고 봅니다. 그러나, 저는 이 기간동안 일손이 부족한 상태로 회사를 떠날 의도가 아닙니다. 저는 이미 제 업무에 대해 팀원 중 두 명, 쿠퍼 씨와 리 씨와 논의했습니다. 그 둘의 개별 일정을 살펴보고, 그들은 모두 고맙게도 제가 사무실에 없는 동안 제 업무를 처리하는데 돕기로 동의했습니다. 추가로, 저는 제 팀원들이 그들이 알아야할 모든 것을 다루는 상세한 지침들을 남겨둘 것입니다. 제 요청을 고려해주셔서 제 여동생 결혼식에 참석할 수 있는 휴가를 허락해 주시길 진심으로 희망합니다. 마크 웹스터 드림

I Vocabulary & Expressions I

appreciate 인식하다 a week-long 일주일 간의 wedding 결혼(식) sibling 형제 자매 merit 받을 만하다, 가치가 있다 expense 비용 significance 중요성 shorthanded 일손이 부족한 work responsibilities(=tasks) 업무 graciously 고맙게도 instructions 지침

Semi-formal 2 문제 풀이 연습

You should spend about 20 minutes on this task.

Your next door neighbour has sent a message to complain about the noise from your home.

Write a letter to your next door neighbour. In your letter
- *describe the reasons for the noise*
- *describe what action you will take*
- *apologise to your neighbour*

Write at least 150 words.

You do **NOT** need to write any addresses.
Begin your letter as follows:

Dear ....,

1 문제 분석

Your next door neighbour has sent a message to complain about the noise from your home.
당신 옆집 이웃이 당신 집에서 나오는 소음에 대해 불만을 제기하는 메시지를 보냈다.
▶ 편지 작성 목적: 사과에 대한 표시

Write a letter to your next door neighbour. In your letter 당신의 이웃에게 편지를 써라. 편지에는
- describe the reasons for the noise
  소음에 대한 이유를 기술한다
- describe what action you will take
  당신이 어떤 조치를 취할지 기술한다
- apologise to your neighbour
  이웃에게 사과한다

2 아웃라인 잡기

톤 선택	Dear로 시작: Semi-formal, 이웃에게 쓰는 편지이므로 Semi-formal 2로, 보다 편하게 작성 (Semi-formal 1으로 작성해도 괜찮음)
편지 쓰는 목적	집에서 나오는 소음에 대해 사과하기 위해: I feel terrible that the noise from my home has been bothering you so much.

WRITING

세가지 중요 항목 답변	• 소음에 대한 이유 – *hosting my whole family for a family reunion*(전 가족의 상봉을 주최함) • 당신이 어떤 조치를 취할지 – *make reservations at a restaurant*(식당에 예약함) • 이웃에게 사과 – *sorry*(사과) – *come over for dinner*(저녁식사 방문)

3 모범답안

Dear Carl, I just read the message you left at my door, and I feel terrible that the noise from my home has been bothering you so much. I'm so sorry about it. It's been a hectic week at my house, but I didn't realise we were being so loud. Please accept my apology. As you've surely noticed from the additional cars parked out front, I have been hosting my whole family for a family reunion this week. We've had a lively dinner every evening with music and quite a bit of socialising. This would explain the chatter and laughter you've heard from our patio, as we have also been outside every evening enjoying the wonderful weather. I still have one more special evening planned with my family, but I do not wish to further inconvenience you. So, I'll make reservations at a restaurant, and we'll meet there so as not to disturb you with any more noise. Sorry again about all of this. Please come over for dinner one evening next week so that I can thank you for your patience and understanding. Best wishes, Scott (187 words)	칼에게, 방금 당신이 우리집 앞에 남긴 메시지를 읽고 우리집에서 나는 소음이 그렇게 많이 당신을 괴롭혀 왔음에 기분이 정말 좋지 않네요. 소음에 대해 정말 죄송해요. 우리집에서 참 바쁜 한주였지만 우리가 그렇게 시끄러웠는지 몰랐어요. 제 사과를 받아주세요. 우리집 앞에 주차된 추가적인 차들을 당신이 분명히 눈치챘듯이, 이번 주에 전 가족 상봉을 우리집에서 하고 있어요. 우리는 매 저녁에 음악과 함께 활기찬 저녁 식사와 꽤 많은 사교시간을 가졌죠. 이것이 우리집 테라스에서 나오는 수다와 웃음을 설명할 거예요. 우리는 매 저녁 아름다운 날씨를 밖에서 즐겼으니까요. 한번 더 가족들과 특별 저녁이 계획되어 있지만 당신에게 더 이상 불편을 끼치길 원치 않아요. 그래서, 더 이상의 소음으로 당신을 방해하지 않기 위해 식당에 예약해서 거기서 모임을 가질 거예요. 이 모든 것에 대해 다시 한번 죄송해요. 당신의 인내와 이해심에 감사드릴 수 있도록 다음 주 저녁에 식사 차 방문해 주세요. 스코트 보냄

| Vocabulary & Expressions |

feel terrible 기분이 안 좋다, 후회하다 **hectic** 정신없이 바쁜 **apology** 사과 **host** 주최하다 **family reunion** 가족 상봉 **socialising** 사교 **chatter** 수다, 재잘거림 **patio** 테라스, 뜰 **inconvenience** 불편하게 하다 **disturb** 방해하다 **patience** 인내 **understanding** 이해심

자가 평가

General Training Task 1 문제를 풀고 나서 아래 채점기준에 맞게 자신의 글을 평가하도록 한다. 이때, 자신의 글에 어떠한 부족한 점이 있고, 어떻게 더 발전시켜야 되는지를 고민해 보자,

General Training Task 1 채점기준

채점 영역	채점기준	확인
Task Achievement 과제 달성	• 과제의 모든 요구사항에 맞게 편지 작성 • 최소 150자 이상 작성 • 처음에 편지 쓰는 목적을 분명히 밝힘 • 3가지 답변 포인트에 대해 분명히, 그리고 충실히 답변 • formal, informal의 톤 일치	Y / N Y / N Y / N Y / N Y / N
Coherence and Cohesion 일관성과 응집성	• 충분한 응집 장치(접속사, 부사 등의 연결어, 한정사 및 대명사) 사용 • 인사 - 글의 목적 - 3가지 답변 포인트 - 마무리 순으로 문단 구성 • 주제 문장과 뒷받침 문장 간의 논리적 연결 • 문단 간의 연속성	Y / N Y / N Y / N Y / N
Lexical Resource 어휘력	• 다양한 어휘를 정확하게 사용 • 같은 단어를 반복 사용하는 대신 동의어 및 패러프레이징 사용 • 철자 오류 없음 • 구동사 등의 평이한 어휘보다 고급 어휘 사용	Y / N Y / N Y / N Y / N
Grammatical Range and Accuracy 문법의 다양성과 정확성	• 다양한 문장 형태(복문, 문장의 5형식)를 완벽하게 사용 • 다양한 문법 사항(접속사, 관계대명사, 명사절, 분사구문 등)을 완벽하게 사용 • 문법 실수가 없음 • 구두점(punctuation) 사용이 완벽함	Y / N Y / N Y / N Y / N

General Training Task 1 다음 기출 변형 문제를 편지 틀에 맞게 영작하자.

You should spend about 20 minutes on this task.

Your company recently had a dinner party at a restaurant to celebrate a special occasion. Participants at the party said that they enjoyed the food, but they were not satisfied with the serving staff at the restaurant.

Write a letter to the manager of the restaurant on behalf of your company. In your letter
- *give details of the reason for the company celebration*
- *explain what was good and bad at the restaurant*
- *suggest what the manager should do to improve the service in the future*

Write at least 150 words.

You do **NOT** need to write any addresses.
Begin your letter as follows:

Dear Sir or Madam,

인사(톤 선택)

____

편지 쓰는 목적

____

____

첫 번째 중요 항목 답변

____

____

____

____

____

____

정답 및 해설 p.068

두 번째 중요 항목 답변

세 번째 중요 항목 답변

마무리 문장

끝맺음

WRITING

UNIT 17 Task 2 - 에세이 핵심 분석

오늘의 학습 목표

1 Task 2 에세이 특징을 파악한다.
2 Task 2 에세이 작성 순서를 익힌다.
3 Task 2 채점기준을 숙지한 후, 채점기준에 따라 에세이를 쓰도록 한다.

Task 2 에세이

Task 2는 에세이 쓰기로 Academic/General Training 공통 유형이다. 에세이(essay)란 '특정 주제에 대해 자신의 의견을 표현하는 짧은 글'로 영어권 국가의 학교에서 가장 기본적인 시험 및 과제 형태이다.

특별히 IELTS Task 2에서는, 특정 주제로 범위가 한정되어 있기에, 주제에서 벗어나지 말고 정확하게 그 주제를 다뤄야 되며, 250자 정도의 짧은 글로 자신의 의견을 표현하는 만큼 논리적이고 일관성 있게, 같은 단어 반복없이 적절한 어휘를 활용하여 글을 작성해야 한다.

Task 2 작문 필수 요소

Task 2 에세이 글을 작성할 때는 반드시 다음의 요소가 들어가야 된다.

- 문제에 제시된 주제에 대한 진술이나 질문을 패러프레이징 하기
  → 문제에 나온 문장 그대로 사용하면 감점
- 주제에 대한 자신만의 의견 진술하기
  → 자신의 명확한 의견 없으면 감점
- 자신의 의견을 뒷받침하는 논리적인 근거 및 이유 제시하기
  → 문제 주제와 연관된 자신만의 개인적 경험을 예시로 들어도 좋음
- 격식을 갖춘 문어체로 글쓰기
  → 축약이나 약자 또는 비격식 어휘·문체 사용시 감점

Task 2 에세이 문제 풀이 방법

Sample Question

You should spend about 40 minutes on this task.

Write about the following topic:

Some parents guide their children's education towards specific careers, such as in engineering, medicine or law.

What are the advantages and disadvantages for the child who has this kind of parental guidance?

Give reasons for your answer and include any relevant examples from your own knowledge or experience.

Write at least 250 words.

WRITING

1 문제 분석

You should spend about 40 minutes on this task. 이 문제에 약 40분을 사용한다.

Write about the following topic: 다음 토픽에 대해 글을 써라:

▶ 첫 두 줄은 모든 Task 2에 항상 똑같이 나오는 문구로 문제 풀이 시간과 이어질 토픽에 대해 언급한다.

Some parents guide their children's education towards specific careers, such as in engineering, medicine or law.
어떤 부모들은 그들의 자녀들 교육을 공학, 의학, 법학 같은 특정 진로에 맞춰서 이끈다.

What are the advantages and disadvantages for the child who has this kind of parental guidance?
이런 종류의 지도를 받는 아이에게 장점과 단점은 무엇인가?

▶ 항상 Task 2 박스 안은 두 부분으로 구분되어 제시되는데, 첫 부분은 토픽 설명, 두 번째 부분은 문제 유형 설명이다.

Give reasons for your answer and include any relevant examples from your own knowledge or experience.
대답에 대한 근거를 제시하고 자신의 지식과 경험을 바탕으로 관련된 예시를 포함한다.

Write at least 250 words.
최소 250자를 적어라.

▶ Task 2에 항상 똑같이 나오는 문장들로, 자신의 대답에 대한 근거와 이에 대한 예시를 바탕으로 250자 이상 작성을 요구한다.

2 브레인스토밍

Task 1 보다 Task 2는 배점이 높고, 특히 특정 주제에 대해 자신만의 의견을 논리적으로 나타내야 되므로, 글을 쓰기 전에 약 1~3분 정도를 어떻게 글을 쓸지 반드시 브레인스토밍을 하면서 아웃라인을 잡도록 한다.

adv(장)	더 많은 경험 more experience – 현명한 결정을 내리는데 있어서 to make informed decisions – 더 좋은 아이디어들 better ideas – 더 믿을 수 있는 more reliable
dis(단)	자율의 중요성을 간과하다 overlook the importance of autonomy – 스스로 자신의 진로를 선택할 자유 the freedom to choose their own career paths – 주인의식과 책임감이 부족하다 lack a sense of ownership and responsibility – 좋아하는 일에서 탁월해지기 위해 더 노력할 가능성 more likely to strive to achieve excellence in a profession they like

3 아웃라인 잡기

서론 – 본론 1 – 본론 2 – 본론 3 (생략 가능) – 결론의 기본 구조로 아웃라인을 잡는다. 일반적으로 아웃라인은 문제 유형별로, 그리고 자신의 논리에 따라 차이가 있는데, 일반적으로는 다음과 같이 아웃라인을 잡는다.

서론 Introduction	서론 첫 문장 – 문제 박스에 제시된 토픽 패러프레이징(*paraphrasing*)을 통해 에세이 주제에 대해 언급 마지막 문장 – 대주제문(*thesis statement*)으로, (*i*) 문제에 대한 자신의 의견, (*ii*) 앞으로 본론에서 어떤 내용을 전개할지, (*iii*) 문제에 대한 재해석 중 하나 적기
본론 Body	본론 1 첫 문장 – 본론 1 문단의 주제 문장(*topic sentence*) 본론 1 두 번째 문장 이후 – 주제 문장을 지지하는 근거 문장(*supporting sentence*) 본론 1 근거문을 뒷받침하는 세부 내용 – 구체적인 예 또는 자신만의 경험(*supporting details: examples or own experience*) 본론 1 마지막 문장(생략 가능) – 본론 1의 키 포인트를 정리하는 결론 문장(*concluding sentence*)
	본론 2 첫 문장 – 본론 2 문단의 주제 문장(*topic sentence*) 본론 2 두 번째 문장 이후 – 주제 문장을 지지하는 근거 문장(*supporting sentence*) 본론 2 근거문을 뒷받침하는 세부 내용 – 구체적인 예 또는 자료(*supporting details: example or research*) 본론 2 마지막 문장(생략 가능) – 본론 2의 키 포인트를 정리하는 결론 문장(*concluding sentence*)
결론 Conclusion	2~3 문장으로 자신의 입장 및 내용 정리

4 글쓰기

① 서론

These days, many parents try to control what their children study in an effort to push them towards specific fields and professions. (paraphrasing)
요즘, 많은 부모들이 특정 분야와 직업에 자녀들을 보내려는 노력의 일환으로 아이들이 무엇을 공부할지 통제하려고 한다. (패러프레이징)

There are both advantages and disadvantages to this kind of parental intervention. (thesis statement)
이러한 종류의 부모 간섭에는 장점과 단점 모두 있다. (대주제문: 문제에 대한 재해석)

② 본론 1: Advantages

On the one hand, the guidance of parents can be extremely beneficial to a child. (topic sentence)
한편으로, 부모의 지도는 아이에게 매우 도움이 될 수 있다. (주제 문장)

Parents who have worked in a variety of jobs have much more experience, so they are generally better equipped to make informed decisions regarding career choices and can give better ideas to their children. (supporting sentence 1)
다양한 일을 해온 부모들은 훨씬 더 많은 경험을 가지고 있기에, 일반적으로 직업 선택에 있어서 현명한 결정을 내림에 있어서 준비가 더 잘 되어 있어서 더 좋은 아이디어들을 그들의 자녀들에게 줄 수 있다. (근거 문장 1)

Another potential benefit is that parents may have connections within their own field. (supporting sentence 2)
또다른 잠재적 혜택은 부모가 자신의 분야 내에서는 연줄이 있을 수 있다는 점이다. (근거 문장 2)

For instance, a friend of mine, whose father is a renowned doctor, was happy to follow in her father's footsteps as she knew that her father's influence and referrals could open many doors for her in the medical profession. (supporting details: example)
예를 들어, 내 친구는 아버지가 유명한 의사인데, 아버지의 영향과 소개가 의료 직종에서 그녀를 많은 길로 인도할 수 있음을 알았기에, 그녀는 기꺼이 아버지의 뒤를 따랐다. (근거 세부 내용: 예)

Such parental assistance leads to a more reliable future. (concluding sentence)
이러한 부모의 도움은 더 믿을 수 있는 미래로 이끈다. (본론 1 마무리 문장)

③ 본론 2: Disadvantages

On the other hand, we cannot overlook the importance of autonomy when it comes to older children. (topic sentence)
반면에, 더 나이가 있는 아이들과 관련해서, 우리는 자율의 중요성을 놓쳐서는 안된다. (주제 문장)

In other words, we should give teenagers the freedom to choose their own career paths so that they feel a greater sense of pride in their efforts and achievements. (supporting sentence 1)
다시 말하면, 우리는 십대들이 자신의 노력에 대한 더 큰 자부심과 성취감을 느낄 수 있도록, 그들 스스로 자신의 진로를 선택할 자유를 주어야 한다. (근거 문장 1)

Moreover, if people enter a profession in which they have no interest, they will lack a sense of ownership and responsibility. (supporting sentence 2)
더욱이, 사람들은 관심이 없는 일을 하게 되면, 주인의식과 책임감이 부족하게 될 것이다. (근거 문장 2)

Instead, children should aim to enter a field that inspires them so that they can live a happy and fulfilling life. (supporting sentence 3)
대신에, 아이들은 행복하고 성취감을 주는 삶을 살 수 있도록 그들에게 영감을 주는 분야에 진입하는 것에 목표를 삼아야 한다. (근거 문장 3)

From what I have seen, children are more likely to strive to achieve excellence in a profession they like. (supporting details: experience)
내가 보아온 바로는, 아이들은 그들이 좋아하는 직업에서 특출 나기 위해 더욱 노력할 가능성이 높다. (근거 세부 내용: 경험)

④ 결론

All in all, there are both pros and cons to consider with regard to parents choosing the career path of a child. While a child can benefit from the advice of his or her parents, that child may also regret the loss of autonomy and control over their future later in their life. (summary)
종합하면, 부모가 아이의 진로를 선택하는 것에 관해 고려할 장단점이 모두 있다. 아이가 부모의 조언으로부터 혜택을 얻을 수 있는 반면, 아이는 또한 자신의 장래에 대한 자율성과 통제권 상실에 대해 후회할 수 있다. (두 문장으로 전체 핵심 내용 요약)

5 교정

다 쓴 글에 대해서 2~3분 동안 시제 일치, 주어-동사 수 일치를 반드시 확인하며 교정(proofreading)을 하자. 이 두 가지는 영문법의 기본으로 짧은 시간에 쉽게 검토 가능한 영역이다.

예문 There ~~is~~ are both advantages and disadvantages to this kind of parental intervention.
복수동사 복수명사 주어

6 최종답안

These days, many parents try to control what their children study in an effort to push them towards specific fields and professions. There are both advantages and disadvantages to this kind of parental intervention.	요즘, 많은 부모들이 특정 분야와 직업에 자녀들을 보내려는 노력의 일환으로 아이들이 무엇을 공부할지 통제하려고 한다. 이러한 종류의 부모 간섭에는 장점과 단점 모두 있다.
On the one hand, the guidance of parents can be extremely beneficial to a child. Parents who have worked in a variety of jobs have much more experience, so they are generally better equipped to make informed decisions regarding career choices and can give better ideas to their children. Another potential benefit is that parents may have connections within their own field. For instance, a friend of mine, whose father is a renowned doctor, was happy to follow in her father's footsteps as she knew that her father's influence and referrals could open many doors for her in the medical profession. Such parental assistance leads to a more reliable future.	한편으로, 부모의 지도는 아이에게 매우 도움이 될 수 있다. 다양한 일을 해온 부모들은 훨씬 더 많은 경험을 가지고 있기에, 일반적으로 직업 선택에 있어서 현명한 결정을 내림에 있어서 준비가 더 잘 되어 있어서 더 좋은 아이디어들을 그들의 자녀들에게 줄 수 있다. 또다른 잠재적 혜택은 부모가 자신의 분야 내에서는 연줄이 있을 수 있다는 점이다. 예를 들어, 내 친구는 아버지가 유명한 의사인데, 아버지의 영향과 소개가 의료 직종에서 그녀를 많은 길로 인도할 수 있음을 알았기에, 그녀는 기꺼이 아버지의 뒤를 따랐다. 이러한 부모의 도움은 더 믿을 수 있는 미래로 이끈다.
On the other hand, we cannot overlook the importance of autonomy when it comes to older children. In other words, we should give teenagers the freedom to choose their own career paths so that they feel a greater sense of pride in their efforts and achievements. Moreover, if people enter a profession in which they have no interest, they will lack a sense of ownership and responsibility. Instead, children should aim to enter a field that inspires them so that they can live a happy and fulfilling life. From what I have seen, children are more likely to strive to achieve excellence in a profession they like.	반면에, 더 나이가 있는 아이들과 관련해서, 우리는 자율의 중요성을 놓쳐서는 안된다. 다시 말하면, 우리는 십대들이 자신의 노력에 대한 더 큰 자부심과 성취감을 느낄 수 있도록, 그들 스스로 자신의 진로를 선택할 자유를 주어야 한다. 더욱이, 사람들은 관심이 없는 일을 하게 되면, 주인의식과 책임감이 부족하게 될 것이다. 대신에, 아이들은 행복하고 성취감을 주는 삶을 살 수 있도록 그들에게 영감을 주는 분야에 진입하는 것에 목표를 삼아야 한다. 내가 보아온 바로는, 아이들은 그들이 좋아하는 직업에서 특출 나기 위해 더욱 노력할 가능성이 높다.
All in all, there are both pros and cons to consider with regard to parents choosing the career path of a child. While a child can benefit from the advice of his or her parents, that child may also regret the loss of autonomy and control over their future later in their life. (304 words)	종합하면, 부모가 아이의 진로를 선택하는 것에 관한 장단점이 모두 있다. 아이가 부모의 조언으로부터 혜택을 얻을 수 있는 반면, 아이는 또한 자신의 장래에 대한 자율성과 통제권 상실에 대해 후회할 수 있다.

문법 정리 3: 분사 - 동사의 형용사화

❶ -ing/-ed 형태의 수식

일반적으로 동사에 -ing가 붙으면 능동의 의미, -ed가 붙으면 수동의 의미이다.

예 Students attending the class have to fill out a survey.
그 수업에 참석하는 학생들은 설문지를 작성해야 한다. (능동)

All the questions asked by the students were relevant.
학생들로부터 받은 모든 질문들이 적절하였다. (수동)

❷ 감정 형용사

감정을 나타내는 동사에 -ing나 -ed를 붙이면 형용사가 된다. 이때, 일반적으로 사람을 수식하면 -ed, 사물을 수식하면 -ing가 붙는다고 생각하면 편하다.

기쁨의 감정: please 기쁘게 하다	The music was pleasing to the ear. 그 음악은 귀를 즐겁게 했다(듣기 좋았다). We are pleased to hear you are feeling better. 우리는 당신의 (건강) 상태가 더 좋아진다고 들어서 기쁩니다.
흥분의 감정: excite 흥분시키다	The school offers an exciting programme. 학교가 흥미로운 프로그램을 제공한다. An excited crowd waited for the band to arrive. 흥분한 관중들이 밴드가 도착하기를 기다렸다.
실망의 감정: disappoint 실망시키다	His essay was somewhat disappointing. 그의 에세이는 다소 실망스러웠다. He was disappointed to see his essay returned with some poor comments. 그는 안 좋은 평가와 함께 되돌려 받은 그의 에세이를 보고 실망했다.
혼란의 감정: confuse 혼란시키다	The instructions are obscure and confusing. 설명이 모호하고 혼란스럽다. I was momentarily confused by the foreign road signs. 외국의 도로 표지에 나는 잠시 혼란스러웠다.
흥미의 감정: interest 흥미를 일으키다	That story is interesting. 그 이야기는 흥미롭다. Some people are not interested in social networking sites. 어떤 사람들은 SNS에 흥미가 없다.
격려의 감정: encourage 격려하다	The sales figures are very encouraging. 그 판매 수치는 매우 고무적이다. I was encouraged by a lot of positive feedback. 나는 많은 긍정적인 피드백에 의해 힘을 얻었다.
당황의 감정: embarrass 당황스럽게 하다	Students can learn how to overcome embarrassing situations. 학생들은 당황스러운 상황들을 극복하는 법을 배울 수 있다. Some people are embarrassed about their weight. 몇몇 사람들은 자신들의 몸무게에 당황스러워한다.

자가 평가

Task 2 문제를 풀고 나서 아래 채점기준에 맞게 자신의 글을 평가하도록 한다. 이때, 자신의 글에 어떠한 부족한 점이 있고, 어떻게 더 발전시켜야 되는지를 고민해 보자,

Academic/General Training Task 2 채점기준

채점 영역	채점기준	확인
Task Response **과제 응답**	• 과제의 모든 요구사항에 맞게 자신의 의견에 대한 근거와 예시 포함	Y / N
	• 최소 250자 이상 작성	Y / N
	• 제시된 토픽에 대한 답변	Y / N
	• 완전하게 전개된 자신의 생각 및 입장을 보여줌	Y / N
	• 결론이 불명확하거나 본론에 대한 반복이 아님	Y / N
Coherence and Cohesion **일관성과 응집성**	• 충분한 응집 장치(접속사, 부사 등의 연결어, 한정사 및 대명사) 사용	Y / N
	• 서론 – 본론 1, 2 – 결론의 문단 구성	Y / N
	• 주제 문장과 뒷받침 문장 간의 논리적 연결	Y / N
	• 문단 간의 연속성	Y / N
Lexical Resource **어휘력**	• 다양한 어휘를 정확하게 사용	Y / N
	• 같은 단어를 반복 사용하는 대신 동의어 및 패러프레이징 사용	Y / N
	• 철자 오류 없음	Y / N
	• 구동사 등의 평이한 어휘보다 고급 어휘 사용	Y / N
Grammatical Range and Accuracy **문법의 다양성과 정확성**	• 다양한 문장 형태(복문, 문장의 5형식)를 완벽하게 사용함	Y / N
	• 다양한 문법 사항(접속사, 관계대명사, 명사절, 분사구문 등)을 완벽하게 사용	Y / N
	• 문법 실수가 없음	Y / N
	• 구두점(punctuation) 사용이 완벽함	Y / N

Academic/General Training Task 2 다음 기출 변형 문제를 서론 - 본론 - 결론 형식에 맞게 영작하자.

You should spend about 40 minutes on this task.

Write about the following topic:

> *Due to the development of intelligent technology, computers will become more intelligent than human beings. Some people say this development will have a positive impact on humans. Others have a negative view on this issue.*
>
> *Discuss both these views and give your own opinion.*

Give reasons for your answer and include any relevant examples from your own knowledge or experience.

Write at least 250 words.

서론

서론 토픽 패러프레이징

____

____

서론 마지막 문장(대주제문)

____

____

정답 및 해설 p.069

본론 1

본론 1 첫 문장(주제 문장)

본론 1 근거 문장 및 세부 내용

본론 2

본론 2 첫 문장(주제 문장)

본론 2 근거 문장 및 세부 내용

결론

UNIT 18

Task 2 - 에세이 토픽 브레인스토밍

오늘의 학습 목표

1 같은 단어를 반복해서 사용하지 않기 위한 방법을 익힌다.
2 논점에서 벗어나는 오프토픽(off-topic)을 피한다.
3 빈출 에세이 주제별 브레인스토밍을 연습해보고 관련 어휘를 알아둔다.

같은 단어 사용 반복 피하기

채점기준인 어휘력(Lexical Resource)에서 다양한 어휘 사용(showing a wide variety of vocabulary)과 함께, 같은 단어 반복을 피하는 것(avoiding repetition)은 가장 중요한 채점 요소이다. 단어 반복을 피하기 위해서는 다음과 같은 방법들이 있다.

1 동의어/유의어 사용

같거나 유사한 의미를 갖고 있는 단어를 사용하여 자신의 다양한 어휘력을 보여주면서 같은 단어 사용 반복을 피한다. 단, Task 2에서 요구하는 에세이는 formal writing에 해당하므로 informal 단어의 사용은 자제한다.

예시 **think**(생각하다) → **believe**(믿다), **argue**(주장하다), **consider**(여기다), **be of the opinion**(생각하다)

▶ reckon(생각하다): informal 단어로 Task 2에서는 사용 자제

school students(학교 학생들) → **pupils**(어린 학생들), **young learners**(어린 학습자들), **children**(아이들)

▶ kids(애들): informal 단어로 Task 2에서는 사용 자제

2 대명사 사용

앞에서 언급된 명사를 지칭하는 대명사를 사용하여, 명사의 반복 사용을 피한다. 대명사의 적절한 사용은 또다른 채점기준인 일관성과 응집성(Coherence and Cohesion)에서 추가 점수를 얻는 요소가 되기도 한다.

예시 **If a** patient **is sufficiently anesthetised,** he or she **will feel no pain during surgery.**

환자가 충분히 마취가 된다면, 그 또는 그녀는 수술 동안에 아픔을 느끼지 않을 것이다.

3 상위 단어 사용

사용된 단어를 포함하는 개념의 상위 단어를 사용하거나 전체를 총괄하여 지칭할 수 있다.

예시 **tiger, lion, wolf**(호랑이, 사자, 늑대) → **predator**(포식자) → **animal**(동물)

oil, gas(기름, 가스) → **fossil fuels**(화석 연료) → **natural resources**(천연 자원)

hospitals, banks, schools, shops(병원, 은행, 학교, 상점) → **amenities**(편의시설들) → **facilities**(시설들)

Off-Topic 피하기

채점기준인 과제 응답(Task Response)에서 자신의 의견에 대한 근거와 예시를 포함하여 250자 이하로 작성하되 과제와 관련 있는 아이디어만 제시하여야 한다. 즉 브레인스토밍을 통해 좋은 아이디어를 생각해내고, 이에 대한 다양한 관련 어휘를 안다고 하여도, 과제와 관련이 없는 아이디어와 어휘라면, 글에 포함하면 안된다.

예제 아래 문장 중 과제 주제와 관련 없는 아이디어를 **두 개** 고르시오.

Topic: Smart phones allow people to stay connected with each other, but they also isolate us.
스마트폰은 사람들이 서로 연결되도록 돕지만, 또한 우리를 고립시키기도 한다.

A Smart phones make it easier to work while we are travelling.
스마트폰은 우리가 이동하면서도 일하기 더 쉽도록 한다.

B People have difficulty escaping from work due to constant communication with work through text messages and e-mail.
사람들은 문자 메시지와 이메일을 통해 업무와 관련된 끊임없는 연락으로 인해 일에서 벗어나기 어렵다.

C Many people often visit social networking sites, but they rarely see their virtual friends.
많은 사람들이 종종 SNS를 이용하지만, 그들의 실제 친구를 거의 만나지는 않는다.

D With more and more technological advances, our society becomes better to live in.
더욱 더 많은 기술적 진보와 함께, 우리 사회는 더 살기 좋아진다.

E Through a smart phone, I can keep in touch with my friends and family every day.
스마트폰을 통해, 나는 내 친구들과 가족과 매일 연락할 수 있다.

여기서 주제는 스마트폰의 장점으로 사람 간의 연결, 단점으로는 고립을 제시한다. 따라서 스마트폰으로 인한 연결(장점)과 고립(단점)에 대해 나타내는 아이디어들이 필요하다.

A는 스마트폰과 사람의 연결로 인한 장점을 언급하므로 관련 아이디어이다.

B는 스마트폰으로 인한 단점이긴 하지만 고립이 아닌 다른 단점을 언급하므로 off-topic이다.

C는 스마트폰과 연관된 고립을 언급하므로 관련 아이디어이다.

D는 주제와 연관없이 너무 일반적인 내용을 언급하므로 off-topic이다.

E는 스마트폰으로 인한 연결의 장점을 언급하므로 관련 아이디어이다.

이렇듯 B처럼 좋은 아이디어가 있어도 과제와 연관이 없다면 사용하면 안된다. 또한 D처럼 주제와 관련 없는 일반적인 아이디어도 off-topic이므로 이러한 문구 사용 역시 자제한다.

WRITING

Task 2 빈출 토픽 관련 어휘 및 아이디어

Task 2는 단순히 영작 실력을 묻는 것이 아니라 글쓴이가 자신의 논리적이며 깊은 사고를 얼마나 보일 수 있는지를 묻는 영역이다. 아이엘츠 시험이 한 국가의 상위 교육기관에 진학할 인재와 그 나라에 도움이 될 이민자를 선별할 목적으로 영어 실력을 측정하는 시험인 만큼, 지적인 아이디어와 어휘들을 최대한 270~290자에 담아낼 수 있어야 한다. 따라서 시험에 빈출되는 토픽에 대한 충분한 브레인스토밍을 통해 폭넓은 아이디어와 그에 대한 어휘를 최대한 습득하도록 한다.

다음은 시험에 자주 나온 문제들을 크게 교육, 정부, 사회의 3개 큰 분야로 나누어 빈출 토픽 소개 및 관련 아이디어와 어휘를 나열한다. 직접 브레인스토밍을 해보면서 자신만의 아이디어나 유용한 어휘가 있으면 추가하도록 하자.

1 교육(Education)

① 교과목이나 직업에 있어서 성별에 따라 구분이 필요한지 논의

- 남녀평등
  gender equality
- 여성과 남성이 같음을 의미하는 것은 아님
  not imply that females and males are the same
- 개별 자질들에 대한 축복을 받다
  be blessed with individual qualities
- 적성을 개발하다(키우다, 찾다)
  develop(nurture, find) one's aptitude
- 한계를 정하다
  define the boundary

② 고등학교 졸업하고 바로 일할 때, 또는 여행을 할 때, 아니면 공부할 때 장단점 논의

- 고등학교 졸업 후 바로 대학에 가지 않고 여행이나 일을 하며 일년을 보내다
  take a gap year
- 시야를 넓히다
  broaden their horizons
- 금전 및 필수적 생활 기술에 대한 책임감
  responsibility for finances and other essential life skills
- 허송세월하다
  waste his or her time
- 경력을 쌓거나 경험을 쌓다
  build one's career or gain experience

③ 타고난 선천적 요소와 경험/교육을 통한 후천적 요소 중 무엇이 더 중요한지 논의

- 타고난 재능과 능력
  innate talents and abilities
- 유전적 자질
  genetic endowment

- 경험으로 배우고 얻다
  be learned and acquired with experience
- 적절한 교육과 훈련의 도움으로
  with the help of proper education and training

④ 대학이 취업에 필요한 기술과 지식 전수에 중점을 맞춰야 되는지, 아니면 취업과 관련 없이 학문적 추구에 중점을 맞춰야 되는지 논의

- 직업과 관련 없는 코스
  non-vocational courses
- 학생들에게 지식을 제공하다
  provide students with knowledge
- 자신의 선호에 따라
  depending on their preference
- 학생들을 인력으로서 준비시키다
  prepare students for the workforce
- 창의력을 증진시키다
  enhance creativity
- 학교는 양쪽의 좋은 점을 고려해야 한다
  schools should consider both qualities

⑤ 아이들 훈육을 부모가 담당해야 할지, 아니면 학교가 담당해야 할지 논의

- 강력한 기여
  a strong contribution
- 다음 세대에게 훌륭한 사회구성원이 되는 방법을 가르치다
  teach the next generation how to be good members of society
- 집에서 시작되다
  begin in the home
- 다음 단계로 나아가다
  advance to the next step
- 규칙에 복종하고 다른 사람들을 존중하다
  obey rules and respect others

⑥ 아이들에게 비싼 선물을 사주는 것이 나쁜 생각인지 논의

- 따스함과 감정이 없는 물질 세계
  a materialistic world devoid of warmth and feeling
- 아이들이 사랑과 우정같이 더 중요한 가치들을 제대로 인식하는 것을 막다
  prevent children from appreciating more important values such as love and friendship

- 돈으로 무엇이든 살 수 있다는 인상을 주다
  give an impression that everything can be bought with money
- 사회에 어울리기 어려운
  difficult to fit in society

⑦ 아이들에게 경쟁심이 장려되어야 될지, 아니면 협동심이 장려되어야 될지

- 경쟁과 협동을 동시에 할 필요가 있다
  need to compete and cooperate simultaneously
- 공부에서 뛰어나거나 운동경기에서 이기면서 경쟁하는 것을 배우다
  learn to compete to excel in studies or win an athletic event
- 축구같은 팀 스포츠나 그룹 과제를 하면서 협동심을 배울 수 있다
  can be taught cooperation when they play team sports like football or work on group assignments
- 다른 팀들과 경쟁하기 위해 자신의 팀원들과 협력하다
  cooperate with their team members to compete with the other teams

⑧ 조기 외국어 교육의 장단점

- 어린 나이에 외국어 공부를 시작하는 것
  starting to learn a foreign language at a young age
- 아이들의 지적 능력
  the intellectual abilities of children
- 더 높은 단계의 유창함을 달성하다
  achieve a higher level of fluency
- 정체성과 모국어에 부정적 영향
  negative impacts on their identity and speaking their mother tongue

⑨ 외국어 학습이 해외 여행이나 해외 근무 외에도 어떤 이유로 필요한지 논의

- 다양한 문화와 전통적 면을 이해하는데 돕다
  help to understand diverse cultural and traditional aspects
- 세계에 대한 이해력을 증가시키다
  increase global understanding
- 인지 능력을 향상시키다
  improve cognitive skills
- 세계 문화, 음악, 예술 그리고 영화를 감상하다
  appreciate international literature, music, art and film

2 정부(Government)

① 가난한 나라에 대한 선진국의 지원 의무가 타당한지 논의

- 양쪽 모두에 긍정적
  a win-win situation for both
- 가난에서 비롯된 많은 사회악
  many social evils resulting from poverty
- 가난한 국가에 재정적 지원을 제공
  providing financial aid to poor nations
- 세상을 살기에 더 평화로운 곳으로 만들다
  make the world a more peaceful place to live in
- 가난한 국가 국민들의 구매력 향상
  the increase in the purchasing power of people living in poor nations
- 부유한 국가의 판매 증가
  rise in the sales of rich nations
- 난민 급증(선진국 지원이 없을 때 일어날 수 있는 일)
  a sudden increase in the number of refugees

② 범죄에 대한 획일적 처벌이 필요한지, 아니면 개별 상황과 동기를 고려하여야 하는지 논의

- 획일적 처벌이 상당한 양의 시간과 돈을 줄일 수 있다
  fixed punishments can save a substantial amount of time and money
- 정상 참작이 가능한 정황들
  extenuating circumstances
- 범죄율에 영향을 미치는 가난과 교육 같은 요인들
  factors influencing crime rates such as poverty and education
- 올바르고 공정한 판결을 내리다
  issue a just and fair verdict
- 사회에 미치는 영향은 비슷하다
  the effects on our society are almost the same
- 상황을 탓하며 쉽게 범죄를 저지를 수 있다
  easily commit crimes, blaming the circumstances

③ 범죄자에 대해 처벌보다 교육이 더 중요하다는 주장에 대한 논의

- 대부분 범죄자들은 환경의 피해자들이다
  most criminals are victims of circumstances
- 사회 빈곤층
  the poor strata of the society
- 교육 부족
  lack of education

- 적은 취업 기회
  not many employment opportunities
- 더 높은 범죄 성향
  higher criminal tendencies
- 사회에 위협이 되다
  pose a threat to society
- 다른 시민들의 안전을 위해 수감되어야 한다
  should be put in prison to ensure the safety of other citizens

④ 교통/오염 문제 해결을 위해 석유 가격 인상이 최선책인지 논의

- 산업에서 아주 중요한 역할을 하다
  play a fundamental role in the industry
- 운송비를 증가시키다
  increase transport costs
- 여러 제품들 가격에 영향을 미치다
  influence the prices of the various goods
- 교통 체증과 공기 오염을 해결하기 위한 다른 방안들
  some other ways to tackle traffic congestion and air pollution
- 대중 교통 수단을 개선하다
  improve the modes of public transport services
- 자가용 운전에 대한 매력적이고 경제적인 대안들
  attractive and affordable alternatives to driving your own car
- 재생 에너지 자원 개발에 투자
  investment in developing renewable energy resources

⑤ 정부가 세금을 도로보다 철도에 투자하는 것에 어느 정도 찬성하는지 논의

- 도로 교통 사고 사상자들
  casualties in road traffic accidents
- 더 안전하고, 빠르고, 믿을 수 있는 교통 수단
  a safer, faster and more reliable means of transport
- 지역의 지질 상태
  the geological condition of an area
- 인구밀도가 높은 지역
  areas of high population density

⑥ 자원 재활용이나 분리수거 시행을 위한 유일한 방법이 정부의 규제인지 논의

- 규제를 시행하다
  impose regulations
- 개인이나 사업체에 벌금을 부과하다
  fine individuals or businesses

- 소셜 미디어나 광고를 통해 대중의 관심(인식)을 고취시키다
  raise public awareness via social media or advertising
- 재활용의 중요성에 대해 시민들을 교육시키다
  educate people about the importance of recycling

⑦ 대중의 건강을 증진하기 위해 스포츠 시설 설립이 최선의 방법일지, 아니면 더 좋은 방법이 있을지 논의

- 건강을 증진시키고 만성 질병의 위험을 줄이기 위한 신체 활동
  physical activity to improve health and reduce the risk of chronic disease
- 흡연, 음주, 사이버 중독과 같은 나쁜 습관을 경고하는 광고
  adverts warning of bad habits such as smoking, drinking and cyber addiction
- 균형 잡힌 식단에 관해 사람들을 교육시키다
  educate people about a balanced diet
- 건강한 삶의 방식과 양질의 의료 시설
  healthy lifestyle and quality healthcare facilities

WRITING

⑧ 사람들의 체중 증가의 원인과 이로 인한 어떠한 건강 문제가 있는지, 그리고 해결책 논의

- 유전자와 생활 방식 같은 요인들
  factors such as genes and lifestyle
- 고혈압, 당뇨, 심장병 그리고 관절 문제
  high blood pressure, diabetes, heart disease and joint problems
- 과체중인 사람들에 대한 반감으로 인한 사회 심리적 스트레스
  psychosocial stress resulting from disapproval of overweight people
- 규칙적인 운동과 건강한 식단
  regular exercise and a healthy eating plan

3 사회(Society)

① 광고가 사람들 소비에 어떻게, 어떠한 영향을 미치는지 논의

- 소비자의 구매 행동에 영향을 미치다
  influence consumers' buying behaviour
- 상품에 대해 긍정적이고 오래 가는 인상을 만들다
  create positive and long-lasting impressions about their products
- 소비자들을 잘못 이끈다
  mislead consumers
- 자신의 예산을 벗어나 소비하도록 사람들을 조종하다
  manipulate people to spend outside of their budget

② 기술 발달로 인한 과거 방식(종이책, 오프라인 몰, 기타 예전 삶의 방식들)이 완전히 사라지게 될지 논의

- 전자책과 실체가 있는 책
  digital books and physical books

- 돈, 시간 그리고 공간을 아끼다
  save money, time and space
- 물건을 직접 보고 만지는 것을 좋아하다 = 실제로 물건을 경험하다 (옷, 화장품 등)
  like to see and touch items in person = actually experience products (e.g. clothes, cosmetics)
- 고객들이 상점들과 개인적 관계를 정립할 기회
  the opportunity for customers to establish personal connections with stores
- 일부는 미래에도 살아남을 것이다
  some of them will survive in the future

③ 소셜 미디어의 장단점

- 현재 벌어지는 사안에 대해 더 많은 정보를 받는
  more informed about current affairs
- 더 쉽게 그룹 토론을 가능하게 하다
  make group discussions easier
- 장애인들이 다른 사람들과 동등하게 소통하도록 돕다
  help people with disabilities interact at the same level with others
- 사이버 괴롭힘에 노출되다
  be exposed to cyberbullying
- 면대면 의사소통과 사회성 능력을 없애다
  erase face-to-face communication and social skills
- 사람들을 고립시키고 실상의 접촉을 방해한다
  isolate people and discourage real interaction
- 너무 많은 개인 세부 정보를 노출하다
  disclose too many personal details

④ 로봇이 인간의 일을 대신하는 것에 대한 장단점 논의

- 기계에 대체되다
  be replaced by machines
- 덜 활동적이 되다
  become less active
- 비만과 같은 건강 문제들
  some health problems like obesity
- 사람의 손길이 닿을 수 없는 곳에서 작업하다
  operate in locations that humans cannot reach
- 해저와 같이 외진 환경을 탐험하다
  explore remote environments like the ocean floor
- 24시간 일하고 최소의 관리가 요구된다
  work twenty-four hours and require minimal maintenance

⑤ 인공 지능이 인간을 능가할 수 있는 미래에 대한 긍정적/부정적 의견 논의

- 휴대폰과 노트북 같은 기계들의 대중성과 보편성
  the popularity and ubiquity of devices such as mobile phones and laptop computers
- 선호도와 인터넷 검색 기록을 통해 우리의 사용자 경험을 극대화해준다
  optimise our user experience based on preferences and browsing history
- 실업 증가
  a rise in unemployment
- 작은 기계적 결함이나 오작동이 전 세계적 재앙이 될 수 있다
  a glitch or malfunction can result in a global catastrophe

⑥ 직업에 따라 받는 급여가 다른데 이에 대한 옹호 또는 정부의 급여 상한제 도입 의견 논의

- 돈은 사람이 성공하기에 필요한 기술과 헌신에 대한 척도가 될 수 있다
  money could be an indicator of the skills and dedication a person needs to be successful
- 높은 봉급은 숙련된 인력이 나라를 떠나는 것을 막는다
  excellent pay packages deter skilled people from leaving a country
- 높은 봉급은 사람들이 위험하고 힘든 일을 하도록 유인한다
  high salaries entice people to do dangerous or unpleasant work
- 급여 상한제는 더 많은 평등을 갖고 올 것이다
  limiting high salaries would bring more equality
- 높은 급여 제한이 아닌 기회의 평등이 중요하다
  equal opportunity is important, not limiting high salaries

⑦ 세계적으로 같은 제품을 구매하고 사용하는 것에 대한 장단점 논의

- 세계화와 규모의 경제로 인해 외국의 좋은 제품을 싼 값에 사용한다
  use good foreign products at low prices because of globalisation and economies of scale
- 수출품을 통해 그 나라의 문화를 접할 수 있다
  can be introduced to a country's culture through its exports
- 문화적 다양성의 상실은 인류에 커다란 손실이다
  the loss of cultural diversity is a great loss for humanity
- 한 나라에서 다른 나라로 제품을 운송하는 것은 엄청난 온실가스 배출 증가를 불러일으킨다
  transporting goods from one country to another country causes a tremendous increase in greenhouse gas emissions

⑧ 과소비에 대한 원인과 해결책 논의

- 군중을 좇아가다
  keep up with the crowd
- 온라인 쇼핑과 신용카드가 소비를 너무 쉽게 만든다
  online shopping and credit cards make spending too easy
- 체크카드 사용
  using a debit card

⑨ 농업의 발달에도 세계적으로 굶는 사람들이 많은데 그 이유와 해결책 논의

- 홍수, 가뭄 그리고 지진과 같은 자연 재해
  natural disasters such as floods, droughts and earthquakes
- 정치적 문제와 내전에 따른 농작과 유통의 어려움
  difficulty in farming and distributing food due to political issues and civil wars
- 과학적 기반으로 땅을 경작하도록 농부들을 훈련시키다
  train farmers to cultivate their lands on a scientific basis
- 유전 공학을 포함한 현대 기술의 사용
  use of modern technologies including genetic engineering
- 냉장고가 필요 없는 말린 식량을 비축하는 것
  storing dry foods that do not need refrigerators

⑩ 수명 연장에 대한 장단점 논의

- 사랑하는 사람들과 있을 수 있음
  being together with their loved ones
- 은퇴를 즐길 시간
  time to enjoy their retirement
- 손주들 돌보는데 도움
  helping look after their grandchildren
- 가족과 사회의 무거운 짐
  a heavy burden on their family and society
- 의료 시설 부족
  a shortage of medical facilities

⑪ 음식물 쓰레기 원인과 해결책 논의

- 싼 음식 가격
  the low cost of food
- 집약적 작물 재배
  intensive crop farming
- 유전자 변형 작물
  genetically modified crops
- 이러한 문제에 대한 경각심을 일깨움
  raising awareness of this issue
- 음식물 쓰레기를 방지하는 법을 시행
  enforcing laws that prevent food waste

문법 정리 4: 접속사 vs. 전치사 vs. 접속부사

수험생들이 많이 틀리는 부분 중 하나로, 접속사를 써야 될 자리에 전치사나 접속부사를 넣는 경우가 있다. 문장에 알맞은 접속사, 전치사, 접속부사를 각각의 특징에 맞게 넣어서 사용하도록 한다.

접속사

각각의 절(주어+동사)을 연결해 주는 연결사로 and, but 등의 등위접속사와 when, although, because 등의 부사절 접속사가 있다. 절+접속사+절, 또는 부사절접속사+절, 절의 구조로 사용된다.

예문 The policy on controlling oil prices has some serious drawbacks although it helps to save energy.
석유 가격 조정 정책이 에너지를 절약하는데 도움이 되지만 몇몇 심각한 문제가 있다.
▶ 절(it helps ~)을 연결하므로 접속사를 써야 됨

전치사

명사 앞에 위치하여 명사와 함께 수식어구 역할을 하는 품사로, 접속사같이 절과 절을 연결하지 못하고 명사만 뒤에 연결해 주는, 전치사+명사의 구조이다.

예문 The policy has some serious drawbacks in spite of some advantages.
몇몇 장점에도 불구하고, 그 정책은 몇몇 심각한 문제가 있다.
▶ 명사(some advantages)를 연결하므로 전치사를 써야 됨

접속부사

접속부사란 문장과 문장, 또는 문단과 문단을 부드럽게 연결해 주는 부사로, 접속사나 전치사가 아니므로 두 개의 절이나 명사를 연결할 수 없고, 쉼표가 접속부사에 따라온다. 예를 들어, 접속부사가 문두에 왔으면 뒤에 쉼표가 오고, 문장 중간에 왔다면 앞뒤에 쉼표가 온다.

예문 However, increasing oil prices can be a severe blow to national competitiveness.
= Increasing oil prices, however, can be a severe blow to national competitiveness.
그러나, 유가 상승이 국가 경쟁력에 심각한 타격을 줄 수 있다.
▶ 두개의 절을 연결하는 것이 아니고 하나의 절만 나오기에 접속부사를 써야 됨

뜻이 유사한 접속사, 전치사, 접속부사 정리

	접속사	전치사	접속부사
시간: ~하는 동안	while	during	
~하자마자	as soon as	upon(=on) ~ing	
~전에	before	before = prior to	previously 이전에
~후에	after	after = following	then 그리고 나서
~까지, ~때쯤	by the time	by	
이유: ~때문에(그래서)	because = as = since = now that	because of = due to = owing to	therefore = thus
양보: 비록 ~이지만	although = even though	despite = in spite of = notwithstanding	nevertheless 그럼에도 불구하고 = nonetheless = notwithstanding
조건: 만일 ~가 아니면 ~인 경우에	unless = if not in case	without ~이 없으면 in case of	otherwise 그렇지 않으면
역접: 그러나 반면에	but while = whereas		however on the other hand

WRITING

PRACTICE TEST

Academic/General Training Task 2 **다음 기출 변형 문제를 채점기준에 맞게 써보자.**

You should spend about 40 minutes on this task.

Write about the following topic:

Studies show that many criminals do not receive enough education. For this reason, some people believe that the best way to reduce crime is to educate them rather than punish them.

To what extent do you agree or disagree with this statement?

Give reasons for your answer and include any relevant examples from your own knowledge or experience.

Write at least 250 words.

서론

서론 토픽 패러프레이징

____

____

서론 마지막 문장(대주제문)

____

____

정답 및 해설 p.071

본론 1

본론 1 첫 문장(주제 문장)

본론 1 근거 문장 및 세부 내용

본론 2

본론 2 첫 문장(주제 문장)

본론 2 근거 문장 및 세부 내용

결론

WRITING

UNIT 19 Task 2 - 에세이 영작 스킬

오늘의 학습 목표

1. 자신의 의견을 나타내는 표현을 익힌다.
2. 서론-본론-결론에 각각 필요한 표현 및 영작 스킬을 익힌다.
3. 글의 일관성과 응집력을 위해 다양한 연결어(linking words)를 적재적소에 사용한다.

자신의 의견/입장 표현 영작 스킬

1 Task 2 필수요소

Task 2 에세이 답안에는 반드시 자신만의 의견이 명확히 나타나야 된다. 많은 수험생들이 답안에 자신의 의견은 없이 일반적 사람들의 의견, 사회 현상만 적고 끝나는 경우가 많은데 이런 경우 채점기준 과제 응답(Task Response) 부분을 이행하지 않은 것이기에 좋은 점수를 받을 수 없다. 따라서 서론 마지막 문장이나 결론에서는 자신만의 의견을 확실히 나타내며, 본론에서 자신의 의견을 뒷받침할 논거 및 자신의 경험을 기술해야 한다.

그리고 이러한 자신의 의견 및 입장에 따라 전체 글의 흐름이 달라진다. 따라서 문제를 읽고 바로 아웃라인을 잡기 전에, 먼저 자신의 입장을 정하고 그에 대한 브레인스토밍을 한 후 아웃라인을 잡도록 한다.

2 자신의 의견/입장 표현 방법

자신의 의견을 표현하는 방법으로는 다음과 같이 4가지 방법이 있다.

의견/추측의 부사 사용	personally 개인적으로, probably 아마도 예문 개인적으로, 나는 이것이 좋은 아이디어라고 믿는다. Personally, I believe this is a good idea. ※ Personally는 I와 함께 짝꿍으로 자주 쓰인다.
가능성/추측의 조동사 사용	would ~일 것이다, could ~일 것이다, might ~일지 모른다 예문 이것은 좋은 아이디어일 것이다. This could be a good idea.
의견/추측의 수식어구 사용	in my view 내 의견으로, in my personal opinion 내 개인적 의견으로 예문 내 의견으로, 이것은 좋은 아이디어이다. In my view, this is a good idea.

의견/이해/추측의 동사 사용	① 자신의 의견을 표현할 때: believe, feel, think, be convinced 예문 나는 이것이 좋은 아이디어라고 생각한다. I feel that this is a good idea. ② 자신의 이해를 나타낼 때: realise, understand 예문 나는 이것이 좋은 아이디어임을 안다. I realise that this is a good idea. ③ 자신의 추측을 나타낼 때: suspect, suppose 예문 나는 이것이 좋은 아이디어라고 추측한다. I suspect that this is a good idea.

문법 정리 5: 명사절 접속사 that

명사절 접속사 that은 주어 + 동사로 이루어진 절을 하나의 명사처럼 묶어서 주어, 목적어, 보어 자리에 사용하도록 도와주는 접속사이다.

예문 매 상황이 다르다는 것은 사실일 것이다.

That every situation is different could be true. ▶ that절이 문장의 주어로 쓰임

나는 매 상황이 다르다는 것을 이해한다.

I understand that every situation is different. ▶ that절이 동사(understand)의 목적어로 쓰임

그 이유는 매 상황이 다르다는 것이다.

The reason is that every situation is different. ▶ that절이 동사(is)의 보어로 쓰임

명사절 접속사 that과 관계대명사 that은 뒤에 절(주어 + 동사)을 이끄는 점에서 비슷해 보이지만, 다음과 같은 차이가 있다.

	명사절 접속사 that이 이끄는 절	관계대명사 that이 이끄는 절
역할	문장의 주어, 목적어, 보어 역할	관계대명사 앞에 있는 명사(선행사)를 수식하는 수식어 역할
형태	주어, 동사, 목적어 등을 갖춘 완전한 절	주어나 목적어가 없는 불완전한 절

예문 나는 최근에 변한 그 상황을 이해한다.

I understand the situation that has recently changed.

▶ that절이 the situation을 수식하는 관계대명사절로 that절에 주어가 따로 있지 않고 관계대명사 that이 주어 역할도 하므로, 여기서 that은 '주격 관계대명사'라고 부름

나는 미래 세대가 맞닥뜨릴지 모르는 그 상황을 이해한다.

I understand the situation that the future generation might encounter.

▶ that절이 the situation을 수식하는 관계대명사절로 that절의 타동사 encounter에 목적어가 없고 대신 관계대명사 that이 목적어 역할을 하므로, 여기서 that은 '목적격 관계대명사'라고 부름

문단 및 문장 영작 스킬

1 서론 패러프레이징 방법

패러프레이징(Paraphrasing), 즉 주어진 말을 다른 표현으로 변형하지만 같은 의미를 전달하는 방법으로 보통 다음의 세 가지 방법이 사용되며, 이 세 가지 방법을 혼용하여 패러프레이징 연습을 하자.

- **단어 변경**: 문제에 제시된 단어와 같거나 유사한 의미의 단어로 대체하여 표현
- **문장 구조 변경**: 능동태와 수동태, 구와 절을 서로 바꿔가며 표현
- **재작성**: 제시된 내용과 큰 틀에서 비슷한 내용으로 완전히 다시 작성

문제에 제시된 문장	패러프레이징
Nowadays, people waste a lot of food that was bought from shops and restaurants. 요즘 사람들은 상점과 식당에서 구매한 많은 음식을 버린다.	• 단어 변경 These days, **people** throw away **a lot of food that was** purchased **from** grocery stores or **restaurants.** 요즘 사람들은 식료품점 또는 식당에서 구매한 많은 음식을 버린다. • 문장 구조 변경 **These days, people throw away a lot of food that** they buy from grocery stores or order at restaurants. 요즘 사람들은 식료품점에서 사거나 식당에서 주문한 많은 음식을 버린다. • 재작성 Every day, millions of tons of food are wasted all over the world. 매일 수만톤의 음식이 전 세계에서 버려진다.

2 서론 대주제문 작성 방법

서론 마지막 문장은 에세이에서 글 전체 핵심 내용을 요약하는 대주제문(thesis statement)이 나온다. 보통 다음의 세 가지 내용 중 하나의 내용으로 대주제문을 작성한다.

- **문제에 대한 자신의 의견**: 두괄식 글의 기본으로 서론에서 자신의 전체적인 입장을 제시하는 부분으로 보통 다음과 같이 시작
  in my opinion 내 생각에는
- **앞으로 본론에서 어떤 내용을 전개할지**: 앞으로 에세이에서 무슨 내용을 다룰지 알려주는 부분으로 보통 다음과 같이 시작
  this essay discusses ~ 이 에세이는 ~에 대해 논한다
  this essay will attempt to look into ~ 이 에세이는 ~에 대해 살펴보도록 하겠다
- **문제에 대한 재해석**: 문제에서 묻는 포인트를 패러프레이징하는 방법으로 보통 다음과 같이 시작
  the question is whether ~ or not 문제는 ~인지 아닌지이다
  there are some advantages and disadvantages to ~에 대한 장점과 단점이 있다

문제에 제시된 문장	패러프레이징
Why do you think people throw away food? What can be done to reduce the amount of food waste? 왜 사람들이 음식을 버린다고 생각하는가? 음식 쓰레기 양을 줄이기 위해 무엇을 할 수 있는가?	• 자신의 의견 In my opinion, **understanding the causes of this phenomenon would lead us to some applicable solutions that will result in reducing food waste.** 내 생각에는, 이러한 현상에 대한 원인을 이해하는 것이 음식 쓰레기를 줄이는 적용가능한 해결방안으로 이끌 것이다. • 본론 전개 내용 This essay discusses **the reasons people waste food and some applicable solutions to this phenomenon.** 본 에세이는 사람들이 음식을 버리는 이유와 이러한 현상에 적용가능한 해결책들에 대해 논한다. • 문제 재해석 There are some causes and solutions related to **this issue.** 이러한 문제에 대한 원인과 해결책이 있다.

WRITING

3 본론 작성 방법

본론은 Task 2에서 가장 중요한 부분으로 자신의 아이디어를 논리적으로 나타내는 것이 관건이다. 즉, 천편일률적인 아이디어가 아닌, 자신만의 아이디어를 논리적으로 작문해야 좋은 점수를 받을 수 있다.

일반적으로 본론 문단은 세 개(본론 1 - 본론 2 - 본론 3) 또는 두 개(본론 1- 본론 2)로 구성되며 각 문단은 주제 문장(topic sentence)으로 시작을 한다. 즉 본론의 모든 문단을 두괄식으로 작성하여, 각 문단이 어떠한 내용인지를 첫 문장에서 알려주도록 한다. 주제 문장은 그 뒤에 바로 나오는 근거 문장(supporting sentence)에 의해 논리적으로 뒷받침되어야 하고, 이어서 구체적인 예 또는 자료(supporting details: example or research)가 추가되어야 한다. 이로 인해 자신의 주장이 추상적 내용이 아닌 현실감 있는 사실적 내용임을 증명한다. 수험생들이 주장을 뒷받침하는 구체적인 내용을 제대로 적지 않는 경향이 많은데, 구체적인 예는 채점기준 중 과제응답(task response)에서 요구하는 사항이므로 반드시 적도록 한다. 추가적으로 각 문단의 마무리 문장(concluding sentence)으로 자신이 하고자 하는 말을 정리할 수 있는데, 이미 본론에서 했던 말을 단순히 반복하거나 본론에서 사용했던 단어를 반복해서 사용할 것 같으면 마무리 문장은 생략하도록 한다.

특별히 본론에서는 각 문단간 또는 각 문장간 연결어(linking words)를 잘 사용하여 글이 논리적이고 체계적으로 흐를 수 있도록 해야 채점기준 중 일관성과 응집성(coherence and cohesion)에서 좋은 점수를 얻을 수 있다. 다음 소개되는 연결어들은 보통 문장 또는 문단 앞에 나와 내용을 연결해 준다.

- on the one hand 한편 (양자 중 첫 의견을 설명할 때)
- on the other hand 다른 한편 (양자 중 남은 다른 의견을 설명할 때)
- in other words 즉, 바꿔 말하면 (앞 내용을 부연할 때)
- in this case 이 경우에 (앞 내용에 이어서 설명할 때)
- first = to begin with 먼저 (첫 번째 근거를 설명할 때)
- second 두 번째로 (두 번째 근거를 설명할 때)

- finally 마지막으로 (마지막 근거를 설명할 때)
- last but not least 마지막으로 (앞 근거들만큼 중요한 마지막 근거를 설명할 때)
- then 그리고 나서 (순차적으로 순서를 들어 설명할 때)
- for example = for instance 예를 들면 (예를 들어 설명할 때)
- take the example of ~의 예를 보자 (예를 들어 설명할 때)
- from my experience 내 경험으로 볼 때 (자신의 경험을 예로 들 때)
- therefore = thus = as a result = consequently = as a consequence = so 따라서 (결과나 결론을 말할 때)
- that is why 주어+동사 그것이 ~하는 이유이다, 그래서 (결과나 결론을 말할 때)
- in contrast = by contrast 반면 (앞 내용과 비교/대조를 하여 강조할 때)
- on the contrary 반대로 (앞 내용과 반대되는 다른 내용을 설명할 때)
- however 그러나 (역접으로 앞 내용과 배치되는 다른 내용을 설명할 때)
- otherwise 그렇지 않으면 (반대되는 상황에 대해 가정할 때)
- nevertheless = nonetheless = even so = in spite of that 그럼에도 불구하고 (배치되는 내용을 주장할 때)
- actually = in fact 실은 (보통 앞 내용과 배치되는 주장이나 근거를 말할 때)
- indeed 실제로, 정말로 (앞 내용을 강조하거나 지지 근거를 말할 때)
- meanwhile 한편 (화제 전환할 때)
- furthermore = moreover = in addition = besides = on top of that 추가로 (추가 정보를 부연할 때)
- when it comes to = regarding = concerning = as to ~에 관한 (화제를 언급하거나 전환할 때)
- to be specific 구체적으로 (앞 내용을 보다 상세하게 설명할 때)
- not only that, but 주어+동사 그뿐 아니라, ~이다 (앞 내용을 부연할 때)
- in this regard 이런 점에서 (앞 내용을 부연할 때)
- in this way 이런 식으로 (앞 내용을 부연할 때)
- as such 이와 같이 (앞 내용에 대한 결론을 말하거나 부연할 때)
- to some extent 어느 정도까지는 (정도를 설명할 때)
- overall = on the whole 전반적으로 (전체 내용을 대략적으로 설명할 때)
- according to ~에 따르면 (인용을 할 때)

4 결론 작성 방법

보통 결론은 두 문장으로 작성하는데, 첫 번째 문장에서 전체 내용을 요약하고, 두 번째 문장에서는 자신의 생각을 명확히 언급해 준다. 결론은 다음 연결어 중 하나로 시작하는 것이 일반적이다.

- all in all = all things considered 모든 것을 고려해 볼 때
- in conclusion 결론으로
- as has been described 앞에서 서술한 것처럼
- to sum up = in summary 요약하면

결론은 앞에서 말한 내용을 요약 또는 강조하며 마무리하는 부분이기에, 단어 반복이 이루어지기 쉬운 부분이다. 만일 서론이나 본론에 사용하였던 동일한 어구를 자주 반복하여 결론에 사용하면 채점자는 단어 수를 늘리기 위해 결론을 쓴다고 판단하고 감점을 주게 된다. 따라서 결론에서는 동의어/유의어 등을 활용과 문장 형식 변형 등을 통해 단순한 반복이 되지 않도록 특별히 유의한다.

또한 결론에서는 절대 본론에서 언급하지 않은 새로운 논제나 내용을 추가하지 않는다. 결론에서 본론에 없는 내용을 언급하거나 본론에서 했던 말과 다른 말을 하는 경우에는 채점기준 중 일관성과 응집성(coherence and cohesion)에서 감점이 된다.

WRITING

문법 정리 6: 분사구문 / with 분사구문 - 동사가 이끄는 수식어구

❶ 분사구문

반복을 싫어하는 영어의 성질에 의거하여 접속사가 이끄는 절을 축약하여 사용하는 것이 분사구문이다.

예문 Satellites in space orbit the Earth while they watch us, whether we like it or not.
우리가 좋든 싫든 우주에 인공 위성이 우리를 지켜보면서 지구 궤도를 돈다.
= Satellites in space orbit the Earth watching us, whether we like it or not.

이 문장에 있는 두 개의 절이 주어가 같으므로(satellites = they), 접속사가 이끄는 절의 접속사(while)와 주어(they)를 삭제하고 그에 대한 표시로 동사를 -ing로 만들어 준다.

참고로 접속사를 생략하지 않고 분사구문의 의미를 보다 명확히 나타내는 경우도 있지만, 생략하는 경우가 더 많다.

예문 Satellites in space orbit the Earth while watching us, whether we like it or not.

❷ with 분사구문

주절과 부사절의 주어가 다른 경우에는 with를 사용하고 그 뒤에 부사절 주어를 써서 분사구문을 만들어 준다.

예문 An improved higher education system can be achieved when more universities offer greater opportunities for more students.
더 많은 대학들이 더 많은 학생들에게 더 큰 기회를 제공할 때, 향상된 고등 교육 시스템이 달성될 수 있다.
= An improved higher education system can be achieved with more universities offering greater opportunities for more students.

PRACTICE TEST

Academic/General Training Task 2 **다음 기출 변형 문제를 서론 - 본론 - 결론 형식에 맞게 영작하자.**

You should spend about 40 minutes on this task.

Write about the following topic:

> ***These days, people throw away a lot of the food that they buy from grocery stores or order at restaurants.***
>
> ***Why do you think people throw away food?***
>
> ***What can be done to reduce the amount of food waste?***

Give reasons for your answer and include any relevant examples from your own knowledge or experience.

Write at least 250 words.

서론

서론 토픽 패러프레이징

____

____

서론 마지막 문장(대주제문)

____

____

정답 및 해설 p.072

본론 1

본론 1 첫 문장(주제 문장)

본론 1 근거 문장 및 세부 내용

본론 2

본론 2 첫 문장(주제 문장)

본론 2 근거 문장 및 세부 내용

결론

UNIT 20

Task 2 - 에세이 아웃라인 잡기

오늘의 학습 목표

1. Task 2에 빈출하는 문제 유형을 파악한다.
2. Task 2 빈출 문제 유형별 아웃라인 잡기를 익힌다.
3. 접속사, 전치사, 접속부사 용법을 제대로 파악하여 영작할 때 올바르게 사용한다.

Task 2 빈출 문제 유형별 출제도 분석

Task 2 문제 박스안에 두 번째 부분에서 문제 유형을 파악할 수 있는데, 보통 다음의 5가지 유형으로 문제가 출제된다.

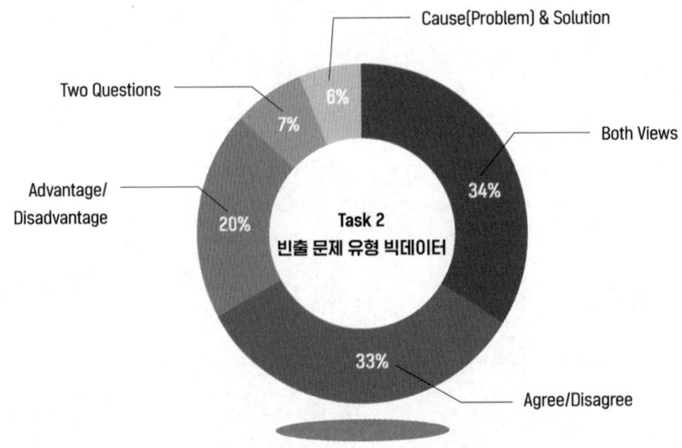

문제 유형마다 답안 글의 구조가 달라질 수 있는데, 본 교재에서는 학습 편의를 위해 각 유형마다 아웃라인을 제공한다. 참고로 정형화된 아웃라인으로 글을 쓰면 7.0이상 고득점을 받는데 오히려 방해가 될 수 있다. 채점관들은 기계적인 형식에 대해서 감점을 주고 있기 때문이다.

따라서 아직 에세이 영작이 서툰 수험생들은 제시된 아웃라인으로 답안 작성 연습을 하고, 에세이 영작이 자연스러운 수험생들은 틀에 얽매이지 말고 자신의 주장을 논리적으로 가장 잘 보여줄 수 있는 방식으로 답안을 작성하자.

Both Views 문제 유형 아웃라인 잡기

1 문제 유형 분석

Both Views(양자 의견)은 Task 2에서 가장 많이 나오는 문제 유형으로 보통 다음과 같이 나온다.

Discuss **both these views** and give **your own opinion.**
이 두 의견들을 모두 논의하고 자신만의 의견을 제시하라.

2 아웃라인 잡기

문제에 나온대로, 양자의 의견을 각각 비중을 두어 다룬 다음에 자신만의 의견도 함께 제시해야 하는데, 다음과 같이 아웃라인을 잡으면 채점 기준인 Task Response에 맞게 글을 쓸 수 있다.

서론	① 문제 패러프레이징(paraphrasing): 문제에서 제시된 사안을 패러프레이징 (이때, 문제에서 나온 단어를 그대로 사용하면 감점) ② 대주제문(thesis statement): 에세이 전체에 대한 자신의 주장을 한 문장으로 진술하거나 어떠한 내용을 에세이에 작성하려 하는지 명시
본론 1	① 주제 문장(topic sentence): 양자 의견 중 내가 덜 지지하는 의견의 타당성 언급 ② 근거 문장(supporting sentence): 주제 문장에 대한 근거 제시 ③ 세부 내용(supporting details): 근거를 뒷받침할 구체적인 예, 자료 언급 ④ 결론 문장(concluding sentence): 본론 1의 전체적인 내용을 정리하여 주제 문장 강조 (결론 문장은 생략 가능)
본론 2	① 주제 문장(topic sentence): 내가 더 지지하는 의견의 타당성 설명(본론 1보다 자세하게) ② 근거 문장(supporting sentence): 주제 문장에 대한 근거 제시 ③ 세부 내용(supporting details): 근거를 뒷받침할 구체적인 예, 자료 언급 ④ 결론 문장(concluding sentence): 본론 2의 전체적인 내용을 정리하여 주제 문장 강조 (결론 문장은 생략 가능)
결론	① 자신의 의견 제시(own opinion) ② 마무리(wrap up): 자신의 의견을 부연 설명하며 마무리

3 기출 문제 연습

You should spend about 40 minutes on this task.

Write about the following topic:

Some people believe that charities and nonprofit organisations should only help people in their own country. Others believe that they should help people regardless of where they live.

어떤 사람들은 자선단체와 비영리 단체가 자국의 사람들만 도와야 한다고 생각한다. 다른 사람들은 어디에 사는지에 관계없이 사람들을 도와야 한다고 생각한다.

Discuss both these views and give your own opinion.

이 두 의견들을 모두 논의하고 자신만의 의견을 제시하라.

Give reasons for your answer and include any relevant examples from your own knowledge or experience.

Write at least 250 words.

모범답안

There are countless people in need, but charities and nonprofit organisations often face resource constraints. For this reason, some feel that these organisations should focus on helping people within their own country. Others think that aid should be given irrespective of location. While there is merit to both sides, this essay will argue that assistance should primarily be directed towards individuals from one's own country.	도움이 필요한 사람들이 무수히 많지만, 자선 단체와 비영리 단체는 종종 자원의 제약에 직면한다. 이러한 이유로, 일부 사람들은 이러한 단체가 자국 내 사람들을 돕는 데 집중해야 한다고 생각한다. 다른 사람들은 지역에 관계없이 지원을 제공해야 한다고 생각한다. 이 에세이는 양쪽 모두의 주장이 모두 타당하지만, 원조는 주로 자국의 사람들을 대상으로 이루어져야 한다고 주장할 것이다.
It is perfectly reasonable to extend assistance to other nations. Doing so is important especially when countries lack the necessary resources or infrastructure to cope with crises. For example, natural disasters such as typhoons, tsunamis and earthquakes often overwhelm the affected countries, leaving them unable to handle the aftermath by themselves. Without help from other countries, the affected nations may struggle to recover and rebuild, prolonging the suffering of their citizens.	다른 국가로 지원을 확대하는 것은 지극히 이성적이다. 특히 국가들이 위기에 대처하는 데 필요한 자원이나 인프라가 부족할 때 그렇게 하는 것은 중요하다. 예를 들어 태풍, 쓰나미, 지진과 같은 자연재해는 피해 국가를 압도하여, 그 여파를 스스로 감당할 수 없게 만드는 경우가 많다. 다른 국가의 도움 없이는, 피해 국가는 복구와 재건에 어려움을 겪게 되어, 국민들의 고통이 장기화될 수 있다.
Despite this, domestic charities and nonprofit organisations should primarily provide aid to individuals within the same country. This is because they would be the ones who best understand community needs, nuances in culture and legal requirements. Therefore, they could make sure that their assistance reaches those who require help while avoiding any infringement on local customs or laws. Foreign charitable organisations, on the other hand, may unintentionally make errors or even cause harm, making it a wiser choice to support local charities instead.	그럼에도 불구하고, 국내 자선 단체와 비영리 단체는 같은 국가 내의 사람들에게 우선적으로 도움을 제공해야 한다. 이는 이 단체들이 지역사회의 필요, 문화의 미묘한 차이, 법적 요건 등을 가장 잘 이해하고 있기 때문이다. 따라서, 현지 관습이나 법률에 대한 침해를 피하면서 도움이 필요한 사람들에게 도움이 전달되도록 할 수 있다. 반면에, 외국 자선 단체는 의도치 않게 실수를 하거나 피해를 입힐 수 있으므로, 현지 자선 단체를 지원하는 것이 더 현명한 선택이 될 수 있다.
In my opinion, international aid should not overshadow domestic problems. If charities and nonprofit organisations are not careful, they may divert valuable resources away from their own citizens. In conclusion, while helping foreign countries has its merits, it is undeniable that the welfare of one's own nation should come first. (269 words)	내 생각에는, 국제 원조가 국내 문제를 무색하게 해서는 안 된다. 자선 단체와 비영리 단체가 조심하지 않으면, 귀중한 자원이 자국민에게 돌아가지 않을 수 있다. 결론적으로, 외국을 돕는 것도 장점이 있지만, 자국의 복지가 우선시되어야 한다는 것은 부인할 수 없는 사실이다.

| Vocabulary & Expressions |

countless 무수히 많은 charity 자선 단체 nonprofit 비영리 resource 자원 constraint 제약 irrespective of ~와 관계없이 merit 마땅히 받을 만한 가치, 장점 direct ~로 향하다 individuals (개별) 사람들 cope with ~에 대처하다 crises 위기들 overwhelm ~을 압도하다 affected 영향을 받은, 피해를 받은 aftermath 여파 prolong 연장시키다, 연장하다 suffering 고통 domestic 국내의 needs 필요, 요구 nuance 미묘한 차이, 뉘앙스 infringement 침해 custom 관습 charitable 자선의 unintentionally 의도치 않게 cause harm 해를 끼치다 overshadow ~에 그늘을 드리우다, ~을 무색하게 하다 undeniable 부인할 수 없는 welfare 복지

Agree/Disagree 문제 유형 아웃라인 잡기

1 문제 유형 분석

어떤 토픽에 대해 Agree/Disagree(동의/반대)를 묻는 문제는, 보통 어느 정도 동의하고 반대하는지 정도를 묻는 방식으로 많이 출제된다.

To what extent do you **agree or disagree** with this statement?
당신은 어느 정도 이 진술에 동의 또는 반대하는가?

2 아웃라인 잡기

답안 문단 구조는 자신이 어느 정도 동의하는지 반대하는지에 따라 달라지는데, 전적으로 동의 또는 동의하지 않는다면 다음과 같이 작성한다.

서론	① 문제 패러프레이징(paraphrasing): 문제에서 제시된 사안을 패러프레이징 (이때, 문제에서 나온 단어를 그대로 사용하면 감점) ② 대주제문(thesis statement): 전적으로 동의 또는 동의하지 않는다는 자신의 의견 명시
본론 1	① 주제 문장(topic sentence): 자신의 의견에 대한 타당성 1 ② 근거 문장(supporting sentence): 주제 문장에 대한 근거 제시 ③ 세부 내용(supporting details): 근거를 뒷받침할 구체적인 예, 자료 언급 ④ 결론 문장(concluding sentence): 본론 1의 전체적인 내용을 정리하여 주제 문장 강조 (결론 문장은 생략 가능)
본론 2	① 주제 문장(topic sentence): 자신의 의견에 대한 타당성 2 ② 근거 문장(supporting sentence): 주제 문장에 대한 근거 제시 ③ 세부 내용(supporting details): 근거를 뒷받침할 구체적인 예, 자료 언급 ④ 결론 문장(concluding sentence): 본론 2의 전체적인 내용을 정리하여 주제 문장 강조 (결론 문장은 생략 가능)
결론	① 요약(summary): 본론 내용 요약 ② 나의 의견 강조(restatement): 요약 내용을 바탕으로 자연스럽게 나의 의견을 강조 (이때, 서론 또는 본론에서 사용했던 단어나 문구를 결론에서 그대로 쓰지 말고 패러프레이징)

만일 좀 더 동의를 하거나 좀 더 반대를 한다면 다음과 같이 본론에 자신이 좀 더 동의 또는 반대하는 의견을 한 문단 더 작성하여 자신의 의견에 무게를 실을 수 있다.

서론	① 문제 패러프레이징(paraphrasing): 문제에서 제시된 사안을 패러프레이징 (이때, 문제에서 나온 단어를 그대로 사용하면 감점) ② 대주제문(thesis statement): 에세이 전체에 대한 자신의 주장을 한 문장으로 진술하거나 어떠한 내용을 에세이에 작성하려 하는지 명시
본론 1	① 주제 문장(topic sentence): 양자 의견 중 내가 덜 지지하는 의견의 타당성 ② 근거 문장(supporting sentence): 주제 문장에 대한 근거 제시 ③ 세부 내용(supporting details): 근거를 뒷받침할 구체적인 예, 자료 언급 ④ 결론 문장(concluding sentence): 본론 1의 전체적인 내용을 정리하여 주제 문장 강조 (결론 문장은 생략 가능)
본론 2	① 주제 문장(topic sentence): 내가 더 지지하는 의견의 타당성 1 ② 근거 문장(supporting sentence): 주제 문장에 대한 근거 제시 ③ 세부 내용(supporting details): 근거를 뒷받침할 구체적인 예, 자료 언급 ④ 결론 문장(concluding sentence): 본론 2의 전체적인 내용을 정리하여 주제 문장 강조 (결론 문장은 생략 가능)
본론 3	① 주제 문장(topic sentence): 내가 더 지지하는 의견의 타당성 2 ② 근거 문장(supporting sentence): 주제 문장에 대한 근거 제시 ③ 세부 내용(supporting details): 근거를 뒷받침할 구체적인 예, 자료 언급 ④ 결론 문장(concluding sentence): 본론 3의 전체적인 내용을 정리하여 주제 문장 강조 (결론 문장은 생략 가능)
결론	① 요약(summary): 본론 내용 요약 ② 나의 의견 강조(restatement): 요약 내용을 바탕으로 자연스럽게 나의 의견을 강조 (이때, 서론 또는 본론에서 사용했던 단어나 문구를 결론에서 그대로 쓰지 말고 패러프레이징)

3 기출 문제 연습

You should spend about 40 minutes on this task.

Write about the following topic:

Changing jobs frequently can help your personal career.
직장을 자주 옮기면 당신의 경력에 도움이 될 수 있다.

To what extent do you agree or disagree with this statement?
당신은 어느 정도 이 진술에 동의 또는 반대하는가?

Give reasons for your answer and include any relevant examples from your own knowledge or experience.

Write at least 250 words.

모범답안

With more people changing jobs every few years, the traditional concept of staying loyal to one company has shifted. Many people believe that joining a new company can lead to better career opportunities. While there are certainly benefits to long-term commitment to a single company, I believe that the given statement is, to a large extent, true.	몇 년마다 직장을 옮기는 사람들이 늘어나면서 한 회사에 충성해야 한다는 전통적인 개념이 바뀌고 있다. 많은 사람들이 새로운 회사에 입사하면 더 나은 커리어 기회를 얻을 수 있다고 생각한다. 한 회사에 장기적으로 헌신하면 분명 이점이 있는 것은 사실이지만, 나는 주어진 진술이 상당 부분 사실이라고 생각한다.
There are several valid reasons for remaining with the same company throughout one's career. One of the biggest benefits is ensuring high job security. This is because working for a long time in a company allows for developing a deep understanding of the culture, values and processes within the workplace. This knowledge helps navigate challenges more effectively, contribute meaningfully to team projects and foster a positive work environment. Thus, there is an opportunity to become an irreplaceable employee within the company.	경력 내내 한 회사에 계속 근무하는 데에는 몇 가지 타당한 이유가 있다. 가장 큰 장점 중 하나는 높은 고용 안정성을 보장한다는 점이다. 이는 한 회사에서 오랫동안 근무하면 직장 내 문화, 가치, 프로세스에 대한 깊은 이해가 가능하기 때문이다. 이러한 지식은 문제를 보다 효과적으로 해결하고, 팀 프로젝트에 의미 있게 기여하며, 긍정적인 업무 환경을 조성하는 데 도움이 된다. 따라서 회사 내에서 대체 불가능한 직원이 될 수 있는 기회가 주어진다.
Nevertheless, changing jobs often allows for developing a broader knowledge base. Each new role exposes one to different industries, leading to the acquisition of a diverse skill set that can be invaluable in any career. This variety of experiences enables rapid skill development and a deeper understanding of how various organisations operate. By encountering and solving different problems across jobs, one can grow into a versatile and knowledgeable professional.	그럼에도 불구하고, 이직은 종종 더 넓은 지식 기반을 개발할 수 있는 기회를 허락한다. 새로운 직무를 맡을 때마다 다양한 산업을 접하게 되므로, 어떤 커리어를 쌓아도 귀중한 다양한 기술을 습득할 수 있다. 이러한 다양한 경험은 빠른 기술 개발과 다양한 조직의 운영 방식에 대한 깊은 이해를 가능하게 한다. 여러 직무에서 다양한 문제를 접하고 해결함으로써, 다재다능하고 지식이 풍부한 전문가로 성장할 수 있다.
Furthermore, job changes can significantly expand a professional network. Moving between different companies or industries leads to meeting and collaborating with a wide array of colleagues, supervisors and industry experts. This extended network not only provides valuable insights but also opens up new career opportunities.	더욱이, 이직은 전문가 네트워크를 크게 확장할 수 있다. 다른 회사나 업계로 옮기는 것은 다양한 동료, 상사, 업계 전문가와의 만남과 협업으로 이어진다. 이렇게 확장된 네트워크는 귀중한 통찰력을 제공할 뿐만 아니라 새로운 커리어 기회도 열어준다.

In conclusion, while job security might be the primary reason some workers stay at one job long-term, I believe that changing jobs often can offer more potential for personal and professional growth. (284 words)	결론적으로, 일부 근로자가 한 직장에 오래 머무는 주된 이유는 고용 안정성일 수 있지만, 나는 직장을 자주 바꾸는 것이 개인적, 직업적 성장을 위한 더 많은 잠재력을 제공할 수 있다고 믿는다.

| Vocabulary & Expressions |

loyal 충성스러운 **shift** 바뀌다 **lead to** ~로 이어지다 **long-term** 장기적인 **commitment** 헌신 **to a large extent** 상당 부분 **valid** 유효한, 타당한 **job security** 고용 안정성 **navigate** (힘든 상황을) 다루다, 처리하다 **contribute to** ~에 도움이 되다, ~에 기여하다 **acquisition** 습득 **invaluable** 귀중한 **versatile** 다재다능한 **expand** ~을 확장하다 **collaborate with** ~와 협업하다 **a wide array of** 다양한 **extend** ~을 연장하다, 확대하다, 확장하다 **insight** 통찰력

Advantage/Disadvantage 문제 유형 아웃라인 잡기

1 문제 유형 분석

어떤 토픽에 대한 Advantage/Disadvantage(장점/단점)를 묻는 문제로, 장점과 단점이 무엇인지 각각 묻거나 장점이나 단점 중 무엇이 더 큰지를 묻기도 한다. 또한 토픽에 따라, Advantage/Disadvantage 대신 Positive/Negative(긍정적/부정적) 영향을 묻기도 한다.

What are the **advantages and disadvantages** of this?
이것의 장점들과 단점들은 무엇인가?

Do the **advantages** of this **outweigh the disadvantages**?
이것의 장점들이 단점들보다 더 큰가?

Do you think this is a **positive or negative** development?
당신은 이것이 긍정적 또는 부정적 발달이라고 생각하는가?

2 아웃라인 잡기

위에서 제시된 3가지 질문이 조금씩 차이가 있지만 답안 틀은 다음과 같이 통일되게 잡을 수 있다. 또한 Agree/Disagree처럼 본론 3을 한 문단 더 작성하여 자신의 의견에 무게를 실을 수도 있다.

서론	① 문제 패러프레이징(paraphrasing): 문제에서 제시된 사안을 패러프레이징 (이때, 문제에서 나온 단어를 그대로 사용하면 감점) ② 대주제문(thesis statement): 장단점이 모두 있지만 장점 또는 단점이 더 많다는 자신의 의견 명시
본론 1	① 주제 문장(topic sentence): 장점이 더 많다고 생각되면 단점을 본론 1에서 먼저 언급 ② 근거 문장(supporting sentence): 주제 문장에 대한 근거 제시 ③ 세부 내용(supporting details): 근거를 뒷받침할 구체적인 예, 자료 언급 ④ 결론 문장(concluding sentence): 본론 1의 전체적인 내용을 정리하여 주제 문장 강조 (결론 문장은 생략 가능)

본론 2	① 주제 문장(topic sentence): 장점 기술(단점보다 구체적으로 기술 및 내용 전개) ② 근거 문장(supporting sentence): 주제 문장에 대한 근거 제시 ③ 세부 내용(supporting details): 근거를 뒷받침할 구체적인 예, 자료 언급 ④ 결론 문장(concluding sentence): 본론 2의 전체적인 내용을 정리하여 주제 문장 강조 (결론 문장은 생략 가능)
결론	① 요약(summary): 본론 내용 요약 ② 나의 의견 강조(restatement): 요약 내용을 바탕으로 자연스럽게 나의 의견을 강조 (이때, 서론 또는 본론에서 사용했던 단어나 문구를 결론에서 그대로 쓰지 말고 패러프레이징)

3 기출 문제 연습

You should spend about 40 minutes on this task.

Write about the following topic:

In some countries, the government has tried to reduce traffic in the city centre by imposing a congestion tax on vehicles during rush hour.
일부 국가에서는 정부가 출퇴근 시간대에 차량에 혼잡세를 부과하여 도심의 교통량을 줄이려고 노력하고 있다.

Do you think this is a positive or negative development?
당신은 이것이 긍정적 또는 부정적 발달이라고 생각하는가?

Give reasons for your answer and include any relevant examples from your own knowledge or experience.

Write at least 250 words.

모범답안

It is a widely known fact that many cities worldwide experience severe traffic congestion, particularly in their city centres. In an effort to alleviate this issue, some governments have enacted a congestion tax on vehicles during rush hour. Although there are some disadvantages in this situation, I personally believe there are more advantages.	전 세계 많은 도시에서 특히 도심의 교통 혼잡이 심각하다는 것은 널리 알려진 사실이다. 이 문제를 완화하기 위해, 일부 정부에서는 출퇴근 시간대에 차량에 혼잡세를 부과하는 정책을 시행하고 있다. 이러한 상황에는 몇 가지 단점도 있지만, 개인적으로 더 많은 장점이 있다고 생각한다.
One negative aspect of implementing a congestion tax is that it can place a financial burden on low-income workers. Many people who have a job in the city cannot afford to live near their workplace because of the high	혼잡세 시행의 한 가지 부정적인 측면은 저소득층 근로자에게 재정적 부담을 줄 수 있다는 것이다. 도시에서 직장을 가진 많은 사람들은 높은 생활비 때문에 직장 근처에 거주할 여유가 없다. 대신 도시 변두리에

WRITING

living costs. Instead, they live on the outskirts of the city and rely on their personal vehicle to drive to work. If the government imposes a congestion tax, these people would be forced to spend more on transport just to maintain their jobs.	거주하며 개인 차량에 의존해 출퇴근한다. 정부가 혼잡세를 부과하면 이 사람들은 직장을 유지하기 위해 더 많은 교통비를 지출해야 할 것이다.
However, the government can use the tax revenue to improve public transport and infrastructure. With additional funding, the government can enhance the reliability of the public transport system. Through this, more individuals would be encouraged to switch from using private vehicles to public transport, reducing congestion. Additionally, policymakers can implement exemptions for low-income workers to ensure that the tax does not burden those who cannot afford it.	하지만, 정부는 이 세수를 대중교통과 인프라 개선에 사용할 수 있다. 추가 자금이 확보되면, 정부는 대중교통 시스템의 신뢰성을 높일 수 있다. 이를 통해, 더 많은 개인이 자가용 대신 대중교통을 이용하도록 장려하여 교통 혼잡을 줄일 수 있다. 또한 정책 입안자들은 저소득층 근로자에 대한 면제를 시행하여 세금을 감당할 수 없는 사람들에게 부담이 되지 않도록 할 수 있다.
Moreover, a congestion tax can reduce pollution levels in urban areas. By discouraging unnecessary car journeys during rush hour, those with flexible schedules would adjust their travel times or seek alternative modes of transport. This decrease in the number of vehicles on the road during rush hour not only alleviates traffic congestion but also generates less air pollution, ultimately leading to cleaner and healthier urban environments.	더욱이, 혼잡세는 도시 지역의 오염 수준을 줄일 수 있다. 출퇴근 시간대에 불필요한 자동차 운행을 억제함으로써, 일정이 유연한 사람들은 이동 시간을 조정하거나 대체 교통수단을 찾게 될 것이다. 이렇게 출퇴근 시간대에 도로를 달리는 차량 수가 감소하면 교통 혼잡이 완화될 뿐만 아니라 대기 오염도 줄어들어, 궁극적으로 더 깨끗하고 건강한 도시 환경으로 이어진다.
In conclusion, while a congestion tax may pose financial challenges for some, the overall benefits of improved public transport, reduced traffic congestion and lower pollution levels make it a worthwhile measure. (299 words)	결론적으로, 혼잡세는 일부 사람들에게는 재정적 어려움을 제기할 수 있지만, 대중교통 개선, 교통 혼잡 감소, 오염 수준 감소라는 전반적인 이점들은 이를 가치 있는 조치로 만든다.

I Vocabulary & Expressions I

severe 심각한 **alleviate** ~을 완화하다 **congestion tax** 혼잡세 **implement** ~을 시행하다 **afford** ~할 여유가 있다 **outskirt** 변두리, 외곽 **impose** ~을 부과하다 **tax revenue** 세수 **funding** 자금 **reliability** 신뢰성 **exemption** 면제 **burden** 부담, 부담을 지우다 **pollution** 오염 **discourage** ~을 억제하다 **flexible** 유연한 **adjust** ~을 조정하다 **alternative** 대체의 **generate** ~을 발생시키다 **pose** ~을 제기하다 **worthwhile** 가치 있는 **measure** 조치

Two Questions 문제 유형 아웃라인 잡기

1 문제 유형 분석

Two Questions(2개의 질문) 유형은 특정 토픽과 관련하여 두 개의 짧은 질문들에 대해 답변하는 문제이다. 일정하게 정

해진 형태의 질문들이 아니고 토픽에 따라 자유롭게 아래와 같은 질문들이 출제된다.

How might having a lot of money make people happy?
돈을 많이 갖는 것이 얼마나 사람들을 행복하게 만들까?

What other things can make people happy?
어떤 다른 것들이 사람들을 행복하게 만들까?

2 아웃라인 잡기

답안은 각 질문에 대한 대답을 본론 각 문단으로 잡아서 구성하면 된다. 즉, 질문이 두 개이므로 본론이 두 개가 된다.

서론	① 문제 패러프레이징(paraphrasing): 문제에서 제시된 사안을 패러프레이징 (이때, 문제에서 나온 단어를 그대로 사용하면 감점) ② 대주제문(thesis statement): 앞으로 전개될 에세이 흐름 정리
본론 1	① 주제 문장(topic sentence): 첫 번째 질문에 대한 답변 ② 근거 문장(supporting sentence): 답변에 대한 근거 제시 ③ 세부 내용(supporting details): 근거를 뒷받침할 구체적인 예, 자료 언급 ④ 결론 문장(concluding sentence): 본론 1의 전체적인 내용을 정리하여 주제 문장 강조 (결론 문장은 생략 가능)
본론 2	① 주제 문장(topic sentence): 두 번째 질문에 대한 답변 ② 근거 문장(supporting sentence): 답변에 대한 근거 제시 ③ 세부 내용(supporting details): 근거를 뒷받침할 구체적인 예, 자료 언급 ④ 결론 문장(concluding sentence): 본론 2의 전체적인 내용을 정리하여 주제 문장 강조 (결론 문장은 생략 가능)
결론	① 요약(summary): 본론 내용 요약 ② 나의 의견 강조(restatement): 요약 내용을 바탕으로 자연스럽게 나의 의견을 강조 (이때, 서론 또는 본론에서 사용했던 단어나 문구를 결론에서 그대로 쓰지 말고 패러프레이징)

3 기출 문제 연습

You should spend about 40 minutes on this task.

Write about the following topic:

Many people believe that learning a foreign language is a very difficult task.
많은 사람이 외국어를 배우는 것은 매우 어려운 일이라고 생각한다.

What are the difficulties of learning a foreign language?
외국어 학습의 어려움은 무엇인가?

What is the best way to overcome them?
이를 극복하는 가장 좋은 방법은 무엇인가?

Give reasons for your answer and include any relevant examples from your own knowledge or experience.

Write at least 250 words.

모범답안

Learning a foreign language is a common goal for many people worldwide. However, the process is often seen as difficult and daunting. As a result, many foreign language learners give up before achieving proficiency. This essay discusses a few challenges and explores solutions for addressing them.

외국어를 배우는 것은 전 세계 많은 사람들의 공통된 목표다. 그러나, 그 과정은 종종 어렵고 벅찬 것으로 여겨진다. 그 결과, 많은 외국어 학습자가 능숙해지기도 전에 포기한다. 이 에세이는 몇 가지 도전 과제에 대해 논의하고 이를 처리할 수 있는 해결책을 모색한다.

There are multiple challenges when learning a foreign language. To begin with, grammar rules vary widely between languages and understanding them requires diligent study and practice. Second, acquiring sufficient vocabulary is essential but can be time-consuming. Even after mastering grammar and vocabulary, however, communicating effectively with native speakers remains a significant challenge since they often use idiomatic expressions and informal language that are not always taught in textbooks. Additionally, expressing one's thoughts and ideas in a foreign language can be difficult, leading to a fear of making mistakes. This fear can cause learners to freeze up when interacting with native speakers.

외국어를 배울 때는 여러 가지 어려움이 있다. 우선, 문법 규칙은 언어마다 매우 다양하고, 이를 이해하려면 부지런한 공부와 연습이 필요하다. 둘째, 충분한 어휘를 습득하는 것은 필수적이지만 시간이 많이 소요될 수 있다. 그러나 문법과 어휘를 익힌 후에도, 원어민은 교과서에서 가르치지 않는 관용적 표현과 비공식적인 언어를 자주 사용하기 때문에 원어민과 효과적으로 의사소통하는 것은 여전히 큰 도전 과제다. 또한, 자신의 사고와 생각을 외국어로 표현하는 것은 어려울 수 있고, 실수에 대한 두려움으로 이어질 수 있다. 이러한 두려움은 학습자가 원어민과 대화할 때 얼어붙게 만들 수 있다.

One of the most effective ways to overcome these difficulties is through constant exposure. One strategy is to watch a TV show with subtitles in the target language. This enables learners to practise their listening and reading comprehension skills at the same time. It also helps familiarise them with common phrases and cultural references. Another effective approach is to practise communicating with native speakers. If possible, immersing oneself in the country where the language is spoken can be invaluable. If this is not an option, finding native speakers online to practise with can also be highly beneficial.

이러한 어려움을 극복하는 가장 효과적인 방법 중 하나는 지속적인 노출이다. 한 가지 전략은 대상 언어로 된 자막이 있는 TV 프로그램을 시청하는 것이다. 이를 통해 학습자는 듣기 및 독해 능력을 동시에 연습할 수 있다. 또한 일반적인 구문과 문화적 언급에 익숙해지는 데 도움이 된다. 또 다른 효과적인 접근 방식은 원어민과 대화하는 연습을 하는 것이다. 가능하다면, 해당 언어가 사용되는 국가에 직접 가보는 것도 큰 도움이 될 수 있다. 이것이 여의치 않다면, 온라인에서 원어민을 찾아 함께 연습하는 것도 큰 도움이 될 수 있다.

In conclusion, while learning a foreign language presents numerous challenges, exposure to the language can help learners tackle these obstacles. Through various strategies, individuals can achieve proficiency and unlock new opportunities. (275 words)	결론적으로, 외국어를 배우는 데는 수많은 어려움이 있지만, 언어에 대한 노출은 학습자가 이러한 장애물을 해결하는 데 도움이 될 수 있다. 다양한 전략을 통해, 개인은 능숙도를 높이고 새로운 기회를 열어 보일 수 있다.

I Vocabulary & Expressions I

daunting 힘든, 벅찬 proficiency 능숙(도) vary 다양하다 diligent 부지런한, 열심인 sufficient 상당한 time-consuming 시간이 많이 소요되는 idiomatic expression 관용적 표현 freeze up 얼어붙게 하다 constant 지속적인 exposure 노출 subtitle 자막 target language 대상 언어 reading comprehension 독해 familiarise ~을 익숙해지게 하다 phrase 구문 reference 언급 immerse oneself in 자신을 ~에 담그다 invaluable 귀중한 unlock ~을 열어 보이다

Cause(Problem) & Solution 문제 유형 아웃라인 잡기

1 문제 유형 분석

Two Questions 문제 유형 중에서 특히 Cause(Problem) & Solution, 즉, 원인 및 문제와 해결책 관련 질문들이 많이 출제되고 있다.

Why is this the case?
원인: 왜 이런 경우가 있는가?

What can be done about this problem?
해결책: 이 문제에 대해서 무엇이 행해질 수 있는가?

2 아웃라인 잡기

일반적으로 Cause(Problem) & Solution 답안은 Two Questions 문제 유형처럼 각각의 질문에 대한 답변을 각각 독립된 문단으로 작성하면 된다. 하지만 문제에 따라서 해결책을 더 자세하게 또는 원인을 더 자세하게 적어야 되는 경우도 있는데, 그렇게 되면 본론 문단이 총 3개가 된다.

서론	① 문제 패러프레이징(paraphrasing): 문제에서 제시된 사안을 패러프레이징 (이때, 문제에서 나온 단어를 그대로 사용하면 감점) ② 대주제문(thesis statement): 앞으로 전개될 에세이 흐름 정리
본론 1	① 주제 문장(topic sentence): 첫 번째 질문(원인 또는 문제점)에 대한 답변 ② 근거 문장(supporting sentence): 답변에 대한 근거 제시 ③ 세부 내용(supporting details): 근거를 뒷받침할 구체적인 예, 자료 언급 ④ 결론 문장(concluding sentence): 본론 1의 전체적인 내용을 정리하여 주제 문장 강조 (결론 문장은 생략 가능)

본론 2	① 주제 문장(topic sentence): 두 번째 질문(해결책)에 대한 답변 ② 근거 문장(supporting sentence): 답변에 대한 근거 제시 ③ 세부 내용(supporting details): 근거를 뒷받침할 구체적인 예, 자료 언급 ④ 결론 문장(concluding sentence): 본론 2의 전체적인 내용을 정리하여 주제 문장 강조 (결론 문장은 생략 가능)
결론	① 요약(summary): 본론 내용 요약 ② 나의 의견 강조(restatement): 요약 내용을 바탕으로 자연스럽게 나의 의견을 강조 (이때, 서론 또는 본론에서 사용했던 단어나 문구를 결론에서 그대로 쓰지 말고 패러프레이징)

3 기출 문제 연습

You should spend about 40 minutes on this task.

Write about the following topic:

Nowadays, the eating habits of people around the world are changing, causing them many health problems, including obesity.
오늘날 전 세계 사람들의 식습관이 변화하면서 비만을 비롯한 많은 건강 문제가 발생하고 있다.

Why do people tend to eat so poorly?
사람들은 왜 그렇게 안 좋게 먹는 경향이 있을까?

What can be done to improve their eating habits?
식습관을 개선하기 위해 무엇을 할 수 있을까?

Give reasons for your answer and include any relevant examples from your own knowledge or experience.

Write at least 250 words.

모범답안

Diets are changing in most regions of the world. More people are consuming nutritionally imbalanced meals in larger amounts, leading to a rise in global obesity rates and other health problems. This essay discusses why this is the case and what we can do to solve this problem.	전 세계 대부분의 지역에서 식단이 변화하고 있다. 더 많은 사람들이 영양 불균형 식사를 더 많이 섭취하고 있으며, 이로 인해 전 세계적으로 비만율과 다른 건강 문제가 증가하고 있다. 이 에세이는 그 이유와 문제를 해결하기 위해 우리가 할 수 있는 일에 대해 논한다.

There are several factors that contribute to poor eating habits. One of the primary reasons people tend to eat poorly is the increased availability and convenience of processed foods, such as ready meals and fast food. In today's fast-paced world, individuals often find it difficult to prepare home-cooked meals and instead opt for quick, easy options that require little to no preparation. These foods, however, typically contain harmful preservatives and are high in calories, sugars and fats while being low in essential nutrients. Additionally, healthier food options, such as fresh fruits and vegetables, are often more expensive than junk food. This makes it harder for lower-income families to afford nutritious meals.

잘못된 식습관에 기여하는 여러 요인이 있다. 사람들이 건강하지 않게 먹는 경향의 주된 이유 중 하나는 즉석식품과 패스트푸드와 같은 가공식품의 가용성과 편의성이 높아졌기 때문이다. 빠르게 변화하는 오늘날의 세상에서, 사람들은 종종 집에서 직접 조리한 식사를 준비하기 어려워하고, 대신 준비가 거의 또는 전혀 필요 없는 빠르고 간편한 옵션을 선택한다. 하지만 이러한 식품은 일반적으로 해로운 방부제를 함유하고 칼로리, 당분, 지방은 높은 반면 필수 영양소는 낮다. 또한 신선한 과일과 채소 등 건강에 좋은 식품은 정크푸드보다 더 비싼 경우가 많다. 이는 저소득층 가정에서 영양가 있는 식사를 하기 어렵게 만든다.

To address this issue, governments can improve eating habits globally by regulating the food industry and implementing policies. This includes limiting the number of calories and the amount of sugar and fat in food products and providing incentives for food companies that improve the nutritional value of their products. Furthermore, governments can impose taxes on sugary drinks to discourage their consumption and use the tax revenue to fund nutrition programmes. Additionally, subsidising fresh produce can make it more affordable and accessible for disadvantaged families. By adopting these measures, governments can play a crucial role in promoting healthier eating habits.

이 문제를 해결하기 위해, 각국 정부는 식품 산업을 규제하고 정책을 시행함으로써 전 세계적으로 식습관을 개선할 수 있다. 이는 식품의 칼로리와 설탕 및 지방의 양을 제한하고 제품의 영양가를 개선하는 식품 회사에 인센티브를 제공하는 것을 포함한다. 더욱이, 정부는 설탕이 함유된 음료에 세금을 부과하여 소비를 억제하고 세수를 영양 프로그램 기금으로 사용할 수 있다. 또한, 신선한 농산물에 보조금을 지급하면 빈곤한 가정들이 더 감당할 수 있으며 쉽게 접근할 수 있다. 이러한 조치들을 채택함으로써, 정부는 더 건강한 식습관을 장려하는 데 중요한 역할을 할 수 있다.

In conclusion, people nowadays tend to eat poorly because it is cheaper and more convenient to do so. As a countermeasure, governments should create legislation that deters companies from selling excessively unhealthy food products and that also helps to make fresh produce more accessible and affordable.

(304 words)

결론적으로, 오늘날 사람들은 음식을 건강하지 않게 먹는 것이 더 저렴하고 편리하기 때문에 그렇게 하는 경향이 있다. 이에 대한 대책으로, 정부는 기업이 건강에 해로운 식품을 과도하게 판매하는 것을 막고 신선한 농산물을 더 저렴하고 쉽게 구할 수 있도록 돕는 법안을 만들어야 한다.

WRITING

| Vocabulary & Expressions |

diet 식단 consume ~을 섭취하다, 소비하다 nutritionally 영양적으로 imbalanced 불균형한 obesity 비만 contribute to ~에 기여하다 eating habits 식습관 availability 가용성 processed foods 가공식품 ready meals 즉석식품 home-cooked meal 집밥 opt for ~을 선택하다 little to no 거의 ~없는 preservative 방부제 nutritious 영양이 풍부한 regulate ~을 규제하다 implement ~을 시행하다 limit ~을 제한하다 impose ~을 부과하다 discourage ~을 막다 subsidise 보조금을 주다 affordable 감당할 수 있는, 저렴한 disadvantaged 빈곤한 adopt ~을 채택하다 crucial 중요한 promote ~을 장려하다, 촉진하다 countermeasure 대책, 보호 조치 legislation 법안 deter ~을 막다 excessively 과도하게

Academic/General Training Task 2 **다음 기출 변형 문제를 서론 - 본론 - 결론 형식에 맞게 영작하자.**

You should spend about 40 minutes on this task.

Write about the following topic:

> *Nowadays, some high-school graduates travel or work for a period of time instead of going directly to study at university.*
>
> *Do the advantages of this outweigh the disadvantages?*

Give reasons for your answer and include any relevant examples from your own knowledge or experience.

Write at least 250 words.

서론

서론 토픽 패러프레이징

____

____

서론 마지막 문장(대주제문)

____

____

정답 및 해설 p.074

본론 1

본론 1 첫 문장(주제 문장)

본론 1 근거 문장 및 세부 내용

WRITING

본론 2

본론 2 첫 문장(주제 문장)

본론 2 근거 문장 및 세부 내용

결론

SPEAKING
MASTER

Unit 21 IELTS SPEAKING에 대한 모든 것

Unit 22 Part 1 - 나의 학업 또는 직업

Unit 23 Part 1 - 내가 사는 곳

Unit 24 Part 1 - 나와 관련된 질문

Unit 25 Part 2 - 사람

Unit 26 Part 2 - 사물

Unit 27 Part 2 - 사건

Unit 28 Part 3 - 사회적 이슈: 브레인스토밍

Unit 29 Part 3 - 사회적 이슈: 채점기준에 따른 답변

Unit 30 Part 3 - 사회적 이슈: 토픽별 표현

UNIT 21

IELTS SPEAKING에 대한 모든 것

오늘의 학습 목표

1 IELTS SPEAKING 시험(진행 방식, Part별 특징, 대답 방식)을 숙지한다.
2 채점기준을 명확히 인지하고 채점기준에 따라 말하도록 연습한다.
3 평상시 브레인스토밍을 통해 어떠한 질문에도 막힘없이 길게 대답할 수 있도록 한다.

IELTS SPEAKING 기본 정보

시험 방식	• 원어민 시험관과 1:1 인터뷰 방식 (IELTS on computer도 마찬가지임) • 화상 스피킹 시험(Video-Call Speaking Test)을 통해 비대면으로 진행할 수 있음 • Writing과 다르게 Speaking 시험에서는 축약 및 구어적 표현들로 자연스럽게 말함
시험 시간	• 약 11~14분 소요 • Speaking 시험 시간은 시험 보는 국가마다 다른데, 보통 시험 접수할 때 또는 Listening, Reading, Writing 시험 당일에 알 수 있음 • 어떤 국가는 다른 과목 시험보다 하루 또는 이틀 전에 보기도 하고, 당일 또는 다음날에 보기도 함 • 국내는 주로 당일에 보는 추세
진행 과정	자신의 Speaking 시험 시간 20분 전까지 대기실에 도착 ⬇ 자신의 이름이 호명되면 시험관이 있는 면접실 앞 의자에서 대기하다가 시험관이 들어오라고 하면 노크하고 들어감(시험관이 직접 문을 열고 들어오라고 하는 경우도 있음) ⬇ 입실 후 가벼운 인사를 하면 시험관이 녹음기의 마이크에 대고 응시자 이름과 수험번호를 말하며 시험 녹음을 시작함(응시자에게 이름과 수험번호를 직접 말하도록 하는 경우도 있음) ⬇ 시험관이 신분증(여권)을 요구하여 시험자 본인임을 확인하고 시험이 시작됨 ⬇ 시험관이 각 Part에 대해 질문을 하며 자연스럽게 인터뷰 방식으로 시험을 진행함 ⬇ 시험이 끝나면 공손히 시험관에게 인사하고 나옴 ※ Video-Call Speaking Test도 진행 과정이 동일하지만 다음과 같은 차이점이 있음 ① 화면을 통해 시험관과 인터뷰 ② 헤드셋을 쓰고 시험관의 질문을 듣고 답변함 ③ Part 2 질문은 화면에 제시됨

각 Part별 특징

Part 1 쉬운 질문	• 직업 또는 학업, 집과 고향, 취미(쇼핑, 독서, 운동 등), 좋아하는 것(색깔, 날씨, TV프로그램 등)과 같은 친근한 주제에 대해 4~5분 정도 6~12개 질문이 주어짐 • 대답을 길게 할수록 질문 수가 줄어들고 고득점 맞을 확률도 올라감
Part 2 토픽 카드	• 하나의 주제와 관련된 4개 질문이 적힌 카드(Topic Card), 답변을 메모할 연필과 노트가 제공됨 • 답변 준비 시간 1분 이후, 2분 동안 제시된 질문에 대한 답변을 말함 • 2분이 넘으면 답변 중간에 시험관이 끊음 • 2분의 답변 시간 이후 시험관이 주제와 관련된 추가 질문을 1~2개 할 수 있음
Part 3 심층 질문	• Part 3에서는 Part 2에서 다루었던 주제에 대해 심도 있는 질문이 나옴 • Part 2에서 다루었던 주제가 개인적인 것이었다면, Part 3에서는 그와 관련된 시사적인 관점이나 사회적인 문제들을 위주로 질문이 나옴 • 자신의 의견을 논리적이고 명확하게 전달하면서, 이를 이유나 근거로 뒷받침해야 함 • Part 1처럼 4~5분 정도 4~8개 질문이 주어지고, 역시 대답을 길게 할수록 질문 수가 줄어들고 고득점 맞을 확률도 올라감

시험 중 돌발상황 대처법

질문을 잘 듣지 못했거나 이해하지 못했을 때

질문 내용에 맞지 않는 대답을 하는 것이 가장 위험하다. 추측하여 답하는 대신 I beg your pardon? 또는 I am sorry but could you repeat the question please? 등으로 되물어라. 단, 너무 자주하면 감점 요인이 될 수 있으므로, 질문할 때 최대한 집중하여 되묻는 일을 최소한으로 하는 것이 좋다.

모르는 내용이거나, 자신의 상황과 맞지 않아 대답하기 곤란한 질문일 때

질문을 바꿔 달라고 하면 감점될 수 있으므로 어떻게든 답변한다. Speaking 시험은 진실성을 테스트하는 것이 아니라 영어 말하기 능력을 테스트하는 시험이므로 주변에서 보고 들은 내용을 자신의 이야기처럼 말하거나, 이러한 간접 체험도 없는 내용이라면 상상해서라도 대답하는 태도를 보이는 것이 좋다. 이러한 경우에는 다음과 같이 시작하며 말해보자.

I am sorry, I don't know much about that, but I would probably say ~
죄송하지만 저는 그것에 대해 잘 모릅니다만, 아마도 ~라고 답변하겠습니다.

시험관이 같은 질문을 다시 할 때

시험관이 같은 질문을 다시 하는 경우가 있는데, 이때는 방금한 나의 답변이 시험관의 질문과는 동 떨어진 동문서답이어서 시험관이 올바른 답변을 듣기 위해 다시 질문을 하는 것이다. 같은 질문을 다시 받았지만 새롭게 답변하기 어렵거나 여전히 질문에 대한 이해가 제대로 되지 않았다면 다음과 같이 말해보자.

I am sorry, but could you phrase that question in a different way please?
죄송하지만 그 질문을 다른 방식으로 표현해 주실 수 있나요?

질문에 단어를 이해하지 못했을 때

질문에 나온 단어를 잘 모르는데도 추측해서 대답하다가 동문서답을 하게 되어 똑같은 질문을 다시 받는 경우가 생길 수 있다. 이때는 시험관에게 그 단어를 설명해달라고 요청하는 것이 좋다.

I am sorry, but I don't quite understand the word A. Could you explain it to me please?
죄송하지만 저는 A라는 단어를 잘 이해하지 못합니다. 그것을 제게 설명해 주실 수 있나요?

IELTS SPEAKING 채점기준

IELTS SPEAKING은 IELTS 공식 홈페이지에서 공개한 채점기준에 따라 채점이 이루어진다. 수험생들은 아래의 채점기준 세부 내용을 숙지하여 최대한 채점기준에 부합하여 말할 수 있도록 한다. Part 1, 2, 3 모두가 다음 4개의 채점기준에 따라 각각 평가되기에, 각 Part 모두 풍부한 어휘와 문법을 사용하면서 될 수 있으면 길게 말하도록 노력하자.

채점 영역	채점기준	채점기준에 맞춰 글 쓰는 팁 및 구체적 평가 점수
Fluency and Coherence **유창성과 일관성**	• 반복이나, 자기 수정없이 유창하게 말함 • 단어나 문법을 찾기 위해 머뭇거리지 않음 • 최적의 연결어로 일관성 있게 말함 • 화제를 완전하고 적절하게 전개함	• Um, Uh 등의 불필요한 말의 사용 자제 • 생각한 후 말하는 것이 아니라 생각나는 대로 바로바로 발화 • hence(이런 이유로), therefore(그러므로), that's why(그 때문에), having said that(그렇긴 해도) 등의 다양한 연결어를 적합하게 사용 • 기출 문제 브레인스토밍으로 적절한 답변 소재를 미리 생각
Lexical Resource **어휘력**	• 모든 화제에서 완전한 유창성 및 정확성을 갖춘 어휘를 사용함 • 영어 특유의 관용적 표현을 자연스럽고 정확하게 사용함	• 상황에 맞는 다양한 고급 단어 구사 • 영어식에 맞는 표현(콜로케이션) 사용 • 같은 단어를 반복하여 말하는 대신에 패러프레이징
Grammatical Range and Accuracy **문법의 다양성과 정확성**	• 다양한 문장 형태(형식)를 자연스럽고 적절하게 사용함 • 일관되게 정확한 문장 형태를 사용함	• 분사구문, 물주구문(주어가 사물인 구문: 시험에서 'I' 주어만 사용하지 말 것), 진주어-가주어, 관계대명사/관계부사, to부정사/동명사, 명사절/부사절 등을 섞어서 사용 • 하나의 절에 주어와 동사가 반드시 하나씩 있도록 하고, 주어/동사 수일치 및 시제 유의
Pronunciation **발음**	• 정확하고 섬세하게 다양한 모든 발음을 사용함 • 시종일관 유연한 발음을 유지함 • 이해하는데 수월함	• 미국식/영국식/호주식 발음 중 어떤 것을 사용해도 무관 • 너무 느리거나 빠르게 말하는 것은 자제 • 얼버무리지 말고 알아듣기 쉽도록 크고 명료하게 발음

IELTS SPEAKING 정복비법

Step 1. 답변 소재 영어로 생각하기(Brainstorming)

영어를 자유롭게 구사하는 원어민급 수험생들이 예상외로 Speaking 점수가 6.0에 멈추는 경우가 있는데, 질문에 대해 답변 소재가 없어서 제대로 답변하지 못하고 얼버무리다 끝나서 그렇다. 반면 발음이 불안하고 문법도 정확하게 구사하지 못하는 수험생이 6.5를 넘는 경우가 자주 있는데, 이는 어색한 영어라도 풍부한 어휘를 사용하며 계속해서 말을 하여 시험관에게 자신의 실력을 어필하는 경우이다.

IELTS가 공개한 채점기준에 따르면, 머뭇거리지 않고 일관성 있게 답변 소재를 전개하며(Fluency and coherence) 풍부한 어휘를 구사하면(Lexical resource), 원어민 같이 문법의 다양성과 정확성(Grammatical range and accuracy), 그리고 자연스러운 발음(Pronunciation)을 갖추지 못하더라도 Speaking에서 어느 정도 좋은 점수를 얻을 수 있다. 물론 여기에 원어민급의 완벽한 문법과 발음을 구사하면 더욱 높은 점수를 받는다.

깊이 있는 내용의 말하기는 연습으로 생기는 것이지 원어민이나 준원어민이라고 할 수 있는 것은 아니다. 따라서 평상시에 IELTS SPEAKING 예상 질문을 떠올리며 답변 소재를 영어로 생각하는 습관을 들이는 것이 필요하다. 이렇게 질문으로 나올 법한 주제에 대해 브레인스토밍을 하다 보면, 그에 필요한 어휘력도 익히게 되고, 결국 Speaking 점수도 향상시킬 수 있다.

Brainstorming 연습 예시 MP3 Unit21_1

질문

What is your favourite colour? (Why?) 당신이 가장 좋아하는 색은 무엇인가? (왜죠?)

Brainstorming

blue(답: 파란색) – reminds me of sky and ocean(이유: 하늘과 바다가 떠오름) – feel relaxed(부연: 긴장을 품) – plenty of blue shirts(예시: 파란색 셔츠 많이 있음) – my favourite(마무리: 가장 좋아함)

시험장에서 나의 답변

Blue is my favourite colour. The reason I like it most is that the colour reminds me of a beautiful blue sky and a spacious blue ocean, which make me feel relaxed and refreshed. Because of that, I have plenty of blue shirts and wear them quite frequently. That's why I can say blue is my favourite.

파란색이 제가 가장 좋아하는 색입니다. 제가 이 색을 가장 좋아하는 이유는 그 색은 제게 아름다운 푸른 하늘과 광활한 푸른 대양을 생각나게 하기 때문인데, 이는 긴장과 피로를 풀어줍니다. 그렇기에, 저는 많은 파란색 셔츠를 갖고 있고 꽤 자주 입는 편입니다. 그래서 파란색을 가장 좋아한다고 말할 수 있습니다.

Step 2. 음원 따라말하기(Shadowing)

Speaking에서 문법의 다양성과 정확성(Grammatical range and accuracy), 그리고 자연스러운 발음(Pronunciation)을 갖추기 위한 최고의 훈련법은 본책에 수록된 Speaking 모범 답안 MP3를 따라말하는 것(shadowing)이다. 쉐도잉은 이미 Listening 정복 비법에서 배웠는데, Speaking에서도 중요하다. 검증된 모범 답안의 예문을 원어민 속도에 따라 쉐도잉하며 암기하다 보면, 실제 시험에서 이러한 문장 패턴을 무의식적으로 자연스럽게 사용할 수 있다.

특히 Speaking에서 쉐도잉을 할 때에는 Listening에서보다 목소리를 더 크게 하고 발음도 더욱 또렷하게 연습을 해야 한다. 수험생 중 입을 작게 벌려가며 조용하게 영어를 말하는 경우가 꽤 있다. 가뜩이나 한국말도 작게 말하는데, 어색한 영어를 말하려니 더 작게 말할 수밖에 없겠지만 언어의 목적, 바로 '의사소통'을 위해서는 정확하고 크게 입을 벌려 말이 입 밖으로 나가 상대에게 전달되어져야 한다. 어색하고 헷갈리는 발음의 영어를 의기소침해서 발음하면, 상대방은 더 못 알아듣는다. 어차피 영어는 외국어이기에 틀리기 쉽다. 틀릴 것을 걱정하지 말고 자신의 생각을 전달하기 위해 언제나 크고 자신 있게 영어를 입 밖으로 내는 연습을 하자.

Step 3. 나의 답변 녹음하여 들어보기(Recording)

쉐도잉에서 한 걸음 더 나아가, 자신의 목소리를 녹음해서 들어보는 것도 좋은 방법이다. 쉐도잉을 통해 어느 정도 자신의 영어 말하기가 자연스럽게 되었다고 생각할 수 있지만, 녹음된 자신의 목소리를 다시 들어보면 어색한 발음의 영어를 구사하는 자신을 발견하게 될 것이다. 특히 질문에 대해 답변을 하는 자신의 목소리를 녹음해서 다시 듣거나, 스터디 팀원들과 서로의 말하기를 평가해 보자.

이렇게 녹음을 통해 우선 자신의 틀리거나 부자연스러운 발음을 파악하고, 반복 연습으로 정확하고 자연스러운 발음으로 완벽하게 고쳐야 한다. 수험생 중에 exhibition[엑써비션]을 [이그지비션]이라고 발음하는 학생이 있었는데 학생 역시 자신의 발음이 잘못된 것을 알고 있었다. 하지만 이 단어를 습관적으로 [이그지비션]이라고 계속 잘못 발음했는데, 이는 충분한 연습을 하지 않아 예전에 잘못 발음하던 습관이 고쳐지지 않은 것이다. 따라서 아는 것에서 끝나는 것이 아니라 확실히 고쳐질 때까지 끊임없는 연습을 해야 한다.

Eye contact의 중요성

영미권에서는 대화 중 눈을 마주치는 것을 매우 중요하게 여긴다. 시선을 피하면 상대방이 진실되지 못하거나 무언가를 숨기려 한다고 생각할 수 있다. 또한, 관심이 없거나 무시하는 듯한 인상을 줄 수도 있다. IELTS 시험에서도 마찬가지다. 응시생이 시험관의 눈을 피하고 다른 곳을 보며 말하면, 시험관은 외운 내용을 그대로 읊거나 시험에 집중하지 못하고 있다고 판단할 수 있다. 이렇게 좋지 않은 인상을 주면 자신의 실력보다 낮은 점수를 받을 가능성이 높아진다. 따라서 시험관의 눈을 편안하고 호감 있게 바라보며 말하는 것이 중요하다. 이는 긍정적인 인상을 남기고, 자신의 영어 실력을 효과적으로 어필하는 데 도움이 된다.

IELTS SPEAKING 고득점 Key Points 정리

지금까지 배운 IELTS SPEAKING에 대한 내용을 바탕으로 7.0이상 고득점으로 가는 Key Points를 정리한다.

1 질문에 정확하게 대답하자

- 정말 기본 중에 기본으로, 복잡하지 않게 질문에 정확하게 대답하자. 괜히 둘러서 말하면 상대방이 못 알아듣는다. 영어권 국가는 두괄식이니, Yes/No 또는 단답형으로 먼저 질문에 대해 확실히 대답하고 나서, 이유나 부연을 말하는 것이 유리하다.
- 질문을 정확하게 이해하지 못했으면, 'I beg your pardon' 또는 'I am sorry but could you repeat the question please?' 등으로 되묻자.

2 채점기준을 생각하며 말하자

- Fluency and Coherence: 흐름이 끊어지지 않게(중간 중간에 'Um, Uh' 등의 불필요한 말을 많이 하지 말고 침묵도 없어야 됨), 그리고 아이디어들을 논리적으로 서로 연결시켜서 질문 당 Part 1은 3문장 이상, Part 3는 5문장 이상으로 말하도록 노력한다.
- Lexical Resource: 정확하게 다양하고 높은 수준의 단어들을 사용하는데, 최대한 내가 아는 많은 단어들을 보여주어야 한다. 아는 단어들을 입안에서 참지 말고 약 13분의 스피킹 시험 시간 동안 최대한 쏟아내자!
- Grammatical Range and Accuracy: 하나의 질문에 대한 답변에도 다양한 문장 구조를 사용해보자. 모든 문장에 제대로 된 시제 및 수 일치는 기본이다.
- Pronunciation: 분명하고 쉽게 이해되도록 또박또박, 강세와 억양을 살려서 말하자. 특히 정확하고 크게 입을 벌려 말이 입 밖으로 나가서 상대에게 전달되도록 한다.

SPEAKING

3 말만큼 행동도 중요하다

- Make eye contact: 자연스럽고 친근하고, 밝게 시험관을 바라본다. 부담스럽게 바라보거나 눈을 피하고, 바닥, 천장, 창문 밖 경치, 면접관 옆을 보는 순간, 0.5가 날라간다.
- Answer in a polite and friendly way: 시험관을 대학 또는 이민 면접관이라 생각하고 친근하고 공손한 어조와 태도로 대답한다.
- Body language is important: 적절한 몸짓을 통해 분위기를 주도하고 전달력도 높이자.
- It is not over until the end: 방을 나서서 완전히 면접관과 헤어지기 전까지 공손하게 행동한다. 끝나고 절대 아쉬워하지 말고 자신있게 다음과 같이 말하고 당당하게 나가자.

  Thank you for your time. I really appreciate it.
  시간 내주셔서 정말 감사합니다.

PRACTICE TEST

Brainstorming 각 질문에 대해 최소 4문장 이상을 만들 수 있도록 답변 소재를 생각해 보자.

1 Do you enjoy being your current age? [Why/Why not?]

2 Describe a woman who is important in your life. Who is she and what is she like?

3 Do people in your country use public transport a lot?

정답 및 해설 p.076

Shadowing 음원을 들으면서 크게 따라 말해 보자.

MP3 Unit21_2

1 Yes, I do. I've just turned 32 years old and feel more confident in myself since I believe that my social skills have greatly improved. Also, I am much more knowledgeable now than I was in my 20s. Of course, I am still quite young, so I have many more things to learn about and experience. But overall, being 32 is good.

MP3 Unit21_3

2 I would like to talk about my mother. She is a calm, mild-mannered woman with a gentle voice that makes me feel comforted. She is also very attentive to her family and always makes sacrifices to put her children first. That's why I am always grateful to her.

SPEAKING

MP3 Unit21_4

3 Yes, we do. In particular, our railway lines are well developed and can efficiently deal with our high population density. Furthermore, the fares are very reasonable. Therefore, many people prefer to use public transport rather than to drive a car.

Recording 앞의 질문에 대한 자신만의 답변을 녹음해 보고 들어 보자.

UNIT 22

Part 1 - 나의 학업 또는 직업

오늘의 학습 목표

1. Part 1 질문 유형과 답변 방식을 숙지한다.
2. Part 1에 반드시 등장하는 자신의 일 또는 공부관련 자기 소개 부분을 완벽히 준비한다.
3. 자신의 신분 소개와 관련된 답변 소재, 고급 어휘, 사용할 문법을 정리한다.

Part 1에 대한 모든 것

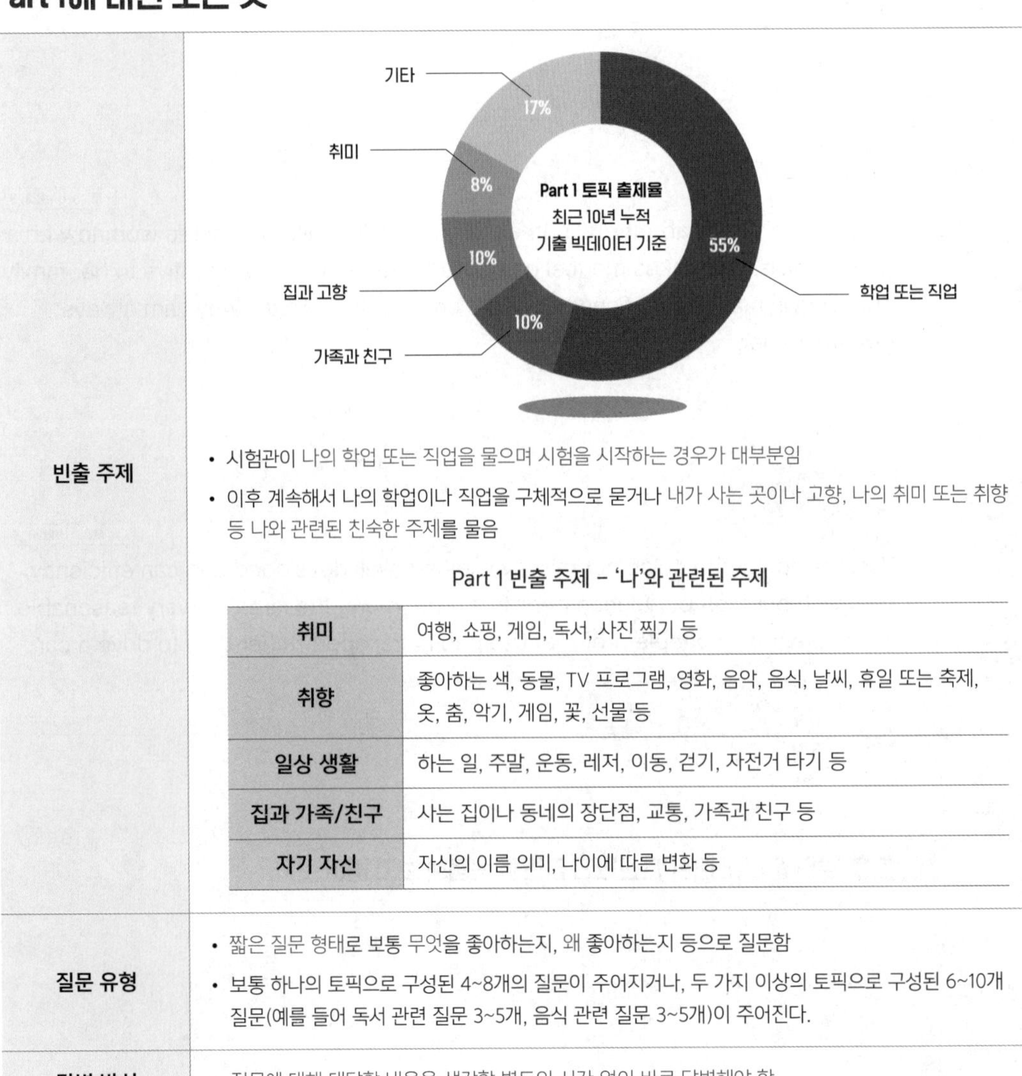

빈출 주제

- 시험관이 나의 학업 또는 직업을 물으며 시험을 시작하는 경우가 대부분임
- 이후 계속해서 나의 학업이나 직업을 구체적으로 묻거나 내가 사는 곳이나 고향, 나의 취미 또는 취향 등 나와 관련된 친숙한 주제를 물음

Part 1 빈출 주제 – '나'와 관련된 주제

취미	여행, 쇼핑, 게임, 독서, 사진 찍기 등
취향	좋아하는 색, 동물, TV 프로그램, 영화, 음악, 음식, 날씨, 휴일 또는 축제, 옷, 춤, 악기, 게임, 꽃, 선물 등
일상 생활	하는 일, 주말, 운동, 레저, 이동, 걷기, 자전거 타기 등
집과 가족/친구	사는 집이나 동네의 장단점, 교통, 가족과 친구 등
자기 자신	자신의 이름 의미, 나이에 따른 변화 등

질문 유형

- 짧은 질문 형태로 보통 무엇을 좋아하는지, 왜 좋아하는지 등으로 질문함
- 보통 하나의 토픽으로 구성된 4~8개의 질문이 주어지거나, 두 가지 이상의 토픽으로 구성된 6~10개 질문(예를 들어 독서 관련 질문 3~5개, 음식 관련 질문 3~5개)이 주어진다.

답변 방식

- 질문에 대해 대답할 내용을 생각할 별도의 시간 없이 바로 답변해야 함

고득점 비법 - 나의 학업/직업

1 나의 학업 또는 직업 소개에 대한 확실한 준비

IELTS SPEAKING에서 신분 소개, 즉 자신의 학업이나 직업에 대한 질문이 첫 문제로 나오는 경우가 99%이다. 신분 관련 질문을 하나만 하고 다른 토픽으로 넘어가는 경우도 있지만, 대부분은 자기 신분 관련해서 조금씩 구체적인 질문이 파생되고, Part 2에서도 가끔 자신의 일과 공부 관련 질문이 주어지기도 한다. 따라서 자신의 공부나 일에 대한 소개를 확실히 할 수 있어야 한다. 성공적인 신분 소개는 고득점으로 가는 첫 단계인 동시에, 응시자에게는 자신감을, 시험관에게는 강렬한 첫인상을 심어줄 수 있다.

2 단답형이 아닌 짜임새 있는 흐름을 가진 여러 문장의 대답

시험관이 학생인지 일하는지를 질문하는데, 이 때 단순히 '일한다' 또는 '공부한다'의 단답형으로 대답하면 안된다. 무엇을 공부하는데, 어디서 공부를 하며, 얼마동안 공부해왔다는 식으로 구체적 흐름이 있는 여러 문장으로 답변을 해야 고득점을 받을 수 있다. 질문 하나하나에 대해 구체적이고 자세히 대답하면 질문 수도 줄어들고 점수도 높아지는 경향이 있다.

3 채점기준에 맞는 나만의 신분 소개 연습

채점에 플러스가 될 수 있는 적절한 고급 어휘와 문법을 함께 생각해 두어 자신만의 모범 답변을 완성해 간다.

학사 학위 / 석사 학위 / 박사 학위	bachelor's degree / master's degree / doctor's degree
대학교 1학년 / 2학년 / 3학년 / 4학년	freshman / sophomore / junior / senior
과제 / 사례 연구 / 시험 / 마감일	assignment / case study / exam / deadline
한 학기 휴학 중입니다.	I'm taking a semester off.
재직 중입니다.	I work at(=for) a company.
관리인으로 재직 중입니다.	I work as a manager.
사업을 하고 있습니다.	I run my own business(=company).
A에게 B를 제공하다	provide A with B = provide B for A = provide B to A
~할 수밖에 없다	cannot help ~ing = cannot help but 동사원형
아침 일찍부터 밤 늦게까지 쉬지 않고 일하거나 공부하다	burn the candle at both ends
인맥을 쌓다	build a strong network
엄청난 양의	the tremendous amount of
상당 수의	a substantial number of
그래서	that's why

기출 문제 - 나의 학업/직업

1 Are you a student or are you a worker? MP3 Unit22_1

당신은 학생입니까 아니면 직장인입니까?

Model Answer brainstorming은 파란색으로 표시

I am a university student, and I am doing a bachelor's degree in business management at Siwon University. This is my final semester of study.

저는 대학생으로 시원 대학교에 다니며 경영학 학사 학위 중에 있습니다. 이번이 제 마지막 학기입니다.

나만의 모범 답변

2 What subject are you studying? MP3 Unit22_2

당신은 어떤 과목을 공부하나요?

Model Answer brainstorming은 파란색으로 표시

I am studying business management, which requires completing various team projects and researching case studies from around the world. Since I have a substantial number of assignments to finish, I spend most of my time studying on campus.

저는 경영학을 공부하고 있는데, 이 과목은 다양한 팀 프로젝트를 끝내야 하고 전 세계의 사례 연구 조사를 필요로 합니다. 끝내야 할 상당한 수의 과제들 때문에, 저는 대부분의 시간을 캠퍼스에서 공부하는 데 보냅니다.

나만의 모범 답변

3 What is something you don't like about your job or study?

MP3 Unit22_3

당신의 일이나 공부에서 좋아하지 않는 점은 무엇입니까?

Model Answer brainstorming은 파란색으로 표시

I dislike that I often have to study until late at night. In particular, if there is an exam or a tight deadline for a project, I cannot help burning my candle at both ends. Nevertheless, it's not that unbearable for me, so I can say it's just a minor issue.

저는 종종 밤늦게까지 공부해야 하는 점이 싫습니다. 특히, 만일 시험이나 긴박한 프로젝트 마감일이 있으면, 하루 종일 공부할 수밖에 없습니다. 그럼에도 불구하고, 그렇게 참지 못할 정도는 아니어서, 단지 작은 문제점이라고 말할 수 있겠네요.

나만의 모범 답변

SPEAKING

4 How long have you been studying English?

MP3 Unit22_4

당신은 얼마나 오랫동안 영어를 공부해오고 있나요?

Model Answer brainstorming은 파란색으로 표시

I've been learning English for more than 10 years ever since I was 10. Even after studying English for over a decade, there are still many things in the English language I don't know because of the tremendous amount of vocabulary and exceptions to grammar rules. I think that's why English is difficult to learn.

저는 열 살 때 이래로 약 10년 동안 영어를 공부해 오고 있습니다. 비록 십 년이 넘도록 영어를 공부해왔지만, 영어에 대해 모르는 것이 너무 많은데, 엄청난 양의 어휘와 예외적인 문법 때문입니다. 그래서 영어가 배우기 어려운 것 같습니다.

나만의 모범 답변

PRACTICE TEST

Part 1 다음 세부 요구 사항에 따라 각 질문의 모범 답변을 만들자.

Q1

MP3 Unit22_5

Why did you choose your job or subject?

- Brainstorming 위 질문에 필요한 핵심어(답변 소재)를 3가지 이상 적어보자.

- Lexical resource 플러스 점수를 위해 반드시 사용해야 할 어휘를 3가지 이상 적어보자.

- Grammatical range 플러스 점수를 위해 반드시 사용해야 할 문법을 적어보자.

- Model Answer 위에 적은 답변 소재, 어휘, 문법을 활용하여 나만의 모범 답변을 만들자.

정답 및 해설 p.077

Q2

MP3 Unit22_6

Do you like your work or study? [Why/Why not?]

- Brainstorming 위 질문에 필요한 핵심어(답변 소재)를 3가지 이상 적어보자.

- Lexical resource 플러스 점수를 위해 반드시 사용해야 할 어휘를 3가지 이상 적어보자.

- Grammatical range 플러스 점수를 위해 반드시 사용해야 할 문법을 적어보자.

- Model Answer 위에 적은 답변 소재, 어휘, 문법을 활용하여 나만의 모범 답변을 만들자.

Q3

MP3 Unit22_7

Where is your workplace or school located?

- Brainstorming 위 질문에 필요한 핵심어(답변 소재)를 3가지 이상 적어보자.

- Lexical resource 플러스 점수를 위해 반드시 사용해야 할 어휘를 3가지 이상 적어보자.

- Grammatical range 플러스 점수를 위해 반드시 사용해야 할 문법을 적어보자.

- Model Answer 위에 적은 답변 소재, 어휘, 문법을 활용하여 나만의 모범 답변을 만들자.

Q4

MP3 Unit22_8

How do most people travel to work where you live?

- Brainstorming 위 질문에 필요한 핵심어(답변 소재)를 3가지 이상 적어보자.

- Lexical resource 플러스 점수를 위해 반드시 사용해야 할 어휘를 3가지 이상 적어보자.

- Grammatical range 플러스 점수를 위해 반드시 사용해야 할 문법을 적어보자.

- Model Answer 위에 적은 답변 소재, 어휘, 문법을 활용하여 나만의 모범 답변을 만들자.

SPEAKING

UNIT 23

Part 1 - 내가 사는 곳

오늘의 학습 목표

1 내가 사는 곳 관련 빈출 질문에 대한 브레인스토밍을 한다.
2 답변을 위한 어휘 및 표현을 익힌다.
3 채점기준에 맞게 나만의 모범 답변을 만들고 연습한다.

고득점 비법 - 내가 사는 곳

1 내가 사는 곳의 주거 형태와 사는 동네

IELTS SPEAKING 시험에서는 Part 2를 제외하고는 브레인스토밍 시간이 따로 주어지지 않기에, '내가 사는 곳'과 같이 자주 시험에 나오는 토픽에 대해서는 미리 브레인스토밍을 해보고 답변을 연습해야 한다.

자신이 공동 주택에 사는지 단독 주택에 사는지(apartment or house), 집의 구조가 어떤지, 도시에 사는지 시골/전원에 사는지(urban or rural area), 도시에 산다면 도심에 사는지 근교에 사는지(city centre or suburb)를 먼저 말할 수 있도록 한다.

보통 아이엘츠 시험에서는 공동 주택을 영국식 표현인 flat으로 지칭하는데, 스피킹 Part 1 문제에서는 flat 대신 apartment로도 자주 묻는다.

2 내가 사는 곳의 위치 및 특징

자신이 사는 곳의 위치 및 얼마나 오래 그곳에서 살았는지에 대해서 설명할 수 있어야 하며, 특별히 사는 곳의 장점과 단점도 미리 하나씩 정리해 두어서 시험장에서 바로 답변이 나올 수 있도록 한다.

3 미래에 대한 질문

미래에 어떠한 집에서 살고 싶은지, 계속해서 그곳에서 살 건지 미래와 관련된 질문도 최근 들어 자주 출제되고 있다. 이러한 질문들은 미리 준비하지 않으면 시험장에서 당황하여 제대로 답변을 하지 못할 수 있으므로, 공부하면서 미리 답변을 생각해 두도록 한다.

유용한 표현 - 내가 사는 곳

고향	hometown
동네, 이웃	neighbourhood
수도	capital city
도시	city, town, urban area
시골, 전원	country, countryside, rural area
집, 단독 주택	house
아파트, 빌라, 공동 주택	apartment(미국식), flat(영국식)
원룸 오피스텔, 원룸 아파트	studio apartment(미국식), studio flat(영국식)
거실, 침실, 화장실, 부엌	living room, bedroom, bathroom, kitchen
~에게 편리한	convenient for
~을 살/할 형편이 되다	afford
~와 방/집을 같이 쓰다	share a house/room with
혼자서 살다	live on my own
최상의 선택	top choice
형제자매	sibling
더 좋은 교육 기회	better educational opportunities
많은	plenty of
경력을 쌓을 기회, 취업 기회	career opportunities
분위기, 기운	atmosphere
예전에 살았지만 지금은 살지 않는다	used to live
~로 이사가다, 옮기다	move to
이사 나가다/들어오다	move out/in
거주자, 주민	resident
동전의 양면	both sides of the coin
최신 유행하는 식당	hip restaurant
신나는 밤문화	exciting nightlife
최적의/완벽한 장소	perfect place
~한 뷰/전경의	with a view of
삶을 누리다, 꿈을 실현하다	live the dream
(방이) 넓은	spacious
~에 전념하는, ~에 전용인	dedicated to
컴퓨터 게임(하기)	gaming

기출 문제 - 내가 사는 곳

1 Do you live in a house or a flat?

MP3 Unit23_1

주택에 거주하나요, 아파트에 거주하나요?

Model Answer brainstorming은 파란색으로 표시

Currently, I live in a flat in Seoul with my family. Like most flats in my country, it has a living room, three bedrooms, two bathrooms and a kitchen. Although I'd prefer to live in a house, I'm satisfied with the convenience of living in a flat.

현재 저는 가족과 함께 서울의 한 아파트에 살고 있습니다. 우리나라 대부분의 아파트와 마찬가지로 거실, 침실 3개, 욕실 2개, 주방이 있습니다. 주택에 살고 싶지만 아파트 생활의 편리함에 만족하고 있습니다.

나만의 모범 답변

2 What is your favourite room in your home?

MP3 Unit23_2

집에서 가장 좋아하는 방은 어디인가요?

Model Answer brainstorming은 파란색으로 표시

Most people would choose their bedroom as their favourite room, but I share mine with my sibling, so it's not my top choice. My favourite room is the living room because I enjoy relaxing on the sofa while watching TV shows.

대부분의 사람들은 가장 좋아하는 방으로 침실을 선택하지만, 저는 동생과 방을 같이 쓰기 때문에, 제 최고의 선택은 아닙니다. 제가 가장 좋아하는 방은 거실인데, 소파에 앉아 TV 프로그램을 보며 휴식을 취하는 것을 즐기기 때문입니다.

나만의 모범 답변

3 How long have you lived there?

그곳에서 얼마나 오래 살았나요?

MP3 Unit23_3

Model Answer brainstorming은 파란색으로 표시

I have lived here for around ten years, ever since my family moved to Seoul when I was eight years old. Before that, we lived in Busan, which is where I was born.

저는 8살 때 가족이 서울로 이사 온 이후 약 10년 동안 이곳에서 살았습니다. 그 전에는 제가 태어난 부산에서 살았어요.

나만의 모범 답변

4 Will you continue living there in the future?

앞으로도 계속 그곳에서 살 것인가요?

MP3 Unit23_4

Model Answer brainstorming은 파란색으로 표시

Yes, I think that I will continue living here in the near future because it would be too expensive for me to move out and live on my own. However, I hope that someday, I will be able to afford a house with a large backyard.

네, 집을 나가서 혼자 살기에는 비용이 너무 많이 들기 때문에 당분간은 여기서 계속 살 것 같습니다. 하지만 언젠가는 넓은 뒷마당이 있는 집을 살 수 있기를 바랍니다.

나만의 모범 답변

PRACTICE TEST

Part 1 다음 세부 요구 사항에 따라 각 질문의 모범 답변을 만들자.

Q1

MP3 Unit23_5

Do you live in the city or the country?

- Brainstorming 위 질문에 필요한 핵심어(답변 소재)를 3가지 이상 적어보자.

- Lexical resource 플러스 점수를 위해 반드시 사용해야 할 어휘를 3가지 이상 적어보자.

- Grammatical range 플러스 점수를 위해 반드시 사용해야 할 문법을 적어보자.

- Model Answer 상기에 적은 답변 소재, 어휘, 문법을 활용하여 나만의 모범 답변을 만들자.

정답 및 해설 p.079

Q2

MP3 Unit23_6

What are some advantages of your neighbourhood?

- Brainstorming 위 질문에 필요한 핵심어(답변 소재)를 3가지 이상 적어보자.

- Lexical resource 플러스 점수를 위해 반드시 사용해야 할 어휘를 3가지 이상 적어보자.

- Grammatical range 플러스 점수를 위해 반드시 사용해야 할 문법을 적어보자.

- Model Answer 위에 적은 답변 소재, 어휘, 문법을 활용하여 나만의 모범 답변을 만들자.

Q3

MP3 Unit23_7

Would you say your hometown is a good place for young people to live?

- Brainstorming 위 질문에 필요한 핵심어(답변 소재)를 3가지 이상 적어보자.

- Lexical resource 플러스 점수를 위해 반드시 사용해야 할 어휘를 3가지 이상 적어보자.

- Grammatical range 플러스 점수를 위해 반드시 사용해야 할 문법을 적어보자.

- Model Answer 위에 적은 답변 소재, 어휘, 문법을 활용하여 나만의 모범 답변을 만들자.

Q4

MP3 Unit23_8

What kind of house do you want to live in in the future?

- Brainstorming 위 질문에 필요한 핵심어(답변 소재)를 3가지 이상 적어보자.

- Lexical resource 플러스 점수를 위해 반드시 사용해야 할 어휘를 3가지 이상 적어보자.

- Grammatical range 플러스 점수를 위해 반드시 사용해야 할 문법을 적어보자.

- Model Answer 위에 적은 답변 소재, 어휘, 문법을 활용하여 나만의 모범 답변을 만들자.

UNIT 24

Part 1 - 나와 관련된 질문

오늘의 학습 목표

1 나의 취미, 취향에 대한 기출 문제를 보며 브레인스토밍을 한다.
2 자신의 답변을 한단계 업그레이드해줄 고급 어휘와 표현들을 반드시 정리한다.
3 채점기준에 맞게 나만의 모범 답변을 만들고 연습한다.

고득점 비법 - 나와 관련된 질문

1 다양한 시제 사용

자기 자신에 대한 질문은 과거/현재/미래 시제가 모두 가능한 주제이므로, 시제 사용에 특히 유의해야 한다. 하지만 반대로 생각하면, 다양한 시제를 사용할 수 있다는 능력을 보여줄 수 있는 기회이기도 하다. 예를 들어, '어떤 음악을 좋아하는가?'라는 질문의 답변으로, 현재시제(클래식-오래도록 변하지 않은 가치 때문에)만 사용할 수도 있지만, '과거완료시제(예전에는 힙합을 좋아했음)-현재완료&과거(대학생때부터 클래식 입문)-현재시제(이유: 오래도록 변하지 않는 가치)'의 3가지 시제를 사용할 수도 있는 것이다.

2 두괄식으로 답변

질문에 대한 답변을 먼저하고 부연설명을 붙이는 두괄식 방식의 답변이 고득점에 유리하다. 즉, Do/Does 등으로 시작하는 일반의문문에는 Yes/No로, WH-Questions같은 경우는 해당하는 내용으로 답변을 시작하도록 한다. 시험관과 인터뷰 시 질문에 대한 대답을 따로 준비할 시간이 없기에, 빈출 질문 사항들에 대해 브레인스토밍을 수시로 하여 시험장에서 바로 답변할 수 있도록 연습을 하는 것이 중요하다.

3 답변에 대한 충분한 부연 설명

반드시 예시나 이유 등으로 답변에 대한 부연 설명을 해야 한다. 고득점을 위해서는 최소 3문장 이상의 추가 정보를 만들도록 한다. 답변에 대한 구체적 예시와 이유로 각각 1~2문장을 붙이는 것이다. 여기에 패러프레이징을 이용한 마무리 문장으로 답변을 끝내면 유창함은 물론 다양한 문법적 지식과 어휘력을 발휘할 수 있다.

부연 설명 만드는 Patterns

예시	For example / For instance / As an example 예를 들어
	An example of this is that **주어 동사** 이것의 예는 ~입니다
이유	This is why **주어 동사** / This is because **주어 동사** 그것은 ~때문입니다
	The reason is that **주어 동사** 이유는 ~입니다
	주어 동사 since **주어 동사** ~은 ~이기 때문입니다
구체적 설명	In other words 다르게 말하면
	What I mean is **주어 동사** 제가 의미하는 것은 바로 ~입니다

유용한 표현 - 나와 관련된 질문

클래식 음악	classical music
그것은 내게 특별하다	it has a special place in my heart
~하는 것이 중요하다	it is important that절: 가주어(it) – 진주어(that절) 구문
~로부터 멀리 떨어져	far away from
특징으로 삼다	feature
아주 멋진	stunning
기묘한	bizarre
정말 그런 A는 어디에도 없다 (정말 그런 영화는 어디에도 없다)	there's really no other A like it (there's really no other film like it)
A에서 B로의 변화/과도 (학생에서 젊은 전문가로의 변화)	transition from A to B (transition from a student to a young professional)
마무리 짓다	wrap up
급격하게 변하다	change dramatically
해외에서 일하다 / 해외에서 공부하다	work abroad / study abroad
대체로 보아	all in all
유명 브랜드 옷	name brand clothing
최신 기기	the latest gizmo
~하는 데 시간을 보내다 (일주일을 스쿠버 다이빙하며 보내다)	spend 시간 ~ing (spend a week scuba diving)
힘들게 번 돈	hard-earned money
저축은 많은 절제를 요한다	saving money requires a lot of discipline
우리의 눈을 사로잡는 물건	an item to catch our eyes
~을 둘러보다, 훑어보다	browse through
나와 같은 나이	the same age as me (=my age)
거의	more or less
단계, 시기, 국면	phase
동료, 동창	peer
초등학교	elementary school(미국식), primary school(영국식)
중고등학교	secondary school

SPEAKING

채점기준에 따른 모범 답변 - 나와 관련된 질문

MP3 Unit24_1

질문

What kind of music do you like?

당신은 어떤 종류의 음악을 좋아하나요?

답변 brainstorming은 파란색으로 표시

Ever since I was a child, my favourite kind of music has been classical music. I'm always amazed that songs written hundreds of years ago can still be so beautiful and powerful today. Bach especially has a special place in my heart, and I listen to him anytime I need to stop, take a deep breath and relax. To me, classical music is the perfect type of music.

제가 아이였을 때 이래로, 제가 가장 좋아하는 음악 종류는 클래식 음악입니다. 저는 수백 년 전에 쓰여진 곡들이 오늘날도 여전히 아름답고 강렬한 점에 항상 놀랍니다. 특히 바흐가 저에게 특별한데요, 멈춰서 심호흡을 하고 느긋하게 할 필요가 있는 언제든지 바흐를 듣습니다. 제게, 클래식 음악은 완벽한 음악 형태입니다.

채점기준에 따른 답변 평가

Fluency and Coherence 유창성과 일관성	반복이나 자기 수정 안함
	단어나 문법을 찾기 위해 머뭇거리지 않음
	연결어를 사용하며 일관성 있게 말함 부사절 접속사(ever since)와 부사(especially)의 적절한 사용으로 내용 일관성 유지
	화제를 완전하고 적절하게 전개 두괄식으로 질문에 먼저 대답을 하고(classical music), 이유(songs written hundreds of years ago can still be so beautiful and powerful)와 구체적 예(Bach), 그리고 마무리 문장까지 이어지는 완벽한 전개를 보임
Lexical Resource 어휘력	상황에 맞는 다양한 고급 단어 구사 classic music이 아닌 classical music
	영어다운 표현을 사용하고 동의어 반복 없이 패러프레이징 [영어다운 표현] has a special place in my heart 나에게 특별하다 take a deep breath 크게 심호흡을 하다 [패러프레이징] favourite kind of music 가장 좋아하는 음악 종류 → perfect type of music to me 내게 완벽한 음악 유형
Grammatical Range and Accuracy 문법의 다양성과 정확성	분사, 관계대명사, 명사절 등의 다양한 문법을 정확하게 사용 <u>부사절접속사</u> ever since ~이래로 줄곧 <u>be amazed that절</u> that절에 대해 놀랍다 <u>과거분사</u> songs written 쓰여진 곡들
	주어/동사 수일치 및 올바른 시제 사용 수일치 및 현재완료 시제를 제대로 사용
Pronunciation 발음	정확한 발음 [바흐]가 아닌 [바크]로 발음
	너무 느리거나 빠르지 않게, 일관된 스피드로 발음
	얼버무리지 않고 알아듣기 쉽도록 크고 명료하게 발음
총 평	충실한 내용의 완벽한 전개, 영어다운 표현들과 패러프레이징, 그리고 다양한 문법을 완벽하게 사용하였기에, 해당 답변은 어려운 고급 어휘를 사용하지 않아도 발음만 주의하면 충분히 고득점 가능

기출 문제 - 나와 관련된 질문

1 How do you usually spend your holidays [Why?] MP3 Unit24_2
당신은 주말을 보통 어떻게 보내나요? [왜죠?]

Model Answer brainstorming은 파란색으로 표시

Like most people, my holidays are all about spending time with family. It's important that, no matter where we live, my siblings, parents and I make the journey to visit my grandparents. But since I live quite far away from my hometown, the holiday can become rather stressful with all the travelling and traffic. Nevertheless, it's all worth it once I'm relaxing in my grandparent's house with my entire family.

대부분의 사람들처럼 저는 휴일을 가족들과 보냅니다. 어디에 살든지 상관없이, 제 형제자매, 부모님과 저는 조부모님 댁을 방문합니다. 그러나 저는 제 고향에서 꽤 멀리 떨어져서 살기에, 이동과 교통으로 다소 스트레스가 되기도 합니다. 그럼에도 그럴 가치가 있는데, 일단 조부모님 댁에서 온 가족과 함께 쉬게 되면 그렇습니다.

나만의 모범 답변

2 What's your favourite TV programme? [Why?] MP3 Unit24_3
당신의 가장 좋아하는 TV 프로는 무엇인가요? [왜죠?]

Model Answer brainstorming은 파란색으로 표시

My favourite TV programme is *Planet Earth*. I'm a nature lover, and every episode features stunning footage that shows just how amazing the natural world is. I'm especially interested in the bizarre creatures living in the ocean depths, so I've probably watched the episode about the deep sea at least a dozen times. There's really no other show like it.

제가 가장 좋아하는 TV 프로는 플래닛 어스입니다. 저는 자연을 정말 사랑하는데, 모든 에피소드는 자연이 얼마나 놀라운지를 보여주는 멋진 영상을 담고 있습니다. 저는 특별히 해양 깊이 사는 기묘한 생물들에 관심이 많기에, 아마도 최소 수십 번은 심해 관련 에피소드를 본 것 같습니다. 정말 이와 같은 쇼는 어디에도 없습니다.

나만의 모범 답변

SPEAKING

3 What will be different about your life in the future? [Why?]

MP3 Unit24_4

당신의 미래 삶에서 무엇이 달라질까요? [왜죠?]

Model Answer brainstorming은 파란색으로 표시

The biggest difference in my future will be my transition from a student to a young professional. Since I'm currently wrapping up my university studies, my life will change dramatically after I graduate and start working. I also plan to work abroad, so I'll be living in a foreign country, too. All in all, I believe that I have a bright future.

제 미래에서 가장 큰 차이는 학생에서 젊은 전문가로의 변화일 것입니다. 현재 저는 대학 공부를 마무리하고 있기에, 제 삶은 졸업하고 일을 시작하면 급격하게 변할 것입니다. 저는 또한 해외에서 일할 계획이기에, 외국에서 살게 될 것입니다. 대체로 보아, 저는 미래가 밝다고 생각합니다.

나만의 모범 답변

4 Do you ever save money to buy something special? [Why?/Why not?]

당신은 전에 특별한 무언가를 사기 위해 돈을 모은 적이 있나요? [왜죠? / 왜 아니죠?]

MP3 Unit24_5

Model Answer brainstorming은 파란색으로 표시

Every year, I save enough money so that I can travel to an exotic location. I'm not a materialistic person, so I choose to spend my hard-earned money on unique experiences rather than name brand clothing or the latest gizmo. For example, last year, I spent a week scuba diving in the Indian Ocean. Even though saving money requires a lot of discipline, the memories I create are priceless.

매년 저는 이국적인 장소로 여행할 수 있도록 충분한 돈을 모읍니다. 저는 물질적인 사람이 아니어서 힘들게 번 돈을 유명 브랜드 옷이나 최신 기기 대신에 독특한 경험에 소비하기로 선택합니다. 예를 들면, 작년에, 저는 인도양에서 스쿠버 다이빙하며 일주일을 보냈습니다. 비록 저축은 많은 절제를 요하지만, 제가 만드는 추억은 너무 소중합니다.

나만의 모범 답변

5 In what kind of places do you like to go shopping [Why?]

MP3 Unit24_6

어떤 유형의 장소로 쇼핑 가는 것을 좋아하나요? [왜죠?]

Model Answer brainstorming은 파란색으로 표시

Personally, I enjoy shopping at large department stores. Everything there is designed to be convenient for the shopper, from the organised floor plans to the friendly service. My wife and I will spend entire afternoons going from floor to floor, waiting for the perfect item to catch our eyes, or simply browsing through the bookstore. No other shopping experience really compares.

개인적으로, 저는 커다란 백화점에서의 쇼핑을 즐깁니다. 잘 배치된 평면도부터 친절한 서비스까지, 그곳의 모든 것은 쇼핑객이 편리하도록 디자인되어 있습니다. 제 아내와 저는 매 층을 다니며, 눈을 사로잡는 멋진 제품을 기다리며 또는 단순히 서점을 둘러보며 오후 내내 보낼 겁니다. 그 어떤 쇼핑 경험도 견줄 수 없습니다.

나만의 모범 답변

SPEAKING

6 Are your friends mostly your age or different ages? [Why?]

MP3 Unit24_7

당신의 친구들은 대개 당신 나이인가요 아니면 다른 나이인가요? [왜죠?]

Model Answer brainstorming은 파란색으로 표시

For the most part, my friends are the same age as me. The majority of my friends are my peers from primary school, secondary school and then university, so we've more or less grown up together through different phases. Now that I'm working, I interact more frequently with coworkers who are older than me, but we aren't exactly close friends. So, yes, most of my friends are my age.

대부분 제 친구들은 저와 같은 나이입니다. 대부분의 제 친구들이 제 초등학교, 중고등학교, 대학교 동창들이기에 우리는 거의 여러 시기를 함께 성장해 왔습니다. 저는 이제 일하기에, 저보다 더 나이 많은 동료들과 더 자주 교류를 하지만, 엄밀하게 친한 친구는 아닙니다. 그래서, 네, 제 대부분의 친구들은 제 나이입니다.

나만의 모범 답변

PRACTICE TEST

Part 1 다음 세부 요구 사항에 따라 각 질문의 모범 답변을 만들자.

Q1

MP3 Unit24_8

How different are the clothes you wear now from those you wore 10 years ago?

- Brainstorming 위 질문에 필요한 핵심어(답변 소재)를 3가지 이상 적어보자.

- Lexical resource 플러스 점수를 위해 반드시 사용해야 할 어휘를 3가지 이상 적어보자.

- Grammatical range 플러스 점수를 위해 반드시 사용해야 할 문법을 적어보자.

- Model Answer 위에 적은 답변 소재, 어휘, 문법을 활용하여 나만의 모범 답변을 만들자.

정답 및 해설 p.081

Q2

MP3 Unit24_9

What is your morning routine?

- Brainstorming 위 질문에 필요한 핵심어(답변 소재)를 3가지 이상 적어보자.

- Lexical resource 플러스 점수를 위해 반드시 사용해야 할 어휘를 3가지 이상 적어보자.

- Grammatical range 플러스 점수를 위해 반드시 사용해야 할 문법을 적어보자.

- Model Answer 위에 적은 답변 소재, 어휘, 문법을 활용하여 나만의 모범 답변을 만들자.

Q3

MP3 Unit24_10

Do you prefer to watch films at home or in the cinema? [Why?]

- Brainstorming 위 질문에 필요한 핵심어(답변 소재)를 3가지 이상 적어보자.

- Lexical resource 플러스 점수를 위해 반드시 사용해야 할 어휘를 3가지 이상 적어보자.

- Grammatical range 플러스 점수를 위해 반드시 사용해야 할 문법을 적어보자.

- Model Answer 위에 적은 답변 소재, 어휘, 문법을 활용하여 나만의 모범 답변을 만들자.

Q4

MP3 Unit24_11

Are you interested in science? [Why/Why not?]

- Brainstorming 위 질문에 필요한 핵심어(답변 소재)를 3가지 이상 적어보자.

- Lexical resource 플러스 점수를 위해 반드시 사용해야 할 어휘를 3가지 이상 적어보자.

- Grammatical range 플러스 점수를 위해 반드시 사용해야 할 문법을 적어보자.

- Model Answer 상기에 적은 답변 소재, 어휘, 문법을 활용하여 나만의 모범 답변을 만들자.

UNIT 25

Part 2 - 사람

오늘의 학습 목표

1. Part 2 문제 유형과 빈출 토픽을 익힌다.
2. 1분 동안 메모하는 방법과 메모 내용 활용법을 익힌다.
3. 사람과 관련된 빈출 토픽의 답변 소재, 고급 어휘 등을 브레인스토밍 한다.

Part 2에 대한 모든 것

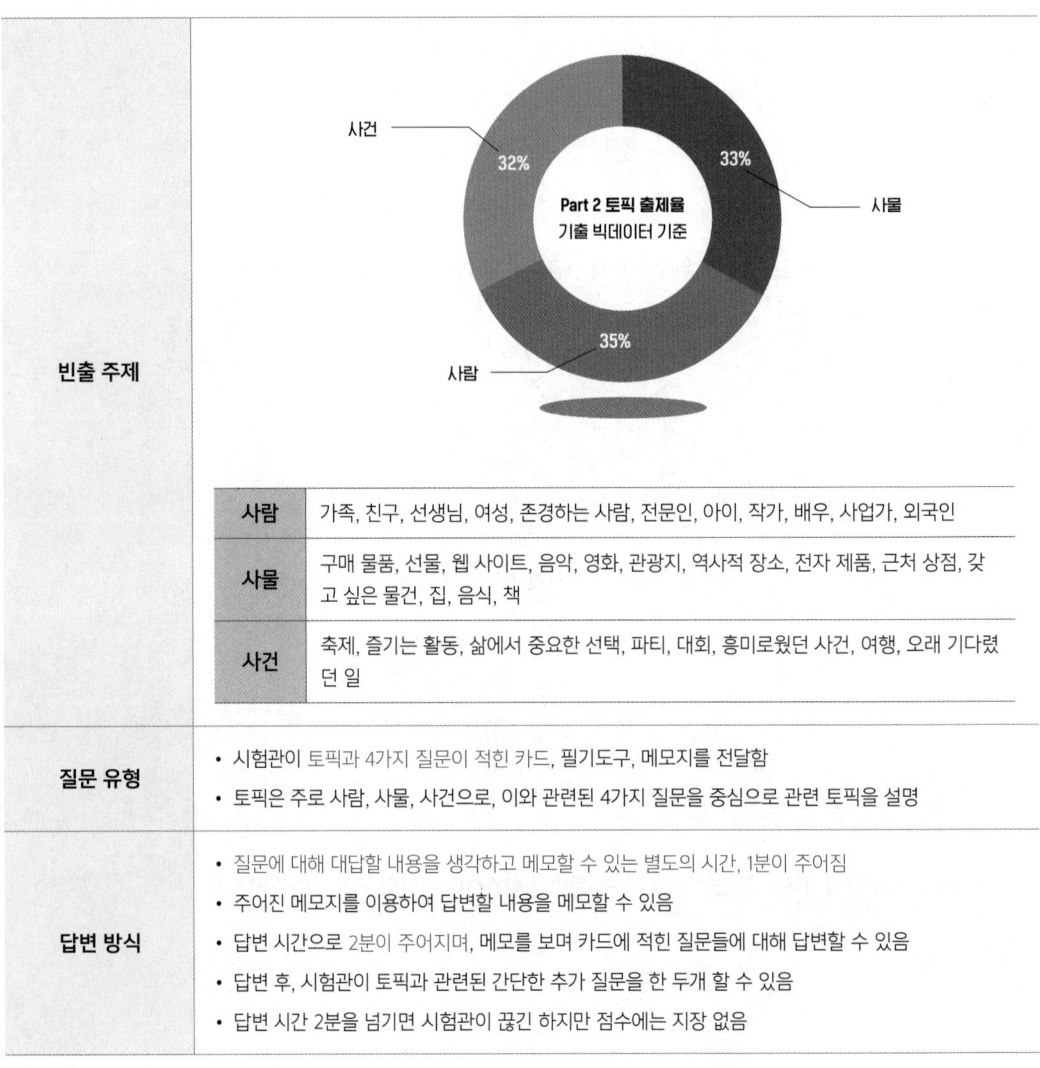

빈출 주제	Part 2 토픽 출제율 (기출 빅데이터 기준): 사람 35%, 사물 33%, 사건 32% **사람**: 가족, 친구, 선생님, 여성, 존경하는 사람, 전문인, 아이, 작가, 배우, 사업가, 외국인 **사물**: 구매 물품, 선물, 웹 사이트, 음악, 영화, 관광지, 역사적 장소, 전자 제품, 근처 상점, 갖고 싶은 물건, 집, 음식, 책 **사건**: 축제, 즐기는 활동, 삶에서 중요한 선택, 파티, 대회, 흥미로웠던 사건, 여행, 오래 기다렸던 일
질문 유형	• 시험관이 토픽과 4가지 질문이 적힌 카드, 필기도구, 메모지를 전달함 • 토픽은 주로 사람, 사물, 사건으로, 이와 관련된 4가지 질문을 중심으로 관련 토픽을 설명
답변 방식	• 질문에 대해 대답할 내용을 생각하고 메모할 수 있는 별도의 시간, 1분이 주어짐 • 주어진 메모지를 이용하여 답변할 내용을 메모할 수 있음 • 답변 시간으로 2분이 주어지며, 메모를 보며 카드에 적힌 질문들에 대해 답변할 수 있음 • 답변 후, 시험관이 토픽과 관련된 간단한 추가 질문을 한 두개 할 수 있음 • 답변 시간 2분을 넘기면 시험관이 끊긴 하지만 점수에는 지장 없음

Part 2 고득점 비법

1 4가지 질문 포인트 이해

Part 1이 끝나면 시험관이 아래와 같이 토픽 및 4가지 질문이 제시된 카드를 주는데, 이때 토픽과 질문 내용을 제대로 숙지하는 것이 중요하다.

> Describe a friend you had when you were a child.
>
> You should say:
> who he/she was
> how you met
> how long you two were friends
> and explain what you liked doing together in your childhood.

2 1분 동안 각 질문 당 2개 정도 메모

토픽 카드와 함께 주어지는 필기구 및 메모장을 이용하여 토픽 및 각 질문에 대한 브레인스토밍을 1분간 충실하게 한다. 이때 메모는 질문 당 2개 정도의 아이디어가 적당한데 이는 단답형이 아닌 여러 문장의 답변을 하기 위함이다. 그리고 가급적 영어로 쓰는 것이 유리한데, 답변 시간에 단어를 떠올리는 시간을 아낄 수 있고 실수 가능성도 줄일 수 있기 때문이다.

> *– Yuri, preschool*
> *– mother helping me ride a bicycle, recently moved*
> *– for a year, moved again to another city*
> *– talk and wander, looking for anything new and interesting*

3 Speaking 시험에서 준비가 가장 많이 필요한 파트

Part 2는 영어를 잘해도 준비가 없으면 원하는 점수를 받을 수 없다. 특히 2분이라는 시간 동안 혼자 말하는 것은 많은 연습이 요구된다. 따라서 앞으로 배우는 모든 문제들을 충분한 시간을 들여 확실히 공부하도록 한다.

유용한 표현 - 사람

교재에 제시된 표현들 이외에, 사람과 관련된 질문에 공통적으로 쓰이는 표현들을 최대한 많이 정리하여 2분 간의 답변 시간 동안 같은 단어를 반복하여 사용하지 않도록 한다.

좋은 친구가 되다	become good friends
동네	neighbourhood
~와 결혼하다	be married to
나에게 가장 많은 영향을 끼치다	influence me the most
담임 선생님	homeroom teacher
내가 처음에 만났던 사람들 중 하나	one of the first people I met
마음이 편해지다	feel relaxed
차분한 몸가짐	calm demeanor
친절한 태도	friendly manner
냉정(침착함)을 잃다	lose one's cool
~에 대해 특별하게 여기게 되다	develop a soft spot for
~을 고대하다	look forward to
조성하다, 발전시키다, 기르다	foster
~을 머리에 떠올리다	think of
나의 교우 범위에서	in my circle of friends
~에 관심을 가지다, ~에 열중하다	be into
죽이 맞다	hit it off
약간의 ~한 요소가 첨가된	with a dash of
~에 대한 (청각적) 재능이 있다	have a great ear for
~에 전념하다	be dedicated to
크게 성공하다	make it big
~이 되는 것에 대해 꿈꿔왔다	have dreamed of being
~하는 것에 영감을 받다, 고취되다	be inspired to부정사
공감할 수 있는	relatable

진짜배기, 굉장한 것	the real deal
~의 팬	a fan of
~에 사로잡힌	obsessed with
~을 내놓다	come up with
~에 근거하여	based on
~의 유일한 선택	one's only option
늦게까지 일하다	work late
능숙한 운전자	confident driver
능숙한 선생님	confident teacher
능숙한 연설가	confident speaker
집으로 가는 길	on one's way home
~로 가는 길	on one's way to ~
A를 차에 태우러 가다	pick A up
도로 밖으로 차를 빼다	pull off the road
아무도 없는 곳에	in the middle of nowhere
~ 얼굴에 안도	the relief on one's face
일정을 잡다, 주선하다	make arrangements
A를 수리되도록 하다	get A fixed
~을 자랑스럽게 여기다	feel proud of
상황을 처리하다	handle the situation
A를 힘든 상황에서 구해내다	get A out of a sticky situation
책임감을 느끼다	feel responsible

채점기준에 따른 모범 답변 - 사람

MP3 Unit25_1

1 4가지 질문 포인트 이해

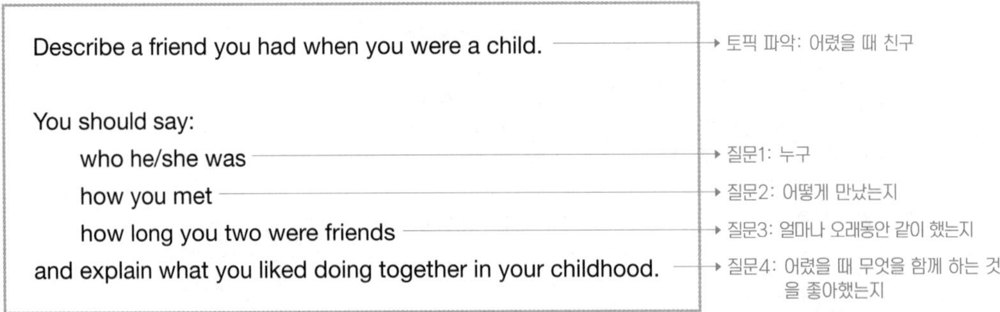
Describe a friend you had when you were a child. → 토픽 파악: 어렸을 때 친구

You should say:
who he/she was → 질문1: 누구
how you met → 질문2: 어떻게 만났는지
how long you two were friends → 질문3: 얼마나 오래동안 같이 했는지
and explain what you liked doing together in your childhood. → 질문4: 어렸을 때 무엇을 함께 하는 것을 좋아했는지

2 1분 동안 각 질문에 2개 정도 메모

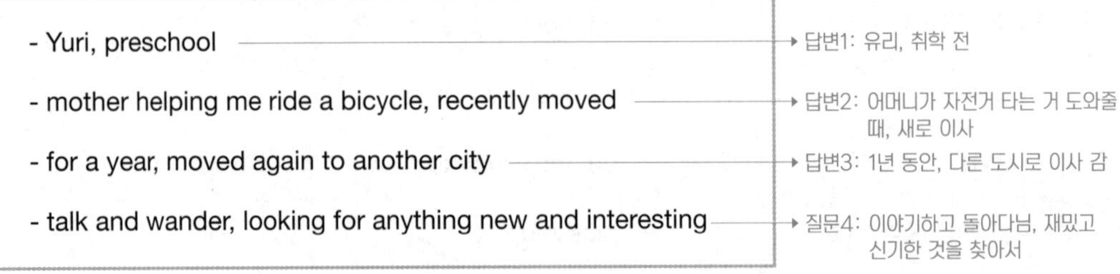
- Yuri, preschool → 답변1: 유리, 취학 전
- mother helping me ride a bicycle, recently moved → 답변2: 어머니가 자전거 타는 거 도와줄 때, 새로 이사
- for a year, moved again to another city → 답변3: 1년 동안, 다른 도시로 이사 감
- talk and wander, looking for anything new and interesting → 질문4: 이야기하고 돌아다님, 재밌고 신기한 것을 찾아서

3 모범 답변

① I remember Yuri, who was my closest friend when I was in preschool.
저는 제 취학 전 가장 친한 친구였던 유리가 생각납니다.

② I met her when my mother was helping me learn how to ride a bicycle. Since I was very young, only 5 years old, it was really hard for me to ride a two-wheeled bicycle; I could only ride a three- or four-wheeled bicycle. While my mother was supporting my bicycle and me, Yuri came and told us that she had recently moved to our neighbourhood and wanted to be friends with me. My mother said OK for me, and from that day, we became good friends.
제가 자전거 타는 법을 배우는 것을 어머니가 도와주실 때 유리를 만났습니다. 저는 단지 5살로 매우 어렸기에, 세 발이나, 네 발이 아닌 두 발 자전거를 타는 것은 정말로 어려웠습니다. 어머니가 제 자전거와 저를 붙잡아주고 계실 때, 유리가 다가와서 최근에 우리 동네로 이사왔다고 말하며 저와 친구가 되고 싶다고 했습니다. 어머니는 저 대신 OK라고 하셨고, 그 날 이후로 우리는 친한 친구가 되었습니다.

③ However, our friendship lasted only for a year because she moved again to another city. At that time, I didn't have any experience of moving so I could not relate to her feelings and difficulties regarding her frequent moving. In addition, I was too young to understand the notion of saying farewell and being separated. Therefore, I was not able to give her an amicable parting.
하지만, 우리의 우정은 단지 1년만 지속되었는데, 그녀가 또다시 다른 도시로 이사했기 때문입니다. 그때, 저는 이사에 대한 어떠한 경험도 없어서 그녀의 감정이나 빈번한 이사에 따른 어려움을 이해할 수 없었습니다. 게다가 너무 어렸기에 작별과 헤어짐의 개념도 이해하지 못했습니다. 그래서, 저는 그녀에게 제대로 된 이별을 선사하지 못했습니다.

④ Well, when it comes to what we liked doing together, I used to visit her house and we talked a lot or maybe just babbled. We also wandered around our houses and neighbourhood looking for anything new and interesting. Sometimes, I think of her and wonder how she is doing, how she has changed and whether she is married.
음, 우리가 함께 하기 즐겼던 것과 관련하여, 저는 그녀의 집에 방문하곤 했고 많은 것을 이야기, 아마도 옹알이하듯이 얘기했겠죠. 우리는 또한 우리들의 집과 동네를 돌아다녔는데, 뭔가 새로운 것과 흥미로운 것을 찾으면서요. 때때로 저는 그녀가 생각나고 그녀가 어떻게 지내는지, 어떻게 변했는지 그리고 결혼은 했는지 궁금합니다.

⑤ That is all that I can say now. → 마지막에 마무리 말을 통해 자신의 답변이 끝났음을 시험관에 알려주자.
이것이 제가 지금 말할 수 있는 전부입니다.

채점기준에 따른 답변 평가

Fluency and Coherence 유창성과 일관성	반복이나 자기 수정 안함
	단어나 문법을 찾기 위해 머뭇거리지 않음
	연결어를 사용하며 일관성 있게 말함 접속사(and, so), 부사절 접속사(when, since, while, because), 접속부사(therefore, however) 등을 적절히 사용하여 글의 일관성 유지
	화제를 완전하고 적절하게 전개 각 질문에 대한 완벽한 대답을 하고, 질문의 대답 흐름상 부자연스럽게 연결될 수 있는 부분에 Well, when it comes to를 넣어서 최대한 자연스럽고 적절하게 전개
Lexical Resource 어휘력	상황에 맞는 다양한 고급 단어 구사 two-wheeled bicycle 두발 자전거 notion of saying farewell and being separated 작별과 헤어짐의 개념 amicable parting 제대로 된 이별 babble (아기들이) 옹알이하다
	영어다운 표현을 사용하고 동의어 반복 없이 패러프레이징 [영어다운 표현] relate to her feelings 그녀의 감정을 이해하다 [패러프레이징] understand 이해하다 → relate to 이해하다(공감하다)
Grammatical Range and Accuracy 문법의 다양성과 정확성	분사, 관계대명사, 명사절 등의 다양한 문법 사용 주격 관계대명사(who) tell 사람 that절 사람에게 that절을 말하다 현재분사 looking for ~을 찾으면서
	주어/동사 수일치 및 올바른 시제 사용 수일치 및 과거완료, 과거, 현재 등의 다양한 시제를 제대로 사용
Pronunciation 발음	정확한 발음
	너무 느리거나 빠르지 않게, 일관된 스피드로 발음 1분 40초~2분이라는 시간 안에 말하기
	얼버무리지 않고 알아듣기 쉽도록 크고 명료하게 발음
총 평	각 질문에 대한 충실한 답변과 자연스러운 내용 전개, 영어다운 표현들과 고급 어휘 및 패러프레이징, 그리고 다양한 문법을 완벽하게 사용하였기에, 본 답변은 발음만 주의하면 충분히 고득점 가능

기출 문제 - 사람

1

Describe a teacher who has influenced you. MP3 Unit25_2

You should say:
where you met him/her
what subject he/she taught
what was special about him/her
and explain why this person influenced you so much.

Model Answer brainstorming은 파란색으로 표시

The teacher who influenced me the most was Mr Elliot, whom I met in middle school.

Mr Elliot was my English teacher for two years. He was also my homeroom teacher, so he was one of the first people I met at my middle school. I had just moved to a new school, so, as you can imagine, I was extremely nervous. But when the bell rang to start the school day, Mr Elliot introduced himself by telling a humorous story about his dog. It made all the students laugh, and I instantly felt more relaxed.

Mr Elliot taught with that same calm demeanor and friendly manner throughout the two years I had him. I don't remember him ever yelling at a student or losing his cool. I always felt comfortable in his classroom, and it helped me develop a soft spot for learning English. I looked forward to his class, so that made me work harder on my assignments.

That's why I think Mr Elliot is the reason I am confident in my English abilities today. On top of that, he also helped foster a love of reading in me. When I think of how important teachers are to their students, I think of how important Mr Elliot was to me.

That is all that I can say now.

나만의 브레인스토밍

당신에게 영향을 준 선생님에 대해 말해 보세요.

당신은 다음에 대해 말해야 합니다:

어디서 당신이 그를/그녀를 만났는지

어떤 과목을 그/그녀가 가르쳤는지

무엇이 그/그녀에 대해 특별했는지

그리고 왜 이 사람이 당신에게 그렇게 많이 영향을 미쳤는지 설명하세요.

모범 답변

저에게 가장 큰 영향을 준 선생님은 중학교 때 만난 엘리엇 선생님이었습니다.

엘리엇 선생님은 2년 동안 저의 영어 선생님이었고, 담임 선생님이기도 해서 제가 중학교에서 처음으로 만난 분들 중 한 명이었습니다. 저는 새로운 학교로 전학을 온 상태라서, 상상할 수 있듯이, 매우 긴장하고 있었습니다. 하지만, 수업 시작을 알리는 종이 울리자마자 엘리엇 선생님은 자신의 강아지에 관한 재미있는 이야기를 하며 자신을 소개했습니다. 그 이야기에 모든 학생들이 웃었고, 저도 즉시 긴장이 풀렸습니다.

엘리엇 선생님은 제가 2년 동안 수업을 들을 때 항상 그 차분하고 친절한 태도로 가르치셨습니다. 저는 그분이 학생들에게 소리를 지르거나 화를 내는 모습을 본 적이 없습니다. 항상 그의 교실에서 편안함을 느꼈고, 그 덕분에 저는 영어 공부에 대해 애정을 가지게 되었습니다. 선생님의 수업이 기다려졌고, 그 덕분에 과제에도 더 열심히 임하게 되었습니다.

그래서 저는 오늘날 제 영어 실력에 자신감을 가질 수 있는 이유가 엘리엇 선생님 덕분이라고 생각합니다. 그뿐만 아니라, 선생님은 제가 독서를 사랑하게 만드는 데도 큰 역할을 했습니다. 교사가 학생들에게 얼마나 중요한지를 생각할 때, 저는 엘리엇 선생님이 저에게 얼마나 중요한 존재였는지를 떠올리게 됩니다.

이것이 제가 지금 말할 수 있는 전부입니다.

나만의 모범 답변

2

Describe someone you know who has a unique or special talent. MP3 Unit25_3

You should say:
- who this person is
- how you know this person
- what he/she does well

and explain why you think this person is so good at doing this.

Model Answer brainstorming은 파란색으로 표시

I'm lucky to have several talented people in my circle of friends, but I think my friend Dave is the most talented.

I first met Dave four years ago, when I first moved here to start my new job. He was friends with some people I went to university with, so we met one night at a party they were having. He was funny, and we were both into the same bands, so we hit it off pretty quick.

Anyways, Dave is a wonderful musician himself. He mostly plays acoustic guitar and the piano, and his style is folksy with a dash of pop. He has a great ear for melody, and he plays shows all over the city. He's already recorded two albums, and he has a lot of fans online. He's extremely dedicated to his craft, so that's why I think he'll make it big soon.

As a person who has always secretly dreamed of being a musician, I'm inspired to see a close friend actually be a talented and successful one. And you know, I think people can connect with his songs because his lyrics are relatable. He's the real deal, and I can't wait for more people to discover his music.

That is all that I can say now.

나만의 브레인스토밍

당신이 아는 사람 중 독특하거나 특별한 재능을 가진 사람에 대해 말해 보세요.

당신은 다음에 대해 말해야 합니다:

이 사람이 누구인지

이 사람을 당신은 어떻게 아는지

그/그녀가 무엇을 잘하는지

그리고 당신 생각에는 왜 이 사람이 그것을 잘하는지 설명하세요.

모범 답변

제 친구들 중 재주 있는 친구들이 몇몇이 있는 것은 행운인데, 데이브는 가장 재능이 있는 친구라고 생각합니다.

저는 처음 데이브를 4년 전, 새로운 일을 시작하기 위해 여기에 처음 왔을 때 만났습니다. 그는 제가 대학을 함께 다녔던 몇몇 사람들과 친구였기에, 우리는 그들이 주최한 파티 밤에 만났습니다. 그는 재밌었고 우리 모두 같은 밴드를 좋아하였기에, 우리는 꽤 빨리 죽이 맞았습니다.

어쨌든, 데이브 자신도 훌륭한 음악가입니다. 그는 대개 어쿠스틱 기타와 피아노를 연주하고, 그의 스타일은 팝 요소를 살짝 가미한 싱어송라이터 스타일(folksy: 기타 하나 들고 노래 부르는 스타일)입니다. 그는 선율에 특별한 재능이 있고, 도시 곳곳에서 쇼를 공연합니다. 그는 이미 두 개의 앨범을 녹음했고 온라인에 많은 팬을 갖고 있습니다. 그는 극도로 그의 기술에 전념하기에, 그가 곧 크게 성공하리라고 생각합니다.

언제나 비밀스럽게 음악가를 꿈꿔왔던 사람으로서, 친한 친구가 실제로 능력 있고 성공적인 사람이 되는 것을 보며 감명을 받습니다. 저는 사람들이 그의 노래와 연결될 수 있다고 생각하는데, 그의 가사는 공감할 수 있기 때문입니다. 그는 진짜배기이고, 저는 더 많은 사람들이 그의 음악을 발견하기를 몹시 바랍니다.

이것이 제가 지금 말할 수 있는 전부입니다.

나만의 모범 답변

3

Describe a writer you would like to meet in the future. MP3 Unit25_4

You should say:
who he/she is
what you know about this writer already
what you would like to find out about this writer
and explain why you would like to meet this writer.

Model Answer brainstorming은 파란색으로 표시

In the future, I would love to meet Stephen King, the famous American horror writer.

I've been a fan of Mr King's ever since high school, when I first read his novel *The Shining*. I had never read a story like it before, and it made me rather obsessed with his work. Then I discovered a lot of his stories are made into terrifying movies, and I loved watching all of them. I especially enjoyed the recent remake of *IT*, even though it kept me awake for several nights.

The thing I most want to find out from Mr King is how he comes up with the ideas for his stories. He's so creative, and he's published over eighty books. I really want to know how he creates so many fantastic stories and characters. Also, I'm curious whether he likes the movies that are made based on his novels.

Mostly, I would like to meet him because I would love to be a writer, too, even though I doubt I could do it. Perhaps if I met Mr King, he could give me the right advice to get me started. I think, although he writes rather dark stories, he'd be an extremely friendly guy, and I could learn a lot from him about writing and even life in general.

That is all that I can say now.

나만의 브레인스토밍

당신이 미래에 만나고 싶은 작가에 대해 말해 보세요.

당신은 다음에 대해 말해야 합니다:

그/그녀는 누구인지

그 작가에 대해 이미 아는 것은 무엇인지

그 작가에 대해 알고 싶은 것은 무엇인지

그리고 왜 그 작가를 만나고 싶은지 설명하세요.

모범 답변

미래에, 저는 유명한 미국 공포 소설 작가, 스티븐 킹을 정말로 만나고 싶습니다.

저는 그의 소설 '샤이닝'을 고등학생 때 처음 읽은 이후로 줄곧 그의 팬입니다. 그의 많은 스토리들이 공포 영화로 만들어지는 것을 발견하고, 저는 그 영화들 전부를 보는 것을 좋아합니다. 비록 여러 날 밤 잠 못 들게 만들었지만, 특히 최근 리메이크인 '잇'을 즐겼습니다.

제가 킹 씨로부터 가장 알기 원하는 것은 어떻게 그의 스토리에 대한 아이디어를 생각해 내는지입니다. 그는 매우 창조적이어서 80권이 넘는 책을 출간했습니다. 저는 정말로 어떻게 그가 그 많은 환상적인 이야기들과 등장 인물들을 창조해 내는지 알기 원합니다. 저는 또한 그의 소설에 기반한 영화들을 그가 좋아하는지도 궁금합니다.

대체로, 제가 그를 만나고 싶은 이유는 저도 작가가 되고 싶기 때문입니다. 비록 제가 그럴 수 있을지 의심스럽긴 하지만요. 아마도 킹 씨를 만나면, 제가 시작할 수 있도록 올바른 조언을 해줄 수 있을 거라고 생각합니다. 그는 다소 어두운 이야기를 쓰지만, 굉장히 친절한 사람일 것 같고, 글쓰기뿐만 아니라 인생 전반에 걸쳐 많은 것을 배울 수 있을 것 같아요.

이것이 제가 지금 말할 수 있는 전부입니다.

SPEAKING

나만의 모범 답변

4

Describe a person who you have helped. MP3 Unit25_5

You should say:
why you helped
how you helped this person
what the result was
and explain how you felt about helping this person.

Model Answer brainstorming은 파란색으로 표시

I recently helped my older brother when he was having car difficulties during a blizzard. I helped him because he's my brother, of course, but because of the severe weather, I was really his only option, too.

Anyways, he had been working late and was driving to his home in the countryside, pretty far outside of the town. This was in January, and there had been a blizzard that day. He's a confident driver in the snow, but while he was on his way home, his engine malfunctioned and his car died. He had to pull off the road into an empty parking lot in the middle of nowhere.

Because of the bad weather, he couldn't get a tow truck to help him. So, he called me, and I had to drive through the blizzard to pick him up. It was stressful, but once I pulled into the parking lot, I could see the relief on his face. I took him home, and the next morning, he made arrangements to get his car fixed.

I was uncomfortable driving in the snow, but I felt proud of myself for handling the situation and getting my brother out of a sticky situation. It made me feel responsible and more confident.

That is all that I can say now.

* anyways(어쨌든)는 anyway와 같은 표현인데 보통 미국에서 구어체로 사용된다.

나만의 브레인스토밍

당신이 도와줬던 사람에 대해 말해 보세요.

당신은 다음에 대해 말해야 합니다:

당신이 왜 도왔는지

당신이 어떻게 이 사람을 도왔는지

결과가 어땠는지

그리고 이 사람을 도운 것에 대해 어떻게 느꼈는지 설명하세요.

모범 답변

저는 최근에 제 형을 도왔는데요, 형이 눈보라 속에서 자동차 문제를 겪을 때였습니다. 저는 물론 제 형이기에 도왔지만, 극심한 날씨로 인해, 제가 정말로 형의 유일한 선택이기도 했습니다.

어쨌든, 형은 늦게까지 일하고 도시에서 멀리 떨어진 시골에 있는 자기 집에 운전하며 가고 있었습니다. 1월이었는데, 그날 눈보라가 있었습니다. 형은 눈 속에서 능숙하게 운전하는데, 집에 오는 길에, 차 엔진이 고장을 일으키며 시동이 꺼졌습니다. 그는 아무도 없는 곳의 빈 주차 공간으로 차를 빼냈습니다.

악천후 때문에, 그는 도와줄 견인 트럭을 부를 수 없었습니다. 그래서 형은 제게 전화를 했고, 저는 형을 태우러 가기 위해 눈보라 속을 운전해야 했습니다. 스트레스가 많았지만, 제가 그 주차 공간에 차를 주차시켰을 때, 저는 형의 얼굴에서 안도감을 볼 수 있었습니다. 저는 그를 집으로 데려갔고 그 다음날 아침에 형은 차를 고치도록 예약을 했습니다.

저는 눈 속을 운전하는 것에 불안했지만, 그 상황을 처리하고 형을 힘든 상황에서 구해내서 스스로를 자랑스럽게 여겼습니다. 그것은 제게 책임감과 더 큰 자신감을 느끼게 했습니다.

이것이 제가 지금 말할 수 있는 전부입니다.

나만의 모범 답변

PRACTICE TEST

Part 2 다음 세부 요구 사항에 따라 각 질문의 모범 답변을 만들자.

Q1

MP3 Unit25_6

Describe an interesting person you met recently.

You should say:
who the person was
where you met the person
what you were doing when you met him/her
and explain why you thought he/she was interesting.

- Brainstorming 1분 동안, 각 질문에 핵심어(답변 소재)를 1가지 이상, 총 4개 이상 메모하자.

- Model Answer 위에 적은 답변 소재를 활용하고 채점기준에 유의하여, 2분 동안 답변해 보자.

유창성과 일관성	반복이나 자기 수정 여부	Y / N
	단어나 문법을 찾기 위해 머뭇거리는지 여부	Y / N
	연결어를 사용하며 일관성 있게 말하는지 여부	Y / N
	화제를 완전하고 적절하게 전개하는지 여부	Y / N
어휘력	상황에 맞는 다양한 고급 단어 구사 여부	Y / N
	영어다운 표현 사용 및 동의어 반복 않고 패러프레이징 여부	Y / N
문법의 다양성과 정확성	분사, 관계대명사, 명사절 등의 다양한 문법 사용 여부	Y / N
	주어/동사 수일치, 올바른 시제 사용 여부	Y / N
발음	틀리지 않고 정확한 발음 사용 여부	Y / N
	너무 느리거나 빠르지 않게, 일관된 스피드로 발음 여부	Y / N
	얼버무리지 않고 알아듣기 쉽도록 크고 명료하게 발음 여부	Y / N

정답 및 해설 p.083

Q2

MP3 Unit25_7

Describe someone you know who owns a business.

You should say:
who he/she is
in what kind of business he/she works
why this person decided to start a business
and explain whether you would like to have your own business, as this person has.

SPEAKING

- Brainstorming 1분 동안, 각 질문에 핵심어(답변 소재)를 1가지 이상, 총 4개 이상 메모하자.

- Model Answer 위에 적은 답변 소재를 활용하고 채점기준에 유의하여, 2분 동안 답변해 보자.

유창성과 일관성	반복이나 자기 수정 여부	Y / N
	단어나 문법을 찾기 위해 머뭇거리는지 여부	Y / N
	연결어를 사용하며 일관성 있게 말하는지 여부	Y / N
	화제를 완전하고 적절하게 전개하는지 여부	Y / N
어휘력	상황에 맞는 다양한 고급 단어 구사 여부	Y / N
	영어다운 표현 사용 및 동의어 반복 않고 패러프레이징 여부	Y / N
문법의 다양성과 정확성	분사, 관계대명사, 명사절 등의 다양한 문법 사용 여부	Y / N
	주어/동사 수일치, 올바른 시제 사용 여부	Y / N
발음	틀리지 않고 정확한 발음 사용 여부	Y / N
	너무 느리거나 빠르지 않게, 일관된 스피드로 발음 여부	Y / N
	얼버무리지 않고 알아듣기 쉽도록 크고 명료하게 발음 여부	Y / N

UNIT 26

Part 2 - 사물

오늘의 학습 목표

1 사물 관련 기출 질문 및 모범 답변을 통해 질문 스타일과 답변 방식을 이해한다.
2 사물 관련 토픽의 답변 소재, 고급 어휘 등을 브레인스토밍한다.
3 Part 2 마스터 훈련법대로 기출 문제와 Practice Test를 풀어본다.

Part 2 마스터 훈련법

1 실전처럼 문제 분석과 아이디어 메모 연습하기

실제 시험처럼 문제를 1분 동안 분석하면서, 각 질문에 대해 최소 2개의 아이디어를 노트에 메모한다. 만약에 1분이라는 시간 동안 메모를 다 하고도 시간이 남으면, 남는 시간 동안 아이디어를 어떻게 연결할지 머릿속으로 연습한다. 절대 1분이라는 시간을 낭비하지 않도록 한다.

2 2분간 앞을 보며 답변해 보기

주어진 1분이 지나면, 바로 메모를 참고하면서 2분 동안 답변을 한다. 메모에 적은 아이디어는 자신의 스토리가 중간에 끊어지거나 잘못된 방향으로 가지 않도록 이끌어줄 가이드이지만, 결국 말하기 답변은 시험관을 보면서 자연스럽게 말해야 한다. 따라서 메모에 너무 의존하면서 말하지 않도록 연습을 한다.

3 녹음 후 다시 듣고 평가하기

답변 시 녹음을 해서 자신의 답변이 2분이라는 시간을 채울 수 있는지 확인하고, 녹음을 들으며 채점기준에 맞게 자신의 답변을 채점해본다.

Part 2 문단 구성 Patterns

다음은 특히 Part 2의 2~4번째 질문에 대한 답변을 구성하기에 좋은 연결어이다. 각 문장의 연결어를 순서대로 넣어서 말하는 연습을 하면 최소 3문장으로 답변할 수 있게 된다.

첫 번째 문장: However / Also / That's why / Mostly / For the most part
두 번째 문장: In addition / On top of that / Plus / Even though / Although
세 번째 문장: Therefore / So I guess that's

유용한 표현 - 사물

교재에 제시된 표현들 이외에, 사물과 관련된 질문에 공통적으로 쓰이는 표현들을 최대한 많이 정리하여 2분 간의 답변 시간 동안 같은 단어를 반복하여 사용하지 않도록 한다.

~의 상징	a symbol of
아주 멋진	stunning
~에 강렬한 충격을 주다	have a strong impact on
복잡한	intricate
~의 팬(열렬한 신자)	a fan of
~에게 특별히 눈에 띄다, 특출나다	stick out to
다른 방식으로	in a different way
A라 불리는	called A
~의 주요소, 중심지	a staple of
가볍게 들르다	run in(=stop in)
각종	an assortment of
사이드 메뉴	side dishes
단골 손님	regular customer
최상급	top-of-the-line
공동체 의식	a sense of community
쇼핑 구역	shopping district
쉽게 이용가능한, 즉시 이용가능한	readily available
~하는 것을 꺼리다	mind ~ing
~로 가득찬	full of
유명 상표	name brand
특징, ~을 특징으로 삼다, 특별히 포함하다, 특징을 이루다	feature
~을 따라잡다	catch up with
~로 가다, ~로 향하다	head to
다양한	a wide array of
길거리 음식	street food
노점상	vendor
엄선된, 훌륭한	a selection of
근접, 가까움	proximity

SPEAKING

채점기준에 따른 모범 답변 - 사물

MP3 Unit26_1

1 4가지 질문 포인트 이해

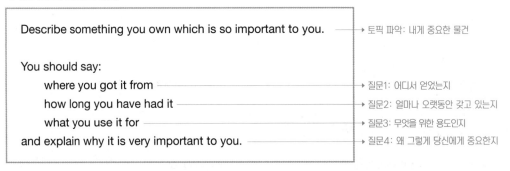

Describe something you own which is so important to you. → 토픽 파악: 내게 중요한 물건

You should say:

where you got it from → 질문1: 어디서 얻었는지

how long you have had it → 질문2: 얼마나 오랫동안 갖고 있는지

what you use it for → 질문3: 무엇을 위한 용도인지

and explain why it is very important to you. → 질문4: 왜 그렇게 당신에게 중요한지

2 1분 동안 각 질문에 2개 정도 메모

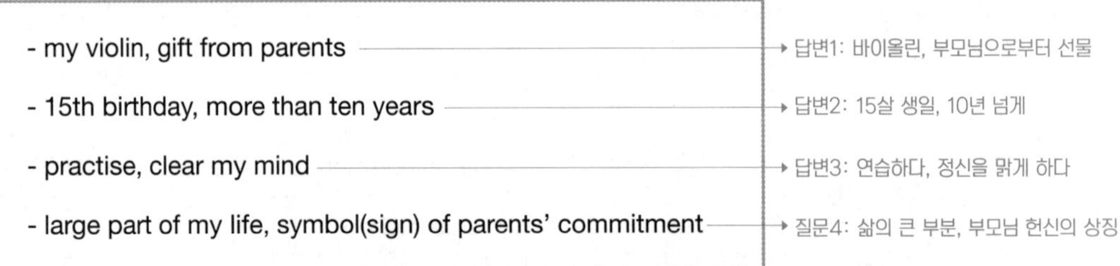

- my violin, gift from parents
답변1: 바이올린, 부모님으로부터 선물
- 15th birthday, more than ten years
답변2: 15살 생일, 10년 넘게
- practise, clear my mind
답변3: 연습하다, 정신을 맑게 하다
- large part of my life, symbol(sign) of parents' commitment
질문4: 삶의 큰 부분, 부모님 헌신의 상징

3 모범 답변

① My most important possession is my violin. It was a gift from my parents, and I believe they bought it at a large instrument department store in Seoul.

제게 가장 중요한 소유물은 제 바이올린입니다. 그것은 부모님으로부터 선물이고 서울에 커다란 악기 백화점에서 그것을 사주셨던 거 같아요.

② They gave it to me for my 15th birthday, so I've had it for more than ten years. I had been playing a beginner violin until I got my new one. My parents really went above and beyond to get me a high-quality violin to replace it, since I had been so focused on practising.

부모님은 그것을 제 15살 생일에 주셨기에, 저는 그것을 10년 넘게 갖고 있습니다. 저는 그 새 바이올린을 갖기 전에 초급용 바이올린으로 연주하고 있었어요. 부모님은 정말로 제 기대를 넘어서는 고품질 바이올린으로 교체해 주셨는데, 그때 제가 정말 연습에 몰두하고 있었기 때문입니다.

③ When I was still a student, I used it every day to practise. I attended a violin academy for years, and I was also a member of the school symphony. Plus, on my own time, I would play my violin alone in my room. It always helped to clear my mind. It still does, actually, but I don't have much free time these days.

제가 아직 학생일 때, 저는 매일 연습하곤 했습니다. 저는 수년간 바이올린 학원을 다녔고 학교 교향악단의 단원이기도 했습니다. 더욱이, 제 자유시간에 혼자 방에서 바이올린을 연주하곤 했습니다. 그것은 항상 정신을 맑게 하는데 도움이 되었습니다. 지금도 그렇지만, 사실 요즘은 자유시간이 거의 없습니다.

④ Music has always been a large part of my life, so I feel strongly connected to my violin. It's a different way that I can express myself, and I can completely change my mood just by playing for fifteen minutes. It's also a symbol of my parents' love for me and how committed they were to my dreams and passions. That is all that I can say now.
음악은 항상 제 삶의 큰 부분이었기에, 저는 제 바이올린과 크게 연결되었음을 느낍니다. 그것은 제 자신을 표현하는 다른 방식이고 단지 15분간 연주함으로 제 기분을 완벽하게 전환시킬 수 있습니다. 그것은 또한 저에 대한 부모님의 사랑과 부모님께서 제 꿈과 열정을 위해 얼마나 헌신하셨는지에 대한 상징입니다. 이것이 제가 지금 말할 수 있는 전부입니다.

채점기준에 따른 답변 평가

Fluency and Coherence 유창성과 일관성	반복이나 자기 수정 안함
	단어나 문법을 찾기 위해 머뭇거리지 않음
	연결어를 사용하며 일관성 있게 말함
	화제를 완전하고 적절하게 전개 각 질문에 대한 완벽한 대답을 하며 내용 전개
Lexical Resource 어휘력	상황에 맞는 다양한 고급 단어 구사 특별히 어려운 단어는 없지만 상황에 맞는 어휘로 말하고자 하는 바를 완벽하게 표현
	영어다운 표현을 사용하고 동의어 반복 없이 패러프레이징 [영어다운 표현] go above and beyond (예상을) 넘어서다 feel strongly connected to ~와 강하게 연결됨을 느끼다 express myself 자신을 표현하다
Grammatical Range and Accuracy 문법의 다양성과 정확성	분사, 관계대명사, 명사절 등의 다양한 문법 사용 부사절, 명사절을 통해 다양한 형태의 복문 사용
	주어/동사 수일치, 올바른 시제 사용 과거완료와 현재완료 등의 다양한 시제를 올바르게 사용
Pronunciation 발음	정확한 발음
	너무 느리거나 빠르지 않게, 일관된 스피드로 발음
	얼버무리지 말고 알아듣기 쉽도록 크고 명료하게 발음
총 평	각 질문에 대한 충실한 답변과 자연스러운 내용 전개, 자연스러운 어휘와 다양한 문장 구조 및 시제로, 8.0 이상 고득점 가능

기출 문제 - 사물

1

> Describe a TV programme or a film which has made a strong impression on you.
>
> MP3 Unit26_2
>
> You should say:
> what kind of film or TV programme it was
> when you saw it
> what the story was about
> and explain why this one made such an impression on you.

Model Answer brainstorming은 파란색으로 표시

A film that had a strong impact on me was *Interstellar*, which was directed by Christopher Nolan. It is a blockbuster sci-fi film with stunning visuals and deep themes.

The movie first came out in 2014, and I saw it on its opening weekend because I was so excited by the trailer. I've always been a fan of sci-fi movies, so *Interstellar* was right up my alley. Still, I didn't expect to like it as much as I did. I ended up seeing it three times at the cinema, and I talked about it with my friends endlessly.

The story is quite intricate, but basically, Earth's environment has become so bad that people can no longer grow crops. Consequently, the human race is doomed unless a new planet is found. So, a team of scientists travels through a mysterious wormhole to find a new habitable planet. It sounds crazy, but the coolest thing about the movie is that it actually features real scientific theories, especially Einstein's theory of relativity and ideas about black holes.

As I said earlier, *Interstellar* is a beautiful movie with a lot of intense action. But the themes are what really stuck out to me. The film made me reflect on how we're damaging the Earth, and what it means for our future. It also made me think about space in a different way.

That is all that I can say now.

나만의 브레인스토밍

당신에게 강렬한 인상을 준 TV 프로그램이나 영화에 대해 말해 보세요.

당신은 다음에 대해 말해야 합니다:

어떤 종류의 영화 또는 TV 프로그램이었는지

언제 보았는지

무슨 내용인지

그리고 왜 당신에게 강렬한 인상을 주었는지 설명하세요.

모범 답변

제게 강렬한 충격을 주었던 영화는 *인터스텔라*였는데, 크리스토퍼 놀란이 감독했습니다. 그것은 굉장히 멋진 영상과 깊이 있는 주제의 블록버스터 공상과학 영화입니다.

영화는 2014년에 처음 나왔는데, 저는 영화 예고편을 보고 매우 들떠, 개봉 주말에 그것을 봤습니다. 저는 언제나 공상과학 영화의 팬인데, *인터스텔라*는 제 취향 저격이었습니다. 저는 제가 그렇게나 좋아할지는 예상 못했습니다. 저는 3번이나 극장에서 보게 되었고 제 친구들과 끊임없이 그 영화에 대해 얘기를 했습니다.

영화 줄거리는 꽤 복잡하지만, 기본적으로 지구 환경이 너무 나빠져서 사람들이 더이상 작물을 재배할 수 없게 됩니다. 결과적으로 새 행성을 찾지 않는다면 인류는 불행할 결말을 맞게 될 운명입니다. 그래서 한 과학자팀이 살 수 있는 새로운 행성을 찾아 신비로운 웜홀을 통해 여행합니다. 이상하게 들리겠지만 영화에서 가장 멋진 부분은 이 영화가 실제 과학 이론들, 특히 아인슈타인의 상대성 이론과 블랙홀에 대한 아이디어를 다룬 점입니다.

이미 말했듯이, *인터스텔라*는 강렬한 액션과 함께 아름다운 영화입니다. 그러나 영화 주제야말로 정말 저에게 특별한 것이었습니다. 이 영화는 얼마나 우리가 지구를 손상시키는지, 그리고 그것이 우리의 미래에 대해 무엇을 뜻하는지를, 저로 하여금 돌아보게 만들었습니다. 그것은 또한 제가 우주를 다른 방식으로 생각하도록 했습니다.

이것이 제가 지금 말할 수 있는 전부입니다.

나만의 모범 답변

2

Describe a useful website you visit.

MP3 Unit26_3

You should say:
- what the website is
- how often you use the website
- what information the website gives you

and explain why it is useful to you.

Model Answer brainstorming은 파란색으로 표시

The most useful website that I visit is Youtube. It's one of the most popular websites in the world, so I'm sure everyone knows what it is, but it's a video-sharing platform that lets people watch videos and share their own.

I would say I visit Youtube at least once a day although it's probably higher than that. I like to put on music videos in the background while I'm at home, and I even use Youtube while I'm commuting to work. It's so easy to play a video on my phone, and it makes my subway ride much more bearable.

I think the best quality of Youtube is that it provides easy and free access to a lot of learning materials. I use it to learn new English phrases, since a lot of channels and Youtubers focus on that topic specifically. Nowadays, a lot of people use these Youtube channels exclusively to brush up on their English, and I think it's an effective method, especially for learning slang or everyday phrases.

So, while I use Youtube to relax by watching my favourite music videos or laughing along with famous Youtube stars, I can also say it has helped improve my language skills. I don't know if I'd be as confident in English today if it weren't for Youtube.

That is all that I can say now.

나만의 브레인스토밍

당신이 방문한 유용한 웹사이트에 대해 말해 보세요.

당신은 다음에 대해 말해야 합니다:

어떤 웹사이트인지

얼마나 자주 웹사이트를 사용하는지

무슨 정보를 그 웹사이트가 주는지

그리고 왜 당신에게 유용한지 설명하세요.

모범 답변

제가 방문하는 가장 유용한 웹사이트는 유튜브입니다. 그것은 세계에서 가장 유명한 웹사이트이기에, 저는 그것이 무엇인지 모두 다 안다고 확신합니다만, 그것은 사람들로 하여금 영상을 보고 그들의 영상을 공유하도록 하는 영상 공유 플랫폼입니다.

비록 그보다 많겠지만, 저는 최소 하루에 한번은 유튜브를 방문한다고 말할 수 있겠네요. 집에 있을 때 뮤직 비디오를 배경으로 틀어 놓는 것을 좋아하고, 심지어 출근하며 유튜브를 사용합니다. 제 휴대폰으로 재생하기가 쉽고, 전철 타는 것을 훨씬 더 견딜만하게 해줍니다.

제가 생각하기로 유튜브의 최고 특징은 많은 학습 자료에 쉽게 그리고 무료로 접속하는 것입니다. 저는 새로운 영어 표현을 배우기 위해 사용하는데, 많은 채널들과 유튜버들이 특히 그러한 주제에 집중합니다. 요즘, 많은 사람들이 영어를 갈고 닦기 위해 이 유튜브 채널들을 전적으로 사용하는데, 저는 속어나 일상 표현을 배우는데 특히 효과적인 방법이라고 생각합니다.

그래서, 제가 가장 좋아하는 뮤직 비디오를 보거나 유명한 유튜브 스타들과 함께 웃으며 휴식을 취하기 위해 유튜브를 사용하는 동시에, 그것이 제 언어 실력을 향상시키는데 도움을 주고 있다고도 말씀드릴 수 있습니다. 만약 유튜브가 없다면, 지금처럼 제가 영어에 자신이 있을지 모르겠습니다.

이것이 제가 지금 말할 수 있는 전부입니다.

나만의 모범 답변

3

Describe a successful family business you know about. MP3 Unit26_4

You should say:

how you know this business
what type of business it is
what kind of people often visit this business

and explain why this family business is successful.

Model Answer brainstorming은 파란색으로 표시

I lived in New York City for a year, and there was a popular family business called Sal's Deli on the same block as my apartment. When I first moved to my apartment, my roommate took me there for lunch, and I instantly recognised why it was a staple of the neighbourhood.

Sal's is a basic corner convenience shop, but it is also a deli and sandwich shop. So, you can run in for a bag of crisps, or you can order one of their delicious sandwiches. They also have an assortment of side dishes, like pasta salad. Most people swear that Sal's has the best coffee in the city, too.

Since it is a small local shop, everyone who goes to Sal's lives in the immediate area. So, all my neighbours were regular customers who went to Sal's at least once a day, maybe more. I think I probably stopped in every morning before work. You can always count on meeting a familiar face when you stop in.

Of course, Sal's is so popular because Sal and his family care about making high-quality food. Their deli meats really are top-of-the-line. But I think people really love Sal's because of how friendly the family are, and how it really brings a sense of community to our little neighbourhood in New York City.

That is all that I can say now.

나만의 브레인스토밍

당신이 아는 성공한 가족 경영(사업체)에 대해 말해 보세요.

당신은 다음에 대해 말해야 합니다:

당신이 어떻게 이 사업체를 아는지

어떤 유형의 사업체인지

어떤 종류의 사람들이 이 사업체를 자주 방문하는지

그리고 왜 이 가족 사업체가 성공하는지 설명하세요.

모범 답변

저는 일년 동안 뉴욕에 살았는데, 살즈 델리라는 유명한 가족 사업체가 제 아파트와 같은 블록에 있었습니다. 제가 처음 아파트로 이사 왔을 때, 제 룸메이트가 저를 점심에 거기로 데려갔고, 저는 즉시 왜 그곳이 동네에서 주요 장소인지 알아챘습니다.

살즈는 기본적인 길모퉁이 편의점이지만 조제식품 및 샌드위치 가게이기도 합니다. 그래서 감자칩을 위해 잠깐 들르거나 맛있는 샌드위치를 주문할 수 있습니다. 그곳은 파스타 샐러드 같은 각종 사이드 메뉴도 있습니다. 대부분의 사람들은 살즈가 도시에서 가장 좋은 커피를 갖고 있다고도 단언합니다.

작은 동네 가게이기에, 살즈에 다니는 모든 이들은 바로 그 지역에 살았습니다. 그래서 모든 동네사람들이 하루에 한번 혹은 그 이상 살즈에 가는 단골들이었죠. 저는 아마 매일 아침 일하기 전에 들렀다고 생각합니다. 당신은 거기에 들르면 아는 사람들을 만날 것이라고 항상 기대할 수 있습니다.

물론, 살과 그의 가족이 고품질 음식을 만드는 것에 신경쓰기 때문에 살스는 정말 유명합니다. 그들의 조제육은 정말 최상입니다. 하지만, 저는 사람들이 살즈를 정말로 좋아하는 이유는 그 가족들이 아주 친절하고, 뉴욕의 작은 동네에 공동체 의식을 정말로 가져다주기 때문입니다.

이것이 제가 지금 말할 수 있는 전부입니다.

SPEAKING

나만의 모범 답변

4

Describe a shopping centre you have visited.

MP3 Unit26_5

You should say:

where it is located

how people travel to the shopping centre

what kinds of shops the place has

and explain whether you think it is a good place to go shopping or not.

Model Answer brainstorming은 파란색으로 표시

I'm not much of a shopper, but my favourite shopping area is Myeongdong. It's less of a shopping centre and more of a shopping district, with a lot of different stores spread out over a close area. It's located in central Seoul.

One of Myeongdong's best features is its convenient location, since it's right in the middle of Seoul. Most people go there simply by bus or subway. For me, it only takes 20 minutes to get there by bus. Of course, as in other busy areas of Seoul, taxis are also readily available if you don't mind spending a little more.

For the most part, Myeongdong is full of fashionable clothing stores. It draws a lot of tourists, too, so it has several name brand stores that are rare in the rest of South Korea, especially ones that feature mainly Western styles. Whenever I need to update my wardrobe and catch up with the latest fashion trends, I just head to Myeongdong and look around. Plus, Myeongdong is also famous for its wide array of street food, too. I've even seen a vendor that sells lobster tail on a stick.

I think Myeongdong is ideal for shopping because of the selection of stores that are all located in proximity to each other. Moreover, it's an active area, and there's always something interesting to see.

That is all that I can say now.

나만의 브레인스토밍

당신이 방문했던 쇼핑 센터에 대해 말해 보세요.

당신은 다음에 대해 말해야 합니다:

어디에 위치하는지

어떻게 사람들이 그 쇼핑 센터로 이동하는지

어떤 종류의 상점들이 있는지

그리고 당신이 생각하기에 그곳이 쇼핑하기 좋은지 아닌지 설명하세요.

모범 답변

저는 쇼핑을 많이 하지는 않지만, 제가 가장 좋아하는 쇼핑 장소는 명동입니다. 그곳은 쇼핑 센터라기보다는 쇼핑 구역으로 많은 다양한 상점들이 근접 지역에 펼쳐져 있습니다. 그곳은 서울 중심에 위치해 있죠.

명동의 최고 특징들 중 하나는 편리한 위치인데, 서울 한복판에 있기 때문입니다. 대부분 사람들은 단순히 그곳에 버스나 지하철로 갑니다. 제게는, 버스로 20분밖에 걸리지 않습니다. 물론, 서울에 다른 붐비는 지역처럼, 돈을 조금 더 소비하는 것을 꺼리지 않는다면 택시도 쉽게 이용 가능합니다.

대부분, 명동은 유행을 따르는 옷 가게들로 가득 차 있습니다. 그곳은 많은 관광객들도 끌어들이기에, 한국의 다른 지역에서는 보기 힘든, 특히 서구 스타일 특징의 여러 유명 브랜드 가게들도 있습니다. 제 옷들을 새롭게 하고 최신 유행을 따라갈 필요가 있을 때마다, 저는 그저 명동으로 가서 둘러봅니다. 추가적으로, 명동은 다양한 길거리 음식으로도 유명합니다. 저는 전에 랍스터 꼬리 꼬치를 파는 노점상도 본 적이 있습니다.

저는 명동이 쇼핑에 이상적이라고 생각하는데 괜찮은 상점들이 모두 서로 근접하게 위치해 있기 때문입니다. 게다가, 활발한 지역이어서 항상 흥미로운 볼거리가 있습니다.

이것이 제가 지금 말할 수 있는 전부입니다.

나만의 모범 답변

PRACTICE TEST

Part 2 다음 세부 요구 사항에 따라 각 질문의 모범 답변을 만들자.

Q1

MP3 Unit26_6

Describe an interesting historic place.

You should say:
- what it is
- where it is located
- what you can do there

and explain why the place is interesting.

- **Brainstorming** 1분 동안, 각 질문에 핵심어(답변 소재)를 1가지 이상, 총 4개 이상 메모하자.

- **Model Answer** 위에 적은 답변 소재를 활용하고 채점기준에 유의하여, 2분 동안 답변해 보자.

유창성과 일관성	반복이나 자기 수정 여부	Y / N
	단어나 문법을 찾기 위해 머뭇거리는지 여부	Y / N
	연결어를 사용하며 일관성 있게 말하는지 여부	Y / N
	화제를 완전하고 적절하게 전개하는지 여부	Y / N
어휘력	상황에 맞는 다양한 고급 단어 구사 여부	Y / N
	영어다운 표현 사용 및 동의어 반복 않고 패러프레이징 여부	Y / N
문법의 다양성과 정확성	분사, 관계대명사, 명사절 등의 다양한 문법 사용 여부	Y / N
	주어/동사 수일치, 올바른 시제 사용 여부	Y / N
발음	틀리지 않고 정확한 발음 사용 여부	Y / N
	너무 느리거나 빠르지 않게, 일관된 스피드로 발음 여부	Y / N
	얼버무리지 않고 알아듣기 쉽도록 크고 명료하게 발음 여부	Y / N

정답 및 해설 p.085

Q2

MP3 Unit26_7

Describe a special food you enjoy.

You should say:
what it is
where you have it
whether the food is popular with other people in your country
and explain how you feel while eating that food.

- Brainstorming 1분 동안, 각 질문에 핵심어(답변 소재)를 1가지 이상, 총 4개 이상 메모하자.

- Model Answer 위에 적은 답변 소재를 활용하고 채점기준에 유의하여, 2분 동안 답변해 보자.

유창성과 일관성	반복이나 자기 수정 여부	Y / N
	단어나 문법을 찾기 위해 머뭇거리는지 여부	Y / N
	연결어를 사용하며 일관성 있게 말하는지 여부	Y / N
	화제를 완전하고 적절하게 전개하는지 여부	Y / N
어휘력	상황에 맞는 다양한 고급 단어 구사 여부	Y / N
	영어다운 표현 사용 및 동의어 반복 않고 패러프레이징 여부	Y / N
문법의 다양성과 정확성	분사, 관계대명사, 명사절 등의 다양한 문법 사용 여부	Y / N
	주어/동사 수일치, 올바른 시제 사용 여부	Y / N
발음	틀리지 않고 정확한 발음 사용 여부	Y / N
	너무 느리거나 빠르지 않게, 일관된 스피드로 발음 여부	Y / N
	얼버무리지 않고 알아듣기 쉽도록 크고 명료하게 발음 여부	Y / N

UNIT 27

Part 2 - 사건

오늘의 학습 목표

1. 사건 관련 기출 질문 및 모범 답변을 통해 질문 스타일과 답변 방식을 이해한다.
2. 사건 관련 토픽의 답변 소재, 고급 어휘 등을 브레인스토밍한다.
3. Unit 26의 Part 2 마스터 훈련법대로 기출 문제와 Practice Test를 풀어본다.

유용한 표현 - 사건

교재에 제시된 표현들 이외에, 사건과 관련된 질문에 공통적으로 쓰이는 표현들을 최대한 많이 정리하여 2분 간의 답변 시간 동안 같은 단어를 반복하여 사용하지 않도록 한다.

졸업식	graduation ceremony
졸업장	certificate of graduation
따뜻한 기온	warm temperature
개회사	opening remark
특별 초대 연사	special guest speaker
내가 ~하는 순간	the moment I ~
내 삶에서 진정한 전환점	real turning point in my life
성취, 업적	achievement
일상, 틀에 박힌 일	routine
정신적 위안	mental relief
강변 공원	riverside park
러닝 머신	treadmill
나 혼자만의 시간	my alone time
정신을 놓다, 멍하게 하다	let my mind wander
몰두해 있다, 빠져 있다	get in the zone
체중 관리	weight management
~에 자리잡고 있다	be nestled in
~하면서 시간/돈을 쓰다	spend time/money ~ing
버스 타고 한 시간	an hour-long bus ride
한번 해보다	give it a go

~을 할 줄 알게 되다	get the hang of
A보다 더	more so than A
~에 큰 영향을 미치다	have a large impact on
그것들(그들)이 나에게 의미하는 것	what they mean to me
~에 전념하다	commit oneself to ~ing
마음을 터놓다	open up
잘 진행되다, 잘 되다	go well
~의 역할을 하다	serve as
~로 가득차다	be full of
곧바로, 즉각	outright
~인지 궁금하다	wonder if
전문 경험을 얻다	get professional experience
~로부터 잠시 쉬다	take a break from
침체되다, 부진해지다	stagnate
일상에 만족하는	content in one's routines
~에 지겨운	bored with
승진하다	move up
결국	eventually
먼 훗날에	later down the road
~에 자신있는	confident in
울렁거리다, 매스껍다	feel sick
꽉 갇힌 느낌이다	feel stuck
원하는 것을 해내다, 참석하다, 시간에 맞춰 가다	make it

채점기준에 따른 모범 답변 - 사건

MP3 Unit27_1

1 4가지 질문 포인트 이해

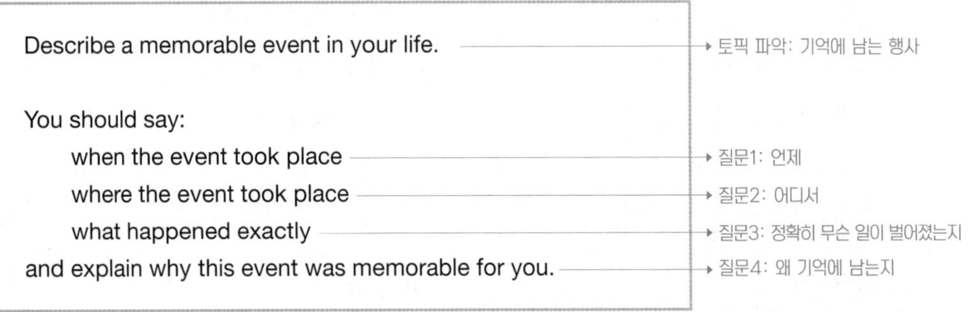

Describe a memorable event in your life.
→ 토픽 파악: 기억에 남는 행사
You should say:
when the event took place
→ 질문1: 언제
where the event took place
→ 질문2: 어디서
what happened exactly
→ 질문3: 정확히 무슨 일이 벌어졌는지
and explain why this event was memorable for you.
→ 질문4: 왜 기억에 남는지

2 1분 동안 각 질문에 2개 정도 메모

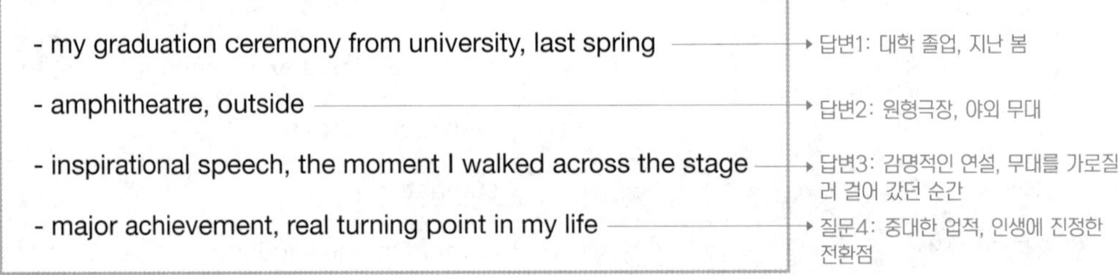

3 모범 답변

① A memorable event in my life was my graduation ceremony from university. It was held last spring after I had completed all the requirements for my course of study.
제 삶에서 기억에 남는 행사는 제 대학 졸업식입니다. 제가 제 학업에 필요한 모든 코스를 끝마친 후, 지난 봄에 열렸습니다.

② The ceremony was held on my university's campus. There's a large amphitheatre near the centre of campus that is used for special events, such as graduation ceremonies and concerts. It is outside but we were lucky to have blue skies and a warm temperature that day. Plus, since my university's campus is well known for its natural beauty, the setting for my graduation ceremony was exceptionally gorgeous.
그 기념식은 대학 캠퍼스에서 열렸습니다. 캠퍼스 중앙 부근에 커다란 원형 극장이 있는데, 졸업식과 콘서트 같은 특별한 행사를 위해 사용됩니다. 야외에 있지만, 그날은 다행히 파란 하늘과 따뜻한 날씨였습니다. 추가로, 저희 대학 캠퍼스는 자연의 아름다움으로 유명한데, 졸업식을 위한 세팅이 유난히 아름다웠습니다.

③ My peers who were also graduating and I sat in seats in front of the stage, and our family members sat around and behind us. We were all dressed in our gowns and hats to show off our achievements. After the dean gave an opening remark, a special guest speaker, who was a famous doctor, gave an inspirational speech. Finally, we were called up to the stage one by one to accept our certificates of graduation. I'll never forget the moment I walked across the stage.
같이 졸업하는 동창들과 저는 무대 앞 자리에 앉았고 가족들은 저희 뒤에 둘러 앉았습니다. 저희는 모두 저희의 업적을 뽐

낼 가운과 모자를 썼습니다. 학장님 개회사 이후 유명한 의사가 특별 초대 연사로 감명적인 연설을 했습니다. 마지막으로, 우리는 졸업장을 받기 위해 한 명씩 무대 위로 호명되었습니다. 저는 제가 무대를 가로질러 걸었던 그 순간을 결코 잊지 못할 것입니다.

④ This day represented all the hard work I had put into my university studies, so it signified a major achievement for me. In a way, I consider it my first professional success because it marked my entry into the real world. It was a real turning point in my life. That is all that I can say now.
이날은 제가 대학 공부에 쏟았던 모든 고된 작업을 의미했기에, 제게는 중대한 업적을 상징했습니다. 어떤 면에서, 졸업을 제 첫 전문적 성공으로 간주하는데, 그것은 제게 진정한 세상으로의 진입을 표했기 때문입니다. 졸업은 제 인생에서 진정한 전환점이었습니다. 이것이 제가 지금 말할 수 있는 전부입니다.

채점기준에 따른 답변 평가

Fluency and Coherence **유창성과 일관성**	반복이나 자기 수정 안함
	단어나 문법을 찾기 위해 머뭇거리지 않음
	연결어를 사용하며 일관성 있게 말함 after, plus, finally, in a way
	화제를 완전하고 적절하게 전개 각 질문에 대한 완벽한 대답 및 내용 전개
Lexical Resource **어휘력**	상황에 맞는 다양한 고급 단어 구사 amphitheatre 원형극장 opening remark 개회사 entry into ~로 진입
	영어다운 표현을 사용하고 동의어 반복 없이 패러프레이징 [영어다운 표현] give an inspirational speech 감명적인 연설을 하다 [패러프레이징] represent → signify, mark
Grammatical Range and Accuracy **문법의 다양성과 정확성**	분사, 관계대명사, 명사절 등의 다양한 문법 사용 부사절, 명사절, 관계대명사절, 분사구문, 수동태 등을 사용
	주어/동사 수일치 및 올바른 시제 사용 수일치 및 미래, 과거완료 등의 다양한 시제를 올바르게 사용
Pronunciation **발음**	정확한 발음
	너무 느리거나 빠르지 않게, 일관된 스피드로 발음
	얼버무리지 않고 알아듣기 쉽도록 크고 명료하게 발음
총 평	모든 채점기준에 부합한 답변으로 발음만 정확하면 8.0 이상 고득점 가능한 답변

기출 문제 - 사건

1

Describe some healthy activity you enjoy doing. MP3 Unit27_2

You should say:
- what the activity is
- where you do it
- who you share the activity with

and explain why this activity is healthy for you.

Model Answer brainstorming은 파란색으로 표시

I've always prioritised my health by staying active and dieting frequently. I do a variety of exercises to keep my routines fresh, but my favourite activity has always been simply running. For me, it's both an effective physical exercise and a stress-reducing mental relief.

I prefer to run outside, so I usually go to a large park near my home or, if it's available, a running track in front of a local high school. On the weekends, I especially love driving to the riverside park and running along its main trail that follows the river through the centre of the city. Of course, if the weather isn't agreeable, I just run on the treadmill at the gym.

The thing I love the most about running is that I do it by myself. I really don't enjoy running with a friend or jogging group. I see it as my alone time. It's very therapeutic for me to just run and let my mind wander. I need to be able to get in the zone and just run.

Of course, running is arguably the best cardio exercise, so it's great for weight management and heart health. As I mentioned earlier, I think it's also great for my mental health. I can forget about my worries and just run, enjoying my runner's high.

That is all that I can say now.

나만의 브레인스토밍

당신이 즐기는 건강한 활동에 대해 말해 보세요.

당신은 다음에 대해 말해야 합니다:

어떤 활동인지

어디에서 하는지

누구와 그 활동을 함께 하는지

그리고 왜 그 활동이 당신에게 건강한지 설명하세요.

모범 답변

저는 항상 활동적으로 움직이고 자주 다이어트를 함으로 제 건강을 우선시합니다. 저는 제 일상을 새롭게 하기 위해 다양한 운동을 하지만, 제가 가장 좋아하는 활동은 항상 그저 달리는 것입니다. 제게, 달리기는 효과적인 신체 운동과 스트레스를 줄이는 정신적 위안입니다.

저는 바깥에서 달리는 것을 선호하기에 보통 집 근처 커다란 공원에 가거나 가능하면 동네 고등학교 앞에 있는 육상 트랙에 갑니다. 주말에, 저는 특히 강변 공원으로 운전하고 가서 도시 중심을 관통하는 강을 끼고 나아가는 주요 길을 따라 달리는 것을 좋아합니다. 물론, 날씨가 좋지 않다면, 저는 그냥 체육관의 러닝머신 위에서 달립니다.

달리기에 대해 제가 가장 좋아하는 것은 저 혼자 하는 것입니다. 저는 정말로 친구나 조깅 단체와 함께 달리는 것을 즐기지 않습니다. 저는 달리기를 제 혼자만의 시간으로 생각합니다. 제가 그냥 달리며 제 정신을 멍하게 하는 것은 매우 힐링이 됩니다. 저는 몰두해서 그냥 달릴 수 있어야 합니다.

물론, 달리기는 거의 틀림없이 최고의 심장 강화 운동이기에, 체중 관리와 심장 건강에 좋습니다. 앞서 말한 대로, 저는 달리기가 제 정신 건강에도 좋다고 생각합니다. 저는 러너즈 하이(격렬한 운동 후 느끼는 황홀감)를 즐기며 근심을 잊고 그냥 달릴 수 있습니다.

이것이 제가 지금 말할 수 있는 전부입니다.

나만의 모범 답변

2

Describe something you did that was exciting. MP3 Unit27_3

You should say:
- what you did
- where and when you did this
- who you did it with

and explain why you think doing this activity was exciting.

Model Answer brainstorming은 파란색으로 표시

I've been busy with my studies lately, but one exciting thing I've done recently is snowboarding. I've been skiing several times, but this was my first time snowboarding. And to me, it really felt like surfing on the snow or riding the mountain like a wave.

I went this winter just a few months ago. There's a popular ski resort outside of Seoul that I went to. The resort is nestled in among some beautiful mountains, and the ski slopes run all along them. Surprisingly, it was easy to get to from the city. It was only an hour-long bus ride.

I went with some of my university friends. For the most part, we spent our winter break studying, but we decided we needed to do something to relax and have some fun. So, we made plans for this three-day stay at the ski resort. We booked a nice room that had a great view of the slopes, and we spent our days snowboarding.

Mostly, it was exciting just to try something new. I thought I had missed the opportunity to ever snowboard, so I was eager to finally give it a go. I struggled to stand at first, but once I got the hang of it, I loved it — maybe more so than skiing. I hope to do it again.

That is all that I can say now.

나만의 브레인스토밍

당신이 했던 흥미로웠던 것에 대해 말해 보세요.

당신은 다음에 대해 말해야 합니다:

무엇을 했는지

어디서, 언제 했는지

누구와 했는지

그리고 왜 당신에게 이 활동이 흥미로웠는지 설명하세요.

모범 답변

저는 최근에 학업으로 바빴지만, 최근 제가 했던 가장 흥미로운 것은 스노보드 타기입니다. 저는 스키를 여러 번 탔지만, 스노보드는 처음이었습니다. 그리고 제게, 그것은 정말로 눈 위를 서핑하거나 파도처럼 산 위를 타는 느낌이었습니다.

저는 단지 몇 달 전인 이번 겨울에 갔습니다. 제가 갔던 곳은 서울 바깥에 있는 유명 스키 리조트입니다. 리조트는 아름다운 산 가운데에 자리하는데, 스키장이 산들을 따라 이어집니다. 놀랍게도, 도시에서 가기 편했습니다. 버스로 단지 한 시간만 걸렸거든요.

저는 제 대학 친구 몇몇과 함께 갔습니다. 대부분, 우리는 겨울 방학을 공부하며 보냈지만 좀 쉬고 즐길 필요가 있다고 결정했습니다. 그래서 우리는 스키 리조트에서 3일을 계획했습니다. 우리는 스키장의 멋진 전경을 볼 수 있는 좋은 방을 예약했고, 스노보드를 타며 우리의 일정을 보냈습니다.

대부분, 단지 새로운 무언가를 시도하는 것에 흥미로웠습니다. 저는 전에 스노보드 탈 기회를 놓쳤다고 생각했기에, 마침내 한 번 해보는 것을 간절히 원했습니다. 처음에는 서기도 힘들었지만, 설 줄 알게 되자 스노보드가 너무 좋았습니다. 어쩌면 스키보다도요. 저는 다시 한번 스노보드를 타기를 희망합니다.

이것이 제가 지금 말할 수 있는 전부입니다.

SPEAKING

나만의 모범 답변

3

Describe an important discussion which influenced your life. MP3 Unit27_4

You should say:

what the subject of the discussion was
when you had this discussion
who you discussed the subject with

and explain why this discussion influenced your life so much.

Model Answer brainstorming은 파란색으로 표시

An important discussion that has influenced my life was the one I had during my interview to get into my university programme. It was just a conversation about literature, but it had a large impact on my life in several ways.

I had this discussion six years ago, when I was applying to university. The final part of my application process was a one-on-one interview with the director of my programme of studies, which I had chosen to be English literature.

I was nervous during the whole process, but once I started talking with the director, I immediately relaxed. It was one of the first times I had a rich and flowing conversation about my favourite authors and books, what they meant to me and why I wanted to commit myself to studying literature. I'd never spoken much about my love for reading before then, so I think I really opened up during the interview.

Anyway, it must have gone well, because I got into the programme. The director I spoke with turned out to teach one of my first classes, and later, she even became my thesis advisor. So, that conversation definitely served as the basis of my university studies. In a way, it reassured me that I had chosen the right subject to study because it proved to me how passionate I was about the subject.

That is all that I can say now.

나만의 브레인스토밍

당신의 삶에 영향을 준 중요한 토론에 대해 말해 보세요.

당신은 다음에 대해 말해야 합니다:

어떤 주제의 토론이었는지

언제 토론을 했는지

누구와 그 주제를 토론했는지

그리고 왜 그 토론이 당신 삶에 그렇게 많은 영향을 주었는지 설명하세요.

모범 답변

제 인생에 영향을 끼쳤던 중요한 토론은 대학교 입학 면접 동안에 있었던 것입니다. 그냥 문학에 대한 대화였지만, 여러 면에서 제 인생에 큰 영향을 주었습니다.

제가 대학에 지원할 때인, 6년전에 이 토론을 했습니다. 제 지원 과정의 마지막 단계는 제 학문 과정인 영문과 학과장님과의 1대1 면접이었습니다.

저는 전체 과정 동안 초조했지만 일단 학과장님과 대화하기 시작하면서 즉시 편안해졌습니다. 제가 가장 좋아하는 저자들과 책들, 그것들이 저에게 어떠한 의미가 있는지, 왜 문학에 전념하기를 원하는지에 대해 제가 거의 처음으로 했던 풍성하고 쉼 없는 대화였습니다. 그 전에 저는 독서에 대한 애호를 전혀 말하지 않았기에 저는 면접 동안 정말 마음을 터놓았습니다.

어쨌든, 그 대화는 잘 되었음에 틀림없는데, 제가 그 학문 과정에 들어갔기 때문입니다. 저와 말했던 학과장님은 제 첫 수업 중 하나를 가르치셨고, 나중에 그녀는 심지어 제 논문의 지도교수가 되었습니다. 그래서, 그 대화는 확실히 제 대학 공부 기반으로써 역할을 했습니다. 어떤 면에서, 그 대화는 제가 저에게 맞는 과목을 선택했음을 다시 한번 확인시켜주었는데, 제가 얼마나 그 과목에 열정적인지를 증명하였기 때문입니다.

이것이 제가 지금 말할 수 있는 전부입니다.

나만의 모범 답변

4

Describe an important choice you had to make in your life. MP3 Unit27_5

You should say:
when you made this choice
what you had to choose between
whether you made a good choice
and explain how you felt when you were making this choice.

Model Answer brainstorming은 파란색으로 표시

Every life is full of hard choices, and mine isn't any different. I'd have to say my last big decision was when I had to choose whether to pursue a graduate degree or continue working at my job. Obviously, this decision would have a huge impact on my life.

Honestly, this was an issue on my mind ever since I graduated from university and accepted a job outright at a small design studio. I always wondered if I should have continued my education right away, but I was happy getting professional experience and taking a break from studying. But last year, I started to stagnate at my job, so that's when I decided to return to school.

It still wasn't an easy choice, though. Most people become content in their routines. Maybe I had become a little bored with my work, but I was still happy doing it. I liked my coworkers, the pay was good and I could see myself moving up in the company. But I knew eventually I would need a graduate degree, and there'd be an opportunity I'd have to give up on if I didn't have it.

I won't really know if it was a good choice until later down the road. Right now, I'm confident in the decision because I saved up enough money to still be financially comfortable, and I'm excited about my prospects in different programmes. But I won't know until I can look back on all of this.

I feel sick when I'm faced with a big decision. I know it will completely change my life, and that's a scary feeling. But feeling stuck is an awful feeling, too. So, I'm glad I made it.

That is all that I can say now.

나만의 브레인스토밍

당신 인생에서 해야했던 중요한 선택에 대해 말해 보세요.

당신은 다음에 대해 말해야 합니다:

언제 이 선택을 했는지

무엇 간에 선택해야 했는지

좋은 선택을 했는지

그리고 당신이 이 선택을 했을 때 어떻게 느꼈는지 설명하세요.

모범 답변

매 삶은 어려운 선택으로 가득 차 있는데 저 또한 다르지 않습니다. 저는 제 마지막 큰 결정이 대학원 진학을 할지 아니면 일을 계속할지 선택하는 것이었다고 말해야 하겠습니다. 확실히, 이 결정은 제 삶에 커다란 영향이 있으니까요.

솔직히, 이것은 제가 대학을 졸업하고 작은 디자인 스튜디오에서의 일자리를 바로 수락한 이래로 언제나 제 생각 속에 있던 문제였습니다. 저는 항상 제 학업을 곧바로 계속 해야할지 궁금했지만, 전문 경험을 쌓는 것과 공부로부터 휴식을 취하는 것에 행복했습니다. 그러나 작년에, 저는 제 일에 침체기를 겪기 시작했고, 그래서 그 때 학교로 되돌아 가기로 결정했습니다.

그것은 여전히 쉬운 결정은 아니었습니다. 대부분 사람들은 그들의 일상에 만족하게 됩니다. 아마도 제가 제 일에 조금 싫증을 느끼게 된 것 같기도 하지만, 여전히 그 일을 하는 것이 행복했습니다. 저는 제 동료들을 좋아했고, 봉급도 좋았고, 제 자신이 회사 내 승진하는 것을 예상할 수 있었습니다. 하지만, 저는 결국 대학원 학위가 필요하고 학위가 없으면 포기해야만 하는 기회가 있을 것임을 알았습니다.

저는 정말로 그것이 좋은 선택이었는지 먼 훗날까지 알지 못할 것입니다. 지금 당장 저는 그 결정에 자신 있는데 여전히 금전적으로 안정적인 충분한 돈을 모아두었고 다른 학문 과정에 대한 기대에 흥분되기 때문입니다. 그러나 저는 이 모든 것을 돌아볼 수 있을 때까지 모를 겁니다.

저는 큰 결정에 마주치면 울렁거립니다. 저는 그것이 제 인생을 완전히 바꿀 것임을 알기에, 무서운 기분이 듭니다. 그러나, 갇혀 있는 기분도 끔찍합니다. 그래서 저는 바라던 일을 하게 되어 기쁩니다.

이것이 제가 지금 말할 수 있는 전부입니다.

나만의 모범 답변

PRACTICE TEST

Part 2 다음 세부 요구 사항에 따라 각 질문의 모범 답변을 만들자.

Q1

MP3 Unit27_6

Describe a memorable journey by car, plane or boat.

You should say:
where you went
how you travelled
why you went on the journey
and explain why you think this journey is so memorable.

- **Brainstorming** 1분 동안, 각 질문에 핵심어(답변 소재)를 1가지 이상, 총 4개 이상 메모하자.

- **Model Answer** 위에 적은 답변 소재를 활용하고 채점기준에 유의하여, 2분 동안 답변해 보자.

유창성과 일관성	반복이나 자기 수정 여부	Y / N
	단어나 문법을 찾기 위해 머뭇거리는지 여부	Y / N
	연결어를 사용하며 일관성 있게 말하는지 여부	Y / N
	화제를 완전하고 적절하게 전개하는지 여부	Y / N
어휘력	상황에 맞는 다양한 고급 단어 구사 여부	Y / N
	영어다운 표현 사용 및 동의어 반복 않고 패러프레이징 여부	Y / N
문법의 다양성과 정확성	분사, 관계대명사, 명사절 등의 다양한 문법 사용 여부	Y / N
	주어/동사 수일치, 올바른 시제 사용 여부	Y / N
발음	틀리지 않고 정확한 발음 사용 여부	Y / N
	너무 느리거나 빠르지 않게, 일관된 스피드로 발음 여부	Y / N
	얼버무리지 않고 알아듣기 쉽도록 크고 명료하게 발음 여부	Y / N

정답 및 해설 p.087

Q2

MP3 Unit27_7

Describe an important festival in your country.

You should say:
- what the festival is
- what people in your country do during the festival
- what you like or dislike about it

and explain why you think this festival is important.

- Brainstorming 1분 동안, 각 질문에 핵심어(답변 소재)를 1가지 이상, 총 4개 이상 메모하자.

- Model Answer 위에 적은 답변 소재를 활용하고 채점기준에 유의하여, 2분 동안 답변해 보자.

유창성과 일관성	반복이나 자기 수정 여부	Y / N
	단어나 문법을 찾기 위해 머뭇거리는지 여부	Y / N
	연결어를 사용하며 일관성 있게 말하는지 여부	Y / N
	화제를 완전하고 적절하게 전개하는지 여부	Y / N
어휘력	상황에 맞는 다양한 고급 단어 구사 여부	Y / N
	영어다운 표현 사용 및 동의어 반복 않고 패러프레이징 여부	Y / N
문법의 다양성과 정확성	분사, 관계대명사, 명사절 등의 다양한 문법 사용 여부	Y / N
	주어/동사 수일치, 올바른 시제 사용 여부	Y / N
발음	틀리지 않고 정확한 발음 사용 여부	Y / N
	너무 느리거나 빠르지 않게, 일관된 스피드로 발음 여부	Y / N
	얼버무리지 않고 알아듣기 쉽도록 크고 명료하게 발음 여부	Y / N

SPEAKING

UNIT 28

Part 3 - 사회적 이슈: 브레인스토밍

오늘의 학습 목표

1. Part 3 질문 유형과 답변 방식을 숙지한다.
2. 각 기출 토픽의 사회적 영향, 중요성, 변화, 장단점 등(예: 쇼핑이 어떻게 사회적 영향을 미치는지, 얼마나 중요한지, 미래에 어떻게 변화하는지)에 대해 브레인스토밍한다.
3. 질문을 패러프레이징 하는 방법으로 첫 문장을 만드는 연습을 해본다.

Part 3에 대한 모든 것

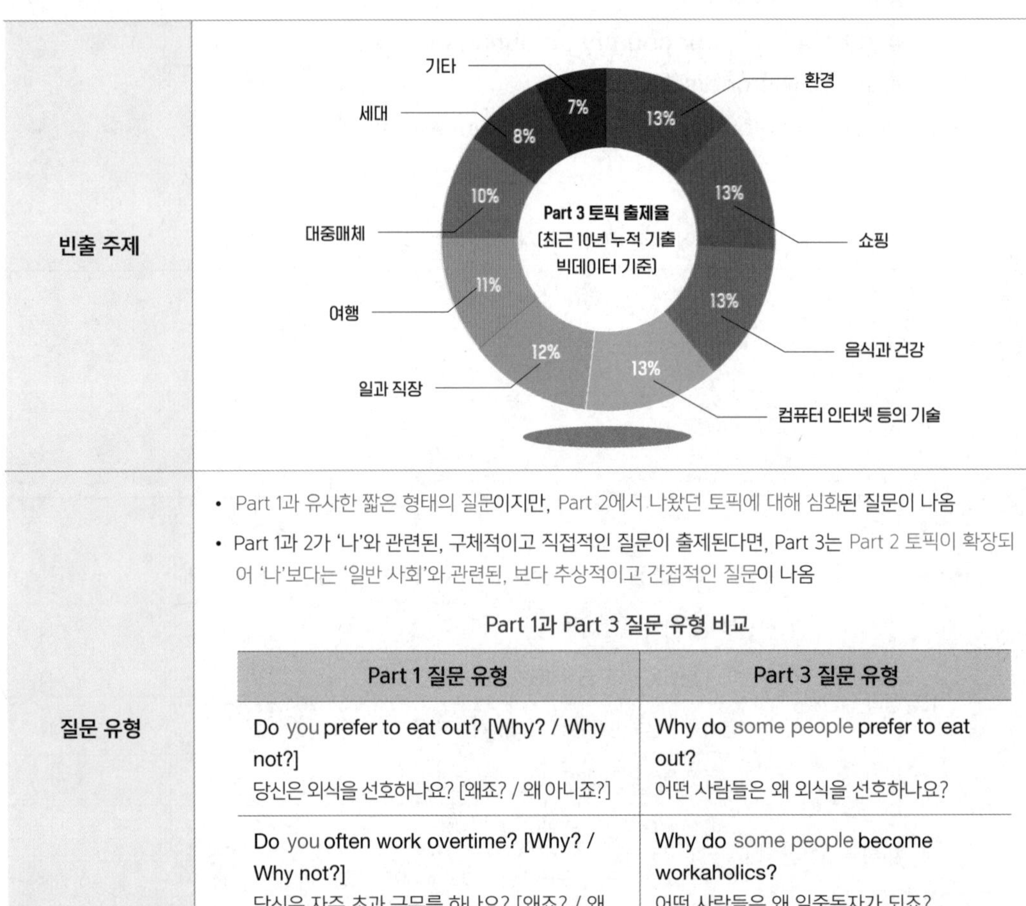

빈출 주제

질문 유형

- Part 1과 유사한 짧은 형태의 질문이지만, Part 2에서 나왔던 토픽에 대해 심화된 질문이 나옴
- Part 1과 2가 '나'와 관련된, 구체적이고 직접적인 질문이 출제된다면, Part 3는 Part 2 토픽이 확장되어 '나'보다는 '일반 사회'와 관련된, 보다 추상적이고 간접적인 질문이 나옴

Part 1과 Part 3 질문 유형 비교

Part 1 질문 유형	Part 3 질문 유형
Do you prefer to eat out? [Why? / Why not?] 당신은 외식을 선호하나요? [왜죠? / 왜 아니죠?]	Why do some people prefer to eat out? 어떤 사람들은 왜 외식을 선호하나요?
Do you often work overtime? [Why? / Why not?] 당신은 자주 초과 근무를 하나요? [왜죠? / 왜 아니죠?]	Why do some people become workaholics? 어떤 사람들은 왜 일중독자가 되죠?

What kind of things do you prefer shopping for? [Why?] 당신은 어떤 종류의 물건을 사는 것을 선호하나요? [왜죠?]	What items are popular to purchase in your country? 당신 국가에서 구매하는 것으로 인기 있는 물건은 무엇인가요?

• 사회적 영향, 변화, 비교, 장단점 등을 묻는 고난도 질문 유형은 Part 1에서 등장하기도 하지만 Part 3에서 보다 자주 등장함

Part 3 고난도 질문 유형

[영향] How does advertising influence what people choose to buy? 광고가 사람들 구매에 어떠한 영향을 주나요?	[변화] Do you think cinemas will close in the future? 당신은 미래에 영화관이 문 닫을 것이라고 생각하나요?
[비교] Do you think young people feel the same about shopping at markets as older people? 당신은 젊은이들이 시장에서 쇼핑할 때 노인들이 느끼는 것과 같다고 생각하나요?	[장단점] What are the advantages to society of a highly developed shopping mall? 잘 발달된 쇼핑몰이 사회에 어떤 이점들이 되나요?
[정도] How important do you think it is for individuals to keep learning after finishing school? 당신은 개인들이 졸업 후 계속 공부하는 것이 얼마나 중요하다고 생각합니까?	[제안] How should tourists behave when they are in a different country? 여행객들은 다른 나라에서 어떻게 행동해야 하나요?

• 고난도 질문은 내용이 어려운 만큼 답변이 바로 생각나지 않기에 기출 문제에 대한 브레인스토밍을 미리미리하여 대비할 필요가 있음
• Part 1과 마찬가지로 보통 시험관이 4~8개 질문을 하는데, 하나의 질문에도 충실하게 답변하면 질문 수가 줄고 점수가 높아지는 경향이 있음

답변 방식

• 질문에 대해 대답할 내용을 생각할 시간 없이 바로 답변함
• 반드시 질문에 대한 답변을 먼저하고 그 답변에 대한 이유를, 그리고 그 이유에 대한 근거(예시)를 말하는 방식으로 충실하게 답변함
• 최소 4문장 이상으로 답변하는 것이 유리함
• 질문이 추상적이고 어렵기에 제대로 집중해서 질문을 들어야 동문서답을 피할 수 있음

Part 3 고득점 비법

1 미리 아이디어 생각해 두기

가장 중요한 고득점 비법이다. Part 3 질문은 일반 사회와 관련된 것이 많기에, 자신이 생각하지 않던 부분이 나오면 답변을 하기 곤란한 경우가 많다. 예를 들면, 애완동물의 장단점에 대해 말하는 것이 질문으로 나왔는데, 애완동물에 전혀 관심이 없는 사람은 애완동물을 좋아하거나 키우는 사람보다 답변할 거리가 없을 것이다.

답변 소재가 없으면 제대로 말하지 못하게 되므로 결국 좋은 점수를 받을 수 없게 된다. 이러한 상황에 대비해서 기출 문제를 보며 다양한 아이디어를 미리 브레인스토밍을 해두는 것이 가장 중요하다.

참고로 Part 3 질문은 Writing Task 2 에세이 토픽과도 유사하기에 이러한 브레인스토밍 연습은 Writing 과목 대비에도 많은 도움이 된다.

2 Paraphrasing(패러프레이징)으로 답변 시작

Part 3 답변의 시작은 질문 문장을 패러프레이징하여 답변할 수 있는데, 이 전략의 장점은 다음과 같이 네 가지가 있다.

① 질문을 패러프레이징 하면서 답변에 필요한 아이디어를 생각할 시간을 벌 수 있다.
② 패러프레이징을 통해 질문을 보다 제대로 이해할 수 있다.
③ 패러프레이징을 통해 짧게 끝날 수 있는 답변을 보다 길게 말할 수 있다.
④ 어휘력 채점기준에 있는 패러프레이징 부분에서 점수를 얻을 수 있다.

Part 3 답변 시작 예시

질문: Why do people enjoy going to the cinema?

답변1: Because they can watch a movie on a big screen with a good sound system.

답변2: <u>People enjoy going to the cinema</u> because they can watch a movie on a big screen with a good sound system.

답변3: <u>I think many people love to go to the cinema</u> because they can watch a movie on a big screen with a good sound system.

답변1과 같이 바로 질문에 답변을 할 수 있지만, 이렇게 하려면 아이디어가 미리 준비되어 있어야 한다. 답변2와 같이 질문을 다시 언급하면서(repeat) 아이디어를 정리할 시간을 벌거나, 더 나아가서 답변3처럼 바꾸어 말하면서(paraphrase) 어휘력 부분의 추가 점수도 획득할 수 있다.

3 답변 생각할 시간이 모자랄 때

문제를 들었을 때, 전혀 답변에 대한 아이디어가 없어서 질문 문장을 패러프레이징하는 시간으로는 충분하지 않은 경우가 있다. 아이디어가 없을 때 얼버무리며 말하다 답변을 흐지부지 끝내서 감점 당하기 보다는, 아래와 같이 말하며 시간을 벌어 보자.

That's a very interesting question. Let me think for a second.
매우 흥미로운 질문이네요. 잠시만 생각해 보겠습니다.

It is difficult to say, but I think ~
대답하기 어려운데요, 제 생각에는 ~

I don't really know for sure, but I would say ~
정말 잘 모르겠는데요, ~인 것 같습니다.

To be honest, I'm not familiar with this subject, but I think ~
솔직히, 이 주제에 대해 잘 모르지만, 제 생각에는 ~

하지만 이러한 말을 여러 번 사용하면 감점이 될 수 있으니 꼭 필요할 때만 사용해야 한다. 가급적 패러프레이징 하는 시간을 활용하여 답변 내용을 생각해내도록 한다. 참고로 답변 아이디어가 없다고 질문을 바꿔 달라고 하면 절대로 안된다. 아이디어가 도무지 떠오르지 않더라도 위 표현을 활용하여 이야기를 지어내서라도 답변하는 연습을 하자.

문법 점수 올리는 Patterns

다음 문법 중 최소 3개 이상을 포함시켜서 답변하는 연습을 하여, 채점기준 중 문법 점수에서 고득점을 받도록 하라.

가주어 it	It is 형용사 that 주어 동사
명사절 주어	What young people mostly think about that is ~
전치사 + 동명사 + 상관접속사	by watching my favourite music videos or laughing along with ~
현재완료시제	It has been popular ~
관계대명사	those who 동사
관계부사	the place where 주어 동사
명사 + 현재분사	long lines of customers waiting outside stores
명사 + 과거분사	areas limited to ~

SPEAKING

Part 3 기출 문제

다양한 Part 3 기출 문제를 통해 미리 아이디어 또는 핵심 어휘를 브레인스토밍해보고 자신만의 답변을 만들어보자. 각 기출 문제에 대한 모범 답변은 해설집에 제시되어 있다.

1 In what ways can people in a family be similar to each other? 정답 및 해설 p.090
어떤 면들을 가족 구성원들이 서로 닮을 수 있나요?

Brainstorming 예시

have something in common 공통점이 있다 – resemble 닮다 – appearance 외모 – character 성격 – behaviour 행동 – gene 유전자 – inherit 물려받다, 유전하다

2 How has the size of the family changed in the last few decades in your country?
당신 국가에서 지난 수십 년 동안 가족의 크기가 어떻게 변해왔나요?

Brainstorming 예시

extended family 대가족 – with close relatives 가까운 친척들과 – nuclear family 핵가족 – a married couple with their children 결혼한 커플과 그들의 자녀 – only child 외동

3 Who should be responsible for the care of the elderly: the family or the government?
당신은 노인 돌봄의 책임이 가족과 국가 중 누구에게 책임이 있다고 생각하나요?

Brainstorming 예시

younger/elderly family member 젊은/나이든 가족 구성원 – sacrifice 희생하다 – support 지원 – government 정부 – look after the senior citizens 노인을 돌보다 – taxpayer 납세자 – public programme 공공사업 – healthcare 건강관리

4 Do you think that society is becoming more materialistic?
당신은 사회가 점점 더 물질주의적이 된다고 생각하나요?

Brainstorming 예시

without a doubt 의심의 여지없이 – advertising 광고 – mentality 사고방식 – consumer culture 소비문화 – inclination to worldly success 세속적 성공에 대한 성향

5 How do large shopping malls affect small local shops?
대형 쇼핑몰이 작은 지역 상점들에 어떠한 영향을 미치나요?

Brainstorming 예시

small local shops toward extinction 종말로 향하는 동네 상점들 – small specialty stores 작은 전문점들 – compete with giant malls 거대 쇼핑몰과 경쟁하다 – window shopping 윈도우 쇼핑(구매는 하지 않고 진열품을 바라보며 다니는 것)

6 What are the most important qualities that people who start a business need?
창업하는 사람들이 필요로 하는 가장 중요한 자질들은 무엇인가요?

Brainstorming 예시

creativity 창의력 - new demands 새로운 수요 - determination to settle matters 문제를 해결할 결단력 - high level of confidence 높은 수준의 자신감 - effective communication skills 효과적인 의사 소통 능력

7 Are there any disadvantages to running a business?
사업을 운영하면 단점들이 있나요?

Brainstorming 예시

financial risk 재정적 위험 - no guaranteed income 보장된 수입이 없음 - financial loss 재정적 손실 - go bankrupt 파산하다

8 Do you agree that people should have a good work-life balance?
당신은 사람들이 일과 삶의 균형을 유지해야 한다는 말에 동의하나요?

Brainstorming 예시

working longer hours 더 길게 일함 - have less time for their families and themselves 가족과 스스로를 위한 시간이 줄어듦 - the disruption in their personal relationships 개인 관계의 분열 - health problems 건강 문제 - overworking 과로

9 How have developments in technology affected employment in your country?
기술 발달이 어떻게 당신 나라의 고용에 영향을 미쳤나요?

Brainstorming 예시

mass unemployment 대규모 실업 - become obsolete 쓸모없게 되다 - automation 자동화 - the advent of AI 인공지능의 출현 - eliminate a vast number of jobs 많은 수의 직업을 없애다

10 How would the way people use the internet change in the future?
사람들이 인터넷을 사용하는 방식이 미래에 어떻게 바뀔까요?

Brainstorming 예시

the internet of things 사물 인터넷 - a usual thing 일상적인 것 - ubiquitous networking 유비쿼터스 네트워킹(어디에나 있는 인터넷 망) - virtual reality 가상 현실 - augmented reality 증강 현실 - be integrated with our everyday lives 일상 생활과 통합되다

11 What are the positive and negative effects of social media?

소셜 미디어의 긍정적, 부정적 영향은 무엇인가요?

Brainstorming 예시

stay in touch with ~와 연락을 유지하다 – advertise 광고하다 – addictive 중독적인 – psychological distress 정신적 고통 – the fear of missing out 정보를 놓치는 것에 대한 두려움

12 What is the typical diet of people in your country?

당신 나라 사람들의 주식은 무엇인가요?

Brainstorming 예시

steamed rice 밥 – staple food 주식 – fermented vegetables 발효된 야채 – spicy, tangy flavour 맵고 칼칼한 맛 – chicken 닭고기 – pork 돼지고기 – beef 소고기

13 Do you think food is important in a festival?

당신은 음식이 축제에서 중요하다고 생각하나요?

Brainstorming 예시

plays a vital role in ~에 있어서 중요한 역할을 하다 – celebration 축하 – mark 기념하다 – feature local foods 지역 음식을 특징으로 하다 – treat 훌륭한 요리 – essential to bringing people together 사람들을 함께 있게 하는데 필수적인

14 How may globalisation affect different festivals around the world?

어떻게 세계화가 전 세계에 서로 다른 축제들에 영향을 끼칠까요?

Brainstorming 예시

easily participate in ~에 더 쉽게 참가하다 – traditions and customs 전통과 관습 – get a full sense of a culture 하나의 문화를 완전히 이해하다 – wonderful gateway 훌륭한 관문 – beneficial for the global community 지구촌에 도움이 되는

15 What kinds of music are popular with young people in your country?

당신 국가의 젊은이들에게 어떤 종류의 음악이 유행인가요?

Brainstorming 예시

K-Pop, Korean pop 한국 대중가요 – idol culture 아이돌 문화 – boy bands and girl groups 소년 밴드와 소녀 그룹 – fandoms of teenagers and young adults 십대들과 20대의 팬덤 – spreading to other countries 다른 나라로 뻗어 나가는

MEMO

PRACTICE TEST

Part 3 다음 세부 요구 사항에 따라 각 질문의 모범 답변을 만들자.

Q1

MP3 Unit28_1

Should companies give compensation to customers who complain about a purchase?

- Brainstorming 위 질문에 필요한 아이디어(답변 소재)를 3가지 이상 적어보자.

- Paraphrasing 질문 패러프레이징을 통해 답변의 첫 문장을 만들어 보자.

Q2

MP3 Unit28_2

Are there any advantages or disadvantages of being famous?

- Brainstorming 위 질문에 필요한 아이디어(답변 소재)를 3가지 이상 적어보자.

- Paraphrasing 질문 패러프레이징을 통해 답변의 첫 문장을 만들어 보자.

정답 및 해설 p.094

Q3

MP3 Unit28_3

What do you think influences young people's taste in music?

- Brainstorming 위 질문에 필요한 아이디어(답변 소재)를 3가지 이상 적어보자.

- Paraphrasing 질문 패러프레이징을 통해 답변의 첫 문장을 만들어 보자.

Q4

MP3 Unit28_4

Have relationships with neighbours in your country changed in recent years?

- Brainstorming 위 질문에 필요한 아이디어(답변 소재)를 3가지 이상 적어보자.

- Paraphrasing 질문 패러프레이징을 통해 답변의 첫 문장을 만들어 보자.

UNIT 29

Part 3 - 사회적 이슈: 채점기준에 따른 답변

오늘의 학습 목표

1 다양한 Part 3 질문에 대해 평상시에 수시로 연습한다.
2 채점기준에 맞게 모범 답변을 연습한다.
3 자신의 답변을 녹음해 보고 들어보면서 부족한 점을 보완한다.

채점기준에 따른 모범 답변

MP3 Unit29_1

질문

What items are popular to purchase in your country?
당신 국가에서 구매하기에 인기 있는 물건은 무엇인가요?

답변 brainstorming은 파란색으로 표시

All kinds of electronics are popular purchases in my country because we have a tech-savvy, modern culture. Korea has one of the most connected societies in the world, and nearly everyone has a smartphone and constant access to the Internet. So, when a new mobile device is released, you can count on seeing long lines of customers waiting outside stores to buy the latest model. This is especially true when Samsung releases a new product. Since that company has such a huge influence in my country, I think people are more likely to support them and purchase their flagship products.

우리나라는 기술에 민감한 현대적 문화를 갖고 있기에 모든 유형의 전자 제품이 인기 있는 구매품입니다. 한국은 세계에서 가장 인터넷이 연결된 국가로 거의 모든 사람들이 스마트폰을 갖고 있고 인터넷에 지속적인 접속을 합니다. 그래서, 새 모바일 기기가 출시되면, 당신은 최신 모델을 사기 위해 상점 밖에서 기다리는 고객들의 긴 줄을 보리라 기대할 수 있습니다. 이것은 특히 삼성이 새 제품을 출시할 때 사실이죠. 삼성은 우리나라에서 정말 큰 영향력을 갖고 있기에, 저는 사람들이 삼성을 더욱 지지하고 삼성의 주력 제품들을 구매하려 한다고 생각합니다.

채점기준에 따른 답변 평가

<table>
<tr><td rowspan="4">Fluency and Coherence
유창성과 일관성</td><td>반복이나 자기 수정 안함</td></tr>
<tr><td>단어나 문법을 찾기 위해 머뭇거리지 않음</td></tr>
<tr><td>연결어를 사용하며 일관성 있게 말함
부사절 접속사(because, since, when)와 접속사(and, so)를 적절히 사용하여 글의 일관성 유지</td></tr>
<tr><td>화제를 완전하고 적절하게 전개
두괄식으로 질문에 대답을 하되(All kinds of electronics), 이유(tech-savvy modern culture),
구체적 예(long lines of customers waiting outside stores, Samsung)로의 짜임새 있는 전개</td></tr>
<tr><td rowspan="2">Lexical Resource
어휘력</td><td>상황에 맞는 다양한 고급 단어 구사
tech-savvy modern culture 기술에 밝은 현대 문화
flagship products 주력 제품들</td></tr>
<tr><td>영어다운 표현을 사용하고 동의어 반복 없이 패러프레이징
[영어다운 표현] has such a huge influence 정말 큰 영향력을 갖고 있다
are more likely to 더 ~할 것이다
[패러프레이징] smartphone → mobile device
Samsung → that company</td></tr>
<tr><td rowspan="2">Grammatical Range and Accuracy
문법의 다양성과 정확성</td><td>분사, 관계대명사, 명사절 등의 다양한 문법 사용
현재분사 long lines of customers waiting outside stores 상점 밖에서 기다리는 고객들의 긴 줄</td></tr>
<tr><td>주어/동사 수일치, 올바른 시제 및 주어-동사 사용
수일치 및 현재완료 시제를 올바르게 사용</td></tr>
<tr><td rowspan="3">Pronunciation
발음</td><td>정확한 발음</td></tr>
<tr><td>너무 느리거나 빠르지 않게, 일관된 스피드로 발음</td></tr>
<tr><td>얼버무리지 않고 알아듣기 쉽도록 크고 명료하게 발음</td></tr>
<tr><td>총 평</td><td>충실한 내용의 완벽한 전개, 영어다운 표현들과 패러프레이징, 그리고 다양한 문법을 완벽하게 사용하였기에, 본 답변은 어려운 고급 어휘를 사용하지 않아도 발음만 주의하면 충분히 8.0 이상 고득점 가능</td></tr>
</table>

SPEAKING

기출 문제

1 **Why do people recycle more these days than in the past?** MP3 Unit29_2

왜 오늘날 사람들이 예전보다 더 재활용을 하나요?

Model Answer brainstorming은 파란색으로 표시

We are more committed to recycling nowadays than we were in the past because we are more aware of our environmental impact. Not so long ago, we didn't pay much mind to what happened to the plastic container we would simply throw away. It was out of sight, out of mind. But now we know that the plastic container will sit in a landfill for years, or float around the ocean until it joins a giant island of trash. Through our past carelessness, we have learned the need for sustainability, and that's why we make more of an effort to recycle nowadays.

요즘 우리는 예전보다 더 재활용에 전념하는데 우리가 환경 영향에 대해 더 많이 인식하고 있기 때문입니다. 얼마 전까지만 해도, 우리는 우리가 쉽게 버리는 플라스틱 용기에 무슨 일이 벌어지는지 신경쓰지 않았죠. 눈에서 멀어지면서 생각에서도 없어졌습니다. 하지만, 이제 우리는 플라스틱 용기가 수년간 매립지에 그대로 있거나 커다란 쓰레기 섬에 합류할 때까지 해양에 떠다니는 것을 압니다. 우리의 지난 부주의를 통해, 우리는 환경파괴 없는 지속가능성에 대한 필요를 배웠고, 이것이 요즘 우리가 재활용에 더 많은 노력을 하는 이유입니다.

나만의 모범 답변

2 Why are rivers important?

왜 강이 중요한가요?

MP3 Unit29_3

Model Answer brainstorming은 파란색으로 표시

Rivers are important for numerous geographical, ecological and economic reasons, but I'm not an expert on these sciences, so I'll focus on why they've been important to humans. Great civilisations have always sprung up around rivers because of the fertile land around them and the easy transportation they provide. For example, Ancient Egypt depended on the bounties of the Nile, and the Yellow River allowed ancient Chinese civilisation to prosper. And today, some of the major cities of the world gained their prominence thanks to their proximity to a river. In short, rivers provide the means for human society to flourish.

강은 수많은 지리적, 생태적, 경제적 이유로 중요하지만, 저는 이러한 과학적인 것에 전문가는 아니기에, 인간에게 왜 강이 중요해 왔는지 초점을 맞추겠습니다. 위대한 문명들은 항상 강가에서 발전했는데 강 주변에 비옥한 땅과 강이 제공하는 편리한 운송 때문입니다. 예를 들면, 고대 이집트는 나일강의 풍부함에 의존하였고, 황허 강은 고대 중국 문명이 번성하도록 했습니다. 그리고 오늘날, 몇몇 세계 주요 도시들은 강 접근성 덕분에 그들의 명성을 얻었습니다. 요약하면, 강은 인간 사회가 번영할 수단을 제공합니다.

나만의 모범 답변

SPEAKING

3 What disadvantages are there if a society has a large gap between the rich and the poor? MP3 Unit29_4

사회에 커다란 빈부 격차가 있다면 어떤 단점들이 있나요?

Model Answer brainstorming은 파란색으로 표시

A society with substantial inequality between the wealthy and the impoverished will become more unstable because of the low quality of life of the poor. Studies have shown that countries with large wealth gaps have higher rates of health and social issues, such as mental illness, crime and incarceration. The poor simply cannot attain the means to support a healthy lifestyle, and this leads to a lack of trust that individuals have in their society. Furthermore, it's worth noting, the stratification of people into 'elites' and 'masses' has been at the core of the collapse of major civilisations in history.

부유한 사람들과 빈곤한 사람들 간에 상당한 불평등이 있는 사회는 더 불안정하게 될 것인데 가난한 사람들의 삶의 낮은 질 때문입니다. 연구들은 커다란 부의 격차를 갖고 있는 국가들이 정신질환, 범죄 그리고 투옥과 같은 건강과 사회 문제의 더 높은 비율을 갖고 있음을 보여왔습니다. 가난한 사람들은 단순히 건강한 삶의 방식을 지탱할 수단을 획득할 수 없고, 이는 개인들이 사회에 갖고 있는 신뢰 부족으로 귀결됩니다. 더욱이, 주목할 점은, 엘리트와 대중의 인구 계층화는 역사상으로 주요 문명 멸망의 핵심이었다는 것입니다.

나만의 모범 답변

4 How do people in your country learn about history?

당신 국가 사람들은 역사를 어떻게 배우나요?

MP3 Unit29_5

Model Answer brainstorming은 파란색으로 표시

I believe most people in my country have a good grasp of history because it's one of the core subjects we learn in school. From an early age, we begin learning about history. At first, we focus mostly on our nation's foundation and major events, and then later we begin learning world history. Plus, it may seem odd, but a lot of popular movies and television shows have historical settings. While these might not be completely reliable sources of information, I think they improve our overall sense of history.

저는 우리나라 대부분 사람들이 역사에 대해 올바른 이해를 한다고 생각하는데 역사는 우리가 학교에서 배우는 핵심 과목 중 하나이기 때문입니다. 어릴 때부터 우리는 역사에 대해 배우기 시작합니다. 먼저, 우리는 대체로 우리나라의 건국과 주요 사건들에 초점을 맞추고, 이후 세계 역사를 배우기 시작합니다. 이외에, 좀 이상해 보이지만, 많은 영화와 TV 쇼들이 역사적 배경을 갖고 있습니다. 이것들이 완전히 믿을 만한 정보는 아니지만, 저는 이러한 것들이 우리의 전반적인 역사적 감각을 향상시킨다고 생각합니다.

나만의 모범 답변

SPEAKING

Part 3 다음 세부 요구 사항에 따라 각 질문의 모범 답변을 만들자.

Q1

MP3 Unit29_6

What is the difference between the role of a teacher and a parent in the education of children?

- Recording 자신의 답변을 녹음하여 들어보면서, 아래 채점기준에 따라 Y/N을 표시하고, 부족한 점을 보완해 본다.

유창성과 일관성	반복이나 자기 수정 안함	Y / N
	단어나 문법을 찾기 위해 머뭇거리지 않음	Y / N
	연결어를 사용하며 일관성 있게 말함	Y / N
	화제를 완전하고 적절하게 전개	Y / N
어휘력	상황에 맞는 다양한 고급 단어 구사	Y / N
	영어다운 표현을 사용하고 동의어 반복 없이 패러프레이징	Y / N
문법의 다양성과 정확성	분사, 관계대명사, 명사절 등의 다양한 문법 사용	Y / N
	주어/동사 수일치, 올바른 시제 및 주어-동사 사용	Y / N
발음	정확한 발음	Y / N
	너무 느리거나 빠르지 않게, 일관된 스피드로 발음	Y / N
	얼버무리지 않고 알아듣기 쉽도록 크고 명료하게 발음	Y / N

정답 및 해설 p.097

Q2

MP3 Unit29_7

Do you think the traditional classroom will disappear in the future?

- Recording 자신의 답변을 녹음하여 들어보면서, 아래 채점기준에 따라 Y/N을 표시하고, 부족한 점을 보완해 본다.

유창성과 일관성	반복이나 자기 수정 안함	Y / N
	단어나 문법을 찾기 위해 머뭇거리지 않음	Y / N
	연결어를 사용하며 일관성 있게 말함	Y / N
	화제를 완전하고 적절하게 전개	Y / N
어휘력	상황에 맞는 다양한 고급 단어 구사	Y / N
	영어다운 표현을 사용하고 동의어 반복 없이 패러프레이징	Y / N
문법의 다양성과 정확성	분사, 관계대명사, 명사절 등의 다양한 문법 사용	Y / N
	주어/동사 수일치, 올바른 시제 및 주어-동사 사용	Y / N
발음	정확한 발음	Y / N
	너무 느리거나 빠르지 않게, 일관된 스피드로 발음	Y / N
	얼버무리지 않고 알아듣기 쉽도록 크고 명료하게 발음	Y / N

Q3

MP3 Unit29_8

What can children learn from playing sports?

- Recording 자신의 답변을 녹음하여 들어보면서, 아래 채점기준에 따라 Y/N을 표시하고, 부족한 점을 보완해 본다.

유창성과 일관성	반복이나 자기 수정 안함	Y / N
	단어나 문법을 찾기 위해 머뭇거리지 않음	Y / N
	연결어를 사용하며 일관성 있게 말함	Y / N
	화제를 완전하고 적절하게 전개	Y / N
어휘력	상황에 맞는 다양한 고급 단어 구사	Y / N
	영어다운 표현을 사용하고 동의어 반복 없이 패러프레이징	Y / N
문법의 다양성과 정확성	분사, 관계대명사, 명사절 등의 다양한 문법 사용	Y / N
	주어/동사 수일치, 올바른 시제 및 주어-동사 사용	Y / N
발음	정확한 발음	Y / N
	너무 느리거나 빠르지 않게, 일관된 스피드로 발음	Y / N
	얼버무리지 않고 알아듣기 쉽도록 크고 명료하게 발음	Y / N

Q4

MP3 Unit29_9

Do you think people today are busier than before?

- Recording 자신의 답변을 녹음하여 들어보면서, 아래 채점기준에 따라 Y/N을 표시하고, 부족한 점을 보완해 본다.

유창성과 일관성	반복이나 자기 수정 안함	Y / N
	단어나 문법을 찾기 위해 머뭇거리지 않음	Y / N
	연결어를 사용하며 일관성 있게 말함	Y / N
	화제를 완전하고 적절하게 전개	Y / N
어휘력	상황에 맞는 다양한 고급 단어 구사	Y / N
	영어다운 표현을 사용하고 동의어 반복 없이 패러프레이징	Y / N
문법의 다양성과 정확성	분사, 관계대명사, 명사절 등의 다양한 문법 사용	Y / N
	주어/동사 수일치, 올바른 시제 및 주어-동사 사용	Y / N
발음	정확한 발음	Y / N
	너무 느리거나 빠르지 않게, 일관된 스피드로 발음	Y / N
	얼버무리지 않고 알아듣기 쉽도록 크고 명료하게 발음	Y / N

UNIT 30 Part 3 - 사회적 이슈: 토픽별 표현

오늘의 학습 목표

1 Part 3 빈출 토픽과 각 토픽에서 사용할 유용한 표현을 익힌다.
2 채점기준에 맞게 모범 답변을 연습한다.
3 자신의 답변을 녹음해 보고 들어보면서 부족한 점을 보완한다.

Environment/Pollution 환경/오염

지속 가능한	sustainable
대체, 대안	alternative
공기 오염	air pollution
~에 대한 부담	strain on
천연자원	natural resources
쓰레기(버려진 휴지·깡통·병 등)	litter
~을 오염시키다	pollute
~에 해를 끼치다, ~에 손상을 입히다	cause damage to
탄소 발자국 (온실 효과를 유발하는 CO2 배출량)	carbon footprint
기후 변화	climate change
배기가스	exhaust fumes
동식물군	flora and fauna
화석연료	fossil fuel
멸종 위기종	endangered species
온실 가스	greenhouse gas
재생 에너지	renewable energy
서식지 파괴	habitat destruction
큰 위협을 가하다	pose a significant threat
지구 온난화	global warming
환경 오염	environmental pollution

Money/Shopping 돈/쇼핑

구매(품), ~을 구매하다	purchase
더 높은 사회적 지위	higher social status
내구성이 있는, 오래가는	durable
엄청난 양의 돈	large amounts of money
특별하게 느끼다	feel special
고급의	high-end
대량 생산된	mass-produced
사치품	luxury goods
친절한 서비스	friendly service
물질(만능)주의의	materialistic
돈을 아끼다, 모으다	save money
열심히 번 돈	hard-earned money

SPEAKING

Food/Cooking 음식/요리

위안을 주는 음식, 소울푸드	comfort food
집밥	home-cooked meal
재료	ingredient
방부제	preservative
화학 물질	chemicals
채식주의자	vegetarian
(우유, 달걀도 먹지 않는) 채식주의자	vegan
식물성의	plant-based
지역 농민들	local farmers
음식 알레르기	food allergy
식단 제한	dietary restriction
식당 음식	restaurant food

Education/Language 교육/언어

~로부터 배우다	learn from
~을 이해해다, 생각해 내다	figure out
또래, 동료	peer
학구적으로, 학업적으로	academically
어려운 과목, 어려운 주제	tough subject
(예의 바르게) 행동하다, 처신하다	behave
교육학적 방법	pedagogical method
학교 교육	schooling
대단히 흥미로운, 매혹적인	fascinating
친한 친구	close friend
언어 장벽	language barrier
학원	private academy

Job/Work 직업/일

재택근무(하다)	work from home
사무직 근로자	office worker
집안일	household chores
일과 연관된 활동들	work-related activities
애쓰다, 몸부림치다	struggle
휴식을 취하다	take breaks
규칙적으로	regularly
이동하다, 옮기다	shift
협업하다	collaborate
생산적인	productive
(주의를) 산만하게 하다	distract
워라벨, 일과 삶의 균형	work-life balance

Travel/Transport 여행/교통

여행, 이동, 여정	journey
자전거, 자전거로 가다	bike
자전거 전용 도로	bike lane
대중교통	public transport (미국식 public transportation)
돌아다니다	get around
출퇴근길	daily commute
극심한 교통(량)	heavy traffic
관광 명소	tourist attraction
여행 계획	travel plan
아름다운 경치	beautiful scenery
잊을 수 없는 경험	unforgettable experience
교통 체증	(traffic) congestion

SPEAKING

Culture/Entertainment 문화/오락

스티리밍 서비스, OTT	streaming service
입소문이 나다	go viral
대중문화	popular culture
온라인 후기	online review
종교 의식, 종교 축제	religious ceremony
어쩌다 한 번, 극히 드물게	once in a blue moon
~을 몰아서보다, 정주행하다	binge-watch
기본 예의	common courtesy
문화적 차이	cultural differences
개인 취향, 개인적 선호도	personal preference
유명인	celebrity
중독	addiction

Generation/Time 세대/시간

태도	attitude
청소년	adolescent
미래 세대	future generations
고령화 인구, 인구 고령화	ageing population
출산율	birth rate
노인들	elderly people
세대 차이	the generation gap
소통의 격차	the communication gap
큰 차이를 만들다	make a big difference
A와 B 사이의 경계를 흐릿하게 하다	blur the line between A and B
기한이 지난	overdue
늦지 않게	in time

Health 건강

건강한	healthy
비만	obesity
체중 증가	weight gain
역효과, 악영향	adverse effect
식습관	dietary habit
건강 보조 식품	dietary supplements
면역 체계	immune system
정신 건강	mental health
우울증	depression
치매	dementia
압박, 부담	pressure
과격한 운동, 힘든 운동	strenuous exercise

Technology 기술

선진의, 진보된	advanced
화상통화	video call
가상 현실 환경	virtual reality setting
사이버 공간	cyberspace
효율적으로	efficiently
효과적으로	effectively
뒤떨어진, 구식의	out of date
과도하게	excessively
절제	moderation
(주의를) 산만하게 하는 것	distraction
첨단의	cutting-edge
~에 대한 최신 정보를 얻다	stay updated on

SPEAKING

Policy 정책

(정책을) 시행하다	implement
세계적인 변화	global shift
(새로운) 계획	initiative
엄격하게	strictly
만장일치의	unanimous
예상치 못한	unexpected
조치	measure
열정적인	passionate
관계 당국, 관청	the authorities
공통점, 타협점	common ground
역할을 하다	play a role
지원, 도움, 보조	aid

기출 문제

1 Why do some cities have less air pollution? MP3 Unit30_1

일부 도시의 대기 오염이 적은 이유는 무엇인가요?

Model Answer brainstorming은 파란색으로 표시

Some cities have lower air pollution levels because they do a great job managing traffic congestion. These cities have an excellent cycling infrastructure, so people can bike across the city using well-connected bike lanes instead of driving. They also implement a congestion tax during rush hour to reduce the number of cars on the road. At the same time, they invest in the public transport system. This makes it more convenient for residents to get around the city without driving. I think all these factors manage to reduce air pollution and keep their air cleaner.

일부 도시는 교통 혼잡을 잘 관리하기 때문에 대기 오염 수준이 낮습니다. 이러한 도시는 자전거 인프라가 잘 갖춰져 있어 사람들이 자동차 대신 잘 연결된 자전거 도로를 이용해 도시를 가로질러 자전거를 탈 수 있습니다. 또한 출퇴근 시간대에는 혼잡세를 시행하여 도로의 차량 수를 줄입니다. 동시에, 대중교통 시스템에도 투자하고 있습니다. 이를 통해 주민들은 자가용을 이용하지 않고도 도시를 더 편리하게 이동할 수 있습니다. 이러한 모든 요소가 대기 오염을 줄이고 공기를 더 깨끗하게 유지하는 데 도움이 된다고 생각합니다.

나만의 모범 답변

2 Do you think tourism causes environmental damage?

MP3 Unit30_2

관광이 환경 파괴를 유발한다고 생각하나요?

Model Answer brainstorming은 파란색으로 표시

Tourists can definitely cause environmental pollution. They often use more water and electricity than the locals, putting a lot of strain on natural resources. Some tourists don't show much respect for the environment, such as by leaving litter behind. This not only ruins the beautiful scenery but also pollutes the soil and water. Plus, their carbon footprint from flights and other modes of transport contributes to air pollution and climate change. It's a shame that tourism can cause so much damage to the environment. I think there should be a global shift towards sustainable travel.

관광객은 분명 환경오염을 일으킬 수 있습니다. 관광객들은 현지인보다 더 많은 물과 전기를 사용하며 천연 자원에 많은 부담을 주기도 합니다. 일부 관광객은 쓰레기를 버리는 등 환경에 대한 존중을 보여주지 않습니다. 이는 아름다운 경관을 망칠 뿐만 아니라 토양과 물을 오염시킵니다. 또한 항공편 및 기타 교통 수단으로 인한 탄소 발자국은 대기 오염과 기후 변화에 기여합니다. 관광업이 환경에 이렇게 많은 피해를 입힐 수 있다는 것은 안타까운 일입니다. 전 세계적으로 지속 가능한 여행으로 전환해야 한다고 생각합니다.

나만의 모범 답변

3 Why do some people like to buy expensive goods?

MP3 Unit30_3

어떤 사람들은 왜 고가의 상품을 구매하길 좋아하나요?

Model Answer brainstorming은 파란색으로 표시

I think some people like to purchase expensive goods because they believe that those items are better quality and reflect a higher social status. Usually, when something is more expensive, we tend to assume that it's made using durable materials. So, the value of these goods increases, making consumers more likely to buy them even if they're expensive. Plus, purchasing luxury goods can make people feel like they've accomplished something. Most of the time, being able to spend large amounts of money is associated with success. It can boost a buyer's self-esteem and make them feel more special compared to others.

어떤 사람들은 비싼 물건이 더 좋은 품질이고 더 높은 사회적 지위를 반영한다고 믿기 때문에 비싼 물건을 구입하는 것을 좋아한다고 생각합니다. 일반적으로, 어떤 물건이 더 비싸면 내구성이 좋은 소재로 만들어졌다고 생각하는 경향이 있습니다. 따라서 이러한 상품의 가치가 높아져 소비자는 비싸더라도 구매할 가능성이 높아집니다. 또한, 비싼 물품을 구매하면 사람들은 자신이 무언가를 성취한 것처럼 느낄 수 있습니다. 대부분의 경우, 많은 돈을 쓸 수 있다는 것은 성공과 관련이 있습니다. 이는 구매자의 자존감을 높이고 다른 사람에 비해 더 특별하다고 느끼게 할 수 있습니다.

나만의 모범 답변

4 Do you think small markets will disappear in the future? MP3 Unit30_4

당신은 앞으로 소규모 시장들이 사라질 것이라고 생각하나요?

Model Answer brainstorming은 파란색으로 표시

It is true that small markets are struggling to compete with supermarkets. However, I don't think that they're going to vanish anytime soon. Small markets offer fresher, tastier and higher-quality produce that is sourced directly from local farmers. This is something that supermarkets can't match with their mass-produced fruits and vegetables. Even though buying from small markets may cost more, there is a strong demand for these superior products, especially from high-end restaurants and customers who care about where their food comes from.

소규모 시장이 대형마트와 경쟁하기 위해 고군분투하고 있는 것은 사실입니다. 하지만 조만간 사라질 것이라고는 생각하지 않습니다. 소규모 시장은 현지 농부가 직접 공급하는 더 신선하고 맛있고 품질 좋은 농산물을 제공합니다. 이는 슈퍼마켓이 대량으로 생산한 과일과 채소와는 비교할 수 없는 부분입니다. 소규모 시장에서 구매하는 것이 더 비쌀 수 있지만, 특히 고급 레스토랑과 음식의 출처에 관심이 많은 고객들 사이에서 이러한 우수한 제품에 대한 수요가 높습니다.

나만의 모범 답변

Part 3 다음 세부 요구 사항에 따라 각 질문의 모범 답변을 만들자.

Q1

MP3 Unit30_5

What are the advantages and disadvantages of eating at a restaurant?

- Recording 자신의 답변을 녹음하여 들어보면서, 아래 채점기준에 따라 Y/N을 표시하고, 부족한 점을 보완해 본다.

유창성과 일관성	반복이나 자기 수정 안함	Y / N
	단어나 문법을 찾기 위해 머뭇거리지 않음	Y / N
	연결어를 사용하며 일관성 있게 말함	Y / N
	화제를 완전하고 적절하게 전개	Y / N
어휘력	상황에 맞는 다양한 고급 단어 구사	Y / N
	영어다운 표현을 사용하고 동의어 반복 없이 패러프레이징	Y / N
문법의 다양성과 정확성	분사, 관계대명사, 명사절 등의 다양한 문법 사용	Y / N
	주어/동사 수일치, 올바른 시제 및 주어-동사 사용	Y / N
발음	정확한 발음	Y / N
	너무 느리거나 빠르지 않게, 일관된 스피드로 발음	Y / N
	얼버무리지 않고 알아듣기 쉽도록 크고 명료하게 발음	Y / N

정답 및 해설 p.100

Q2

MP3 Unit30_6

How do you think the way we eat will change in the future?

- Recording 자신의 답변을 녹음하여 들어보면서, 아래 채점기준에 따라 Y/N을 표시하고, 부족한 점을 보완해 본다.

유창성과 일관성	반복이나 자기 수정 안함	Y / N
	단어나 문법을 찾기 위해 머뭇거리지 않음	Y / N
	연결어를 사용하며 일관성 있게 말함	Y / N
	화제를 완전하고 적절하게 전개	Y / N
어휘력	상황에 맞는 다양한 고급 단어 구사	Y / N
	영어다운 표현을 사용하고 동의어 반복 없이 패러프레이징	Y / N
문법의 다양성과 정확성	분사, 관계대명사, 명사절 등의 다양한 문법 사용	Y / N
	주어/동사 수일치, 올바른 시제 및 주어-동사 사용	Y / N
발음	정확한 발음	Y / N
	너무 느리거나 빠르지 않게, 일관된 스피드로 발음	Y / N
	얼버무리지 않고 알아듣기 쉽도록 크고 명료하게 발음	Y / N

Q3

MP3 Unit30_7

How has technology changed the society we live in now?

- Recording 자신의 답변을 녹음하여 들어보면서, 아래 채점기준에 따라 Y/N을 표시하고, 부족한 점을 보완해 본다.

유창성과 일관성	반복이나 자기 수정 안함	Y / N
	단어나 문법을 찾기 위해 머뭇거리지 않음	Y / N
	연결어를 사용하며 일관성 있게 말함	Y / N
	화제를 완전하고 적절하게 전개	Y / N
어휘력	상황에 맞는 다양한 고급 단어 구사	Y / N
	영어다운 표현을 사용하고 동의어 반복 없이 패러프레이징	Y / N
문법의 다양성과 정확성	분사, 관계대명사, 명사절 등의 다양한 문법 사용	Y / N
	주어/동사 수일치, 올바른 시제 및 주어-동사 사용	Y / N
발음	정확한 발음	Y / N
	너무 느리거나 빠르지 않게, 일관된 스피드로 발음	Y / N
	얼버무리지 않고 알아듣기 쉽도록 크고 명료하게 발음	Y / N

Q4

MP3 Unit30_8

Does technology distract people?

• Recording 자신의 답변을 녹음하여 들어보면서, 아래 채점기준에 따라 Y/N을 표시하고, 부족한 점을 보완해 본다.

유창성과 일관성	반복이나 자기 수정 안함	Y / N
	단어나 문법을 찾기 위해 머뭇거리지 않음	Y / N
	연결어를 사용하며 일관성 있게 말함	Y / N
	화제를 완전하고 적절하게 전개	Y / N
어휘력	상황에 맞는 다양한 고급 단어 구사	Y / N
	영어다운 표현을 사용하고 동의어 반복 없이 패러프레이징	Y / N
문법의 다양성과 정확성	분사, 관계대명사, 명사절 등의 다양한 문법 사용	Y / N
	주어/동사 수일치, 올바른 시제 및 주어-동사 사용	Y / N
발음	정확한 발음	Y / N
	너무 느리거나 빠르지 않게, 일관된 스피드로 발음	Y / N
	얼버무리지 않고 알아듣기 쉽도록 크고 명료하게 발음	Y / N

ACTUAL
TEST

Actual Test 1 IELTS on paper

- Writing [Academic]
- Writing [General Training]
- Reading [Academic]
- Reading [General Training]
- Listening [Academic / General Training]
- Speaking [Academic / General Training]

Actual Test 2 IELTS on computer

- Listening [Academic / General Training]
- Reading [Academic]
- Reading [General Training]
- Writing [Academic]
- Writing [General Training]
- Speaking [Academic / General Training]

Actual Test 1

IELTS on paper

- 연필과 지우개로 답안 작성 (고사장에 따라 연필과 지우개가 지급되기도 함)
- 국내에서는 2019년 4월부터 Writing - Reading - Listening - Speaking 순서로 시험 진행됨
- Writing 답안 작성시 채점관이 수월하게 읽을 수 있도록 깔끔하게 글씨를 쓸 필요가 있음
- 2020년 1월부터 컴퓨터 시험과 동일하게 Listening 영역은 Section 대신 Part로 구분을 하고, 예제(Example) 풀이 부분 없이 바로 1번 문제부터 시험이 시작됨
- Listening은 방송이 끝나고 답안 작성을 위한 10분의 추가 시간이 주어짐 (Reading은 추가 시간이 주어지지 않음에 유의)
- 시험 시간이 끝나고 감독관이 연필을 내려놓으라고 지시하는데도 답안 작성을 하면 부정행위로 간주되어 시험이 취소될 수 있음

WRITING **[Academic]**

TASK 1

You should spend about 20 minutes on this task.

The pie charts below show the electricity generation by source in China and Spain in 2005 and 2015.

Summarise the information by selecting and reporting the main features, and make comparisons where relevant.

Write at least 150 words.

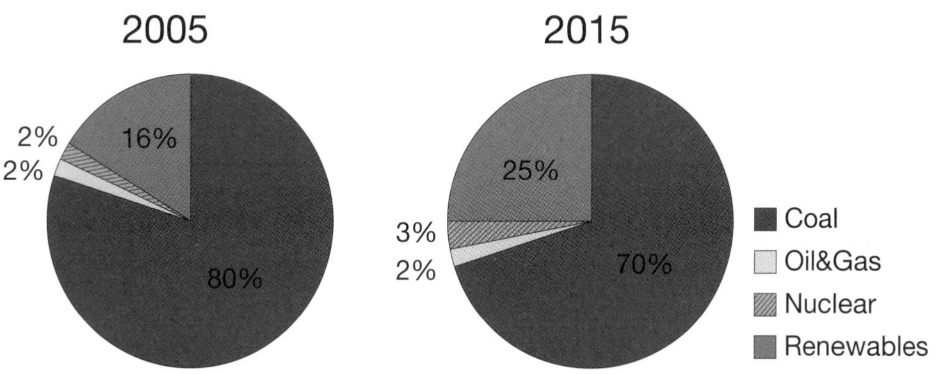

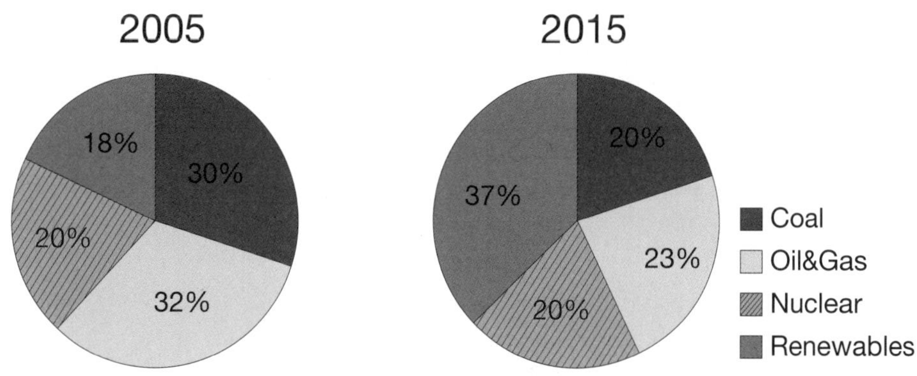

ACTUAL TEST 1

TASK 2

You should spend about 40 minutes on this task.

Write about the following topic:

Once children start school, teachers have more influence on their intellectual and social development than parents.

To what extent do you agree or disagree with this opinion?

Give reasons for your answer and include any relevant examples from your own knowledge or experience.

Write at least 250 words.

TASK 1

You should spend about 20 minutes on this task.

You have heard that your supervisor is retiring from his job. You are planning to buy a present for him and your colleague would like to get a gift with you.

Write a letter to your colleague. In your letter
- ***describe your feelings about your supervisor retiring from his job***
- ***say what item you plan to buy for the supervisor***
- ***suggest when you would meet your colleague to buy a present***

Write at least 150 words.

You do **NOT** need to write any addresses.

Begin your letter as follows:

Dear ....,

TASK 2

You should spend about 40 minutes on this task.

Write about the following topic:

Social media sites have negatively impacted both individuals and society.

To what extent do you agree or disagree with this statement?

Give reasons for your answer and include any relevant examples from your own knowledge or experience.

Write at least 250 words.

READING PASSAGE 1

You should spend about 20 minutes on ***Questions 1-13,*** *which are based on Reading Passage 1 below.*

Isambard Kingdom Brunel: A genius of naval engineering

British engineer Isambard Kingdom Brunel is typically revered for his accomplishments on land, such as the construction of Britain's Great Western Railway and its numerous tunnels and bridges. However, it is important to remember the impressive naval vessels that Brunel designed during his illustrious career, as his contributions to shipbuilding had a profound impact on steamship technology from the late 1830s to the late 1850s. While completing work on the railway in 1836, Brunel jested with his colleagues that he would like to extend the railroad all the way to the United States by establishing a transatlantic steamship company. What began as a humorous notion soon manifested in reality when Brunel drafted a design for his first steamship, which he named the *Great Western*. The design was mocked by some of Brunel's fellow engineers, who proclaimed that the ship was too large for efficient travel. Brunel insisted that, while a vessel's carrying capacity increases as the cube of its dimensions, its water resistance only increases as the square of its dimensions. With this firm belief, Brunel contended that large vessels were more fuel efficient and perfectly adapted to lengthy voyages across oceans.

Once construction of the *Great Western* was complete, it immediately became the longest ship in the world. Although the general structure of the vessel was constructed with wood, Brunel used iron bolts and bars to reinforce the keel of the ship. It was primarily powered by steam, but the ship also boasted four conventional masts and sails in order to save on fuel required for steam power. Brunel himself missed the *Great Western's* maiden voyage from Bristol to New York on 8 April 1838, having been injured in a fire aboard the ship as the vessel was undergoing its final preparations. The fire necessitated a delay to the ship's scheduled launch date, which resulted in the *Great Western* failing to claim the title of the first steam-powered ship to cross the Atlantic. Setting off a full four days before the *Great Western*, the *Sirius* reached America only one day ahead of the *Great Western*, and the vessel had completely run out of fuel. The *Great Western*, on the other hand, reached American shores with a third of its coal supplies unused. The *Great Western* had proven not only that Brunel's assertions had been correct, but also that transatlantic steamship service was a commercially viable business. The Great Western Steamboat Company used the *Great Western* in regular service between Bristol and New York from 1838 to 1846. However, the company later filed for bankruptcy after enduring countless financial hardships, and the *Great Western* was eventually scrapped in 1856 after briefly serving as a troop carrier during the Crimean War.

Brunel's second innovation in naval engineering was the *Great Britain*, a steamship launched in the summer of 1843 to significant fanfare, and lauded as a breakthrough in technology. Having carried out tests aboard the propeller-driven steamship *Archimedes*, Brunel had become certain that propeller-driven ships were vastly superior to those using paddle wheels. As such, he installed a massive six-bladed propeller to power the 98-meter-long *Great Britain*. To this day, naval engineers consider it to be the first truly modern ship, by virtue of its being constructed by metal and utilizing an engine and propellers rather than wind, steam, or paddle wheels.

The *Great Britain* experienced problems during its maiden voyage from Liverpool to New York, despite completing the crossing in an impressive time of just over 14 days. For instance, the vessel proved to be unstable in the choppy waters of the North Atlantic, which resulted in seasickness in a large number of passengers. A few years later, in 1846, a navigational error resulting from an unforeseen interaction between the ship's iron hull and its magnetic compass led to the ship running aground on the coast of Ireland. It took almost one year before the hulking vessel was eventually dragged back into the water and sailed back to its port of origin. In that time, the company operating the ship had folded due to financial issues, and the *Great Britain* was sold, having made only eight Atlantic crossings of the Atlantic. It was later converted into a sailing ship, ferrying immigrants to Australia for a number of years before finding a permanent home in the UK as a tourist attraction.

It was not until the early 1850s that Brunel put his previous disappointments behind him and turned his attention back to naval engineering. He designed the *Great Eastern* to be capable of non-stop travel between London and Sydney and back, and at nearly 700 feet long and accommodating four thousand passengers, it was the largest ship built until the start of the 20th century. Tragically, Brunel, who had been suffering from ill health, died due to a stroke just a few hours after inspecting the unfinished ship in 1859. As was the case with many of Brunel's ambitious endeavors, the ship ran over budget and behind schedule due to financial and technical problems. After making a handful of successful, though unprofitable voyages, the *Great Eastern* was given a more suitable purpose in the late 1860s when it was used to lay the transatlantic telegraph cable that would enable telecommunication between Europe and North America.

Although the *Great Eastern* was sometimes described as a 'white elephant' in its day – that is, something whose cost and maintenance outweigh its value or usefulness – it has since been argued that Brunel's vessels were simply decades ahead of their time, and their perceived failure was only a result of the poor economic conditions of the era. Indeed, Brunel's technological innovations paved the way for the construction of massive, propeller-driven, all-metal passenger ships, and he is now rightly recognized as one of the world's most influential and inspiring engineers.

Questions 1-8

Do the following statements agree with the information given in Reading Passage 1?

In boxes 1-8 on your answer sheet, write

TRUE	*if the statement agrees with the information*
FALSE	*if the statement contradicts the information*
NOT GIVEN	*if there is no information on this*

1 Brunel is primarily well-known for his achievements in shipbuilding.

2 Brunel's first ship design was deemed inefficient by some of his peers.

3 The *Great Western* was the heaviest ship in the world for many years.

4 The *Great Western* was the first steamship to successfully cross the Atlantic.

5 Brunel drew inspiration from the design of the propeller-driven *Archimedes*.

6 The *Great Britain* was left stranded on land for more than a year.

7 Brunel passed away prior to the launch of the *Great Eastern*.

8 The *Great Eastern* experienced mechanical faults during its maiden voyage.

ACTUAL TEST 1

Questions 9-13

Complete the sentences below.

Choose ***ONE WORD ONLY*** *from the passage for each answer.*

Write your answers in boxes 9-13 on your answer sheet.

9 Brunel first conceived of transatlantic steamship travel while working on a ....

10 Due to a ...., the *Great Western's* launch date was pushed back.

11 Brunel concluded that paddle wheels were inferior to .... as a means of powering ships.

12 The *Great Britain* transported .... for a brief time before moving to the UK.

13 The *Great Eastern* played a pivotal role in facilitating .... between America and Europe.

READING PASSAGE 2

*You should spend about 20 minutes on **Questions 14-26**, which are based on Reading Passage 2 below.*

The Water of San Joaquin Valley

In most of the developed world, access to safe drinking water is taken for granted. So why is this not the case in parts of Northern California?

A In Northern California, the provision of readily available, safe water for residences and businesses requires the management of a wide variety of water quality challenges, many of which are proving difficult to overcome. These problems result from both naturally occurring processes and human actions. Many of the contaminants present in the region, such as minor traces of mercury resulting from mining, originate from past industrial activities, but some sources of pollution are more recent and increasingly problematic. In fact, new contaminants are being frequently identified in the wells of the people of Northern California.

B Water quality regulation began in the state in the 1960s and 1970s when the Porter-Cologne Water Quality Control and the Safe Drinking Water Acts were implemented by the government. These acts were designed to prevent companies from polluting local water and ensure that drinking water supplies met appropriate safe standards. Over subsequent decades, numerous laws and regulations have been introduced to control and manage other issues such as pesticide use on farms and the depositing of hazardous substances at waste sites. However, despite these efforts, a critical situation exists in Northern California, where some communities have not enjoyed clean, safe drinking water for several decades.

C In the State of California, the highest rates of drinking water contamination can be found in the San Joaquin Valley. The most prevalent contaminants detected in wells of drinking water and the surrounding groundwater are nitrates. Contamination levels are particularly high in the Central Valley, a region that is home to more than 1.3 million people, many of whom reside in communities that are completely dependent on the contaminated groundwater. Although some contaminants result from naturally occurring processes in the groundwater, the dire circumstances seen in Central Valley are primarily a direct result of intensive agricultural and industrial practices that involved the application of fertilizers and pesticides on a massive scale for a prolonged period of time.

D Nitrate, an inorganic substance used in the manufacture of fertilizers, is by far the most prevalent and problematic contaminant in Central Valley. The hazardous levels found in the Valley have been caused by more than five decades of careless use of industrial fertilizers, as well as the improper storage and disposal of animal waste products. Nitrate concentrations gradually built up in local groundwater and eventually tainted supply wells built to serve both residences and businesses. The high levels of nitrate currently present in the Central Valley have been attributed to the death of infants and the birth of stillborn babies. Thyroid illnesses, reproductive ailments, and some cancers have also been linked to the ingestion of nitrate-rich water.

E The discovery of high levels of nitrate left many communities with no choice but to abandon their supply wells and drill further underground in search of uncontaminated water. Their efforts proved fruitless, as they discovered that deeper pockets of water were contaminated with arsenic. Arsenic naturally occurs in soil and rocks and is also a byproduct of fertilizers, pesticides, and mining activities. In the San Joaquin Valley, it was historically used in pesticides that were applied to orchards and cotton fields. Medical research has shown a connection between arsenic poisoning and reduced mental function in children, and it has also been flagged as a carcinogen and a contributor to Type 2 Diabetes. These deep pockets of groundwater were also found to contain DBCP (dibromochloropropane), a pesticide that was once commonly used on tomatoes and grapes. Although it was banned several years ago, high levels of DBCP persist in San Joaquin Valley water sources, even in the present day.

F People who reside in low-income, underdeveloped communities are disproportionately affected by groundwater contamination in the San Joaquin Valley. Members of such communities are at a disadvantage, as their wells are typically shallower than wells in affluent areas, which leaves them more susceptible to contaminations. In addition, solutions available to ensure safe drinking water tend to be expensive, and people in these communities often do not have the means to take advantage of them. Furthermore, recent studies have shown that disadvantaged communities with nitrate-contaminated groundwater pay almost triple the recommended cost for water. So far, government-led plans for water management and effective land use have failed to adequately decontaminate sources of drinking water in underprivileged communities. One reason that the eradication of contaminants has proven difficult is that most of them do not have a distinct taste or smell, so expensive, continuous water quality testing is the only viable long-term solution.

G Currently, more than 500 rural communities in Northern California are unable to provide safe drinking water, and it is estimated that statewide solutions that would benefit these communities would require a budget increase of between $60 million and $150 million per year. At present, approximately $10 billion is spent annually on water pollution control in California, with most of it allocated for site-specific sources of pollution such as wastewater treatment. The US Environmental Protection Agency (EPA) recently committed to providing additional funding, with a goal of bringing 20 communities into compliance with safety regulations per year over the next ten years. It also plans to work directly with community leaders and provide funding for education and training to San Joaquin Valley residents in an effort to raise awareness and knowledge about preventing water pollution.

Questions 14-17

Complete the summary below.

*Write **ONE WORD ONLY** from the passage for each answer.*

Write your answers in boxes 14-17 on your answer sheet.

The water problem in Northern California

Water sources in Northern California contain a wide variety of **14** .... , such as mercury and nitrates. Starting in the 1960s, the government established two **15** .... in an effort to regulate water quality. The majority of water pollution in Central Valley region is a result of industrial and **16** .... activities.

The US EPA has taken measures to provide additional **17** .... that will be used to educate members of rural communities and bring rural water systems into compliance with safety regulations.

Questions 18-21

*Complete each sentence with the correct ending, **A-F,** below.*

*Write the correct letter, **A-F**, in boxes 18-21 on your answer sheet.*

18 Mercury detected in Northern Californian water sources

19 The dangerous levels of nitrates found in Central Valley water sources

20 Residents in low-income communities

21 Arsenic in deep pockets of groundwater

A may contribute to excessive groundwater pollution.
B may have been caused by poor animal waste management.
C may not be detected by any currently-known methods.
D may lead to mental problems in children.
E may be more at risk of drinking contaminated water.
F may have resulted from mining activities in the past.

ACTUAL TEST 1

Questions 22-26

*Reading Passage 2 has seven paragraphs, **A-G**.*

Which section contains the following information?

*Write the correct letter, **A-G**, in boxes 22-26 on your answer sheet.*

***NB** You may use any letter more than once.*

22 a description of an attempt to locate water further beneath the ground

23 a reason why some people cannot take advantage of safe water solutions

24 an example of a substance that has since been banned from use

25 an overview of laws intended to address the problem of water contamination

26 an outline of a plan to improve knowledge about water pollution

READING PASSAGE 3

*You should spend about 20 minutes on **Questions 27-40**, which are based on Reading Passage 3 below.*

THE EVOLUTION OF MOVIE TRAILERS

Movie trailers have transformed significantly over a period spanning several decades, from their very simplistic origins during Hollywood's Golden Age to the high-technology marketing tools they are today. The evolution of trailers mirrors the artistic and business-oriented transformations that have taken place within the film industry as a whole. In fact, these previews have become an industry unto themselves, with numerous Web sites and awards shows dedicated solely to celebrating the year's best trailers. These days, the announcement of a trailer for a hotly-anticipated movie garners as much attention as the release of the movie itself. However, it wasn't always this way. Early trailers were nothing more than a series of still images, crudely spliced together and attached onto the end of movies. These served their purpose of enticing some cinemagoers to return for coming features, but by today's standards, the previews were barely effective as wide-reaching marketing tools.

During the silent era of cinema, trailers did not evolve much further past the initial concept of showing a title card, a tagline, a handful of film clips, and a cast list. However, the introduction of sound in motion pictures threw open the door on the potential of trailers. The preview for the 1927 Al Jolson musical *The Jazz Singer* was a seven-minute trailer that partly served to announce this revolutionary change in the film industry to the public. In the promo, a man stands in front of a curtain, audibly clears his throat, and states, "Ladies and gentlemen, I am privileged to say a few words to you." The trailer elicited intense excitement among audience members throughout the US, all of whom were amazed by the man's direct address to the audience and the voiceover narration of movie scenes.

The 1930s saw a shift in attitudes toward movie marketing, with the majority of film studios gradually moving toward a more sophisticated format for trailers, and a stark difference in quality is evident when comparing the trailers for 1932's *Tarzan The Ape Man* and 1939's *Gone With The Wind*. It wasn't until the 1940s, however, that many of the characteristic flourishes we now associate with classic Hollywood trailers were introduced. The breathtakingly innovative trailer for John Ford's adaptation of John Steinbeck's novel *The Grapes of Wrath* was heralded as a landmark in the transition between the relatively simple trailers of the 20s and 30s and the technical prowess exhibited by those produced in the 40s. The promo begins by focusing on how Steinbeck's book has completely sold out across the country, with footage of desperate customers demanding a copy to no avail at various bookstores. The lead actor of the movie, Henry Fonda, is not introduced until approximately the two-minute mark when footage of the movie is finally unveiled at the end of the clip. This "peer pressure" approach was tremendously effective, as audience members became convinced of the popularity of the book and did not want to be the ones who missed out on seeing its big screen adaptation.

The majority of trailers produced during the 1940s and 1950s generally emphasized the fame of the lead actors and lavished praise upon the dramatic or heartfelt narratives. In the case of the psychological horror film *Psycho*, released in 1960, director Alfred Hitchcock decided to take a more indirect approach, concerned that a typical trailer would inadvertently reveal one of the film's shocking twists. Hitchcock had already become a recognizable public persona due to his prominent appearances on television, so he decided that he would insert himself into the trailer for the film. The resulting six-and-a-half-minute promo clip features Hitchcock giving viewers a personal tour of the Bates Motel, the setting of the majority of the film's scenes. The director teases viewers by alluding to horrific events that unfolded in the motel – events apparently too disturbing to describe in detail. The trailer proved extremely compelling, with those who viewed it instantly curious to find more about the events that transpired at the Bates Motel, and thus flocking to cinemas in droves.

The creators of movie trailers continued to innovate throughout the 1960s, with two trailers particularly standing out as landmarks in the evolution of the industry. In 1964, director Stanley Kubrick and Pablo Ferro, a Cuban artist, collaborated on sketch-like title cards that featured in Kubrick's film, *Dr. Strangelove.* Kubrick was so impressed with the result that he enlisted Ferro to helm work on the trailer for his movie. Ferro flashed simple black-and-white title cards, each bearing a single word, at a rapid rate, only pausing occasionally to present a brief image or piece of dialogue from the movie. The trailer presents a total of 220 shots in only 97 seconds, having the effect of a camera shutter rapidly opening and closing. Although quick edits became commonplace by the 1990s, the effect was highly unique and memorable to viewers at the time of the trailer's release. In the same year, the trailer for a relatively obscure Western movie, *Gunfighters of Casa Grande*, was notable for being the first to feature a voiceover by Don LaFontaine, who coined the phrase, "In a world...," which would be used in countless trailers to come. At the time of LaFontaine's passing in 2008, it was estimated that he had lent his voice to more than five thousand movie trailers.

In the ensuing decades, movie trailers continued to become increasingly elaborate and artful, with most film studios allocating sizable budgets and production teams for the creation of each trailer. In the 1970s, trailers were frequently aired on television networks, with the trailer for Steven Spielberg's *Jaws* being shown several times per day on all major networks in the weeks leading up to the film's release. These days, as technology continues to evolve, so too does the art of trailer production and the means by which trailers are delivered, and the Internet serves as the most important marketing tool for generating public interest in both movies and the trailers that precede them.

Questions 27-31

Choose the correct letter, ***A, B, C*** *or* ***D.***

Write the correct letter in boxes 27-31 on your answer sheet.

27 In the first paragraph, the writer says that the first trailers ever created

A were nominated for a wide variety of awards.

B were attached to the start of movies as previews.

C were less successful as a promotion method than today's trailers.

D were comprised of a series of short animated film sequences.

28 According to the third paragraph, the trailer for *The Grapes of Wrath*

A drew direct influence from the trailer for *Gone With The Wind*.

B included spoken excerpts from a popular novel of the era.

C was the first movie promo to incorporate sound.

D was more technically advanced than the trailers of the 1930s.

29 What does the writer suggest about Alfred Hitchcock's strategy?

A It showed that Hitchcock expected his film to be a box office success.

B It was an effort to prevent viewers from learning too much about the movie.

C Its main aim was to introduce potential viewers to the film's main character.

D It was not the first time that Hitchcock had taken such an approach.

30 What point is made about the trailer for *Gunfighters of Casa Grande*?

A It featured more film clips than any other trailers of the 1960s.

B It helped a relatively small-scale film to find an international audience.

C It was the first trailer to be directed by Don LaFontaine.

D It marked the beginning of a narrator's successful career.

31 What was notable about the trailer for *Jaws*?

A It was one of the first movie trailers to be screened via the Internet.

B It received the largest production budget ever allocated for a trailer.

C It took advantage of the medium of television to reach a potential audience.

D It introduced several technical innovations that are still used today.

Questions 32-37

Look at the following statements (Questions 32-37) and the list of movie trailers below.

Match each statement with the correct film, ***A, B, C*** *or* ***D.***

Write the correct letter, ***A, B, C*** *or* ***D,*** *in boxes 32-37 on your answer sheet.*

NB *You may use any letter more than once.*

32 It featured the director himself directly communicating with the viewers.

33 It was created by an artist who had previously worked with the film's director.

34 It introduced one of the film's performers near the end of its runtime.

35 It was notable for helping to usher in the era of sound in Hollywood movies.

36 It utilized a fast-visual style that would gain widespread popularity decades later.

37 It highlighted the popularity of the movie's original literary source.

List of Movie Trailers

A	The Jazz Singer
B	The Grapes of Wrath
C	Psycho
D	Dr. Strangelove

Questions 38-40

Do the following statements agree with the information given in Reading Passage 3?

In boxes 38-40 on your answer sheet, write

TRUE	*if the statement agrees with the information*
FALSE	*if the statement contradicts the information*
NOT GIVEN	*if there is no information on this*

38 John Ford was disappointed with the trailer for *The Grapes of Wrath*.

39 Trailers of the 1950s placed emphasis on the popularity of the actors.

40 The 1970s saw a decrease in studio demand for expensive movie trailers.

SECTION 1 *Questions 1-14*

Read the text below and answer Questions 1-7

OUR RECOMMENDED RUCKSACKS

A Blacks Travel Daypack

A rucksack designed for short daytrips that's still surprisingly large enough to accommodate large loads. The innovative fabric is 100 percent water resistant, so you don't need to worry should inclement weather occur.

B Kozlowski Supreme

Boasting a distinctive golden logo, this is the first rucksack to be launched by the renowned fashion designer, Mia Kozlowski. You had better start saving up if you want this bag, as the desirable Kozlowski brand comes at a price.

C Startrek Omega

From one of the most well-established brands in the market, this rucksack is perfect for those who like to be organized during a trip. With six separate zippered pockets and four side pouches, you'll always find a place to store your things.

D Bower Summit

Affordably priced, the Bower range offers a great selection of well-designed rucksacks. They come in a wide variety of neon colors, such as yellow, green, and pink, which means you'll definitely be visible on the mountain when wearing this bag.

E Matterhorn Pro

For those who want something reliable. With a titanium frame and double-stitched material, this bag comes with an impressive 15-year warranty covering manufacturing defects and damage through general usage. It also includes a free water bottle to help you stay hydrated.

F Sunrise Montero

From a relatively new manufacturer, this rucksack features innovative cushioned straps that provide optimal comfort to the wearer. At a fairly spacious 40-liters, this bag is suitable for moderate one- or two-day trips.

G Rader Stride

This 80-liter bag is best suited to serious hikers who plan to be on the mountain for several days at a time. Available in black/grey or black/blue, this stylish rucksack is the top choice for many renowned mountaineers.

Questions 1-7

Look at the seven reviews of suitcases, ***A-G****.*

For which suitcase are the following statements true?

Write the correct letter, ***A-G****, in boxes 1-7 on your answer sheet.*

NB *You may use any letter more than once.*

1 This rucksack comes with a complimentary item.

2 This rucksack contains several additional storage compartments.

3 It is easy to be seen while hiking when wearing this rucksack.

4 This rucksack is for those who are willing to purchase an expensive bag.

5 Belongings carried in this rucksack will not be damaged in heavy rain conditions.

6 The manufacturer guarantees that this rucksack will last a long time.

7 Those who plan to go on long excursions will like this rucksack.

Read the text below and answer Questions 8-14.

Prescott Business School

Three-Day Sales Course

This is an intensive course which is designed for those who have worked in the sales industry for several years and wish to augment their current skillset with advanced, modern techniques. In order to be accepted you should have a proven record in the industry and a desire to improve yourself through hard work.

1st Day: Advanced lessons in delivering on-site sales demonstrations and establishing strong rapport with potential customers. The day ends with each participant submitting a draft sales pitch for a fictional product assigned to them by the instructor.

2nd Day: The day begins with each participant delivering their sales pitch in front of the other participants. Afternoon classes will focus on collaborative selling techniques and include several group activities.

3rd Day: The session focuses on methods for adding value to a product or service in order to make it more attractive. Several noted business leaders will share their insights with participants. The day concludes with a personal evaluation for each attendee.

Application Guidelines

Spaces at this popular workshop are limited, and in an effort to maintain a high standard of participants, acceptance is by interview only. Please note, however, that academic qualifications are irrelevant and do not factor into our decision-making process.

Within one week of receiving your application form and registration fee, we will schedule an interview with you and send you additional information about the workshop via e-mail. For your initial interview, you will need to tell us about your achievements in the sales industry and present some form of evidence of your accomplishments. You will also be asked to describe your current role and your thoughts on the industry in general.

For those currently based abroad who wish to apply, you will be able to participate in your first interview by using our video chat program that can be accessed through our homepage. Those who successfully pass the first interview stage will be invited to a second and final session which must be attended in person at our campus. We will provide temporary free parking permits to anyone attending the second session.

Questions 8-14

Do the following statements agree with the information given in the text?

In boxes 8-14 on your answer sheet, write

TRUE *if the statement agrees with the information*

FALSE *if the statement contradicts the information*

NOT GIVEN *if there is no information on this*

8 People can sign up for the three-day course without any previous sales experience.

9 Participants will perform a sales pitch in front of other workshop members at the end of the first day.

10 Instructors will use successful companies as case studies on the second day.

11 Participants will receive feedback from instructors on the last day of the workshop.

12 During their first interview session, applicants will be asked about their academic qualifications.

13 Prescott Business School will send participants driving directions after scheduling an interview.

14 Overseas applicants can take part in the first interview session via a website.

SECTION 2 *Questions 15-27*

Read the text below and answer Questions 15-20.

Decontamination and clearance instructions for laboratories

This Laboratory Decontamination and Clearance Guide is designed for laboratories that plan to relocate to new premises or completely cease operations. This information will help you with your transition and ensure that you conform to all state health and safety regulations.

There are several things you must do prior to the clearance activities outlined below. First and foremost, you must notify the Environmental Safety Association (ESA) of your intent to close or transfer the laboratory. When doing so, you should send the ESA a timeline of activities regarding the movement and disposal of laboratory equipment and chemicals. Next, you must arrange a waste pickup service for all chemicals, sharp objects, and general waste, and an appropriate transportation service for any chemicals and equipment that will be moved to a new location.

Clearance activities can be performed either by in-house laboratory employees or an ESA-approved company. Begin with the decontamination of all laboratory equipment that has been used in conjunction with radioactive, chemical, or biological materials, regardless of whether the equipment will be moved or left in place. Use the soap solution detailed in your laboratory manual, followed by a water rinse. Remove tape and non-slip mats from all laboratory benches and wash all horizontal surfaces as well as the fronts and sides of cabinets with the same soap solution as above. Wash these surfaces starting with the highest areas in the room and proceeding to the lowest. Any surfaces that may potentially be contaminated should be treated with disinfectant. Place all chemicals and cultures in leak-proof containers and arrange them in single layers in heavy-duty cardboard boxes. Finally, notify the ESA to inform them that the clearance activities are complete.

ESA agents will arrive on-site to check chemical inventories and perform a full clearance inspection in order to ensure that the laboratory is completely free from contamination. They will also perform checks for specific environmental hazards, including faulty electrical wiring or mold. If the results from the clearance inspection fail to meet the standards set by the ESA, additional cleaning must be carried out by the laboratory staff or by an ESA-approved contractor, at the laboratory supervisor's expense.

Questions 15-20

Complete the flowchart below.

*Choose **NO MORE THAN TWO WORDS** from the text for each answer.*

Write your answers in boxes 15-20 on your answer sheet.

Procedure for laboratory relocation or closure

Pre-clearance activities

Inform the Environmental Safety Association (ESA) of your intention to move or close the lab. Provide them with a **15** .... detailing activities related to the transfer of lab equipment and materials.

Clearance activities

All laboratory equipment that has come into contact with biological or chemical substances must undergo **16** ....

Equipment and laboratory surfaces must be washed using a **17** .... and then rinsed.

Put all chemicals in **18** .... arranged in single layers in cardboard boxes.

ESA activities

After you inform the ESA of the completion of clearance activities, an ESA inspection team will visit the laboratory. The team will review your **19** .... of chemicals and inspect the laboratory. The team will also determine whether any other potential **20** .... are present.

Follow-up activities

If there is a problem with the inspection, the laboratory supervisor will be told to clean the premises again, or pay to have an ESA-approved company carry out the work.

Read the text below and answer Questions 21-27.

Appendix: Settling staff disputes in the workplace

This appendix details the causes of disputes between employees and offers advice about how employers can take measures to reduce and resolve workplace conflict.

Employers should be aware that there are many different potential reasons for conflict between workers, and each reason may require a different approach. Causes of conflict can range from clashes of personality to communication breakdowns between staff and management. Almost all cases result in lower productivity in the workplace and therefore should be addressed as soon as they arise to prevent serious consequences such as project failures. The most common reasons for disputes are behaviours that coworkers find irritating, a feeling that needs are not being met and adequate resources are not being provided, differences over work methods, competition between highly-motivated workers, and unclarified workplace roles, such as cases in which a nonsupervisory worker is asked to supervise other employees.

Employers can mitigate the frequency and severity of workplace conflict by creating a work environment designed to preclude conflict wherever possible, and by dealing with any disputes that do arise promptly and fairly. The most important thing is to ensure that work policies are clear, and that the reasoning behind dispute mediation decisions is consistent from one case to the next. When attempting to settle a conflict, an employer should always focus on the actions of the employees, and the consequences of those actions, rather than the personalities of the individuals involved. In addition, the HR department should develop and implement conflict resolution training workshops that all managers should regularly attend. In extreme cases where conflict escalates to the point of physical violence, theft, or threatening behaviour, employers should consider notifying the police.

Questions 21-27

Complete the notes below.

Choose ***ONE WORD ONLY*** *from the text for each answer.*

Write your answers in boxes 21-27 on your answer sheet.

Staff disputes in the workplace

Disputes: Causes and Effects

- each type of conflict requires a specific **21** .... in order to reach a resolution
- disputes can arise when **22** .... between employees and supervisors is poor
- unresolved conflict can lead to a decrease in **23** .... and even more significant consequences
- conflict can occur when employees' **24** .... in the workplace are not clearly defined

Recommended Actions

- make sure that all **25** .... are clearly outlined for employees
- refrain from focusing on the **26** .... of employees when resolving disputes
- have the HR department establish **27** .... that will help managers with conflict resolution

SECTION 3 *Questions 28-40*

Questions 28-36

*The text has nine paragraphs, **A-I**.*

Choose the correct heading for each paragraph from the list of headings below.

*Write the correct number, **i-xi**, in boxes 28-36 on your answer sheet.*

List of Headings	
i	An error on the bidding floor
ii	The quality assurance process
iii	Commonly traded seafood products
iv	The adoption of an electronic system
v	Education and online trading
vi	A market of incredible size and scope
vii	A method for trading flowers
viii	An investment for the future
ix	Overcoming financial difficulties
x	An introduction to our guide
xi	How to check the freshness of seafood

28 Paragraph **A**

29 Paragraph **B**

30 Paragraph **C**

31 Paragraph **D**

32 Paragraph **E**

33 Paragraph **F**

34 Paragraph **G**

35 Paragraph **H**

36 Paragraph **I**

A Trip to Sydney Fish Market

A In the entire Southern Hemisphere, no other fish market comes close to the size and scale of Sydney Fish Market. Every year, the market trades almost 15,000 tonnes of seafood comprised of more than 500 different sustainable species. Around 70 employees are on-site to ensure the smooth operation of the wholesale auction and Sydney Seafood School, which is promoted as an institution of seafood excellence.

B If you hope to see the fishermen bringing in their fresh catches, you have to visit the market very early in the morning. Daily tours begin at 6.30 a.m., so my friends and I are up bright and early to meet our guide, Henry, at a restaurant just outside the market entrance. Henry starts off by briefing us on a few facts regarding the market. We are impressed to hear that not only is it the largest of its type in the Southern Hemisphere, but it is also considered the second most diverse market in the world after Tokyo's famous Tsukiji Market.

C Henry leads us onto the auction floor, where buyers are seated in rows, eyes fixated on three large monitors. We hear sounds of disappointment coming from a few of the buyers following a completed sale. Henry guesses that an inexperienced bidder possibly paid over the odds for the sale, inadvertently raising the average sale price for other sales in that category. We are all fascinated by the rapid pace and high energy on the auction floor, and urge Henry to explain it to us.

D According to Henry, the market implemented a digital auction system in 1989, marking a significant landmark in the evolution of seafood sales. Auction prices are set at least $3 above the expected market price per kilo, and rows of buyers type feverishly on keyboards, making numerous sales in quick succession. Henry points out that the system is much more efficient than the previous traditional voice auction, with barely any stock going unsold on any given day.

E The system draws direct inspiration from a 'reverse auction' system that has been used for more than a century to buy and sell tulips in flower markets in the Netherlands. In 2004, the market installed advanced digital video projectors to improve the visibility and presentation of the auction clocks. Up to 200 buyers will watch these screens each day, and this reverse auction system has gained a deserved reputation as the fastest and most efficient method of trading seafood.

F On the day of our visit, there are 60 tonnes of fish stacked or laid out on the auction floor, delivered in the early morning by more than 1,000 suppliers based throughout the Asia-Pacific region. As early as 2 a.m., products begin arriving and a team of quality assurance inspectors grade them based on their size, weight, and expected shelf life. Henry gives each of us a high-visibility jacket to put on before we step out onto the auction floor ourselves to get a closer look at the wide variety of fish and shellfish.

G Henry shows us a B+-grade lobster caught hours earlier, and informs us that when buying shellfish, it is crucial to check that the shells are strong as it indicates that the creature is in good health and will yield higher quality meat. As instructed by Henry, we then smell the gills of a massive fish, almost as long as a human, to test for freshness. To our surprise, he also tells us that the freshness of seafood is mainly related to the way it has been treated since being caught, and not necessarily the length of time that has passed since it was caught.

H We finish our tour with a visit to the marketplace, where we see all manner of seafood available for purchase, and then a look at the prestigious Sydney Seafood School. The school was established in 1989 and now attracts over 10,000 students per year, due in part to its impressive list of guest chefs and speakers from the culinary world. We also have a chance to check out the innovative new online-based seafood trading system that the fish market's technology team launched in 2001. Operating alongside the on-site Dutch auction, the Web-based trading facility takes fish trading to a whole new level by reaching a wider range of buyers.

I Before we leave the market, Henry tells us about some of the modifications planned for the building. He first notes that the existing market is one of the most popular tourist attractions in Sydney, with around two million people taking a tour of the premises each year. Not only does the market generate approximately $20 million annually for the local economy, but it also generates almost $70 million through tourist spending. With this in mind, the local government has allocated $250 million to renovate the old space and create a modernized destination with a focus on retail and tourism. Henry shows us the proposed blueprint and explains how the building will integrate various attractive features while still housing a bustling auction floor and market. One thing is for sure: we all agreed that we would love to return for another tour once modifications are complete!

Questions 37-40

Complete the summary below.

Choose ***ONE WORD ONLY*** *from the text for each answer.*

Write your answers in boxes 37-40 on your answer sheet.

Sydney Fish Market's auction system

In 1989, Sydney Fish Market introduced a new auction system that was considered a **37** .... in the development of seafood trading. The system is a significant improvement over the old **38** .... auction method. It was modelled on a system used to trade **39** .... in flower markets in the Netherlands. **40** .... were later installed on the auction floor in order to improve the visibility of the clocks.

LISTENING **[Academic / General Training]**

PART 1 *Questions 1-10*

Complete the table below.

Write ***ONE WORD AND/OR A NUMBER*** *for each answer.*

Summer Festival Programmes

Place	Main Focus	Additional Details
Marina Art Institute	making **1** .... and learning about ancient tools and weapons	• free admission • also includes complimentary **2** .... on site • participants receive a **3** .... % discount in a gift store
Digby Garden Centre	planting and **4** .... flowers	• participants are given a selection of **5** .... and a vase • a **6** .... is available at 9 am and noon
7 .... Music Hall	learning how to **8** .... in a variety of styles	• located opposite the **9** .... • appropriate **10** .... is recommended

PART 2 *Questions 11-20*

Questions 11-13

*Choose the correct letter, **A**, **B** or **C**.*

Orientation Day at Faraday Farm

11 What is Faraday Farm most well-known for?

A The diversity of its livestock

B The efficiency of its farming methods

C The freshness of its produce

12 According to the speaker, previous temporary workers have complained about

A low hourly rates.

B unsafe working conditions.

C access to public transport.

13 The orientation will finish earlier than scheduled because

A important tasks need to be performed.

B inclement weather is expected.

C the speaker has an appointment.

Questions 14-20

Label the map below.

*Write the correct letter **A-I**, next to Questions 14-20.*

Faraday Farm Layout

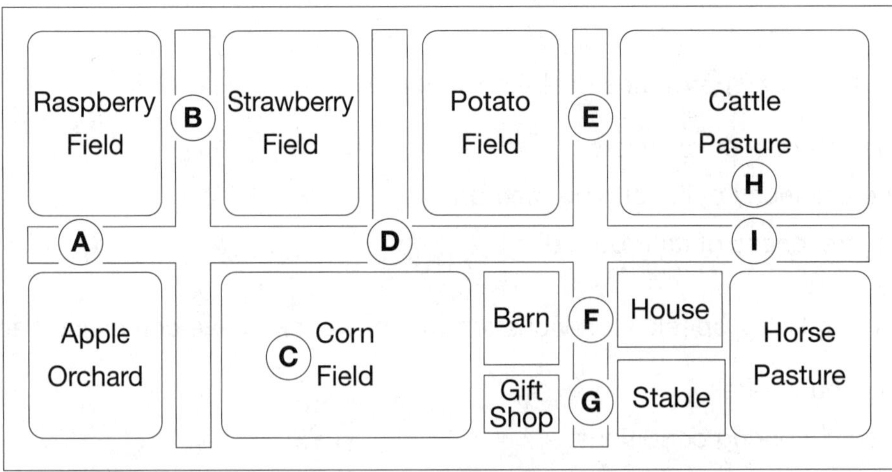

14 Changing footwear ....

15 Quality testing ....

16 Meeting coworkers ....

17 Machinery introduction ....

18 Lunch break ....

19 Soil maintenance talk ....

20 Feeding animals ....

PART 3 *Questions 21-30*

Questions 21-25

Choose the correct letter, ***A, B*** *or* ***C.***

21 Why is Kevin interested in investigating the psychology of marketing?

A He completed a module in it last year.

B He thinks it will be a straightforward topic.

C He thinks it will help him with future coursework.

22 Kevin and Sara agree that one benefit of their study topic is that it involves

A primarily Internet-based research.

B direct interaction with consumers.

C collaboration with local businesses.

23 What do they decide to check with their course leader?

A whether a deadline can be extended

B whether a topic is acceptable

C whether project allowance will be provided

24 Sara recommends reserving a copy of Hopper's book on visual marketing because

A many students have requested to borrow it.

B there are not many copies available.

C it has won several industry awards.

25 What does Kevin say about Professor Bush's lecture notes?

A They can be obtained upon request.

B They detail failed marketing strategies.

C They include information relevant to the study.

Questions 26-30

Complete the flowchart below.

Choose ***FIVE*** *answers from the box and write the correct letter,* ***A-H****, next to Questions 26-30.*

A incentives	**B** payments	**C** images	**D** graph
E database	**F** location	**G** stores	**H** survey

Main Research Steps

Gather relevant **26** .... of specific products from the Internet

⬇

Prepare a concise **27** .... for participants in the study

⬇

Select a suitable **28** .... in order to interact with a diverse range of people

⬇

Provide **29** .... to encourage participation in the study

⬇

Compile all data gathered during the study

⬇

Present findings in a **30** .... based on demographic variables

PART 4 *Questions 31-40*

Complete the notes below.

Write ***ONE WORD ONLY*** *for each answer.*

The Importance of Sustainable Transport

Introduction

— Sustainable transport is a key component of sustainable development, and it offers three types of benefits: environmental, social and **31** ....

The LEDS GP Report

— The Low Emission Development Strategies Global Partnership (LEDS GP) report states that sustainable transport can create more **32** .... and improve commuter safety.

— The report lists three main goals:

- Expand public transportation coverage and utilise new **33** .... to make systems more dependable
- Encourage biking and walking by providing bike share stations, improving pedestrian routes and limiting **34** .... in downtown areas
- Increase costs associated with **35** .... ownership and use funds collected to improve public transit

New developments and future prospects

— Much current research focuses on modifying motor vehicles and the way we drive them, including:

- Reducing the **36** .... of vehicles
- Reducing the friction of tires
- Developing sustainable driving methods

— Until new clean sources of electricity are established, production of **37** .... in electric cars will be similar to that of petrol cars.

— Researchers in Korea unveiled new technology which allows a vehicle's **38** .... to be charged even during transit.

— Successful developments have also been made in hybrid vehicles, which feature a combination of two types of **39** ....

— However, **40** .... are expected to be costly in the long-term and have little impact on reducing greenhouse gas emissions.

SPEAKING **[Academic / General Training]**

Part 1

[Your Life]
Let's talk about what you do.
Do you work or are you a student?

[If you work]
What kind of job do you do?
What do you particularly like about your job?

[If you are a student]
What subject are you studying?
Why did you want to study that subject?

[Hometown or city]
Let's go on to talk about your hometown or city.
What is the most interesting part of your town or city? [Why?]
Has your hometown changed in any way in your lifetime? [How?]
Do you think your town is a good place for young people to live? [Why/Why not?]

Part 2

Describe the first mobile phone that you had.
You should say:
  when it was that you had your own mobile phone
  why you had your own phone
  what features the mobile phone had
and explain how this phone made changes in your life.

Rounding-off Question:
In general, how often do you think people change their mobile phone?

Part 3

[Mobile phones and Smartphones]
Should children have their own mobile phone?
What would the world be like without mobile phones?
Do you think that the way people use smartphones may change in the future?

[Technology and Work]
What kinds of machines are used for office work nowadays?
Do you think technology has brought more stress than benefits to employees? [Why/Why not?]

MEMO

Actual Test 2

IELTS on computer

- Listening - Reading - Writing 순서로 본 시험이 진행되며, Speaking은 본 시험 전 또는 후에 진행됨
- Section(리딩 제너럴), Passage(리딩 아카데믹), Task(라이팅) 대신 Part란 용어로 통일
- CTRL+C(복사), CTRL+V(붙이기), CTRL+Z(실행취소) 사용 가능
- 표시하고 싶은 글씨를 마우스로 드래그한 후 오른쪽 클릭을 하면 하이라이트 또는 메모 가능
- Listening의 경우 개인 Headset을 이용하여 청취하고 Part 1이 Example(예제) 없이 바로 1번부터 시험 시작하며, Part 4 끝나고 10분 대신 2분 답안 정리 시간 주어짐
- 컴퓨터 시험은 시간이 다 되면 자동으로 시험 화면이 전환되므로, 종이 시험과 달리 시험 종료 후 답안 작성할 여지가 전혀 없음
- Speaking은 시험장에 따라 실제 면접 또는 화상(Video-call)으로 진행

※ Actual Test 2는 실제 컴퓨터 화면을 최대한 지면에 구현한 모의고사이기에 일반 종이 모의고사와 레이아웃이 다름을 알려드립니다.

XXXXX-1234 29 minutes left Settings Help Hide

PART 1

Listen and answer questions **1-10**.

Complete the notes. Write **ONE WORD AND/OR A NUMBER** in each gap.

Edward's Property Advice

About Edward:

- Purchased his house in 2017.
- Come across his house on a [1].
- Wanted to find a house with at least two [2].
- Houses viewed: oldest one was built in [3].
- Thinks he should have taken a mortgage term of [4] years.

Benefits of searching for property online:

- Lots of property websites that provide extensive, diverse ranges of properties.
- Having a certified listing on a website boosts a seller's [5].
- New technology allows prospective buyers to take a virtual tour.
- Property websites show the nearest [6] to a property.
- Websites also estimate the cost of [7] per month.

Advice for property viewing:

- Inspect [8]
- Take several [9]
- Speak with [10]

PART 1 1 2 3 4 5 6 7 8 9 10 PART 2 11 12 13 14 15 16 17 18 19 20
Review PART 3 21 22 23 24 25 26 27 28 29 30 PART 4 31 32 33 34 35 36 37 38 39 40

ACTUAL TEST 2

XXXXX-1234 22 minutes left

PART 2

Listen and answer questions **11-20**.

Questions 11-16

Choose the correct answer.

The Watersports Centre

11 Louise mentions that when kayaking, the visitors are allowed to

A ○ stop to feed local wildlife.

B ○ take pictures of the beautiful scenery.

C ○ move away from the regular routes.

13 What does Louise say about the archery competition?

A ○ No safety gear is required.

B ○ It will be held inside the centre.

C ○ The winner will receive a prize.

15 The campground facilities are free except for

A ○ laundry facilities.

B ○ cooking facilities.

C ○ entertainment facilities.

Questions 17-20

What information does Louise give about kayaking on each of the following river routes?

Choose the correct answer and move it into the gap.

Kayak routes

Brody River	17
East River	18
White River	19
Merry River	20

PART 1 1 2 3 4 5 6 7 8 9 10 PART 2 11 12 13 14 15 16 17 18 19 20

Review PART 4 31 32 33 34 35 36 37 38 39 40

12 What does Louise tell the group about this morning's hiking trip?
A ○ The group will stop briefly for refreshments.
B ○ Footwear is available for those who need it.
C ○ Group members can choose a different activity.

14 Regarding the waterskiing lesson, Louise says that
A ○ participants must be above a certain age.
B ○ swimming ability is not important.
C ○ an extra fee will be requested.

16 If there is heavy rain while the visitors are in their tents, they should
A ○ move to a nearby dormitory.
B ○ remain in the tent until morning.
C ○ contact one of the centre's employees.

Information

A It passes by a wildlife zone.
B It is suitable for beginners.
C It requires additional equipment.
D It contains several rare species of fish.
E It requires road transportation.
F It has some unsafe sections.

PART 3 21 22 23 24 25 26 27 28 29 30

ACTUAL TEST 2

XXXXX-1234 15 minutes left

PART 3

Listen and answer questions **21-30**.

Questions 21-26

Choose the correct answer.

Utilising Music in Advertising

21 What was Nick's attitude to music in advertisements before this project?

A ○ He thought it was an integral factor.
B ○ He didn't give it much consideration.
C ○ He found most of it irritating.

23 When discussing the music in a sandwich company's advertisement, Nick agrees with Susan that

A ○ it misleads consumers.
B ○ it incorporates well-known melodies.
C ○ it is indicative of a new trend.

25 What surprised both students about the advertisement made by the electronics manufacturer?

A ○ Its music was nominated for several industry awards.
B ○ Its music directly referenced the products being advertised.
C ○ Its music was written exclusively for the advertisement.

Questions 27 and 28

Choose **TWO** correct answers.

Which **TWO** things surprised the students about the Peterson study on music in advertising?

A ○ the criticism it received from experts
B ○ its similarity to other studies
C ○ the duration of the research involved
D ○ the narrow age range of participants
E ○ the wide range of musical genres it covered

PART 1 1 2 3 4 5 6 7 8 9 10 PART 2 11 12 13 14 15 16 17 18 19 20
Review PART 4 31 32 33 34 35 36 37 38 39 40

22 Susan says that before doing this project,
A ○ she was unaware of how advertisement music influenced her.
B ○ she generally enjoyed all music in advertisements.
C ○ she often purchased products endorsed by celebrities.

24 Nick prefers jingles to full-length songs in advertising because they are
A ○ more memorable.
B ○ more melodic.
C ○ more relevant.

26 In what way do the students think music in advertising will change in the future?
A ○ It will feature more well-known artists.
B ○ It will be governed by stricter regulations.
C ○ It will be more psychologically manipulative.

Questions 29 and 30

Choose **TWO** correct answers.

What were **TWO** of the findings presented in the Peterson study?

A ○ Acoustic guitars make people feel excited.
B ○ Vocal music is likely to make people feel relaxed.
C ○ A correlation exists between string music and happiness.
D ○ Percussion makes people feel motivated.
E ○ Brass instruments arouse negative emotions.

XXXXX-1234 8 minutes left

PART 4

Listen and answer questions **31-40**.

Complete the notes. Write **ONE WORD ONLY** for each answer.

The History of Cotton

Cotton in The Old World

- Ancient civilisations used cotton to produce [31] that had several uses.
- 5th BCE: Herodotus wrote that cotton was better than [32] in terms of both its appearance and feel.
- Alexander the Great's soldiers preferred [33] manufactured from cotton.

Cotton in the Middle Ages

- Cotton became popular throughout many parts of the world.
- 6th CE: Equipment used to produce cotton in India was introduced to other countries by [34].
- 16th CE: Dual-roller gins became commonplace and were sometimes powered by [35].

Cotton Spreads Throughout Europe

- Various conquests facilitated the spread of cotton production throughout Europe.
- 14th CE: The spinning wheel improved the European cotton industry due to its high [36].
- Cities such as Venice and Antwerp emerged as important [37] for cotton trading.
- As trade with India increased, secretive [38] of cotton processing were told to European traders.
- The European middle class turned to cotton when people became more interested in [39] and new fashion.

The American Cotton Industry

- 19th CE: The US had become the largest producer of cotton in the world.
- Consequently, increased demand for cotton led to a rise in [40], particularly in cotton-rich southern states.

PART 1 1 2 3 4 5 6 7 8 9 10 PART 2 11 12 13 14 15 16 17 18 19 20

Review PART 4 31 32 33 34 35 36 37 38 39 40

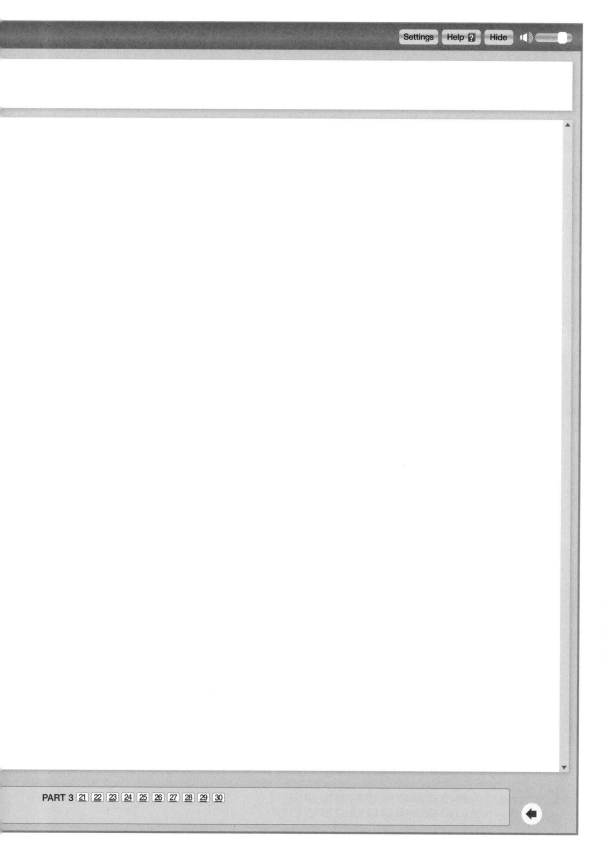

ACTUAL TEST 2

XXXXX-1234

PART 1

Read the text below and answer questions **1-13**.

Bamboo

Bamboo is a fast-growing, versatile, flowering plant that is found throughout many regions of the world. With up to a thirty percent annual increase in biomass, compared to only five percent for trees, bamboo's rate of biomass generation is unmatched by any other plants. As such, it gives rise to larger yields of raw material, which is utilized extensively for a wide variety of functions. Bamboo shoots are called culms, and their strength and diversity of size historically made them ideal for use in construction. To this day, bamboo culms are laminated, cut into sheets, and laid as flooring in China and Japan. As civilizations evolved, the true versatility of bamboo was gradually uncovered, and all parts of the plant are now utilized in a growing range of industries.

In Asian medicine, particularly Chinese medicine, the leaves of the bamboo plant are commonly crushed and added as an active ingredient in medicinal teas. These teas are consumed by millions of people who wish to lose weight while cleansing their body. Bamboo leaves contain relatively high levels of protein and minerals such as riboflavin, thiamine, and iron, which are known for their health benefits. An additional advantage of medications containing crushed bamboo leaves is that they suppress allergies and promote blood circulation. Aside from their use in medicine, the leaves are also pressed flat and used to wrap steamed dumplings in several Asian cultures.

Bamboo's versatility is most evident in its myriad uses within the culinary field. The plant's sap can be extracted from the culms and then fermented to produce numerous beverages, both alcoholic and non-alcoholic. The spongy white tissue, called the pith, which lines the interior of the culms, is often pickled to create a condiment that is served alongside many dishes throughout Asia. The whole culms themselves are the most frequently used part of the plant. When bamboo culms are utilized in cooking, they are first placed in boiling water in order to remove any toxins and render them safe for consumption. In some cultures, the culms of larger bamboo are not only used as an ingredient, but also as a means to cook certain foods. Soups are often boiled in the hollowed bamboo culms directly over a flame. It is said that food prepared in such a manner has a subtle, unique taste. In addition to their association with cooking, bamboo culms are burned in ovens – a process called pyrolysis – to produce bamboo charcoal, a fuel that is still in common usage in China and Japan. As an alternative fuel, bamboo benefits the environment by reducing pollutant residue.

PART 1 1 2 3 4 5 6 7 8 9 10 11 12 13

Review PART 3 27 28 29 30 31 32 33 34 35 36 37 38 39 40

Settings Help Hide

Questions 1-7

Complete the table. Write **ONE WORD ONLY** from the text in each gap.

BAMBOO PREPARATION & USES		
Part	**Preparation Method**	**Uses**
Leaves	Crushed	Used in medications to promote weight loss and inhibit [1]
	Flattened	Used as wrappers for [2]
Sap	Fermented	Used to make a wide variety of [3]
Culms	Pickled	The pith is pickled to produce a [4]
	Boiled	Culms are boiled to remove [5], before being used as ingredients
	Hollowed	Empty culms are used for boiling [6] throughout Asia
	Burned	Undergo pyrolysis to produce charcoal used for a [7]

PART 2 14 15 16 17 18 19 20 21 22 23 24 25 26

In order to reap the full benefits of strong, healthy bamboo, the plant must be cultivated and harvested under very precise conditions. Bamboo crops grow optimally in warm temperate climates. Since the bamboo plant has thin roots, care must be taken to protect it from strong winds, which can pull plants out of the soil in extreme circumstances. Another reason that regions of high wind are undesirable for bamboo crops is that strong gusts can damage the tips of bamboo leaves.

When it comes to soil types, bamboo can be grown and cultivated on a wide variety of soils, as long as they are free from excess rocks and roots of other plants. The optimal soil conditions for cultivating bamboo are well-drained sandy soil with a pH range of around 5.5. In order to ensure high quality and yield, animal manure and fertilizers are typically applied to bamboo crops. Bamboo plants have voracious appetites, and fertilizers prevent the soil from being washed out of nutrients too quickly. Bamboo flourishes well when fertilizers containing potassium and nitrogen are used, but it is also essential to provide other minerals and nutrients by adding manure and organic compost to the soil.

Harvesting of bamboo is carried out based on three cycles: life cycle, annual cycle, and daily cycle. Each culm of bamboo experiences a life cycle of 5 to 7 years, and they are generally allowed to reach this level of maturity before being harvested. If any of the older culms in a crop show signs of decay, they will be cut down and removed to ensure adequate light and resources for the healthy culms. The annual cycle pertains to the season in which bamboo is harvested. As bamboo predominantly grows during the wet season, disturbing the culms at this time could potentially disrupt growth and damage the crop. Likewise, right before the wet season presents a risk of damaging brand-new culms that have recently sprouted. As a result, the optimal time to harvest bamboo is three or four months before the wet season begins. The final consideration when harvesting bamboo is the daily cycle. Most farmers harvest bamboo crops at dawn or dusk, as this is the time of day when photosynthesis occurs at its slowest rate, resulting in lower levels of sugar in the sap.

PART 1 1 2 3 4 5 6 7 8 9 10 11 12 13

Review PART 3 27 28 29 30 31 32 33 34 35 36 37 38 39 40

Questions 8-13

Choose **TRUE** if the statement agrees with the information given in the text, choose **FALSE** if the statement contradicts the information, or choose **NOT GIVEN** if there is no information on this.

8 Bamboo has naturally evolved to withstand strong winds.

○ TRUE
○ FALSE
○ NOT GIVEN

9 A soil pH of 5.5 is desirable for optimal growth of bamboo.

○ TRUE
○ FALSE
○ NOT GIVEN

10 The roots of the bamboo plant are highly susceptible to damage.

○ TRUE
○ FALSE
○ NOT GIVEN

11 Some chemical fertilizers are more important than organic compost when growing bamboo.

○ TRUE
○ FALSE
○ NOT GIVEN

12 Most bamboo culms are harvested near the end of their life cycle.

○ TRUE
○ FALSE
○ NOT GIVEN

13 Sugar levels of bamboo sap are at their highest during dawn and dusk.

○ TRUE
○ FALSE
○ NOT GIVEN

PART 2 14 15 16 17 18 19 20 21 22 23 24 25 26

ACTUAL TEST 2

PART 2

Read the text below and answer questions **14-20**.

Fingerprint Identification

A Although ancient civilizations most likely did not fully comprehend that fingerprints could accurately identify individuals, there is historical evidence of them being used for broad identification purposes. For instance, records dating back to China's Qin Dynasty indicate that investigators sometimes took fingerprints as evidence from crime scenes, and around 300 CE, fingerprints were being presented during criminal trials in China. The Chinese historian Kia Kung-Yen even suggested in the year 650 that the comparison of fingerprints could be used as a valid method of identity verification.

B It was not until the mid-17th century that scientific interest in fingerprints began to truly grow, particularly throughout Europe. In 1665, the research notes of Italian physician Marcello Malpighi described patterns of ridges that exist on the fingertips. Approximately two decades later, Malpighi's contemporary, the English botanist Nehemiah Grew, published the first scientific paper to detail the ridge structure of the skin covering the palms and fingers. However, even then, it was not known that fingerprints were unique to each individual. This hypothesis was not officially put forward until 1788 when the German anatomist Johann Christoph Andreas Mayer declared that no two people can possibly share the same fingerprint patterns.

C In 1823, the Czech scientist Jan Purkinje expanded on Mayer's work, publishing a thesis that described numerous distinct fingerprint patterns, but he did not believe the patterns could be used to credibly identify individuals. When the British politician Lord William Russell was murdered in 1840, a doctor named Robert Blake Overton recommended that the Metropolitan Police check the crime scene and victim for fingerprints. Although the police did follow Overton's advice, fingerprints did not play a role in the identification of the murderer, and fingerprint collection and analysis would not become a routine police practice for several decades.

D Several important landmarks in the evolution of fingerprint identification occurred in the second half of the 19th century. In 1863, a chemistry professor based at Val-de-Grâce military hospital in Paris made a breakthrough in the detection of fingerprints on paper and other smooth surfaces. Professor Paul-Jean Coulier discovered that the presence of iodine fumes caused fingerprints to be revealed in great detail. Later, in 1877, Sir William James Herschel instituted the use of fingerprints on contracts and property deeds that were prepared in Calcutta and the surrounding towns. This practice helped to prevent conflict and doubts over the authenticity of

PART 1 1 2 3 4 5 6 7 8 9 10 11 12 13
Review PART 3 27 28 29 30 31 32 33 34 35 36 37 38 39 40

Questions 14-17

The text has six paragraphs (**A-F**). Which paragraph contains the following information?

	A	B	C	D	E	F
14 reference to fingerprints to complement written verification						
15 mention of the first hypothesis to state that all fingerprints are unique						
16 mention of a trial that resulted in a successful conviction based on fingerprint evidence						
17 reference to a method for detecting fingerprints using a chemical						

Questions 18-20

Look at the following research findings (Questions 18-20) and the list of researchers below.
Match each accomplishment with the correct researcher, **A-F**.

18 Published the first paper to identify ridges on the hands and fingertips

19 First person to recommend fingerprint identification to the Metropolitan Police

20 Devised a model of fingerprint analysis based on another researcher's concepts

List of Researchers

A Marcello Malpighi
B Nehemiah Grew
C Jan Purkinje
D Robert Blake Overton
E Dr. Henry Faulds
F Francis Galton

PART 2 14 15 16 17 18 19 20 21 22 23 24 25 26

signatures. By registering the fingerprints of the elderly, he also prevented false financial claims from non-beneficiaries after an individual had passed away.

E With research into fingerprint detection and analysis continuing at a rapid pace, attention began to shift toward the need for a comprehensive classification and storage system. In 1880, Dr. Henry Faulds, a Scottish surgeon based in Japan, published a paper in the well-respected scientific journal *Nature*. In his paper, he emphasized the high accuracy of fingerprint identification and put forward a technique that could be used to record fingerprints with ink. Upon returning to the United Kingdom, Faulds met with officials from the Metropolitan Police, hoping that they would embrace and adopt his concept, but was disappointed when it was rejected at the time. Still believing in the effectiveness of his method, he described it in a letter he sent to Charles Darwin. Unfortunately, due to waning health, Darwin was unable to assist Faulds with the further improvement of the method, and instead passed on the information to his cousin, a young anthropologist named Francis Galton. Galton was immediately impressed with the concepts proposed by Faulds and worked diligently to refine them over the next ten years. The culmination of his efforts was a comprehensive statistical model of fingerprint analysis and identification that he had designed explicitly for application in the field of forensic science. Galton estimated that the likelihood of two different individuals having the same fingerprint patterns was approximately 1 in 65 billion.

F Global advancements in fingerprint identification research led to the establishment of the first official Fingerprint Bureau in Calcutta in 1897. The Council of the Governor General set up the bureau after approving a committee report recommending that fingerprints be used for the classification of criminal records. Two fingerprint experts who were employed by the bureau, Azizul Haque and Hem Chandra Bose, are recognized as the main contributors to a revolutionary fingerprint classification system. The Henry Classification System, named for their project supervisor Sir Edward Richard Henry, was later approved by the Metropolitan Police in the UK, and adopted by its own newly-established fingerprint bureau in 1901. Joseph Faurot, the Deputy Commissioner of the New York Police Department, is credited with establishing the fingerprinting of criminals as a routine practice in the United States. In 1902, the first arrest and conviction based on fingerprint evidence occurred. Henri Leon Scheffer was identified as the perpetrator of a murder after Alphonse Bertillon discovered his fingerprints on a glass display cabinet and matched them with copies of Scheffer's prints that had been taken previously. The Scheffer case received much publicity, and the effectiveness of fingerprint identification in criminal trials received worldwide recognition.

Questions 21-26

Complete the summary. Write **ONE WORD ONLY** from the text in each gap.

Fingerprint Identification Research

Fingerprints were being used for general identification purposes during criminal trials in [21] around 300 CE. In the mid-17th century, European scientists studied the patterns of the [22] found on the skin of the fingers and palms. Research into fingerprint identification continued over the next two centuries, and true progress occurred in the 19th century. Sir William James Herschel used fingerprints to verify official documents and prevent dishonest [23] from being made with regards to the finances of the deceased. In the late-19th century, Dr. Henry Faulds took his fingerprint classification method to Charles Darwin, who was unable to help due to poor [24]. Two employees of the first fingerprint [25] in Calcutta developed a successful fingerprint classification system that was later implemented by the Metropolitan Police in the UK. Meanwhile, in the United States, fingerprints left on a [26] played a role in the conviction of a crime, proving the effectiveness of fingerprint identification.

PART 2 14 15 16 17 18 19 20 21 22 23 24 25 26

PART 3

Read the text below and answer questions **27-40.**

Ice Age Theory

A Throughout the lifespan of the Earth, five ice ages are known to have occurred thus far. These are referred to as the Huronian, Cryogenian, Andean-Saharan, Karoo, and the Quaternary Ice Ages, the last of which is ongoing in the present day. Each ice age is characterized by alternating periods of temperate conditions and more extreme conditions. The harsher, colder periods are referred to as glacial periods, while the relatively mild periods are called interglacial periods. The Quaternary Ice Age started about 2.5 million years ago when ice sheets in the Northern Hemisphere began to spread outwards. The Earth is presently going through an interglacial period, with the previous glacial period ending approximately 10,000 years ago.

B The geographical findings that would eventually form the foundation of ice age theory largely came about in the mid-18th century. After spending time in the valley of Chamonix in the Alps in 1742, Pierre Martel, an engineer from Geneva, published his travel journal. In it, he noted that the residents of towns within the valley explained that the oddly random dispersal of boulders was a result of the gradual extension of nearby glaciers. Several similar reports would soon come to light regarding this region in the Alps. Eventually, researchers began to note that the same explanations regarding glacier extension were also given by residents in the Val de Ferret in the Valais and the Seeland in western Switzerland, among numerous other regions throughout the world. For instance, during a trip to the Andes in Chile, the German naturalist Ernst von Bibra learned from the indigenous people that the irregular dispersal of boulders and debris could be correlated with the movement of local glaciers.

C In a paper published in 1824, the Danish-Norwegian geologist Jens Esmark proposed that erratic boulder patterns near glaciers indicated that the Earth had experienced a sequence of prolonged ice ages. Esmark believed that extreme climate change had given rise to periods of glaciation. The concepts introduced in Esmark's paper were of great interest to the scientific community, and several of his peers sought to refine his ideas further. The German geologist Albrecht Bernhardi referenced Esmark's theory in his paper published in 1832. Bernhardi hypothesized that, at certain points over millions of years, ice caps had been of such a size that they had even reached the temperate regions of the planet.

D Around the same time, the German botanist Karl Schimper was carrying out research on mosses which were growing on randomly dispersed boulders not far from a glacier in Bavaria.

Settings Help ? Hide

Questions 27-31

The text has seven paragraphs (**A-G**). Which paragraph contains the following information?

	A	B	C	D	E	F	G
27 the first known use of the term ice age							
28 the rejection of a theory developed by two former fellow students							
29 a reference to the ice age that the Earth is currently experiencing							
30 a proposal for a relationship between the Earth's orbit and climate							
31 findings taken from a traveling researcher's journal							

Questions 32-36

Complete the summary. Choose **ONE WORD ONLY** from the text in each gap.

Evidence for the occurrence of ice ages

Pierre Martel was one of the first people to propose the extension of [32] based on irregular patterns of nearby boulders. Several researchers made similar observations, and further refined Martel's theory. Karl Schimper studied [33] growing on the boulders, and then co-developed a theory with Louis Agassiz. Many of their peers disagreed with the theory, believing that the Earth had been [34] ever since it was originally formed. James Croll later proposed that accumulation of snow could impact [35] and marine currents, giving rise to an ice age. Parts of Croll's research were later discredited, but his proposed relationship between orbital variations and [36] was later modified by Milutin Milankovitch.

PART 2 14 15 16 17 18 19 20 21 22 23 24 25 26

Based on moss patterns, he concluded that the boulders must have been transported by moving ice. During the summer of 1836, Schimper took a trip to the Swiss Alps with his former university classmate Louis Agassiz. Together, they worked on a detailed theory of a sequence of global glaciations, drawing heavily from the concepts presented in Bernhardi's earlier paper, in addition to their own extensive field studies. The following year, Schimper coined the term "ice age" in reference to a period of glaciation.

E When Agassiz presented their findings to an annual meeting of leading European scientists in July 1837, the audience expressed criticism and openly cast doubts over the theory due to its disregard for established theories related to climate change. A large proportion of scientists still insisted that the planet had been gradually cooling ever since its birth. Following the rejection from the scientific community, Agassiz threw himself into intensive geological fieldwork. In 1840, he published a book titled *Study on Glaciers*. Due to a series of personal quarrels, Agassiz elected not to mention any of Schimper's research or contributions in his book, which further soured relations between the two.

F Ice age theory was not fully embraced by the international science community until the late-1870s, when the Scottish scientist James Croll published *Climate and Time, in Their Geological Relations*, in which he put forward his astronomical-based theory of climate change. Croll's theory took into account the effects of Earth's orbital variations on climate cycles. He effectively proved that decreases in sunlight during winter months resulted in increased accumulation of snow, and subsequently correlated this with the idea that ice caps change in size in response to solar variations. Croll also presented data that indicated that snow accumulation could alter the trade winds and warm ocean currents, eventually leading to a prolonged ice age. He suggested that when a significant orbital variation occurs in winter, the Earth will experience colder temperatures due to its distance from the Sun, resulting in an ice age approximately every 22,000 years. According to Croll's theory, multiple ice ages must have occurred throughout the Earth's history, and the last of which should have ended roughly 80,000 years ago.

G Concurrent with Croll's investigations, other researchers were presenting similar evidence of multiple ice ages, and several leading geologists began investigating sediments in each hemisphere to corroborate existing data. Analysis of sediments around Niagara Falls suggested that the last ice age ended between 6,000 and 35,000 years ago, and those who accepted these measurements were quick to discredit Croll's theory regarding ice age timelines. However, his general idea of orbital variations influencing Earth's climate remained undisputed and was further enhanced by the work of Milutin Milankovitch, a Serbian climatologist and mathematician. Many years later, in 1976, a modified form of Croll's theory, now known as Milankovitch Cycles, gained widespread acceptance within the scientific community.

Review

PART 1 1 2 3 4 5 6 7 8 9 10 11 12 13

PART 3 27 28 29 30 31 32 33 34 35 36 37 38 39 40

Questions 37-40

Look at the following statements (Questions 37-40) and the list of researchers below.
Match each statement with the correct researcher, **A, B, C** or **D**.

37 Some accepted theories of climate change in the 1800s were not important.

38 Randomly scattered rocks are a result of glacial extension.

39 Ice caps may once have stretched into warmer regions of the planet.

40 A build-up of snow is indicative of variations in the Earth's orbit.

List of Researchers

A Pierre Martel

B Albrecht Bernhardi

C Louis Agassiz

D James Croll

PART 2 14 15 16 17 18 19 20 21 22 23 24 25 26

ACTUAL TEST 2

XXXXX-1234 59 minutes left

PART 1

Read the text below and answer questions **1-7**.

Rideshare Offer: Orlando to Chicago

We are looking for someone who wants to travel from Orlando to Chicago and would be willing to share gas and accommodation costs. The distance between the two cities is 1,154 miles, and the journey will require a driving time of approximately 18 hours. Ideally, we will drive for 9 hours per day, plus refreshment stops, and stay in a motel for one night. The plan is to set off at around 9 a.m. on Thursday, March 19th. Please note that this is a one-way rideshare offer, as we are not certain when we will return to Orlando.

About us: I'm Brigitte! I'm Swedish, but I moved to Orlando with my family a few years ago. I'm 25 years old and am pursuing a career in acting. The reason for my trip is to attend an audition for a film that will be primarily shot in Chicago. A Swedish friend of mine, Agatha, will be accompanying us on the trip, just to do some sightseeing. Originally, our Mexican friend, Lola, planned to join us, but she is unable to as she will be playing a concert with her band in Orlando that particular weekend. Agatha and I are very easy-going and friendly, and we love to meet new people.

The vehicle itself is an RV (Recreational Vehicle) and comes equipped with a bathroom, a stove, pots, pans, plates, and cutlery, a microwave, and a television. It used to include a bed, but the previous owner of the vehicle removed this to enlarge the comfortable seating area.

Agatha and I will handle all of the driving, so there's no need for you to have a license. All gas and accommodation costs will be split three ways and paid immediately in cash, so make sure you bring enough money along for the trip. As we are two females, we would prefer to have a third female companion, but we will still consider any men who request to join us on the trip. Please send an introductory e-mail to bsvensson@greenmail.net if you are interested.

Review

PART 1 1 2 3 4 5 6 7 8 9 10 11 12 13 14

PART 3 28 29 30 31 32 33 34 35 36 37 38 39 40

Settings Help Hide

Questions 1-7

Choose **TRUE** if the statement agrees with the information given in the text, choose **FALSE** if the statement contradicts the information, or choose **NOT GIVEN** if there is no information on this.

1 The travelers will arrive in Chicago on Friday.

- TRUE
- FALSE
- NOT GIVEN

2 Brigitte and Agatha will stay in Chicago for one week.

- TRUE
- FALSE
- NOT GIVEN

3 Brigitte's friend Agatha is a musician.

- TRUE
- FALSE
- NOT GIVEN

4 The vehicle that will be used has cooking facilities.

- TRUE
- FALSE
- NOT GIVEN

5 The RV has had new features added since being purchased.

- TRUE
- FALSE
- NOT GIVEN

PART 2 15 16 17 18 19 20 21 22 23 24 25 26 27

PART 1 1 2 3 4 5 6 7 8 9 10 11 12 13 14

Review

PART 3 28 29 30 31 32 33 34 35 36 37 38 39 40

6 Brigitte will drive the vehicle for the entire duration of the journey.

○ TRUE
○ FALSE
○ NOT GIVEN

7 Gas costs will be paid equally by all three travelers.

○ TRUE
○ FALSE
○ NOT GIVEN

PART 2 15 16 17 18 19 20 21 22 23 24 25 26 27

ACTUAL TEST 2

XXXXX-1234 50 minutes left

PART 1

Read the text below and answer questions **8-14**.

TV Streaming Services

A Orion

Plans: For $8.99 a month, subscribers can sign up for the Orion Basic plan. For $12.99 a month, viewers have access to the Orion Plus Live TV plan, which features more than 30 live and on-demand channels and allows streaming on two screens simultaneously. Add-ons available include unlimited screens and no commercials. However, those unlimited screens come at an extra cost, with the add-on costing an additional $14.99 per month. Removal of ads costs an extra $4.99 per month. Another drawback is that the service does not allow offline viewing.

B Streamflix

Plans: Starting at $7.99 a month for a Basic Plan, viewers can watch in standard definition on one device at a time. The $10.99 per month Premium Plan gives a high definition option and allows streaming on one more device. Not only are the base prices low, but Streamflix gains a slight edge over the competition by not charging an added fee to remove ads. It also allows you to download shows to watch offline. Potential subscribers should note, however, that there is a relatively long wait period for some TV shows to be added to the service after they originally air.

C Blast TV

Plans: The basic plan, Blast Standard, gives viewers more than 25 channels for $9.99 per month. You can get Blast Silver and an extra 20 channels for an extra $5 per month. If that's still not enough, get the Blast Gold plan, which comes with more than 60 channels for $19.99 per month. Blast TV offers a wide range of add-ons, including country- and language-specific packages. However, offline viewing is out of the question, and network sports broadcasts are pretty hard to come by with Blast TV. It's also debatable whether the price tag provides true value for money.

D Digital Prime

Plans: This service currently offers only one plan, which runs for $12.99 per month. The main perk of this relatively new service is that it allows you to watch your shows in virtual reality using the cutting-edge Digital Prime VR app. You also won't have to sit through any ads, as they are already removed by the service provider. One downside is that the service doesn't allow you to download shows to watch offline. The service also provides less content than the others, although it does have a large number of channels devoted to live concerts and sporting events.

PART 1 1 2 3 4 5 6 7 8 9 10 11 12 13 14

Review PART 3 28 29 30 31 32 33 34 35 36 37 38 39 40

Settings Help Hide

Questions 8-14

Look at the four reviews of TV streaming services, **A-D**. For which service are the following statements true?

	A	B	C	D
8 This service is useful for people with more than two viewing devices.				
9 You can download content with this service and watch it offline.				
10 This service is cheaper than the other three listed services.				
11 You can use an innovative app in conjunction with this service.				
12 This service is ideal for people who want programming from another country.				
13 You must pay an extra fee to have adverts taken off this service.				
14 This service would suit someone seeking a range of sports content.				

PART 2 15 16 17 18 19 20 21 22 23 24 25 26 27

XXXXX-1234 

PART 2

Read the text below and answer questions **15-20**.

Why you should encourage socializing in your workplace

Socializing at work used to be viewed as a negative thing, and managers were quick to discourage staff from gathering around the water cooler to indulge in gossip. These days, however, business owners recognize the advantages of workplace socializing, spending more time and effort encouraging productive social interaction rather than disciplining staff for having a quick chat.

One of the clear benefits of a sociable workforce is the sharing of knowledge. When a business sends several communications to staff during the workday, some employees may fail to notice one of them. While socializing with one another, employees will often discuss such communications, alerting those individuals who missed them. Social interaction also gives workers a chance to hear different perspectives on issues such as new policies or project proposals. Management can take advantage of informal environments, such as a break room, to encourage discussion about work issues and answer any questions employees may have.

When new employees come into a busy work environment, they can understandably feel overwhelmed. Encouraging the new employees to socialize helps them to settle in and feel confident. Managers should lead a new employee through all work departments and introduce them individual to all of the staff, or in larger companies, the department supervisors. While doing so, the manager should mention the new employee's hobbies and take time to introduce him or her to likeminded workers with whom the new employee has several things in common.

Socializing has clear benefits when it comes to teamwork and healthy competition. In several fields of business, particularly in sales-oriented companies, sales teams will often compete against each other to reach a monthly target and win a bonus or other incentive. Allowing these teams to celebrate their successes in the workplace, giving each other high-fives and boasting about their achievements, can have a positive effect on team spirit. Managers can encourage teamwork by congratulating winning teams in the workplace and discussing their performance. Not only will it encourage the winners to maintain their hard work, but other teams will find inspiration in your words and double their efforts.

Lastly, one of the most important, yet often overlooked, advantages of socialization is that it can result in strong, unexpected alliances within your company. For instance, a member of the

Review

PART 1 1 2 3 4 5 6 7 8 9 10 11 12 13 14

PART 3 28 29 30 31 32 33 34 35 36 37 38 39 40

Settings Help ? Hide

Questions 15-20

Complete the sentences. Choose **ONE WORD ONLY** from the text in each gap.

- Managers should encourage socializing instead of [15] staff who spend time talking.
- Socializing enables staff to find out about any [16] they have not noticed during the day.
- Let other staff know about a new worker's [17] so that they can form a friendship.
- Allow sales teams to [18] their achievements in the workplace.
- Congratulate winning teams in order to provide [19] for competing teams to do better.
- Build [20] between staff by organizing inter-department gatherings.

PART 2 15 16 17 18 19 20 21 22 23 24 25 26 27

accounting department might forge a friendship with a member of the production department, and this alliance could result in a collaborative effort that successfully cuts the company's production costs. The same thing can arise when a customer service employee has a social relationship with a production worker.

When a customer complains about a design fault in a product, the two workers can come up with an ideal solution and response. Managers should plan inter-department social gatherings so that such alliances have a chance to be formed.

Review

PART 1 1 2 3 4 5 6 7 8 9 10 11 12 13 14

PART 3 28 29 30 31 32 33 34 35 36 37 38 39 40

PART 2 15 16 17 18 19 20 21 22 23 24 25 26 27

ACTUAL TEST 2

XXXXX-1234 33 minutes left

PART 2

Read the text below and answer questions **21-27**.

Data-gathering approaches for your project

When planning an important work project, it is often beneficial to collect information from consumers, company stakeholders, employees, or competitors. Here are four of the most effective data-gathering approaches, and an outline of their advantages and disadvantages:

Benchmarking

This technique involves evaluating the leading companies within your field or industry and determining what factors have contributed to their success. By doing so, you can learn a lot from the successes of other companies, at no risk to you or your own firm. Benchmarking allows you to set standards for your outcomes by analyzing those of demonstrably effective past projects. It can also be useful to help you validate your project approach in the eyes of management when the time comes to seek final approval. However, in order for it to be worthwhile, you need to find benchmarks that closely match your own project, and this is easier said than done.

Focus Groups

You can create a focus group by assembling several people, typically between 8 and 15 per group, who broadly represent your target consumer base. This method is designed to help you understand the real, current needs of your end users, instead of simply making assumptions based on possibly outdated data. Note that it is crucial to have an experienced group leader, which can involve an extra expense. External experts will demand a sizable sum, and internal employees may require costly training beforehand.

Surveys

Surveys have long been an effective way to gather data and ascertain the perceptions and opinions of a group of people. This method saves you time, as participants can receive the surveys by e-mail and send them back to you within a specified timeframe. This means that you do not need to attend meetings or record information first-hand. Additionally, questions can be tailored in order to fit the objectives you have set for your project. The biggest drawback of surveys is that some recipients may give the task low priority, or forget about it altogether.

Prototypes

A prototype is typically an early, simplified version of your proposed end product or service. Once created, this can be made available to selected consumers, who will then provide feedback that you can utilize to make improvements. Unfortunately, building prototypes can be extraordinarily expensive, and the approach is typically only suitable for companies developing and utilizing new technology, such as those in the construction or electronics industries.

Review

PART 1 1 2 3 4 5 6 7 8 9 10 11 12 13 14

PART 3 28 29 30 31 32 33 34 35 36 37 38 39 40

Questions 21-27

Complete the notes. Choose **ONE WORD ONLY** from the text in each gap.

Information gathering techniques

There are many effective ways to gather information, including:

Benchmarking

- requires the analysis of successful companies in your field
- allows you to gather data without any [21] to your company
- [22] may look to these past successes and approve your project approach
- finding projects similar to your own may be difficult

Focus Groups

- requires a group of between 8 and 15 people
- useful for identifying the genuine [23] of a consumer base
- can generate additional [24] when sourcing a suitable external or internal group leader

Surveys

- saves time by having respondents do much of the work themselves
- allows you to design survey questions focused on the specific [25] of your project

Prototypes

- allows modifications to be made based on [26]
- normally only useful in industries where [27] is used

PART 2 15 16 17 18 19 20 21 22 23 24 25 26 27

ACTUAL TEST 2

XXXXX-1234 

PART 3

Read the text below and answer questions **28-40**.

Animal Extinction in Australia

Researcher and ecologist Professor James Sutton continues to investigate the reasons behind Australia's high rate of animal extinction

I first took an interest in Australia's animal extinction problem, and the various reasons behind it, when I joined a team of paleontologists who were searching for fossilized remains of the thylacine.

More than 90% of Australia's larger terrestrial vertebrates had become extinct by around 40 thousand years ago, with the notable exceptions being the kangaroo and the thylacine. Humans are likely to be one of the major factors in the extinction of many species in Australia, but one-factor explanations are overly simplistic, as climate change and bushfires are sure to have played a part.

The thylacine was once the largest known carnivorous marsupial animal. It is often referred to as the Tasmanian Tiger, due to its striped lower back, although it shared more physical characteristics with a wolf. It was native to the Australian mainland, Tasmania, and New Guinea, and is thought to have become near-extinct on the mainland around two thousand years ago, although reliable accounts of small thylacine groups place them in parts of South Australia as late as the 1830s.

Some experts believe that a major contributing factor to the decline in thylacine populations was the introduction of dingoes – a type of dog – by European settlers. Proponents of this theory argue that the thylacine directly competed with the dingo for food, based on the similar appearance of the two species. This is a plausible explanation, as examinations of thylacine skulls indicate that the animal was a less effective predator than the dingo. Furthermore, the thylacine's diet was far less versatile than that of the dingo, which would consume seeds, berries, and fish in the absence of mammals. However, a counter-argument can be made that the two animals were never in direct competition for prey, as the thylacine mainly hunted at night, while the dingo hunted during the day. A broader theory is that a combination of competition for food, hunting by indigenous populations, and habitat erosion, eventually led to the absolute extinction of the thylacine.

Review

PART 1 1 2 3 4 5 6 7 8 9 10 11 12 13 14

PART 3 28 29 30 31 32 33 34 35 36 37 38 39 40

Settings Help Hide

Questions 28-32

Complete the summary. Write **ONE WORD ONLY** from the text in each gap.

The fate of the thylacine

The thylacine and [28] were two of the only land vertebrates in Australia that were not already extinct 40,000 years ago. Despite being dubbed the Tasmanian tiger, the thylacine more closely resembled a [29]. Some researchers have argued that [30] are to blame for the decline in thylacine population, as they introduced dingoes to their habitat. It is believed that, because the dingo was a better predator and had more variety in its [31], it was able to thrive more easily than the thylacine. However, other factors such as hunting and the degradation of [32] most likely also played a part in the extinction of the thylacine.

PART 2 15 16 17 18 19 20 21 22 23 24 25 26 27

ACTUAL TEST 2

The introduction of invasive species, both deliberately and accidentally, has been a recurring problem in Australia's history of animal extinction, especially in the case of native birds. One incident that had a catastrophic impact on biodiversity was the grounding of the SS Makambo in June, 1918. While repairs were underway, black rats left the ship and invaded the land. The rat population thrived, and, within only six years, directly caused the extinction of several endemic ground-nesting birds such as the Lord Howe thrush. The issue was exacerbated when an ecological solution was proposed and executed: the deliberate introduction of Tasmanian masked owls. This move was designed to eradicate the rat population, but in actual fact, the introduction of the predatory owls led to the extinction of yet more bird species, including the Lord Howe boobook.

While carrying out my research into Australia's extinct species, one of the most troubling and mindless examples of direct human involvement I have come across is the case of the King Island emu. This subspecies of emu was endemic to King Island, situated between mainland Australia and Tasmania, and a sizable population had long thrived on the island's abundant berries and seaweed, with barely any threat from predators.

In 1802, the French naturalist Francois Peron visited the island as part of an expedition. Much of what we know about the King Island emu comes from an interview Peron conducted with seal hunters who had settled on the island. These sealers boasted that they had killed and eaten an estimated 3,600 emus during their six-month stay on the island. Fires that they had started also contributed to a decline in the emu population. Although Peron reported that the island was still swarming with emus at the time of his visit, the population had been decimated by 1805, and the species was considered extinct in 1836 when English settlers found no trace of the birds. This example of human selfishness, and the impact of indiscriminate hunting practices, is something we should keep in mind in our modern age.

This brings me to my most recent research, which concerns the Bramble Cay melomys, a species of rodent that was endemic to a vegetated region at the northern tip of the Great Barrier Reef. While species such as the King Island emu were wiped out due to human action, it can be argued that human inaction played a role in the extinction of the melomys.

The habitat of the melomys rises only a few meters above sea level, making it vulnerable to severe weather conditions. The root cause of the mammal's extinction was sea-level rise as a result of global warming, but this loss was entirely foreseeable and preventable. It had been known for many years that flooding of the creature's habitat was becoming more

PART 1 1 2 3 4 5 6 7 8 9 10 11 12 13 14
PART 3 28 29 30 31 32 33 34 35 36 37 38 39 40

Review

Questions 33-37

Choose the correct answer.

33 What does the writer suggest about animal extinction in Australia?

A ○ It is a trend that is slowing down.

B ○ It is less severe than in other countries.

C ○ There are typically several factors involved.

D ○ There is a lack of useful information.

34 One significant difference between the thylacine and the dingo is their

A ○ preferred time for seeking food.

B ○ physical appearance.

C ○ reproduction cycle.

D ○ ideal habitat.

35 In the fifth paragraph, what does the writer suggest about the Tasmanian masked owls?

A ○ They successfully caused a decline in the rat population.

B ○ They competed with the Lord Howe thrush for food.

C ○ Their extinction was caused by invasive rats.

D ○ Their introduction caused more harm than good.

36 When describing the theory of how the King Island emu became extinct, the writer is

A ○ surprised that the species did not vanish sooner.

B ○ disheartened by a past display of human ignorance.

C ○ confused about which predators preyed on the species.

D ○ disappointed that conservation efforts proved unsuccessful.

37 Which of the following best summarises the writer's point in the final paragraph?

A ○ Public awareness about environmental issues is at an all-time low.

B ○ Humans should refrain from encroaching on vulnerable habitats.

C ○ The government should do more to combat extinction.

D ○ The extinction of the Bramble Cay melomys was inevitable.

PART 2 15 16 17 18 19 20 21 22 23 24 25 26 27

frequent and severe. My own efforts, and those of my peers, to secure government funding for conservation programs were in vain. Part of the reason is that the animal is not as iconic or charismatic as a koala or kangaroo, so it does not receive much attention from the public or the government. Unfortunately, the fate of the melomys is emblematic of the failures in Australia's management of endangered species, which has seen the country record the highest rate of mammalian extinction in the world over the last two centuries.

Review

PART 1 1 2 3 4 5 6 7 8 9 10 11 12 13 14

PART 3 28 29 30 31 32 33 34 35 36 37 38 39 40

Questions 38-40

Look at the following statements (Questions 38-40) and the list of prehistoric animals below.
Match each statement with the correct animal, **A**, **B**, **C** or **D**.

38 Humans actively killed off many of this species for food.

39 This species became extinct as a result of climate change.

40 A sailing accident led to the extinction of this species.

List of Extinct Species

A Tasmanian tiger

B Lord Howe thrush

C King Island emu

D Bramble Cay melomys

PART 2 15 16 17 18 19 20 21 22 23 24 25 26 27

ACTUAL TEST 2

XXXXX-1234 59 minutes left

PART 1

You should spend about 20 minutes on this task. Write at least 150 words.

The tables below give information about production and consumption of coffee in 2017 and 2018 in five coffee-exporting countries.

Summarise the information by selecting and reporting the main features, and make comparisons where relevant.

Production and consumption of coffee (millions of coffee bags*)

Production	2017	2018
Brazil	52.7	61.7
Columbia	13.8	14.2
Indonesia	10.8	10.2
Mexico	4.4	4.5
Vietnam	30.5	29.5

Consumption	2017	2018
Brazil	21.2	22.0
Columbia	1.7	1.8
Indonesia	4.7	4.7
Mexico	2.4	2.5
Vietnam	2.4	2.4

* One bag is 60 kg

Review PART 1 1 PART 2 2

Settings
Help
Hide
Word count: 0

XXXXX-1234 42 minutes left

PART 2

You should spend about 40 minutes on this task. Write at least 250 words.

Write about the following topic:

Natural resources, such as oil, forests and freshwater, are being consumed at an alarming rate all around the world.

What problems does this cause?

How can we solve these problems?

Give reasons for your answer and include any relevant examples from your own knowledge or experience.

Review PART 1 1 PART 2 2

Settings
Help
Hide
Word count: 0

XXXXX-1234 59 minutes left

PART 1

You should spend about 20 minutes on this task. Write at least 150 words.

Your local council has a plan to build some tourist facilities to attract more tourists to the town. The council has advertised for the residents to suggest ideas for the plan.

Write a letter to your local council. In your letter
- **describe the importance of the tourism in your town**
- **explain what kind of facility you recommend**
- **say why you think the facility could be appropriate for the plan**

You do **NOT** need to write any addresses.

Begin your letter as follows:

Dear Sir or Madam,

Review PART 1 1 PART 2 2

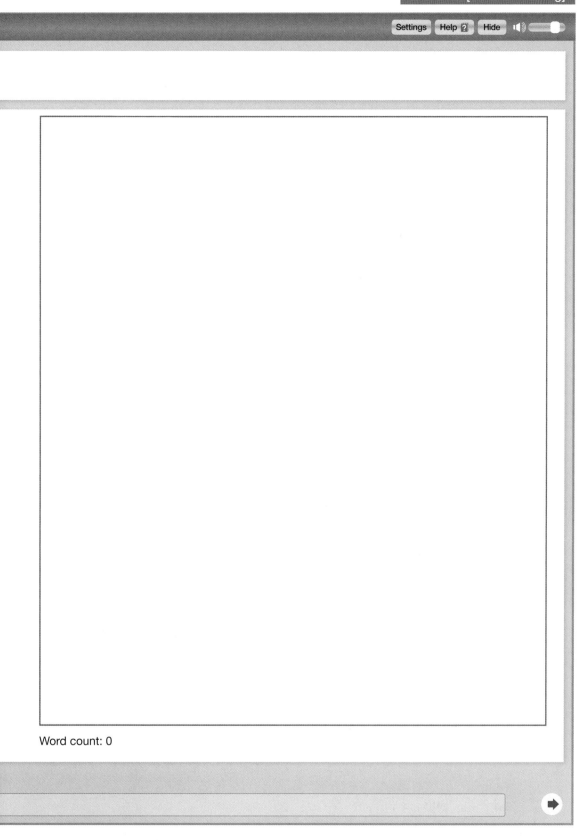
Settings
Help
Hide
Word count: 0

XXXXX-1234 42 minutes left

PART 2

You should spend about 40 minutes on this task. Write at least 250 words.

Write about the following topic:

Some people say that a product's success in the market does not reflect the real needs of consumers, but rather just the power of advertising.

What is your opinion about this?

Give reasons for your answer and include any relevant examples from your own knowledge or experience.

Review PART 1 1 PART 2 2

Settings Help ? Hide

Word count: 0

Part 1

[Weather]

Let's talk about weather.
What kind of weather do you like? [Why?]
How often is the weather cold in your country?

[Food and Cooking]

Let's go on to talk about food and cooking.
What sorts of food do you like most? [Why?]
Do you prefer to eat out or eat at home? [Why?]
What kind of new food would you like to try? [Why?]
Do you watch cookery programmes on TV? [Why/Why not?]

Part 2

Describe something you bought and like.

You should say:
- what you purchased
- where you bought it
- why you like it

and explain why it is so memorable to you.

Rounding-off Question:
Is this item famous in your country or other countries?

Part 3

[Buy Things]

What are the advantages of internet shopping?
What are the differences between shopping at large department stores and small local shops?

[Local Business]

Do large shopping malls and commercial centres affect small local businesses? [How?]
What types of local business are in your neighbourhood?
How important is customer service to the success of a shop?

MEMO

MEMO

Writing & Speaking 공식 채점 기준표

IELTS WRITING TASK 1: Band Descriptors

Band Score	Task Achievement	Coherence & Cohesion
9	All the requirements of the task are fully and appropriately satisfied. There may be extremely rare lapses in content.	The message can be followed effortlessly. Cohesion is used in such a way that it very rarely attracts attention. Any lapses in coherence or cohesion are minimal. Paragraphing is skilfully managed.
8	The response covers all the requirements of the task appropriately, relevantly and sufficiently. (Academic) Key features are skilfully selected, and clearly presented, highlighted and illustrated. (General Training) All bullet points are clearly presented, and appropriately illustrated or extended. There may be occasional omissions or lapses in content.	The message can be followed with ease. Information and ideas are logically sequenced, and cohesion is well managed. Occasional lapses in coherence or cohesion may occur. Paragraphing is used sufficiently and appropriately.
7	The response covers the requirements of the task. The content is relevant and accurate – there may be a few omissions or lapses. The format is appropriate. (Academic) Key features which are selected are covered and clearly highlighted but could be more fully or more appropriately illustrated or extended. (Academic) It presents a clear overview, the data are appropriately categorised, and main trends or differences are identified. (General Training) All bullet points are covered and clearly highlighted but could be more fully or more appropriately illustrated or extended. It presents a clear purpose. The tone is consistent and appropriate to the task. Any lapses are minimal.	Information and ideas are logically organised and there is a clear progression throughout the response. A few lapses may occur. A range of cohesive devices including reference and substitution is used flexibly but with some inaccuracies or some over/under use.
6	The response focuses on the requirements of the task and an appropriate format is used. (Academic) Key features which are selected are covered and adequately highlighted. A relevant overview is attempted. Information is appropriately selected and supported using figures/data. (General Training) All bullet points are covered and adequately highlighted. The purpose is generally clear. There may be minor inconsistencies in tone. Some irrelevant, inappropriate or inaccurate information may occur in areas of detail or when illustrating or extending the main points. Some details may be missing (or excessive) and further extension or illustration may be needed.	Information and ideas are generally arranged coherently and there is a clear overall progression. Cohesive devices are used to some good effect but cohesion within and/or between sentences may be faulty or mechanical due to misuse, overuse or omission. The use of reference and substitution may lack flexibility or clarity and result in some repetition or error.

Scoring criteria for Academic and General Training tests

A script must fully fit the positive features of the descriptor at a particular level. **Bolded text** indicates negative features that will limit a rating.

Lexical Resource	Grammatical Range & Accuracy
Full flexibility and precise use are evident within the scope of the task. A wide range of vocabulary is used accurately and appropriately with very natural and sophisticated control of lexical features. Minor errors in spelling and word formation are extremely rare and have minimal impact on communication.	A wide range of structures within the scope of the task is used with full flexibility and control. Punctuation and grammar are used appropriately throughout. Minor errors are extremely rare and have minimal impact on communication
A wide resource is fluently and flexibly used to convey precise meanings within the scope of the task. There is skilful use of uncommon and/or idiomatic items when appropriate, despite occasional inaccuracies in word choice and collocation. Occasional errors in spelling and/or word formation may occur, but have minimal impact on communication.	A wide range of structures within the scope of the task is flexibly and accurately used. The majority of sentences are error free, and punctuation is well managed. Occasional, non-systematic errors and inappropriacies occur, but have minimal impact on communication.
The resource is sufficient to allow some flexibility and precision. There is some ability to use less common and/or idiomatic items. An awareness of style and collocation is evident, though inappropriacies occur. There are only a few errors in spelling and/or word formation, and they do not detract from overall clarity.	A variety of complex structures is used with some flexibility and accuracy. Grammar and punctuation are generally well controlled, and error free sentences are frequent. A few errors in grammar may persist, but these do not impede communication.
The resource is generally adequate and appropriate for the task. The meaning is generally clear in spite of a rather restricted range or a lack of precision in word choice. If the writer is a risk taker, there will be a wider range of vocabulary used but higher degrees of inaccuracy or inappropriacy. There are some errors in spelling and/or word formation, but these do not impede communication.	A mix of simple and complex sentence forms is used but flexibility is limited. Examples of more complex structures are not marked by the same level of accuracy as in simple structures. Errors in grammar and punctuation occur, but rarely impede communication.

Band Score	Task Achievement	Coherence & Cohesion
5	The response generally addresses the requirements of the task. The format may be inappropriate in places. (Academic) Key features which are selected are not adequately covered. The recounting of detail is mainly mechanical. **There may be no data to support the description.** (General Training) All bullet points are presented but one or more may not be adequately covered. The purpose may be unclear at times. The tone may be variable and sometimes inappropriate. There may be a tendency to focus on details (without referring to the bigger picture). The inclusion of irrelevant, inappropriate or inaccurate material in key areas detracts from the task achievement. There is limited detail when extending and illustrating the main points.	Organisation is evident but is not wholly logical and there may be a lack of overall progression. Nevertheless, there is a sense of underlying coherence to the response. The relationship of ideas can be followed but the sentences are not fluently linked to each other. There may be limited/overuse of cohesive devices with some inaccuracy. The writing may be repetitive due to inadequate and/or inaccurate use of reference and substitution.
4	The response is an attempt to address the task. (Academic) Few key features have been selected. **(General Training) Not all bullet points are presented.** (General Training) The purpose of the letter is not clearly explained and may be confused. **The tone may be inappropriate.** **The format may be inappropriate.** Key features/bullet points which are presented may be irrelevant, repetitive, inaccurate or inappropriate.	Information and ideas are evident but not arranged coherently, and there is no clear progression within the response. Relationships between ideas can be unclear and/or inadequately marked. There is some use of basic cohesive devices, which may be inaccurate or repetitive. There is inaccurate use or a lack of substitution or referencing.
3	The response does not address the requirements of the task (possibly because of misunderstanding of the data/diagram/situation). Key features/bullet points which are presented may be largely irrelevant. Limited information is presented, and this may be used repetitively.	There is no apparent logical organisation. Ideas are discernible but difficult to relate to each other. Minimal use of sequencers or cohesive devices. Those used do not necessarily indicate a logical relationship between ideas. There is difficulty in identifying referencing.
2	The content barely relates to the task.	There is little relevant message, or **the entire response may be off topic.** There is little evidence of control of organisational features.
1	**Responses of 20 words or fewer are rated at Band 1.** The content is wholly unrelated to the task. Any copied rubric must be discounted.	**Responses of 20 words or fewer are rated at Band 1.** The writing fails to communicate any message and appears to be by a virtual non writer.
0	Should only be used where a candidate did not attend or attempt the question in any way, used a language	

Lexical Resource	Grammatical Range & Accuracy
The resource is limited but minimally adequate for the task. Simple vocabulary may be used accurately but the range does not permit much variation in expression. There may be frequent lapses in the appropriacy of word choice, and a lack of flexibility is apparent in frequent simplifications and/or repetitions. Errors in spelling and/or word formation may be noticeable and may cause some difficulty for the reader.	The range of structures is limited and rather repetitive. Although complex sentences are attempted, they tend to be faulty, and the greatest accuracy is achieved on simple sentences. Grammatical errors may be frequent and cause some difficulty for the reader. Punctuation may be faulty.
The resource is limited and inadequate for or **unrelated to the task**. Vocabulary is basic and may be used repetitively. There may be inappropriate use of lexical chunks (e.g. memorised phrases, formulaic language and/or language from the input material). Inappropriate word choice and/or errors in word formation and/or in spelling may impede meaning.	A very limited range of structures is used. **Subordinate clauses are rare and simple sentences predominate.** Some structures are produced accurately but grammatical errors are frequent and may impede meaning. Punctuation is often faulty or inadequate.
The resource is inadequate (which may be due to the response being significantly underlength). Possible over-dependence on input material or memorised language. Control of word choice and/or spelling is very limited, and errors predominate. These errors may severely impede meaning.	Sentence forms are attempted, but errors in grammar and punctuation predominate (except in memorised phrases or those taken from the input material). This prevents most meaning from coming through. **Length may be insufficient to provide evidence of control of sentence forms.**
The resource is extremely limited with few recognisable strings, apart from memorised phrases. There is no apparent control of word formation and/or spelling.	There is little or no evidence of sentence forms (except in memorised phrases).
Responses of 20 words or fewer are rated at Band 1. No resource is apparent, except for a few isolated words.	**Responses of 20 words or fewer are rated at Band 1.** No rateable language is evident.

other than English throughout, or **where there is proof that a candidate's answer has been totally memorised.**

IELTS WRITING TASK 2: Band Descriptors

Band Score	Task Response	Coherence & Cohesion
9	The prompt is appropriately addressed and explored in depth. A clear and fully developed position is presented which directly answers the question/s. Ideas are relevant, fully extended and well supported. Any lapses in content or support are extremely rare.	The message can be followed effortlessly. Cohesion is used in such a way that it very rarely attracts attention. Any lapses in coherence or cohesion are minimal. Paragraphing is skilfully managed.
8	The prompt is appropriately and sufficiently addressed. A clear and well developed position is presented in response to the question/s. Ideas are relevant, well extended and supported. There may be occasional omissions or lapses in content.	The message can be followed with ease. Information and ideas are logically sequenced, and cohesion is well managed. Occasional lapses in coherence and cohesion may occur. Paragraphing is used sufficiently and appropriately.
7	The main parts of the prompt are appropriately addressed. A clear and developed position is presented. Main ideas are extended and supported but there may be a tendency to over generalise or there may be a lack of focus and precision in supporting ideas/material.	Information and ideas are logically organised, and there is a clear progression throughout the response. (A few lapses may occur, but these are minor.) A range of cohesive devices including reference and substitution is used flexibly but with some inaccuracies or some over/under use. Paragraphing is generally used effectively to support overall coherence, and the sequencing of ideas within a paragraph is generally logical.
6	The main parts of the prompt are addressed (though some may be more fully covered than others). An appropriate format is used. A position is presented that is directly relevant to the prompt, although the conclusions drawn may be unclear, unjustified or repetitive. Main ideas are relevant, but some may be insufficiently developed or may lack clarity, while some supporting arguments and evidence may be less relevant or inadequate.	Information and ideas are generally arranged coherently and there is a clear overall progression. Cohesive devices are used to some good effect but cohesion within and/or between sentences may be faulty or mechanical due to misuse, overuse or omission. The use of reference and substitution may lack flexibility or clarity and result in some repetition or error. Paragraphing may not always be logical and/or the central topic may not always be clear.

Scoring criteria for Academic and General Training tests

A script must fully fit the positive features of the descriptor at a particular level. **Bolded text** indicates negative features that will limit a rating.

Lexical Resource	Grammatical Range & Accuracy
Full flexibility and precise use are widely evident. A wide range of vocabulary is used accurately and appropriately with very natural and sophisticated control of lexical features. Minor errors in spelling and word formation are extremely rare and have minimal impact on communication.	A wide range of structures is used with full flexibility and control. Punctuation and grammar are used appropriately throughout. Minor errors are extremely rare and have minimal impact on communication.
A wide resource is fluently and flexibly used to convey precise meanings. There is skilful use of uncommon and/or idiomatic items when appropriate, despite occasional inaccuracies in word choice and collocation. Occasional errors in spelling and/or word formation may occur, but have minimal impact on communication.	A wide range of structures is flexibly and accurately used. The majority of sentences are error free, and punctuation is well managed. Occasional, non-systematic errors and inappropriacies occur, but have minimal impact on communication.
The resource is sufficient to allow some flexibility and precision. There is some ability to use less common and/or idiomatic items. An awareness of style and collocation is evident, though inappropriacies occur. There are only a few errors in spelling and/or word formation and they do not detract from overall clarity.	A variety of complex structures is used with some flexibility and accuracy. Grammar and punctuation are generally well controlled, and error-free sentences are frequent. A few errors in grammar may persist, but these do not impede communication.
The resource is generally adequate and appropriate for the task. The meaning is generally clear in spite of a rather restricted range or a lack of precision in word choice. If the writer is a risk taker, there will be a wider range of vocabulary used but higher degrees of inaccuracy or inappropriacy. There are some errors in spelling and/or word formation, but these do not impede communication.	A mix of simple and complex sentence forms is used but flexibility is limited. Examples of more complex structures are not marked by the same level of accuracy as in simple structures. Errors in grammar and punctuation occur, but rarely impede communication.

Band Score	Task Response	Coherence & Cohesion
5	The main parts of the prompt are **incompletely addressed**. The format may be inappropriate in places. The writer expresses a position, but the development is not always clear. Some main ideas are put forward, but they are limited and are not sufficiently developed and/or there may be irrelevant detail. There may be some repetition.	Organisation is evident but is not wholly logical and there may be a lack of overall progression. Nevertheless, there is a sense of underlying coherence to the response. The relationship of ideas can be followed but the sentences are not fluently linked to each other. There may be limited/overuse of cohesive devices with some inaccuracy. The writing may be repetitive due to inadequate and/or inaccurate use of reference and substitution. **Paragraphing may be inadequate or missing.**
4	The prompt is tackled in a minimal way, or the answer is tangential, possibly due to some misunderstanding of the prompt. **The format may be inappropriate.** A position is discernible, but the reader has to read carefully to find it. Main ideas are difficult to identify and such ideas that are identifiable may lack relevance, clarity and/or support. Large parts of the response may be repetitive.	Information and ideas are evident but not arranged coherently and there is no clear progression within the response. Relationships between ideas can be unclear and/or inadequately marked. There is some use of basic cohesive devices, which may be inaccurate or repetitive. There is inaccurate use or a lack of substitution or referencing. There may be no paragraphing and/or no clear main topic within paragraphs.
3	No part of the prompt is adequately addressed, or the prompt has been misunderstood. No relevant position can be identified, and/or there is little direct response to the question/s. There are few ideas, and these may be irrelevant or insufficiently developed.	There is no apparent logical organisation. Ideas are discernible but difficult to relate to each other. There is minimal use of sequencers or cohesive devices. Those used do not necessarily indicate a logical relationship between ideas. There is difficulty in identifying referencing. Any attempts at paragraphing are unhelpful.
2	The content is barely related to the prompt. No position can be identified. There may be glimpses of one or two ideas without development.	There is little relevant message, or the **entire response may be off topic.** There is little evidence of control of organisational features.
1	**Responses of 20 words or fewer are rated at Band 1.** **The content is wholly unrelated to the prompt.** Any copied rubric must be discounted.	**Responses of 20 words or fewer are rated at Band 1.** The writing fails to communicate any message and appears to be by a virtual non writer.
0	Should only be used where a candidate did not attend or attempt the question in any way, used a language	

Lexical Resource	Grammatical Range & Accuracy
The resource is limited but minimally adequate for the task. Simple vocabulary may be used accurately but the range does not permit much variation in expression. There may be frequent lapses in the appropriacy of word choice and a lack of flexibility is apparent in frequent simplifications and/or repetitions. Errors in spelling and/or word formation may be noticeable and may cause some difficulty for the reader.	The range of structures is limited and rather repetitive. Although complex sentences are attempted, they tend to be faulty, and the greatest accuracy is achieved on simple sentences. Grammatical errors may be frequent and cause some difficulty for the reader. Punctuation may be faulty.
The resource is limited and inadequate for or **unrelated to the task**. Vocabulary is basic and may be used repetitively. There may be inappropriate use of lexical chunks (e.g. memorised phrases, formulaic language and/or language from the input material). Inappropriate word choice and/or errors in word formation and/or in spelling may impede meaning.	A very limited range of structures is used. **Subordinate clauses are rare and simple sentences predominate.** Some structures are produced accurately but grammatical errors are frequent and may impede meaning. Punctuation is often faulty orinadequate.
The resource is inadequate (which may be due to the response being significantly underlength). Possible over-dependence on input material or memorised language. Control of word choice and/or spelling is very limited, and errors predominate. These errors may severely impede meaning.	Sentence forms are attempted, but errors in grammar and punctuation predominate (except in memorised phrases or those taken from the input material). This prevents most meaning from coming through. **Length may be insufficient to provide evidence of control of sentence forms.**
The resource is extremely limited with few recognisable strings, apart from memorised phrases. There is no apparent control of word formation and/or spelling.	There is little or no evidence of sentence forms (except in memorised phrases).
Responses of 20 words or fewer are rated at Band 1. No resource is apparent, except for a few isolated words.	**Responses of 20 words or fewer are rated at Band 1.** No rateable language is evident.

other than English throughout, or **where there is proof that a candidate's answer has been totally memorised.**

IELTS Speaking: Band Descriptors

Band Score	Fluency and coherence	Lexical resource
9	Fluent with only very occasional repetition or self-correction. Any hesitation that occurs is used only to prepare the content of the next utterance and not to find words or grammar. Speech is situationally appropriate and cohesive features are fully acceptable. Topic development is fully coherent and appropriately extended.	Total flexibility and precise use in all contexts. Sustained use of accurate and idiomatic language.
8	Fluent with only very occasional repetition or self-correction. Hesitation may occasionally be used to find words or grammar, but most will be content related. Topic development is coherent, appropriate and relevant.	Wide resource, readily and flexibly used to discuss all topics and convey precise meaning. Skilful use of less common and idiomatic items despite occasional inaccuracies in word choice and collocation. Effective use of paraphrase as required.
7	Able to keep going and readily produce long turns without noticeable effort. Some hesitation, repetition and/or self-correction may occur, often mid sentence and indicate problems with accessing appropriate language. However, these will not affect coherence. Flexible use of spoken discourse markers, connectives and cohesive features.	Resource flexibly used to discuss a variety of topics. Some ability to use less common and idiomatic items and an awareness of style and collocation is evident though inappropriacies occur. Effective use of paraphrase as required.
6	Able to keep going and demonstrates a willingness to produce long turns. Coherence may be lost at times as a result of hesitation, repetition and/or self-correction. Uses a range of spoken discourse markers, connectives and cohesive features though not always appropriately.	Resource sufficient to discuss topics at length. Vocabulary use may be inappropriate but meaning is clear. Generally able to paraphrase successfully.

Scoring criteria for Academic and General Training tests

Grammatical range and accuracy	Pronunciation
Structures are precise and accurate at all times, apart from 'mistakes' characteristic of native speaker speech.	Uses a full range of phonological features to convey precise and/or subtle meaning. Flexible use of features of connected speech is sustained throughout. Can be effortlessly understood throughout. Accent has no effect on intelligibility.
Wide range of structures, flexibly used. The majority of sentences are error free. Occasional inappropriacies and non systematic errors occur. A few basic errors may persist.	Uses a wide range of phonological features to convey precise and/or subtle meaning. Can sustain appropriate rhythm. Flexible use of stress and intonation across long utterances, despite occasional lapses. Can be easily understood throughout. Accent has minimal effect on intelligibility.
A range of structures flexibly used. Error-free sentences are frequent. Both simple and complex sentences are used effectively despite some errors. A few basic errors persist.	Displays all the positive features of band 6, and some, but not all, of the positive features of band 8.
Produces a mix of short and complex sentence forms and a variety of structures with limited flexibility. Though errors frequently occur in complex structures, these rarely impede communication.	Uses a range of phonological features, but control is variable. Chunking is generally appropriate, but rhythm may be affected by a lack of stress timing and/or a rapid speech rate. Some effective use of intonation and stress, but this is not sustained. Individual words or phonemes may be mispronounced but this causes only occasional lack of clarity. Can generally be understood throughout without much effort.

Band Score	Fluency and coherence	Lexical resource
5	Usually able to keep going, but relies on repetition and self-correction to do so and/or on slow speech. Hesitations are often associated with mid sentence searches for fairly basic lexis and grammar. Overuse of certain discourse markers, connectives and other cohesive features. More complex speech usually causes disfluency but simpler language may be produced fluently.	Resource sufficient to discuss familiar and unfamiliar topics but there is limited flexibility. Attempts paraphrase but not always with success.
4	Unable to keep going without noticeable pauses. Speech may be slow with frequent repetition. Often self-corrects. Can link simple sentences but often with repetitious use of connectives. Some breakdowns in coherence.	Resource sufficient for familiar topics but only basic meaning can be conveyed on unfamiliar topics. Frequent inappropriacies and errors in word choice. Rarely attempts paraphrase.
3	Frequent, sometimes long, pauses occur while candidate searches for words. Limited ability to link simple sentences and go beyond simple responses to questions. Frequently unable to convey basic message.	Resource limited to simple vocabulary used primarily to convey personal information. Vocabulary inadequate for unfamiliar topics.
2	Lengthy pauses before nearly every word. Isolated words may be recognisable but speech is of virtually no communicative significance.	Very limited resource. Utterances consist of isolated words or memorised utterances. Little communication possible without the support of mime or gesture.
1	Essentially none. Speech is totally incoherent.	No resource bar a few isolated words. No communication possible.
0	Does not attend	

Notes: (i) A candidate must fully fit the positive features of the descriptor at a particular level.
(ii) A candidate will be rated on their average performance across all parts of the test.

Grammatical range and accuracy	Pronunciation
Basic sentence forms are fairly well controlled for accuracy. Complex structures are attempted but these are limited in range, nearly always contain errors and may lead to the need for reformulation.	Displays all the positive features of band 4, and some, but not all, of the positive features of band 6.
Can produce basic sentence forms and some short utterances are error-free. Subordinate clauses are rare and, overall, turns are short, structures are repetitive and errors are frequent.	Uses some acceptable phonological features, but the range is limited. Produces some acceptable chunking, but there are frequent lapses in overall rhythm. Attempts to use intonation and stress, but control is limited. Individual words or phonemes are frequently mispronounced, causing lack of clarity. Understanding requires some effort and there may be patches of speech that cannot be understood.
Basic sentence forms are attempted but grammatical errors are numerous except in apparently memorised utterances.	Displays some features of band 2, and some, but not all, of the positive features of band 4.
No evidence of basic sentence forms.	Uses few acceptable phonological features (possibly because sample is insufficient). Overall problems with delivery impair attempts at connected speech. Individual words and phonemes are mainly mispronounced and little meaning is conveyed. Often unintelligible.
No rateable language unless memorised.	Can produce occasional individual words and phonemes that are recognisable, but no overall meaning is conveyed. Unintelligible.

MEMO

MEMO

lab.siwonschool.com

단 하나의 교재를 만들기 위해 아이엘츠 전문가 총 출동!
국내 최정상 정통 영국파 강사, 10년 이상 경력의 아이엘츠 전문 강사, 원어민 시험영어 전문가,
호주/영국 명문대 졸업 기획자는 물론 아이엘츠 리딩/리스닝 만점 연구원까지

시원스쿨이 제대로 만든 아이엘츠를 직접 확인하세요

시 작 을 고 민 하 고 있 는 모 든 분 들 에 게

그냥 따라만 오세요

아이엘츠 커리큘럼

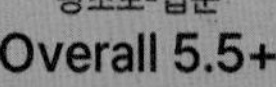

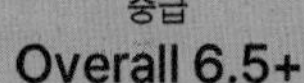

왕초보-입문
Overall 5.5+
딱딱한 내용의 원서보다 유형별 공략을
단계적으로 돕는 아이엘츠 교재를
저자 직강으로 학습해 보세요.

중급
Overall 6.5+
기초를 갖춘 수강생이라면
실전까지 빠르게 끝낼 수 있는 교재로
체계적인 학습이 가능합니다.

실전
Overall 7.0+
실제 아이엘츠 시험과 가장 유사한 문제를
풀어 보고 접근법에 대해 학습하며
목표를 달성할 수 있습니다.

CAMBRIDGE
학습 전
필독서

한 권으로 끝내는

IELTS MASTER

정답 및 해설

 Listening

 Reading

 Writing

 Speaking

 Academic Module

 General Training Module

 IELTS on paper

 IELTS on computer

시원스쿨 LAB

한 권으로 끝내는

IELTS MASTER

정답 및 해설

시원스쿨 LAB

PRACTICE TEST ANSWERS

LISTENING UNIT 1 ~ UNIT 5

READING UNIT 6 ~ UNIT 12

WRITING UNIT 13 ~ UNIT 20

SPEAKING UNIT 21 ~ UNIT 30

PRACTICE TEST LISTENING

Unit 01 IELTS LISTENING에 대한 모든 것

▪ 철자

1. magazine	2. behavio(u)r	3. excellent	4. manager	5. disease
6. nursery	7. waitress	8. garage	9. drawer	10. pollution
11. oxygen	12. college	13. competition	14. deliveries	15. environments

해설 garage는 보통 영국에서는 [개라-쥐] 또는 [개리쥐], 미국에서는 [거라-쥐]라고 발음한다.

▪ 문법

1. The consumption of .... in China increased in 2015.
중국에서 ....의 소비가 2015년에 증가했다.

A tea B teas C a tea

정답 A
해설 일반적인 차(tea)를 나타내는 불가산명사 tea가 정답이다.

2. Do not wear ....
....................................를 입지 마시오.

A jean B jeans C a jean

정답 B
해설 청바지는 jeans, 복수를 사용한다.

3. The Industrial Revolution had a significant impact on social and .... parts.
산업혁명은 사회적이고 .... 부분들에 중대한 영향을 주었다.

A politic B politics C political

정답 C
해설 social과 빈칸은 and로 병렬 연결되어 명사 parts를 수식하고 있다. 따라서 social과 동일한 품사인 형용사로 뜻이 자연스럽게 연결되는 political(정치적인)이 정답이다.

▪ 따라 말하기

It's my pleasure to welcome you all to Lilydale.
릴리데일에 오신 것을 환영합니다.

I'm sure you'll all enjoy your stay here in our beautiful town.
여러분 모두 이곳 아름다운 마을에서 즐겁게 지내실 겁니다.

I know that most of you are here to go kayaking on our local lakes and rivers.
저는 여러분 대부분이 우리 지역 호수와 강에서 카약을 타기 위해 이곳에 오신 것을 알고 있습니다.

I'll tell you more about the kayak routes in a moment.
잠시 후 카약 루트에 대해 더 말씀드리겠습니다.

First, I'll briefly describe how to get around town, and where to find some local amenities you might need.
우선, 시내를 돌아다니는 방법과 여러분이 필요할지도 모를 편의시설들은 어디서 찾을 수 있는지 간략히 설명하겠습니다.

| Vocabulary & Expressions |

disease 병, 질병 nursery 탁아소, 보육시설 garage 차고 drawer 서랍 pollution 오염 oxygen 산소 college 전문학교 competition 경쟁, 대회 deliveries 배달, 배달품 environment 환경 politic 현명한, 신중한 politics 정치 political 정치적인 briefly 간략히 describe 설명하다 amenities 편의시설

LISTENING

Unit 02 Part 1 - 두 사람 간 시설, 주거, 여행 관련 질의 응답

▪ 파트 1

1. Waverley	2. friend	3. castles	4. beach	5. monument
6. mountains	7. 800	8. admission	9. 2,500	10. flights

출제 포인트 **난이도: 중하**

실제 시험에서 출제율이 높은 여행 예약 내용에, 가장 전형적인 문제 유형인 Note/Table Completion이 출제된 가장 기본적인 Part 1 문제임

음원 남 - 호주 / 여 - 영국 / 속도 - 실제 원어민 대화 속도

* IELTS MASTER Listening 음원의 모든 소개 부분은 영국인 성우들이 진행하고, 본문은 실전 대비를 위해 실제 시험에서 빠르게 나올 때 속도를 기준으로 음원이 녹음됨

You will hear a phone conversation between a tour company representative and Maria, who wants some information on motorbike tours in Scotland. First, you have some time to look at questions 1 to 6.

여러분은 여행사 직원과 스코틀랜드 오토바이 투어에 대한 정보를 원하는 마리아 사이의 전화 통화를 듣게 됩니다. 먼저 여러분은 1-6번 문제를 살펴볼 시간이 있습니다.

Now listen carefully and answer questions 1 to 6.

이제 주의 깊게 듣고 1-6번 문제에 답하세요.

TOUR REP: Thanks for calling Wild Bike Tours. My name is Anthony. How can I help you?
MARIA: Hi. I was hoping to find out about your motorbike tours of Scotland. Do you have any pamphlets you could send to me?
TOUR REP: Yes, we do. First, can I take your name, please?
MARIA: Sure, it's Maria Smith.
TOUR REP: Thanks. And what address should I mail them to?
MARIA: 38 Q1 Waverley Street, London.
TOUR REP: Would you mind spelling that for me?
MARIA: Okay. W-A-V-E-R-L-E-Y Street.
TOUR REP: And the postal code?

여행사 직원: 와일드바이크 투어에 전화 주셔서 감사합니다. 제 이름은 앤서니입니다. 무엇을 도와 드릴까요?
마리아: 안녕하세요. 귀사의 스코틀랜드 오토바이 투어에 관해서 알아보려고 합니다. 저에게 보내주실 수 있는 어떤 안내 책자라도 있나요?
여행사 직원: 네, 있습니다. 우선, 성함을 말씀해 주시겠습니까?
마리아: 그럼요, 마리아 스미스입니다.
여행사 직원: 감사합니다. 그리고 어느 주소로 우송해 드리면 될까요?
마리아: 런던 Q1 웨이벌리가 38번지입니다.
여행사 직원: 철자를 알려주시겠습니까?
마리아: 네. W-A-V-E-R-L-E-Y 가입니다.
여행사 직원: 그리고 우편번호는요?

MARIA: It's E1 6AN.
TOUR REP: Great. And how can I get in touch with you? By phone?
MARIA: That's fine, yeah.
TOUR REP: Can I take your number?
MARIA: It's 07215 667883.
TOUR REP: Okay, and lastly, how did you find out about Wild Bike Tours? Did you see an advertisement online?
MARIA: No, actually a Q2 friend of mine recommended you.
TOUR REP: I'm glad to hear that! Well, I'll send those pamphlets to you today, but I'd also be happy to tell you about our tours while you're on the phone right now. What type of tour are you interested in?
MARIA: Well, I'm interested in touring Lowlands and Highlands of Scotland with my husband. We've heard that the scenery is wonderful, and we'd love to experience it on motorbikes.
TOUR REP: You won't regret it. We have a couple of motorbike tours that include many places of interest in those regions. The first one begins in the Dunblane area, where there are many Q3 castles that were used in the popular *Outlander* TV programme.
MARIA: Oh, really? I'd love to see those. I'm a big fan of that programme.
TOUR REP: Perfect. Then you ride to Glenfinnan. From Glenfinnan, you'll drive out west to picturesque Morar on the west coast. There, you can visit several craft shops.
MARIA: I'd prefer to relax on the Q4 beach, if possible. I read that it's beautiful.
TOUR REP: No problem! And the tour returns to Dunblane at the end.
MARIA: Sounds good.
TOUR REP: The other tour is a little different. It begins and ends in the capital city, Edinburgh. You'll start by heading north to Fort William.
MARIA: Oh, I'm sure I read an article about an impressive Q5 monument in Edinburgh city centre. Will we have a chance to see it?
TOUR REP: Yes, you'll have some time in the city before setting off, so you can see the Scott Monument.
MARIA: Great! Does this trip only go north?
TOUR REP: No, it also goes out west to Ullapool, where you'll have a chance to leave your bike and take a cruise on the ferry.
MARIA: Oh, I'm afraid I can't go on any boats. I get really seasick.
TOUR REP: In that case, you could skip Ullapool and head straight up to Inverness.

마리아: E1 6AN입니다.
여행사 직원: 아주 좋습니다. 그럼 제가 어떻게 연락드릴 수 있나요? 전화로 하면 될까요?
마리아: 네, 그러시면 됩니다.
여행사 직원: 번호를 알려주시겠습니까?
마리아: 07215 667883입니다.
여행사 직원: 네, 그리고 마지막으로, 와일드바이크 투어에 관해 어떻게 알게 되셨나요? 온라인으로 광고를 보셨나요?
마리아: 아뇨, 실은 제 Q2 친구 한 명이 추천해 주었어요.
여행사 직원: 그 말씀을 들으니 기쁘네요! 저, 오늘 그 안내 책자들을 보내 드리겠지만, 지금 전화 통화 동안에도 저희 투어에 관해서 말씀드리고 싶네요. 어떤 종류의 투어에 관심이 있으신가요?
마리아: 저, 제 남편과 스코틀랜드의 저지대와 산악지대들을 여행하는 데 관심이 있습니다. 듣기로는 경치가 매우 아름다워서, 오토바이로 경험해 보고 싶어요.
여행사 직원: 후회하지 않으실 겁니다. 저희에게 그 지역들 내에 있는 흥미로운 많은 곳들을 포함하는 두가지 오토바이 투어가 있습니다. 첫 번째 것은 던블레인 지역에서 출발하는데, 그곳은 인기 있는 아웃랜더 TV 프로그램에 이용되었던 많은 Q3 성들이 있는 곳입니다.
마리아: 오, 그래요? 그 성들을 꼭 보고 싶네요. 제가 그 프로그램을 정말 좋아하거든요.
여행사 직원: 완벽하네요. 그 다음에 글렌피넌으로 이동합니다. 글렌피넌에서부터, 서부 해안의 그림 같은 모로를 향해 서쪽으로 가죠. 그곳에서 여러 공예품 매장을 방문하실 수 있습니다.
마리아: 가능하면 Q4 해변에서 편하게 쉬고 싶어요. 그곳이 아름답다는 글을 봤어요.
여행사 직원: 문제없습니다! 그리고 이 투어는 마지막에 던블레인으로 돌아옵니다.
마리아: 좋네요.
여행사 직원: 다른 투어 하나는 약간 다릅니다. 수도인 에든버러에서 시작하고 끝납니다. 포트 윌리엄을 향해 북쪽으로 떠나는 것으로 시작되죠.
마리아: 오, 에든버러 도심에 있는 인상적인 Q5 기념물에 관한 기사를 분명히 읽었어요. 그것을 볼 기회가 있을까요?
여행사 직원: 네, 출발 전에 그 도시에서 약간의 시간을 가지실 것이기 때문에, 스캇 기념탑을 보실 수 있습니다.
마리아: 좋아요! 이 여행은 북쪽으로만 가나요?
여행사 직원: 아뇨, 울라풀을 향해 서쪽으로도 떠나는데, 그곳에 오토바이를 두고 유람선을 타고 여행할 기회를 가져요.
마리아: 오, 저는 어떤 보트도 탈 수 없을 것 같아요. 뱃멀미가 정말 심하거든요.
여행사 직원: 그러시면, 울라풀은 건너뛰고 곧장 인버네스로 가실 수 있습니다.

MARIA: Ah, that's home to a lot of Q6 mountains, right?
TOUR REP: Yes, and not only are they impressively tall, but they are beautiful all year round.
MARIA: Well, my husband might be interested in checking those out.

마리아: 아, 그곳은 많은 Q6 산들의 본고장이죠?
여행사 직원: 네, 그리고 그 산들은 인상적일 정도로 높을 뿐만 아니라 일년 내내 아름답죠.
마리아: 저, 제 남편이 그 산들을 보는데 관심있을지도 몰라요.

Before you hear the rest of the conversation, you have some time to look at questions 7 to 10.

Now listen and answer questions 7 to 10.

여러분은 대화의 나머지 부분을 듣기 전에, 7-10번 문제를 살펴볼 시간이 주어집니다.

이제 주의 깊게 듣고 7-10번 문제에 답하세요.

MARIA: So how many days are the trips and how much do they cost?
TOUR REP: The first motorbike tour I described, the one that starts from Dunblane, lasts nine days and has a total riding distance of Q7 800 miles. So, you cover less than 100 per day, which isn't too exhausting. The cost is £2,000 per person for that tour. That includes all hotel rooms, a motorbike and Q8 admission to several sites of interest. Unfortunately, you need to pay for all your own food.
MARIA: OK. And how about the other tour?
TOUR REP: That one takes ten days, and you'll ride for approximately one thousand miles in total.
MARIA: So I guess that one is more expensive, right?
TOUR REP: Yes, it's £ Q9 2,500 per person, which is actually a bargain when you consider everything that it covers.
MARIA: So that covers accommodation and motorbike hire. How about food?
TOUR REP: Yes, even meals are included. And you get Q10 flights to and from Edinburgh in the price.
MARIA: Oh, that does sound like good value. Thanks for the information. I'll give you a call once I've looked over the pamphlets.
TOUR REP: I look forward to hearing from you.
MARIA: Talk to you soon.

That is the end of Part 1. You now have one minute to check your answers to Part 1.

마리아: 그럼 그 여행들은 며칠 동안 진행되고 비용은 얼마인가요?
여행사 직원: 던블레인에서 출발하는 것으로 설명해 드린 첫 번째 오토바이 투어는 9일 동안 지속되고 총 운행거리가 Q7 800마일입니다. 따라서 하루에 100마일 미만을 소화하기 때문에, 그렇게 지치지 않죠. 이 투어에 대한 비용은 1인당 2,000파운드입니다. 여기에는 모든 호텔 객실과 오토바이, 그리고 흥미로운 몇몇 장소에 대한 Q8 입장료가 포함됩니다. 안타깝지만, 모든 음식에 대해서는 직접 비용을 지불하셔야 합니다.
마리아: 좋아요. 그럼 나머지 투어는 어떤가요?
여행사 직원: 그 투어는 10일이 소요되며, 대략 총 1천 마일을 오토바이로 이동합니다.
마리아: 그럼 그 투어가 더 비싸겠네요?
여행사 직원: 네, 1인당 Q9 2,500파운드인데, 포함하는 모든 것을 고려하면 실제로는 아주 저렴한 것입니다.
마리아: 그럼 그 가격에 숙박 시설과 오토바이 대여는 포함되어 있겠네요. 음식은요?
여행사 직원: 네, 심지어 식사도 포함되어 있죠. 그리고 이 가격에 에든버러를 오가는 Q10 항공편도 이용하시게 됩니다.
마리아: 아, 그럼 분명 좋은 가격인 것 같네요. 정보 알려주셔서 감사합니다. 안내 책자들을 살펴보는 대로, 전화 드릴게요.
여행사 직원: 연락 주시기를 기다리고 있겠습니다.
마리아: 곧 연락 드리겠습니다.

이것으로 파트 1이 끝납니다. 여러분은 이제 자신의 답을 체크할 1분의 시간을 갖습니다.

| Vocabulary & Expressions |

spell ~의 철자를 말해주다 get in touch with ~와 연락하다 advertisement 광고 be interested in ~에 관심이 있다 scenery 경치 of interest 흥미로운 region 지역 ride to 운전해서 ~로 가다 picturesque 그림 같은 craft 공예품 head north 북쪽으로 향하다 impressive 인상적인 monument 기념비, 기념물 set off 출발하다, 떠나다 leave ~을 남겨 놓다 cruise 유람선 여행 get seasick 뱃멀미를 하다 skip ~을 건너뛰다 head straight to ~로 곧장 가다 home to ~의 본고장, 본거지 all year round 일년 내내 describe ~을 설명하다 last 지속되다 cover 포함하다 less than ~ 미만의 exhausting 지치게 하는 admission 입장(료) unfortunately 안타깝게도, 아쉽게도 approximately 약, 대략 in total 전부, 총 ~의 bargain 저렴한 것, 싸게 산 것 accommodation 숙박 시설 hire 대여, 임대 value 가격, 값어치 once ~하자마자 look over ~을 살펴보다, 검토하다 look forward to -ing ~하기를 고대하다

문제 1-6

다음 노트 내용을 완성하시오.

각 답변에 대해 **1개의 단어만**을 쓰시오.

MOTORBIKE TOURS OF SCOTLAND

스코틀랜드 오토바이 투어

Name 성명: Maria Smith 마리아 스미스

Address 주소: 38 **1** .... Street, London 런던 **1** .... 가 38번지

Postcode 우편번호: E1 6AN E1 6AN

Phone 전화번호: (mobile) 07215 667883 (휴대전화) 07215 667883

How did the customer find out about our company? **2** ....

회사에 관해 어떻게 알게 되었는지? **2** ....

Recommended motorbike tours 추천 오토바이 투어

Tour A 투어 A:

- Dunblane area: the customer wants to visit some **3** .... where TV shows were filmed
  던블레인 지역: 고객은 TV 프로그램이 촬영되었던 **3** ....을 방문하기를 원한다
- Morar: the customer wants to spend time on a **4** ....
  모로: 고객이 **4** ....에서 시간을 보내기를 원한다

Tour B 투어 B:

- The customer wants to see the **5** .... in downtown Edinburgh
  고객이 에든버러 시내에서 **5** ....을 보기를 원한다
- At Ullapool: the customer would prefer not to take a cruise
  울라풀에서: 고객은 여객선을 타고 싶어하지 않는다
- At Inverness: her husband probably is interested in visiting **6** ....
  인버네스에서: 고객의 남편이 아마 **6** ....을 방문하는 데 관심이 있을 것이다

1. 방송에서 여자는 "Waverley Street"이라고 말하고, 철자를 정확히 "W-A-V-E-R-L-E-Y"라고 말한다. 이때 여자가 r을 영국식으로 [아]라고 발음함에 유의한다. 따라서 정답은 Waverley로 전부 소문자 또는 대문자로 써도 된다.

2. 여행사 직원이 "how did you find out about Wild Bike Tours?"라며 회사에 관해 어떻게 알았는지 묻자, "a friend of mine"이라고 답한다. 정답은 한 단어이므로 friend가 정답이다.

3. 던블레인 지역에는 TV에서 나온 성들(castles)이 많다고 하였으므로(in the Dunblane area, where there are many castles that were used in the popular *Outlander* TV programme), 정답은 castles이다. 방송에서 정확히 castles라고 나왔고, 문제에 문법상 복수(관계부사의 동사가 복수명사를 받는 were)명사 자리이므로 단수형인 castle은 오답 처리됨에 유의한다.

4. "I'd prefer to relax on the beach, if possible"이라며 고객(여성)은 모로에서 방문하기 원하는 곳을 해변이라고 말한다. 따라서 정답은 beach이다.

5. 고객(여성)은 "impressive monument in Edinburgh city centre"라고 말하며 에든버러 도심에서 기념물을 보기 원하므로 정답은 monument이다.

Paraphrasing downtown(시내) → city centre(도심)

6. 여행사 직원이 인버네스(Inverness)에 대해 말하자 고객은 산들에 대해 언급하고(that's home to a lot of mountains, right?) 남편이 관심있다고 하므로(my husband might be interested in checking those out), 정답은 mountains이다.
Paraphrasing visiting(방문) → checking out(살펴봄)

문제 7-10

다음 표를 완성하시오.

각 답변에 대해 **1개의 단어** 또는 숫자를 쓰시오.

	Duration 기간	Distance travelled 이동 거리	Price (per person) 가격 (1인당)	Price Covers (per person) 가격에 포함되는 것 (1인당)
Tour A 투어 A	9 days 9일	**7** .... miles	£2,000	• accommodation 숙박 • motorbike 오토바이 • **8** ....
Tour B 투어 B	10 days 10일	1,000 miles 1000마일	**9** £	• accommodation 숙박 • motorbike 오토바이 • meals 식사 • two **10** .... 2개의 **10** ....

7. 9일 동안 총 이동 거리가 800마일(nine days and has a total riding distance of 800 miles)이라고 답하므로 정답은 800 또는 eight hundred이다.

8. 여행사 직원이 호텔방, 오토바이, 입장료가 포함된다고 말하므로(That includes all hotel rooms, a motorbike and admission), 정답은 admission이다.
Paraphrasing price covers(가격이 포함한다) → That(the cost) includes(비용이 포함한다)
accommodation(숙박) → hotel rooms(호텔방들)

9. 인당 2500파운드이므로(it's £2,500 per person), 정답은 2,500 또는 2500이다. 단, 표에 나온 £(파운드)를 또 쓰면 오답이다.

10. 에든버러 왕복 항공편도 얻는다고 말하므로(you get flights to and from Edinburgh in the price), 비용에 포함되는 2개의 무엇은 flights이다.
Paraphrasing two flights(두개의 항공편) → flights to and from(왕복 항공편)

Unit 03 Part 2 - 한 사람의 시설, 장소, 정책 관련 설명

■ 파트 2

11. C	12. B	13. C	14. B	15. E
16. D	17. F	18. G	19. I	20. C

출제 포인트 **난이도: 중**

실제 시험에서 출제율이 높은 도시의 정책 변화 내용에, 가장 전형적인 문제 유형인 Multiple Choice와 Labelling Map이 출제된 가장 기본적인 Part 2 문제임. 특히 Labelling Map의 경우, 난이도는 평이하지만, 문제 정답이 방송에서 연이어 나오기에 한번 흐름이 끊기거나 잠깐 딴 생각을 하면 틀리기 쉬움.

음원 남 - 영국 / 속도 - 실제 원어민 독백 속도

You will hear the chairman of the Urban Planning Department in Waterfield addressing local residents about proposed changes to cycling facilities in the city centre. First, you have some time to look at questions 11 to 13.

워터필드 지역 도시계획국장이 도심 지역의 자전거 시설물에 대해 제안된 변화와 관련해 지역 주민들에게 연설하는 내용을 들어보세요. 먼저 여러분은 11-13번 문제를 살펴볼 시간이 있습니다.

Now listen carefully and answer questions 11 to 13.

이제 주의 깊게 듣고 11-13번 문제에 답하세요.

Welcome, ladies and gentlemen. My name is Donald Paterson, and I'm the head of the Urban Planning Department at Waterfield City Council. We've called this meeting to inform members of the public about some changes we are planning to implement for the benefit of cyclists here in Waterfield. I'll begin by giving you details about these improvements, and then I'll be happy to answer any questions you might have.

환영합니다, 신사 숙녀 여러분. 제 이름은 도널드 패터슨이며, 워터필드 시의회 도시계획국장입니다. 이곳 워터필드 지역의 자전거 이용자들의 편의를 위해 저희가 계획하고 있는 몇몇 변화와 관련해 일반 주민들께 알려 드리고자 이 회의를 소집했습니다. 이 개선 사항에 관한 상세 정보를 제공해 드리는 것으로 이야기를 시작할 것이며, 그런 다음에 여러분께서 가지고 계실 수 있는 어떤 질문에도 답변해 드리도록 하겠습니다.

First of all, why have we decided to make so many significant changes now? Well, of course, such changes are always welcome, as they give residents a better quality of life. Q11 But the main reason is that we want Waterfield, and its residents, to be more caring about the environment. In fact, we hope that improvements to cycling amenities will lead to a reduction in motor transportation over the next decade or so.

가장 먼저, 저희가 왜 지금 이렇게 많은 중요한 변화를 주기로 결정했을까요? 자, 물론, 이와 같은 변화는 언제나 반가운 일인데, 주민 여러분에게 더 나은 삶의 질을 제공해주기 때문이죠. Q11 하지만 주된 이유는 저희가 워터필드 지역과 주민 여러분이 환경에 대해 더욱 관심을 가지길 원하고 있다는 점입니다. 사실, 저희는 자전거 편의시설 개선이 향후 10년 정도 기간에 걸쳐 자동차 교통 감소로 이어지기를 바랍니다.

Also, at last month's public forum, we received several requests and complaints from many of the cycling enthusiasts among you. Q12 People were rather upset at how narrow the existing cycle paths are, and urged us to widen them. So, we're taking steps to address that issue, as well as several others. Fortunately, we have an excellent road safety record here in Waterfield, so we know that an increased number of cyclists will not result in any safety concerns, especially once we implement all of the changes.

또한, 지난 달에 있었던 공개 토론회에서, 저희는 여러분 중 많은 자전거 애호가들로부터 여러 요청 사항과 불만 사항을 들었습니다. Q12 사람들이 기존의 자전거 도로가 얼마나 좁은지에 대해 다소 불만스러워했으며, 저희에게 확장해 달라고 촉구했습니다. 따라서, 저희는 이 문제뿐만 아니라 여러 다른 문제들도 처리하기 위한 조치를 취하고 있습니다. 다행히, 워터필드는 훌륭한 도로 안전 기록을 갖고 있기에, 증가된 자전거 이용자 숫자가 어떠한 안전 우려도 야기하지 않을 것임을 알고 있습니다. 특별히 모든 변화를 시행하면 말이죠.

We think the proposed changes are all highly beneficial to our city. We have even allocated funding to start a bike rental programme and are ready to construct the first of several rental stations. Q13 But, of course, it's no good giving people access to free bikes if they attempt to steal them, so we are looking at measures to prevent that. GPS tracking technology and additional CCTV cameras will most likely be utilised.

저희는 이 제안된 변화가 시에 매우 유익하리라 생각합니다. 저희는 자전거 대여 프로그램을 시작하기 위한 자금도 할당해 두고 여러 자전거 대여소들 중 첫 번째를 지을 준비도 되어 있습니다. Q13 하지만, 당연히, 사람들이 훔치려고 할 경우에는 무료 자전거 이용 권한을 제공하는 것이 좋지 않기 때문에, 이를 방지하기 위한 조치들을 살펴보고 있습니다. GPS 추적 기술과 추가 CCTV 카메라가 활용될 가능성이 가장 높습니다.

Before you hear the rest of the talk, you have some time to look at questions 14 to 20.

여러분은 대화의 나머지 부분을 듣기 전에, 14-20번 문제를 살펴볼 시간이 주어집니다.

Now listen and answer questions 14 to 20.

이제 주의 깊게 듣고 14-20번 문제에 답하세요.

OK, now I'd like you all to take a look at this map of downtown Waterfield, particularly the area around Main Street. Now, Q14 one of the biggest new additions will be the bike rental station, which will be in front of the hotel on Eden Road. This will include 40 bikes at the beginning, with a plan to add more later in the year.

좋습니다, 이제 여러분 모두가 이 워터필드 시내 지도를 봐주셨으면 하는데, 특히 중심가 주변 구역을 봐주십시오. 자, Q14 가장 큰 새로운 추가 사항들 중의 하나가 자전거 대여소인데, 이는 에덴로에 있는 호텔 앞에 위치하게 될 것입니다. 이곳에 처음에는 40대의 자전거가 포함될 것이며, 올 하반기에 더 많이 추가될 계획입니다.

We've also decided to construct an underpass to allow walkers and bikers to safely pass under busy Main Street. Q15 This will be located between the theatre and the department store. Construction should take approximately 3 months.

저희는 또한 보행자들과 자전거 이용자들이 분주한 중심가 밑으로 안전하게 통행할 수 있도록 지하도도 건설하기로 결정했습니다. Q15 이는 극장과 백화점 사이에 위치하게 될 것입니다. 건설 공사는 약 3개월이 소요될 것입니다.

Next, we already have bike lanes on most streets, Q16 and we are finally going to add them to Finn Street as well. These should be ready for use within a couple of weeks.

다음으로, 우리는 대부분의 거리에 자전거 전용 도로를 이미 보유하고 있으며, Q16 드디어 핀가에도 추가할 예정입니다. 이는 2주 안으로 준비가 될 것입니다.

Q17 We will be adding new bicycle storage rails outside the department store at its Clarence Road entrance. There will be space for at least 70 bicycles.

Q17 우리는 클라렌스로 쪽 입구가 있는 백화점 외부에 새로운 자전거 보관대를 추가할 것입니다. 최소 70대의 자전거를 놓을 수 있는 공간이 생길 것입니다.

Q18 Speaking of Clarence Road, we are aware that some potholes have formed at the junction with Main Street, so we will be repairing these and resurfacing that part of the road.

Q18 클라렌스로를 말씀드린 김에, 중심가와 맞닿은 교차로에 몇몇 움푹 패인 곳이 형성되어 있다는 사실을 알고 있으므로, 이를 수리하고 도로의 해당 부분을 재포장할 것입니다.

Q19 We also plan to set up a small bicycle repair booth just outside the café on Main Street. Cyclists can stop by there if they have a puncture or wish to have their brakes or gears checked.

Q19 저희는 또한 중심가에 위치한 카페 바로 바깥쪽에 작은 자전거 수리소도 설치할 계획입니다. 자전거 이용자들은 타이어 펑크가 나거나 브레이크 또는 기어를 점검 받기를 원할 때 그곳에 들르시면 됩니다.

Oh, and I almost forgot one of the biggest changes! In addition to the underpass, Q20 we will be constructing a pedestrian bridge at the section of Main Street between the hotel and the bank. So, cyclists and pedestrians will no longer have such difficulty crossing the busy street. OK. So, does anyone have any questions?...

오, 그리고 가장 중요한 변화들 중의 한 가지를 잊을 뻔 했습니다! 지하도 외에도, Q20 저희는 중심가 구역의 호텔과 은행 사이에 보행자용 다리도 건설할 예정입니다. 따라서, 자전거 이용자들과 보행자들은 분주한 그 거리를 건너는 것과 같은 어려움을 더 이상 겪지 않을 것입니다. 좋습니다. 그럼 질문 있으신 분 계신가요?

That is the end of Part 2. You now have 30 seconds to check your answers to Part 2.	이것으로 파트 2가 끝납니다. 여러분은 이제 자신의 답을 체크할 30초의 시간을 갖습니다.

| Vocabulary & Expressions |

urban planning 도시 계획 inform A of B A에게 B를 알리다 implement ~을 시행하다 benefit 혜택, 이득 details 세부 사항, 상세 정보 improvement 개선, 향상 significant 중요한 resident 주민 caring about ~에 대해 관심 갖는 amenities 편의시설 lead to ~로 이어지다 reduction in ~의 감소 transportation 교통 decade 10년 enthusiast 애호가 upset 불만스러운, 화난 narrow 좁은 existing 기존의 urge 촉구하다 widen ~을 확장하다 take steps 조치를 취하다 address ~을 처리하다 result in ~을 야기하다 concern 우려 once 일단 ~하면 highly 매우, 대단히 beneficial to ~에게 유익한 allocate ~을 할당하다 funding 자금 rental 대여, 임대 access to ~에 대한 이용 (권한) attempt to do ~하려 시도하다 measures 조치, 방법 prevent ~을 방지하다 most likely ~할 가능성이 가장 높은 utilise ~을 활용하다 particularly 특히 addition 추가(된 것) approximately 약, 대략 as well ~도, 또한 storage rail 보관대 at least 최소한, 적어도 be aware that ~임을 알다 pothole 움푹 패인 곳 form 형성되다 junction 교차로 resurface (도로 등) ~을 재포장하다 set up ~을 설치하다 repair booth 수리소 stop by ~에 들르다 puncture 타이어 펑크 have A p.p. A가 ~되게 하다 in addition to ~외에도, 뿐만 아니라 pedestrian 보행자 no longer 더 이상 ~ 않다 have difficulty -ing ~하는데 어려움을 겪다 cross ~을 건너다

문제 11-13

A, B, C 중에서 알맞은 글자를 고르시오.

Cycling Changes in Waterfield 워터필드의 자전거 이용 관련 변화

11. Why were changes to cycling amenities proposed in Waterfield?
워터필드 지역에서 왜 자전거 편의시설에 대한 변화가 제안되었는가?

A To reduce the number of road accidents 도로 사고의 숫자를 줄이기 위해
B To attract a greater number of tourists 더 많은 수의 관광객들을 끌어들이기 위해
C To make the city more environmentally-friendly 도시를 더욱 환경친화적으로 만들기 위해

변화의 주된 이유로 워터필드 지역 주민들이 환경에 대해 더욱 관심을 가지길 원한다고 말하므로(the main reason is that we want Waterfield, and its residents, to be more caring about the environment), 정답은 C이다.
Paraphrasing more environmentally-friendly(더 친환경적인) → more caring about the environment(환경에 더 관심 갖는)

12. At a recent public forum, local residents strongly demanded
최근의 공개 토론회에서, 지역 주민들이 ....을 강력히 요구했다

A safer city roads. 더 안전한 시내 도로
B wider cycle paths. 더 넓은 자전거 전용 도로
C access to free bicycles. 무료 자전거의 이용

주민들이 자전거 길을 확대해 달라 요구하므로(People were rather upset at how narrow the existing cycle paths are, and urged us to widen them), 정답은 B이다.
Paraphrasing recent(최근에) → last month(지난 달)
strongly demand(강하게 요구하다) → urge(촉구하다)

13. According to the speaker, one problem with the new amenities will be
화자의 말에 따르면, 새 편의시설에 대한 한 가지 문제점은 ....일 것이다.

A securing funding for annual maintenance. 연간 유지 관리에 필요한 자금을 확보하는 일
B making them accessible to all age groups. 모든 연령대의 사람이 이용 가능하도록 만드는 일
C finding a way to prevent bicycle theft. 자전거 절도를 방지하는 방법을 찾는 일

좋지 않은 점, 즉 문제점으로 도난을 언급하고 있기에(it's no good giving people access to free bikes if they attempt to steal them), 정답은 C이다.

Paraphrasing problem(문제) → no good(좋지 않음)
finding a way(방법을 찾다) → looking at measures(조치를 살피다)
bicycle theft(자전거 절도) → steal them(bikes)(자전거를 훔치다)

문제 14-20

다음 지도에 표기하시오.

A에서 I까지 알맞은 글자를 14번에서 20번 문제 옆에 기입하시오.

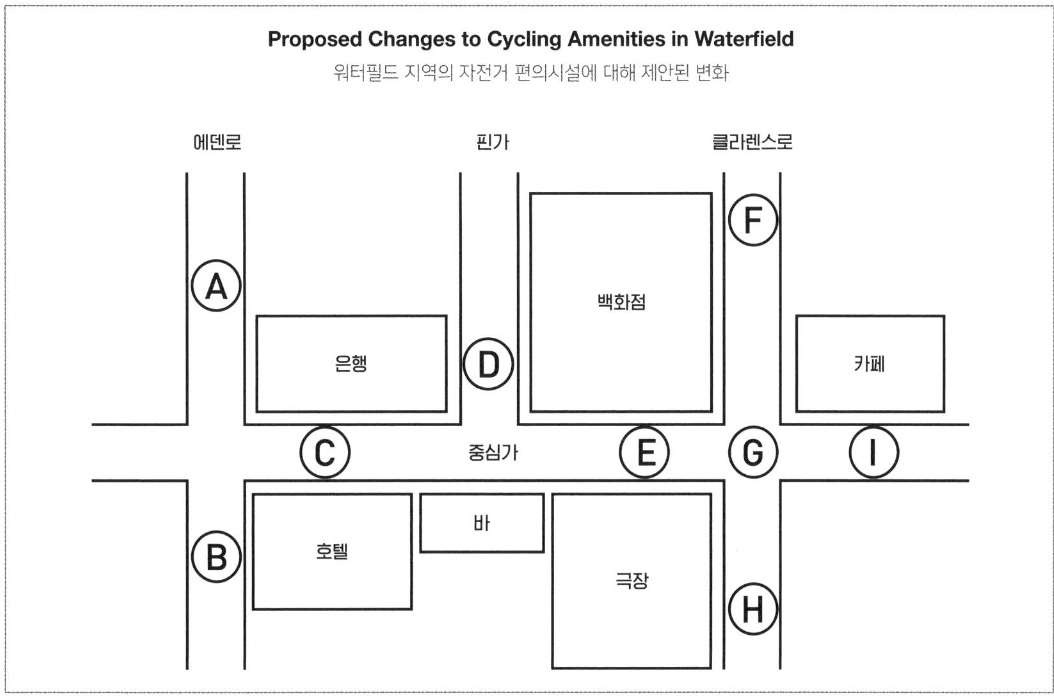

14. New bike rental station 신규 자전거 대여소 ………………………………

새로운 자전거 대여소는 호텔 앞 에덴로(one of the biggest new additions will be the bike rental station, which will be in front of the hotel on Eden Road)이므로 정답은 B이다.

15. Pedestrian/cyclist underpass 보행자/자전거 이용자 지하도 ………………………………

중심가 밑에 보행자와 자전거 이용자에게 안전한 지하도(an underpass to allow walkers and bikers to safely pass under busy Main Street)가 극장과 백화점 사이에 위치(This will be located between the theatre and the department store)하므로 정답은 E이다.

Paraphrasing pedestrian(보행자) → walker(걷는 사람)
cyclist(자전거 이용자) → biker(오토바이나 자전거 이용자)

16. Designated bicycle lanes 지정된 자전거 도로 ………………………………

자전거 도로가 핀가에 추가되므로(bike lanes on most streets, and we are finally going to add them to Finn Street as well), 정답은 D이다.

17. Bicycle storage rails 자전거 보관대 ....

클라렌스로에 있는 백화점 입구 바깥에 자전거 보관대가 추가되므로(We will be adding new bicycle storage rails outside the department store, at its Clarence Road entrance), 정답은 F이다.

18. Resurfaced road 재포장된 도로 ....

재포장된 도로는 클라렌스로와 중심가 교차로의 움푹 파인 구멍을 수리하여 생기므로(Speaking of Clarence Road, we are aware that some potholes have formed at the junction with Main Street, so we will be repairing these and resurfacing that part of the road), 정답은 G이다.

19. Bicycle repair booth 자전거 수리소 ....

중심가 카페 밖에 자전거 수리소가 설치될 예정이므로(We also plan to set up a small bicycle repair booth just outside the café on Main Street), 정답은 I이다.

20. Pedestrian/cyclist bridge 보행자/자전거 이용자 다리 ....

보행자 다리가 중심가 부분에서 호텔과 은행 사이에 생기므로(we will be constructing a pedestrian bridge at the section of Main Street between the hotel and the bank), 정답은 C이다.

Unit 04 Part 3 – 두 사람 이상의 학업 관련 대화

▪ 파트 3

21&22. B, D	**23&24.** A, E	**25&26.** C, E	
27. C	**28.** B	**29.** B	**30.** A

출제 포인트 **난이도: 중상**

실제 시험 Part 3에서 출제율이 높은 두 대학생 간 과제 내용에, 가장 전형적인 문제 유형인 Multiple Choice가 나온 가장 기본적인 Part 3 문제임. Multiple Choice의 경우, 방송에 등장하는 단어가 보기에서 오답으로 유인하는 경우가 많아 난이도가 높음.

음원 남 - 영국 / 여 - 영국 / 속도 - 실제 원어민 대화 속도

You will hear a student called Matthew talking to his course leader about some research he has done on nutrition and sport. First, you have some time to look at questions 21 to 26.	매튜라는 이름의 학생이 영양과 스포츠에 관해 실시한 조사 내용에 관해 지도 교수와 나누는 이야기를 들어보세요. 먼저 여러분은 21-26번 문제를 살펴볼 시간이 있습니다.
Now listen carefully and answer questions 21 to 26.	이제 주의 깊게 듣고 21-26번 문제에 답하세요.
COURSE LEADER: Hi, Matthew. Well, the deadline for your dissertation is just one month away, so I just wanted to check that everything is on schedule. Can you tell me how your research on nutrition and sport has gone so far? Last time, you mentioned that you were surveying some athletes. How did that go?	**지도 교수:** 안녕, 매튜. 네 논문 마감 기한이 불과 한 달밖에 남지 않았기 때문에, 모든 것이 일정대로인지 확인해 보려고 해. 영양과 스포츠에 관한 네 연구가 지금까지 어떻게 되어 가고 있는지 얘기해 주겠니? 지난 번에, 일부 운동 선수들에게 설문 조사를 하고 있는 중이라고 했는데. 그 일은 어떻게 되었니?

MATTHEW: Very well, I think. I selected fifty athletes, half male and half female. Twenty-five of them play football, ten of them play rugby and fifteen of them play tennis. Q21&22 They are all very experienced in their respective sports and play for professional teams. Some of them have even won medals and awards in competitions.
COURSE LEADER: Sounds good. And how old were these athletes?
MATTHEW: I chose a fairly wide age range, so the youngest was 20 years old, while some of them were as old as 33. Q21&22 And although I didn't set out to choose athletes who regularly take a nutrient supplement, that practice is so common these days, so it turned out that they all did anyway.
COURSE LEADER: Yes, that's not surprising. So, you gathered your information through questionnaires, right?
MATTHEW: Yes. Because I was using a relatively large group of subjects, Q23&24 face-to-face interviews would have been too time-consuming, so I went with questionnaires instead. I made contact with each participant by e-mail, after receiving permission from team owners and managers, and asked them to send them back within two weeks.
COURSE LEADER: Do you think it was a good way to collect meaningful data?
MATTHEW: I do, because the respondents had plenty of time to fill it out, Q23&24 so they generally provided very thorough answers to each question. I think an interview would have been more rushed, resulting in just quick responses.
COURSE LEADER: Good point. And your main focus was the connection between nutrition and exercise, right?
MATTHEW: Yes. But my focus shifted a little once my research was underway. Q25&26 At first, I was planning to only concentrate on the way certain foods and beverages affect athletes' performances. But then, the more I looked into the subject, Q25&26 I decided to branch out and also look at how easy or difficult it is for different athletes to receive sound nutritional advice.
COURSE LEADER: Oh, I'm surprised that it wouldn't be the same for all athletes.
MATTHEW: I was surprised, too! But it really depends on each team's manager and owner.

Before you hear the rest of the discussion, you have some time to look at questions 27 to 30.

Now listen and answer questions 27 to 30.

매튜: 아주 잘된 것 같아요. 제가 50명의 운동 선수를 골랐는데, 반은 남성이고 나머지 반은 여성이었어요. 이들 중에서 25명은 축구를, 10명은 럭비를, 그리고 15명은 테니스를 해요. Q21&22 이 선수들은 전부 각자의 스포츠에서 아주 경험이 많고 프로팀에서 활동해요. 일부 선수들은 심지어 대회에서 메달과 상을 받기도 했어요.
지도 교수: 잘된 것 같구나. 그럼 이 선수들은 나이가 어떻게 되니?
매튜: 제가 꽤 다양한 연령대를 선택했기 때문에, 가장 어린 사람은 20살이었고, 반면에 일부는 33살이나 되기도 했어요. Q21&22 그리고 제가 처음부터 영양 보충제를 주기적으로 섭취하는 운동 선수들을 선택하려고 했던 것은 아니었지만, 그 관행이 요즘에는 아주 흔하기 때문에, 어쨌든 선수들 모두 그렇게 했던 것으로 드러났어요.
지도 교수: 맞아, 그것은 놀라운 일이 아니지. 그럼, 설문지를 통해서 정보를 수집한 것이 맞지?
매튜: 네. 제가 비교적 큰 규모의 대상자 그룹을 이용했기 때문에 Q23&24 대면 인터뷰는 너무 시간이 많이 소비되는 것 같아서, 대신에 설문지로 했어요. 구단주와 감독들로부터 허락을 받은 후에 이메일로 각 참가자에게 연락했고, 2주 내에 다시 돌려보내도록 요청 드렸어요.
지도 교수: 의미 있는 자료를 수집하는 데 있어 좋은 방법이었다고 생각하나?
매튜: 네, 왜냐하면 응답자들에게 작성할 시간이 충분했기 때문에, Q23&24 대부분 각 문제에 대해 매우 철저한 답변을 제공해 주었어요. 제 생각에 인터뷰는 좀 더 성급하게 진행되어서 결과적으로 즉각적인 답변만을 만들어 냈을 것 같아요.
지도 교수: 좋은 지적이야. 그리고 주된 초점은 영양과 운동 사이의 관계였었지?
매튜: 네. 하지만 일단 연구가 시작되자 제 초점이 약간 바뀌었어요. Q25&26 처음에는, 특정 음식과 음료가 운동 선수들의 성적에 영향을 미치는 방식에만 집중할 계획이었어요. 하지만, 그 후에, 주제 내용을 더 살펴보다가, Q25&26 그 범위를 더 확장해서 서로 다른 운동 선수들이 좋은 영양상의 조언을 얻는 것이 얼마나 쉬운지 또는 어려운지도 살펴보기로 결정했어요.
지도 교수: 오, 모든 운동 선수들에게 동일하지 않을 거라니 놀랍구나.
매튜: 저도 놀랐어요! 하지만 정말로 각 팀의 감독과 구단주에게 달려 있는 부분이에요.

여러분은 대화의 나머지 부분을 듣기 전에, 27-30번 문제를 살펴볼 시간이 주어집니다.

이제 주의 깊게 듣고 27-30번 문제에 답하세요.

COURSE LEADER: So, you decided to have an equal number of men and women in your study. Why was that? Many of those sports are largely dominated by men.
MATTHEW: Well, that is true, but I made a decision early on to study both genders equally, because Q27 I figured that my findings would be applicable to all individuals, regardless of sex, and not only to serious athletes.
COURSE LEADER: I think it was a smart choice. Now, when conducting your study, did you refer to Frank Allen's research paper on sports nutrition?
MATTHEW: No, I've never heard of it.
COURSE LEADER: Well, in the paper, he suggests that the greatest impact on a professional athlete's performance is not linked to diet or exercise, but to hydration. Q28 He found that fluid loss accounted for a significant drop in overall performance, and that regular intake of water or energy drinks resulted in better performances.
MATTHEW: Interesting. Well, luckily, I did look into that as part of my research, and I drew a pretty similar conclusion.
COURSE LEADER: That sounds promising then.
MATTHEW: Yes, and I had no idea that it had such an impact.
COURSE LEADER: So did you find out anything else interesting about the role of nutrition in sport?
MATTHEW: What I noticed is that all of my subjects tended to combine several strategies in order to achieve the best results. In other words, Q29 no two people had the same diet, and each plan was specifically tailored to each athlete's needs.
COURSE LEADER: I guess that would make sense, as every person's body is different, and different sports require different types of performance.
MATTHEW: Exactly.
COURSE LEADER: And while studying your subjects, were you surprised by any of their responses?
MATTHEW: Yes, Q30 I was very shocked that barely any of them had been informed just how crucial it is to look after your body after an exhausting sports match. Most of them would simply have a drink, and had no idea about recovering carbohydrates, protein and electrolytes, and this can have really negative consequences.
COURSE LEADER: Right, it's astounding that team managers don't educate their players more about that.

That is the end of Part 3. You now have 30 seconds to check your answers to Part 3.

지도 교수: 그럼, 연구 내용에 동일한 숫자의 남성과 여성들을 포함하기로 결정했구나. 왜 그렇게 한 것이지? 많은 스포츠가 대부분 남성이 지배적인데.
매튜: 음, 맞는 말씀이긴 하지만, 두 성별을 동일하게 연구하기 위해 일찍부터 그렇게 결정하였고, Q27 제 연구 결과물이 성별에 상관없이 전문 운동 선수들뿐만 아니라 모든 사람들에게 적용 가능할 것이라고 생각했기 때문이에요.
지도 교수: 현명한 선택이었던 것 같구나. 그럼, 연구를 실시할 때, 스포츠 영양학에 관한 프랭크 앨런의 연구 논문을 참고하였니?
매튜: 아뇨, 그건 들어본 적이 없었어요.
지도 교수: 음, 논문에서 그 교수는 전문 운동 선수의 성적에 가장 큰 영향을 미치는 것이 식단이나 운동 연습이 아니라 수분 섭취와 관련되어 있다고 제시하고 있어. Q28 그는 수분 손실이 전반적인 운동 능력의 상당한 감소 원인이 된다는 점과, 물 또는 에너지 음료의 주기적인 섭취가 더 나은 경기력을 만들어주었다는 점을 발견했지.
매튜: 흥미롭네요. 저, 다행히도, 제 연구의 일환으로 그 부분을 확실히 살펴봤는데, 꽤 비슷한 결론을 이끌어냈어요.
지도 교수: 그럼 조짐이 좋을 것 같구나.
매튜: 네, 그리고 그게 그렇게 영향이 있었는지는 몰랐어요.
지도 교수: 그럼 스포츠에서 영양의 역할에 관해 다른 흥미로운 것도 찾았니?
매튜: 제가 알아차린 것은 저의 연구대상자 모두가 가장 좋은 결과를 이루기 위해 여러 전략들을 결합하는 경향이 있었다는 점이에요. 다시 말씀드리면, Q29 그 어떤 두 사람도 동일한 식사를 하지 않았고, 각각의 식사 계획은 각 운동 선수의 필요에 특정하게 맞춰져 있었어요.
지도 교수: 모든 사람의 신체가 다르고 서로 다른 스포츠마다 다른 종류의 능력을 필요로 하기 때문에 이해가 되는구나.
매튜: 맞습니다.
지도 교수: 그리고 주제 내용을 연구하면서, 어떤 것이든 그 선수들의 응답에 놀라지는 않았니?
매튜: 놀랐어요, Q30 그들 중 누구도 지치게 만드는 스포츠 경기 후에 신체를 돌보는 일이 얼마나 중요한지를 알고 있었던 사람이 거의 없었다는 점에 매우 충격을 받았어요. 그 선수들 중 대부분은 단순히 음료를 마시면서 탄수화물과 단백질, 그리고 전해질을 회복하는 것에 대해 전혀 알지 못했는데, 이건 정말로 부정적인 결과를 만들 수 있거든요.
지도 교수: 그렇지, 팀 감독들이 그 부분에 대해 더 소속 선수들을 교육하지 않는다는 점이 매우 놀라운 일이구나.

이것으로 파트 3가 끝납니다. 여러분은 이제 자신의 답을 체크할 30초의 시간을 갖습니다.

| Vocabulary & Expressions |

deadline 마감 기한 dissertation 논문 nutrition 영양 so far 지금까지 survey ~을 설문 조사하다 athlete 운동 선수 respective 각각의 win (상 등) ~을 타다, 받다 competition (경기) 대회 fairly 꽤, 상당히 set out 시작하다 nutrient supplement 영양 보충제 practice 관행, 관례 turn out ~으로 드러나다 questionnaire 설문지 face-to-face 면대면의 time-consuming 시간 소모가 큰 participant 참가자 respondent 응답자 fill out ~을 작성하다 thorough 철저한 rushed 성급한, 서두르는 result in ~의 결과를 낳다 shift 바뀌다 underway 진행 중인 concentrate on ~에 집중하다 affect ~에 영향을 미치다 performance 능력, 성과 look into ~을 살펴보다, 조사하다 subject 대상자, 피실험자 branch out 확장하다, 다각화하다 sound 좋은, 잘 된 nutritional 영양상의 depend on ~에 달려 있다 dominate 우세하다 figure 생각하다, 파악하다 applicable 적용 가능한 individual 사람, 개인 regardless of ~와 상관없이 conduct ~을 실시하다, 수행하다 refer to ~을 참고하다 impact on ~에 대한 영향 be linked to ~와 연관되어 있다 hydration 수분 섭취 fluid loss 수분 손실 account for ~의 원인이 되다 significant 상당한 drop in ~의 감소 intake 섭취 draw a conclusion 결과를 이끌어내다 promising 조짐이 좋은, 유망한 tend to do ~하는 경향이 있다 strategy 전략 be tailored to ~에 맞춰져 있다 make sense 이해가 되다, 말이 되다 barely 거의 ~ 않다 informed 알고 있는 crucial 중대한, 중요한 look after ~을 돌보다 carbohydrate 탄수화물 protein 단백질 electrolyte 전해질 negative 부정적인 consequence 결과 astounding 매우 놀라운 regimen 요법, 관리

문제 21-22

A와 E 사이에서 **두 개의 글자**를 고르시오.

Which **TWO** characteristics were shared by the athletes involved in Matthew's sport research?
어떤 **두 가지** 특징이 매튜의 스포츠 연구에 관련된 운동 선수들에 의해 공통적으로 나타났는가?

A They had all won important sports competitions. 모두 중요한 스포츠 경기 대회에서 우승했다.
B They had all taken nutrition supplements. 모두 영양 보충제를 섭취했다.
C They were all under 20 years old. 모두 20세 미만이었다.
D They had all played sports professionally. 모두 전문적으로 스포츠를 했다.
E They all played for the same sports team. 모두 동일한 스포츠 팀에서 활동했다.

매튜가, 운동선수들 모두 전문 팀에서 스포츠를 하고(They are all very experienced in their respective sports and play for professional teams), 영양 보충제를 섭취한다고 하였으므로(And although I didn't set out to choose athletes who regularly take a nutrient supplement, that practice is so common these days, so it turned out that they all did anyway), 정답은 각각 D(They had all played sports professionally)와 B(They had all taken nutrition supplements)이다. 이때 순서를 바꿔서 21에 B, 22에 D라고 써도 정답 처리된다.

문제 23-24

A와 E 사이에서 **두 개의 글자**를 고르시오.

Which **TWO** points does Matthew make about his use of questionnaires?
매튜는 자신의 설문지 활용과 관련해 어떤 **두 가지** 주장을 하는가?

A It resulted in comprehensive responses. 포괄적인 응답이라는 결과를 낳았다.
B It meant that he could not ask follow-up questions. 그가 후속 질문을 할 수 없었음을 의미했다.
C It enabled him to easily compare various data. 그가 다양한 자료를 쉽게 비교할 수 있게 해주었다.
D It had been successful in previous studies. 이전의 연구에서는 성공적이었다.
E It allowed him to save some research time. 일부 조사 시간을 절약할 수 있게 해주었다.

매튜가, 시간 소비가 많은 인터뷰 대신에 설문지를 사용했고(face-to-face interviews would have been too time-consuming, so I went with questionnaires instead), 응답자들이 매우 자세한 답변을 했다고 하므로(they generally provided very thorough answers to each question), 정답은 각각 E(It allowed him to save some research time)와 A(It resulted in comprehensive responses)이다. 이때 순서를 바꿔서 23에 A, 24에 E라고 써도 정답 처리된다.

Paraphrasing comprehensive responses(포괄적인 응답) → thorough answers(철저한 대답)

문제 25-26

A와 E 사이에서 **두 개의 글자**를 고르시오.

Which **TWO** topics did Matthew focus on in his research?
매튜는 자신의 연구에서 어느 **두 가지** 주제에 초점을 맞췄는가?

A the side effects of nutritional supplements 영양 보충제의 부작용
B the effects of dehydration on athletes 탈수가 운동 선수에게 미치는 영향
C the relationship between diet and performance 식단과 성과 사이의 관계
D the benefits of high-calorie foods in sports 스포츠에서 고칼로리 음식이 주는 장점
E the availability of nutritional information 영양 정보의 이용 가능성

매튜가 처음에는 음식과 음료가 운동 성과에 어떻게 영향을 미치는지에 초점을 맞추려고 했지만(At first, I was planning to only concentrate on the way certain foods and beverages affect athletes' performances), 이후 좋은 영양상의 조언을 얻는 것이 얼마나 쉬운지 또는 어려운지에 대해 조사가 확대되었다고 하였으므로(I decided to branch out and also look at how easy or difficult it is for different athletes to receive sound nutritional advice), 정답은 각각 C(the relationship between diet and performance), E(the availability of nutritional information)이다. 이때 순서를 바꿔서 25에 E, 26에 C라고 써도 정답 처리된다.

Paraphrasing focus on(~에 집중하다) → concentrate on(~에 집중하다)
diet(식사, 식습관) → certain foods and beverages(특정 음식과 음료)
availability(이용 가능성) → how easy or difficult it is to receive(얼마나 쉽게 또는 어렵게 얻을 수 있는지)
nutritional information(영양 정보) → nutritional advice(영양 조언)

문제 27-30

A, B, C 중에서 알맞은 글자를 고르시오.

27. Matthew included both male and female subjects in his study because
매튜가 자신의 연구에 남성과 여성 대상자를 모두 포함했는데, 그 이유는

A he wanted to focus primarily on sports that are played by both sexes.
두 성별 모두가 경기하는 스포츠에 주로 초점을 맞추고 싶었기 때문이다.

B he predicted there would be a large data discrepancy between the two sexes.
두 성별 사이에 데이터 상의 큰 차이가 있을 것으로 예측했기 때문이다.

C he thought his research would be of interest to both men and women.
자신의 연구가 남성과 여성 모두에게 흥미로울 것으로 생각했기 때문이다.

매튜는 남성과 여성 모두를 포함시킨 이유로 자신의 연구결과가 모두에게 적용 가능하다고 하였는데(I figured that my findings would be applicable to all individuals, regardless of sex, and not only to serious athletes), 보기 A와 B는 전혀 방송과 관련이 없는 내용으로, 이 중에서 가장 유사하게 패러프레이징 된 C가 정답이다.

Paraphrasing of interest to both men and women(남녀 모두에 관심있는)
→ applicable to all individuals, regardless of sex(성별에 상관없이 모두에게 적용가능한)

28. Frank Allen's research paper suggests that in professional sport, an athlete's performance is significantly influenced by
프랭크 앨런의 연구 논문은 프로 스포츠에서 운동 선수의 경기력이 ....에 의해 상당히 영향을 받음을 암시한다.

A their pre-match exercise regimen. 경기 전의 운동법
B their consumption of fluid. 수분 소비
C their intake of nutrient supplements. 영양 보충제 섭취

수분 손실이 성적에 상당한 하락을 설명하고, 정기적인 수분섭취가 더 나은 성적으로 귀결된다고(He found that fluid loss accounted for a significant drop in overall performance, and that regular intake of water or energy drinks resulted in better performances) 하였으므로, B가 정답이다.

Paraphrasing significantly influenced(상당한 영향을 받는) → greatest impact(가장 큰 영향)
fluid(수분) → hydration(수분)

29. What did Matthew note about the diet plans of his subjects?
매튜는 대상자의 식단 계획과 관련해 무엇에 주목했는가?

A They were created by qualified dietitians. 자격을 갖춘 영양사에 의해 만들어졌다.
B They were highly personalised. 개인의 필요에 크게 맞춰져 있었다.
C They included regular light meals. 주기적으로 먹는 가벼운 식사를 포함했다.

아무도 같은 식단을 갖지 않고 각 운동선수의 필요에 맞게 식단이 짜여 졌다고 하므로(no two people had the same diet, and each plan was specifically tailored to each athlete's needs), 정답은 B이다.
Paraphrasing highly personalised(매우 개별화된) ➔ specifically tailored(특별히 맞춰진)

30. According to the speakers, athletes are still not given enough information on
화자들의 말에 따르면, 운동 선수는 ....에 관한 충분한 정보가 여전히 주어지지 않는다.

A the importance of post-exercise recovery techniques. 운동 후의 회복 기술이 지니는 중요성
B the negative impact of carbohydrates on fitness. 탄수화물이 신체 단련에 미치는 부정적인 영향
C the benefits of a balanced daily diet. 균형 잡힌 일일 식단의 장점

거의 아무도 운동 후 자신의 몸을 돌보는 것이 중요한지를 모른다고 말하므로(barely any of them had been informed just how crucial it is to look after your body after an exhausting sports match), 정답은 A이다.
Paraphrasing importance of post-exercise recovery techniques(운동 후 회복 기법의 중요성)
➔ how crucial it is to look after your body after an exhausting sports match(지친 운동 경기 후 자신의 몸을 돌보는 것의 중요성)

Unit 05 Part 4 - 한 사람의 강의 또는 발표

▪ 파트 4

31. North	**32.** religious	**33.** palaces	**34.** gold	**35.** limbs
36. clay	**37&38.** individualism, abstraction		**39&40.** wood, seashells	

출제 포인트 **난이도: 상**

실제 Part 4 시험에서 호주 원주민 예술(Aboriginal art) 등의 토속 예술이 출제된 적이 있는데, 자기가 모르는 주제 또는 단어와 마주쳤을 경우를 대비하기 위한 연습으로 난이도가 높게 출제되었지만 Part 4에 가장 전형적인 note completion 문제 유형과 Part 4에 가끔씩 등장하는 short-answer 문제 유형으로 문제가 제작됨

음원 여 - 영국 / 속도 - 실제 시험과 유사

You will hear a lecture about African Art. First, you have some time to look at questions 31 to 40.	아프리카 예술에 관한 강연을 들어보세요. 먼저 여러분은 31-40번 문제를 살펴볼 시간이 있습니다.
Now listen carefully and answer questions 31 to 40.	이제 주의 깊게 듣고 31-40번 문제에 답하세요.
Good morning, everyone. Today, I will be continuing our lecture series on ethnic art by talking specifically about the art produced by various African cultures.	안녕하세요, 여러분. 오늘, 다양한 아프리카 문화에서 만들어진 예술에 관해 구체적으로 이야기함으로써 민족 예술에 관한 강연 시리즈를 이어가도록 하겠습니다.

A wide variety of art forms are prevalent throughout the African continent, including sculpture, painting, fibre art, metalwork, ceramics, and dance. When scholars use the term 'African art', they generally do not consider or include the art of the Q31 North African countries along the Mediterranean coast. Surprisingly, the art of Ethiopia is also different from most African art, so it is usually not included under the term African art.

Perhaps one of the most recognisable and characteristic forms of African art is sculpture, and in particular, the sculpting of masks. Masks play an important role among many indigenous populations, often being worn during important events such as funerals and weddings. It is very uncommon for sculptors to create masks that serve as direct images of gods, even though many masks are made exclusively for use in Q32 religious ceremonies.

African sculptors are renowned for their skills, which they utilise for many more things in addition to mask art. For instance, West African cultures developed bronze casting techniques in order to create decorative elements in royal Q33 palaces in countries like Benin and Togo in the 12th and 13th centuries. Starting in the 13th century, the Akan people of West Africa began sculpting intricate brass weights, known as Akan goldweights, which were used for weighing merchandise and Q34 gold. Many of the Akan goldweights apparently depict African proverbs, even though it is rare to see such narrative elements in African sculpture. As a result, scholars have been able to study the goldweights to gain valuable insights into the Akan culture and its history.

When it comes to the sculpting of figurines and statuettes, which are common throughout Africa, the Mande-speaking people of West Africa usually carve figurines from wood, and the finished article typically has cylinder-shaped Q35 limbs. East Africans are known for their Makonde sculptures, including wood figurines with large heads and exaggerated features. Southern Africa is best known for its Q36 clay figurines that have cylindrical heads and a combination of human and animal features.

African art can be broadly characterised as possessing three key thematic elements. First, there is a strong focus on expressive Q37&38 individualism, especially in West African art. A good example of this is seen in the highly-stylised art produced by the Dan people of Ivory Coast

아주 다양한 예술 형태들이 아프리카 대륙 전역에서 널리 퍼져 있는데, 여기에는 조각품, 그림, 섬유 예술, 금속 가공, 도자기 공예 그리고 춤이 포함되어 있습니다. 학자들이 "아프리카 예술"이라는 용어를 사용할 때, 일반적으로 지중해 연안을 따라 위치한 Q31 북아프리카 국가들의 예술을 고려하거나 포함하지는 않습니다. 놀랍게도, 에티오피아의 예술도 대부분의 아프리카 예술과 다르기 때문에, 보통 아프리카 예술이라는 용어에 포함되지 않습니다.

아마도 가장 알아보기 쉽고 특징적인 유형의 아프리카 예술 중의 하나는 조각일 것이며, 특히, 가면 조각이 그렇습니다. 가면은 많은 토착민들 사이에서 중요한 역할을 하며, 흔히 장례식이나 결혼식 같은 중요한 의식 중에 착용합니다. 조각가들이 신들의 정확한 이미지로서 역할을 하는 가면을 만드는 일이 아주 흔하지는 않습니다. 비록 많은 가면들이 오로지 Q32 종교적인 의식에서 사용되기 위해 만들어지지만요.

아프리카 조각가들은 그들이 지닌 기술로 유명한데, 이는 가면 예술 외의 여러 많은 것에도 활용됩니다. 예를 들어, 서아프리카 문화는 12세기와 13세기에 베냉과 토고 같은 국가의 Q33 왕궁에 장식적 요소를 만들기 위해 청동 주물 기술을 발전시켰습니다. 13세기부터, 서아프리카의 아칸족 사람들은 아칸족 금 저울추라고 알려진 복잡한 놋쇠 저울추를 조각하기 시작했고, 이는 상품과 Q34 금의 무게를 재는 데 사용되었습니다. 아칸족의 많은 금 저울추는 분명히 아프리카의 속담들을 묘사하고 있습니다. 비록 아프리카 조각품에서 이 같은 서술적인 요소들을 찾아보기는 쉽지 않지만요. 그 결과, 학자들은 아칸 문화와 그 역사에 대한 귀중한 통찰력을 얻기 위해 금 저울추를 연구할 수 있었습니다.

아프리카 전역에서 일반적으로 나타나는 조각 인형 및 소형 조각품들과 관련해서, 만데어를 사용하는 서아프리카 사람들은 보통 나무를 이용해 조각 인형을 조각하며, 완성품은 일반적으로 원기둥 형태의 Q35 팔다리가 있습니다. 동아프리카 사람들은 마콘데족 조각품으로 잘 알려져 있으며, 여기에는 큰 머리와 과장된 특징들을 지닌 나무 조각 인형이 포함됩니다. 남아프리카는 원통형 머리와 함께 사람과 동물의 특징이 조합된 모습을 한 Q36 점토 조각 인형으로 가장 잘 알려져 있습니다.

아프리카 예술은 크게 세 가지 핵심 주제 요소를 지니고 있는 것으로 특징지어질 수 있습니다. 우선, 표현적인 Q37&38 개인주의에 크게 중점을 두는 것인데, 특히 서아프리카 예술에서 잘 나타납니다. 이에 대한 좋은 예가 코트디부아르와 라이베리아의 단족 사람들에 의해 만들어진 대단히 양식화된 예술에서 보여집니다. 아프리카 예술의 두 번째 주제 요소는 인간 형상에 대한 강조입니

and Liberia. A second thematic element of African art is its emphasis on the human figure. The human figure serves as the primary focus for most African art, and this theme was even adopted by some European cultures. For instance, in the 1400s, Portuguese merchants traded with the Sapi culture in West Africa, who carved intricate ivory salt containers that resembled human figures. When the traders returned to Portugal with the salt containers, local craftsmen were quick to imitate the style, and salt containers depicting human figures soon became commonplace throughout Portugal. The final thematic element of African art is Q37&38 abstraction. African artists generally tend to avoid naturalistic representation in favour of visual abstraction, and this is generally true throughout the entire continent.

I now like to focus on the many materials that are used in African art. The vast majority of African artworks are wood sculptures, as Q39&40 wood is such an abundant material and requires little or no treatment or processing prior to it being used in art. Masks are sometimes adorned with parrot feathers, precious gemstones and Q39&40 seashells, the latter of which being a near-limitless resource in coastal regions.

Now, let's take a look at some pictures of the artworks I've discussed...

That is the end of Part 4. You now have one minute to check your answers to Part 4.

다. 인간의 형상은 대부분의 아프리카 예술에 대한 일차적인 초점의 역할을 하며, 이 주제는 심지어 일부 유럽 문화에서도 차용되었습니다. 예를 들어, 1400년대에 포르투갈 상인들은 서아프리카의 사피 문화와 교역했는데, 사피 문화는 사람의 형상을 닮은 복잡한 상아 소금 용기를 조각했습니다. 상인들이 소금 용기를 가지고 포르투갈로 돌아왔을 때 현지 장인들은 재빨리 이 스타일을 모방했고, 곧 포르투갈 전역에서 사람 형상을 묘사한 소금 용기가 일반화되었습니다. 아프리카 예술의 마지막 주제 요소는 Q37&38 추상적 개념입니다. 아프리카 예술가들은 보통 시각적 추상성을 위해 자연주의적 표현을 피하는 경향이 있는데, 이는 일반적으로 아프리카 대륙 전체에 걸쳐 사실로 나타납니다.

이제 아프리카 예술에 사용되는 많은 재료들에 초점을 맞춰 보겠습니다. 대부분의 아프리카 예술품들은 나무 조각품들인데, Q39&40 나무는 아주 풍부한 재료이며, 예술품에 사용되기에 앞서 처리나 가공이 거의 필요 없거나 전혀 필요로 하지 않습니다. 가면은 종종 앵무새 깃털과 귀중한 원석, 그리고 Q39&40 조개 껍질로 장식되는데, 이 중에서 마지막 것은 해안 지역에서 거의 무한한 자원입니다.

이제, 제가 말씀드린 작품들의 사진 몇 장을 살펴 보겠습니다...

이것으로 파트 4가 끝납니다. 여러분은 이제 자신의 답을 체크할 1분의 시간을 갖습니다.

I Vocabulary & Expressions I

ethnic 민족의 prevalent 널리 퍼져 있는 fibre 섬유 ceramics 도자기, 도예 term 용어 hold ~을 유지하다 recognisable 인식 가능한 sculpture 조각(품) indigenous 토착의 ceremony 의식, 예식 depending on ~에 따라 다른 serve as ~의 역할을 하다 exclusively 오로지, 독점적으로 religious 종교적인 be renowned for ~로 잘 알려져 있다 utilise ~을 활용하다 bronze casting 청동 주물 decorative 장식적인 element 요소 intricate 복잡한 weight (무게를 재는) 추, 무게 weigh ~의 무게를 재다 depict ~을 묘사하다 proverb 속담 narrative 묘사적인 insight 식견 when it comes to ~와 관련해서 figurine 조각 인형 statuette 작은 조각품 article 물품 cylinder-shaped 원기둥 모양의 limbs 사지, 팔다리 distinctive 독특한 marked with ~로 표기된, ~가 찍혀 있는 including ~을 포함하여 clay 점토, 찰흙 feature 특징 combination 결합, 조합 characterise ~을 특징짓다 possess ~을 소유하다 thematic 주제의 expressive 표현적인 individualism 개인주의 highly-stylised 대단히 양식화된 emphasis on ~에 대한 강조 human figure 인간의 형상 adopt ~을 차용하다 resemble ~을 닮다 craftsman 공예가 imitate ~을 모방하다 abstraction 추상(성) representation 표현 abundant 풍부한 treatment 처리 processing 가공 prior to ~에 앞서 adorned with ~로 장식된 parrot feather 앵무새 깃털 gemstone 원석 near-limitless 거의 무한한 resource 자원

문제 31-36

다음 노트 내용을 완성하시오.
각 답변에 대해 **1개의 단어만** 작성하시오.

African Art 아프리카 예술

An overview of African art 아프리카 예술의 개요

- Diverse art forms are common in Africa
  아프리카에서는 아주 다양한 예술 형태가 흔하다
- The term generally exclude the art of **31** .... Africa and Ethiopia
  그 용어는 일반적으로 **31** ....아프리카와 에티오피아의 예술을 제외한다

African mask art and sculpture 아프리카 가면 예술과 조각품

- Masks are often used in **32** .... ceremonies but rarely resemble gods
  가면은 흔히 **32** .... 의식에 사용되었지만, 좀처럼 종교 신들을 닮지 않았다
- Bronze was used to decorate **33** .... in some countries
  청동은 일부 국가에서 **33** ....을 장식하는 데 사용되었다.
- Akan goldweights were used to measure the weight of goods and **34** ....
  아칸족 금 저울 추는 상품과 **34** ....의 무게를 측정하는 데 사용되었다

African figurine art 아프리카의 조각 인형 예술

- The **35** .... of West African figurines are distinctively cylindrical.
  서아프리카 조각 인형의 **35** ....은 독특하게 원통형이다
- South African figurines mixed human and animal features and are made from **36** ....
  남아프리카의 조각 인형에는 인간과 동물의 특징이 섞여 있으며, **36** ....로 만들어진다

31. 학자들은 지중해 연안을 따라 있는 북아프리카 국가들은 아프리카 예술로 여겨지거나 포함되지 않는다고(When scholars use the term 'African art', they generally do not consider or include the art of the North African countries along the Mediterranean coast)하므로 정답은 North이다.
Paraphrasing exclude(제외하다) → do not consider or include(고려하거나 포함하지 않는다)

32. 많은 가면들이 오로지 종교적인 의식에서 사용되기 위해 만들어지지만, 조각가들이 신들의 직접적인 이미지와 같은 역할을 하는 가면을 만드는 일이 아주 흔치 않다고 하였으므로(It is very uncommon for sculptors to create masks that serve as direct images of gods, even though many masks are made exclusively for use in religious ceremonies), 정답은 religious이다.

참고로 실제 시험에서 자신이 모르는 단어가 정답으로 나오는 경우가 있는데, 우선 한글로 들은 대로 적어보고 다음 문제에 집중한다. 시험이 끝나고 시간이 남을 때 다시 그 문제로 돌아와서 단어를 제대로 적어보자.
Paraphrasing rarely(드문) → uncommon(드문)
resemble(닮다) → serve as direct images(정확한 이미지로서 역할을 하다)

33. 청동 주물 기술이 왕궁을 장식하는 요소를 만드는 데 사용되었으므로(bronze casting techniques in order to create highly naturalistic reliefs, which were commonly used as decorative elements in royal palaces), 정답은 palaces이다. royal palaces라고 쓰면 두 단어가 되므로 오답이다.
Paraphrasing in some countries(일부 국가에서) → in countries like Benin and Togo(베냉과 토고 같은 국가에서)

34. 무게 재는 것과 관련하여, 아칸족은 금저울추로 상품과 금의 무게를 재는데 사용하였으므로(the Akan people of West Africa began sculpting intricate brass weights, known as Akan goldweights, which were used for weighing merchandise and gold), 정답은 gold이다.

Paraphrasing measure the weight(무게를 재다) → weigh(무게를 재다)
goods(상품) → merchandise(상품)

35. 서아프리카에서 만데어를 사용하는 사람들이 원기둥 형태의 팔다리를 가진 작은 나무 인형을 조각한다고 하므로(The Mande-speaking people of West Africa usually carve figurines from wood, and the finished article typically has cylinder-shaped limbs), 정답은 limbs이다.

Paraphrasing cylindrical(원기둥의) → cylinder-shaped(원기둥 형태의)

36. 남아프리카는 원통형 머리, 사람과 동물 특징이 조합된 점토 조각 인형으로 유명하다고 하였으므로(Southern Africa is best known for its clay figurines that have cylindrical heads and a combination of human and animal features), 인형의 재질은 점토이다. 따라서 정답은 clay이다.

Paraphrasing mixed(혼합된) → a combination of(~의 조합)

문제 37-40

다음 문제에 답변하시오.

각 답변에 대해 **1개의 단어만** 작성하시오.

What are the three main thematic elements of African art?
아프리카 예술의 세 가지 주요 주제 요소는 무엇인가?

- **37** ....
- human figure 인간의 형상
- **38** ....

순서대로(first, second, final) 개인주의, 인간 형상, 추상성(individualism, human figure, abstraction)을 말하므로, 빈칸에 정답은 각각 individualism과 abstraction이다. 이때 37, 38번에 정답 순서를 바꿔 써도 된다.

What two materials are mentioned as being in plentiful supply?
충분히 공급되는 것으로 언급된 두 가지 재료는 무엇인가?

- **39** ....
- **40** ....

풍성한 공급이 이루어지는 재료로 나무와(wood is such an abundant material) 조개껍데기(parrot feathers, precious gemstones and seashells, the latter of which being a near-limitless resource)가 나왔으므로 빈칸에 정답은 wood와 seashells이며, 이 역시 정답 순서를 바꿔 써도 된다.

Paraphrasing plentiful supply(풍성한 공급) → abundant material(풍성한 재료)
near-limitless resource(거의 끝없는 자원)

Unit 06 IELTS READING에 대한 모든 것

Sustainable Development

A [Q1] The beginnings of sustainable development can be traced back to 17th and 18th century England, where the country's depleting timber resources led to new forest management practices. The idea became more prominent throughout 19th century Europe in response to the environmental concerns brought on by industrialization. From here, sustainable development continued to evolve, [Q4] influencing both economic development and [Q5] social progress while also highlighting the importance of safeguarding the environment for future generations.

B [Q2] The modern concept of sustainable development was defined within the report *Our Common Future*, commonly called the Brundtland Report, which was released by the United Nations World Commission on Environment and Development in 1987. The Brundtland Report defines sustainable development as development that meets the needs of the present without compromising the ability of future generations to meet their own needs. This is the most frequently cited definition of the concept to date. Since the Brundtland Report, the concept of sustainable development has developed beyond this initial intergenerational framework to also [Q5] focus on the goal of socially inclusive and environmentally sustainable economic growth.

C [Q3] In 2015, the United Nations General Assembly adopted the 2030 Agenda for Sustainable Development and its 17 Sustainable Development Goals (SDGs). The SDGs are a call to action by all countries – poor, rich and middle-income – to promote prosperity while protecting the planet. [Q6] These long-term goals recognize that ending poverty, encouraging economic growth, and improving social conditions must go hand-in-hand with those of curbing and adapting to climate change and ensuring environmental protection.

지속가능한(친환경) 발전

A [Q1] 지속가능한 발전의 시작은 17, 18세기 영국으로 거슬러 올라갈 수 있는데, 영국의 고갈되는 목재가 새로운 산림 관리 실행을 이끌었다. 이 아이디어는 산업화가 가져온 환경 우려에 대한 반응으로, 19세기 유럽 전역에서 더욱 뚜렷해졌다. 여기서, 지속가능한 발전은 계속해서 진화하여, [Q4] 미래 세대를 위한 환경 보호의 중요성을 강조하는 한편 경제 발전과 [Q5] 사회적 진전 모두에 영향을 주었다.

B [Q2] 지속가능한 발전의 현대적 개념은 보통 브룬틀란드 보고서라 불리는 *우리의 공통된 미래* 보고서에 정의되었는데, 이 보고서는 1987년에 유엔환경개발위원회에 의해 발행되었다. 브룬틀란드 보고서는 지속가능한 발전을, 미래 세대가 자신들의 필요를 충족하기 위한 능력을 손상시키지 않으면서 현재 세대의 필요를 충족시키는 발전으로 정의한다. 이것은 지금까지 가장 자주 인용되는 개념이다. 브룬틀란드 보고서 이후, 지속가능한 개발의 개념은 이 첫 세대 간 체계를 뛰어넘어 발전해왔는데, 이는 또한 [Q5] 사회적으로 포괄적이고 환경적으로 지속가능한 경제 성장 목표에 중점을 맞춘다.

C [Q3] 2015년에 유엔총회는 지속가능한 발전을 위한 2030 행동 강령과 그에 대한 17개의 지속가능한 발전 목표들(SDGs)을 채택했다. SDGs는 지구를 보호하면서도 번영을 촉진하기 위해, 가난하거나 부유하거나 중간층 모든 국가들의 행동을 요구한다. [Q6] 이러한 장기 목표들은 가난 종결시키기, 경제 성장 장려하기, 그리고 사회적 환경 개선하기가, 기후 변화를 억제하며 적응하는 목표들, 환경 보호를 보장하는 목표들과 함께 가야함을 공인한다.

| Vocabulary & Expressions |

trace back 거슬러 올라가다 depleting 고갈되는 prominent 두드러진 in response to ~에 응하여 concerns 걱정, 우려 industrialization 산업화 evolve 진화하다 progress 진보, 진척 safeguard 보호하다 generation 세대 release 내보내다, 발행하다 compromise 양보하다, 손상하다 cite 인용하다 initial 처음의 intergenerational 세대 간의 framework 틀, 체계, 뼈대 inclusive 포함한, 포괄적인 adopt 채택하다 agenda 계획, 행동 강령, 안건 call 요구 promote 촉진하다 prosperity 번영 planet 행성, 지구 recognize 인식하다, 공인하다 poverty 가난 go hand-in-hand 함께 가다 curb 억제하다 adapt 맞추다, 적응하다 ensure 보장하다, 확실히 하다

▪ 스키밍

1. v　　**2.** vi　　**3.** iii

List of Headings 제목 목록

- **i** The methods of sustainable forest management 지속가능한 산림 관리 방법
- **ii** The importance of protecting natural systems 자연 보호의 중요성
- **iii** The United Nations' plans for sustainable development 지속가능한 발전을 위한 유엔의 계획
- **iv** The technology behind sustainable development 지속가능한 발전 이면의 기술
- **v** The birth of the concept of sustainable development 지속가능한 발전 개념의 탄생
- **vi** The report defining sustainable development 지속가능한 발전을 정의하는 보고서

1. A 문단

A 문단은 지속가능한 발전의 시작(beginnings of sustainable development)에 대한 설명부터 출발하여, 이 개념의 변화(continued to evolve)를 설명한다. 따라서 제시된 목록 중 v가 가장 적합한 정답이다.

참고로 i의 지속가능한 산림 관리가 언급은 되지만 구체적 방법(methods)은 본문에 없고, ii의 자연 보호 중요성이 언급되지만 전체 제목으로 잡기에는 한계가 있다.

Paraphrasing birth(탄생) → beginnings(시작)

2. B 문단

B 문단은 브룬틀란드 보고서가 현대적 지속가능한 발전 개념을 정립했음을 주 내용으로 다루기에, 정답은 vi이다.

Paraphrasing the report(보고서) → Brundtland Report(브룬틀란드 보고서)

3. C 문단

C 문단은 전체적으로 지속가능한 발전을 위한 유엔의 행동 강령(agenda)과 관련 목표(goals)가 소개되므로, 정답은 iii이다.

Paraphrasing plans(계획) → agenda(계획, 행동 강령), goals(목표)

▪ 스캐닝

4. NOT GIVEN　　**5.** FALSE　　**6.** TRUE

4. In the 19th century, environmental protection was a higher priority than economic development.
19세기에, 환경 보호는 경제 개발보다 더 높은 우선순위였다.

19세기를 키워드로 잡고 스캐닝을 하면 A 문단 중간부터 관련 내용이 있는데, 환경 보호의 중요성이 강조되었다는 말은 있지만, 경제 개발보다 더 우선순위인지 제시된 정보만으로는 판단할 수 없으므로, 정답은 NOT GIVEN이다.

5. Before the Brundtland Report, social aspects were not considered in the concept of sustainable development.
브룬틀란드 보고서 전에, 사회적 측면들은 지속가능한 발전의 개념에 고려되지 않았다.

사회적 측면들(social aspects)을 키워드로 잡고 스캐닝을 하면 A 문단에 19세기 이후 지속가능한 발전 개념이 진화되어 사회적 진전(social progress)에 영향을 주었다는 이야기가 나오고, 그 이후 B 문단에 브룬틀란드 보고서에도 사회적으로 포괄적(socially inclusive) 내용이 나온다. 즉, 문제에 나온 진술과 달리, 본문에서는 브룬틀란드 보고서 이전에 이미 사회적 진전 개념이 고려되었으므로, 정답은 FALSE이다.
Paraphrasing social aspects(사회적 측면들) → social progress(사회적 진전), socially inclusive(사회적으로 포괄적인)

6. Addressing the issue of climate change is one of the Sustainable Development Goals.
기후 변화 문제를 다루는 것은 지속가능한 발전 목표들 중 하나이다.

지속가능한 발전 목표들(SDGs)과 기후 변화(climate change)를 키워드로 잡고 스캐닝을 하면, C 문단 마지막에서 나열한 여러 목표들 중 기후 변화 억제와 적응이 언급되므로, 정답은 TRUE이다.
Paraphrasing addressing the issue of climate change(기후 변화 문제를 다루기)
→ curbing and adapting to climate change(기후 변화를 억제하고 적응하기)

Unit 07 READING Skills 1 – T/F/NG, Matching Features, Summary/Note/Table/Sentence Completion

▪ 패시지

1. NOT GIVEN	2. TRUE	3. FALSE	4. TRUE	
5. C	6. A	7. B	8. B	9. A
10. E	11. A	12. C	13. D	

출제 포인트 **난이도: 중**

독해 지문 구조는 보통 특정 주제에 대해 다양한 연구자와 그들의 연구가 소개되면서 각 연구의 특징을 설명하는 형태로 많이 출제되고 있기에, 각 연구의 연도와 사람 이름을 확인하여 각 연구의 특징과 차이점을 파악하며 읽는 것이 핵심임

참고로 아동 교육과 육아 관련 주제도 자주 출제되는 편임

기출 2024년 5월 - 어린이 심리 발달
2024년 4월 - 아동기 행동
2019년 1월 - 첫째와 다른 자녀 간에 차이점

The Effects of Birth Order on Personality	**출생 순서가 성격에 미치는 영향**
One of the first theorists to argue that birth order influences personality was the Austrian psychiatrist Alfred Adler (1870 – 1937). Adler, who was a contemporary of Sigmund Freud, firmly believed that birth order can have a significant impact on an individual's personality and emotional responses, including the ways in which they deal with love, friendship, and stress. According to Adler, the introduction of a new baby into a family unit has a profound and lasting	출생 순서가 성격에 미치는 영향을 주장한 첫 번째 이론가들 중의 한 명은 오스트리아의 정신과 의사 알프레드 아들러(1870–1937)였다. 아들러는 지그문트 프로이드와 동시대 사람이었으며, 출생 순서가 개인의 성격과 정서 반응에 중요한 영향을 미칠 수 있다고 굳게 믿었으며, 여기에는 사랑과 우정, 그리고 스트레스를 대하는 방식들도 포함된다. 아들러에 따르면, 한 가정에 새로 태어난 아이의 진입은 기존의 아이(들)에게 엄청나고 지속적인

influence on the older child or children, who will experience feelings of diminished privilege and value. Q1 Adler theorized that the extra parental attention that younger children typically receive greatly affects their personalities later in life. In a three-child family, for example, the youngest child would tend to be pampered, which can result in poorly-developed social skills. Q6 The middle child, who would not experience such pampering, was most likely to enjoy a successful and fulfilling life, but would also be most likely to argue with other siblings. Adler believed that the oldest child would be most likely to succumb to substance abuse and experience anxiety due to feelings of excessive responsibility for younger siblings and the lack of parental attentiveness. Q9 As a result, he reasoned that this child would be most likely to end up in jail or suffer from severe mental health conditions.

The effect of birth order has become a controversial issue in psychology in the years since Alfred Adler first presented his theory. Q7 In 1996, an American psychologist named Frank Sulloway published a book in which he outlined his theory that birth order had clear effects on the 'Big Five' personality traits: agreeableness, neuroticism, openness, extraversion, and conscientiousness. Sulloway believed that first-borns were less agreeable and less receptive to new ideas than later-borns, but on the other hand, were more socially assertive and conscientious. Q8 However, fellow psychologists such as Judith Rich Harris and Toni Falbo published rigorously researched papers that were highly critical of Sulloway's theories and findings. Brian Sutton-Smith, a psychologist who spent most of the career analyzing the cultural and developmental effects of children's playing habits, argued that Q2 any perceived effects of birth order would likely be eliminated by experiences that an individual has later in life, as each human being continually adapts to a unique combination of societal and environmental factors.

Researching the possible effects of birth order is a challenge due to the near-impossible task of controlling the vast number of social and demographic Q10 variables associated with birth order. Family Q11 size, for example, plays a crucial role in any study of the topic. On average, large families are lower on the socioeconomic ladder than small families, which means third-born children involved in a study are more likely to come from poorer families than first-born children. If a researcher identifies a specific Q12 trait related to third-born children, it may be a result of family size or other variables rather than birth order. Such problems are virtually unavoidable, which leads to

영향을 미치며, 이들은 특권과 가치가 줄어든 느낌을 경험하게 된다. Q1 아들러는 더 어린 아이들이 일반적으로 받는 부모의 추가적인 관심이 나중 삶에서 성격에 크게 영향을 미친다는 이론을 제시했다. 예를 들어, 3명의 아이가 있는 가정에서 가장 어린 아이는 응석받이가 될 경향이 있을 수 있는데, 이는 결과적으로 형편없이 개발된 사교 능력을 야기할 수 있다. Q6 둘째 아이는, 이와 같은 애지중지함을 경험하지 못할 수 있는 아이인데, 성공적이고 성취감 있는 삶을 즐길 가능성이 가장 크지만, 다른 형제들과 다툴 가능성도 가장 클 수 있다. 아들러는 첫째 아이가 동생들에 대한 과도한 책임감과 부모의 관심 부족으로 인해 약물 남용에 빠지고 불안감을 겪을 가능성이 가장 클 수 있다고 생각했다. Q9 결과적으로, 이 첫째 아이가 결국 감옥에 가거나 심각한 정신 건강 질환을 앓을 가능성이 가장 클 수 있다고 아들러는 추론했다.

알프레드 아들러가 자신의 이론을 처음 제시한 이후로 출생 순서에 따른 영향은 수년간 심리학 분야에서 논란이 많은 문제가 되어 왔다. Q7 1996년에, 프랭크 설로웨이라는 이름의 미국 심리학자가 책을 한 권 출간했는데, 이 책에서 그는 출생 순서가 '5대' 성격 특성에 분명한 영향을 미친다는 자신의 이론을 기술했다: 상냥함, 신경과민성, 개방성, 외향성, 성실성. 설로웨이는 처음 태어난 아기가 나중에 태어난 아기보다 새로운 생각에 대해 덜 호의적이고 덜 수용적인 반면, 사회적으로 더 자신감 있고 성실하다고 생각했다. Q8 하지만, 주디스 리치 해리스나 토니 팰보와 같은 동료 심리학자들은 설로웨이의 이론과 결과물에 대해 매우 비판적인 내용으로 치밀하게 연구한 논문을 펴냈다. 브라이언 서튼-스미스는 아이들 놀이 습관의 문화적이고 발달적 영향을 분석하는 데 대부분의 경력을 보낸 심리학자인데, Q2 출생 순서의 어떠한 인지된 영향도 삶의 나중에 겪는 경험에 의해 없어질 가능성이 있고 이는 각각의 인간은 사회적인 요소와 환경적인 요소의 고유한 조합에 지속적으로 적응하기 때문이라고 주장했다.

출생 순서가 미칠 가능성이 있는 영향들을 연구하는 것은 출생 순서와 관련되어 있는 매우 많은 사회적이고 인구통계적 Q10 변수들을 통제하는 거의 불가능한 과제이기 때문에 하나의 도전이다. 예를 들어, 가족의 Q11 규모는 이 주제에 대한 어떠한 연구에서도 중요한 역할을 한다. 평균적으로, 대가족은 소가족보다 사회경제학적인 지위에서 더 낮은 위치에 있는데, 이는 연구 과정에 관련된 셋째 아이가 첫째 아이보다 더 가난한 가정에 속해 있을 가능성이 더 높다는 것을 의미한다. 만일 한 연구자가 셋째 아이와 관련된 특정 Q12 성격을 발견한 경우, 출생 순서가 아닌 가족 규모나 기타 변수들에 따른 결과일 수 있는 것이다. 이러한 문제점들은 사실상 불가피한 것이며, Q13 비평가들에 의해 쉽게 반박되는 결정적이지 못한 연구와 결과물을 야기한다.

inconclusive studies and findings that are easily disputed by Q13 critics.

Q3 Swiss researchers Cecile Ernst and Jules Angst evaluated all of the birth order research published between 1946 and 1980 and attempted to control for variables. They concluded that birth order had minimal effects on personality, and even suggested that further research into birth order would be a waste of time and resources. More recently, researchers have analyzed data based on wide-reaching surveys related to the Big Five personality traits, but no evidence was found to support Sulloway's theory that a significant correlation exists between birth order and self-reported personality.

Some smaller studies have partially supported Sulloway's predictions. Delroy Paulhus of the University of British Columbia found that later-borns have a tendency to be rebellious but score higher on agreeableness and openness, while first-borns are more parent-oriented and score higher on conscientiousness and conservatism. Paulhus and his contributors assert that the effect can be seen quite clearly within families, but they concede that results are weak when comparing individuals from different families due to the prevalence of genetic and socioeconomic factors. Q5 Paulhus also claims that children who do not have any siblings are not significantly different from those who have siblings. In fact, they share many characteristics with first-borns, particularly the high regard they have for their parents.

Q4 Judith Rich Harris concurs that birth order effects may be apparent within a family unit, but she argues that they are not long-lasting personality traits. Harris pointed out that, while first-borns and later-borns behave differently when in the company of their parents and siblings, even in adulthood, the majority of people move out of their childhood home relatively early in their life. Harris' research findings indicate that personality traits adopted in the childhood home have little to no bearing on an individual's behavior outside the home, even during childhood.

Q3 스위스의 연구자 세실 에른스트와 쥘 앙스트가 1946년에서 1980년 사이에 출간된 모든 출생 순서 연구 내용을 평가해 변수들을 통제하려 했다. 이들은 출생 순서가 성격에 아주 적은 영향을 미친다고 결론을 내렸으며, 심지어 출생 순서에 대한 추가적인 연구는 시간과 자원 낭비일 수 있다고까지 시사했다. 더 최근에는, 연구자들이 5대 성격 특성과 관련된 광범위한 설문 조사를 바탕으로 데이터를 분석했지만, 출생 순서와 자가 보고된 성격 사이에 중요한 상관 관계가 존재한다는 설로웨이의 이론을 지지할 수 있는 그 어떠한 단서도 찾지 못했다.

일부 소규모 연구가 설로웨이의 예측을 부분적으로 지지한 적은 있다. 브리티시 콜럼비아 대학의 델로이 폴허스는 나중에 태어난 아이들이 반항적인 경향이 있지만 상냥함과 개방성 부분에서 더 높은 점수를 기록하였고, 반면에 첫째로 태어난 아이들은 더욱 부모 중심적이고 성실성과 보수성 부분에서 더 높은 점수를 기록한 사실을 발견했다. 폴허스와 그의 조력자들은 그 영향이 가정 내에서 꽤 분명하게 보여질 수 있다고 주장하지만, 여러 가정 출신의 개인들을 비교할 때는 유전적이고 사회경제학적 요소들의 우세함으로 인해 결과가 설득력이 부족하다는 점을 인정하고 있다. Q5 폴허스는 형제가 전혀 없는 아이들이 형제가 있는 아이들과 크게 다르지 않다고도 주장한다. 실제로, 그 아이들은 첫째로 태어난 아이들과 많은 특성을 공유하는데, 특히 부모에 대한 높은 존경심이 그렇다.

Q4 주디스 리치 해리스는 출생 순서 영향이 가족 단위 내에서는 분명할 수 있다는 데 동의하지만, 그것이 장기간 지속되는 성격 특성은 아니라고 주장한다. 해리스가 지적한 점은, 첫째로 태어난 아이들과 나중에 태어난 아이들이 심지어 성년기에도 부모 및 형제와 함께할 때 다르게 행동하긴 하지만 대부분의 사람들이 삶에서 비교적 이른 시기에 유년 시절의 집을 떠난다는 것이다. 해리스의 연구 결과물은 유년 시절의 집에서 채택된 성격 특성은 유년기일지라도 집 밖에서 보이는 행동과는 거의 관련이 없다는 것을 시사한다.

I Vocabulary & Expressions I

effect on ~에 미치는 영향 birth order 출생 순서 personality 성격 influence ~에 영향을 미치다 contemporary 동시대의 사람 significant 상당한 emotional response 정서 반응 deal with ~을 대하다, 다루다 profound 엄청난, 깊이 있는 lasting 지속적인 diminished 줄어든, 약해진 privilege 특혜, 특권 theorize 이론을 제시하다 parental attention 부모의 관심 affect ~에 영향을 미치다 pampered 응석받이가 된 poorly-developed 형편없이 발달된 fulfilling 성취감을 주는 sibling 형제자매 succumb to ~에 빠지다, 굴복하다 substance abuse 약물 남용 excessive 과도한 reason 추론하다 end up 결국 ~하게 되다 suffer from (병 등) ~을 앓다 controversial 논란이 많은 trait (성격적인) 특성 agreeableness 상냥함 neuroticism 신경증적 성격 extraversion 외

향성 conscientiousness 성실성 agreeable 호의적인 receptive 수용적인 assertive 적극적인 rigorously 엄밀히 be critical of ~에 대해 비판적이다 eliminate 제거하다, 없애다 adapt to ~에 적응하다 combination 조합, 결합 demographic 인구 통계적인 variable 변수 associated with ~와 관련된 play a role 역할을 하다 pivotal 중추적인, 중요한 socioeconomic 사회경제학적인 ladder (사회적인) 지위 lead to ~을 초래하다 inconclusive 결정적이지 못한 dispute ~을 반박하다 evaluate ~을 평가하다 wide-reaching 광범위한 correlation 상관 관계 self-reported 자가 보고된 a tendency to do ~하는 경향 rebellious 반항적인 parent-oriented 부모 중심적인 conservatism 보수성 assert 주장하다 concede 인정하다 prevalence 우세함, 널리 퍼짐 concur 동의하다 point out 지적하다 in the company of ~와 함께 하는 adopt ~을 받아들이다, 채택하다 have no bearing 관련이 없다

문제 1-4

다음 내용이 독해 지문에 주어진 정보와 일치하는가?
답지 1-4번 칸에 다음을 쓰시오.

TRUE 문제 진술이 정보와 일치하면
FALSE 문제 진술이 정보와 다르면
NOT GIVEN 문제 진술에 대한 정보를 독해 지문에서 찾을 수 없으면

1. Alfred Adler encouraged parents to show more attention to all children in a family unit.
알프레드 아들러는 부모들에게 가정 내의 모든 아이들에게 더 많은 관심을 보이도록 권했다.

알프레드 아들러가 부모들에게 모든 아이에게 더 많은 관심(more attention)을 보이라고 권장했다는 내용이다. 첫 번째 문단에서 어린 아이들이 일반적으로 받게 되는 추가적인 부모의 관심이(extra parental attention) 아이들의 성격에 영향을 미친다는 이론을 제시하였다는 내용이 나오지만, Adler가 부모가 모든 아이들에게 더 많은 관심을 보여야 한다고 권장하였다는 내용은 지문 어디에도 없으므로 정답은 NOT GIVEN이다.

Paraphrasing parents(부모) → parental(부모의)
more(더) → extra(추가적인)

2. Brian Sutton-Smith predicted that birth order effects present in an individual will eventually vanish.
브라이언 서튼-스미스는 개인에게 존재하는 출생 순서 영향이 결국 사라질 것이라고 예측했다.

브라이언 서트-스미스는 출생 순서(birth order effects)가 개인(individual)에게 존재하는 영향이 결국 사라진다고(vanish) 예측했다는 내용이다. 학자 이름과 vanish가 가장 중요한 핵심어가 된다. 두 번째 문단에서 effects of birth order와 individual 그리고 vanish에 상응하는 eliminate가 나오는 문장 내용이 정답 근거가 된다. 즉, 출생 순서의 어떠한 영향도 삶에서 겪는 경험으로 인해 없어질 수 있다는 내용과 일치하므로 정답은 TRUE이다.

참고로 문제 문장에서 present는 동사가 아닌 형용사(존재하는)로 사용되었다. present 앞에 which is가 생략되어 있는 구조로, that절의 주어는 birth order effects이고 동사는 will vanish이다.

Paraphrasing predict(예상하다) → would likely(~일 가능성이 있다)
eventually(결국에) → later in life(나중에, 장래에)
vanish(사라진다) → be eliminated(제거되다)

3. The research evaluated by Ernst and Angst showed a clear relationship between birth order and personality.
에른스트와 앙스트에 의해 평가된 연구는 출생 순서와 성격 사이의 명확한 관계를 보여주었다.

에른스트와 앙스트가 평가한 연구들은 출생 순서(birth order)와 성격(personality) 사이에 명확한 관계(clear relationship)가 있다는 것을 보여주었다는 내용이다. 학자 이름, personality와 clear를 가장 중요한 핵심어로 잡는다. 네 번째 문단에서 birth order와 personality가 나온 문장 내용이 정답 근거가 된다. 출생 순서가 성격에 미치는 영향이 아주 적다는(minimal effects) 결론을 냈다는 내용이고, 이는 clear와 상반된다. 따라서 정답은 FALSE이다.

참고로 사람 이름은 '이름+성'이 모두 언급되기도 하지만, 문제처럼 이름 혹은 성 하나만 언급될 수도 있음을 기억한다.

4. The findings of Judith Rich Harris show that birth order affects personality within the family home.
주디스 리치 해리스의 연구 결과는 출생 순서가 가정 내에서의 성격에 영향을 미친다는 것을 보여준다.

주디스 리치 해리스의 연구 결과가 가정 내에서의(within the family home) 성격(personality)은 출생 순서의 영향이 있다는 것을 보여준다는 내용이다. 학자 이름과 within the family home이 가장 중요한 핵심어가 된다. 마지막 문단에서 within a family unit이 나오는 문장 내용이 정답 근거가 된다. 즉, 출생 순서의 영향이 가족 단위에서는 분명하다는 것에 동의하긴 하지만 이것이 오래 지속되지는 않는다는 내용과 일치하므로 정답은 TRUE이다.

바로 뒤에 나오는 내용인, 부모나 형제자매와 함께 있을 때 첫째나 막대들이 다르게 행동하기는 한다는 것을 해당 학자가 지적했다는 내용으로도 정답이 TRUE인 것을 알 수 있다.

Paraphrasing within the family home(가족 내에서) → within a family unit(가족 단위 내에서)

| Vocabulary & Expressions |

encourage A to do A가 ~하도록 권하다 predict 예상하다 eventually 결국 vanish 사라지다 relationship 관계

문제 5-9

다음 진술(문제 5-9번)과 아래의 인물 목록을 살펴보시오.
각 진술에 A, B, 또는 C 중 알맞은 연구자를 연결하시오.
A, B, 또는 C 중 알맞은 기호를 답지 5-9번 칸에 적으시오.
유의 어떤 글자든 한 번 이상 사용해도 된다.

List of Researchers 연구가 명단

A Alfred Adler 알프레드 아들러
B Frank Sulloway 프랭크 설로웨이
C Delroy Paulhus 델로이 폴허스

5. Noted that an only child shares personality traits with first-born children.
외동이 첫째로 태어난 아이들이 보이는 성격 특성을 지닌다는 점에 주목했다.

외동이 첫째 아이들과 성격 특성이 같다는 내용을 찾아야 한다. 다섯 번째 문단의 마지막 두 문장에서 외동을 묘사하는 내용이 처음 언급된다. 형제자매가 없는 아이들(they)은 첫째로 태어난 아이들과 많은 특징을 공유한다는 내용이고 이를 언급한 사람은 Paulhus이다. 따라서 정답은 C이다.

Paraphrasing an only child(외동) → children who do not have any siblings(어떠한 형제자매도 없는 아이들)
personality traits(성격 특성) → characteristics(특징)

6. Theorized that middle children are more likely to succeed than their siblings.
둘째로 태어난 아이들이 형제들보다 성공할 가능성이 더 높다는 이론을 제시했다.

둘째 아이들이 다른 형제자매보다 더 성공할 것이라는 내용을 찾아야 한다. middle child가 언급된 문장 내용을 살펴보자. 둘째 아이들은 가장 성공적이고 성취감 있는 삶을 즐길 가능성이 크다는 내용이며 이는 Adler가 제시한 이론인 앞 문장의 예시이다. 세 아이들 중에서 둘째가 가장 성공적일 것이라는 내용은 둘째 아이가 다른 형제들보다 더 성공적일 것이라는 내용과 일치한다. 따라서 정답은 A이다.

Paraphrasing succeed(성공하다) → enjoy a successful life(성공적인 삶을 즐기다)

7. Argued that birth order affects five distinctive personality traits.
출생 순서가 다섯 가지 구별되는 성격 특성에 영향을 미친다고 주장했다.

다섯가지 성격을 출생순서와 관련시켜 언급한 내용을 찾아야 한다. 지문에서 Big five가 언급된 문장 내용을 살펴보자. 출생 순서가 5대 성격 특징에 분명한 영향을 미친다는 내용이고 이를 언급한 사람은 Sulloway이므로 정답은 B이다.

숫자는 패러프레이징하기 어려우므로 five를 핵심어로 잡고 지문을 스캐닝한다면 금방 정답을 찾을 수 있다.

Paraphrasing birth order affects(출생순서가 영향을 미치다)
→ birth order had clear effects on(출생순서가 ~에 분명한 영향을 미치다)

8. **Received several criticisms from peers in the psychology field.**
심리학 분야의 동료들로부터 여러 비판을 받았다.

동료의 비판을 받은 학자를 찾아야 한다. 지문에서 fellows와 critical이 언급된 문장 내용을 살펴보자. 동료 심리학자들이 Sulloway의 이론과 결론에 대해 비판적인 연구물을 출간했다는 내용이므로 정답은 B이다.

Paraphrasing criticisms(비판) → critical(비판적인)
peers(동료) → fellows(동료)

9. **Believed that the oldest of three siblings is more likely to commit a crime.**
세 명의 형제들 중 첫째가 범죄를 저지를 가능성이 가장 높다고 생각했다.

첫째 아이가 다른 형제자매들보다 더 범죄를 저지를 가능성이 크다는 내용을 찾아야 한다. 첫 번째 문단의 마지막 문장에 나오는 어휘, jail(감옥)을 범죄를 저지르는 것과 연관시킬 수 있어야 한다. 범죄를 저지른 사람들을 가두는 곳이 jail이기 때문이다. 이 문장의 주어인 this child는 앞 문장에서 언급된 the oldest child이고 이를 언급한 사람은 Adler이므로 정답은 A이다.

Paraphrasing commit a crime(범죄를 저지르다) → end up in jail(결국 감옥에 갇히다)

I Vocabulary & Expressions I

note 주목하다 share 공통으로 갖다 trait 특성, 특징 succeed 성공하다 distinctive 독특한, 구별이 되는 peer 동료 field 분야 commit (범죄 등을) 저지르다 crime 범죄

문제 10-13

아래의 A-F 단어 목록을 사용하여 요약문을 완성하시오.

A-F 중 알맞은 기호를 답지 10-13번 칸에 적으시오.

Problems with birth order research 출생 순서 관련 연구가 지니는 문제점

The effects of birth order are difficult to study due to the wide variety of **10** .... that need to be considered. For example, the **11** .... of families greatly affects the research and results. Third-born children are more likely to come from poorer families, so any **12** .... that is discovered might be a result of socioeconomic factors, and not a result of birth order. Because of this, **13** .... view such studies as being flawed and inconclusive.

출생 순서에 따른 영향은 고려해야 하는 아주 다양한 **10** ....로 인해 연구하기 어렵다. 예를 들어, 가족의 **11** ....는 연구 내용과 결과물에 크게 영향을 미친다. 셋째로 태어난 아이들은 더 가난한 집안 출신일 가능성이 더 높기 때문에, 발견되는 어떠한 **12** ....도 사회경제학적인 요소에 따른 결과일 수 있으며, 출생 순서로 인한 결과가 아닐 수 있다. 이로 인해, **13** ....는 이와 같은 연구를 결점이 있고 결정적이지 못한 것으로 여긴다.

A size 규모	**B** survey 설문 조사	**C** trait 특징
D critics 비평가들	**E** variables 변수	**F** parents 부모들

10. 빈칸에 들어갈 단어는 출생 순서 관련 연구가 어려운(difficult) 이유로서(due to), 고려되어야 하는 다양한 '무엇'이다. 세 번째 문단의 첫 문장에서 difficult에 상응하는 challenge가 나오고 due to도 있으므로 due to 뒤에 나오는 내용을 살펴보자. 출생 관련된 사회적이고 인구통계적인 아주 많은 '변수(variables)'를 통제하는 것이 거의 불가능하므로 어렵다는 내용이다. 따라서 빈칸에 알맞은 단어는 E이다.

Paraphrasing difficult(어려운) → challenge(어려움)
the wide variety of(매우 다양한) → the vast number of(아주 많은)

11. 빈칸에 들어갈 단어는 다양한 변수의 예시인, 가족(families)의 '무엇'이다. 가족 규모(Family size)가 출생 순서와 관련된 주제의 모든 연구에 중요한 역할을 한다는 내용이 근거가 되어 빈칸에 들어갈 단어는 size에 해당하는 A이다.

Paraphrasing the size of families(가족 규모) → family size(가족 규모)

12. 빈칸 문장의 내용은 셋째로 태어난(Third-born) 아이들은 더 가난한 집안 출신일 가능성이 크므로 '무엇'이 사회경제학적인(socioeconomic) 요소에 따른 결과일 수 있다는 것이다. 세 번째 지문에서 third-born과 socioeconomic이 언급된 문장 내용을 살펴보자. 대가족은 사회경제학적으로 더 낮은 위치에 있을 수 있으므로 첫째들보다는 셋째들이 가난한 가정 출신일 가능성이 크며, 이 때문에 셋째 아이들과 관련된 특정한 '성격(trait)'은, 출생 순서가 아닌 가족 규모나 다른 요소에 의한 결과, 즉 사회경제학적인 요소의 결과일 수도 있다는 내용이다. 따라서 빈칸에 들어갈 단어로 알맞은 것은 C이다.
Paraphrasing discover(발견하다) ➜ identify(발견하다)

13. 빈칸에 들어갈 단어는 출생 순서 관련된 연구가 결점이 있고 확실하지 않다고 보는 '사람들'이다. inconclusive studies가 나온 문장 내용을 살펴보자. 결정적이지 못한 연구와 결과물로 이어져서 'critics (비평가들)'에 의해 쉽게 반박된다는 내용이 근거가 되어 빈칸에 들어갈 단어는 D이다.
Paraphrasing view such studies as being flawed(그러한 연구를 결점이 있다고 보다)
➜ findings that are easily disputed by(~에 의해 연구 결과물들이 쉽게 반박되다)

I Vocabulary & Expressions I
the variety of 다양한 discover 발견하다 flawed 결함이 있는

Unit 08 READING Skills 2 – Sentence Completion, Matching Information

▪ **패시지**

1. E	2. C	3. F	4. D	
5. anesthetic	6. physician	7. dominant	8. right-handed	9. surgery
10. F	11. A	12. E	13. B	14. H

출제 포인트 **난이도: 중**

언어학 주제와 인간의 신체 중 뇌와 관련된 주제 모두 아이엘츠에서 빈출되고 있기에, 비록 난해한 주제들이지만 이와 관련된 지문을 자주 접하면 실제 시험에서 의외로 어렵지 않게 풀 수 있음

기출 2024년 5월 - 냄새와 기억력
2018년 11월 - 언어 표현과 비언어 표현
2017년 1월 - 대뇌의 좌우 분화와 관련된 왼편/오른편 운전

Lateralization and Language
How hemispheric lateralization of the human brain affects the expression of language

A One of the first theories of hemispheric language lateralization was put forth by the French physician Jean-Baptiste Bouillaud. Q1 Bouillaud believed that, because the majority of individuals perform most tasks with their right hand, including writing, the right hand might be controlled by the left hemisphere of the brain. Based on this theory, language, which is fundamental

대뇌 기능 분화와 언어
인간 두뇌의 좌우 기능 분화가 어떻게 언어 표현에 영향을 미치는가

A 대뇌의 좌우 언어 기능 분화에 대한 최초 이론들 중 하나는 프랑스인 의사 장 밥티스트 브이요에 의해 제시되었다. Q1 브이요는 대다수의 사람들이 글쓰기를 포함해 오른손으로 대부분의 일을 하기 때문에 오른손이 좌뇌의 통제를 받을 수 있다고 생각했다. 이 이론에 따르면, 글쓰기의 근본이 되는 언어 또한 좌뇌에 의해 대체로 지배될 수 있다. Q11 브이요의 이론

to writing, would also be largely governed by the left hemisphere. Q11 Bouillaud's theory was investigated further by his son-in-law Simon Alexandre Ernest Aubertin, who collaborated with the leading French neurologist Paul Broca.

B In 1861, Q13 a 51-year-old patient named Leborgne visited Paul Broca. After examining Leborgne, who could understand language but had major difficulties expressing it, Broca determined that a lesion must have formed on the patient's left frontal lobe, a diagnosis that was soon proven to be accurate based on autopsy notes released after Leborgne passed away. Broca studied several other individuals who had lesions or other abnormalities affecting the left frontal lobe and found that all of them had problems articulating themselves through spoken language. Meanwhile, he found that right frontal lesions in other patients had barely any effect on language expression. Subsequently, Broca theorized that language expression is governed only by one hemisphere, predominantly the left.

C Q2 Broca's theory of language lateralization was further supported by the findings of the German anatomist Carl Wernicke. In 1874, Wernicke examined a large number of patients whose language capabilities had been severely disrupted. In each of them, he identified lesions in the temporal lobe of the left hemisphere, but in different sections of the lobe from those that Broca had studied, which inhibited the individual's ability to form language. Q2 Building on these findings, Wernicke created a map that depicted the organization of language processes in the left hemisphere.

D In 1949, Juhn Wada, a researcher at the Montreal Neurological Institute, devised a test that proved invaluable to early studies of lateralization. The Wada Test involves the injection of an Q5 anesthetic into one side of the brain, which will effectively turn off that side for roughly 10 minutes. While one side of the patient's brain is anesthetized, a Q6 physician will evaluate the person's language capabilities. In most cases, the left hemisphere is anesthetized. If the left hemisphere is the Q7 dominant hemisphere, then the patient will lose his or her ability to express language. Conversely, if the patient's right hemisphere is dominant, then he or she will have no difficulty in continuing to speak with the physician.

위 시몬 알렉산드레 어니스트 오베르탱에 의해 한층 더 연구되었으며, 오베르탱은 프랑스의 선구적인 신경학자 폴 브로카와 공동으로 연구했다.

B 1861년에, Q13 레보른이라는 이름의 51세 환자가 폴 브로카를 방문했다. 언어를 이해할 수는 있지만 그것을 표현하는 데 심각한 문제를 겪던 레보른을 진찰한 후, 브로카는 이 환자의 좌측 전두엽에 장애가 일어난 것이 분명하다는 결론을 내렸는데, 이 진단은 레보른이 사망한 후에 공개된 부검 자료를 토대로 정확했던 것으로 곧 밝혀졌다. 브로카는 좌측 전두엽에 발생한 장애나 기타 이상이 있는 여러 다른 사람들을 연구했고, 그들 모두가 구어로(말하는 것으로) 스스로를 표현하는 데 문제를 겪고 있음을 알게 되었다. 한편, 다른 환자들의 우측 전면부의 장애는 언어 표현에 거의 어떠한 영향을 미치지 않는다는 점도 알게 되었다. 그 후, 브로카는 언어 표현이 한쪽 뇌, 주로 좌뇌에 의해서만 지배된다는 점을 이론으로 제시했다.

C Q2 언어 기능 분화에 대한 브로카의 이론은 독일 해부학자 칼 베르니케의 연구 결과에 의해 한층 더 뒷받침되었다. 1874년에, 베르니케는 언어 능력이 심각하게 지장을 받은 다수의 환자들을 진찰했다. 그들 각각에게서, 베르니케는 좌뇌의 측두엽에서 장애를 발견했지만 브로카가 연구했던 사람들의 엽 내 다른 부분이었고, 그 장애는 그 사람들의 언어 형성 능력을 억제했다. Q2 이 발견을 바탕으로, 베르니케는 좌뇌에서 이뤄지는 언어 처리 구조를 묘사하는 도해를 만들었다.

D 1949년에, 몬트리올 신경학회의 연구원인 준 와다는 대뇌 기능 분화의 초기 연구에 있어 매우 유용한 것으로 입증된 테스트 하나를 고안해냈다. 이 와다 테스트는 뇌의 한쪽 면에 Q5 마취제를 주사하는 것이 수반하는데, 이는 약 10분 동안 효과적으로 해당 부분의 신경을 끄게 한다. 환자 뇌의 한쪽 면이 마취된 상태로 있는 동안, Q6 의사는 그 사람의 언어 능력을 평가한다. 보통의 경우, 왼쪽 뇌를 마취한다. 만약 좌뇌가 Q7 우세한 쪽일 경우, 그 환자는 언어를 표현하는 능력을 잃게 된다. 반대로, 환자의 우뇌가 우세할 경우, 그 사람은 의사와 지속적으로 이야기하는 데 어려움이 없을 것이다.

E [Q3] The effectiveness of the Wada Test was documented in a 1977 study conducted by Brenda Milner. By using the process outlined above, [Q12] Milner found that the left hemisphere is dominant in terms of language expression for 70% of left-handed people and 98% of [Q8] right-handed people. Her findings also showed that 2% of right-handed people have a dominant right hemisphere. This finding was significant as it correlated with the percentage of individuals whose speech capabilities are disrupted when they develop a lesion on the right hemisphere of their brain. As a result of Milner's research, the Wada Test became accepted by the scientific community, and it began to be implemented as a preliminary procedure in brain [Q9] surgery, as it allows surgeons to keep the hemisphere associated with speech turned on throughout a surgical procedure.

F Another procedure that has helped to provide crucial information about language lateralization is commissurotomy. [Q10] During this procedure, the hemispheres of a patient (referred to as a split-brain patient) are disconnected by severing the corpus callosum, a nerve tract which connects both hemispheres. The aim of the procedure is to eliminate communication between hemispheres so that each one carries out processes independently. Roger Sperry conducted some of the most widely publicized split-brain studies throughout the 1970s at the California Institute of Technology, concluding definitively that hemispheric lateralization affects language expression.

G [Q4] Sperry worked with numerous split-brain patients, asking each of them to identify objects held in each hand without looking at them. Split-brain patients whose left hemisphere remained functional were able to easily describe items placed in their right hand, but could not verbally identify any items placed in their left hand. Meanwhile, patients using their right hemisphere were only able to give a basic description of each object, rather than an accurate identification. For example, some were unable to identify a ruler but could express that the item was long and flat.

H Sperry's research conclusively showed that, in the vast majority of individuals, major language processes are carried out by the left hemisphere of the brain. However, it is wrong to say that the right hemisphere has absolutely zero capacity for language. As shown in Sperry's research, some test subjects were able

E [Q3] 와다 테스트의 유효성은 브렌다 밀너가 1977년에 실시한 연구에서 문서화되었다. 위에 간단히 설명된 과정을 활용해, [Q12] 밀너는 언어 표현이라는 면에서 왼손잡이의 70퍼센트, 그리고 [Q8] 오른손잡이의 98퍼센트에 해당하는 사람들에게 있어 좌뇌가 우세하다는 점을 알게 되었다. 이 연구 결과물은 오른손잡이 사람들의 2퍼센트가 우세한 우뇌를 갖고 있다는 점도 보여주었다. 이 결과는 우뇌에 장애가 발생할 때 언어 구사 능력이 손상되는 사람들의 비율과 연관성이 있다는 점에서 상당한 의미가 있었다. 밀너의 연구 결과로 인해 와다 테스트는 과학계에서 인정받게 되어 뇌 [Q9] 수술의 한 예비 절차로 시행되기 시작했다, 이는 외과 수술 내내 의사들이 언어 구사와 관련된 한쪽 뇌가 기능하는 상태를 유지하는 것을 가능하게 해주기 때문이다.

F 언어 기능 분화에 관한 중요한 정보를 제공하는 데 도움을 준 또 다른 수술은 교련절개술이다. [Q10] 이 수술 중에, 환자(분할 뇌 환자라고 일컬어지는)의 양쪽 뇌는 양쪽 뇌를 서로 연결해주는 신경계인 뇌량을 절단함으로써 연결이 끊긴다. 이 수술의 목적은 양쪽 뇌 사이의 소통을 제거함으로써 각각의 반구가 처리 과정을 독립적으로 수행하도록 만들기 위함이다. 로저 스페리는 1970년대 전반에 걸쳐 캘리포니아 공과대학에서 가장 널리 알려진 분할 뇌 연구의 일부를 실시했으며, 대뇌 좌우 반구의 언어 기능 분화가 언어 표현에 영향을 미친다고 확실하게 결론 내렸다.

G [Q4] 스페리는 다수의 분할 뇌 환자와 연구했는데, 그들 각각에게 눈으로 보지 않은 채로 각 손에 들려진 물체를 파악하도록 요청했다. 좌뇌가 기능하는 상태로 유지된 분할 뇌 환자는 자신의 오른손에 놓인 물체를 쉽게 설명할 수 있었지만, 왼손에 놓인 어떠한 물체도 말로 확인해주지 못했다. 반면, 우뇌를 사용하는 환자는 정확한 확인 대신 오직 각 물체에 대한 기본적인 설명만 할 수 있었다. 예를 들면, 일부 환자는 '자'라는 것을 알아차릴 수는 없었지만 이 물체가 길고 납작하다는 것은 표현할 수 있었다.

H 스페리의 연구는 대다수의 사람들에게 있어 주요 언어 처리 과정이 좌뇌에 의해 수행된다는 것을 결과적으로 보여주었다. 하지만, 우뇌가 언어에 대해 전적으로 아무런 능력도 없다고 말하는 것은 옳지 않다. 스페리의 연구가 보여주는 것처럼, 일부 실험 대상자들은 우뇌를 사용할 때 물체의 기본적인 설명을 제공할 수 있었는데, 이는 어떤 사람들의 우뇌는 보통 수준으로 언어를 표현할 수 있다는 것을 나타낸다. [Q14] 실상은, 우리가 오직 좌뇌만을 이용해 말로 의사 소통한다는 브로카의 초기 이론은 완전히 정확한 것이 아니라는 것이다. 우리가 우뇌보다 좌뇌를 통해 훨씬 더

to provide rudimentary descriptions of objects when using the right hemisphere, showing that the right hemisphere in some individuals is able to express language to a modest degree. Q14 As such, Broca's earlier theory that we verbally communicate only with our left brain is not entirely accurate. While it is true that we express language much more effectively with our left hemisphere than with our right, the right hemisphere still plays a role in the emotional shading of our speech.	효과적으로 언어를 표현한다는 것은 맞지만, 우뇌도 여전히 우리가 하는 말에서 감성적인 음영을 나타내는 데 일조하고 있다.

I Vocabulary & Expressions I

lateralization 대뇌 좌우 기능 분화 hemispheric 반구(체)의 be put forth by ~에 의해 제시되다 the majority of 대다수의 fundamental 근본적인 govern 통제하다 investigate ~을 조사하다 collaborate with ~와 공동 작업하다 neurologist 신경학자 lesion (병리) 장애, 손상 must have p.p. ~한 것이 분명하다 frontal lobe 전두엽 diagnosis 진단 autopsy (사체의) 부검 pass away 사망하다 abnormality 이상, 기형 articulate ~을 분명히 표현하다 barely 거의 않는 subsequently 그 후에, 나중에 theorize that ~라는 이론을 제시하다 predominantly 대개 findings 결과(물) anatomist 해부학자 disrupt ~에 지장을 주다 temporal lobe 측두엽 inhibit ~을 억제하다, 저해하다 building on ~을 바탕으로 depict ~을 설명하다 devise ~을 고안하다 invaluable 매우 귀중한 injection 주사, 주입 an(a)esthetic 마취제 an(a)esthetize ~을 마취시키다 dominant 지배적인 correlate with ~와 상관 관계가 있다 develop ~을 발생시키다 scientific community 과학계 implement ~을 시행하다 preliminary 예비의 procedure 절차, 수술 surgeon 외과 전문의, 의사 associated with ~와 관련된 surgical 외과의, (외과) 수술의 commissurotomy 교련절개술 referred to as ~라고 일컬어지는 split-brain 분할 뇌의 sever ~을 절단하다 corpus callosum 뇌량 nerve tract 신경계 eliminate ~을 없애다, 제거하다 widely publicized 널리 알려진 conclude that ~라고 결론 내다 identify ~을 확인하다 functional 기능하는 verbally 말로, 구두로 accurate 정확한 conclusively 결정적으로 vast 막대한 rudimentary 기본적인 to a modest degree 보통 수준으로 as such 실상은 shading 음영(법)

문제 1-4

A-F 중 맞는 것으로 아래의 각 문장을 완성하시오.

답지의 1-4번 칸에 상자 안의 A-F 중 올바른 기호를 기입하시오.

1. Jean-Baptiste Bouillaud theorized that
장 밥티스트 브이요가 이론으로 제시한 것은

고유명사인 사람 이름이 가장 중요한 핵심어이다. A 문단에서 문제에서 언급된 학자의 이름인 Jean-Baptiste Bouillaud와 함께 theories가 나왔으므로 해당 문단 내용을 살펴보자. 장 밥티스트 브이요가 이론화시킨 내용을 골라야 한다. 세 번째 문장이 based on this theory라고 시작하므로 두 번째 문장 내용이 바로 브이요의 이론 내용이다. 보기 중 이와 일치하는 것은 오른손으로 수행되는 일은 좌뇌에 의해 통제된다는 내용인 E이다. 따라서 정답은 E이다.

2. Carl Wernicke contributed to the field of language lateralization by
칼 베르니케는 대뇌의 좌우 언어 기능 분화 연구 분야에 기여했는데, 그 방법은

Carl Wernicke가 언급된 C 문단 내용을 살펴보자. 베르니케가 언어 기능 분화 연구에 기여한 방법을 찾아야 한다. 첫 문장 내용이 브로카의 언어 기능 분화가 베르니케의 연구 결과물에 의해 뒷받침되었다고 하는 것이다. 그리고 베르니케 연구의 상세 내용이 나온다. 이 내용을 보기에서 찾아보면, 좌뇌의 언어 처리 과정에 대한 도해를 설계하였다는 내용인 C이다. 따라서 정답은 C이다.
Paraphrasing designing a map(도해를 설계한 것) → created a map(도해를 만들었다)

READING

3. Brenda Milner's work showed that
브렌다 밀너의 연구가 보여준 것은

Brenda Milner가 언급된 E 문단 내용을 살펴보자. 브렌다 밀너의 연구가 밝혀낸 것을 찾아야 한다. 첫 문장 내용이 와다 테스트의 효력이 브렌다 밀너의 연구로 문서화되었다는 것이다. 그리고 나머지 내용은 이 연구의 상세 내용이다. 이를 바탕으로 정답을 보기에서 찾아보면, 한쪽 뇌의 우세함에 대한 한 시험(=와다 테스트)이 효과적이었다는 F가 정답이다. 이전 내용을 바탕으로 a test for hemispherical dominance를 와다테스트로 연결시킬 줄 알아야 한다.

참고로 이 문제는 지문에 언급된 바가 내용적으로 패러프레이징되었다. 즉, 연구가 한 시험이 효과적이었다는 것을 밝혀냈다는 내용(work showed that ~ effective)을, 한 실험의 효력을 문서화했다는 내용으로 패러프레이징되었다.

4. Roger Sperry tested for hemisphere dominance by
로저 스페리는 한쪽 뇌의 우세함에 대해 실험했는데, 그 방법이

Roger Sperry가 언급된 F와 G, H 문단 내용을 살펴보자. 스페리가 한쪽 뇌 우세함을 실험한 방법을 찾아야한다. F 문단의 후반부에서 스페리가 분할 뇌 연구를 통해 언어 기능 분화가 언어 표현에 영향을 미친다는 것을 결론을 내렸다는 내용이 나오고, 이 결론을 내리게 한 실험 내용은 G 문단에서 나온다. 분할 뇌 환자에게 손에 있는 물체를 파악하도록 요청하는 실험이었다. 이는 실험 방법에 해당하므로 이 내용을 보기에서 찾아본다. 손을 이용해 특정 물체를 파악하게 했다는 내용인 D가 지문 내용과 일치한다. 따라서 정답은 D이다.

참고로 A는 오답이다. 교련절개술로 인해 언어 기능 분화에 대해 실험할 수 있는 것은 맞지만 이 수술을 고안한 사람이 Roger Sperry라고 언급되지 않았고, 더욱 중요한 것은 스페리가 시행한 실험은 분할 뇌 연구라고 언급되었을 뿐이다. 즉, 스페리가 실험한 분할 뇌 연구가 교련절개술을 포함하는지 아닌지는 지문 내용만으로는 알 수 없다.

Paraphrasing identify specific objects by hand(손으로 특정 물체를 알아맞히다)
→ identify objects held in each hand without looking at them(손에 들려 있는 물건을 보지 않고 무엇인지 알아맞히다)

A devising a test for blocking communication between brain hemispheres.
양쪽 뇌 사이의 소통을 막는 것에 대한 테스트를 고안한 것이다.

B lesions on brain hemispheres have little to no effect on language expression.
양쪽 뇌에 발생한 장애가 언어 표현에 거의 영향을 미치지 않는다.

C designing a map of language processes controlled by the left hemisphere.
좌뇌에 의해 통제되는 언어 처리 과정의 도해를 설계한 것이다.

D having split-brain patients identify specific objects by hand.
분할 뇌 환자들에게 손으로 특정 물체를 확인하게 한 것이다.

E tasks performed with the right hand are controlled by the left hemisphere.
오른손으로 수행되는 일은 좌뇌에 의해 통제된다.

F a test for hemispherical dominance was an effective technique.
한쪽 뇌의 우세함에 대한 한 시험은 효과적인 기술이었다.

| Vocabulary & Expressions |

contribute 기여하다 field 분야 block 막다 by hand 손으로, 손을 이용하여 task 업무, 일 effective 효과적인 hemisphere (뇌, 지구의) 반구 dominance 우세, 지배

문제 5-9

다음 요약문을 완성하시오.

각 정답은 지문에서 한 단어로 고르시오.

답지의 5-9번 칸에 정답을 기입하시오.

The Wada Test 와다 테스트

The Wada Test was developed by Juhn Wada and requires the injection of an **5** .... into one hemisphere of the brain. Language capabilities are then assessed by a **6** .... for a period of around ten minutes. The test helps to show which hemisphere of an individual's brain is more **7** .... Brenda Milner used the test to show that the left hemisphere is primarily in control of language expression in ninety-eight percent of **8** .... individuals studied. The Wada Test gained widespread acceptance and was eventually used in brain **9** .... so that patients could remain communicative.

와다 테스트는 준 와다에 의해 개발되었으며, 한쪽 뇌에 **5** ....을 주사하는 일을 필요로 한다. 그런 후에 약 10분의 시간 동안 **6** ....에 의해 언어 능력이 평가된다. 이 테스트는 사람 뇌의 어느 한쪽이 더 **7**.. 보여주는 데 도움이 된다. 브렌다 밀너는 연구된 **8** .... 사람들의 98퍼센트에서 좌뇌가 주로 언어 표현을 통제한다는 점을 보여주기 위해 그 테스트를 활용했다. 와다 테스트는 널리 인정 받았으며, 결국 환자들이 뇌 **9** ....에서 의사 전달 가능 상태로 유지될 수 있도록 하는 데 활용되었다.

5. 빈칸에 들어갈 단어는 전치사 of가 앞에 있으므로 명사이고, 와다 테스트에서 한쪽 뇌에 주사하는 '무엇'이다. injection이 나오는 문장 내용을 살펴보자. 와다 테스트에 뇌의 한쪽에 '마취제'를 주사하는 것이 포함한다고 하므로 정답은 anesthetic이다.

6. 빈칸에 들어갈 단어는 부정관사 a가 앞에 있으므로 단수명사이고, 10분의 시간 동안 언어능력을 평가하는 '무엇'이다. 숫자 정보인 10 minutes가 가장 중요한 핵심어이다. 10 minutes와 assess에 상응하는 evaluate가 나오는 문장 내용을 살펴보자. 10분 정도 한쪽의 신경을 끄는 것이 와다테스트이고, '의사'가 언어 능력을 평가한다는 내용이므로 정답은 physician이다.
Paraphrasing assessed by a physician(의사에 의해 평가되는) ➔ a physician will evaluate(의사가 평가할 것이다)

7. 빈칸에 들어갈 단어는 is more가 앞에 있으므로 형용사이고, 와다 테스트가 어느 쪽의 뇌가 '어떠하다고' 보여주는 것이다. 즉 와다 테스트를 통해 알 수 있는 정보이다. which hemisphere에 상응하는 left hemisphere와 right hemisphere가 한 문장에 나오는 내용을 살펴보자. '좌뇌가 우세한 쪽일 경우, ~ 반대로, 환자의 우뇌가 우세할 경우, ~'라고 전개되므로 한쪽 뇌가 '우세'한지에 대한 정보를 얻을 수 있음을 알 수 있으므로 정답은 dominant이다.

8. 빈칸에 들어갈 단어는 전치사 of와 명사 individuals 사이에 있으므로 형용사이고, '어떠한' 98퍼센트의 사람들은 좌뇌가 주로 언어 표현을 통제한다는 내용이다. 숫자 정보인 ninety-eight percent가 가장 중요한 핵심어이다. 98%가 나오는 문장 내용을 살펴보자. '오른손잡이'의 98퍼센트에 해당하는 사람들에게 있어 좌뇌가 지배적이라는 점을 알게 되었다는 내용이므로 정답은 right-handed이다.

참고로 right-handed와 같이 하이픈(-)으로 연결된 단어는 한 단어로 취급한다는 것을 알아 두자.
Paraphrasing is primarily in control of language expression(언어 표현 조절을 주로 통제한다)
➔ is dominant in terms of language expression(언어 표현과 관련해 좌뇌가 우세하다)

9. 빈칸에 들어갈 단어는 brain과 복합 명사를 이루는 명사이고, 와다 테스트가 널리 인정을 받아서 뇌 '무엇'에서 의사 전달 가능 상태로 유지하는 데 활용한다는 내용이다. gained acceptance에 상응하는 became accepted가 나오는 문장 내용을 살펴보자. 과학계의 인정을 받게 되었고 뇌 '수술'에 있어서 예비 절차의 하나로 시행되기 시작했다는 내용이므로 정답은 surgery이다.
Paraphrasing gained widespread acceptance(널리 인정받았다) ➔ accepted by(~의 인정을 받는)

I Vocabulary & Expressions I

capability 능력 assess 평가하다 widespread 광범위한 acceptance 인정, 승인 eventually 결국 communicative 의사 전달의

문제 10-14

독해 지문은 A-H의 8개 문단을 갖고 있다.

어떤 문단이 다음 정보를 포함하는가?

A-H 중 알맞은 기호를 답지 10-14번 칸에 적으시오.

NB 어떤 문자든 한번 이상 사용할 수 있음

10. a description of a method for disrupting hemispheric communication via nerves
신경을 통한 양쪽 뇌 사이의 소통에 지장을 주는 방법에 대한 묘사

양쪽 뇌 사이의 신경 소통 방해가 언급된 문단을 찾아야 한다. disrupting과 nerves가 가장 중요한 핵심어이다. F 문단에서 nerve tract이 언급된 문장을 살펴보자. 뇌량 절단(severing)을 통해 신경 소통 방해(disrupting)을 유발한다는 내용이므로 문제 내용과 일치한다. 따라서 정답은 F이다.

11. a reference to the continuation of an individual's work by a family member
한 사람의 연구가 가족의 일원에 의해 지속된 것에 대한 언급

가족 일원에 의해 지속된 연구가 언급된 문단을 찾아야 한다. family member가 가장 중요한 핵심어이다. A 문단에서 가족 일원을 나타내는 호칭인 son-in-law가 언급된 문장을 살펴보자. 브이요의 이론이 사위에 의해 한 층 더 연구되었다는 내용이므로 문제 내용과 일치한다. 따라서 정답은 A이다.

Paraphrasing continuation(지속된 것) → was investigated further(한층 더 연구되었다)
a family member(가족 일원) → son-in-law(사위)

12. the results of a study on hemisphere dominance in relation to handedness
잘 쓰는 어느 한쪽 손과 관련된 한쪽 뇌의 우세함에 관한 연구 결과

handedness와 한쪽 뇌의 우세함의 관련성이 언급된 문단을 찾아야 한다. E 문단에서 right-handed와 언급된 문장을 살펴보자. 왼손잡이와 오른손잡이 사람들의 수치를 좌뇌 우세와 연관시키고 있는 내용으로 문제 내용과 일치한다. 따라서 정답은 E이다.

Paraphrasing handedness(잘 쓰는 어느 한쪽 손) → right-handed(오른손잡이), left-handed(왼손잡이)
dominance(우세함) → dominant(우세한)

13. a reference to a specific individual whose speech was affected by a brain lesion
뇌 장애에 의해 언어 구사에 문제가 생긴 특정한 사람에 대한 언급

뇌 장애가 있어서 발화 문제가 생긴 특정 사람을 찾아야 한다. specific individual와 speech was affected가 가장 중요한 핵심어인데, 이것을 patient와 연결시킬 수 있어야 한다. 발화 문제가 생긴 어떠한 사람을 '환자'라고 칭할 수 있기 때문이다. patient가 언급된 B 문단 내용을 살펴보자. 레보른이라는 특정 사람이 언급되며 이 사람은 언어를 표현하는 데 문제가 있었다고 한다. 사후 부검 결과 왼쪽 뇌에 장애가 있었다고 하므로 문제 내용과 일치한다. 따라서 정답은 B이다.

참고로 affect(영향을 미치다)는 질병과 함께 쓰이면 '병에 걸리다, (장애가) 발생하다' 등의 뜻으로 쓰이고, 재해 등과 쓰이면 '피해를 주다' 뜻으로 주로 사용된다.

Paraphrasing individual whose speech was affected(언어 구사에 문제가 생긴 사람) → patient(환자)
speech was affected(언어 구사에 문제가 생긴)
→ had major difficulties expressing language(언어를 표현하는 데 심각한 문제가 있다)

14. a conclusion that a previous theory was flawed
이전의 이론에 결점이 있었다는 결론

이전 이론에 결함이 있다는 언급을 찾아야 한다. flawed가 가장 중요한 핵심어인데, 이것을 theory ~ is not entirely correct와 연결시킬 수 있어야 한다. 이론이 결함이 있다는 건, 그 이론이 정확하지 않다는 의미이기 때문이다. 이 문구가 나오는 H 문단 내용을 살펴보자. 브로카의 초기 이론이 완전히 정확한 것은 아니라는 내용으로, 문제 내용과 일치한다. 따라서 정답은 H이다.

Paraphrasing a previous theory(이전의 이론) → Broca's earlier theory(브로카의 초기 이론)
flawed(결함이 있는) → not entirely accurate(완전히 정확하지 않은)

I Vocabulary & Expressions I

via ~을 통해 reference 언급, 참조 in relation to ~과 관련된 flawed 결함이 있는 handedness 잘 쓰는 손

■ 패시지

1. ix	2. iii	3. vi	4. i	5. vii
6. iv	7. viii			
8. YES	9. NOT GIVEN	10. NO	11. YES	12. NOT GIVEN
13. NO				

출제 포인트 난이도: 중

매출을 상승시키는 마케팅 관련 주제의 지문이 심심치 않게 아이엘츠에 출제되기에, 이러한 내용의 지문에 익숙해질 필요가 있음

기출 2024년5월 - 브랜드 로열티
2019년 10월 - 마트에서 판매 촉진 방법
2019년 6월 - 영업의 새로운 ABC: Attunement, Buoyance, Clarity
2018년 12월 - 비주얼 머천다이징: 당신의 상점에서 제품을 전시하는 방법

The Art of Visual Merchandising

Visual merchandising is becoming increasingly important in the retail sector. But what are the most crucial psychological elements of this approach?

A In order to promote products and boost sales, owners of retail businesses employ a wide variety of visual merchandising strategies. Q8 The overall aim of visual merchandising is to make the shopping experience more engaging and enjoyable for consumers while driving profits for the business itself. One of the first visual marketing techniques, which remains just as effective today, was the notion that Q1 the area surrounding a cash register is of utmost importance. While standing in line, customers have a tendency to make last-minute purchases. Business owners began noticing this and setting up displays of low-cost products designed to appeal to 'impulse buyers'. From a psychological perspective, this type of point of sale (POS) visual merchandising must be discreet in order to be effective; if the display is too large or intrusive, it might disrupt the customer's checkout experience.

B A crucial factor in visual merchandising in the retail sector is finding a way to showcase as many products as possible without making the display look cluttered. The most common way to display items in a clothing store is to use mannequins. However, some retailers make the mistake of failing to properly utilize their mannequins. For instance, dressing a mannequin in

비주얼 머천다이징 기술

비주얼 머천다이징이 소매 부문에서 점점 더 중요해지고 있다. 하지만 이 접근 방식의 가장 중요한 심리학적 요소들은 무엇인가?

A 제품을 홍보하고 매출을 촉진시키기 위해, 소매 업체 주들은 아주 다양한 비주얼 머천다이징(시각 판촉: 디자인이나 장식 등의 시각적 효과를 중시하는 판매 촉진 방법) 전략을 활용한다. Q8 비주얼 머천다이징의 전반적인 목표는 업체 자체를 위한 수익을 촉진함과 동시에 소비자들에게 더욱 매력적이고 즐거운 쇼핑 경험을 만들어 주는 것이다. 최초의 비주얼 마케팅 기술 중 하나는, 오늘날에도 그만큼 효과적인 것인데, Q1 계산대 주변의 공간이 가장 중요하다는 개념이었다. 줄을 서 있는 동안에, 고객들은 마지막 구매를 하는 경향이 있다. 업체주들은 이를 알아차리고 '충동 구매자들'의 마음을 끌도록 계획된 저가 상품의 진열을 놓기 시작했다. 심리학적인 관점에서, 이와 같은 유형의 판매 시점(POS) 비주얼 머천다이징이 효과를 거두려면 반드시 신중해야 한다; 진열품이 너무 크거나 거슬리면, 고객의 계산대 경험에 지장을 줄 수도 있기 때문이다.

B 소매 부문의 비주얼 머천다이징에 있어 중요한 한 요소는 제품 진열이 어수선해 보이지 않도록 하면서 가능한 한 많은 제품을 진열할 방법을 찾는 것이다. 의류 매장에서 제품을 진열하는 가장 일반적인 방법은 마네킹을 이용하는 것이다. 하지만, 일부 소매업체들은 마네킹을 적절히 활용하지 못하는 실수를 저지른다. 예를 들어, 오직 한 가지 옷으로만 마네킹에게 옷

only one garment is a missed opportunity to present numerous items of clothing that go together well. Q2 To make the most of store mannequins, it is recommended to create a theme for each one and dress it in items for sale, from head to toe, even including accessories such as watches, hats, and gloves. Another effective way that apparel retailers can make their merchandise more visible is to have staff members wear in-season garments while working on the shop floor.

C Q10 Grouping multiple products together helps customers to envisage how a product will look, function, and feel before they buy it. Stores such as IKEA show how different products complement one another in a home setting. Q3 Exemplary real-life bedrooms, kitchens, and living rooms are created on the shop floor, with each one encompassing several products that are available for purchase. This represents a perfect example of the powerful effect of using visual merchandising to paint an appealing picture for shoppers. When grouping products in such a way, it is vital to make sure that displays have a simple and accessible arrangement. If the merchandise is somewhat visually bland, eye-catching items – such as a colorful teddy bear on a bed – are often added to attract the attention of shoppers.

D Aside from merchandise displays, business owners incorporate Q4 many other visual elements to appeal to consumers. Flowers are a common addition, as they have been shown to promote relaxation and a sense of calm. This results in shoppers who are happy to linger and peruse the items on display, and more inclined to make a casual purchase. Flowers are commonly given and received as gifts, so the brain connects the image of flowers with feelings of happiness and satisfaction. Q11 Studies have shown that even looking at a picture of flowers, or any natural scene, can have the same calming and relaxing effect. Therefore, if a business simply does not have the budget for continually buying fresh flowers, they can strategically place pictures of flowers in the vicinity of product displays.

E On a similar note, Q5 unique artwork is known to contribute to a memorable shopping experience. Artwork has been shown to have beneficial effects in a wide variety of different businesses, from boutique hotels to retail stores. In terms of visual merchandising in retail, one-off paintings or sculptures give a sense of

을 입히는 것은 함께 잘 어울리는 다수의 의류 제품을 보여줄 기회를 놓치는 것이다. Q2 매장 내 마네킹을 가장 잘 활용하기 위해서는, 각 마네킹에 대해 하나의 주제를 정해 머리부터 발 끝까지 판매용 제품으로 입히는 것이 권장되며, 심지어 시계와 모자, 장갑 같은 액세서리들도 여기에 포함된다. 의류 소매업체들이 상품을 더 잘 보이도록 만들 수 있는 또 다른 효과적인 방법은 매장 내에서 근무하는 직원들에게 해당 시즌의 의류를 착용하게 하는 것이다.

C Q10 다수의 제품들을 한데로 모으는 것은 고객들이 구매하기에 앞서 제품이 어떻게 보이고 기능하며 느껴질지를 예상하는 데 도움이 된다. 이케아 같은 매장들은 다양한 제품들이 자택 환경에서 서로 어떻게 보완이 되는지를 보여준다. Q3 좋은 예가 되는 실생활의 침실과 주방, 거실이 매장 내에 만들어지고, 이들 각각은 구매 가능한 여러 제품들을 포함한 채로 있다. 이것은 쇼핑객이 매력적인 그림을 그리게 하는 비주얼 머천다이징을 활용한 것에 대한 강력한 효과를 보여주는 완벽한 예시에 해당한다. 이러한 방식으로 제품을 한데 모을 때, 상품 진열은 간단하고 다가가기 쉬운 배열로 이루어지는 것이 필수적이다. 상품이 다소 시각적으로 단조롭다면, 쇼핑객들의 관심을 끌기 위해 눈길을 끄는 제품들이 (침대 위의 알록달록한 곰 인형 같은) 종종 추가되기도 한다.

D 상품 진열 외에도, 업체 소유주들은 Q4 소비자들의 마음을 끌기 위해 많은 다른 시각적 요소들을 포함시킨다. 꽃이 흔하게 추가되는 요소인데, 편안함과 차분한 느낌을 고취시키는 것으로 보이기 때문이다. 이는 쇼핑객들이 기꺼이 오래 머물러 진열 중인 상품을 잘 살펴보도록 하게 하고, 가벼운 구매를 더욱 하고 싶어지도록 한다. 꽃은 선물로 흔히 주고받는 것이기 때문에, 사람의 뇌가 꽃의 이미지를 행복감과 만족감으로 연관 짓게 된다. Q11 다수의 연구는 다음을 보여주는데, 심지어 꽃의 사진이나 그 어떠한 자연 경관을 보는 것조차도 차분하고 편안함을 주는 동일한 효과를 가질 수 있다고 한다. 따라서, 만약 업체가 단지 신선한 꽃을 지속적으로 구매할 예산을 보유하고 있지 않다면, 제품 진열 주변에 꽃 사진을 전략적으로 배치하면 된다.

E 비슷한 관점에서, Q5 독특한 예술품은 기억에 남을 만한 쇼핑 경험에 일조하는 것으로 알려져 있다. 예술품은 부티크 호텔에서부터 소매 판매점에 이르기까지 아주 다양하게 다른 업체에 유익한 효과가 있는 것으로 알려져 왔다. 소매 부문의 비주얼 머천다이징과 관련해, 단 하나뿐인 그림이나 조각품은 매장에 고급스럽고 특수한 느낌을 제공해준다. 예술품은 잘 알려진 예술가들로부터 의뢰될 수 있고 그러면 브랜드와 제

exclusivity and distinctiveness to a store. Pieces of art can be commissioned from well-known artists and have a visual connection to your brand and products. In addition, highly visible abstract works of art help to create intrigue and draw potential customers into a store. Some business leaders with a keen eye for visual merchandising take it to the next level, having artworks created from the actual products that a business sells.

F Whatever approach a business owner opts for, they should tailor their displays or store designs to appeal to the age range of their target market. In the case of many clothing retailers, the primary target market is relatively young – generally from 17 to 35 – so Q6 it is effective to use common social media language in their visual merchandising strategies. Expressions such as "OMG!" and "Like!" are brief and impactful, and help to attract millennials to merchandise displays. Using Internet-derived language in visual merchandising promotes feelings of familiarity and inclusiveness in younger consumers. They will view the store or brand as being trendy, and might then share images of it with their friends online. Many businesses utilize this strategy in their visual merchandising so that customers make a subconscious connection between the physical store and its online presence, resulting in a higher number of Web site visitors.

G Q7&13 Another way to keep up with the changing times and stay relevant is to incorporate technology into visual merchandising. The majority of customers appreciate innovation and interactivity. Recently, companies such as Bloomingdale's and Ralph Lauren have installed window displays comprised of high-definition touchscreens that allow consumers to customize specific items of clothing, place an order, then pick it up in-store. As technology continues to evolve, an increasing number of retailers are turning to virtual reality as a way to attract customers and improve their retail experience. By donning VR headsets, customers can see how a piece of furniture would look in their home, or explore the interior and exterior of a vehicle that is not physically available for viewing. And with retailers allocating more and more of their marketing budget for high-tech visual merchandising, and demand for such technology increasing, these innovations are just the tip of the iceberg.

품에 대한 시각적 연관성을 지닐 수 있다. 추가로, 매우 눈에 잘 띄는 추상 예술 작품은 흥미진진함을 만들어주어 잠재 고객들을 매장으로 끌어들이는 데 도움이 된다. 비주얼 머천다이징에 대해 예리한 시각을 지닌 일부 업체주들은 이를 한 단계 더 끌어올려 업체에서 판매하는 실제 제품으로 예술품을 만들어낸다.

F 업체주가 어떤 접근 방식을 취하든, 목표 시장의 연령대에 속한 고객들의 마음을 끌 수 있도록 진열 방식이나 매장 디자인을 조정해야 한다. 많은 의류 소매업체들의 경우에, 주요 목표 시장이 비교적 젊기 때문에(일반적으로 17세에서 35세 사이), Q6 비주얼 머천다이징 전략에 있어 흔한 소셜 미디어 언어를 활용하는 것이 효과적이다. "OMG!"나 "Like!" 같은 표현들은 짧으면서 강한 인상을 주며, 상품 진열 공간으로 밀레니얼 세대(1980년대 초부터 2000년대 초에 출생한 세대)의 고객들의 마음을 끌도록 도와준다. 비주얼 머천다이징에 인터넷에서 파생된 언어를 활용하는 것은 젊은 소비자들에게 친근하고 포용적인 느낌을 촉진시킨다. 그 소비자들은 해당 매장 또는 브랜드를 최신 유행하는 것으로 보게 되며, 그 후 친구들과 온라인으로 그 이미지들을 공유할 수도 있다. 많은 업체들이 비주얼 머천다이징에 이러한 전략을 활용하는데, 이로 인해 고객들이 물리적인 매장과 그 매장의 온라인상 존재 사이에 잠재 의식적인 연결을 형성하고, 그 결과 더 많은 수의 웹 사이트 방문객을 유발한다.

G Q7&13 변화하는 시대에 발맞춰 가고 밀접하게 관련되어 있는 상태를 유지하는 또 다른 방법은 비주얼 머천다이징에 기술력을 포함시키는 것이다. 대부분의 고객들은 혁신과 상호작용을 높이 평가한다. 최근, 블루밍데일이나 랄프 로렌 같은 회사들은 고화질 터치스크린으로 구성된 진열창을 설치했는데, 이 진열창은 소비자들이 특정 의류 제품을 원하는 대로 만들고 주문한 다음에 매장에서 찾아갈 수 있게 한다. 기술은 지속적으로 발전하므로, 점점 더 많은 소매업체들이 고객들을 끌어들이고 구매 경험을 개선하기 위한 방법의 일환으로 가상 현실로 관심을 돌리고 있다. VR 헤드셋을 착용함으로써, 고객들은 한 가구가 자택에서 어떻게 보일지 확인할 수 있으며, 실제로 보는 것이 불가능한 차량의 실내와 외부를 살펴볼 수도 있다. 그리고 소매업체들이 점점 더 많은 마케팅 예산을 첨단 기술의 비주얼 머천다이징에 할당하고 이러한 기술에 대한 수요가 증가하고 있는 것으로 볼 때, 이와 같은 혁신은 빙산의 일각에 불과하다.

| Vocabulary & Expressions |

retail 소매 (판매) psychological 심리학적인 element 요소 boost ~을 촉진하다 employ ~을 활용하다 strategy 전략 engaging 매력적인 utmost 극도의 appeal to ~의 마음을 끌다 impulse 충동 perspective 관점 point of sale 판매 시점 discreet 신중한 intrusive 거슬리는 disrupt ~에 지장을 주다 showcase ~을 진열하다 cluttered 어수선한 utilize ~을 활용하다 garment 의류, 옷 make the most 최대한 활용하다 in-season 해당 시즌의, 제철의 envisage ~을 상상하다, 예상하다 complement 보완이 되다 exemplary 좋은 예가 되는 with A -ing A가 ~하는 채로 encompass ~을 아우르다, 포괄하다 represent ~을 나타내다, 해당하다 bland 단조로운 aside from ~ 외에도 incorporate ~을 포함하다, 통합하다 addition 추가(되는 것) relaxation 편안함 sense of calm 차분한 느낌 linger 오래 머무르다 peruse ~을 잘 살펴보다, 정독하다 inclined 마음이 내키는 strategically 전략적으로 in the vicinity of ~ 주변에, 인근에 on a similar note 비슷한 관점에서 contribute to ~에 일조하다, 기여하다 beneficial 유익한 one-off 한 개 뿐인, 한 번 뿐인 exclusivity 고급스러움 distinctiveness 특수성 commission ~을 의뢰하다, 주문하다 abstract 추상적인 intrigue 흥미진진함 keen eye 예리한 시각 opt for ~을 선택하다 tailor ~을 맞추다, 조정하다 primary 주요한, 일차적인 impactful 강한 인상을 주는 Internet-derived 인터넷에서 파생된 familiarity 친근감 inclusiveness 포용성, 포괄성 subconscious 잠재 의식의 physical 물리적인 presence 존재(감) appreciate ~을 높이 평가하다 innovation 혁신(적인 것) interactivity 교류, 상호 작용 install ~을 설치하다 comprised of ~로 구성된 customize ~을 맞춤 제작하다 place an order 주문하다 evolve 발전하다, 진화하다 turn to ~로 관심을 돌리다 don ~을 착용하다 explore ~을 살펴보다 allocate ~을 할당하다 tip of the iceberg 빙산의 일각

문제 1-7

독해 지문 1에 A-G, 7개의 문단이 있다.

다음 제목 목록에서 각 문단에 알맞은 제목을 고르시오.

답안지 1-7번 상자에 i-x 중에서 알맞은 기호를 기입하시오.

List of Headings 제목 목록

i	Visual cues to trigger positive emotions 긍정적인 감정을 촉발하는 시각적 신호
ii	Wall color and its effect on psychology 벽 색상과 그것이 심리에 미치는 영향
iii	Make full use of your display models 진열 제품 모델 최대한 활용하기
iv	Speak the language of your consumers 소비자의 언어로 말하기
v	The appeal of offers and discounts 제공 서비스와 할인의 매력
vi	Telling a story to consumers 소비자들에게 이야기 들려주기
vii	Catching attention through art 예술을 통해 관심 사로잡기
viii	Visual merchandising and technology 비주얼 머천다이징과 기술
ix	Utilizing the checkout to boost sales 판매를 촉진시키기 위해 계산대 활용하기
x	Promoting your products in publications 출판물로 상품 홍보하기

1. A 문단

A 문단 전체 내용은 비주얼 머천다이징 전략의 첫 번째 예시로 계산대의 중요성을 언급하며 계산대 근처에서 소비자로 하여금 마지막 소비를 유도한다는 것이다. 제시된 목록 중에서 checkout(계산대)을 언급한 Utilizing the checkout to boost sales가 제목으로 적합하다. 따라서 정답은 ix이다.

Paraphrasing checkout(계산대) → cash register(계산대)

2. B 문단

B 문단 전체 내용은 제품 진열 방법에 관한 것으로 어수선하지 않으면서도 많은 제품을 진열할 수 있는 마네킹을 잘 활용하라는 것이다. 제시된 목록 중에서 마네킹을 뜻하는 display models를 언급한 Make full use of your display models가 제목으로 적합하다. 따라서 정답은 iii이다.

Paraphrasing make full use of(~을 충분히 활용하다) → make the most of(~을 최대한 활용하다)
display models(제품 진열 모델) → mannequins(마네킹)

3. C 문단

C 문단 전체 내용은 다수의 제품을 한데 진열하면 소비자가 그 상품을 어떻게 사용할지에 대해 예상하기 쉽다는 것이다. 즉, 이 제품으로 실생활의 침실이나 거실에서 이런 식으로 사용하면 된다는 것을 보여줄 수 있다는 것이다. 이 문단은 핵심어를 잡기 어려운 경우로, 내용으로 접근해야 한다. 지문에서 실생활 물품들을 전시하면서 쇼핑객이 매력적인 그림을 그리게 하도록 한다는 내용이, 제시된 목록 중에서 '이야기를 들려준다'는 은유적으로 바꿔 표현된 Telling a story to consumers가 제목으로 적합하다. 따라서 정답은 vi이다.

4. D 문단

D 문단 전체 내용은 시각적 요소들(visual elements)에 관해, 예시로 행복감과 만족감을 유발시키는 꽃이 있다면 소비자들이 가벼운 구매를 더 하게 된다는 것이다. 제시된 목록 중에서 꽃을 뜻하는 Visual cues와 꽃이 유발하는 감정을 뜻하는 positive emotions를 언급한 Visual cues to trigger positive emotions가 제목으로 적합하다. 따라서 정답은 i이다.

Paraphrasing visual cues(시각적 신호들) → visual elements(시각적 요소들), flowers(꽃)
trigger(촉발시키다) → promote(고취시키다)
positive emotions(긍정적인 감정) → relaxation and a sense of calm(편안함과 차분함),
feelings of happiness and satisfaction(행복감과 만족감)

READING

5. E 문단

E 문단 전체 내용은 시각적 요소의 또다른 예로 제시된 예술품 활용에 관한 것으로, 예술품은 소비자에게 기억에 남은 쇼핑 경험을 갖게 해주고 잠재 고객을 매장으로 끌어들인다는 것이다. 제시된 목록 중에서 예술품을 뜻하는 art가 언급된 Catching attention through art가 제목으로 적합하다. 따라서 정답은 vii이다.

6. F 문단

F 문단 전체 내용은 목표 소비자층에 맞추어 소셜 미디어 언어, 인터넷 파생어를 사용한다는 것이다. 제시된 목록 중에서 고객과 언어가 언급된 Speak the language of your consumers가 제목으로 적합하다. 따라서 정답은 iv이다.

7. G 문단

G 문단의 전체 내용은 첨단 기술 활용에 관한 것으로, 소비자의 구매 경험을 개선할 수 있는 가상 현실 기술이 예시로 제시된다. 제시된 목록 중에서 기술을 나타내는 technology가 언급된 Visual merchandising and technology가 제목으로 적합하다. 따라서 정답은 viii이다.

| Vocabulary & Expressions |

cue 신호 trigger 촉발시키다, 작동시키다 positive 긍정적인 emotion 감정 wall 벽 make full use of ~을 최대한 활용하다 utilize 활용하다 checkout 계산대 boost 촉진하다 publication 출판물

문제 8-13

다음 내용이 독해 지문 1의 글쓴이 견해와 일치하는가?

답지 8-13번 칸에 다음을 쓰시오.

YES 글쓴이 견해와 일치하면
NO 글쓴이 견해와 상반되면
NOT GIVEN 글쓴이가 문제 진술에 대해 어떻게 생각하는지 말하는 것이 불가능하다면

8. Visual merchandising is an effective way to boost earnings.
비주얼 머천다이징은 수익을 신장시킬 수 있는 효과적인 방법이다.

문제 진술(비주얼 머천다이징이 수익을 신장시키는 데 효과적) 관련하여, A 문단에서 글쓴이는 비주얼 머천다이징의 목표는 '수익을 촉진'시키는 것이고 여전히 '효과적'이라고 언급하고 있다. 즉, 글쓴이 견해와 일치하므로 정답은 YES이다.

Paraphrasing boost earnings(수익을 신장시키다) → driving profits(수익을 촉진하다)

9. **Mannequin displays should be set up near a store's entrance.**
마네킹 진열은 매장 입구 근처에 설치되어야 한다.

마네킹의 위치에 대한 내용으로, 마네킹에 대해 언급된 B 문단 내용을 살펴보자. 마네킹을 권장하는 이유 및 활용방법에 대해 언급되고 있긴 하지만, 마네킹의 매장 내 위치에 관해서는 언급되지 않았다. 따라서 정답은 NOT GIVEN이다.

10. **Displaying multiple products closely together is confusing to consumers.**
다수의 제품을 서로 가까이 진열하는 것은 소비자들을 혼란스럽게 한다.

다수의 제품을 서로 가까이 진열하는 것이 소비자들을 혼란스럽게 한다는 내용이다. 그러나 C 문단에서 다양한 제품을 한데 모으면 구매 전의 소비자들에게 도움이 된다고 언급하고 있다. 글쓴이 견해와 상반되므로 정답은 NO이다.
Paraphrasing Displaying multiple products closely together(다수의 제품을 서로 가까이 진열하는 것)
→ Grouping multiple products together(다수의 제품을 한데 모으는 것)

11. **Photographs of flowers can have the same level of appeal as fresh flowers.**
꽃 사진은 생화와 동일한 수준의 매력을 지닐 수 있다.

꽃 사진과 생화가 동일한 수준의 매력을 지닌다는 내용이다. D 문단에서 꽃(생화)이 편안함과 차분한 느낌을 고취시킨다며 소비자들의 마음을 끌기 위해 사용되는 시각적 요소 중 하나라는 내용이 나온다. 이어서 꽃 사진을 보는 것도 '동일한' 효과를 가질 수 있다고 언급하고 있다. 동일한 수준의 매력을 갖는다는 건 동일한 효과를 가진다고 볼 수 있다. 즉, 글쓴이 견해와 일치하므로 정답은 YES이다.
Paraphrasing have the same level of appeal(동일한 수준의 매력을 지니다)
→ have the same calming and relaxing effect(차분하고 편안함을 주는 동일한 효과를 가지다)

12. **Having an attractive Web site is a key part of visual merchandising.**
매력적인 웹 사이트가 있는 것은 비주얼 머천다이징의 핵심 요소이다.

매력적인 웹사이트를 갖는 것이 비주얼 머천다이징의 핵심 요소라는 내용이다. F 문단에서 웹사이트가 언급되기는 하지만, 인터넷에서 파생된 단어를 쓰는 전략의 결과로 웹사이트의 방문객이 증가한다는 내용 뿐이다. 즉, 글쓴이 견해를 파악할 수 있는 내용이 부재하므로 정답은 NOT GIVEN이다.

13. **Consumers are increasingly unimpressed with high-tech marketing methods.**
소비자들은 첨단 기술의 마케팅 방법에 대해 점점 더 인상적이지 않다고 생각한다.

첨단 기술의 마케팅 방법에 소비자들이 점점 인상을 받지 않는다는 내용이다. 그러나 G 문단에서 변화하는 시대에 발맞추기 위해 비주얼 머천다이징에 기술력을 포함시킨다며 대부분의 고객들은 '혁신'과 상호작용을 '높이 평가'한다는 내용이 언급된다. 그리고 바로 이어서 혁신과 상호작용에 해당하는 첨단기술의 예(고화질 터치 스크린)가 주어진다. 즉, 앞에서 말한 '혁신'은 첨단기술을 말하는 것이다. 이 내용을 바탕으로 글쓴이 견해와 상반된다는 것을 알 수 있으므로 정답은 NO이다.

I Vocabulary & Expressions I

entrance 입구 confusing 혼란스러운 increasingly 점점 더

Unit 10	READING Skills 4 – Short-answer Questions, Diagram Label Completion, Multiple Choice

▪ 패시지

1. willows	2. Siberia	3. (mammoth) bones	4. dwellings
5. foraging	6. grasslands	7. (geographic) barriers	8. drowning
9&10. C, E	11&12. B, D	13. C	

출제 포인트 | 난이도: 중

고대 동물들(공룡, 매머드, 시조새, 거대 포유동물, 고대 개구리 등)과 관련된 고생물학, 고인류학, 화석이나 빙하기 및 이와 관련된 기후 변화(climate change) 주제가 빈번하게 출제되므로 관련 내용 및 어휘에 대한 숙지 필요

기출 2024년 5월 – 최초의 인류 화석, 루시
2019년 6월 – 뉴질랜드 고대 개구리
2019년 2월 – 매머드 화석
2019년 1월 – 곤충의 화석
2018년 12월 – 빙하기

The Woolly Mammoth

The definitive factor that caused the extinction of the woolly mammoth has been highly controversial for a long time. When the last glaciation period ended approximately 15,000 years ago, woolly mammoth populations were flourishing. Although the glaciers were melting, temperatures were still low enough to be comfortable for the mammoth, and for the plant life on which it depended. In fact, the conditions were perfect for growing the mammoth's preferred foods, and the cold temperatures prevented the development of terrain that could impede the Q5 foraging routes of mammoth populations.

Q6 The transition from the Late Pleistocene epoch to the Holocene epoch, around 12,000 years ago, saw a marked reduction in the distribution range of mammoth populations. A steady increase in global temperature brought about significant changes to the mammoth's environment. Q6 Grasslands rich in herbs and nutrients were gradually replaced by forested areas, Q9&10 leading to a shortage of viable habitat for several megafaunal species such as the woolly mammoth. The rising temperatures were unsuitable for growth of the mammoth's preferred foods, such as Q1 willows, and instead allowed nutrient-deficient conifers to grow and thrive. In addition to impenetrably dense forests, soft marshlands formed, creating Q7 geographic barriers that greatly limited the movement and foraging range of mammoths.

털매머드

털매머드의 멸종을 초래한 명확한 요인은 오랜 기간 크게 논란이 되어 왔다. 마지막 빙하 시대가 약 15,000년 전에 끝났을 때, 털매머드의 개체수는 늘어나고 있었다. 빙하가 녹고 있기는 했지만, 기온은 여전히 털매머드와 그들이 의존하는 초목이 편안할 정도로 충분히 낮았다. 사실, 이 환경은 털매머드가 선호하는 먹이들이 자라기에 완벽한 것이었으며, 차가운 기온은 털매머드들이 Q5 먹이 찾기 경로를 방해할 수 있는 지형의 발달을 막아주었다.

약 12,000년 전, Q6 플라이스토세 후기에서 홀로세로의 변천 과정에서 털매머드 개체수의 분포 범위에 있어 뚜렷한 감소세가 나타났다. 전 세계 기온의 지속적인 증가는 털매머드의 서식 환경에 상당한 변화를 초래하였다. 허브와 영양분이 풍부한 Q6 초원은 점차적으로 숲으로 뒤덮인 지역으로 대체되었는데, Q9&10 이는 털매머드 같은 여러 초대형 동물 종이 생존 가능한 서식지의 부족 문제로 이어졌다. 이러한 기온 상승은 Q1 버드나무와 같은 털매머드가 좋아하는 먹이의 성장에 부적합했으며, 이 대신에 영양분이 부족한 침엽수가 자라고 번성하게 해주었다. 관통할 수 없을 정도로 빽빽한 숲 뿐만 아니라, 부드러운 늪지대가 형성되었는데 이는 털매머드의 이동과 식량 채집 범위를 크게 제한했던 Q7 지리적 장애물을 만들었다.

The warming trend that continued throughout the Holocene epoch was accompanied by a significant shrinking of glaciers and rising sea levels, and many scientists have argued that these were contributing factors to the extinction of the mammoth. Studies have shown that the mammoths that lived on the isolated Saint Paul Island off the coast of Alaska gradually died out as the rising sea levels caused a decrease of as much as 90% of total land area. Several scientists have proposed that a cause of mammoth population decline in Siberia was largely Q8 drowning due to significant changes to glaciers. It is believed that, while traveling to new grazing areas, hundreds of thousands of mammoths broke through the melting ice and drowned.

However, such notable warming periods had occurred several times throughout the previous ice age and had never resulted in any megafaunal extinctions, so it would be shortsighted to say that climate change alone led to the extinction of the mammoth. Another significant contributing factor was the spread of human populations throughout northern Eurasia and the Americas, and the development and refinement of new hunting techniques.

Evidence has been found that indicates that humans learned to adapt themselves to the harsher climates of the regions where mammoths resided. Once humans had figured out how to survive in the cold temperatures, then it was possible for them to hunt mammoths everywhere. Although humans had hunted woolly mammoths in Q2 Siberia for thousands of years, it wasn't until the last ice age that hunters crossed the Bering Strait and began killing mammoths in Alaska and the Yukon. As early as 1.8 million years ago, Homo erectus is known to have consumed mammoth meat, although it cannot be proven that this was a result of successful hunting rather than simple scavenging.

More conclusive proof of humans hunting mammoths can be found when studying later human populations. A 50,000-year-old site in England, and various sites dating from 15,000 to 45,000 years old throughout Europe, have yielded Q3 mammoth bones whose condition indicates that early man did indeed become adept at hunting and butchering mammoths. Evidence has also been found that primitive Q4 dwellings were often constructed by Neanderthals using the bones of mammoths. However, several leading paleontologists have argued that bones of dead mammals that have been trampled by other large mammals may bear the same appearance of those that

홀로세 전반에 걸쳐 지속된 이와 같은 온난화 경향은 상당한 빙하 감소 및 해수면 상승을 동반하였고, 많은 과학자들은 이것이 털매머드 멸종에 기여한 요인이라고 주장하고 있다. 연구에 따르면 알래스카 해안에서 떨어져 고립된 세인트 폴 섬에 서식하던 털매머드가 점차 멸종되었고 이는 해수면 상승이 전체 육지 면적의 90퍼센트에 달하는 정도의 감소를 초래하였기 때문이었다. 여러 과학자들은 시베리아의 털매머드 개체수 감소 원인이 대체로 빙하의 상당한 변화로 인한 Q8 익사였다는 의견을 제시했다. 새로운 목초지를 찾아 이동하는 동안 수 십만 마리의 털매머드가 녹아 내리는 얼음 사이를 지나가다가 익사한 것으로 알려져 있다.

하지만, 이런 주목할 만한 온난화 기간이 이전의 빙하기에 여러 차례 나타났어도, 어떠한 초대형 동물의 멸종을 초래한 적은 없었기 때문에, 기후 변화 하나만으로 털매머드의 멸종이 초래되었다고 말하는 것은 근시안적인 생각일 수 있다. 또 다른 중요한 기여 요인은 유라시아 북부와 아메리카 지역 전체에 걸친 인간 집단의 확산과 새로운 사냥 기술의 발전 및 개선이었다.

인간이 그들 스스로를 털매머드가 살았던 지역의 더욱 가혹한 기후에 적응하는 법을 터득했음을 나타내는 증거가 발견되었다. 인간이 추운 기온에서 생존하는 법을 알게 되자, 어디서든 털매머드를 사냥하는 것이 가능했다. 인간이 수천 년 동안 Q2 시베리아 지역에서 털매머드를 사냥하기는 했지만, 사냥꾼들이 베링 해협을 건너 알래스카와 유콘 지역에서 털매머드를 죽이기 시작한 것은 마지막 빙하 시대나 되어서였다. 일찍이 180만년 전에도, 호모 에렉투스가 매머드 고기를 소비한 것으로 알려져 있기는 하지만, 이것이 단순히 죽은 고기를 먹은 것이 아닌 성공적인 사냥의 결과인지는 입증될 수 없다.

인간이 털매머드를 사냥한 더욱 결정적인 증거는 더 나중의 인간 집단에 대한 연구에서 찾아볼 수 있다. 잉글랜드의 5만년 역사를 지닌 한 장소와 유럽 전역의 1만 5천 년에서 4만 5천 년까지 시대를 거슬러 올라가는 다양한 장소에서 Q3 매머드 뼈가 발견되었는데 이 뼈들의 상태는 고대 인류가 매머드를 사냥하고 도살하는 데 확실히 능숙해졌음을 나타내었다. 네안데르탈인에 의해 원시 사회의 Q4 집이 종종 매머드 뼈를 이용해 지어졌음을 보여주는 증거도 발견되었다. 하지만, 여러 선구적인 고생물학자들은 다른 거대 포유류에 의해 짓밟혀 죽은 포유류의 뼈는 도살 당한 동물에게서 나온 것과 유사한 모양

have come from a butchered animal, and therefore it is impossible to rule out trampling when studying bones from seemingly butchered mammoths.

In the past, theories about the extinction of the woolly mammoth generally focused on one factor as the underlying cause, whether that be climate change, hunting by humans, or something different entirely such as a meteor impact. Q11&12 However, recent paleontological research in North America paints a clearer picture of the demise of woolly mammoths. By creating the most comprehensive maps to date of all the changes that occurred during the mammoth's existence, researchers have shown beyond all doubt Q9&10 that the extinction did not result from any single factor, but from a combination of habitat loss as a result of climate change and overhunting by humans.

Q11&12 Using radiocarbon dating of fossils, scientists have created maps of the changing locations of mammoth herds, human settlements, forests, marshlands, and plant species over several thousand years, and then cross-referenced this data with corresponding data related to climate change. The research takes into account more than one thousand mammoth radiocarbon dates, approximately six hundred peatland dates, and almost five hundred tree and plant species dates, as well as a large number of dates taken from known Paleolithic archaeological sites. After obtaining samples from each site, and radiocarbon dating each of them, scientists were able to create a database that could be used to learn more about thousands of previously dated mammoth samples. This extensive research allowed the researchers to develop a definitive map that unites paleobotanical, paleontological, genetic, archaeological and paleoclimate data to give us an accurate representation of the combined factors leading to the extinction of the woolly mammoth.

으로 되어 있을 수 있으며, 그러므로 도살된 것으로 보여지는 매머드에게서 나온 뼈를 연구할 때 짓밟힘을 배제하는 것이 불가능하다고 주장했다.

과거에, 털매머드의 멸종에 관한 이론은 일반적으로 근본적인 원인으로서 한 가지 요인에만 초점을 맞췄는데, 그것이 기후 변화, 인간에 의한 사냥, 혹은 운석 충돌과 같은 뭔가 완전히 다른 원인인지를 밝히는 것이었다. Q11&12 하지만, 북미 지역에서 있었던 최근 고생물학 연구는 털매머드의 종말에 대해 더욱 명확하게 묘사한다. 털매머드가 존재하는 동안 발생되었던 모든 변화들에 대한 현존하는 가장 종합적인 지도를 제작함으로써, 연구가들은 Q9&10 그 멸종이 어떠한 단 하나의 요인이 아닌, 기후 변화와 인간의 과도한 사냥으로부터 비롯된 서식지 소실이라는 복합적인 원인으로 생겨났다는 점을 의심의 여지 없이 보여주었다.

Q11&12 화석에 대한 방사선 탄소 연대 측정법을 활용해, 과학자들은 수천 년에 걸친 매머드 떼와 인간의 정착지, 숲, 습지대, 그리고 초목 종의 위치 변화를 보여주는 지도를 만든 다음, 이 데이터를 기후 변화와 관련된 상응하는 데이터와 교차 참조했다. 이 연구는 1천 개가 넘는 매머드 관련 방사선 탄소 연대 측정 날짜와 대략 600개의 이탄지대(습지 등에서 수생식물의 유해가 미분해 또는 약간 분해된 상태로 퇴적된 토지) 관련 날짜, 그리고 거의 500개에 달하는 나무 및 식물 종 관련 날짜뿐만 아니라 구석기 시대의 고고학적인 유적지들로 알려진 곳에서 얻은 수많은 날짜까지 고려한 것이다. 각 장소에서 샘플을 얻은 후, 각각에 대해 방사선 탄소 연대 측정을 거쳐, 과학자들은 수천 개의 과거 날짜로 된 매머드 샘플들에 관해 더 많은 것을 알아보는 데 사용될 수 있었던 데이터베이스를 만들어낼 수 있었다. 이 광범위한 연구를 통해 연구가들은 하나의 최종적인 지도를 개발할 수 있었고, 이 지도는 털매머드의 멸종을 초래한 복합적인 요소들을 정확히 나타내기 위해 원시 식물 데이터와 고생물학 데이터, 유전학 데이터, 고고학 데이터, 그리고 고기후 데이터를 통합시킨 것이었다.

| Vocabulary & Expressions |

definitive 명확한, 최종적인 extinction 멸종 controversial 논란이 많은 glaciation period 빙하기 population (동물) 개체 수, 집단 flourish 늘다, 번창하다 terrain 지형 impede ~을 지연시키다, 방해하다 foraging 먹이 찾기, 채집 transition 변화, 변천 marked 뚜렷한 distribution range 분포 범위 bring about ~을 초래하다, 유발하다 nutrient 영양분 viable 생존 가능한 habitat 서식지 megafaunal 초대형 동물의 unsuitable 부적합한 nutrient-deficient 영양분이 부족한 conifer 침엽수 impenetrably 꿰뚫을 수 없을 정도로 geographic 지리적인 barrier 장애물, 장벽 warming trend 온난화 경향 be accompanied by ~을 동반하다 shrinking 축소 contributing factor 기여 요인 isolated 외딴, 고립된 die out 자취를 감추다, 멸종되다 drown 익사하다 break through ~을 뚫고 지나가다 notable 주목할 만한 result in ~의 결과를 낳다 shortsighted 근시안적인 refinement 개선, 향상 adapt oneself to ~에 적응하다 reside 살다, 거주하다 consume ~을 소비하다, 먹다 scavenge 죽은 고기를 먹다 yield ~을 산출하다 adept at ~에 능숙한 butcher ~을 도살하다 primitive 원시 시대의 dwelling 주택, 집 paleontologist 고생물학자 trample ~을 짓밟다 rule out ~을 배제하다 seemingly 겉보기에, 보아하니 underlying 근본적인 meteor impact 운석 충돌

paleontological 고생물학적인 demise 종말, 죽음 comprehensive 종합적인 to date 현재까지 existence 존재 beyond all doubt 의심의 여지 없이 result from ~로부터 비롯되다 a combination of 복합적인 radiocarbon dating 방사선 탄소 연대 측정 herd (동물의) 떼, 무리 settlement 정착지 cross-reference ~을 교차 참조하다 corresponding 상응하는 related to ~와 관련된 take into account ~을 고려하다 peatland 이탄지대 Paleolithic 구석기 시대의 archaeological 고고학의 extensive 광범위한 paleobotanical 고식물의 genetic 유전학의 paleoclimate 고기후의 representation 묘사 lead to ~을 초래하다

문제 1-4

각 정답은 지문에서 두개 이하의 단어로 고르시오.

답지 1-4번 칸에 다음을 쓰시오

1. What was known to be a plant commonly eaten by mammoths?
매머드가 흔히 먹었던 식물로 알려진 것은 무엇인가?

매머드가 흔히 먹었던 특정 식물을 찾아야 한다. 흔히 먹은 것은 선호하는 음식(preferred food)이라고 볼 수 있으므로 preferred food를 핵심어로 정답을 찾아보자. 이것이 언급된 부분의 내용 중에서도 특정 식물의 이름이 언급된 부분을 찾아야 한다. 두 번째로 언급된 두 번째 문단의 중반부를 보면, such as와 함께 버드나무가 언급되었다. 따라서 정답은 willows이다.

Paraphrasing commonly eaten(흔히 먹었던) → preferred food(선호하는 음식)

2. Where were mammoths known to be hunted before they were hunted in Alaska?
매머드가 알래스카에서 사냥되기 전에 어디에서 사냥된 것으로 알려졌는가?

매머드가 사냥된(hunted) 특정 지역이되, 알래스카보다 이전 시대에 사냥된 지역을 찾아야 한다. hunted와 Alaska를 핵심어로 잡고 정답을 찾아보자. 즉, 알래스카와 hunted가 모두 언급되면서도 시간적인 비교가 이루어진 문장을 찾아야 한다. 다섯 번째 문단의 중반부를 보면, 시베리아 지역에서 사냥하긴 했지만 알래스카와 유콘 지역에서는 마지막 빙하시대가 되어서야 사냥했다고 한다. 단순하게 시제만 보아도 시베리아(Siberia)에는 과거완료시제가 사용되고, 알래스카는 과거시제가 사용되었으므로 시간관계를 따질 수 있다. 과거완료시제가 과거시제보다 더 먼저 일어난 일을 나타내므로 정답은 Siberia이다.

3. What were found at sites throughout Europe?
유럽 전역에 걸친 장소에서 발견된 것은 무엇인가?

유럽(Europe) 전역에서 발견된 것을 찾아야 한다. Europe을 핵심어로 잡고 정답을 찾아보자. 여섯 번째 문단에서 throughout Europe이 언급된 문장 내용을 살펴보자. 유럽 전역의 오래된 장소에서 매머드 뼈(mammoth bones)가 발견되었다고 하므로, 정답은 mammoth bones이다. 이 지문에서 언급된 뼈는 모두 매머드 뼈이므로, bones만 써도 정답이 된다.

4. What did early humans build using parts from mammoths?
고대 인류가 매머드의 일부를 이용하여 지은 것은 무엇인가?

고대 인류(early humans)가 매머드의 일부로 지은(build) 것을 찾아야 한다. early humans에 상응하는 Neanderthals과 build에 상응하는 constructed가 나온 문장 내용을 살펴보자. 네안데르탈인이 매머드 뼈로 집(dwellings)을 지었다고 하므로 정답은 dwellings이다.

Paraphrasing build(짓다) → construct(건설하다)
parts from mammoths(매머드의 일부) → the bones of mammoths(매머드 뼈)

| Vocabulary & Expressions |

commonly 흔하게

문제 5-8

아래의 도해에 이름을 붙이시오.

각 정답은 지문에서 두개 이하의 단어로 고르시오.

답지 5-8번 칸에 정답을 적으시오.

플라이스토세 후기		홀로세	

Mammoth populations thrive due to an abundance of plant life, and **5** ……….. is easy due to the absence of difficult terrain. 매머드 개체수는 초목의 풍부함으로 인해 번성하고, 험난한 지형의 부재로 인해 **5** ……………………가 쉽다.	Rising temperatures result in forested areas taking the place of nutrient-rich **6** ……….. that contained the mammoth's preferred food. 기온 상승은 매머드가 선호하는 먹이를 포함했던 영양이 풍부한 **6** ……………………를 숲으로 뒤덮인 지역이 대체하는 결과를 낳았다.	**7** ……….. such as forests and marshlands increasingly restrict the movement of mammoth populations searching for food. 숲과 습지대 같은 **7** ……………………가 먹이를 찾아 다니는 매머드들의 움직임을 점점 더 제한했다.	Vast number of mammoths perish due to **8** ……….. as a result of melting ice and rising sea levels. 아주 많은 매머드들이 녹아내리는 얼음과 해수면 상승에 따른 결과로 생긴 **8** ……………………로 인해 죽었다.

5. 빈칸에 들어갈 단어는 be동사 is 앞에서 주어 역할을 할 수 있는 명사이고, 험난한 지형(difficult terrain)의 부재를 이유로 쉬워진 '무엇'이다. terrain과 difficult에 해당하는 impede가 언급된 첫 번째 문단의 문장을 살펴보자. 차가운 기온이 털매머드가 먹이 찾기(foraging) 경로를 방해할 수 있는 지형이 발달하는 것을 막아주었다는 내용이다. 문제에서 언급된 '험난한 지형'은 먹이를 찾는 경로를 '방해할 수 지형'으로 볼 수 있으므로, 정답은 foraging이다.

참고로 foraging(먹이 찾기, 채집)은 funding(자금, 자금 제공)처럼 명사로 사용되는 단어이다. 또다른 -ing형 명사로 warning(경고, 주의), breeding(사육, 번식), reasoning(추리) 등이 있으며 모두 아이엘츠에 빈번히 출제되는 단어들이다.

Paraphrasing difficult terrain(험난한 지형) → terrain that could impede(~을 방해할 수 있는 지형)

6. 빈칸에 들어갈 단어는 nutrient-rich의 수식을 받는 명사이고, 숲으로 뒤덮인 지역이 생기면서 없어진 장소의 종류이다. 도해에서 해당 문장은 플라이스토세 후기와 홀로세 사이에 위치하므로, The transition from the Late Pleistocene epoch to the Holocene epoch이 언급된 두 번째 문단 내용을 살펴보자. 지속적인 기온 상승으로 인해 허브와 영양분이 풍부한 초원(grasslands)은 점차적으로 숲으로 뒤덮인 지역으로 대체되었다는 내용이다. 즉, 숲이 생기고 초원이 없어졌다는 내용이므로 정답은 grasslands이다.

7. 빈칸에 들어갈 단어는 문장의 주어 역할을 하는 명사로, 숲(forests)과 늪지(marshlands)를 지칭하는 단어이며 털매머드의 먹이를 찾는 이동을 제한한 '무엇'이다. 숲과 늪지가 함께 언급된 문장 내용을 살펴보자. 빽빽한 숲과 부드러운 늪지의 형성이 털매머드의 이동과 먹이를 찾는 범위를 크게 제한했던 지리적 장애물(geographic barriers)을 만들었다는 내용이므로 정답은 geographic barriers이다. 지문에서 언급된 barriers는 지리적인 장애물 뿐이므로, barriers만 써도 정답이 된다.

Paraphrasing restrict the movement(이동을 제한하다) → limited the movement(이동을 제한하였다)

8. 빈칸에 들어갈 단어는 전치사 due to 뒤에 위치한 명사로, 매머드가 죽게 만든, 녹아내리는 얼음(melting ice)과 해수면 상승(rising sea levels)이 유발한 '무엇'이다. 도해에서 해당 문장은 마지막에 위치하므로, 앞 문장의 정답 근거가 된 지문의 다음 문단 내용을 살펴보자. 홀로세 전반적으로 있었던 온난화 경향으로 인해 빙하 감소와 해수면 상승이 유발되어 매머드가 멸종되었다는 내용이다. 그 중에서도 due to에 상응하는 a cause of를 찾아보면 매머드가 죽은 원인을 찾을 수 있다. 매머드는 빙하가 녹은 물에 익사했다는 (drowning) 내용이므로 정답은 drowning이다.

Paraphrasing due to(~때문에) → a cause of(~의 원인)
perish(죽는다) → population decline(개체 수 감소)

I Vocabulary & Expressions I

thrive 번성하다 absence 부재 contain 포함하다 search for ~을 찾다 vast 방대한 perish 소멸하다, 죽다

문제 9-10

A-E 중에서 두 개 보기를 고르시오.

답지 9-10번 칸에 올바른 기호를 적으시오.

According to the information in the passage, which **TWO** factors contributed to mammoth extinction?
지문의 정보에 따르면, 어느 **2가지** 요소가 매머드 멸종의 원인이 되었는가?

A competition between animal species
동물 종 사이의 경쟁

B strains of new diseases
여러 새로운 질병 유형

C a decrease in viable habitat
생존 가능한 서식지의 감소

D periods of low temperatures
낮은 기온 기간

E interaction with humans
인간과의 상호 작용

매머드의 멸종에 기여한 원인을 찾아야 한다. 이렇게 문제 내용이 지문의 주제인 경우는 보기를 핵심어로 잡고 정답을 찾아야 하며, 정답은 지문 전체에 퍼져 있을 가능성이 높다.

동물간의 경쟁이나 질병에 대해서는 언급된 바 없으므로 A와 B는 우선 제외시키고, 보기 C부터 확인해보자. 두 번째 문단을 보면 viable habitat이 그대로 언급된 문장이 있다. 내용을 살펴보면 초원이 숲으로 대체되면서 생존 가능한 서식지 부족을 유발하게 되었다는 내용이다. 따라서 이는 매머드 멸종의 원인으로 적합하다.

보기 D는 첫 번째 문단에서 차가운 기온이 매머드가 살기 좋다는 내용이 나오므로 매머드 멸종의 원인이 될 수 없다.

마지막 보기 E는 일곱 번째 문단에서 관련된 내용을 찾을 수 있다. 인간의 과도한 사냥을 포함한 복합적인 요인으로 매머드 멸종이 생겨났다고 하므로 E도 멸종의 원인으로 적합하다.

따라서 정답은 C와 E이다.

Paraphrasing decrease(감소) → shortage(부족)

I Vocabulary & Expressions I

competition 경쟁 species 종 strain 유형 interaction with ~와의 상호작용

문제 11-12

A-E 중에서 두 개 보기를 고르시오.

답지 11-12번 칸에 올바른 기호를 적으시오.

Which **TWO** types of data does the writer mention that scientists have recently used to study the extinction of mammoths in North America?
글쓴이는 과학자들이 북미 지역에서 매머드의 멸종을 연구하기 위해 최근에 어느 **2가지** 유형의 데이터를 활용했다고 언급하는가?

A ice cores removed from glaciers
빙하에서 추출한 얼음 핵

B carbon dating of plant species
식물 종에 대한 방사선 탄소 연대 측정

C changes to mammoth bone structure
매머드 뼈 구조의 변화

D historical data related to changes in climate
기후 변화 관련 있는 역사적 자료

E analysis of primitive tools and weapons
원시 도구 및 무기에 대한 분석

북미(North America)에서 매머드 멸종 연구를 위해 과학자들이 사용한 데이터의 특정 종류를 찾아야 한다. 일곱 번째 문단의 중반에서 North America가 처음으로 언급되고 여덟 번째 문단에서 using과 함께 특정한 데이터가 언급된다. 화석에 대한 방사선 탄소 연대 측정법을 활용하여 초목 종의 위치 변화를 지도에 표시하여 이를 기후 변화 데이터와 상호 참조했다고 한다. 이 내용 중에서 보기와 일치하는 것은 B와 D이다.

Paraphrasing historical(역사적) → over several thousancd years(수천 년에 걸쳐)

| Vocabulary & Expressions |

tool 도구, 장비 weapon 무기

문제 13

A–D 중에서 올바른 보기를 고르시오.

답지 13번 칸에 올바른 기호를 적으시오.

What would be the most suitable subtitle for the article?
기사에 가장 적합한 부제는 무엇인가?

A How mammoths evolved to adapt to increasingly harsh climates
점점 더 가혹해진 기후에 적응하기 위해 매머드가 어떻게 진화했는가

B The mutually beneficial relationship between humans and mammoths
인간과 매머드 사이의 상호 이익 관계

C Searching for a definitive reason for the disappearance of the mammoth
매머드의 멸종에 대한 명확한 이유 찾기

D New evidence shows that mammoths survived longer than previously thought
새로운 증거는 이전에 생각했던 것보다 매머드가 더 오래 생존했음을 보여준다

전체 글에 대한 부제를 고르는 것이므로, 먼저 지문 전체 내용이 무엇이었는지 생각해봐야 한다. 이 지문은 문단마다 각각 매머드 멸종의 다양한 원인을 다루고 있다. 즉, 기후 온난화로 인한 서식지 및 먹이 감소, 익사를 초래, 인간의 매머드 사냥, 그리고 여러 요인들을 통합하여 멸종의 원인을 정확히 분석하려는 과학자들의 시도가 언급되고 있다. 따라서 부제로는 매머드 멸종과 이유 찾기가 언급된 C가 가장 적합하다.

Paraphrasing disappearance(사라짐) → extinction(멸종)

| Vocabulary & Expressions |

suitable 적합한 evolve 진화하다 harsh 가혹한 mutually 상호적으로 beneficial 유익한 disappearance 사라짐, 소실

■ 섹션 1

1. A	2. F	3. E	4. D	5. A
6. B	7. C			
8. TRUE	9. NOT GIVEN	10. FALSE	11. TRUE	12. NOT GIVEN
13. FALSE	14. TRUE			

■ Questions 1-7

출제 포인트 **난이도: 중**

관광 정보지에 Matching information 유형의 전형적인 제너럴 트레이닝 섹션 1의 첫 번째 지문 문제로, 세부적 내용까지도 읽어 두어야 정보를 놓치지 않음

기출 2024년 5월 - 호주 관광
2017년 12월 - 오클랜드 관광 명소
2009년 2월 - 런던 시티 투어

Things to See and Do in the Scottish Highlands!

A. Glen Corrie Eco Park
At Glen Corrie Eco Park we not only care for animals that are indigenous to Scotland, but [Q5] many other birds, mammals, and reptiles from all corners of the planet! Visitors can watch our scheduled feedings and [Q1] have their picture taken with some of our most impressive creatures for a small fee.

B. Fraser Manor
Fraser Manor was the family home of the renowned Fraser family, whose most notable member was the 18th-century architect James Fraser. Fraser designed the manor himself and it remains unchanged and immaculate to this day. [Q6] Many of his original blueprints are on display throughout the home.

C. Scottish Heritage Centre
This is a fun, educational attraction for the whole family. You can enjoy more than 150 indoor exhibits that include historical tools and weapons, artwork, and children's games and toys, and then stroll around [Q7] the recreated 16th-century village in the grounds behind the building.

D. Loch Marr Nature Trails
Visitors can enjoy the stunning views of Loch Marr while walking along the nature trails [Q4] during any season. Even

스코틀랜드 하이랜드에서 보고 할 수 있는 일들!

A. 글렌 코리 에코 파크
글렌 코리 에코 파크에서 저희는 스코틀랜드 토종 동물뿐만 아니라 [Q5] 지구의 모든 곳에서 온 다른 많은 조류와 포유류, 그리고 파충류들도 보살피고 있습니다! 방문객들은 예정된 먹이 주는 것을 볼 수 있으며, [Q1] 소정의 요금을 내시면 가장 인상적인 생물체들과 함께 사진 촬영하실 수 있습니다.

B. 프레이저 대저택
프레이저 대저택은 유명한 프레이저 가문의 집이었으며, 이 가문에서 가장 주목할 만한 인물은 18세기의 건축가 제임스 프레이저입니다. 그가 직접 이 저택을 디자인했으며, 오늘날까지도 전혀 변경되지 않은 채로 티 하나 없이 깔끔한 상태로 유지되어 있습니다. [Q6] 저택 곳곳에 그의 많은 원본 도면이 전시되어 있습니다.

C. 스코틀랜드 문화 유산 센터
이곳은 가족 모두에게 재미있고 교육적인 명소입니다. 150가지가 넘는 실내 전시물을 즐기실 수 있으며, 역사적인 도구와 무기, 예술품, 그리고 아동용 게임과 장난감들을 포함합니다. 그리고 나서는 [Q7] 건물 뒤편 구역에 재현된 16세기 마을 주변을 산책하실 수 있습니다.

D. 마르 호 자연 탐사 오솔길
[Q4] 어느 계절에라도 방문객들은 마르 호의 굉장히 아름다운 경관을 즐기며 자연 탐사 오솔길을 따라 걸을 수 있

in winter, appropriate hiking gear can be rented from the visitor center. Picnic areas are available on some of the trails, and Q4 you can even stay there overnight for a small fee per tent.

습니다. 심지어 겨울에는, 방문객 센터에서 적절한 등산 장비를 대여할 수 있습니다. 소풍 구역들은 오솔길의 몇몇 지점에서 이용 가능하며, Q4 텐트당 소정의 이용료로 그곳에서 숙박할 수도 있습니다.

E. Carnegie Castle
This castle is little more than a ruin these days, but it still carries much cultural significance. Q3 It played a pivotal role in several historical conflicts, and many of the original structures were destroyed. However, visitors can learn a lot during a guided tour, and the area is known as a popular spot for fishing and birdwatching.

E. 카네기 성
요즘 이 성은 하나의 폐허에 지나지 않지만, 여전히 큰 문화적 중요성을 지니고 있습니다. Q3 여러 역사적 전투에서 중추적인 역할을 했으며, 많은 본래의 구조물들은 파괴되었습니다. 하지만, 방문객들은 가이드 투어 중에 많은 것을 배우실 수 있으며, 낚시와 조류 관찰로 인기가 많은 장소로 알려진 곳입니다.

F. Melrose Hall
Melrose Hall is an impressive 19th-century mansion that hosts a wide variety of cultural performance all year round. Check the schedule online and buy tickets for Scottish country dancing performances or the annual Highland Games. Q2 It can also be hired out for weddings and large-scale celebrations.

F. 멜로즈 홀
멜로즈 홀은 인상적인 19세기 대저택으로 연중 아주 다양한 문화 공연을 주최하고 있습니다. 온라인으로 일정을 확인하고 스코틀랜드 컨트리 댄스 공연이나 연례 하일랜드 게임의 입장권을 구매해 보세요. Q2 결혼식이나 대규모 기념 행사 장소로 대관도 됩니다.

I Vocabulary & Expressions I

care for ~을 돌보다, 보살피다 indigenous to ~에 토종인 mammal 포유류 reptile 파충류 planet 지구 feeding 먹이 주기 impressive 인상적인 for a small fee 소액의 요금을 내고 renowned 유명한 notable 주목할 만한 immaculate 티 하나 없이 깔끔한 blueprint 도면, 설계도 on display 전시 중인, 진열 중인 attraction 명소 exhibit 전시(물) stroll around ~ 주변에서 산책하다 recreate ~을 재현하다 grounds (건물 등의) 구내 appropriate 적합한 gear 장비 ruin 폐허 carry significance 중요성을 지니다 pivotal role 중추적인 역할 conflict 충돌, 교전, 갈등 structure 구조물 a wide variety of 아주 다양한 hire out ~을 대여하다 celebration 기념 행사

문제 1-7

A에서 F까지 스코틀랜드 고지대에 위치한 6곳의 방문객 명소들을 확인하시오.
어느 방문객 명소에 대해 다음 문제 진술들이 옳은가?
답지 1-7번 칸에 A-F 중 알맞은 기호를 기입하시오.
유의 어떤 글자든 한 번 이상 사용해도 된다.

1. People can pay to have their photograph taken here.
사람들이 이곳에서 사진 촬영을 하기 위해 비용을 지불할 수 있다.

사진을 찍으려면 비용을 지불해야 하는 곳을 찾아야 한다. picture taken과 fee가 언급된 문장 내용이 근거가 되어 정답은 A이다.
Paraphrasing pay(지불하다) → for a small fee(소정의 요금으로)
photograph(사진) → picture(사진)

2. People can hold a social event at this location.
사람들이 이곳에서 사교 행사를 개최할 수 있다.

사교 행사를 열 수 있는 장소를 찾아야 한다. social event에 상응하는 weddings와 celebrations가 언급된 문장 내용을 살펴보자. 행사를 위해 대관이 된다는 것은, 행사를 열 수 있다는 것이므로 정답은 F이다.

hire는 '고용하다, 대여하다'라는 두가지 뜻을 가지고 있는 동사이고, 명사(대여, 임대, 신입사원)로도 사용가능한 단어이므로 독해할 때 문맥을 주의 깊게 살펴야 한다.
Paraphrasing social event(사교 행사) → weddings and large-scale celebrations(결혼식과 대규모의 기념행사)

3. Visitors can see a building that was damaged during a battle here.
방문객들이 이곳에서 전쟁 중에 손상된 건물을 볼 수 있다.

전쟁 중에 손상된 건물을 볼 수 있는 곳을 찾아야 한다. historical conflict와 destroyed가 나온 문장이 정답 근거이다. conflict는 '갈등, 충돌' 이외에 '교전, 전투'라는 뜻도 있다. 따라서 정답은 E이다.

Paraphrasing damaged(손상된) → destroyed(파괴된)
battle(전쟁) → conflicts(교전, 전투)

4. Camping is available all year round here.
이곳에서 일년 내내 캠핑이 가능하다.

일년 내내 캠핑이 가능한 곳을 찾아야 한다. 소개된 명소 중에서 캠핑이 가능한 자연 환경을 지닌 장소를 위주로 'camping'에 상응하는 것을 찾아보도록 한다. 텐트를 빌려 숙박할 수 있다는 내용이 Loch Marr Nature Trails에서 나온다. 일년 내내 가능한지 확인하기 위해 앞 부분을 확인해보면, during any season이라고 언급되어 있다. 따라서 정답은 D이다.

참고로 F에 문제의 표현과 동일한 all year around가 나오지만 캠핑 관련된 이야기는 언급되지 않으므로 F는 오답이다.

Paraphrasing Camping is available(캠핑이 가능하다)
→ you can even stay there overnight for a small fee per tent(텐트당 소정의 이용료로 그곳에서 숙박도 할 수 있다)
all year around(일년 내내) → during any season(일년 내내)

5. Visitors can see animals from various countries here.
방문객들이 이곳에서 다양한 나라에서 온 동물들을 볼 수 있다.

다양한 나라에서 온 동물을 볼 수 있는 곳을 찾아야 한다. animals와 all corners of the planet이 언급된 문장 내용이 근거가 되어 정답은 A이다.

지문에 나온 세부적인 정보(birds, mammals, and reptiles)가 문제에 이 세부 정보들을 통칭하는, 일반적인 하나의 단어(animal)로 표현될 수 있음을 기억하자.

Paraphrasing animals(동물) → birds, mammals, and reptiles(조류, 포유류, 파충류)
from various countries(다양한 나라에서) → from all corners of the planet(전 세계에서)

6. Building designs are exhibited to the public here.
이곳에 일반인들을 대상으로 건물 도면이 전시되어 있다.

건물의 도면이 전시되어 있는 장소를 찾아야 한다. 소개된 명소 중에서 건물을 위주로 'building design'에 상응하는 것을 찾아보도록 한다. Fraser Manor의 내용 중 마지막 문장에 blueprints를 도면과 연관시킬 수 있어야 한다. 이 문장의 his가 건축가 프레이저를 가리키므로 blueprints는 건물에 대한 설계도임을 확인할 수 있다. 따라서 정답은 B이다.

Paraphrasing building designs(건물 도면) → blueprints(설계도)
are exhibited(전시되어 있다) → are on display(전시 중이다)

7. Visitors can see modern replicas of old buildings here.
방문객들이 이곳에서 옛 건물들에 대한 현대적인 복제물을 볼 수 있다.

옛 건물을 복제한 것을 볼 수 있는 곳을 찾아야 한다. recreated와 16th-century가 언급된 문장 내용을 살펴보자. 16세기 마을이 재현되어 있는 곳이라고 하는데, village는 기본적으로 건물들(buildings)이 있는 곳이므로, 정답은 C이다.

old가 '오래된, 낡은' 뜻도 있지만, 시대적으로 '옛날'의 것을 나타내기도 하므로 16세기와 같은 특정 시대도 old와 패러프레이징 가능하다는 것을 알아둔다.

Paraphrasing replicas of old buildings(옛 건물의 복제물) → recreated 16-century village(재현된 16세기의 마을)

| Vocabulary & Expressions |

hold (행사 등을) 개최하다 damage 손상시키다 battle 전쟁, 투쟁 exhibit 전시하다 the public 대중, 일반인 replica 복제품, 모형

▪ Questions 8-14

출제 포인트 | 난이도: 중하

생활 정보글에 T/F/NG 유형의 전형적인 제너럴 트레이닝 섹션 1의 두 번째 지문 문제로, 문제가 지문 흐름 순서대로 나오기에 생각보다 정답 내용을 찾기 쉬움

기출 2019년 1월 - 영국 GP 예약

Brisbane Health Clinic, Australia
Making an Appointment with a GP

Please phone or e-mail our clinic as far in advance as possible if you wish to schedule an appointment. When we schedule a doctor's appointment for you, we will automatically schedule a 10-minute appointment. Q8 If you are concerned that you will require more time, please let us know and we will do our best to accommodate you. For example, if you are a newly registered family meeting your GP for the first time, 30 minutes is recommended. When making the appointment, please state whether you would prefer to see a health professional of the same gender. Q9 Also, if you feel that you may require a translator, this can be arranged for you in advance, for most languages. We understand that emergencies come up and your plans may change. Q10 If you cannot keep your appointment, please call us no later than the day before.

How can you prepare for your appointment?
A little preparation can help you to get the most out of your appointment. Think about what outcomes you hope to achieve from your meeting with the doctor. Q11 It can be beneficial to bring some written records about specific symptoms you are experiencing. It is very useful to the doctor if you write down when the symptoms occurred, how long they lasted and whether any activities make them worse. Also, make sure that you know the medical history of your family. If you are not sure, then ask your family members. Gather all current or recent prescriptions or medication containers and bring them to show to the doctor, and if you have had any recent medical tests, bring the results of those with you as well. Lastly, allow plenty of time to travel to the clinic so that you do not miss your appointment.

How should you pay for your appointment?
We are pleased to inform you that our clinic uses the Australian bulk billing system, Q13 which means that all standard services at our clinic are covered fully by Medicare. In other words, when you come to an

브리즈번 진료소, 호주
지역일반의 예약

예약 일정을 잡기를 원하시면 가능한 한 미리 저희 진료소로 전화하시거나 이메일을 보내시기 바랍니다. 저희가 진료 의사 예약 일정을 잡을 때, 자동으로 10분간의 예약 시간을 잡아 드립니다. Q8 만약 귀하는 더 많은 시간이 필요할 것 같다고 우려된다면, 저희에게 알려주세요. 그러면 최선을 다해 귀하에게 협조하겠습니다. 예를 들어, 담당 지역일반의를 처음으로 만나는 신규 등록된 가족일 경우는 30분이 권장됩니다. 예약하실 때, 동일한 성별의 의사와 보길 원하는지에 대한 여부를 언급해주십시오. Q9 또한, 통역사가 필요하다고 생각되면, 대부분의 언어가 미리 주선될 수 있습니다. 저희는 긴급 상황이 생겨 귀하의 일정이 변경될 수 있다는 점을 알고 있습니다. Q10 예약을 지킬 수 없을 경우, 늦어도 예약일의 하루 전까지는 전화 주시기 바랍니다.

어떻게 예약 시간에 대한 준비를 해야 할까요?
약간의 준비가 귀하의 예약 시간을 최대한 활용하는 데 도움이 될 수 있습니다. 의사와의 진료에서 어떤 결과를 얻기를 바라시는지 생각해 보십시오. Q11 경험하고 있는 특정 증상에 관한 일부 서면 기록을 지참하고 오시면 도움이 될 수 있습니다. 언제 해당 증상이 발생되었는지, 얼마나 오래 지속되었는지, 그리고 어떠한 움직임이 증상을 악화시키는지 적어 오시면 의사에게는 매우 유용합니다. 또한, 반드시 가족 병력을 알고 계시도록 하십시오. 확실치 않으실 경우, 가족 일원에게 물어보시기 바랍니다. 현재 혹은 최근에 받은 모든 처방전이나 약품 용기들을 모아 가져와서 의사에게 보여주세요, 그리고 최근에 받은 모든 의료 검사가 있다면, 그 결과도 가지고 오십시오. 마지막으로, 진료소까지 오는 시간을 넉넉히 잡으셔서 예약 시간을 놓치지 않으시기 바랍니다.

예약에 대해 어떻게 비용을 지불해야 하는가?
저희 진료소는 호주 정부 의료비 청구 시스템(환자의 자기 부담금 없이 진료소에서 호주 정부로 진료비를 청구하는 제도)을 이용하고 있다는 점을 알려 드리게 되어 기쁩니다, Q13 이는 저희 진료소의 모든 일반 서비스들이 전적으로 국민 건강 보험에 의해 비용이 처리된다는 것을 의미합니다. 다시 말해, 예약 진료에 오시면, 국민 건강 보험에 바로 청구하며 귀하에게는 어떠한 것도 요청하지 않습니

appointment, we will bill Medicare directly and will not ask you for anything. Q14 However, certain treatments and procedures such as travel vaccinations and mole removal are not covered, nor are prescribed items such as hearing aids, glasses, or contact lenses.	다. Q14 하지만, 여행 대비 예방 접종이나 점 제거와 같은 특정 치료와 시술은 보험 처리되지 않으며, 보청기나 안경, 또는 콘택트 렌즈와 같이 처방된 제품도 보험 처리되지 않습니다.

I Vocabulary & Expressions I

appointment 예약, 약속 GP 지역일반의(=general practitioner) far 아주, 훨씬 in advance 미리 be concerned 우려하다 accommodate ~을 수용하다 translator 통역사 arrange ~을 준비하다 no later than 늦어도 ~까지는 get the most out of ~을 최대한 활용하다 outcome 결과 symptom 증상 occur 발생되다 last 지속되다 make sure that 반드시 ~하도록 하다 prescription 처방전 bulk 대부분, 대규모 bill 청구하다 cover (비용) ~을 부담하다, 충당하다 treatment 치료 procedure 수술 vaccination 예방 접종 mole (피부에 있는) 점 removal 제거 prescribed 처방된 hearing aids 보청기

문제 8-14

다음 내용이 지문에서 주어진 정보와 일치하는가?
답지 8-14번 칸에 다음을 쓰시오.

TRUE 문제 진술이 정보와 일치하면
FALSE 문제 진술이 정보와 다르면
NOT GIVEN 문제 진술에 대한 정보를 독해 지문에서 찾을 수 없으면

8. Extended appointments are available upon request.
요청 시에 연장된 예약 시간으로 가능하다.

요청하면 더 길게 진료 보는 것이 가능하다는 내용으로, extended appointments에 상응하는 more time이 있는 문장 내용이 정답 근거가 된다. '최선을 다해 귀하에게 협조하겠다'는 것은 '귀하의 요청에 따르겠다'는 의미이다. 그리고 여기에서 말하는 요청은 시간이 더 필요하다는 것이므로 정답은 TRUE이다.

appointments가 미리 예약된 진료나 회의를 뜻하는 경우, 이 단어를 extended(확장된, 연장된)가 수식하고 있다면 '시간적'인 개념이 확장되는 것으로 이해하고 독해한다.

Paraphrasing extended appointment(연장된 예약 시간) → more time(더 많은 시간)

9. Doctors at the clinic can speak a variety of languages.
해당 진료소의 의사들이 다양한 언어를 말할 수 있다.

지역일반의가 여러 나라의 말을 구사할 줄 안다는 내용으로, 의사의 외국어 능력에 대해서 언급된 바가 없으므로 정답은 NOT GIVEN이다.

참고로 speaking a variety of languages와 내용적으로 관련시킬 수 있는 translator가 있는 문장 내용을 살펴보아도 진료소에서 통역사가 주선한다는 내용이지 의사가 통역사 역할을 한다는 내용은 아니다.

10. Appointments must be canceled at least two days in advance.
예약은 반드시 최소 2일 전에 미리 취소되어야 한다.

예약 취소는 '2일' 전에는 이루어져야 한다는 내용으로, 예약 취소와 관련된 문장에서 상세 정보를 확인해야 한다. cannot keep your appointment가 있는 문장 내용이 정답 근거가 된다. 예약 취소는 예약일의 하루 전까지 가능하다고 제시되어 있는 반면 문제 내용은 2일 전이므로 정답은 FALSE이다.

Paraphrasing at least ~ in advance(최소한 ~ 전에) → no later than(늦어도 ~까지는)

11. Patients are encouraged to bring notes about their condition.
환자들은 그들의 상태에 관한 기록을 가지고 오도록 권장된다.

환자는 건강 상태에 대한 노트를 가져오라고 권장된다는 내용으로, notes about their condition에 상응하는 written records about specific symptoms가 있는 문장 내용이 근거가 되어 정답은 TRUE이다.

Paraphrasing encouraged to bring(~을 가져오는 것이 권장되는) → beneficial to bring(~을 가져오는 것이 유익한)
their condition(환자의 상태) → specific symptoms you are experiencing(경험하고 있는 특정 증상들)

12. Prescriptions can be picked up by a family member.
처방전은 가족이 가져갈 수 있다.

가족은 처방전 수령이 가능하다는 내용으로, 지문 어디에도 처방전 수령 자격에 대해 언급된 바가 없으므로 정답은 NOT GIVEN이다.

참고로 지문에서 가족 관련해 언급된 내용은 가족 병력(the medical story of your family)에 관한 내용으로 처방전 내용과는 무관하다.

13. The clinic has opted out of the Australian Medicare program.
해당 진료소는 호주 의료 보험 프로그램에 참여하지 않고 있다.

호주 의료보험 프로그램에 참여하지 않고 있다는 것은, 이 진료소의 환자들이 호주 의료보험(Australian Medicare program) 처리를 받을 수 없다는 의미이다. 하지만 지문을 살펴보면 이 진료소가 국민건강보험(Medicare)에 의해 전적으로 보험 처리된다는(fully covered) 내용이 나오므로 정답은 FALSE이다.

Australian Medicare program이 Medicare로 나타낼 수 있는 것처럼, 고유 명사도 상위 개념으로 패러프레이징 가능하다는 것을 기억해둔다.

14. Patients will need to pay for travel vaccinations themselves.
환자들이 직접 여행 대비 예방 접종 비용을 지불해야 할 것이다.

여행 대비 예방 접종의 비용은 환자가 직접 내야 한다는 것은 해당 비용은 보험 처리가 되지 않는다는 의미이다. 문제의 핵심어인 travel vaccinations가 제시된 문장이 근거가 되어 정답은 TRUE이다.

Paraphrasing Patients will need to pay for ~ themselves(환자들이 직접 ~비용을 내야 한다)
→ are not covered(보험 처리되지 않는다)

I Vocabulary & Expressions I

extended 연장된, 확장된 upon request 요청시에 a variety of 다양한 patient 환자 encourage 권장하다 prescription 처방전 pick up 수령하다, 가져가다 opt out of ~에 참여하지 않기로 하다

Unit 12 READING Skills 6 – General Training Section 2

■ 섹션 2

15. name	16. personal statement	17. gaps	18. hobbies	19. clichés
20. font	21. spacing	22. spelling		
23. conflict	24. clutter	25. productivity	26. chair	27. exercise

▪ **Questions 15-22**

출제 포인트 **난이도: 중하**

비즈니스/취업 토픽에 Sentence completion 문제 유형의 전형적인 섹션 2 첫 지문 문제로, 비즈니스/취업 관련 용어들을 알고 있으면 쉽게 풀 수 있음

기출 2017년 7월 - CV 작성 팁

Tips for Writing an Effective CV

What information should I include?
Although your goal should be to make your CV stand out from others, there is some information that should be always be included. First of all, never forget to include all of your personal details at the top of the page. You might be surprised at the number of people who have missed out on a job because they forgot to include their name, e-mail address, phone number and address on their CV. In fact, your Q15 name should be right at the top in large font; there is no need to write Curriculum Vitae! Next, add a short Q16 personal statement that clearly describes who you are, what you can offer, and what your professional and personal goals are. Keep it succinct! Limit this to one paragraph, and try to capture the attention of prospective employers.

The next section should detail all of your relevant work experience, including your job titles, the names of the companies you worked for, your dates of employment, and your main job duties. If you have any Q17 gaps in employment history, add a brief explanation. Also, always list your academic qualifications, including all relevant details related to courses and institutions. It is not always relevant to mention your Q18 hobbies, but if you feel that the information backs up your skills and helps you stand out, by all means, include this.

What vocabulary should I use?
Certain words always look attractive in any CV, such as hard-working, responsible, adaptable, reliable, and confident. On the other hand, there are some words that are seen as Q19 clichés by most employers and are best left out. These include multi-tasker, goal-driven, self-motivated, detail-oriented, and flexible.

How should my CV be presented?
In addition to the information contained on the CV, the way that it is presented is equally important. Limit the length to two sides of A4 paper. Any longer and a potential employer might get bored or irritated. Choose a clear, professional

효과적인 이력서 작성 팁

어떠한 정보를 포함해야 하는가?
당신의 목표가 자신의 이력서를 다른 이력서보다 두드러지게 하는 것일지라도, 항상 포함되어야 하는 몇몇 정보가 있다. 가장 먼저, 페이지 맨 위에 개인 상세 정보 모두를 포함해야 한다는 점을 절대 잊지 말아라. 이름과 이메일 주소, 전화번호, 그리고 집 주소를 이력서에 포함시키는 것을 잊음으로써 일자리를 놓치는 사람들의 숫자에 당신은 놀랄 수도 있다. 사실, 당신의 Q15 이름은 큰 글씨로 맨 위쪽에 있어야 하고, '이력서'라는 단어는 기입할 필요가 없다! 다음으로, 당신이 누구인지, 무엇을 할 수 있는지, 그리고 직업적 목표와 개인적 목표가 무엇인지 명확히 설명하는 짧은 Q16 자기 소개를 추가하라. 이는 간결해야 한다! 길이를 한 단락으로 제한하고 잠재 고용주의 관심을 끌도록 노력하라.

다음 부분은 모든 관련 직장 경력을 상세히 설명해야 하며, 여기에는 직위, 근무했던 회사명, 재직 기간, 그리고 주요 직무가 포함되어야 한다. 근무 경력에 Q17 공백이 있을 경우, 간단한 설명을 추가하라. 또한, 학과 과정 및 학교와 모든 관련 세부 내용을 포함하는 학력 사항도 열거하라. Q18 취미를 언급하는 것이 항상 적절한 것은 아니지만, 그 정보가 자신의 능력을 뒷받침해주고 두드러져 보이게 하는 데 도움이 된다고 생각하면, 기꺼이 포함시켜라.

어떠한 어휘를 사용해야 하는가?
어떤 이력서에서도 특정 단어들은 항상 매력적으로 보이는데 예를 들면, 근면한, 책임감 있는, 적응력이 좋은, 신뢰할 수 있는, 자신감 있는 등이다. 반면에, 대부분의 고용주들에게 Q19 상투적인 문구로 보여서 제외되는 것이 최선인 단어들도 있다. 여기에는 다중 업무 처리 가능, 목표 중심적인, 자율적인, 꼼꼼한, 융통성 있는 등이 포함된다.

이력서가 어떻게 보여야 하는가?
이력서에 포함되는 정보뿐만 아니라, 그것이 보여지는 방식도 똑같이 중요하다. 이력서의 길이를 A4 용지 2페이지로 제한하라. 더 길다면 잠재 고용주가 지루해하거나 짜증을 낼 수도 있다. 개러몬드 또는 캘리브리와 같이 깔끔하고 전문적으로 보이는 Q20 서체를 선택하고, 이

Q20 font such as Garamond or Calibri and use size 10.5-12 to ensure that your CV can be easily read. Give the document a well-defined structure, with sufficient Q21 spacing between sections and clear headings. Finally, never forget to make sure your Q22 spelling is correct before submitting your CV.

력서가 쉽게 읽힐 수 있도록 10.5-12의 크기를 사용하라. 항목 간 충분한 Q21 공간과 명확한 제목으로 이해하기 쉬운 구조를 문서에 적용하라. 마지막으로, 이력서를 제출하기 전에 Q22 철자가 정확한지 확인하는 것을 잊지 말아라.

| Vocabulary & Expressions |

CV 이력서(=Curriculum Vitae) stand out from ~중에서 두드러지다 detail 상세 사항, 상세히 기술하다 at the top of ~의 상단에, ~위에 miss out (기회 등을) 놓치다 font 서체 personal statement 자기 소개(서) succinct 간결한 limit 제한하다 capture 사로잡다 attention 관심, 주의 prospective 장래의, 장차의 employer 고용주 relevant 관련된 employment history 경력 brief 간단한 academic qualifications 학력 related to ~와 관련된 institution (대학 등 특정 목적의) 기관 back up 뒷받침하다, 보조하다 skill 기술 by all means 기꺼이 hard-working 근면한 adaptable 적응할 수 있는 cliché 상투적인 문구 be left out 버려지다 goal-driven 목표 지향적인 self-motivated 자율적인 detail-oriented 꼼꼼한 flexible 유연한 length 길이 bored 지루함을 느끼는 irritated 짜증이 난 such as ~와 같은 ensure that ~임을 확실히 하다 well-defined 이해하기 쉬운 structure 구조 sufficient 충분한 spacing 간격, 자간 submit 제출하다

문제 15-22

각 문장을 완성하시오.

각 정답에 대해 지문에서 **2개 단어** 이하로 고르시오.

답지 15-22번 칸에 정답을 기입하시오.

15. Instead of writing Curriculum Vitae, add your .... to the top of the page.
'이력서'라는 말을 쓰는 대신, 페이지 상단에 ....을 추가하라.

빈칸에 들어갈 단어는 소유격 your가 앞에 있으므로 명사이고, 페이지 상단(top)에 써야하는 '무엇'이다. 문제에서 top of the page에 상응하는 문장 내용을 살펴보자. 이력서 맨 위에 '이름'을 크게 써야 한다는 내용이므로 정답은 name이다.

Paraphrasing instead of writing(~을 쓰는 대신에) → there is no need to write(~을 쓸 필요 없다)

16. Add a .... below your contact details to explain your strengths and goals.
장점과 목표를 설명할 수 있도록 상세 연락처 다음에 ....을 추가하라.

빈칸에 들어갈 단어는 관사 a가 앞에 있으므로 명사이고, 연락처(contact details) 아래에 쓰는 '무엇'이다. 연락처에 상응하는 personal details가 있는 문장을 보면 앞에 first of all이 있다. 그리고 스캐닝을 하다 보면 next가 나온다. 연락처 정보 다음에 '자기 소개'를 쓰라고 하므로 정답은 personal statement이다.

위치 정보인 '아래'를 Next라는 부사와 의미적으로 연결시킬 수 있다면 정답을 쉽게 찾을 수 있다.

Paraphrasing contact details(연락처 상세) → personal details(세부 개인정보)

17. Provide explanations for any noticeable .... in your professional career.
직업 경력에 있어서 눈에 띄는 그 어떠한 ....에 대한 설명을 제공하라.

빈칸에 들어갈 단어는 any noticeable의 수식을 받는 명사이고, 설명을 제공해야 하는 경력상의 '무엇'이다. 경력에 상응하는 employment history가 있는 문장에서 어떠한 '공백'도 간단한 설명을 붙이라고 하므로 정답은 gaps이다.

문법적으로 단수형인 gap도 가능하지만, 지문에서 복수형으로 제시되었으므로 gaps로 써야함에 유의하자.

Paraphrasing professional career(경력) → employment history(경력)

18. While not always necessary, describe your .... if you think they are relevant to the job.
항상 필요한 것은 아니지만, 해당 일자리와 관련된다고 생각하는 경우에 ....을 설명하라.

빈칸에 들어갈 단어는 소유격 your 앞에 있으므로 명사이고, 항상 필요한 건 아니지만 직업과 관련되었다면 설명할 '무엇'이다. 항상 필요하지 않다는 내용에 상응하는 not always relevant to mention이 있는 문장에서 언급한 것은 '취미'이다. 능력을 뒷받침한다는 것은 직업과 관련되어 있는 것이라고 볼 수 있으므로 정답은 hobbies이다.

Paraphrasing not always necessary(항상 필수적이지 않은) → not always relevant to mention(~을 언급하는 것이 항상 적절하지는 않은)

19. Avoid using vocabulary that some employers might consider ....
일부 고용주들이 ....라고 여길 수 있는 어휘 사용을 피하라.

빈칸에 들어갈 단어는 이력서에서 피해야 하는 어휘를 설명하는 말이다. 부제에 vocabulary가 포함된 단락 내용을 살펴보자. 피해야 한다는 내용에 상응하는 left out이 있는 문장에서, 고용주가 '상투적인 문구'로 볼 수 있는 말은 제외하는 것이 좋다고 하므로 정답은 clichés이다.

Paraphrasing avoid using(~을 사용하는 것을 피하다) → are best left out(제외하는 것이 최선이다)
consider(~라고 여기다) → are seen as(~로 보이다)

20. Make sure the information is easy to read by selecting an appropriate .... size.
반드시 적절한 .... 크기를 선택해 정보가 쉽게 읽히도록 하라.

빈칸에 들어갈 단어는 size와 함께 복합명사를 이루어 appropriate의 수식을 받는 명사로, 정보를 읽기 쉽도록 선택해야 하는 '무엇'이다. 읽기 쉬운 것에 상응하는 easily read가 있는 문장에서, 쉽게 읽히기 위해 권장되는 '서체' 크기를 알려준다. use size라고만 나왔지만 앞부분 내용으로 이것이 font의 크기를 말하는 것임을 알 수 있으므로 정답은 font이다.

Paraphrasing easy to read(읽기 쉬운) → be easily read(쉽게 읽히는)

21. Use clear headings and adequate .... to ensure the CV is structured well.
이력서의 구조가 반드시 잘 갖춰지도록 하기 위해 명확한 제목과 충분한 ....을 사용하라.

빈칸에 들어갈 단어는 adequate의 수식을 받는 명사로, 구조를 잘 갖추기 위해 명확한 제목(clear headings)와 함께 필요한 '무엇'이다. clear headings가 그대로 사용된 문장에서 adequate에 상응하는 sufficient를 찾으면 쉽게 정답을 찾을 수 있다. 이해하기 쉬운 구조를 위해 충분한 '공간'을 적용하라는 내용이므로 정답은 spacing이다.

Paraphrasing adequate(충분한) → sufficient(충분한)
structured well(구조가 잘 갖춰진) → a well-defined structure(이해하기 쉬운 구조)

22. Check the .... on the CV before you send it to a prospective employer.
잠재 고용주에게 보내기 전에 이력서에 있는 ....를 확인하라.

빈칸에 들어갈 단어는 관사 the가 앞에 있으므로 명사이고, 이력서를 보내기 전에 반드시 확인해야 하는 '무엇'이다. 이력서를 보낸다는 것에 상응하는 before submitting your CV가 있는 문장 내용이 근거가 된다. 제출하기 전에 '철자'가 정확한지 확실히 하라는 내용이므로 정답은 spelling이다.

Paraphrasing check the spelling(철자를 확인하다) → make sure your spelling is correct(철자가 정확한지 확실히 하다)
send(보내다) → submitting(제출하는 것)

I Vocabulary & Expressions I

contact details 연락처 strength 장점 noticeable 뚜렷한, 눈에 띄는 necessary 필수적인 make sure (that) 반드시 ~하다
select 선택하다 appropriate 적절한 adequate 적절한, 충분한

▪ Questions 23-27

출제 포인트 **난이도: 중하**

비즈니스/업무 정보글에 Note completion 문제로, 문제가 지문 흐름 순서대로 나오기에 생각보다 정답 내용을 찾기가 쉬움

기출 2024년 5월 - 사업장에서 CCTV 규정
2018년 3월 - 직장 스트레스 관리법

How to Manage Work Stress

Many people arrive at work already stressed due to a hectic morning routine. This might include getting one's children ready for school, enduring rush hour traffic, and skipping breakfast for a quick cup of coffee. If you start off the day with proper planning and good nutrition, your workday will be much more manageable.

With so many people in one workplace, it is inevitable that people will disagree with one another from time to time. Perhaps you have had experiences where Q23 conflict has arisen between you and a coworker, resulting in communication problems and stress. One way to avoid this is to refrain from sharing personal opinions with coworkers about subjects like religion and politics, which can be extremely sensitive topics for some people.

One of the key contributors to stress both at home and in a work environment is a lack of organization. Make sure that your workstation is free from unnecessary Q24 clutter and you will immediately feel the psychological benefits. A tidy desktop leads to higher Q25 productivity, so keep it clear by making use of your drawers for storage.

Another significant stressor at work is physical discomfort. If you work in a job that requires you to remain seated for most of the day, make sure that your employer provides a high-quality, comfortable Q26 chair for you. Not only will this boost your mood and limit your stress, but it will reduce your risk of back pain and injury.

Despite your best efforts, you might still have had a stressful morning at work. This is why an increasing number of workers are utilizing their lunch hours for Q27 exercise. Burning some calories and working up a sweat can work wonders for people who have work stress building up inside them. Try to organize a regular routine with a group of coworkers, either at a local gym or outside when the weather is nice.

When it is finally time for you to leave work, you might dread your journey home, whether it be in a cramped subway car, or on a congested road. Listening to music has been proven to be an effective way to stay relaxed in chaotic environments, and is a surefire way to rid you of any remaining stress before you get back to your home.

업무 스트레스 관리 방법

많은 사람들이 너무 바쁜 오전의 일상으로 인해 이미 스트레스를 받은 상태로 직장에 도착한다. 여기에는 아이 등교 준비시키기, 출근 시간대 교통 혼잡 견디기, 간단한 커피 한 잔으로 아침 식사 대신하기 등이 포함될 수 있다. 적절한 계획과 좋은 영양으로 하루를 시작한다면, 근무일이 훨씬 더 감당이 될 것이다.

직장 한 곳에 아주 많은 사람들이 있기 때문에, 때때로 사람들이 서로 맞지 않는 경우가 발생하는 것은 불가피하다. 아마도 동료와의 사이에서 Q23 갈등이 발생되어 의사 소통 문제나 스트레스가 초래되는 경험을 한 적이 있을 것이다. 이를 피하는 한 가지 방법은 종교나 정치와 같은 주제에 대해 동료와 개인적인 의견을 나누는 것을 자제하는 것인데, 어떤 사람들에게는 대단히 민감한 주제일 수 있기 때문이다.

집과 업무 환경에서 모두 스트레스가 되는 주된 원인들 중의 하나가 정리의 부족이다. 반드시 업무 공간에서 불필요한 Q24 잡동사니가 없도록 해야 하며, 그 즉시 심리적인 이점을 느끼게 될 것이다. 말끔히 정리된 책상은 더 높은 Q25 생산성으로 이어지므로, 저장 공간으로서 서랍을 활용해 책상을 깔끔하게 유지하라.

직장에서 스트레스를 유발하는 또 다른 중요한 요인은 신체적인 불편함이다. 하루 대부분을 앉은 채로 있도록 만드는 업무를 하는 경우, 반드시 고용주에게 고품질의 편안한 Q26 의자를 제공받도록 해야 한다. 이는 기분을 끌어올리고 스트레스를 제한해줄 뿐만 아니라, 허리 통증과 부상 위험을 줄여줄 것이다.

최선의 노력에도 불구하고, 여전히 직장에서 스트레스가 많은 아침 시간을 보냈을 수도 있다. 이것이 바로 점점 더 많은 직장인들이 Q27 운동을 위해 점심 시간을 활용하는 이유이다. 칼로리를 소모하고 땀을 내는 일은 마음 속에 쌓이는 업무 스트레스가 있는 사람들에게 엄청난 효과가 있을 수 있다. 동료 직원들과 팀을 만들어 지역 체육관이나 날씨가 좋을 때 야외에서 주기적인 운동 시간을 마련하도록 시도하라.

마침내 퇴근할 시간이 되면, 비좁은 지하철이든 아니면 혼잡한 도로든 집으로 돌아가는 길이 두려울 수 있다. 음악을 듣는 것이 혼란스러운 환경에서 편안한 상태로 유지하는 효과적인 방법으로 입증되었으며, 집으로 돌아가기 전에 남아 있는 어떤 스트레스든 없앨 수 있는 확실한 방법이다.

I Vocabulary & Expressions I

how to do ~하는 법 hectic 정신 없이 바쁜 endure ~을 견디다 skip ~을 건너뛰다 proper 적절한 nutrition 영양 inevitable 불가피한 from time to time 때때로 conflict 갈등, 의견 불일치 arise 발생되다 result in ~을 초래하다 refrain from ~을 자제하다 religion 종교 politics 정치 sensitive 민감한 contributor 원인 (제공자) lack of ~의 부족 free from ~이 없는 clutter 잡동사니, 어수선함 psychological 심리적인 benefit 이점, 혜택 physical 신체적인 discomfort 불편함 boost ~을 촉진하다 reduce ~을 감소시키다 injury 부상 utilize ~을 활용하다 work up a sweat 땀을 내다 work wonders 엄청난 효과가 있다 organize ~을 마련하다 dread ~을 두려워하다 cramped 비좁은 congested 혼잡한 chaotic 혼란스러운 surefire 확실한 rid ~에게서 없애다

문제 23-27

아래의 노트를 완성하시오.

각 답변에 대해 지문에서 **1개의 단어**만을 고르시오.

답지 23-27번 칸에 정답을 기입하시오.

Managing Work Stress 업무 스트레스 관리하기

- Start your day well with good planning and a healthy breakfast.
- Try to avoid **23** .... at work by keeping your opinions about sensitive issues to yourself.
- Remove **24** .... from your work area to increase your **25** ....
- Ask your boss to give you a suitable **26** .... that will not result in any health issues.
- During your lunch break, enjoy some **27** .... with coworkers, either indoors or outdoors.
- Listen to music on your way home so that you can relax during your commute.

- 좋은 계획과 건강에 좋은 아침 식사로 하루를 잘 시작하기
- 민감한 문제에 대한 의견을 말하지 않음으로써 직장에서 **23** ....을 피하도록 노력하기
- **25** ....을 증가시키기 위해 업무 공간에서 **24** .... 없애기
- 어떠한 건강 관련 문제도 초래하지 않는 적합한 **26** ....을 제공하도록 상사에 요청하기
- 점심 시간 중에, 동료 직원들과 실내에서 또는 바깥에서 **27** .... 즐기기
- 퇴근 시간 중에 긴장을 풀 수 있도록 집으로 가는 길에 음악 듣기

23. 빈칸에 들어갈 단어는 avoid의 목적어가 되는 명사로, 예민한 주제에 대한 본인의 의견을 말하지 않음으로써 피할 수 있는 '무엇'이다. 지문에서 avoid와 sensitive가 그대로 나온 문장이 문제와 동일한 내용을 가지고 있긴 하지만, avoid의 목적어가 this로 명시되어 있다. 앞 문장을 살펴보면, 동료와의 사이에서 '갈등'이 발생된 경험을 갖고 있을 것이라고 하므로, this가 지칭하는 것은 갈등인 것을 알 수 있다. 따라서 정답은 conflict이다.

근거가 되는 문장에 this와 같은 지시대명사가 나온다면, 대부분 바로 앞 문장 혹은 앞 절에 이 지시대명사가 지칭하는 단어가 나온다.

Paraphrasing keeping your opinions about ~ to yourself(자신의 의견을 스스로만 알고 있는 것)
→ refrain from sharing personal opinions(개인적인 의견을 공유하는 것을 피하다)
issues(문제) → topics(주제)

24. | 25. 24번 빈칸에 들어갈 단어는 remove의 목적어가 되는 명사이고, 25번 빈칸에 들어갈 단어는 your 뒤에 올 명사이다. 의미적으로 이 둘의 관계를 살펴보면, '25번 단어'를 향상시키기 위해 업무 공간에서 '24번 단어'를 치우는 것이다. work area와 remove에 상응하는 workstation과 free가 있는 문장을 살펴보자. 업무 공간에 '잡동사니'가 없어야 하고 이는 심리적 이점과 더 높은 '생산성'의 결과를 낳는다고 내용이다. 다시 말해, 잡동사니를 치우면 생산성이 높아진다는 것이므로 24번 정답은 clutter, 25번 정답은 productivity이다.

Paraphrasing remove(제거하다) → free(~이 없는)
work area(업무 공간) → workstation(업무 공간)
increase your productivity(생산성을 높이다) → higher productivity(더 높은 생산성)

26. 빈칸에 들어갈 단어는 suitable의 수식을 받는 명사로, 건강 문제를 야기하지 않도록 상사에게 요청할 '무엇'이다. boss에 상응하는 employer가 있는 문장과 suitable에 상응하는 high-quality와 comfortable이 있는 문장을 살펴보자. 고용주에게 고품질의 편안한 '의자'를 제공받도록 확실히 하며 이는 허리 통증과 부상의 위험을 줄여줄 것이라는 내용이 이어진다. 고용주에게 반드시 제공받으라는 것은 요청하라는 것으로 볼 수 있고, 허리 통증과 부상의 위험을 줄여준다는 것은 해당하는 건강 문제들을 야기되지 않도록 하는 것으로 볼 수 있다. 따라서 정답은 chair이다.

Paraphrasing ask your boss to give you(당신에게 ~을 주도록 상사에게 요청하라)
→ make sure that your employer provides ~ for you(고용주가 당신에게 ~을 제공하도록 확실히 하라)
a suitable chair(적합한 의자) → a high-quality, comfortable chair(고품질의 편안한 의자)
health issues(건강 문제) → back pain and injury(허리 통증과 부상)

27. 빈칸에 들어갈 단어는 some과 함께 enjoy의 목적어가 되는 명사로, 점심 시간에 동료와 함께 즐길 '무엇'이다. 점심 시간에 상응하는 lunch hours가 나오는 문장에, 더 많은 직장인들이 '운동'을 위해 점심 시간을 활용한다는 내용이 나오므로 정답은 exercise이다. 문제의 coworkers가 나오고 either indoor or outdoor에 상응하는 either at a local gym or outside도 나오는 문장의 내용이 정답을 확실히 해준다.

Paraphrasing lunch break(점심 휴식 시간) → lunch hours(점심 시간)
indoors(실내에서) → at a local gym(지역 체육관에서)

| Vocabulary & Expressions |

keep 간직하다, 지니다 remove 제거하다, 치우다 result in ~을 초래하다 break 휴식 (시간) on one's way home 집에 가는 길에 commute 통근하다

READING

PRACTICE TEST WRITING

Unit 13 IELTS WRITING에 대한 모든 것

▪ 교정

1. has → had
2. leads → led *or*
   recently leads → has recently led
3. however, → but *or*
   increased, however, → increased; however, *or*
   increased, however, → increased. However,
4. are → is
5. decreased → have decreased
6. tends → tend
7. ; → ,
8. result → results

1. 2012년 시제에 과거(dropped)가 쓰였는데, 2011년은 현재완료(has increased)가 쓰였다. 2011년은 2012년보다 이전이고 by(~까지)라는 완료시제와 친한 전치사가 사용됨을 고려하여 과거완료 시제(had increased)를 쓰는 것이 자연스럽다.

2. recently(최근에)라는 부사는 현재시제보다는 현재완료 또는 과거 시제와 어울린다. 따라서 leads를 has led 또는 led로 바꿔준다. 현재완료로 바꿀 때 부사 recently는 has와 led 사이에 들어감에 유의한다.

3. however는 부사로 두 개의 절(주어+동사)을 연결할 수 없다. 두 개의 절을 연결하려면 접속사(but)나 접속사 역할을 하는 구두점인 세미콜론(;)이 필요하다. 아니면 마침표를 써서 각각의 개별 문장으로 만들 수 있다.

The oil price increased, but taxi fares remained unchanged.
The oil price increased; however, taxi fares remained unchanged.
The oil price increased. However, taxi fares remained unchanged.

4. 주어가 3인칭 단수(The reason)이므로 동사가 is가 되어야 한다. are는 복수 주어를 받는 be동사이다.

5. since가 '~이래로'라고 해석될 때는 since 뒤에는 과거시제, 주절은 현재완료 시제가 자연스러운데, 문제의 주절에 시제가 과거(decreased)이므로 현재완료인 have decreased로 고쳐야 된다.

6. 주어가 복수(people)이므로 동사도 이에 따라 tend가 되어야 한다. tends는 3인칭 단수 주어와 어울리는 동사 형태이다.

7. 세미콜론은 절과 절을 연결하는 접속사의 역할을 한다. 문제처럼 주어와 동사로 이루어지지 않은 말 덩어리인 구(compared to adults)는 콤마(,)를 사용하여 연결한다.

8. which는 앞에 절 전체를 하나로 취급하여 받는 관계대명사다. 따라서 which는 단수 주어이고 그 뒤의 동사 역시 단수 주어를 받는 동사이므로 results가 되어야 한다.

▪ 아카데믹 태스크 1

출제 포인트 **난이도: 중**

실제 시험에서 표와 다른 그래프(선, 막대, 파이) 하나가 함께 출제되는 경우가 빈번함

기출 2024년 7월 - 표와 막대 그래프 출제
2024년 6월 - 표와 선 그래프 출제
2024년 5월 - 표와 선 그래프 출제
2024년 5월 - 표와 파이 차트 출제

The table and chart below show the total number of cruise passengers and their percentage by age group in 1975 and 2003 in the UK.
아래 표와 차트는 1975년과 2003년 영국의 총 크루즈 승객 수와 연령대별 비율을 보여준다.

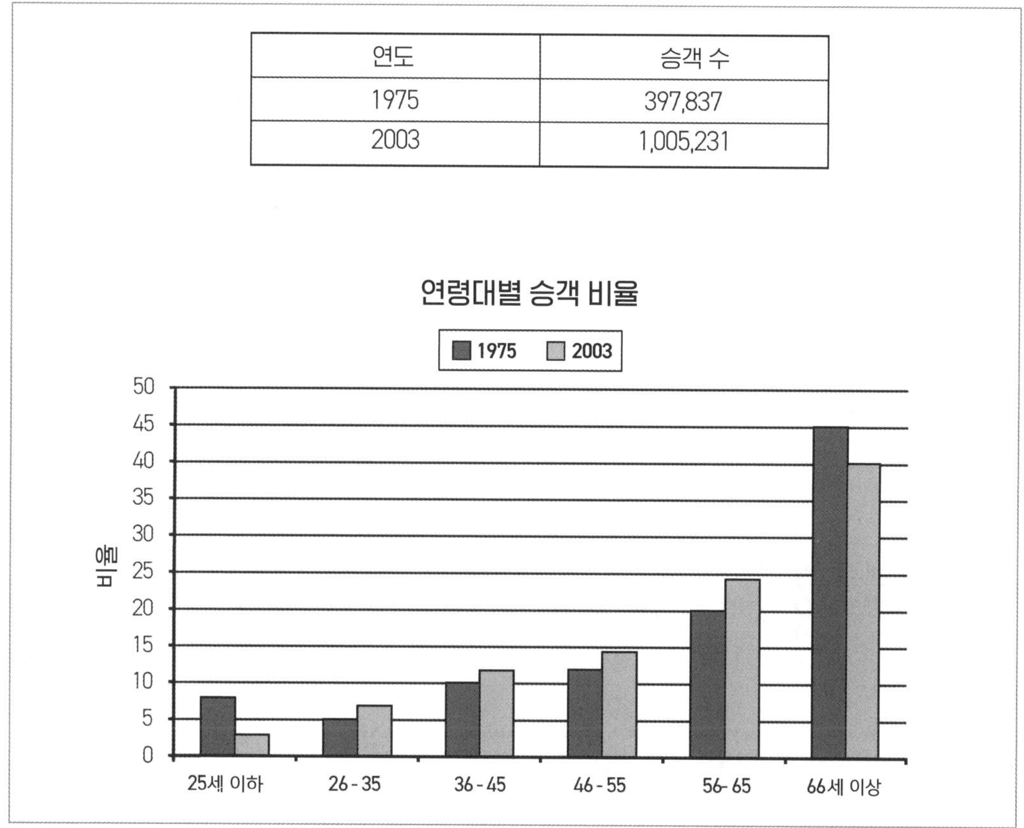

연도	승객 수
1975	397,837
2003	1,005,231

서론 첫 문장 (문제 박스 안 첫 문장 패러프레이징) The charts provide information on the total number of cruise passengers in the UK and the distribution by age group for the years 1975 and 2003. 서론 두 번째 문장(전체적인 추세) Overall, the total number of passengers rose drastically, and the percentage of passengers tended to increase with age.	이 도표들은 1975년과 2003년에 영국의 총 크루즈 승객 수와 연령대별 분포에 대한 정보를 제공한다. 전반적으로, 총 승객 수는 크게 증가했으며, 승객의 비율은 연령이 높아질수록 증가하는 경향을 보였다.

본론 1(주요 정보) Between the two years, the figure for cruise guests grew by approximately 2.5 times, from 397,837 to 1,005,231. Those aged 66 or older made up the largest share in both years, representing 45% in 1975 and 40% in 2003. Conversely, the proportion of younger travellers was relatively low. In 1975, the age group with the smallest percentage of passengers was the 26-35 age group, whereas in 2003, it was those aged 25 or under.

두 해 사이에, 크루즈 승객 수는 397,837명에서 1,005,231명으로 약 2.5배 증가했다. 두 해 모두 66세 이상이 승객의 대부분을 이뤘으며, 1975년에는 45%, 2003년에는 40%로, 두 해 모두, 다수가 66세 이상이었다. 반대로, 젊은 여행객의 비율은 상대적으로 낮았다. 1975년에는 승객 중 가장 적은 비율을 차지한 연령대는 26~35세였지만 2003년에는 25세 이하 연령대였다.

본론 2(세부 정보) Additionally, compared to 1975, the year 2003 saw about 2% more individuals aged 36-45 and 46-55. Similarly, the percentage of travellers aged 56-65 expanded slightly, from 20% in 1975 to 24% in 2003. In contrast, in 1975, the youngest and oldest age groups were greater in percentage by 5% compared to those of 2003.

추가적으로, 1975년에 비해 2003년에는 35~45세와 46~55세 연령대의 여행객이 약 2% 증가했다. 마찬가지로, 56~65세 여행객의 비율은 1975년 20%에서 2003년 24%로 소폭 커졌다. 반면, 1975년에는 2003년에 비해 최연소 연령대와 최고령 연령대의 비율이 5%씩 더 높았다.

(171 words)

| Vocabulary & Expressions |

cruise passenger 크루즈 승객 distribution 분포 drastically 급격하게, 크게 make up ~을 이루다, 형성하다 traveller 여행객(미국식 traveler) expand 확장하다 slightly 약간, 소폭으로

Unit 15 Task 1 - 도해

▪ 아카데믹 태스크 1

출제 포인트 **난이도: 중상**

개발 전후를 비교하여 서술하는 전형적인 지도/배치도 문제임

기출 2018년 12월 - 공장 지역이 미래 주거지로 재개발 계획

The plans below show the layout of a community centre now, and how it will look after development.

아래 평면도는 현재의 주민회관과 배치도와 개발 후 어떻게 될지를 보여준다.

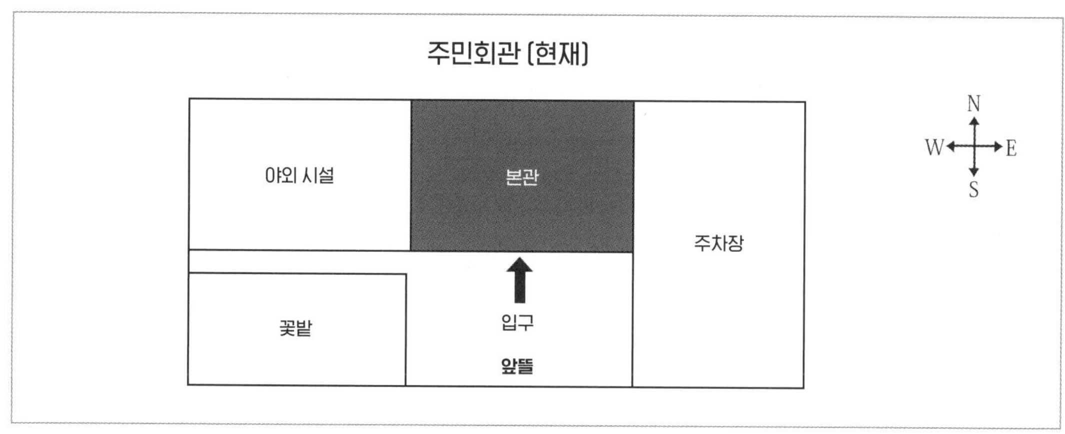

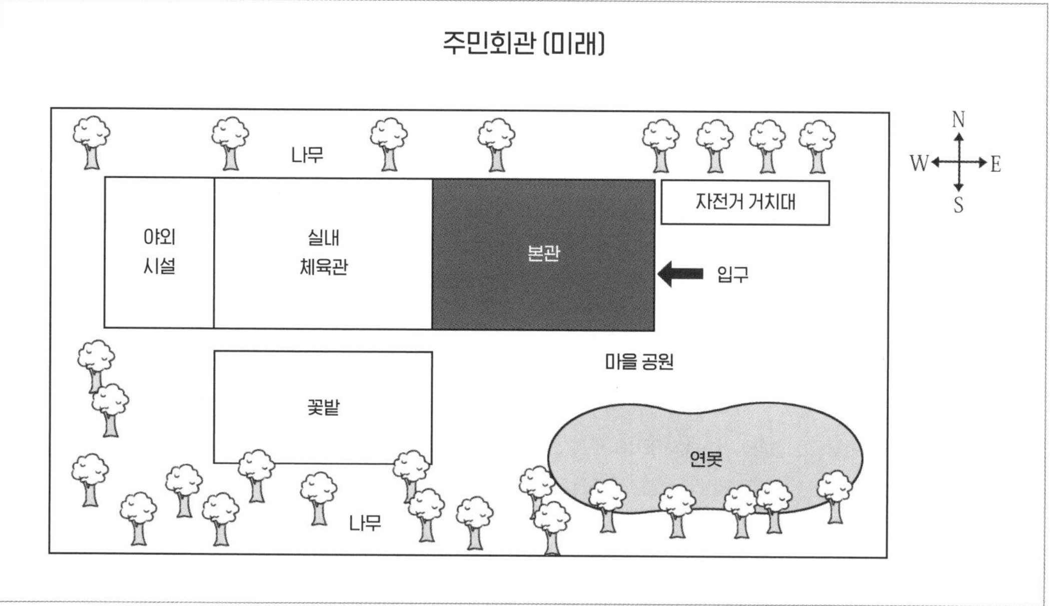

서론 첫 문장 (문제 박스 안 첫 문장 패러프레이징) The maps below display the current and future layouts of a community centre. 서론 두 번째 문장(지도 전체 주요 내용 요약) Overall, an indoor gym will be connected to the main building, and extensive landscaping features will be added.

본론 1(첫 번째 지도 주요 특징) Presently, the community centre consists of the main building with various outdoor areas around it. A flower garden takes up the western area of the front yard of the main building. To the west of the main building is an area for outdoor facilities, and a car park fills the eastern quarter of the layout.

본론 2(두 번째 지도 주요 특징) The future plan will expand and improve the outdoor area while also adding an indoor

아래 지도들은 현재와 미래 주민회관의 배치도를 보여준다. 전체적으로, 실내 체육관이 본관에 연결되고 광범위한 조경 특징들이 추가될 것이다.

현재, 주민회관은 본관과 그 주변의 여러 야외 구역들로 이루어져 있다. 꽃밭은 본관 앞뜰의 서쪽 지역을 차지하고 있다. 본관 서쪽에 야외 시설들이 있고, 주차장은 배치도의 동쪽 구역을 메우고 있다.

미래 계획은 실내 체육관을 추가하면서 야외 구역들이 팽창되고 개선되어질 것이다. 가장 눈에 띄게, 커다란 주차장과 앞뜰이 마을 공원과 연못으로 대체될 것이다. 자전거 거치대가 또한 새 입구 옆에 설치될 것인데, 입구는 건물 남쪽에서 동쪽으로 옮겨질 것이다. 실내 체육관이 야외 시설을 대체하는데, 야외 시설은 새 건물(실내 체

gym. Most notably, the large car park and front yard will be replaced by a community park and a pond. A cycle rack will also be installed next to the new entrance, which will be moved from the southern side of the building to the eastern side. An indoor gym will replace the outdoor facilities, which will then be to the west of the new building. Finally, many trees will be planted around the property. (176 words)	육관)의 서편으로 갈 것이다. 마지막으로, 많은 나무들이 그 부지 주변에 심어질 것이다.

I Vocabulary & Expressions I

below 아래에 community centre 주민회관 indoor 실내의 connect 연결하다 extensive 광범위한 landscaping 조경 feature 특징 add 추가하다 presently 현재 consist of ~으로 구성되다 various 다양한 take up 차지하다 yard 뜰, 마당 facility 시설 quarter 구역, 4분의 1 layout 평면도, 배치도 plan 지도, 평면도 be replaced by ~으로 대체되다 pond 연못 rack 거치대 entrance 입구 plant (나무 등을) 심다 property 부지, 부동산

Unit 16 Task 1 - 편지

▪ 제너럴 트레이닝 태스크 1

출제 포인트 **난이도: 중하**

시험에 가장 많이 출제되는 전형적인 formal letter 문제 스타일

기출 2024년 2월 - 지역 의회에 해변가 쓰레기 문제 설명 및 해결 제안
2018년 12월 - 호텔 매니저에게 두고 온 물건 관련하여 요청
2018년 10월 - 인터넷 쇼핑몰 매니저에게 물품에 대한 불만

Your company recently had a dinner party at a restaurant to celebrate a special occasion. Participants at the party said that they enjoyed the food, but they were not satisfied with the serving staff at the restaurant. Write a letter to the manager of the restaurant on behalf of your company. In your letter • give details of the reason for the company celebration • explain what was good and bad at the restaurant • suggest what the manager should do to improve the service in the future	당신의 회사는 특별한 일을 축하하기 위해 한 식당에서 최근에 저녁 파티를 가졌다. 파티 참석자들은 음식을 즐겼지만 식당 종업원들에 만족하지 못했다고 말했다. 당신의 회사를 대신해서 식당 매니저에게 편지를 써라. 편지에는 · 회사 축하연 이유를 자세하게 기술한다 · 식당에 좋은 점과 나쁜 점을 설명한다 · 장래에 서비스를 향상시키기 위해 매니저가 무엇을 해야 할지 제안한다
인사(톤 선택) Dear Sir or Madam, 편지 쓰는 목적 I am writing to inform you that I had a disappointing experience at your restaurant: we had some issues with the staff that I would like to bring to your attention.	관계자분께, 저는 당신 식당에서 실망스러운 경험을 했음을 알리기 위해 편지를 씁니다: 우리는 종업원들 관련한 몇몇 문제가 있었고 이 점에 대해 제가 귀하의 주목을 끌고자 합니다.

첫 번째 중요 항목 답변 As you might recall, my co-workers at Langdon Advertising and I recently had dinner at your establishment to celebrate our agency's fifth anniversary. We reserved your banquet room, and we had about 20 people in our party.

두 번째 중요 항목 답변 Upon arrival, the host was unaware of our reservation and visibly annoyed by our large party. His demeanor shifted once we confirmed the reservation, but it was a poor first impression. The elegant décor of the dining room helped improve the situation, as did the calming music. However, when we ordered, our server struggled to remember everything. It was of no surprise, then, when our meals arrived with several items missing. I would like to note, though, that the food was delicious.

세 번째 중요 항목 답변 You should be aware that additional training sessions for your front of house staff would surely improve your patrons' experience at your restaurant.

마무리 문장 I look forward to your serving staff meeting the standards suggested by your restaurant's other qualities.

끝맺음 Yours faithfully,

Karen Fuller

(197 words)

귀하가 기억해 내실지 모르겠지만, 랭던 광고 회사의 저와 제 동료들은 최근에 귀하의 식당에서 회사의 5주년을 기념하기 위해 저녁 만찬을 가졌습니다. 우리는 연회실을 예약했고, 약 20명이 파티에 참석했습니다.

도착하자마자, 식당 종업원은 우리 예약에 대해 몰랐고 우리 대규모 일행에 눈에 띄게 짜증을 냈습니다. 우리가 예약을 확인하자 그의 태도는 바뀌었지만, 그것은 안좋은 첫인상이었습니다. 조용한 음악과 함께 우아한 식당의 장식이 이러한 상황을 호전시키는데 도움이 되었습니다. 하지만, 우리가 주문했을 때, 우리의 웨이터가 모든 것을 기억하는데 어려워했습니다. 몇몇 음식이 빠진 채 우리 식사가 나왔을 때, 놀랄 일이 아니었죠. 그래도 음식은 맛있었다고 특별히 말씀드리고 싶네요.

귀하께서는 입구 종업원들의 추가적인 교육은 식당에서 고객들의 경험을 확실히 향상시킬 것임을 알아야 됩니다.

귀하의 종업원들이 식당의 다른 품질들이 보여준 기준들에 맞추길 기대합니다.

캐런 풀러 올림

I Vocabulary & Expressions I

special occasion 특별한 경우, 특별한 일 inform A that절 A에게 that절을 알리다 bring to one's attention 누군가의 주목을 끌다 establishment 영업소 anniversary 기념일 annoyed 짜증이 난 demeanor 태도 elegant 우아한 décor 장식 calming 진정시키는, 안정시키는 note 특별히 언급하다, 주목하다 patron 고객 meet the standards 기준에 맞추다

WRITING

Unit 17 Task 2 – 에세이 핵심 분석

▪ 아카데믹/제너럴 트레이닝 태스크 2

출제 포인트 **난이도: 중상**

최근 시험에 빈출하는 주제로 긍정적/부정적 영향에 대한 충분한 브레인스토밍이 이루어져야 됨

기출 2024년 4월 – 대형 쇼핑몰이 작은 상점들을 대체하는 것이 긍정적 또는 부정적 발달인지 기술
2019년 7월 – 지능화 기술 발달로 인한 긍정적/부정적 의견 모두 및 자신만의 의견 기술
2019년 6월 – 미래에 로봇이 일하는 것에 대한 장점이 단점을 능가하는지 기술
2019년 2월 – 로봇이 우리 삶에 긍정적 또는 부정적인지 기술

Due to the development of intelligent technology, computers will become more intelligent than human beings. Some people say this development will have a positive impact on humans. Others have a negative view on this issue. Discuss both these views and give your own opinion.	인공지능 기술의 발달로 인해, 컴퓨터는 인간보다 더 지능화될 것이다. 몇몇 사람들은 이러한 발달이 인간에게 긍정적인 영향을 미칠 것이라고 말한다. 다른 사람들은 이러한 사안에 대해 부정적인 관점을 갖고 있다. 두 관점을 논하고 자신만의 의견을 진술하라.
서론 토픽 패러프레이징 As intelligent technology continues to be developed, the day will come when computers are even smarter than human beings. Whether or not this development will have a positive or negative effect on humans remains to be seen, and many people have opposing views on this issue. 서론 마지막 문장(대주제문) Personally, I have some concerns about how this might affect our society. 본론 1 첫 문장(주제 문장) Those who believe that the development of intelligent technology will have a positive impact on our lives often cite the popularity and ubiquity of devices such as mobile phones and laptop computers. 본론 1 근거 문장 및 세부 내용 These devices utilise many forms of intelligent technology that have rapidly evolved over the past decade or so. For example, our devices can make recommendations for us and optimise our user experience based on our preferences and browsing history. As computers and devices get more intelligent, they make life more convenient for human beings. 본론 2 첫 문장(주제 문장) However, if intelligent technology evolves to the point where computers are much smarter than us, we could face a number of problems. 본론 2 근거 문장 및 세부 내용 First, more industries will become fully automated as computers and robots perform tasks more efficiently than humans. This will result in a worrying rise in unemployment, especially for unskilled workers. Second, we should be concerned about allowing artificial intelligence to control military weapons and facilities, as one glitch could result in a global catastrophe. 결론 In my opinion, even though increasingly intelligent computers make our lives more comfortable, we should be wary about making them too smart, as this could negatively impact human workers and global safety. Therefore, I think we should place limits on the potential power and functional capacity of the machines we develop. (271 words)	인공지능 기술이 계속해서 발달됨에 따라, 컴퓨터가 인간보다 훨씬 더 똑똑해지는 날이 올 것이다. 이러한 발달이 인간에게 긍정적 또는 부정적 영향을 영향을 가질지 지켜볼 일이고, 많은 사람들은 이 사안에 대립하는 의견을 갖고 있다. 개인적으로, 나는 이것이 얼마나 우리 사회에 영향을 미칠지에 대해 우려가 있다. 인공지능 기술 발달이 우리 삶에 긍정적 영향을 갖고 있다고 믿는 사람들은 종종 휴대폰과 노트북같은 기계의 대중성과 보편성을 언급한다. 이러한 기계들은 지난 십여년동안 급격하게 발전해온 많은 형태의 인공지능 기술을 이용한다. 예를 들어, 우리의 기계들은 우리의 선호도와 인터넷 검색 기록을 근거로 우리에게 제안을 하고 우리의 사용자 경험을 극대화할 수 있다. 컴퓨터와 기계들이 더 지능적이 될수록, 그것들은 인간에게 삶을 더 편리하게 만들어 준다. 그러나, 인공지능 기술이 컴퓨터가 인간보다 훨씬 더 똑똑한 지점까지 발전하면, 우리는 많은 문제들에 직면할 수 있다. 먼저, 인간보다 컴퓨터와 로봇이 더 효율적으로 업무를 수행하므로 더 많은 산업들이 완전히 자동화될 것이다. 이것은 우려되는 실업 증가로 이어질 것인데, 특히 비숙련 노동자들에게서 말이다. 두 번째, 우리는 작은 결함이 전 세계 재앙으로 이어질 수 있기에, 우리는 인공지능이 군무기와 시설을 통제하도록 하는 것에 대해 우려해야 한다. 내 의견으로는, 비록 지능화 컴퓨터들이 점점 더 우리 삶을 안락하게 만들지라도, 우리는 그것들이 너무 똑똑해지는 것에 대해 경계해야 되는데, 인간 근로자와 세계 안보에 부정적 영향을 미칠 수 있기 때문이다. 그러므로, 나는 우리가 발달시키는 기계의 잠재력과 가동력에 대해 제한을 두어야 한다고 생각한다.

I Vocabulary & Expressions I

human being 인간 whether or not ~인지 아닌지 remain to be seen 두고 볼 일이다 cite 인용하다 popularity 대중성 ubiquity 보편성, 어디에나 있음 evolve 진화하다, 발달하다 automated 자동화된 perform tasks 업무를 수행하다 efficiently 효율적으로 worrying 우려되는 unemployment 실업 unskilled 비숙련의 concerned 우려되는 military 군 glitch 작은 기계적 결함 catastrophe 대재앙 increasingly 점점 더 wary 경계하는 place limits 제한을 두다 potential 잠재적인 functional 기능적인, 가동의 capacity 능력, 용량

Unit 18 Task 2 - 에세이 토픽 브레인스토밍

▪ 아카데믹/제너럴 트레이닝 태스크 2

출제 포인트 **난이도: 중상**

동의 또는 비동의 정도(to what extent)를 묻는 문제로, 완전히 동의하는지/동의하지 않는지 또는 일부 동의하는지/동의하지 않는지 등에 대해 자신의 확실한 입장과 그에 대한 근거를 기술해야 됨

기출 2024년 10월 - 일반적으로 조직의 리더들은 나이가 많은데, 젊은 리더가 더 나을 거라는 의견에 동의하는지
2024년 5월 - 정부가 대체 에너지원을 장려하기 위해 더 노력해야한다는 의견에 동의하는지
2024년 4월 - 문화와 역사에 대한 거의 모든 정보를 온라인으로 찾을 수 있으므로 박물관이 더 이상 필요 없다는 의견에 동의하는지
2023년 9월 - 미래를 준비하는 최선의 방법이 젊은 세대에 투자하는 것이라는 의견에 동의하는지
2019년 2월 - 범죄자들에 대한 처벌보다는 교육을 통한 교화에 대해 동의하는지

Studies show that many criminals do not receive enough education. For this reason, some people believe that the best way to reduce crime is to educate them rather than punish them. To what extent do you agree or disagree with this statement?	많은 범죄자들이 충분한 교육을 받지 못함을 연구들이 보여준다. 이러한 이유로 일부 사람들은 범죄를 줄이는 최고의 방법은 그들을 처벌하는 것보다 교육시키는 것이라고 생각한다. 당신은 이 진술에 대해 어느 정도까지 동의하거나 동의하지 않는가?
서론 토픽 패러프레이징 Research indicates that criminals are poorly educated, so many people think that crime rates could be reduced if there were more focus on education rather than punishment. 서론 마지막 문장(대주제문) Although I think that it is still important to punish offenders for their crimes, I do agree that providing them with proper education is even more crucial in the long run. 본론 1 첫 문장(주제 문장) When people argue that criminals should be harshly punished and that educating them would be a waste of time, they are failing to see the bigger picture. 본론 1 근거 문장 및 세부 내용 A lack of education is one of the main reasons that people commit crimes in the first	범죄자들이 교육을 제대로 받지 않음을 연구 조사가 시사하기에, 많은 사람들은 처벌보다 교육에 더 초점을 맞춘다면 범죄율이 감소할 수 있을 것이라고 생각한다. 비록 나는 범죄자들을 그들의 범죄에 따라 처벌하는 것이 여전히 중요하다고 생각하지만, 적절한 교육을 그들에게 제공하는 것이 결국에는 훨씬 더 중요함에 동의한다. 범죄자들은 가혹하게 처벌받아야 되고 그들을 교육시키는 것은 시간 낭비일 것이라고 주장할 때, 그들은 더 큰 그림을 보지 못하는 것이다. 교육 부족은 애초에 사람들이 범죄를 저지르는 주된 이유 중 하나이다. 빈곤층의 많은 사람들이 자격이나 고용 가능성없이 학교를 일찍 떠나기에, 그들은 범죄의 길에 빠져 감옥에 가기 쉽다. 이

place. A lot of people from underprivileged backgrounds leave school early with no qualifications or employment prospects, so it is easy for them to fall into a life of crime and end up in prison. I believe that it is our moral duty to provide these incarcerated criminals with the education they missed earlier in their lives.

본론 2 첫 문장(주제 문장) Furthermore, we need to consider the issue of reoffending. 본론 2 근거 문장 및 세부 내용 The majority of criminals reoffend following their release from prison. The main reason for this is that they are thrust right back into the same circumstances they were in before: jobless, often homeless and penniless. If anything, they are even less employable than they were, thanks to their criminal record. If we focused more on the education and rehabilitation of criminals, they would be better equipped to re-enter society and start a new, honest life.

결론 In conclusion, while no crime should go unpunished, I do agree that we could reduce crime rates more significantly by educating criminals. Indeed, educating prisoners is one of the best things we can do for their successful induction into society.

(283 words)

러한 투옥된 범죄자들에게 그들 삶에서 초기에 놓쳤던 교육을 제공하는 것이 도덕적 의무라고 나는 믿는다.

추가로, 우리는 재범 문제에 대해 고려해볼 필요가 있다. 대다수 범죄자들은 감옥으로부터 석방 이후에 다시 범죄를 저지른다. 이러한 주된 이유는 그들이 전과 같은 바로 그 상황(무직, 종종 노숙, 그리고 무전)으로 다시 내몰리는 것이다. 오히려 범죄 기록으로 인해, 그들은 이전보다 심지어 더 적은 고용 가능성에 있다. 만일 우리가 범죄자들의 교육과 재활에 더 많은 집중을 한다면, 그들은 사회에 재진입하여 새롭게 정직한 삶을 시작하기 위해서 준비가 더 잘 될 것이다.

결론으로, 범죄는 처벌되지 않으면 안되지만, 범죄자들을 교육시킴으로써 더 현저하게 범죄율을 줄일 수 있음에 나는 동의한다. 참으로, 재소자에 대한 교육은 우리가 그들의 성공적인 사회로의 인도를 위해 할 수 있는 최선의 것들 중 하나이다.

| Vocabulary & Expressions |

indicate 나타내다, 시사하다 offender 범죄자 provide A with B A에게 B를 제공하다 crucial 중요한 in the long run 결국에는 harshly 가혹하게 a waste of time 시간 낭비 commit crimes 범죄를 저지르다 in the first place 애초에 underprivileged backgrounds 빈곤층 qualification 자격, 자격증 prospect 전망, 가망 fall into a life of crime 범죄의 길에 빠지다 end up 결국 (어떠한 처지에) 처하게 되다 moral 도덕적인 incarcerated 투옥된 reoffend 다시 범죄를 저지르다 following ~이후에 release 석방 be thrust 내몰리다 circumstance 상황 penniless 무일푼인 if anything 오히려 employable 고용자격을 갖춘 thanks to ~로 인해 rehabilitation 재활 better equipped 더 준비가 잘 된 go unpunished 처벌받지 않다 significantly 현저하게 induction 인도, 소개

Unit 19 Task 2 - 에세이 영작 스킬

▪ 아카데믹/제너럴 트레이닝 태스크 2

출제 포인트 **난이도: 중상**

원인 및 결과 관련하여 최근 가장 많이 출제되는 토픽 문제로 충분한 브레인스토밍이 이루어져야 됨

기출 2024년 5월 - 요즘 많은 학생들이 학교에서 집중하지 못하는 것에 대한 원인과 해결책
2019년 1월 - 음식물 낭비가 많은 것에 대한 원인 및 해결책
2018년 11월 - 한 번 쓰고 버리는 사회에 대한 원인 및 해결책

These days, people throw away a lot of the food that they buy from grocery stores or order at restaurants. Why do you think people throw away food? What can be done to reduce the amount of food waste?	요즘, 사람들은 식료품점에서 사거나 식당에서 주문한 음식을 많이 버리고 있다. 왜 사람들이 음식을 버린다고 생각하는가? 음식물 쓰레기 양을 줄이기 위해 무엇을 해야 할까?
서론 토픽 패러프레이징 Food waste is a significant issue in both households and restaurants, where large amounts of food are discarded regularly, ultimately ending up in landfills and harming the environment. 서론 마지막 문장(대주제문) In my opinion, it is important that we identify the numerous reasons behind this behaviour before we explore ways to remedy the situation. 본론 1 첫 문장(주제 문장) There are multiple factors contributing to the growing problem of food waste. 본론 1 근거 문장 및 세부 내용 First of all, overconsumption has increased as people enjoy a better quality of life and benefit from lower food costs. Many individuals purchase more food than they need from markets, often due to discounts, bulk buying or poor meal planning, resulting in excess food that spoils before it can be eaten. Additionally, large portion sizes and multi-course meals in restaurants lead to significant amounts of food scraps and leftovers being discarded. Substantial quantities of edible food are also thrown away at the end of the day. 본론 2 첫 문장(주제 문장) The food waste issue can be addressed in various ways. 본론 2 근거 문장 및 세부 내용 One method is to raise public awareness about food waste through social media and advertising, encouraging people to be more considerate and less wasteful. This will lead to more mindful purchasing at grocery stores. Furthermore, I believe the government should facilitate the collection of food waste from homes and restaurants to convert into fertiliser. Additionally, tax incentives could be offered to restaurants that produce little food waste or donate unsold meals that are still safe to eat, such as baked goods, salads and soups. 결론 In conclusion, more food is being wasted these days because individuals buy more food than necessary, and restaurants frequently discard food without hesitation. With increased public awareness and government regulations, I believe these issues could be effectively addressed. (281 words)	음식물 쓰레기는 가정과 식당 모두에서 중요한 문제이며, 많은 양의 음식물이 정기적으로 버려져, 결국 매립지로 가서 환경에 해를 끼친다. 내 생각에는, 이러한 행동이 발생하는 여러 가지 이유를 파악하는 것이 중요한데, 이후 이러한 상황을 고치기 위한 방법을 모색한다. 음식물 쓰레기 문제가 증가하는 데에는 여러 가지 요인이 있다. 우선, 사람들이 더 나은 삶의 질을 누리고 낮은 식품 비용의 혜택을 누리면서 과소비가 증가했다. 많은 개인들이 할인, 대량 구매 또는 잘못된 식사 계획으로 인해 필요한 양보다 많은 음식을 시장에서 구매하여, 그 결과 먹기도 전에 상한 음식이 남는 경우가 많다. 또한, 식당에서 많은 양의 음식과 여러 코스로 구성된 식사를 제공하면 상당한 양의 음식 찌꺼기와 남은 음식이 버려진다. 하루가 끝나는 때에 상당한 양의 먹을 수 있는 음식도 버려진다. 음식물 쓰레기 문제는 다양한 방법으로 해결할 수 있다. 한 가지 방법은 소셜 미디어와 광고를 통해 음식물 쓰레기에 대한 대중의 인식을 높이고, 사람들이 더 사려 깊고 낭비를 줄이도록 장려하는 것이다. 이는 식료품점에서 더 신중한 구매로 이어질 것이다. 더욱이, 정부는 가정과 식당에서 발생하는 음식물 쓰레기를 수거하여 비료로 전환할 수 있도록 장려해야 한다고 생각한다. 추가적으로, 음식물 쓰레기를 거의 배출하지 않거나 제빵, 샐러드, 수프 등 먹어도 안전한 미판매 음식을 기부하는 식당에 세금 인센티브를 제공할 수도 있다. 결론적으로, 요즘 개인들이 필요 이상으로 많은 음식을 구매하고 식당에서 망설임 없이 음식을 버리는 일이 잦아지면서 더 많은 음식이 낭비되고 있다. 대중의 인식이 높아지고 정부의 규제가 강화되면, 이러한 문제를 효과적으로 해결할 수 있다고 생각한다.

I Vocabulary & Expressions I

food waste 음식물 쓰레기 significant 중요한, 상당한 household 가정 discard 버리다 end up 끝나다 landfill 매립지 harm 해를 끼치다, 손상하다 identify 확인하다 remedy 치료하다, 고치다 contribute to ~에 기여하다 overconsumption 과소비 bulk buying 대량 구매 excess 여분의, 과도한 spoil 상하다 scrap 찌꺼기 leftover 남은 음식 substantial 상당한 edible 먹을 수 있는 throw away 버리다 address 해결하다 public awareness 대중의 인식 considerate 사려 깊은 mindful 주의하는, 신중한 facilitate 촉진하다 collection 수거 covert 전환하다 fertiliser 비료 donate 기부하다 hesitation 망설임 regulation 규제

Unit 20 Task 2 - 에세이 아웃라인 잡기

▪ 아카데믹/제너럴 트레이닝 태스크 2

출제 포인트 **난이도: 중상**

단순히 장점과 단점을 나열하는 것이 아니고 장점이 더 많은지 아니면 단점이 더 많은지, 또는 상황에 따라 다른지 자신만의 의견을 기술해야 함

기출 2024년 8월 - 커뮤니케이션 기술 발전에 따라 사람들이 다양한 방식으로 서로 소통하는데 이러한 추세의 장점과 단점
2024년 5월 - 사람들이 점점 더 종이책보다 e북을 선택하는 것이 더 많은 장점을 갖고 있는지
2018년 12월 - 졸업 후 바로 대학에 가는 것 대신에 여행이나 일하는 것의 장점이 더 많은지

Nowadays, some high-school graduates travel or work for a period of time instead of going directly to study at university. Do the advantages of this outweigh the disadvantages?	요즘 일부 고등학교 졸업생들이 곧바로 대학에 가는 것 대신에 일정기간 동안 여행을 가거나 일을 한다. 이에 대한 장점이 단점을 능가하는가?
서론 토픽 패러프레이징 These days, more and more high school students are choosing to spend some time travelling or working after they graduate, rather than going straight to university. 서론 마지막 문장(대주제문) I think this decision has both advantages and disadvantages, and overall, it depends on individual circumstances. 본론 1 첫 문장(주제 문장) The advantages of taking a year or so out from one's education for work or travel are obvious. 본론 1 근거 문장 및 세부 내용 First of all, it gives you a chance to refresh yourself before embarking on your next step in education. It also allows you to experience new cultures around the world and meet people from a wide variety of backgrounds. In my case, I spent a year working and travelling around Europe before starting my university course. In addition to making new friends, the experience taught me how to manage my finances, learn new languages and adapt to new social settings. In my view,	요즘, 점점 더 많은 학생들이 졸업 후에 바로 대학에 가는 것보다, 여행하거나 일하는데 시간을 보내기로 선택하고 있다. 나는 이러한 결정이 장점과 단점 모두 있으며, 전체적으로 각 개인의 상황에 따라 다르다고 생각한다. 일이나 여행을 위해 1년 정도 학업을 쉬는 것의 장점들은 분명하다. 무엇보다 먼저, 그것은 당신의 다음 단계 학업을 시작하기 전에, 재충전할 수 있는 기회를 준다. 그것은 또한 전 세계 새로운 문화를 경험하고 다양한 배경의 사람들을 만날 수 있게 해준다. 내 경우, 나는 대학 과정을 시작하기 전에, 유럽에서 일하고 여행하는데 1년을 보냈다. 새 친구를 만드는 것 외에, 그 경험은 어떻게 내 돈을 운용하고, 새 언어를 배우고, 새로운 사회적 상황에 적응해야 하는지 가르쳐줬다. 내 생각에, 이러한 인생 기술들은 대학에서 내 삶을 더 잘 준비하도록 만들어줬다.

these life skills made me better prepared for my life at university.

본론 2 첫 문장(주제 문장) On the other hand, it can be argued that taking a gap year has some detrimental effects. 본론 2 근거 문장 및 세부 내용 If you choose to take a year out to travel, you might struggle to regain the mentality required for studying after a prolonged absence from the world of education. For example, with so much free time, the student could develop several bad habits or lose the motivation to study hard. Also, it can prove to be a significant drain on your finances. When you choose to travel and work simultaneously, you will only generally be offered minimum wage jobs, such as bartending or serving in restaurants and pubs, and these do very little to offset the costs of travel.

결론 In conclusion, there are several advantages and disadvantages to taking a gap year. I believe whether it is a good idea or not depends on each individual's academic discipline and financial circumstances.

(303 words)

반면에, 1년 학업 중단이 해로운 영향을 준다고도 볼 수 있다. 1년을 여행하는데 보내기로 선택한다면, 당신은 교육 세계에 장기간 불참 후 공부에 필요한 사고방식을 다시 갖추는데 힘겨워할지도 모른다. 예를 들면, 많은 자유시간 속에, 안 좋은 습관을 갖거나 열심히 학업 하겠다는 동기도 잃을 수 있다. 또한 당신의 재정에 심각한 낭비가 될 수 있다. 여행과 일을 동시에 하기로 선택하면, 보통 당신은 식당이나 술집에서 바텐더나 서빙과 같은 최저 임금 일자리만 제공받을 것이고, 이것들은 여행 경비를 거의 벌충하지 못한다.

결론적으로, 1년간 학업 중단은 장단점이 있다. 나는 이것이 좋은지 나쁜지는 각 개인의 학업적 기강과 재정 상황에 달려있다고 믿는다.

I Vocabulary & Expressions I

or so 쯤, 정도 obvious 분명한 embark on ~에 착수하다 in addition to ~이외에 take a gap year 고등학교 졸업 후 1년 쉬다 adapt to ~에 적응하다 setting 상황, 환경 detrimental 해로운 prolonged 장기의 absence 부재, 결핍, 불참 drain 배수관, 낭비 motivation 동기 simultaneously 동시에 offset 상쇄하다, 벌충하다 discipline 훈련, 자제, 기강 circumstance 상황

PRACTICE TEST SPEAKING

Unit 21 IELTS SPEAKING에 대한 모든 것

▪ 브레인스토밍

1. Do you enjoy being your current age? [Why/Why not?]
당신은 당신의 현재 나이를 즐기나요? [왜죠/왜 아니죠?]

Yes(대답) - 32 (구체적 나의 나이를 언급) - more confident in myself (이유: 보다 자신감 있음) - improved social skills(부연1: 향상된 사교 능력) - more knowledgeable (부연2: 더 많은 지식) - still young(부연2에 대한 추가설명: 아직도 젊음) - overall good(마무리: 대체로 좋음)

2. Describe a woman who is important in your life. Who is she and what is she like?
당신 삶에서 중요한 여성에 대해 말해 보세요. 그녀는 누구이고 그녀의 성격(외모를 묻는 것이 아님)은 어떻죠?

유의 **외모**를 묻는 질문은 What does she **look** like? 이다.

mother(대답: 어머니) - calm, mild(이유1: 조용하고 온화함) - gentle voice(이유1의 부연: 조용한 목소리) - attentive(이유2: 세심함) - sacrifices(이유2의 부연: 희생) - grateful(마무리: 고마움)

3. Do people in your country use public transportation a lot?
당신 국가 사람들은 대중교통을 많이 이용하나요?

Yes(대답) - railway lines(구체적 답변: 철도망) - well developed(이유1: 잘 발달) - high population density(이유1의 부연: 높은 인구밀도) - very reasonable fares(이유2: 매우 비싸지 않은 요금) - prefer to use(마무리: 선호함)

▪ 쉐도잉

1. Yes, I do. I've just turned 32 years old and feel more confident in myself since I believe that my social skills have greatly improved. Also, I am much more knowledgeable now than I was in my 20s. Of course, I am still quite young, so I have many more things to learn about and experience. But, overall, being 32 is good.
네 그렇습니다. 저는 이제 막 32살이 되었고 스스로에게 더 자신감을 느끼는데요, 왜냐하면 저의 사회적 기술은 많이 향상되었다고 생각하기 때문입니다. 또한 제가 20대였을 때보다 훨씬 더 아는 것이 많습니다. 물론 여전히 어려서 배우고 경험할 것이 더 많습니다. 그러나 전반적으로 32살인 것이 좋습니다.

2. I would like to talk about my mother. She is a calm, mild-mannered woman. with a gentle voice that makes me feel comforted. She is also very attentive to her family and always makes sacrifices to put her children first. That's why I am always grateful to her.
저는 제 어머니에 대해 말씀드리고 싶습니다. 어머니는 조용하고 온화한 부류의 여성으로 조용한 목소리를 갖고 계시는데 이는 저를 편안하게 해줍니다. 또한 어머니는 가족에게 매우 세심하시고 언제나 자식을 먼저 생각하시어 희생하십니다. 이것이 제가 항상 어머니에게 감사하는 이유입니다.

3. Yes, we do. In particular, our railway lines are well developed and can efficiently deal with our high population density. Furthermore, the fares are very reasonable. Therefore, many people prefer to use public transport rather than to drive a car.
네 그렇습니다. 특히 철도가 매우 발달되어 있어서 높은 인구밀도를 효율적으로 처리할 수 있습니다. 게다가 요금이 매우 합리적입니다. 그래서 많은 사람들이 자동차를 운전한 것보다 대중 교통을 이용하는 것을 선호합니다.

Unit 22 Part 1 - 나의 학업 또는 직업

▪ 파트 1

Q1 Why did you choose your job or subject?
왜 당신의 직업 또는 과목을 선택했나요?

브레인 스토밍	• 대답: 경영학 business management • 이유: 내꿈을 실현시키다 make my dream come true • 구체적 설명: 장래희망은 성공한 사업가, 자기만의 사업, 많은 직업 창출 successful businessman, run my own company, provide many good jobs for people	
어휘	**business management** 경영(학) **run one's own company** 자기 회사를 경영하다 **successful businessman** 성공한 사업가	
문법	• **help + 동사원형**: ~하는 것을 돕다 • **5형식:** make(5형식동사)+my dream(목적어)+come true(동사원형) 내 꿈이 실현되도록 만들다 • **provide B for A**: A에게 B를 제공하다(= provide B to A = provide A with B)	
모범 답변	I decided to study business management because the course will help make my dream come true, which is to become a successful businessman. My goal is to run my own company and provide many good jobs for people.	저는 경영학을 공부하기로 결정했는데 이는 그 코스가 성공한 사업가가 되는 제 꿈을 이루는 데 도움이 될 것이라고 생각하기 때문입니다. 제 꿈은 자신의 회사를 경영하며 사람들에게 많은 좋은 직업을 제공하는 것입니다.

Q2 Do you like your work or study? [Why/Why not?]
당신의 직업 또는 공부 과목을 좋아합니까? [왜죠?/왜 아니죠?]

브레인 스토밍	• 대답: Yes • 이유1: 정보와 지식 information and knowledge • 부연: 취업 전 before working • 이유2: 인맥 build a strong network • 부연: 입사지원 apply for a job	
어휘	**build a strong network** 인맥을 쌓다 **essential** 필수적인 **apply for** ~을 신청하다, 지원하다	
문법	• **목적격 관계대명사 생략**: information and knowledge **(which) ~** ~한 정보와 지식들 • **주격 관계대명사**: network **that ~** ~한 인맥 • **시간절 접속사**: before, while, when • **시제**: 내용이 미래시제(will be)라도 when절은 현재 (apply) 사용	
모범 답변	Yes, I love my subject, business management, because it gives me the useful information and knowledge I must know before I start working in my field. In addition, while I study my course, I can build a strong network that will be essential to me when I apply for a job.	네, 저는 제 과목, 경영학을 정말 좋아하는데, 제 분야에서 일을 시작하기 전에 반드시 알아야 하는 유용한 정보와 지식을 주기 때문입니다. 게다가, 공부하면서 제가 입사 지원할 때 꼭 필요한 인맥을 쌓을 수 있습니다.

Q3 Where is your workplace or school located?
당신의 직장 또는 학교는 어디에 위치해있나요?

브레인 스토밍	• 대답: 서울 남쪽에 in the southern part of Seoul 가파른 언덕 꼭대기에 on top of a steep hill 우리 아파트 블록 바로 옆에 right next to my block of flats • 구체적 설명: 내가 도착하는 데 10분밖에 걸리지 않는다 only takes me ten minutes to arrive	
어휘	**steep hill** 가파른 언덕 **challenging** 힘든 **on the bright side** 긍정적인 면으로 **a block of flats** 아파트 블록 **school gate** 교문	
문법	• **be located in**: ~에 위치하다 • **so + 주어 + can**: 그래서 ~할 수 있다 • **it take + 사람 + 시간 + to부정사**: 사람이 to부정사 하는 데 시간이 걸리다	
모범 답변	My school is located in the southern part of Seoul. It is on top of a steep hill, so the climb can be challenging on some mornings. But on the bright side, it is right next to my block of flats, so it only takes me ten minutes to arrive at the school gate.	우리 학교는 서울 남쪽에 위치해 있습니다. 가파른 언덕 꼭대기에 있어서 아침에는 오르기가 힘들 수 있습니다. 하지만 긍정적인 면으로, 제가 사는 아파트 블록 바로 옆에 있어서 제가 교문까지 도착하는 데 10분밖에 걸리지 않습니다.

Q4 How do most people travel to work where you live?
당신이 사는 곳에 대부분 사람들은 어떻게 출근하나요?

브레인 스토밍	• 대답: 대중교통을 통해 via public transport • 이유: 편리 convenient • 구체적 설명: 45분만 걸림 it only takes 45 minutes • 마무리: 최선의 방법 the best way	
어휘	**via** ~을 통해 **commute** 통근하다 **surrounding** 주변의 **suburb** 근교 **fairly** 꽤 **get to** ~에 도착하다 **definitely** 확실히 **[영어다운 표현]** surrounding suburbs 주변 근교 **[패러프레이징]** travel to work 일하러 이동하다 → commute 통근하다 people 사람들 → workers 근로자들 public transport 대중교통 → the subway and buses 지하철과 버스	
문법	• **접속사 where(+ 주어 + 동사)**: ~한 곳에서 • **가주어(it) – 의미상주어(for me) – 진주어(to get to my office)** • **분사구문: using the subway and buses** 지하철과 버스를 이용해서	
모범 답변	Where I live, most people travel to work via public transport. Like most cities, workers commute into the city from the surrounding suburbs, and luckily, our public transport system is quite convenient. I use it, too, and it's fairly simple for me to get to my office using the subway and buses, and it only takes 45 minutes. It's definitely the best way for most people.	제가 사는 곳에서, 대부분 사람들은 대중교통을 통해 직장으로 이동합니다. 대부분 도시들처럼, 근로자들은 주변 근교에서 도시로 출근하는데, 다행히 대중교통 체계가 매우 편리합니다. 저도 이용하는데, 전철과 버스를 이용해서 사무실 출근이 꽤 쉽고 45분밖에 안 걸립니다. 대중교통은 확실히 대부분 사람들에게 최선의 방법입니다.

▪ 파트 1

Q1 Do you live in the city or the country?
당신은 도시에 사나요 아니면 시골에 사나요?

브레인 스토밍	• 대답: 수도 서울 Seoul, the capital city • 과거: 시골에 살았음 used to live in the country • 이사 이유: 더 나은 교육 better educational opportunities	
어휘	capital city 수도 move to ~로 이사가다 better educational opportunities 더 나은 교육	
문법	• used to + 동사원형: 과거에 ~하곤 했었다(현재는 아님)	
모범 답변	I currently live in Seoul, which is the capital city of Korea. I used to live in the country when I was little, but my family moved to the city for better educational opportunities.	저는 현재 대한민국의 수도인 서울에 살고 있습니다. 어렸을 때는 시골에서 살았지만 더 나은 교육 기회를 위해 가족 모두 도시로 이사했습니다.

Q2 What are some advantages of your neighbourhood?
당신 동네의 장점들은 무엇인가요?

브레인 스토밍	• 장점 1: 평화롭고 조용한 분위기로 안전 safe, with a peaceful and quiet atmosphere • 장점 2: 지하철역과 버스 정류장들로 편리 a subway station and bus stops, convenient	
어휘	atmosphere 분위기 nearby 근처에 convenient 편리한 resident 주민, 거주자	
문법	• 분사구문: making it = and make it 그곳을 만들며 • 5형식: making(5형식동사)+it(목적어)+convenient(형용사 목적보어) 그곳을 편리하게 만들다	
모범 답변	I live in a great neighbourhood. First of all, it's safe, with a peaceful and quiet atmosphere. Also, there is a subway station and several bus stops nearby, making it convenient for residents.	저는 아주 좋은 동네에 살고 있습니다. 우선 평화롭고 조용한 분위기로 안전합니다. 또한 지하철역과 여러 버스 정류장이 근처에 있어 주민들이 편리하게 이용할 수 있습니다.

Q3 Would you say your hometown is a good place for young people to live?
당신의 고향이 젊은이들이 살기 좋은 곳이라고 생각하나요?

브레인 스토밍	• 대답: 이상적인 곳 ideal place • 이유 1: 많은 취업 기회 plenty of career opportunities • 이유 2: 최신 유행의 식당들과 신나는 밤문화 hip restaurants and exciting nightlife • 마무리: 완벽한 곳 perfect place

SPEAKING

어휘	ideal 이상적인 somewhere 어딘가 plenty of 많은 career opportunities 취업 기회, 경력을 쌓을 기회 hip restaurant 최신 유행의 식당 exciting nightlife 신나는 밤문화 both sides of the coin 동전의 양면 live the dream 삶을 누리다, 꿈을 실현하다 **[패러프레이징]** good place → ideal place → perfect place
문법	• **분사구문**: living the dream = and live the dream 삶을 누리며
모범 답변	I think my hometown is the ideal place for young people to live. Young people need to live somewhere with plenty of career opportunities, but they also want to live somewhere with hip restaurants and exciting nightlife, and my hometown has both sides of the coin. I work hard and play hard in my hometown, living the dream. It really is the perfect place for young people. 제 고향은 젊은이들이 살기에 이상적인 곳이라고 생각합니다. 젊은이들은 취업 기회가 많은 곳에서 살아야 하지만, 또한 최신 유행의 식당들과 신나는 밤문화가 있는 곳에서 살기를 원하는데, 제 고향은 동전의 양면과도 같은 곳입니다. 저는 고향에서 열심히 일하고 열심히 놀며 삶을 누리고 있습니다. 젊은이들에게 정말 완벽한 곳입니다.

Q4 What kind of house do you want to live in in the future?
당신은 장래에 어떤 집에서 살고 싶은가요?

브레인 스토밍	• 대답: 한강 뷰 a view of the Han River • 부연: 큰 창문이 있는 넓은 거실 a spacious living room with large windows • 추가: 게임 전용 방 a room dedicated to gaming
어휘	a view of ~한 뷰/전망 spacious (방이나 집이) 넓은 living room 거실 ideal 이상적인 additionally 게다가, 추가로 dedicated to ~에 전용인 gaming (컴퓨터) 게임하기
문법	• **콤마(,) + 주격 관계대명사**: hobby, **which** ~ ~한 취미(취미에 대한 부연 설명)
모범 답변	In the future, I would like to live in a house with a view of the Han River. A spacious living room with large windows would be ideal. Additionally, I want my house to have a room dedicated to my hobby, which is gaming. 장래에, 저는 한강이 보이는 집에서 살고 싶습니다. 큰 창문이 있는 넓은 거실이 가장 이상적일 것 같네요. 추가로, 제 취미인 게임을 위한 전용 방이 있는 집이었으면 좋겠습니다.

Unit 24 Part 1 – 나와 관련된 질문

▪ 파트 1

Q1 How different are the clothes you wear now from those you wore 10 years ago?
당신은 10년전 입었던 것과 지금의 복장이 어떻게 다른가요?

브레인 스토밍	• 대답: 더 전문가답게 입는다 dress more professionally • 구체적 설명1: 청바지와 후드티 jeans and hoodies • 구체적 설명2: 정장(넥타이, 자켓, 구두) business attire(ties, jackets, shoes) • 부연: 불편한 uncomfortable	
어휘	wardrobe 옷장 consist of ~로 구성되다, ~이 있다 get home 집에 도착하다 cosy(미국식 cozy) 아늑한 **[영어다운 표현]** without a doubt 의심의 여지없이 jump back into ~로 급히 되돌아가다 **[패러프레이징]** wear 입다 → dress 차려 입다 clothes 옷 → attire 의복, 복장	
문법	• now that**절**: 이제 ~이기 때문에 • look + **형용사**: ~처럼 보이다 • as soon as**절**: ~하자마자	
모범 답변	Well, I definitely dress more professionally these days. Ten years ago, I was still a university student, and my wardrobe consisted mostly of jeans and hoodies. Now that I'm working, I wear business attire every day, like ties, jackets and nice shoes. I look sharp, but, honestly, it can be uncomfortable. Without a doubt, as soon as I get home, I jump back into my cosy hoodie and sweatpants.	음, 저는 확실히 더 전문가답게 요즘 옷을 입습니다. 10년 전에, 저는 여전히 대학생이었고, 제 옷장에는 대부분 청바지와 후드티가 있었습니다. 이제는 일하기 때문에, 저는 정장(넥타이, 자켓, 구두)을 매일 입습니다. 예리하게 보이지만 사실 불편합니다. 의심의 여지없이, 집에 오자마자, 저는 아늑한 후드티와 운동복 바지로 급히 되돌아갑니다.

Q2 What is your morning routine?
당신의 아침 일과(루틴)은 어떻게 되나요?

브레인 스토밍	• 답변: 기상 – 샤워 – 머리 손질 – 옷 입기 – 가벼운 아침 식사 get up – shower – do my hair – get dressed – light breakfast • 부연: 늦으면 건너뜀 skip – running late	
어휘	for starters (구어체) 우선 do one's hair 머리를 손질하다 get dressed 옷을 입다 light breakfast 가벼운 아침 식사 skip 건너뛰다 running late 늦은	
문법	• **4형식**: make(4형식 수여동사)+myself(간접 목적어)+a light breakfast(직접 목적어) 내 자신에게 가벼운 아침을 만들어주다	
모범 답변	For starters, I get up at 7 am and go for a shower. After that, I do my hair and get dressed. I usually make myself a light breakfast with a cup of coffee, but I skip that when I'm running late.	우선 아침 7시에 일어나 샤워를 하러 갑니다. 그런 다음 머리를 손질하고 옷을 입습니다. 보통은 커피 한 잔과 함께 가벼운 아침 식사를 하지만 늦을 때는 건너뜁니다.

SPEAKING

Q3 Do you prefer to watch films at home or in the cinema? [Why?]
당신은 영화를 집에서 보는 것을 선호하나요 아니면 극장에서 보는 것을 선호하나요? [왜죠?]

브레인 스토밍	• 대답: 내 집에서 my home • 이유: 여러 스트리밍 서비스 구독 subscribe to multiple streaming services • 예외: 정말 가끔 극장에 cinema once in a blue moon	
어휘	in the comfort of ~에서 편안하게, ~의 편안함 속에서 subscribe to ~을 구독하다 streaming service 스트리밍 서비스 unlimited access 무제한 접속 at a small cost 적은 비용으로 that said 그렇긴 하지만 once in a blue moon 정말 가끔, 드물게	
문법	• **enjoy + 동명사**: ~하는 것을 즐기다	
모범 답변	I prefer to watch films in the comfort of my home. I subscribe to multiple streaming services, so I have unlimited access to films at a small cost. That said, I enjoy going to the cinema once in a blue moon.	저는 집에서 편안하게 영화 보는 것을 선호합니다. 여러 스트리밍 서비스를 구독하고 있기 때문에 적은 비용으로 영화를 무제한으로 볼 수 있습니다. 그렇긴 하지만, 저는 드물게 극장에 가는 것도 즐깁니다.

Q4 Are you interested in science? [Why/Why not?]
당신은 과학에 관심이 있나요? [왜죠/왜 아니죠?]

브레인 스토밍	• 대답: 네 yes • 부연: 자연 다큐멘터리 시청과 최신 정보 얻는 것을 즐김 enjoy watching nature documentaries and staying updated	
어휘	keen 열렬한 incredibly 믿을 수 없이 fascinating 흥미로운 particularly 특히 nature 자연 stay updated on ~에 대한 최신 정보를 얻다 latest 최신의 advancements in ~의 발전 cutting-edge 첨단의 **[패러프레이징]** be interested in ~에 관심이 있다 → have a keen interest in ~에 관심이 많다	
문법	• **5형식**: find(5형식동사)+it(목적어)+fascinating(목적보어) 그것이 흥미롭다고 여기다 • **enjoy + 동명사**: enjoy watching ~ and staying ~	
모범 답변	Yes, I have a keen interest in science. While it's not my major, I find it incredibly fascinating. I particularly enjoy watching nature documentaries and staying updated on the latest advancements in cutting-edge technology.	네, 저는 과학에 관심이 많습니다. 제 전공은 아니지만 저는 과학이 매우 흥미롭다고 여깁니다. 저는 특히 자연 다큐멘터리를 시청하고 첨단 기술의 최신 발전에 대한 정보를 얻는 것을 즐깁니다.

▪ 파트 2

Q1 Describe an interesting person you met recently. 최근에 만난 사람 중 흥미로운 사람에 대해 말해 보세요.
You should say: 당신은 다음에 대해 말해야 합니다:
who the person was 그 사람이 누구인지
where you met the person 어디서 그 사람을 만났는지
what you were doing when you met him/her 그/그녀를 만났을 때 당신은 무엇을 하고 있었는지
and explain why you thought he/she was interesting. 그리고 왜 그/그녀가 흥미롭다고 생각했는지 설명하세요.

브레인 스토밍	• 누구: Kamal, stand-up comedian • 어디서: flight from Amsterdam to London, sat in the seat next to mine • 만났을 때 무엇을: in-flight meals, said one of the funniest things I ever heard, kept making jokes • 왜 흥미로운지: his career, stand on stage and make an entire audience laugh, real challenge
어휘	it turned out 알고 보니 travel for work 출장 가다 keep to myself 남들과 어울리지 않다 pay attention 관심을 갖다 in-flight meal 기내식 obviously 분명히 something along those lines 그와 같은 것 make jokes 농담하다 go on a streak 계속해서 하다 pull oneself back together 다시 정신을 차리다 do A for a living 생계를 위해 A를 하다 career 직업, 경력
문법	• not only A but (also) B: A 뿐만 아니라 B도 (모범답변처럼 A, B 부분에 전치사 by도 함께 반복됨에 유의) • **동명사 주어**: Being able to stand on stage and make an entire audience laugh 무대에 서서 모든 관중을 웃길 수 있는 것은

모범 답변		
	I recently met an interesting person named Kamal. It turned out that he is a stand-up comedian.	저는 최근에 카말이라는 흥미로운 사람을 만났습니다. 알고 보니 그는 스탠드 업 코미디언이었습니다.
	I met Kamal on a flight from Amsterdam to London. I travel frequently for work, and I usually keep to myself during flights. I guess I can seem cold, but it's just how it goes. Anyways, when Kamal sat in the seat next to mine on the flight, I didn't pay much attention to him.	저는 암스테르담에서 런던으로 가는 비행기에서 카말을 만났습니다. 저는 자주 출장을 다니며 비행기에서 보통 남들과 어울리지 않습니다. 차갑게 보일 수 있겠지만, 그냥 그렇게 되었네요. 어쨌든, 비행기에서 카말이 제 옆에 앉았을 때, 저는 그에게 관심을 거의 기울이지 않았습니다.
	It wasn't until the in-flight meals were delivered that I noticed Kamal was unique. I don't remember exactly what it was, but he said one of the funniest things I ever heard when he received his meal. Obviously, in-flight meals aren't great, so it was something along those lines. I started laughing, and then he kept making jokes. He really went on a streak. I introduced myself after I pulled myself back together, and then he told me what he does for a living.	기내식이 배달될 때가 되어서야 저는 카말이 독특하다고 눈치챘습니다. 저는 정확히 무엇이었는지 기억은 나지 않지만, 그가 기내식을 받으며 말했던 것은 제가 들었던 것들 중 가장 웃긴 것 중 하나였습니다. 분명히 기내식은 그렇게 좋지 않기에, 그와 관련된 내용이었습니다. 저는 웃기 시작했고 그는 계속해서 농담을 했습니다. 그는 정말 계속해서 웃겼죠. 저는 제 정신을 차리고 나서 제 소개를 했고, 그는 생계를 위해 무엇을 하는지 말했습니다.
	I was really impressed, not only by how funny he was on the spot like that, but by his career. Being able to stand on stage and make an entire	저는 기내 같은 곳에서 그가 너무 재미있어서 뿐만 아니라, 그의 직업에 정말로 깊은 인상을 받았습니다. 무대에 서서 모든 관중을 웃길 수 있는 것은 정말로 어려운 일이며, 카말은 분명히 그러한 독특한 재주가 있

SPEAKING

모범 답변	audience laugh is a real challenge, and Kamal definitely has a unique talent for it. Maybe I'll go to one of his shows someday. That is all that I can say now.	습니다. 아마도 저는 언젠가 그의 쇼에 갈 것 같습니다. 이것이 제가 지금 말할 수 있는 전부입니다.

Q2 Describe someone you know who owns a business. 지인 중 사업체를 소유한 사람에 대해 말해 보세요.
You should say: 당신은 다음에 대해 말해야 합니다:
who he/she is 그/그녀가 누구인지
in what kind of business he/she works 그/그녀가 무슨 업종에 종사하는지
why this person decided to start a business 왜 이 사람이 사업을 시작하기로 결정했는지
and explain whether you would like to have your own business, as this person has.
그리고 당신이 이 사람처럼 자기 사업체를 갖고 싶은지 설명하세요.

브레인 스토밍	• 누구: my best friend's father • 무슨 업종: restaurant, simple, home-cooked style • 왜 사업 시작: took it over from his grandmother, to stay in the family • 자기 사업 희망 여부: benefits of having your own business but extremely stressful, not handle that kind of burden	
어휘	run 운영하다 traditional meal 전통 요리 home-cooked style 집밥 스타일 cater 음식을 제공하다 as far as I know 내가 알기로는 take over 인계 받다 close with ~와 가까운 liberating 해방되는, 자유로운 take care of ~을 돌보다 burden 짐	
문법	• **주격 관계대명사**: place **that** ~ ~한 곳 • **주격 관계대명사**: customers **who** ~ ~한 고객들 • **전치사 뒤 동명사**: benefits **of having** ~ ~을 갖는 것의 혜택들	
모범 답변	I don't know many business owners, but when I was growing up, my best friend's father owned his own business. He ran a small restaurant. It wasn't a franchise or anything. It was just a simple place that served traditional meals in a home-cooked style. It catered to mostly older customers who didn't want to cook for themselves. As far as I know, he didn't start the business himself. Rather, he took it over from his grandmother. She had started it when she was younger, and as she got older, she wanted the restaurant to stay in the family. My friend's father was always close with his grandmother, so he took over the restaurant for her. There are a lot of great benefits of having your own business. You can be your own boss, and you can	저는 많은 사업주들을 알지 못하지만, 제가 자랄 때, 제 가장 친한 친구 아버지께서 자신의 사업체를 갖고 있었습니다. 그는 작은 식당을 경영했습니다. 그것은 프랜차이즈 같은 것이 아니었습니다. 그것은 집밥 스타일의 전통 요리를 제공하는 단지 작은 곳이었습니다. 대부분 자신을 위해서 요리하기를 원치 않는 나이 많은 고객들에게 음식을 공급했습니다. 제가 알기로는, 그는 직접 사업을 시작하지 않았습니다. 더 정확히 말하자면, 그는 그의 할머니로부터 인계 받았습니다. 할머니는 젊었을 때 식당을 시작했고, 나이가 들어감에 따라, 식당이 가족에게 남아있기를 원했습니다. 제 친구의 아버지는 항상 그의 할머니와 가까운 관계였기에 그는 그녀를 대신해 그 식당을 인계 받았습니다. 자신의 사업을 갖고 있으면 많은 이점이 있습니다. 자기가 자신의 보스가 되어 사업의 모든 사항을 결정

모범 답변	decide on every detail of the business. That all sounds very liberating. However, I know it was extremely stressful for him, and when they didn't have any customers, he'd worry about taking care of his family. I don't know if I could handle that kind of burden. That is all that I can say now.	할 수 있습니다. 그것은 매우 자유롭게 들립니다. 하지만, 저는 그것이 친구 아버지에게 극도의 스트레스였음을 압니다. 고객이 전혀 없을 때, 그는 가족을 부양하는 것에 걱정했을 것입니다. 저는 그러한 짐을 감당할 수 있을지 모르겠습니다. 이것이 제가 지금 말할 수 있는 전부입니다.

Unit 26 Part 2 - 사물

▪ 파트 2

Q1 Describe an interesting historic place. 흥미로운 역사적 장소에 대해 말해 보세요.
You should say: 당신은 다음에 대해 말해야 합니다:
what it is 무엇인지
where it is located 어디에 있는지
what you can do there 거기서 무엇을 할 수 있는지
and explain why the place is interesting. 그리고 왜 장소가 흥미로운지 설명하세요.

브레인 스토밍	• 무엇: Bukchon Hanok Village, preserved section of a 14th century Korean village • 어디: north-central Seoul, near other famous historic sites • 할 수 있는 것: walk around the traditional village, enjoy a cup of coffee or tea • 왜 흥미로운지: how well this slice of history has been preserved, beautiful mix of the past and present	
어휘	preserved 보존된 school trip 학교 소풍 appreciate 진가를 알아보다 palace 궁 royal shrine 왕가의 사당(종묘) restore 복구하다 mix of A and B A와 B의 혼합 urban environment 도시 환경	
문법	• **목적격 관계대명사 생략**: place (which) I've been to 제가 가봤던 곳 • **현재분사구문**: imagining = and imagine 상상하며 • **과거분사구문**: while seated = while you are seated 앉아 있으면서	
모범 답변	I think the most interesting historic place I've been to is Bukchon Hanok Village, which is a preserved section of a 14th century Korean village. I first went there on a school trip as a child, but I didn't really appreciate it until I returned earlier this year. Bukchon Hanok Village is located in north-central Seoul. It's also near other famous historic sites in Seoul, such as Gyeongbokgung Palace and the	제가 가봤던 곳 중 가장 흥미로운 역사적 장소는 북촌 한옥 마을이라고 생각하는데, 그곳은 한국에 14세기 마을의 보존 구역입니다. 저는 아이였을 때 처음 학교 소풍으로 그곳에 갔지만, 올해 초 다시 방문했을 때까지 그곳의 진가를 실제로 알아보지 못했습니다. 북촌 한옥 마을은 서울 북부 중심에 위치해 있습니다. 그곳은 또한 경복궁과 종묘와 같은 다른 유명한

모범 답변		
	Jongmyo Royal Shrine, so you can visit all these sites in the same day, which is quite convenient. You can walk around the traditional village and get a sense of what life was like back then. The traditional houses, called Hanok, have all been restored, and it's fascinating to stroll through them, imagining how people in the past lived. Stylish cafés have also established businesses in some of the traditional houses, and you can enjoy a cup of coffee or tea while seated in these unique buildings. Bukchon Hanok Village is truly a unique experience, and it's amazing how well this slice of history has been preserved. It's a beautiful mix of the past and present because the village is located in the middle of Seoul's super modern urban environment. When visiting Bukchon, it becomes clear just how far we've come, and just how much has changed. That is all that I can say now.	서울의 역사적 장소들 근처에 있어서, 이 모든 장소들을 같은 날 방문할 수 있기에 꽤 편리합니다. 당신은 전통 마을을 걸어 다니며 그 당시 삶이 어땠는지 엿볼 수 있습니다. 한옥이라 불리는 전통 가옥들은 모두 복원되었고 과거에 사람들이 어떻게 살았는지 상상하며 한옥들 사이로 거니는 것은 환상적입니다. 우아한 카페들이 이러한 전통 가옥들 일부에서 영업을 하고 있어서, 당신은 이 독특한 건물에 앉아서 커피나 차를 즐길 수 있습니다. 북촌 한옥 마을은 정말로 독특한 경험이며, 이 역사의 단편이 얼마나 잘 보존되고 있는지 놀라울 뿐입니다. 북촌은 과거와 현재의 아름다운 혼합물인데, 그 마을은 서울의 가장 현대적인 도심 환경 한가운데에 있기 때문입니다. 북촌을 방문할 때, 우리가 얼마나 발전했고 얼마나 변했는지 분명해집니다. 이것이 제가 지금 말할 수 있는 전부입니다.

Q2 Describe a special food you enjoy. 당신이 즐기는 특별한 음식에 대해 말해 보세요.
You should say: 당신은 다음에 대해 말해야 합니다:
what it is 무엇인지
where you have it 어디서 그것을 먹는지
whether the food is popular with other people in your country 당신 나라 다른 사람들에게 인기 있는지
and explain how you feel while eating that food. 그 음식을 먹으면 기분이 어떤지 설명하세요.

브레인 스토밍	• 무엇: carbonara, Italian pasta dish • 어디서: favourite Italian restaurant, Napoli's, cooking it myself at home • 인기 여부: quite popular in my country, in a different style • 기분: feel like I'm on holiday, away from my everyday life
어휘	dish 요리 ingredient 재료 chef 요리사 a glass of wine 와인 한 잔 turn out 드러나다 tricky 어려운, 곤란한 just right 딱 맞게 authentic 진짜의, 정통의 slip away 슬며시 빠져나가다 a plate of carbonara 카르보나라 한 접시 scenery 경치
문법	• **목적격 관계대명사**: food **that** I enjoy 제가 좋아하는 음식 • **분사구문**: made from = which is made from ~으로 만들어진 • **비교급 강조 구문**: much creamier than ~보다 훨씬 크림이 많은 • **to부정사 주격보어**: is to enjoy 즐기는 것이다 • **분사구문**: surrounded by = where it is surrounded by ~으로 둘러싸인

모범 답변	A special food that I enjoy is spaghetti carbonara. It's an Italian pasta dish made from simple ingredients like cheese, egg, and fatty pork, such as thick bacon.	제가 즐기는 특별 음식은 카르보나라 스파게티입니다. 그것은 치즈, 계란 그리고 두꺼운 베이컨처럼 기름진 돼지고기와 같은 간단한 재료들로 만드는 이탈리아의 파스타 요리입니다.
	I always have this dish when I go to my favourite Italian restaurant, Napoli's. The chef there knows me well, and the waitress knows I always order the same thing: spaghetti carbonara with a glass of red wine. Eventually, I became curious and tried cooking it myself at home. I'm not the best cook, though, so it didn't turn out so well. It was a bit tricky to cook the egg just right.	저는 항상 제가 가장 좋아하는 이탈리아 레스토랑 나폴리즈를 갈 때 이 요리를 먹습니다. 그곳 요리사는 저를 잘 알고 종업원도 제가 항상 같은 것을 주문하는 것을 압니다: 적포도주 한 잔과 카르보나라요. 결국, 저는 궁금해져서 집에서 직접 그것을 요리해 보았습니다. 비록 요리를 잘하지 못해서 그렇게 잘 하지는 못했지만요. 계란을 알맞게 요리하는 것이 약간 어려웠어요.
	Anyways, carbonara has become quite popular in my country, and you can find it at many Italian restaurants and even some fusion restaurants. However, it's prepared in a different style in my country, and it's much creamier than it should be. I'm not sure why it's so different, but I suppose people prefer it. Personally, I much prefer the authentic style.	어쨌든, 카르보나라는 꽤 우리나라에서 유명해서 많은 이탈리아 레스토랑과 심지어 몇몇 퓨전 레스토랑에서도 찾을 수 있습니다. 그러나 우리나라에서는 다른 방식으로 음식이 마련되는데요, 원래보다 훨씬 더 크림이 많습니다. 저는 왜 이렇게 다른지 잘 모르지만 아마도 사람들이 그것을 더 좋아해서 그런 것 같습니다. 개인적으로 저는 정통 방식을 훨씬 더 좋아합니다.
	When I eat carbonara, I feel like I'm on holiday in a far-away place. I have it with a glass of wine, and for a single meal, I can slip away from my everyday life. In truth, my dream is to enjoy a plate of carbonara in Italy, surrounded by the beautiful scenery of the Tuscan countryside.	카르보나라를 먹을 때, 저는 먼 곳에서 휴가를 보내는 느낌을 받습니다. 저는 와인 한 잔과 함께 먹는데, 단 한끼의 식사로, 저는 제 일상으로부터 슬며시 벗어날 수 있습니다. 사실, 제 꿈은 이탈리아에서 카르보나라 한 접시를 즐기는 것인데, 투스카나 시골의 아름다운 경치에 둘러싸여서요.
	That is all that I can say now.	이것이 제가 지금 말할 수 있는 전부입니다.

Unit 27 Part 2 – 사건

▪ 파트 2

Q1 Describe a memorable journey by car, plane or boat. 차, 비행기 또는 배를 통한 기억에 남는 여정에 대해 말해 보세요.
You should say: 당신은 다음에 대해 말해야 합니다:
where you went 어디로 갔는지
how you travelled 어떻게 이동했는지
why you went on the journey 왜 여행을 떠났는지
and explain why you think this journey is so memorable. 그리고 왜 이 여정이 기억에 남는지 설명하세요.

브레인 스토밍	• 어디로: the United States, first flight overseas • 어떻게 이동: flew out from Incheon Airport, short transfer in Tokyo, long flight from Tokyo to Chicago • 왜 여행: study abroad, experience life abroad • 왜 기억: major moment in my life, completely new country
어휘	**journey** 여행, 이동, 여정 **travel** 장거리 여행하다, 이동하다 (영국식 과거형 travelled, 미국식 과거형 traveled) **transfer** 환승 **board** 타다 **reputable** 명성 있는 **transcript** 성적증명서 **jump at** (기회 등에) 덤벼들다, 기꺼이 응하다 **land** 착륙하다 **completely** 완전히 **intimidating** 겁나는
문법	• **콤마 주격 관계대명사**: flight overseas**, which** was to the US 해외 비행이었는데, 미국행이었다 • **remember + 동명사**(~한 것을 기억하다): **remember** feel**ing** excited 흥분을 느끼던 것을 기억하다 비교 **remember + to부정사**(~할 것을 기억하다): **remember to** study 공부할 것을 기억하다

모범 답변

The most memorable journey I've taken was my first flight overseas, which was to the United States. I had never travelled outside of Korea before, let alone on such a long flight.	가장 기억에 남는 여정은 해외로 첫 비행이었는데, 미국행이었습니다. 저는 전에 한국을 전혀 떠나본 적이 없었는데, 혼자서 그렇게 긴 비행은 전혀 없었죠.
I flew out from Incheon Airport, and then I had a short transfer in Tokyo. I remember feeling excited about being in Japan, but, of course, I had to stay in the airport. Then, I boarded the plane for the long flight from Tokyo to Chicago. That flight alone was about twelve hours long.	저는 인천 공항에서 떠나 도쿄에서 짧은 환승을 가졌습니다. 일본에 있는 것 자체에 흥분되었지만, 물론 공항에만 머물러야만 했습니다. 그리고나서, 저는 도쿄에서 시카고로 긴 비행을 위해 비행기를 탔습니다. 그 비행만 약 12시간 걸렸죠.
I made this journey because I had accepted an opportunity to study abroad in Chicago for six months. The programme was at a reputable university, so I thought it would look great on my university transcripts. More than that, I wanted to experience life abroad. I had always dreamed of going to the States, and I jumped at the chance to do it.	저는 6개월간 시카고에서 유학할 기회를 얻어서 이 여행을 하게 되었습니다. 그 유학 프로그램은 명성 있는 대학에서였기에, 저는 제 대학 성적 증명서에 좋아 보이리라 생각했습니다. 그보다 더, 저는 해외에서 생활해 보기를 원했습니다. 저는 항상 미국에 가는 것을 꿈꿔왔기에, 유학 기회에 기꺼이 응했습니다.
So, for all these reasons, the trip was memorable since it was such a major moment in my life. I especially remember looking out the window when we were landing, and knowing I was seeing a completely new country for the first time in my life. It was an exciting but intimidating feeling.	그래서, 이러한 모든 이유들로, 제 삶에서 정말 중대한 순간이었기 때문에 그 여행은 기억에 남았습니다. 저는 특히 착륙 시 창밖을 봤던 것을 기억하는데, 제 삶에서 처음으로 완전히 새로운 나라를 보고 있다는 것을 알았습니다. 흥분되지만 겁도 났었죠.
That is all that I can say now.	이것이 제가 지금 말할 수 있는 전부입니다.

Q2 Describe an important festival in your country. 당신 국가에 중요한 축제에 대해 말해 보세요.
You should say: 당신은 다음에 대해 말해야 합니다:
what the festival is 무엇인지
what people in your country do during the festival 축제 기간 사람들이 무엇을 하는지
what you like or dislike about it 축제에 무엇을 좋아하고 싫어하는지
and explain why you think this festival is important. 왜 이 축제가 중요하다고 생각하는지 설명하세요.

브레인 스토밍	• 무엇: Seoul Lantern Festival, held every fall along Cheonggye Stream • 무엇 하는지: making their own lanterns, observing the lanterns and taking fantastic photos • 좋고 싫은 점: vibrant artwork, rather crowded • 왜 중요: whole family, traditional craft
어휘	beloved 사랑받는, 인기 많은 lantern 등, 초롱 stream 천 run through 관통해 흐르다 owntown 시내, 마을중심 participant 참가자 vibrant 생기 넘치는 craftsmanship 솜씨 mechanise 기계화하다 wait in line 줄 서서 기다리다 shuffle 이리저리 움직이다 aspect 면, 양상 marvel 경탄하다 appreciate 바르게 인식하다, 감상하다 sustain 유지시키다, 지탱하다 otherwise 그렇지 않으면
문법	• **주격 관계대명사**: displays **that** are placed on the water 물 위에 놓인 전시물들 • **현재분사**: several community groups **making** their own lanterns 자신만의 등을 만드는 여러 단체들 • **분사구문**: **observing** the lanterns and **taking** fantastic photos 등을 관찰하고 환상적인 사진을 찍으면서 • **분사구문**: **being** in Seoul(=since it is in Seoul) 그것이 서울에 있기에

모범 답변

An important and beloved festival in my country is the Seoul Lantern Festival. It's held every fall along Cheonggye Stream, which runs through the downtown area.

우리 나라에서 중요하고 인기 많은 축제는 서울 빛초롱 축제입니다. 그것은 청계천을 따라 매년 가을에 개최되는데, 청계천은 시내를 관통해 흐릅니다.

For the festival, artists from around the world design and create lantern displays that are placed on the water and lit. Local citizens also participate, with several community groups making their own lanterns, too. Participants can then walk along the stream, observing the lanterns and taking fantastic photos. Plus, the festival is completely free.

축제 기간 동안, 전 세계 예술가들이 물에 설치되어 빛이 비춰질 등 전시물을 디자인하고 만듭니다. 자신만의 등을 만드는 여러 단체들과, 지역 시민들도 참여합니다. 그후 참가자들은 청계천을 따라 걸으며 등들을 보고 환상적인 사진을 찍습니다. 게다가 이 축제는 완전히 무료입니다.

Everyone enjoys the vibrant artwork on display during the Seoul Lantern Festival. You might see your favourite animation character brought to life through amazing craftsmanship. Some of the lantern displays are even mechanised, which adds a whole extra level of creativity to the event. Of course, being in Seoul, it can become rather crowded, so if you're not a fan of waiting in line or shuffling through large groups of people, you might not enjoy that aspect of the festival.

모든 사람들이 서울 빛초롱 축제 기간 전시된 생기 넘치는 예술작품을 즐깁니다. 당신은 놀라운 솜씨에 의해 생명을 얻은 당신이 가장 좋아하는 만화 캐릭터를 볼지도 모릅니다. 몇몇 등 전시는 기계화되어 있어서, 전체적으로 한 단계 추가적인 창의성을 행사에 부여합니다. 물론 서울이기에, 꽤 붐빌 수 있어서, 줄 서서 기다리거나 많은 무리의 사람들 속을 이리저리 움직이는 것을 좋아하지 않는다면, 축제의 그런 면을 즐기지 않을지도 모릅니다.

Without a doubt, the Seoul Lantern Festival is one of the best events in my country. The whole family can come and marvel at some truly inspired artwork. On top of that, the festival is a fantastic way to appreciate and sustain a traditional craft that may otherwise be lost.

의심의 여지없이, 서울 빛초롱 축제는 우리나라에서 가장 큰 행사 중 하나입니다. 온 가족이 와서 정말 감명 깊은 작품을 보며 경탄할 수 있습니다. 게다가, 축제는 잃어버리게 될 수도 있는 전통 공예를 감상하고 유지시키는 환상적인 방법입니다.

That is all that I can say now.

이것이 제가 지금 말할 수 있는 전부입니다.

Unit 28 Part 3 - 사회적 이슈: 브레인스토밍

- **Part 3 사회적 이슈 기출 문제**

1. In what ways can people in a family be similar to each other?
어떤 면들을 가족 구성원들이 서로 닮을 수 있나요?

Family members can be similar to each other in both how they look and how they act. Since they share genetic information, parents and their children will likely resemble each other. Physical traits like facial structure, hair and eye colour and body size are inherited by children. Aside from appearance, family members mirror each other's behaviours. Children learn how to act from their parents, and as they grow older, they may even pick up peculiar behaviours from their parents.

가족 구성원들은 그들의 생김새와 행동 모두 서로서로 닮을 수 있습니다. 그들은 유전 정보를 공유하기에, 부모와 자녀들은 서로 닮을 가능성이 높습니다. 얼굴 구조, 머리카락과 눈 색깔, 그리고 체형과 같은 신체적 특징들은 아이들에게 유전됩니다. 외모 이외에, 가족 구성원들은 서로의 행동을 거울처럼 반영합니다. 아이들은 그들의 부모로부터 어떻게 행동해야 되는지를 배우고, 자라면서 그들 부모의 독특한 행동까지도 익힐 수 있습니다.

2. How has the size of the family changed in the last few decades in your country?
당신 국가에서 지난 수십 년 동안 가족의 크기가 어떻게 변해왔나요?

A few decades ago, it was much more common for extended families to live together. This meant that several generations would live in the same household. Additionally, families would have more children, so families were larger in terms of both who lived together and how many individuals were in them. But, nowadays, the structure of the nuclear family has become the norm. A married couple will live in their own home, and they will likely only have one or two children.

수십년 전, 대가족이 함께 사는 것은 훨씬 더 흔했습니다. 이는 여러 세대가 같은 식구로 사는 것을 의미했죠. 게다가 가족에는 더 많은 아이들이 있었기에, 가족은 누구와 같이 사는지 그리고 가족에 얼마나 많은 사람들이 있는지에 대한 관점 모두에서 훨씬 더 컸었습니다. 그러나, 요즘, 핵가족 구조가 일반적인 것이 되었습니다. 결혼한 커플들은 그들만의 집에서 단지 한두명의 아이들만 갖습니다.

*** 조동사 will은 습관이나 특정한 경우의 진실을 표현할 때 사용한다. 과거의 습관 및 과거의 진실을 표현할 때는 would를 사용한다.**

3. Who should be responsible for the care of the elderly: the family or the government?
당신은 노인 돌봄의 책임이 가족과 국가 중 누구에게 책임이 있다고 생각하나요?

I do believe that younger family members have a responsibility to make sure their elderly family members are taken care of and that they have a high quality of life. However, this sometimes requires a lot of sacrifice on the family's behalf, and there needs to be ample support from the government, too, to help take care of senior citizens. For instance, a public programme could provide healthcare and security to the elderly once they reach a certain age.

저는 젊은 가족 구성원들이 그들의 나이 많은 가족들이 잘 돌봄 받도록, 그리고 높은 수준의 삶을 갖도록 할 책임이 있다고 생각합니다. 그러나, 이러한 돌봄은 때때로 가족을 대표하여 많은 희생을 요구하기에, 노인들을 돌보는 것을 돕기 위해 정부로부터 충분한 지원도 요구됩니다. 예를 들어, 공공사업은 의료서비스와 안전을 일정 나이에 도달한 노인들에게 제공할 수 있습니다.

4. Do you think that society is becoming more materialistic?
당신은 사회가 점점 더 물질주의적이 된다고 생각하나요?

Without a doubt, society is becoming more materialistic. The countless billboard's along highways and various commercials on television are proof enough of this trend. In modern life, advertising is everywhere, and it has definitely affected our mentality. Whether we want to admit it or not, we live in a consumer culture, and our feelings of self-worth and value to society are enmeshed with how much we can purchase. So, our materialistic culture has caused a lot of other problems for us. I don't think we're moving in the right direction.

의심의 여지없이, 사회는 더욱더 물질주의적이 되어가고 있습니다. 차도를 따라 늘어선 수없이 많은 광고판과 TV에 다양한 광고들은 이러한 현상의 충분한 증거입니다. 현대 삶에서, 광고는 도처에 있는데, 확실히 우리의 사고방식에 영향을 미쳐왔습니다. 우리가 인정하길 원하든 원하지 않든, 우리는 소비문화 속에 살고 우리의 자부심과 사회의 가치에 대한 감정은 얼마나 많이 우리가 구매할 수 있는가와 얽혀 있습니다. 그래서, 우리의 물질주의적 문화는 우리에게 많은 다른 문제들을 야기해 오고 있습니다. 저는 우리가 올바른 방향으로 나아가고 있다고 생각하지 않습니다.

* be enmeshed with ~와 얽혀 있다

5. How do large shopping malls affect small local shops?

대형 쇼핑몰이 작은 지역 상점들에 어떠한 영향을 미치나요?

The rise of large shopping malls has pushed small local shops toward extinction. Now that you can find everything you need in one megastore, there's no need to go to small specialty stores. It's a shame, because local shopping areas and markets used to be lively community areas. But nowadays, they're empty, and a lot of stores have had to close. It's impossible for small shops to compete with giant malls where people can spend hours just window shopping, finding everything they could ever need.

대형 쇼핑몰의 성공은 작은 동네 상점들을 멸종의 길로 몰아넣고 있습니다. 이제 하나의 대형 매장에서 필요한 모든 것을 찾을 수 있기에, 작은 전문점을 갈 필요가 없습니다. 안타까운 현실인데요, 동네 쇼핑 지역과 시장은 활기찬 지역사회 장소였습니다. 그러나 요즘, 그곳들은 비어 있고, 많은 상점들이 문닫아야만 했습니다. 사람들이 필요로 할 만한 모든 것을 찾으며 윈도우 쇼핑하는 데만 몇시간을 보낼 수 있는 거대한 쇼핑몰들과 작은 상점들이 경쟁하는 것은 불가능합니다.

6. What are the most important qualities that people who start a business need?

창업하는 사람들이 필요로 하는 가장 중요한 자질들은 무엇인가요?

I feel that creativity is an extremely important quality for a person who starts a business. You need to be able to come up with ways to fulfil new demands on the market. Also, a successful businessperson needs to have the determination to see a problem through to its solution, since giving up would lead to terrible financial consequences. Finally, I'd say a high level of confidence and effective communication skills are needed, especially when meeting with possible investors.

저는 창의력이 비즈니스를 시작하는 사람에게 극도로 중요한 자질이라고 생각합니다. 시장에서 새로운 수요를 충족시킬 방안들을 생각해 낼 필요가 있습니다. 또한 성공한 사업가는 문제를 끝까지 해결할 결단력을 갖고 있어야 하는데, 포기하는 것은 심각한 재정적 결과로 이어질 수 있기 때문입니다. 마지막으로 높은 수준의 자신감과 효과적인 의사 소통 능력이 요구되는데, 특히 미래의 투자자들과 미팅을 할 때 그렇습니다.

* see a problem through to its solution 끝까지 문제를 해결하다

7. Are there any disadvantages to running a business?

사업을 운영하면 단점들이 있나요?

I think there are numerous disadvantages to running a business since choosing to start your own business involves tons of financial risk. You'll probably have to take out a large loan to start it, and then you won't have any guaranteed income until your business gains traction, which could take a while. And, if it doesn't, then you'll suffer huge financial losses, and you could end up bankrupt. There are surely plenty of benefits, but running your own business is extremely risky.

자기만의 사업을 하기로 선택하는 것은 수많은 금융 위기를 포함하기에 사업을 운영하는데 많은 단점들이 있다고 생각합니다. 사업을 시작하기 위해 수많은 융자를 받아야 할 것이고, 사업이 힘을 받기까지 어떠한 보장된 수입도 없고 이것은 한참이 될 수도 있죠. 그리고 사업이 힘을 받지 못하면 커다란 금융 손실로 고통받을 것이고 파산으로 끝날 수 있죠. 확실히 많은 장점이 있지만, 자기 사업을 하는 것은 대단히 위험합니다.

* gain traction 힘을 받다, 탄력을 받다

8. Do you agree that people should have a good work-life balance?
당신은 사람들이 일과 삶의 균형(워라벨)을 유지해야 한다는 말에 동의하나요?

I wish everyone could have a healthy work-life balance, but it's just not possible for a lot of us. More people are working longer hours nowadays, often spending over twelve hours a day at the office. This means they have less time for their families and for themselves. It causes a real disruption in their personal relationships and becomes a constant point of conflict for married couples. And, with extra stress and exhaustion, health problems also arise. Overworking is actually a very serious issue.

저는 모든 사람들이 건강한 워라벨을 가질 수 있기를 바라지만, 우리 중 많은 이에게 불가능합니다. 더 많은 사람들이 요즘 더 길게 일하고 있는데요, 종종 사무실에서 12시간 넘게 하루를 보내면서 말입니다. 이것은 사람들이 가족들과 스스로를 위해 더 적은 시간을 갖고 있음을 뜻합니다. 이것은 개인 관계에 실질적인 분열을 불러일으키고 결혼한 커플 간 끊임없는 갈등 포인트가 됩니다. 그리고 추가적인 스트레스와 피로로, 건강 문제 또한 발생합니다. 과로는 실제로 매우 심각한 이슈입니다.

9. How have developments in technology affected employment in your country?
기술 발달이 어떻게 당신 나라의 고용에 영향을 미쳤나요?

While advances in technology have helped establish some of my country's corporations as global leaders, it has also led to mass unemployment. More and more blue-collar factory jobs are becoming obsolete due to technology and automation, and this gravely affects a large part of the population. Plus, looking ahead, this problem will only worsen with the advent of AI. Even more jobs will be eliminated, especially in the information sector, which has so far been bolstered by technological advances.

기술에서 진보가 우리 나라 기업들이 글로벌 리더가 되도록 도왔지만, 기술은 또한 대규모 실업을 초래해왔습니다. 기술과 자동화로 인해 점점 더 많은 육체 노동 공장직들이 쓸모없게 되고, 이는 많은 사람들에게 중대한 영향을 미칩니다. 추가로, 앞을 내다봐도, 이 문제는 인공지능의 출현과 함께 더 악화될 것입니다. 심지어 더 많은 직업들이 없어질 것인데, 특히 정보 분야에서요. 이 분야는 지금까지 기술 진보에 의해 강화되어 왔죠.

* be bolstered by ~에 의해 강화되다

10. How would the way people use the internet change in the future?
사람들이 인터넷을 사용하는 방식이 미래에 어떻게 바뀔까요?

I think we'll all continue to be more and more connected to each other and to the world around us. We already have smart homes and digital assistants, so I think we'll interact more with the internet of things. This means we'll be able to influence physical items from incredibly far away thanks to ubiquitous networking. Probably a lot more people will be engaged in virtual reality, too, whether for work or for play. I figure both virtual and augmented reality will become completely integrated with our everyday lives.

저는 우리 모두 서로 간 그리고 전 세계와 더욱 연결되리라 생각합니다. 우리는 이미 스마트 홈과 디지털 보조장치를 갖고 있기에, 사물 인터넷과 더 많은 상호교환이 있을 거라 생각합니다. 이는 우리가 유비쿼터스 네트워킹 덕분에 아주 멀리 떨어진 사물에 영향을 미칠 수 있음을 의미하죠. 또한, 아마도 훨씬 많은 사람들은 가상 현실에 몰두하게 될 것입니다. 일 또는 놀이 때문에요. 저는 가상 현실과 증강 현실 둘 다 우리의 일상 생활과 완전히 통합될 것으로 봅니다.

* be engaged in ~에 몰두하다, 종사하다

11. What are the positive and negative effects of social media?
소셜 미디어의 긍정적, 부정적 영향은 무엇인가요?

For one thing, social media has made it easier than ever to connect with new friends, network with professionals and stay in touch with family. It has also made it far simpler for small business owners to advertise their products and services. On the other hand, social media has led to an array of serious issues due to its addictive nature, and psychological distress can occur in people as they constantly compare their lives to those of others. For example, there's the fear of missing out, which is the anxiety that you're not enjoying the same rewarding experiences that others are on social media.

우선, 소셜 미디어는 새 친구들과 연락하거나 전문인들과 인적 교류를 하고 가족과 연락을 유지하는 것을 이전보다 더 쉽게 만들었습니다. 그것은 또한 소상공인들이 자신의 제품과 서비스를 훨씬 간단하게 광고하도록 만들었죠. 반면에, 소셜 미디어는 중독적인 속성으로 여러 심각한 문제들을 불러일으켰고, 사람들은 끊임없이 그들의 삶을 다른 사람들과 비교함에 따라 정신적 고통이 발생할 수 있습니다. 예를 들어, 정보를 놓치는 것에 두려움이 있는데, 이는 다른 사람들이 소셜 미디어에서 즐기는 가치 있는 경험을 똑같이 즐기지 않는다는 것에 대한 염려이죠.

12. What is the typical diet of people in your country?

당신 나라 사람들의 주식은 무엇인가요?

People in my country typically stick to a diet based on steamed rice and a few staple foods. Many dishes are made from fermented vegetables and prepared with red pepper paste, which causes most foods to have a spicy, tangy flavour. As far as meat goes, most dishes include chicken or pork, with beef appearing less frequently. We try to avoid salty and fatty foods, but some foods like fried chicken and pizza have become increasingly popular over the past few decades.

우리나라 사람들은 쌀밥과 몇몇 주요 식품을 기반으로 한 식사를 고수합니다. 많은 요리들이 발효된 야채로 만들어지고 고추장과 함께 조리되는데, 이러한 이유로 대부분 음식들이 맵고 칼칼한 맛이 있습니다. 고기와 관련해서, 대부분 요리들은 닭고기와 돼지고기를 포함하며, 소고기는 덜 자주 등장하죠. 우리는 짜고 지방이 많은 음식을 피하려고 하지만, 후라이드 치킨이나 피자와 같은 몇몇 음식들은 지난 수십 년간 점점 유명해지고 있습니다.

13. Do you think food is important in a festival?

당신은 음식이 축제에서 중요하다고 생각하나요?

Yes, food plays a vital role in any festival. Whether it's with family or friends, any celebration needs to be marked by a memorable meal. Most regional festivals even feature special foods that are unique to that area, so everyone who attends the festival is sure to order that specific dish or treat. And if it's more of a family festival, then the family members will gather at one home to cook and eat together. Food is essential to bringing people together.

네, 음식은 축제에서 중요한 역할을 합니다. 가족과 있든 친구와 있든 간에, 어떠한 축하도 인상깊은 식사에 의해 기념되어집니다. 대부분 지역 축제는 그 지역에 독특한 특별 요리를 특징으로 하기에, 축제에 참가하는 모두가 그 특정 음식이나 훌륭한 요리를 주문하죠. 그리고 가족 축제에 가깝다면, 식구가 한 집에 모여 같이 요리하고 식사합니다. 음식은 사람들을 함께 있게 하는데 필수적입니다.

14. How may globalisation affect different festivals around the world?

어떻게 세계화가 전 세계에 서로 다른 축제들에 영향을 끼칠까요?

Globalisation has encouraged more people to travel, so now it's easier for people to participate in traditions and customs that are different from their own. I firmly believe that people cannot get a full sense of a culture until they are able to participate in it. So, festivals are a wonderful gateway for foreigners to truly experience a culture that's new to them. This means cultural festivals will have more of a foreigner presence, which I think is beneficial for the global community.

세계화는 더 많은 사람들이 여행하도록 장려하기에, 이제 사람들은 자신들과 다른 전통과 관습에 참여하기가 더 쉽습니다. 저는 사람들이 참여할 수 있을 때까지는 한 문화를 완전히 이해할 수 없다고 생각합니다. 그래서 축제는 외국인들이 그들에게 새로운 문화를 참되게 경험하는 훌륭한 관문입니다. 이는 문화적 축제에 더 많은 외국인 참여가 있을 것이고, 이는 지구촌에 도움이 된다고 생각합니다.

15. What kinds of music are popular with young people in your country?

당신 국가의 젊은이들에게 어떤 종류의 음악이 유행인가요?

K-Pop, or Korean pop, is easily the most popular kind of music with young people in my country. It's about more than the music, too: the mass obsession with K-pop has created an idol culture where young people become devoted to their favourite pop stars. The various boy bands and girl groups enjoy their own fandoms of teenagers and young adults who purchase their records, attend their concerts and even learn their dance moves. It's a cultural phenomenon, and this passion for K-Pop is spreading to other countries, too.

케이팝 또는 한국 대중 가요는 우리나라 젊은이들에게 필시 가장 인기있는 음악 종류입니다. 그것은 음악 이상이기도 합니다. 케이팝에 대한 대중의 집착이 아이돌 문화를 창출해서, 젊은이들이 자신의 가장 좋아하는 대중음악 스타에 헌신적이 되죠. 다양한 소년 밴드나 소녀 그룹들은 십대와 젊은 성인들의 팬덤을 누리는데 이들은 음반을 구매하고 콘서트에 참가하고, 심지어 댄스 동작도 배웁니다. 이것은 문화적 현상이고, 이러한 케이팝에 대한 열정은 다른 나라들에도 퍼져 나가고 있습니다.

* be(become) devoted to ~에 헌신하다, 전념하다

▪ 파트 3

Q1 Should companies give compensation to customers who complain about a purchase?

회사들은 구매에 대해 불만이 있는 고객에게 보상을 해줘야 하나요?

브레인 스토밍	• 대답: Yes
	• 이유 1: 고객 서비스 평판 reputation for customer service
	  └ 부연: 단골 repeat customers
	• 이유 2: 장기적으로 가치 있는 worth more in the long run
	  └ 부연: 브랜드 충성도 brand loyalty	

패러 프레이징	companies should give refunds to customers who have a problem with their purchase because good customer service is important. 회사들은 제품에 문제가 있는 고객들에게 환불을 해줘야 되는데, 좋은 고객 서비스가 중요하기 때문입니다.	
어휘	establish 확립하다 promote 촉진하다	
문법	• **가주어**(it)-**진주어**(to establish repeat customers) • **분사구문**: a customer **satisfied** with = a customer who was satisfied with 만족한 고객 • **동명사 주어**: **keeping** customers happy 계속 고객을 행복하게 하는 것이	
모범 답변	Yes, companies should give refunds to customers who have a problem with their purchase because good customer service is important. Of course, the company may lose a little profit by doing so, but it will improve its reputation for having good customer service. And for a successful business, it's vital to establish repeat customers. A customer satisfied with how his or her complaint was handled will be more likely to buy from that company again. So, it's worth more to the company in the long run because keeping customers happy will promote brand loyalty.	네, 회사들은 제품에 문제가 있는 고객들에게 환불을 해줘야 되는데, 좋은 고객 서비스가 중요하기 때문입니다. 물론, 회사는 이렇게 함으로 수익을 조금 잃을 것이지만, 좋은 고객 서비스를 갖고 있다는 평판이 상승할 것입니다. 그리고 성공하는 업체에게, 단골 고객을 확보하는 것은 중요합니다. 자신의 불만이 처리된 방식에 만족한 고객은 그 회사에서 다시 구매할 가능성이 높을 것입니다. 그래서, 장기적으로 회사에 더 가치가 있는데, 고객을 계속 행복하게 하는 것이 브랜드 충성도를 촉진시킬 것이기 때문입니다.

Q2 Are there any advantages or disadvantages of being famous?

유명해지는 것에 유리한 점과 불리한 점이 있나요?

브레인 스토밍	• 장점 1: 많은 팬들에게 사랑받다 be beloved by so many fans • 장점 2: 부유하고 호화로운 삶 the wealthy and luxurious lifestyle • 단점 1: 사생활과 평범한 삶 없음 no privacy, no normal life • 단점 2: 유명세를 유지하려는 스트레스 stress of maintaining their fame
패러 프레이징	There are both benefits and drawbacks to being famous because your life goes through so many changes when you become a celebrity. 유명해지는 것에 이점과 단점 모두 있는데, 유명인이 되면 아주 많은 변화들을 겪기 때문입니다.
어휘	celebrity 유명인 incredible 믿을 수 없는 anonymity 익명성 Joe Bloggs 일반인 in the limelight 각광받는, 세상의 이목 하에 crave 갈망하다 addiction 중독
문법	• **there are 구문**: there are both benefits and drawbacks / there are serious drawbacks • **가주어**(it) – **진주어**(to be beloved by so many fans) • **동명사 주어**: **having** the wealthy and luxurious lifestyle 부유하고 호화로운 삶을 사는 것이
모범 답변	There are both benefits and drawbacks to being famous because your life goes through so many changes when you become a celebrity. For one thing, it must feel incredible to be beloved by so many fans. And it goes without saying, having the wealthy and luxurious lifestyle of a celebrity would be a dream come true. However, there are serious drawbacks, too. Famous people lose the anonymity that the Joe Bloggs of the world enjoy. They don't have privacy, and they can't have a normal life, even if 'normal' seems boring to us. Moreover, they have the stress of maintaining their fame. I think once you're in the limelight, a part of you will always crave it, like an addiction. 유명해지는 것에 이점과 단점 모두 있는데, 유명인이 되면 아주 많은 변화들을 겪기 때문입니다. 하나는, 많은 팬들에게 사랑받는 것은 굉장하게 느껴질 것임에 틀림없습니다. 말할 필요없이, 유명인의 부유하고 호화로운 삶을 사는 것이 현실이 될 것입니다. 그러나 여러 심각한 단점도 있습니다. 유명인들은 전 세계 평범한 사람들이 즐기는 익명성을 잃습니다. 그들은 사생활이 없고, 평범한 삶을 가질 수 없습니다. 비록 우리에게 '평범함'은 지겨워 보이지만요. 더욱이, 그들은 그들의 명성을 유지하느라 스트레스를 받습니다. 일단 세상의 이목을 갖게 되면, 중독처럼 자신의 일부가 항상 세상의 관심을 갈망한다고 저는 생각합니다.

SPEAKING

Q3 What do you think influences young people's taste in music?
당신은 젊은이들의 음악 기호에 무엇이 영향을 준다고 생각하나요?

브레인 스토밍	• 답변 1: 음악 산업과 대중 문화 music industry and pop culture ㄴ 이유 1: 대중음악 스타에 끊임없는 노출 constant exposure to pop stars ㄴ 이유 2: 또래 압박 peer pressure • 답변 2: 부모의 음악적 취향 parents' musical tastes
패러 프레이징	There are a few powerful influences on young people's taste in music. 젊은이 음악 기호에 몇몇 강력한 영향들이 있습니다.
어휘	be skilled at ~에 숙련되다, 노련하다 constantly 끊임없이 be exposed to ~에 노출되다 play a big role 큰 역할을 하다

문법	• **관계대명사 which**: the music industry itself, **which** has become very skilled • **현재완료시제**: which **has become** very skilled • **복합관계대명사 whomever**: **whomever** the biggest pop star is at the moment • **복합관계대명사 whatever**: **whatever** his or her friends like
모범 답변	There are a few powerful influences on young people's taste in music. I think the strongest influence is the music industry itself, which has become very skilled at both producing and marketing 'pop culture'. Young people nowadays are constantly exposed to whomever the biggest pop star is at the moment. Then, of course, peer pressure plays a big role. Tastes in music are usually shared among social groups, so a young person will probably listen to whatever his or her friends like. Finally, I think the parents' musical tastes can be an influence, too, but not as frequently. | 젊은이들의 음악 기호에 미치는 몇몇 강력한 영향들이 있습니다. 제 생각에는 가장 큰 영향은 음악 산업 자체인데, 이 산업은 '대중 문화'를 생산하고 마케팅 하는데 있어서 매우 노련합니다. 요즘 젊은이들은 현재 가장 유명한 대중음악 스타가 누구든지 간에 이들에게 끊임없이 노출되어 있습니다. 그리고, 물론 또래 압박도 중요한 역할을 합니다. 음악에 대한 취향은 대체로 사회적 집단 속에서 공유되기에, 어린 사람들은 아마도 그의 친구들이 좋아하는 것이 무엇이든지 들을 것입니다. 마지막으로, 부모의 음악적 취향도 영향이 될 수 있지만, 그렇게 자주는 아니겠죠.

Q4 Have relationships with neighbours in your country changed in recent years?
당신 나라에서 최근에 이웃 간 관계가 변화해오고 있나요?

브레인 스토밍	• 대답: 덜 우호적이다 have become less friendly • 부연 1: 자신의 독립된 삶에 집중하다 focus on our separate lives • 부연 2: 아파트 건물의 수많은 이웃 the sheer number of people who live near you • 원인: 개인적으로 모든 사람을 아는 것이 불가능한 impossible to know everyone personally
패러 프레이징	The typical interaction between neighbours has changed in my country recently. 우리나라에서 이웃 간의 전형적인 관계가 최근 변했습니다.
어휘	separate life 독립된 삶 the sheer number of 어마어마한 수의 perfunctory 형식적인
문법	• **분사구문**: lives, **thinking** only of ourselves 자신만을 생각하면서 산다 • **관계대명사 who**: people **who** live near you 당신 주변에 사는 사람들 (neighbours의 패러프레이징)
모범 답변	The typical interaction between neighbours has changed in my country recently. Relationships among neighbours have become less friendly in recent years. We're all so busy that we focus on our separate lives, thinking only of ourselves and our family. So, there isn't as much of an emphasis on community as there was in the past. But, if you think about the sheer number of people who live near you in a crowded city like Seoul, then it would be impossible to know everyone personally. Maybe that's why relationships among neighbours are so perfunctory nowadays. | 우리나라에서 이웃 간의 전형적인 관계가 최근 변했습니다. 이웃 간의 관계는 최근에 덜 우호적으로 되었습니다. 우리 모두 너무 바빠서 자신의 독립된 삶에 집중하고, 우리 자신과 가족만을 생각합니다. 그래서, 과거에 그랬던 것 만큼 공동체에 대한 강조가 많지 않습니다. 그러나, 서울처럼 붐비는 도시에서 당신 근처에 사는 어마어마한 수의 사람들을 생각해보면, 개인적으로 모든 사람을 아는 것은 불가능하겠죠. 아마도 그것이 오늘날 이웃 간에 관계가 왜 그렇게 형식적인지 이유가 될 것입니다.

Unit 29 Part 3 – 사회적 이슈: 채점기준에 따른 답변

■ 파트 3

Q1 What is the difference between the role of a teacher and a parent in the education of children?
아이들 교육에서 선생님과 부모님의 역할 차이는 무엇인가요?

브레인 스토밍	• 대답: 뚜렷이 다른 업무 distinct duties • 구체적 설명 1 – 부모: 어떻게 행동하고 타인을 대해야 하는지 how to behave and treat others 　└ 부연: 부모에 의해 정해진 모범 the model set by parents • 구체적 설명 2 – 선생님: 확립된 교육 방법들 established teaching methods	
패러 프레이징	Teachers and parents have distinct duties when it comes to educating a child. 아이들 교육과 관련해서, 선생님들과 부모님들은 뚜렷이 다른 업무를 갖고 있습니다.	
어휘	distinct 뚜렷이 다른 when it comes to ~과 관련하여 behave 행동하다 treat 대하다 set by 정해진 in a manner that ~한 방법으로 established 확립된	
문법	• **how to + 동사원형**: 어떻게 ~하는지, ~하는 방법 • **분사구문**: model **set by** 정해진 모델	
모범 답변	Teachers and parents have distinct duties when it comes to educating a child because the child will learn from them in different ways. A child needs to learn how to behave and treat others through the model set by his or her parents. So, a parent needs to act in a manner that will influence the child positively. On the other hand, a teacher can follow established teaching methods to educate the child objectively.	아이들 교육과 관련해서, 선생님들과 부모님들은 뚜렷이 다른 업무를 갖고 있는데, 아이는 다른 방식으로 그들에게 배우기 때문입니다. 아이는 어떻게 행동하고 어떻게 다른 이들을 대해야 하는지 자신의 부모님에 의해 정해진 모범을 통해 배울 필요가 있습니다. 그래서, 부모님은 아이에게 긍정적으로 영향을 미치는 방법으로 처신할 필요가 있습니다. 반면에, 선생님은 아이를 객관적으로 가르칠 확립된 교육 방법들을 따를 수 있죠.

Q2 Do you think the traditional classroom will disappear in the future?
당신은 전통적 교실이 장래에 사라질 것이라고 생각하나요?

브레인 스토밍	• 대답: 줄어든 역할 diminished role • 이유: 온라인 교육 online education • 반론: 숙련되고 자격있는 선생님의 실강 actual class with a trained and certified teacher • 재반론: 양질의 강의를 배포하다 distribute quality lessons • 전망: 커다란 도움 great aid
패러 프레이징	I don't believe the traditional classroom will ever completely disappear, but it will have a diminished role. 저는 전통적 교실이 완전히 사라질 것이라고 생각하지 않지만, 전통적 교실의 역할은 줄어들 것입니다.
어휘	certified 자격있는 schooling 학교 교육 distribute 배포하다, 분배하다 simplify 간소화하다 complexity 복잡함 administer 관리하다, 운영하다 aid 지원, 도움, 보조

SPEAKING

문법	• **동명사 주어**: **attending** an actual class with a trained and certified teacher 숙련되고 자격있는 선생님이 가르치는 실제 강의를 참석하는 것이 • **be of 추상명사 구문**: **be of** great **aid** 커다란 도움이 되다 추가 '유용하다, 도움이 되다'란 표현으로 be of aid 대신 다음의 표현들도 사용 가능하다. = be of help = be of use = be of assistance = be of service

모범 답변	I don't believe the traditional classroom will ever completely disappear, but it will have a diminished role as online education improves and becomes more accessible. I'm sure attending an actual class with a trained and certified teacher will always be a part of schooling. However, advances in online education will help distribute quality lessons to students all around the world, especially in poor or remote regions. I think this will simplify some of the complexities of providing quality education fairly and, if administered properly, be of great aid to the traditional classroom.	저는 전통적 교실이 완전히 사라질 것이라고 생각하지 않지만, 온라인 교육이 향상되고 더 접근성이 좋아지면서 전통적 교실의 역할은 줄어들 것입니다. 숙련되고 자격있는 선생님이 가르치는 실제 강의를 참석하는 것이 학교 교육의 일부로 항상 남아 있을 것이라고 생각합니다. 하지만 온라인 교육의 진보는 전 세계, 특히 가난하고 외딴 지역의 학생들에게 수준 높은 강의를 전파하는데 도움이 될 것입니다. 저는 이 방식이 양질의 교육을 제공하는 데 있어서 복잡한 문제들을 간결하게 해주고, 잘 관리되면, 전통적 교실에 커다란 도움이 될 것입니다.

Q3 What can children learn from playing sports?
아이들은 스포츠를 통해 무엇을 배울 수 있나요?

브레인 스토밍	• 대답: 여러 가지 소중한 교훈 a variety of valuable lessons • 구체적 설명 1: 팀워크 teamwork └ 부연: 협력하고 소통하는 방법 how to collaborate and communicate • 구체적 설명 2: 노력 hard work └ 부연: 포기하지 않기 not to give up • 추가: 학업에도 도움 help academically as well
패러 프레이징	Children can learn a variety of valuable lessons from playing sports. 아이들은 스포츠를 통해 여러 가지 소중한 교훈을 배울 수 있습니다.
어휘	**a variety of** 여러 가지 **valuable** 소중한 **figure out** 터득하다 **collaborate** 협력하다 **communicate** 소통하다 **peer** 동료 **hard work** 노력 **master** 숙달하다 **take** 필요하다 **give up** 포기하다 **on the field** 운동장에서 **academically** 학업적으로 **as well** 역시 **work on** 착수하다, 애쓰다 **tough subject** 어려운 과목 **make a big difference** 큰 차이를 만들다
문법	• **목적격 관계대명사 생략**: One of the most important lessons **(which)** they can learn 아이들이 배울 수 있는 가장 중요한 교훈 중 하나는 • **동명사 주어: Mastering** a skill in sports 스포츠 기술을 숙달하는 것은 • **세미콜론(;)**: 절과 절을 연결하는 접속사 역할 • **목적격 관계대명사 생략**: the lessons **(which)** they learn from sports 아이들이 스포츠에서 배우는 교훈들은

모범 답변	Children can learn a variety of valuable lessons from playing sports. One of the most important lessons they can learn is teamwork. When playing team sports, like football or basketball, they figure out how to collaborate and communicate with their peers. Sports also show children the importance of hard work. Mastering a skill in sports takes a lot of practice, so they learn not to give up. These lessons aren't just useful on the field; they help academically as well. Whether they're working on group projects or studying a tough subject, the lessons they learn from sports can make a big difference.	아이들은 스포츠를 통해 여러 가지 소중한 교훈을 배울 수 있습니다. 아이들이 배울 수 있는 가장 중요한 교훈 중 하나는 팀워크입니다. 축구나 농구와 같은 팀 스포츠를 할 때 아이들은 동료들과 협력하고 소통하는 방법을 터득하게 됩니다. 또한 스포츠는 아이들에게 노력의 중요성을 보여줍니다. 스포츠 기술을 숙달하는 것은 많은 연습이 필요하기 때문에, 아이들은 포기하지 않는 법을 배우게 됩니다. 이러한 교훈은 운동장에서만 유용한 것이 아니라 학업에도 도움이 됩니다. 그룹 프로젝트를 수행하든 어려운 과목을 공부하든 아이들이 스포츠에서 배우는 교훈들은 큰 차이를 만들 수 있습니다.

Q4 Do you think people today are busier than before?
당신은 요즘 사람들이 예전보다 더 바쁘다고 생각하나요?

브레인 스토밍	• 대답: 요즘 사람들이 더 바쁨 people nowadays are busier • 예시: 평균적인 사무직 직장인 average office worker └ 이유 1: 9시부터 5시까지를 넘어 근무 work beyond the traditional 9 to 5 └ 이유 2: 처리해야 할 집안일 household chores to tend to └ 이유 3: 일과 개인 생활의 경계가 모호 blur the line between work and personal life	
패러 프레이징	I believe people nowadays are busier compared to the past. 저는 요즘 사람들이 과거에 비해 더 바쁘다고 생각합니다.	
어휘	**compared to** ~에 비해 **average** 평균적인 **office worker** 사무직 직장인 **take up** ~을 차지하다 **extend** 연장하다, 확대하다 **beyond** ~을 넘어 **traditional** 전통적인, 기존의 **9 to 5** 9시-5시 근무, 정시근무 **household chores** 집안일 **tend to** 처리하다, 돌보다 **plus** 또한, 추가적으로 **improve** 향상시키다 **most likely** (가능성 높게) 아마도 **worker productivity** 근로자 생산성 **stay connected** 연결 상태를 유지하다 **all the time** 항상 **blur** 모호하게 만들다, 흐릿하게 만들다 **be expected to** ~하는 것으로 기대되다 **available** 시간이 되는, 이용할 수 있는 **outside of** ~ 외에 **regular working hours** 정규 근무 시간	
문법	• **주격 관계대명사**: hours **that** often extend 종종 연장한 시간들(hours를 수식) • **동명사 주어: staying connected** all the time has blurred ~ 항상 연결 상태를 유지하는 것은	
모범 답변	I believe people nowadays are busier compared to the past. When we look at the average office worker, most of their day is taken up by work-related activities. They wake up, get ready for work and then work for hours that often extend beyond the traditional 9 to 5. When they get home, there are household chores to tend to. Plus, while technology has most likely improved worker productivity, staying connected all the time has blurred the line between work and personal life. Workers are expected to check emails on their phones and be available outside of regular working hours.	저는 요즘 사람들이 과거에 비해 더 바쁘다고 생각합니다. 평균적인 사무직 직장인을 보면, 하루의 대부분을 업무와 관련된 활동으로 보내게 됩니다. 아침에 일어나 출근 준비를 한 다음, 기존의 9시부터 5시까지를 넘어서 종종 연장한 시간 동안 일을 합니다. 집에 돌아오면 처리해야 할 집안일이 있습니다. 또한 기술이 아마도 근로자의 생산성을 향상시켜 왔지만, 항상 연결 상태를 유지하는 것은 일과 개인 생활의 경계를 모호하게 만들었습니다. 직장인들은 휴대폰으로 이메일을 확인하고 정규 근무 시간 외에도 업무를 볼 수 있어야 합니다.

SPEAKING

▪ 파트 3

Q1 What are the advantages and disadvantages of eating at a restaurant?
식당에서 식사할 때의 장점과 단점은 무엇인가요?

브레인 스토밍	• 장점 1: 편한 convenient • 장점 2: 사교에 좋은 great for socialising • 단점 1: 비싼 expensive • 단점 2: 건강에 해 health hazard	
패러 프레이징	There are both benefits and drawbacks to dining at a restaurant. 아이들은 스포츠를 통해 여러 가지 소중한 교훈을 배울 수 있습니다.	
어휘	**dine** 식사하다 **for one thing** 우선 **socialise** 사교적으로 하다 **fun** 재미있는 (cf. funny 웃긴) **venue** 장소 **on the flip side** 반면에 **prepare** 준비하다 **allergy** 알레르기 **dietary restriction** 식단 제한 **health hazard** 건강에 해	
문법	• **동명사 주어: eating at a restaurant** is ~ 식당에서 식사하는 것은 ~ 이다 • **세미콜론(;)**: 절과 절을 연결하는 접속사 역할 • **to부정사 형용사적 용법**: a nice way **to spend** time ~ 시간을 보낼 좋은 방법 • **동명사 주어: dining out** can be ~ 식사하는 것은 ~ 일 수 있다	
모범 답변	There are both benefits and drawbacks to dining at a restaurant. For one thing, eating at a restaurant is convenient and great for socialising. You don't have to cook; you can just walk in, sit down and enjoy your meal. It's also a nice way to spend time with friends and family, and restaurants can be fun venues for parties, too. On the flip side, dining out can be expensive compared to cooking at home. Also, you can't always know for certain how your food was prepared at a restaurant. For people with allergies or dietary restrictions, restaurant food might even be a health hazard.	식당에서 식사하는 것에 이점과 단점이 모두 있습니다. 우선, 식당에서 식사하는 것은 편리하고 사교에 좋습니다. 요리를 할 필요 없이 그냥 들어가 앉아서 식사를 즐기면 되니까요. 또한 친구나 가족과 함께 시간을 보낼 좋은 방법이며, 레스토랑은 파티를 위한 재미있는 장소가 될 수도 있습니다. 반면에, 외식은 집에서 요리하는 것에 비해 비용이 많이 들 수 있습니다. 또한, 식당에서 음식이 어떻게 준비되었는지 항상 확실하게 알 수 있는 것은 아닙니다. 알레르기가 있거나 식단 제한이 있는 사람에게는 식당 음식이 건강에 해가 될 수도 있습니다.

Q2 How do you think the way we eat will change in the future?
당신은 앞으로 우리가 먹는 방식이 어떻게 바뀔 것이라고 생각하나요?

브레인 스토밍	• 대답: 재료에 대해 더 많이 의식하게 됨 become more conscious about the ingredients • 이유 1: 건강하고 지속 가능한 식단 트렌드 a trend of a healthy and sustainable diet ㄴ 부연: 요즘 방부제와 화학 물질 these days, preservatives and chemicals • 이유 2: 채식과 비건 식단을 따름 follow a vegetarian and vegan diet ㄴ 부연: 더 많은 식물성 대체 식품 more plant-based alternatives
패러 프레이징	In the future, I think people will become ~ that go into their food. 미래에는 사람들이 음식에 들어가는 ~하게 될 것이라고 생각합니다.

어휘	conscious 의식하는 ingredient 재료 sustainable 지속 가능한 considering ~을 고려해 볼 때 preservative 방부제 questionable 의심스러운 chemicals 화학 물질 call for ~을 요구하다 over time 시간이 갈수록 vegetarian 채식주의자 vegan (우유, 달걀도 먹지 않는) 채식주의자 plant-based 식물성의 alternative 대체, 대안
문법	• **주격 관계대명사**: the ingredients **that** go into their food 그들의 음식에 들어가는 재료(ingredients를 수식) • **주격 관계대명사**: chemicals **that** are found in our food 우리의 음식에서 발견되는 화학 물질들(chemicals를 수식) • **전치사구**: 전치사(Considering)+명사(all the preservatives and questionable chemicals) • **전치사구**: 전치사(With)+명사(the increasing number of people) • **주격 관계대명사**: people **who** follow a vegetarian or vegan diet 채식이나 비건 식단을 따르는 사람들 (people을 수식)
모범 답변	In the future, I think people will become more conscious about the ingredients that go into their food. There's no doubt that a healthy and sustainable diet is already a trend among most modern-day consumers. Considering all the preservatives and questionable chemicals that are found in our food these days, I think people will probably start to call for cleaner products over time. In addition, with the increasing number of people who follow a vegetarian or vegan diet, I expect that more plant-based alternatives will be developed over time, too. | 미래에는 사람들이 음식에 들어가는 재료에 대해 더 많이 의식하게 될 것이라고 생각합니다. 건강하고 지속 가능한 식단이 이미 대부분의 현대 소비자들 사이에서 트렌드라는 것은 의심할 여지가 없습니다. 요즘 식품에서 발견되는 모든 방부제와 의심스러운 화학 물질을 고려할 때, 사람들은 시간이 갈수록 더 깨끗한 제품을 요구하기 시작할 것이라고 생각합니다. 또한 채식이나 비건 식단을 따르는 사람들이 늘어나면서, 저는 더 많은 식물성 대체 식품이 시간이 갈수록 개발될 것으로 예상합니다.

SPEAKING

Q3 How has technology changed the society we live in now?

기술은 현재 우리가 살고 있는 사회를 어떻게 변화시켜 왔나요?

브레인 스토밍	• 대답: 우리가 서로 소통하는 방식에 있어서 in terms of how we can communicate with each other • 구체적 설명 1: 사람들이 즉각적으로 서로 소통하고 정보를 공유 interact and share information with each other instantaneously • 구체적 설명 2: 화상 전화, 실시간 외국어 번역, 가상 현실 환경에서 협업 make a video call, translate foreign languages in real time and collaborate in a virtual reality setting • 마무리: 인간의 커뮤니케이션은 완전히 사이버 공간으로 옮겨감 human communication has completely shifted toward cyberspace
패러 프레이징	Technology has changed our society 기술은 우리 사회를 변화시켰습니다.
어휘	in terms of ~한 점에서, ~에 있어서 communicate 소통하다 thanks to ~ 덕분에 all over the world 전 세계 interact 소통하다 instantaneously 즉각적으로 advanced 선진의, 진보된 video call 화상통화 translate 번역하다 in real time 실시간으로 collaborate 협업하다 virtual reality setting 가상 현실 환경 normalise 일상화하다 completely 완전히 shift 이동하다, 옮기다 cyberspace 사이버 공간 for better or worse 좋든 싫든

문법	• **how 명사절**: how+주어(we)+동사(can communicate) 우리가 소통하는 방식 • **주격 관계대명사**: advanced technology **that** allows us 우리가 ~하도록 하는 선진 기술 • **5형식**: allow(5형식동사)+us(목적어)+to make a voice call(목적보어), translate~(목적보어) and collaborate~(목적보어) 우리가 화상 전화를 하고 번역을 하고 협업할 수 있도록 한다 • **동명사 주어**: **building** online relationships has become ~ 온라인으로 관계를 구축하는 것이 ~
모범 답변	Technology has changed our society in terms of how we can communicate with each other. Thanks to the internet, people from all over the world can interact and share information with each other instantaneously. Nowadays, there's advanced technology that allows us to make a video call, translate foreign languages in real time and collaborate in a virtual reality setting, such as the metaverse. So, building online relationships has become easier and more normalised. I believe that human communication has completely shifted toward cyberspace these days, for better or worse. 기술은 우리가 서로 소통하는 방식에 있어서 우리 사회를 변화시켰습니다. 인터넷 덕분에 전 세계 사람들이 즉각적으로 서로 소통하고 정보를 공유할 수 있게 되었습니다. 오늘날에는 화상 전화, 실시간 외국어 번역, 메타버스와 같은 가상 현실 환경에서 협업할 수 있는 선진 기술이 있습니다. 따라서 온라인으로 관계를 구축하는 것이 더욱 쉽고 일상화되었습니다. 좋든 싫든 오늘날 인간의 커뮤니케이션은 완전히 사이버 공간으로 옮겨갔다고 생각합니다.

Q4 Does technology distract people?

기술이 사람들의 주의를 산만하게 하나요?

브레인 스토밍	• 대답: 사용자에 따라 다르다 depends on the user • 구체적 설명 1: 생산적인 방식으로 사용 used in a productive way └ 부연: 편리하고 유용한 도구 a convenient and helpful tool • 구체적 설명 2: 절제가 중요 moderation is key └ 부연: 인터넷에서 보는 모든 것을 믿어서는 안 되며, 규칙적으로 휴식을 취하기 shouldn't believe everything we see on the internet, taking breaks regularly • 구체적 설명 3: 과도하게 사용 used excessively └ 부연: 주의를 산만하게 함 become a distraction
패러 프레이징	whether technology is distracting or not depends on the user. 기술이 주의를 산만하게 하는지 아닌지는 사용자에 따라 다르다
어휘	**distract** (주의를) 산만하게 하다 **depend on** ~에 따라 다르다, ~에 달려 있다 **productive** 생산적인 **when it comes to** ~에 관하여 **efficiently** 효율적으로 **effectively** 효과적으로 **tool** 도구 **moderation** 절제 **key** 중요한 **take breaks** 휴식을 취하다 **regularly** 규칙적으로 **excessively** 과도하게 **definitely** 분명히 **distraction** (주의를) 산만하게 하는 것
문법	• **whether 명사절**: whether+주어(technology)+동사(is distracting) 기술이 주의를 산만하게 하는지 • **접속사 + 분사구문**: 접속사(If)+분사구문(used in a productive way) 생산적인 방식으로 사용된다면 • **When it comes to + 명사**: ~에 관하여 • **5형식**: help(5형식동사)+us(목적어)+work(목적보어) 우리가 일하는 것을 돕는다 • **목적격 관계대명사 생략**: everything **(that) we see** 우리가 보는 모든 것 (선행사가 everything인 경우 관계대명사는 which가 아닌 that이 사용됨) • **동명사 주어: taking breaks regularly** is ~ 규칙적으로 휴식을 취하는 것이

모범 답변	I believe whether technology is distracting or not depends on the user. If used in a productive way, I don't think technology is distracting. When it comes to sharing information or learning at school, technology can help us work more efficiently and effectively. It can be used as a convenient and helpful tool, but of course, moderation is key. We shouldn't believe everything we see on the internet, and for those who are always connected to their phones or computers, taking breaks regularly is important. If used excessively, technology will definitely become a distraction.	저는 기술이 주의를 산만하게 하는지 아닌지는 사용자에 따라 다르다고 생각합니다. 생산적인 방식으로 사용된다면, 기술은 주의를 산만하게 하지 않다고 생각합니다. 학교에서 정보를 공유하거나 학습할 때 기술은 우리가 더 효율적이고 효과적으로 일할 수 있도록 도와줄 수 있습니다. 편리하고 유용한 도구로 사용할 수 있지만 물론 절제가 중요합니다. 인터넷에서 보는 모든 것을 믿어서는 안 되며, 항상 휴대폰이나 컴퓨터에 연결되어 있는 사람들에게는 규칙적으로 휴식을 취하는 것이 중요합니다. 과도하게 사용하면 기술은 분명 주의를 산만하게 할 것입니다.

SPEAKING

ACTUAL TEST ANSWERS

Actual Test 1 IELTS on paper

- Writing [Academic]
- Writing [General Training]
- Reading [Academic]
- Reading [General Training]
- Listening [Academic / General Training]
- Speaking [Academic / General Training]

Actual Test 2 IELTS on computer

- Listening [Academic / General Training]
- Reading [Academic]
- Reading [General Training]
- Writing [Academic]
- Writing [General Training]
- Speaking [Academic / General Training]

ACTUAL TEST 1 IELTS on paper

Test 1 WRITING [Academic]

▪ 태스크 1

출제 포인트 **난이도: 중하**

두 개의 특정 연도 간 비율 변화와 함께 두 대상 간에도 비교가 필요한 문제로 총 4개의 파이 차트가 등장

기출 2024년 2월 - 두 국가의 남녀별 산업 종사 비율
2019년 2월 - 한 국가의 1985년과 2003년 에너지 원천 비율
2017년 1월 - 4개 국가의 전기 생산에 들어가는 원천 자원 비율

The pie charts below show the electricity generation by source in China and Spain in 2005 and 2015.
아래 파이 차트는 2005년과 2015년에 중국과 스페인에서 원천 자원에 따른 전기 생산을 보여준다.

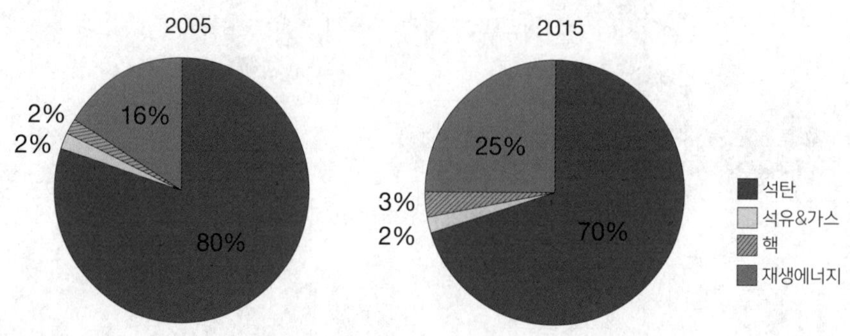

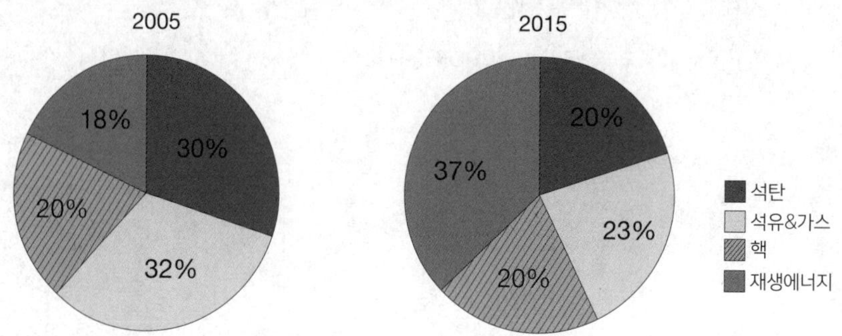

The charts display the means used to produce electrical power in China and Spain in 2005 and 2015. It is evident that China relied more heavily on coal than Spain for its energy needs, and both countries introduced more renewable sources of energy between 2005 and 2015. In China, coal made up the vast majority of China's sources for electricity, comprising 80% in 2005, which decreased moderately to 70% in 2015. In contrast, the amount of electricity generated from renewable sources rose from 16% to 25% between the two years. Oil, gas and nuclear energy combined accounted for less than 5% in both years, showing little to no change over the period. Spain, on the other hand, featured much more balance in its proportions. Notably, the change in percentage for coal mirrored China's trend: electricity sourced from coal fell by 10%. However, renewable energy saw a more substantial rise, increasing by 19%. Electricity generation by oil and gas declined from 32% to 23% over the decade. Meanwhile, nuclear power remained constant at 20%, showing no change. (176 words)	이 차트들은 2005년과 2015년에 중국과 스페인에서 전력을 생산하는 데 사용된 방법들을 보여준다. 중국은 스페인보다 에너지 수요를 석탄에 더 많이 의존하고 있으며, 2005년과 2015년 사이에 두 나라 모두 더 많은 재생에너지원을 도입한 것이 분명하다. 중국의 경우, 2005년에는 석탄이 80%로 중국 전력 공급원의 대부분을 차지했지만, 2015년에는 70%로 다소 감소했다. 반면, 재생에너지원에서 생산된 전기의 양은 2년 사이에 16%에서 25%로 증가했다. 석유, 가스, 원자력을 합친 전력은 두 해 모두 5% 미만을 차지해 이 기간 동안 거의 변화가 없었다. 반면, 스페인은 훨씬 더 균형 잡힌 비율을 보였다. 눈에 띄는 점으로, 석탄과 재생에너지의 비율 변화는 중국의 추세를 반영하여 석탄에서 공급되는 전기는 10% 감소하였다. 하지만, 재생에너지는 19% 증가하여 더 큰 폭의 증가세를 보였다. 석유와 가스에 의한 전력 생산은 10년 동안 32%에서 23%로 감소했다. 한편, 원자력은 20%를 유지하며 변동이 없었다.

I Vocabulary & Expressions I

coal 석탄 renewable 재생 가능한 make up 구성하다, 이루다 comprise 구성하다, 차지하다 moderately 다소 generate 발생시키다, 만들어 내다 combined 합친 account for 차지하다 feature 특징을 보이다 proportion 비율 mirror 반영하다, 비추다 generation 생산 constant 변함없는

▪ 태스크 2

출제 포인트 **난이도: 중상**

학교와 부모의 아이 교육 책임은 빈출 토픽으로 이에 대해 충분한 브레인스토밍이 요구됨

기출 2019년 2월 - 학교가 학생들이 자신의 건강을 돌보는 것에 대해 충분히 교육시키는지
2018년 11월 - 부모가 자녀들의 사회적 교육을 담당해야 하는지 아니면 학교의 몫인지

Once children start school, teachers have more influence on their intellectual and social development than parents.
일단 아이들이 학교에 입학하면, 교사들이 아이들의 지적 그리고 사회적 발달에 부모들보다 더 영향이 있다.

To what extent do you agree or disagree with this opinion?
당신은 이 의견에 어느 정도 긍정 또는 부정하는가?

Some people believe that schoolteachers have more influence than parents when it comes to the intellectual and social development of children. Although I think that teachers play a crucial role in a child's development, I disagree that their contribution is as influential or significant as that of a child's parents.

Teachers contribute to the development of children in many important ways. Teachers are tasked with educating children in areas such as mathematics and language, but their impact is not limited to intellectual development only. A good teacher will also instil positive values and habits in their students, such as a strong work ethic and the importance of both teamwork and using one's own initiative to complete tasks. For example, my teacher always emphasised how important it is to work together with classmates on group projects, and I still use what I learned from her to communicate well with others to this day.

With that said, I think that parents have an even greater impact on the development of their children. They teach them how to do countless invaluable things in everyday life, such as crossing the road safely, eating healthily, maintaining good personal hygiene and being polite and well-mannered at all times. In my own experience, I feel that my parents brought me up exceptionally well, and the values they instilled in me at home have helped me to succeed both in my social and academic lives. I will always be grateful to my parents for teaching me the true value of working hard and achieving my goals.

In the end, teachers and parents both play a significant role in the development of children. However, I feel that parents have more of an impact on their development because they teach their children a vast number of invaluable life lessons.

(299 words)

어떤 사람들은 아이들의 지적, 사회적 발달 관련하여 교사들이 부모들보다 더 영향을 준다고 믿는다. 나는 비록 교사들이 아이들 발달에서 중요한 역할을 한다고 생각하지만, 그들의 기여가 아이 부모들의 그것만큼 영향력이 있거나 중요하다는 것에는 동의하지 않는다.

교사들은 많은 중요한 방법으로 아이들의 발달에 기여한다. 교사들이 아이들을 수학과 언어 같은 분야에서 아이들을 가르치는 업무를 수행하지만, 그들의 영향은 지적 발달에만 제한되지 않는다. 훌륭한 선생님은 또한 굳건한 노동관과 과제들을 끝내기 위한 팀워크와 개인의 자주성의 중요함 같은 긍정적인 가치들과 습관들을 학생들에게 심어줄 것이다. 예를 들어, 나의 선생님은 항상 그룹 프로젝트에서 급우들과 함께 작업하는 것이 얼마나 중요한지를 강조했고, 나는 여전히 그녀로부터 배운 것을 다른 사람들과 잘 의사소통하기 위해 지금까지 사용한다.

그렇지만, 나는 부모들이 아이들 발달에 훨씬 더 큰 영향을 갖는다고 생각한다. 부모들은 안전하게 길을 건너고, 건강하게 식사하고, 개인 위생을 유지하고, 항상 친절하고 매너 있게 하는 것과 같이 일상에서 셀 수 없이 많은 매우 중요한 것들을 어떻게 해야 하는지 아이들에게 가르쳐 준다. 내 경험으로 나의 부모님이 나를 매우 잘 기르셨고, 집에서 그분들이 내게 심어준 가치들은 사회적인 삶과 학문적 삶, 둘 다에서 성공하도록 도와주었다. 근면과 목표 달성의 진정한 가치를 내게 알려주셔서 나는 항상 부모님께 감사할 것이다.

결국, 교사와 부모 모두 아이 발달에 중요한 역할을 한다. 하지만, 나는 부모들이 그들의 자녀들에게 폭넓은 삶의 중대한 교훈들을 가르쳐주기에 부모들이 아이들 발달에 더 영향이 있다고 생각한다.

| Vocabulary & Expressions |

development 발달, 성장 contribute to ~에 기여하다 be tasked with ~의 임무를 갖다 instil 심어주다(미국식 instill) work ethic 노동관, 직업 의식 initiative 자주성, 계획 complete 끝마치다 emphasise 강조하다 with that said 그렇지만 countless 셀 수 없이 많은 invaluable 매우 중요한 hygiene 위생 well-mannered 예절 바른 at all times 항상 bring up 양육하다 exceptionally 매우 grateful 감사하는 in the end 결국 significant 중대한, 상당한

▪ 태스크 1

출제 포인트 난이도: 중하

전형적인 Semi-formal letter 문제들 중 하나로 각 포인트를 놓치지 말고 모두 다 기술해야 됨

기출 2017년 12월 - 그만 두는 상사를 위해 직장 동료와 선물 구매

You have heard that your supervisor is retiring from his job. You are planning to buy a present for him and your colleague would like to get a gift with you.
당신은 당신의 상관이 은퇴한다는 것을 들었다. 당신은 그에게 선물을 사줄 계획이고 당신의 동료는 당신과 함께 선물을 사길 원한다.

Write a letter to your colleague. In your letter
당신의 동료에게 편지를 써라. 편지에는

- describe your feelings about your supervisor retiring from his job
  상관의 은퇴에 대한 당신의 감정을 기술한다
- say what item you plan to buy for the supervisor
  상관에게 어떤 물품을 사줄 계획인지 말한다
- suggest when you would meet your colleague to buy a present
  선물을 사기 위해 동료를 언제 만날지 제안한다

Dear Jesse,

Yesterday at lunch, I mentioned that I wanted to buy a gift for Mr Yeager since he's retiring. You said that you'd like to get him something together, so let's figure out what we should do.

I'm still shocked that Mr Yeager will retire next month. I had no idea he has been at the company for more than 25 years. He looks so young! I'll be sad to see him go, too. His cheerful and relaxed attitude has always kept the mood in the office light and friendly.

So, that's why we should get him something special. As everyone knows, Mr Yeager is an avid golf enthusiast, and after retiring, he'll spend his free time at the golf club. Therefore, some new golfing attire would be the perfect gift, such as a new hat or pair of gloves that he could wear while on the course.

There's a well-known athletic clothing store downtown on Putnam Street. Let's meet there on Saturday afternoon, and then we can pick something out for Mr Yeager together.

제시에게,

어제 점심에, 내가 이에거 씨가 은퇴하기에 그에게 선물을 사드리길 원한다고 말했지. 네가 그에게 무언가를 함께 사길 원한다고 말했으니, 우리가 무엇을 해야될지 생각해보자.

나는 여전히 이에거 씨가 다음달에 은퇴한다는 것에 충격이야. 난 그가 25년 이상을 이 회사에서 일해왔다는 것을 전혀 몰랐어. 그는 너무 어려 보이잖아! 나는 또한 그가 떠나는 것을 보면 슬플 거야. 그의 쾌활하고 편안한 태도가 항상 사무실 분위기를 가볍고 친근하게 해줬으니까.

그래서 우리는 그에게 무언가 특별한 것을 드려야 해. 모두가 알다시피, 이에거 씨는 열렬한 골프광이니, 은퇴 후에 그는 자유시간을 골프 클럽에서 보낼거야. 그러므로, 그가 필드에 있는 동안 착용할 새 모자나 장갑과 같은 새 골프 의류가 완벽한 선물이 될 것 같아.

시내 퍼트넘 가에 잘 알려진 운동 의류점이 있어. 토요일 오후에 그곳에서 만나서 함께 이에거 씨를 위한 무언가를 골라보자.

Best wishes, Anne (179 words)	앤 보냄

I Vocabulary & Expressions I

figure out 생각해내다 cheerful 쾌활한 attitude 태도 avid 열렬한 enthusiast 광, 열렬한 지지자 attire 의류

▪ 태스크 2

출제 포인트 **난이도: 중상**

최근 들어 소셜 네트워킹 사이트의 피해 문제가 빈출되므로 이에 대한 충분한 브레인스토밍이 이루어져야 됨

기출 2019년 1월 - 페이스북같은 소셜네트워킹 사이트가 유해한지
2018년 12월 - 온라인 미팅 또는 강의에 장단점

Social media sites have negatively impacted both individuals and society.
SNS는 개인과 사회 모두에 부정적인 영향을 준다.

To what extent do you agree or disagree with this statement?
당신은 이 진술에 어느 정도 긍정 또는 부정하는가?

These days, social networking sites play a major role in the lives of billions of people worldwide, but many people think such sites harm people and society at large. I strongly agree with this opinion, as I think the negative effects of these social media platforms far outweigh any positive aspects.	요즘, SNS(친구관계를 넓힐 것을 목적으로 개설된 커뮤니티형 웹사이트)가 전 세계 수십억 사람들의 삶에서 중요한 역할을 하고 있지만, 많은 사람들은 이러한 사이트들이 사람들과 사회에 전반적으로 해를 끼친다고 생각한다. 나는 이러한 소셜 미디어 플랫폼의 부정적 영향이 긍정적 측면보다 훨씬 더 크다고 생각하기에, 이 의견에 강하게 동의한다.
First of all, it is worth noting that sites such as Facebook and Twitter do have some benefits. In our modern society, many people have hectic schedules, and it is more common for people these days to go overseas for work or travel. Social networking sites allow users to maintain contact with their friends and family through instant messaging and the sharing of photographs, no matter where they are in the world. Another positive aspect is that these sites provide an inexpensive form of entertainment, as they include news stories, comedic clips, inspirational messages and more.	먼저, 페이스북과 트위터 같은 사이트들에 이점들이 있음을 주목할 가치가 있다. 우리 현대 사회에서, 많은 사람들은 바쁜 일정이 있으며 일이나 여행을 위해 해외에 가는 것이 더 보편화 되어있다. SNS는 사용자들이 세계 어디에 있든지 상관 없이, 즉각적인 메시지 교환과 사진 교환을 통해 그들의 친구들, 가족들과 연락이 유지되도록 한다. 또다른 긍정적인 면은 이러한 사이트들이 뉴스거리, 재밌는 영상, 영감을 주는 메시지 등등, 저렴한 형태의 오락거리를 제공한다는 점이다.
In the long run, however, I believe that these sites have a detrimental effect on people and the society in which we live. To begin with, addiction to social media has become a major problem. Some people waste several hours on social networking sites every day, and it has an adverse effect on	장기적으로, 하지만, 나는 이러한 사이트들이 사람들과 우리가 사는 사회에 해로운 영향을 준다고 믿는다. 우선, 소셜 미디어 중독이 중요한 문제가 되고 있다. 어떤 사람들은 매일 SNS에 수시간을 허비하면서, 그들의 학업과 업무 성과에 부정적인 영향을 준다. 게다가, 이러한 소셜 미디어 중독은 개인 관계 와해의 원인이 된다. 예를 들어,

their studies or job performance. In addition, this addiction to social media contributes to the breakdown of personal relationships. For example, my older brother spent so much time online that his real-life friendships deteriorated, and his social skills have also declined as a result.

Overall, while the benefits of social networking sites are obvious, the detrimental effects they have on human relationships are too serious to ignore. Therefore, I think these sites are harmful not only to individuals but also to society as a whole.

(285 words)

나의 형은 너무 많은 시간을 온라인에 쏟아서 현실 친구들과 관계가 악화되었고, 결과적으로 현실 사회 능력 또한 감퇴되었다.

전반적으로 SNS의 혜택들이 분명히 있지만, 그것들이 인간 관계에 갖는 해로운 영향들이 무시하기에는 너무 심각하다. 그러므로, 나는 이러한 사이트들이 개인뿐만 아니라 사회 전체에도 해롭다고 생각한다.

I Vocabulary & Expressions I

at large 전반적으로, 일반적으로 A outweigh B A가 B보다 더 중대하다 be worth -ing ~할 가치가 있다 note 주목하다 hectic 매우 바쁜 clip 짧은 영상 inspirational 감명을 주는 in the long run 장기적으로 detrimental 해로운 for a start 우선 adverse 부정적인 addiction 중독 contribute to ~에 기여하다 breakdown 와해, 붕괴 deteriorate 악화되다 decline 감퇴하다 as a result 결과적으로 obvious 분명한 ignore 무시하다 society as a whole 사회 전체

Test 1 READING [Academic]

1. FALSE	2. TRUE	3. NOT GIVEN	4. FALSE	5. TRUE
6. FALSE	7. TRUE	8. NOT GIVEN	9. railway	10. fire
11. propellers	12. immigrants	13. telecommunication		
14. contaminants	15. acts	16. agricultural	17. funding	18. F
19. B	20. E	21. D	22. E	23. F
24. E	25. B	26. G		
27. C	28. D	29. B	30. D	31. C
32. C	33. D	34. B	35. A	36. D
37. B	38. NOT GIVEN	39. TRUE	40. FALSE	

▪ 패시지 1 [문제 1-13]

출제 포인트 **난이도: 중**

엔지니어링이나 과학 기술과 관련된 지문이 자주 출제되고 있는데, 과학 원리보다는 특정 엔지니어링이나 발명품의 역사 혹은 그와 관련된 인물에 대한 이야기가 주로 등장함

기출 2024년 6월 - AI 발달
2024년 5월 - 연의 역사
2019년 10월 - 승강기 역사
2018년 12월 - 레코드 역사
2018년 11월 - 구리와 아연

2011년 1월 - 라디오 발명
2010년 6월 - 이점바드 킹덤 브루넬의 조선 디자인

Isambard Kingdom Brunel: A genius of naval engineering

British engineer Isambard Kingdom Brunel is Q1 typically revered for his accomplishments on land, such as the construction of Britain's Great Western Railway and its numerous tunnels and bridges. However, it is important to remember the impressive naval vessels that Brunel designed during his illustrious career, as his contributions to shipbuilding had a profound impact on steamship technology from the late 1830s to the late 1850s. While completing work on the Q9 railway in 1836, Brunel jested with his colleagues that he would like to extend the railroad all the way to the United States by establishing a transatlantic steamship company. What began as a humorous notion soon manifested in reality when Brunel drafted a design for his first steamship, which he named the *Great Western*. Q2 The design was mocked by some of Brunel's fellow engineers, who proclaimed that the ship was too large for efficient travel. Brunel insisted that, while a vessel's carrying capacity increases as the cube of its dimensions, its water resistance only increases as the square of its dimensions. With this firm belief, Brunel contended that large vessels were more fuel efficient and perfectly adapted to lengthy voyages across oceans.

Q3 Once construction of the *Great Western* was complete, it immediately became the longest ship in the world. Although the general structure of the vessel was constructed with wood, Brunel used iron bolts and bars to reinforce the keel of the ship. It was primarily powered by steam, but the ship also boasted four conventional masts and sails in order to save on fuel required for steam power. Brunel himself missed the *Great Western's* maiden voyage from Bristol to New York on 8 April 1838, having been injured in a fire aboard the ship as the vessel was undergoing its final preparations. The Q10 fire necessitated a delay to the ship's scheduled launch date, which resulted in Q4 the *Great Western* failing to claim the title of the first steam-powered ship to cross the Atlantic. Setting off a full four days before the *Great Western*, the *Sirius* reached America only one day ahead of the *Great Western*, and the vessel had completely run out of fuel. The *Great Western*, on the other hand, reached American shores with a third of its coal supplies unused. The *Great Western* had proven

이점바드 킹덤 브루넬: 천재 조선 공학자

영국의 공학자 이점바드 킹덤 브루넬은 Q1 보통 영국의 그레이트 웨스턴 철도를 비롯한 수많은 터널 및 교량 건축과 같이 육상에서 이룬 업적으로 칭송받고 있다. 하지만, 눈부셨던 활동 기간 중에 브루넬이 고안한 인상적인 선박들을 기억하는 것이 중요한데, 조선 분야에 대한 그의 공헌이 1830년대 후반에서 1850년대 후반까지의 증기선 건조 기술에 엄청난 영향을 미쳤기 때문이다. 1836년에 그레이트 웨스턴 Q9 철도 공사를 완료하면서, 브루넬은 대서양 항로 증기선 회사를 설립해 미국까지 그 철로가 죽 이어지도록 연장시키고 싶다고 동료들과 농담하듯 말했다. 재미있는 생각에서 시작된 이 일은 곧 브루넬이 그레이트 웨스턴이라고 명명한 자신의 첫 증기선에 대한 디자인 초안을 만들면서 현실로 나타나게 되었다. Q2 이 디자인은 브루넬의 동료 공학자 몇몇에 의해 조롱을 당했는데, 그들은 이 배가 효율적인 항해를 하기에 너무 크다는 뜻을 분명히 나타냈다. 브루넬은 배의 적재량이 입방 면적에 따라 증가하는 반면에 물 저항력은 오직 평방 면적에 따라 증가한다고 주장했다. 이 확고한 믿음과 함께, 브루넬은 큰 선박이 더 연료 효율적이며 대양을 가로질러 이동하는 긴 항해에 완벽하게 적합하다고 주장했다.

Q3 그레이트 웨스턴의 건조가 완료되자마자, 곧바로 세계에서 가장 긴 선박이 되었다. 이 선박의 전반적인 구조는 나무를 통해 만들어졌지만, 브루넬은 선박의 용골을 강화하기 위해 철제 볼트와 봉을 사용했다. 주로 증기로 동력을 얻기는 했지만, 이 선박은 또한 증기 동력을 얻는 데 필요한 연료를 절약하기 위해 네 개의 전통적인 돛대와 돛도 지니고 있었다. 브루넬 자신은 이 선박이 마지막 준비 과정을 거치는 동안 선상에서 발생된 화재로 인해 부상을 입으면서 1838년 4월 8일에 브리스틀에서 뉴욕으로 가는 그레이트 웨스턴 호의 첫 항해를 보지 못했다. 이 Q10 화재로 인해 불가피하게 이 선박의 예정된 출항 날짜가 지연되었는데, 이로 인해 Q4 그레이트 웨스턴 호가 대서양을 가로지르는 첫 증기선이라는 타이틀을 얻지 못하는 결과가 초래되었다. 그레이트 웨스턴 호보다 꼬박 4일 먼저 출항한 시리우스 호가 그레이트 웨스턴 호보다 겨우 하루 앞서 미국에 도착했는데, 이 선박은 연료가 완전히 떨어졌다. 반면에 그레이트 웨스턴 호는 석탄 연료의 3분의 1일을 사용하지 않은 채로 미국 해안에 도달했다. 그레이트 웨스턴 호는 브루넬의 주장이 옳았을 뿐만 아니라, 대서양을 가로지르는 증기선 서비스가 상업적으로 실현 가능한 사업이라는 점을 입증해주었다.

not only that Brunel's assertions had been correct, but also that transatlantic steamship service was a commercially viable business. The Great Western Steamboat Company used the *Great Western* in regular service between Bristol and New York from 1838 to 1846. However, the company later filed for bankruptcy after enduring countless financial hardships, and the *Great Western* was eventually scrapped in 1856 after briefly serving as a troop carrier during the Crimean War.

Brunel's second innovation in naval engineering was the *Great Britain*, a steamship launched in the summer of 1843 to significant fanfare, and lauded as a breakthrough in technology. Q5 Having carried out tests aboard the propeller-driven steamship *Archimedes*, Brunel had become certain that Q11 propeller-driven ships were vastly superior to those using paddle wheels. As such, he installed a massive six-bladed propeller to power the 98-meter-long *Great Britain*. To this day, naval engineers consider it to be the first truly modern ship, by virtue of its being constructed by metal and utilizing an engine and Q11 propellers rather than wind, steam, or paddle wheels.

The *Great Britain* experienced problems during its maiden voyage from Liverpool to New York, despite completing the crossing in an impressive time of just over 14 days. For instance, the vessel proved to be unstable in the choppy waters of the North Atlantic, which resulted in seasickness in a large number of passengers. A few years later, in 1846, a navigational error resulting from an unforeseen interaction between the ship's iron hull and its magnetic compass led to Q6 the ship running aground on the coast of Ireland. It took almost one year before the hulking vessel was eventually dragged back into the water and sailed back to its port of origin. In that time, the company operating the ship had folded due to financial issues, and the *Great Britain* was sold, having made only eight Atlantic crossings of the Atlantic. It was later converted into a sailing ship, ferrying Q12 immigrants to Australia for a number of years before finding a permanent home in the UK as a tourist attraction.

It was not until the early 1850s that Brunel put his previous disappointments behind him and turned his attention back to naval engineering. He designed the *Great Eastern* to be capable of non-stop travel between London and Sydney and back, and at nearly 700 feet long and accommodating four thousand passengers, it was the largest ship built until the start of the 20th century. Q7 Tragically, Brunel, who had been suffering from ill health, died due to a stroke just

그레이트 웨스턴 증기선 회사는 1838년부터 1846년까지 브리스틀에서 뉴욕 사이를 오가는 정기 운항 서비스를 제공하는 데 그레이트 웨스턴 호를 활용했다. 하지만, 이 회사는 나중에 수많은 재정적 난관을 견디다 못해 파산 신청을 했으며, 그레이트 웨스턴 호는 크림 전쟁 중에 잠시 병력 수송선으로서 역할을 한 후에 결국 1856년에 폐기되었다.

조선 공학 분야에서 브루넬이 이룬 두 번째 혁신은 그레이트 브리튼 호였는데, 이는 1843년 여름에 아주 화려하게 데뷔해 기술의 획기적인 발전으로 극찬을 받은 증기선이었다. Q5 프로펠러로 움직이는 증기선이었던 아르키메데스 호에 승선해 테스트를 실시한 브루넬은 Q11 프로펠러로 움직이는 선박이 외륜을 활용하는 선박보다 훨씬 더 우수하다는 점에 확신을 갖게 되었다. 그에 따라, 브루넬은 98미터 길이의 그레이트 브리튼 호에 동력을 제공하기 위해 6개의 대형 날개가 달린 프로펠러를 설치했다. 오늘날까지도 조선 공학자들은 이것을 진정으로 현대적인 첫 번째 선박으로 여기고 있는데, 강철로 만들어졌을 뿐만 아니라 바람과 증기, 또는 외륜이 아닌 엔진과 Q11 프로펠러를 활용했기 때문이다.

그레이트 브리튼 호는 14일을 약간 초과하는 인상적인 기간 만에 횡단을 완료했음에도 불구하고 리버풀에서 뉴욕으로 떠나는 첫 항해 중에 문제를 겪었다. 예를 들어, 이 선박은 북대서양의 일렁이는 바닷물에서 안정적이지 못한 것으로 드러났으며, 이로 인해 아주 많은 탑승객들이 뱃멀미를 겪는 결과가 초래되었다. 몇 년이 지난 1846년에, 철제 선체와 자기 나침반 사이에서 예기치 못하게 발생된 상호 영향에 의해 초래된 경로 탐색 오류 문제로 인해 Q6 이 선박이 아일랜드 해안에 좌초되는 일로 이어졌다. 이 거대 선박이 마침내 물로 다시 옮겨져 처음 출발했던 항구로 항해해 되돌아가기까지 거의 1년의 시간이 걸렸다. 그 사이에, 이 배를 운영하던 회사는 재정 문제로 인해 사업을 접었으며, 그레이트 브리튼 호는 매각되었는데, 오직 여덟 차례만 대서양 횡단을 완료했다. 이 배는 나중에 범선으로 개조되어 수년 간 호주로 Q12 이민자들을 운송하는 데 쓰였다가 영국에서 관광 명소로 영구히 자리잡게 되었다.

브루넬이 이전의 실망감을 뒤로 하고 조선 공학 분야로 다시 눈길을 돌리게 된 것은 1850년대 초가 되어서였다. 그는 런던과 시드니를 도중에 쉬지 않고 왕복 여행할 수 있도록 그레이트 이스턴 호를 고안했으며, 거의 700피트의 길이로 4천 명의 승객들을 수용해 20세기 초가 되기 전까지 제작된 가장 큰 선박이었다. Q7 비극적이게도, 좋지 못한 건강으로 고생했던 브루넬은 1859년에 미완성 상태였던 이 배를 점검한지 불과 몇 시간 뒤에 뇌졸중으로 인해 사망했다. 브루넬의 많은 야심 찬 노력에 나타났던 경우와 마찬가지로, 이 배도 Q8 재정적인 문

a few hours after inspecting the unfinished ship in 1859. As was the case with many of Brunel's ambitious endeavors, the ship ran over budget and Q8 behind schedule due to financial and technical problems. After making a handful of successful, though unprofitable voyages, the *Great Eastern* was given a more suitable purpose in the late 1860s when it was used to lay the transatlantic telegraph cable that would enable Q13 telecommunication between Europe and North America.

Although the *Great Eastern* was sometimes described as a 'white elephant' in its day – that is, something whose cost and maintenance outweigh its value or usefulness - it has since been argued that Brunel's vessels were simply decades ahead of their time, and their perceived failure was only a result of the poor economic conditions of the era. Indeed, Brunel's technological innovations paved the way for the construction of massive, propeller-driven, all-metal passenger ships, and he is now rightly recognized as one of the world's most influential and inspiring engineers.

제와 기술적인 문제들로 인해 예산을 초과하고 일정에 뒤처졌었다. 성공적이었지만 수익은 없었던 소수의 항해 끝에, 그레이트 이스턴 호에 1860년대 후반에 더 적합한 용도가 주어졌는데, 당시에 유럽과 북미 지역 사이의 Q13 통신을 가능하게 했던 대서양 횡단 전신 케이블을 설치하는 데 이용되었다.

비록 그레이트 이스턴 호가 당시에 때때로 '하얀 코끼리'로 묘사되기는 했지만(말하자면, 비용과 유지 관리가 가치나 유용함을 넘어서는 것), 브루넬의 선박들은 그야말로 10년은 앞서 간 것들이었으며, 사람들에게 인식된 실패는 그저 그 시대의 좋지 못했던 경제 상황에 따른 결과였을 뿐이라는 주장이 그 이후로 제기되어 왔다. 실제로, 브루넬의 기술적인 혁신은 거대하고 프로펠러로 움직이면서 전체가 금속으로 된 여객선 건조의 기틀을 마련해 주었으며, 그는 현재 세계에서 가장 영향력 있고 영감을 주는 엔지니어들 중의 한 사람으로 제대로 인정받고 있다.

| Vocabulary & Expressions |

naval engineering 조선 공학 be revered for ~로 칭송받다 accomplishment 업적, 성취 illustrious 빛나는, 눈부신 contribution 공헌, 기여 profound 엄청난 jest 농담하다 extend ~을 연장하다, 확장하다 transatlantic 대서양 횡단의 notion 생각, 개념 manifest in reality 현실로 나타나다 mock 조롱하다 proclaim 분명히 나타내다 carrying capacity 적재량, 수용량 cube of one's dimensions 입방 면적 resistance 저항(력) square of one's dimensions 평방 면적 contend 주장하다 fuel efficient 연료 효율적인 adapted to ~에 적합한 voyage 항해, 여행 structure 구조(물) reinforce ~을 강화하다 keel 용골(선박 바닥 중앙 재목) conventional 전통적인 mast 돛대 maiden 최초의 injured 부상 당한 undergo ~을 겪다 necessitate ~을 필요하게 만들다 result in ~의 결과가 초래되다 cross ~을 가로지르다 set off 출발하다 run out of ~가 다 떨어지다 with A p.p. A가 ~된 채로 coal supplies 석탄 연료 공급 assertion 주장 commercially 상업적으로 viable 실현 가능한 file for bankruptcy 파산 신청을 하다 endure ~을 견디다 countless 수많은 hardship 난관, 어려움 eventually 결국 scrap ~을 폐기하다 serve as ~의 역할을 하다 troop carrier 병력 수송선 launch (배) ~를 물에 띄우다 to significant fanfare 아주 화려하게 laud ~을 극찬하다 breakthrough 획기적인 발전, 돌파구 carry out ~을 실시하다 propeller-driven 프로펠러로 움직이는 vastly 대단히, 엄청나게 superior to ~보다 우수한 six-bladed 6개의 날개가 있는 power ~에 동력을 제공하다 by virtue of ~에 의해, ~ 덕분으로 utilize ~을 활용하다 crossing 횡단 choppy (파도가) 일렁이는 seasickness 뱃멀미 unforeseen 예기치 못한 interaction 상호 영향 hull 선체 magnetic compass 자기 나침반 lead to ~로 이어지다 run aground 좌초하다 hulking 거대한 be dragged into ~로 이끌려지다 fold (사업 등을) 접다, 중단하다 be converted into ~로 전환되다 ferry ~을 나르다, 수송하다 immigrant 이민자 permanent 영원한 attraction 명소 disappointment 실망(감) accommodate ~을 수용하다 tragically 비극적이게도 suffer from ~로 고생하다 stroke 뇌졸중 As was the case with ~의 경우와 마찬가지로 ambitious 야심 찬 endeavor 노력 run over ~을 넘어서다 budget 예산 a handful of 소수의, 조금의 A though B A이지만 B한 unprofitable 수익성이 없는 telegraph 전신 outweigh ~보다 더 크다 era 시대 pave the way 기틀을 마련하다 inspiring 영감을 주는

문제 1-8

다음 내용들이 독해 지문 1에 제시된 정보와 일치하는가?

답안지 1-8번 상자에 다음 사항을 작성하시오.

참 지문의 정보와 일치하는 경우

거짓 지문의 정보와 일치하지 않는 경우

해당 없음 정보가 존재하지 않는 경우

1. Brunel is primarily well-known for his achievements in shipbuilding.
브루넬은 주로 조선 분야의 업적으로 잘 알려져 있다.

첫 번째 문단에 브루넬은 그의 육상에서 업적으로(his accomplishments on land: railways, tunnels and bridges) 존경받지, 조선(shipbuilding)으로 유명한 것은 아니기에, 정답은 FALSE이다.
Paraphrasing primarily well-known(주로 알려진) → typically revered(일반적으로 칭찬받는)

2. Brunel's first ship design was deemed inefficient by some of his peers.
브루넬의 첫 번째 선박 디자인은 일부 동료들에 의해 비효율적인 것으로 여겨졌다.

첫 번째 문단에 동료들이 브루넬의 디자인에 대해 비효율적이라고 조롱했다는 내용이 있으므로(The design was mocked by some of Brunel's fellow engineers, who proclaimed that the ship was too large for efficient travel), 정답은 TRUE이다.
Paraphrasing inefficient(비효율적인) → too large for efficient travel(효율적인 이동을 위해서는 너무 큰)
peers(동료들) → fellow engineers(동료 기술자들)

3. The *Great Western* was the heaviest ship in the world for many years.
그레이트 웨스턴 호는 여러 해 동안 세계에서 가장 무거운 선박이었다.

두 번째 문단에서, 그레이트 웨스턴 호가 세상에서 가장 긴(longest) 선박이라는 내용만 나오고 가장 무겁다는(heaviest) 내용은 다른 문단에서도 찾을 수 없으므로, 정답은 NOT GIVEN이다.

4. The *Great Western* was the first steamship to successfully cross the Atlantic.
그레이트 웨스턴 호는 성공적으로 대서양을 횡단한 첫 번째 증기선이었다.

두 번째 문단에서, 그레이트 웨스턴 호가 대서양을 횡단한 첫 번째 증기선으로 불리는 것을 실패했다고(the *Great Western* failing to claim the title of the first steam-powered ship to cross the Atlantic) 나오므로, 정답은 FALSE이다.

5. Brunel drew inspiration from the design of the propeller-driven *Archimedes*.
브루넬은 프로펠러로 움직였던 아르키메데스 호의 디자인에서 영감을 얻었다.

세 번째 문단에서, 브루넬이 프로펠러 동력 증기선 아르키메데스 호에 승선하여 시험을 하고, 프로펠러 동력 증기선의 뛰어남을 확신하였다는 내용이 있으므로(Having carried out tests aboard the propeller-driven steamship *Archimedes*, Brunel had become certain that propeller-driven ships were vastly superior to those using paddle wheels), 아르키메데스 호의 디자인에서 영감을 얻었다고 볼 수 있다. 따라서 정답은 TRUE이다.

6. The *Great Britain* was left stranded on land for more than a year.
그레이트 브리튼 호는 일년 이상 동안 육지에 좌초된 상태로 있었다.

네 번째 문단에서, 배가 해안에 좌초되고 거의 일년이 걸렸다고(the ship running aground on the coast of Ireland. It took almost one year) 소개되었다. 즉 일년이 안 걸린 것을 의미하지만, 문제에서는 일년이 넘게(more than a year) 좌초되었다고 하므로, 정답은 FALSE이다.
Paraphrasing be stranded(좌초되다) → run aground(좌초되다)

7. Brunel passed away prior to the launch of the *Great Eastern*.
브루넬은 그레이트 이스턴 호의 진수식 이전에 사망했다.

다섯 번째 번째 문단에서, 브루넬이 미완성된 배를 점검한 후에 죽었다라고(Tragically, Brunel, who had been suffering from ill health, died due to a stroke just a few hours after inspecting the unfinished ship) 나오므로, 정답은 TRUE이다.
Paraphrasing pass away(세상을 떠나다) → die(죽다)

8. The *Great Eastern* experienced mechanical faults during its maiden voyage.
그레이트 이스턴 호는 첫 항해 중에 기계적인 결함을 겪었다.

다섯 번째 번째 문단에서, 지문에는 기계적 결함(mechanical faults)이라는 언급 대신 기술적 문제들(technical problems)이라는 말만 등장하고, 이러한 기술적 문제로 일정이 뒤쳐졌다는 내용이므로(behind schedule due to financial and technical problems), 첫 항해(maiden voyage) 중에 기계적 결함을 겪었는지는 알 수 없다. 따라서 정답은 NOT GIVEN이다.

I Vocabulary & Expressions I

primarily 주로 be deemed ~로 여겨지다 peer 동료 inspiration 영감 be left 놓여지다 stranded 좌초된, 오도가도 못하는 fault 결함

문제 9-13

다음 문장을 완성하시오.

각 답변에 대해 지문에서 **오직 1개의 단어만** 선택하시오.

답안지 9-13번 상자에 답변을 작성하시오.

9. Brunel first conceived transatlantic steamship travel while working on a ....

브루넬은 ....에 대한 일을 하던 중에 처음으로 대서양 횡단 증기선 여행을 구상했다.

첫 번째 문단에서, 브루넬은 대서양 횡단 증기선 여행을 철도 공사를 끝마치는 동안 언급했으므로(While completing work on the railway in 1836, Brunel jested with his colleagues that he would like to extend the railroad all the way to the United States by establishing a transatlantic steamship company), 정답은 railway이다.

10. Due to a ...., the *Great Western's* launch date was pushed back.

..............................로 인해, 그레이트 웨스턴 호의 진수식 날짜가 미뤄졌다.

두 번째 문단에서, 화재가 배의 예정된 진수일에 대한 지연을 필요하게 하였으므로(The fire necessitated a delay to the ship's scheduled launch date), 정답은 fire이다.

Paraphrasing due to(~때문에) → necessitate(~을 필요하게 하다)
be pushed back(뒤로 미뤄지다) → delay(지연)

11. Brunel concluded that paddle wheels were inferior to .... as a means of powering ships.

브루넬은 선박에 동력을 제공하는 수단으로서 외륜이 ....보다 더 좋지 않다는 결론을 내렸다.

세 번째 문단에서, 프로펠러 동력의 배가 외륜을 사용하는 배보다 뛰어나다고(propeller-driven ships were vastly superior to those using paddle wheels) 나오는데, 빈칸에 들어갈 단어는 형용사가 아닌 명사이므로 propeller-driven이 정답이 될 수는 없다. IELTS Reading에서 정답은 지문에 나온 단어를 그대로 적는 것이 원칙이므로, 조금 더 관련 지문을 읽어보면 다시 한번 외륜과 프로펠러에 대한 비교가 나오므로(utilizing an engine and propellers rather than wind, steam, or paddle wheels), 여기서 정답 명사 propellers를 찾으면 된다.

참고로 paddle wheels란 물레방아 같은 커다란 바퀴를 말한다.

12. The *Great Britain* transported .... for a brief time before moving to the UK.

그레이트 브리튼 호는 영국으로 옮겨지기 전에 잠시 동안 ....을 수송했다.

네 번째, 문단에서, 영국에 정착하기 전에 호주로 이민자들을 수송하였다고 나오므로(It was later converted into a sailing ship, ferrying immigrants to Australia for a number of years before finding a permanent home in the UK as a tourist attraction), 그레이트 브리튼 호는 영국으로 옮겨지기 전에 이민자들을 수송했다. 따라서 정답은 immigrants이다.

참고로 문제에서 잠시동안(for a brief time)은, 영구히 영국(a permanent home in the UK)에서 있게 되는 상황과 비교할 때 일시적이라는 의미로 사용되었다.

Paraphrasing transport(수송하다) → ferry(수송하다)
moving to the UK(영국으로 이동) → finding a permanent home in the UK(영국에서 영원한 안식처를 찾음)

13. The *Great Eastern* played a pivotal role in facilitating .... between America and Europe.

그레이트 이스턴 호는 아메리카 지역과 유럽 사이의 ....을 용이하게 하는 데 있어 중추적인 역할을 했다.

다섯 번째 문단에서, 유럽과 북미 사이에 통신이 가능하게 대서양 횡단 전신 케이블 설치에 사용되었으므로(used to lay the transatlantic telegraph cable that would enable telecommunication between Europe and North America), 정답은 telecommunication이다.

Paraphrasing facilitate(용이하게 하다) → enable(가능하게 하다)

| Vocabulary & Expressions |
conceive 구상하다 steamship 증기선 be pushed back 연기되다 paddle wheel 외륜 means 수단 transport 수송하다
pivotal 중추적인 facilitate 용이하게 하다

■ **패시지 2** [문제 14-26]

출제 포인트 **난이도: 중상**

환경 관련 내용은 전통적으로 아이엘츠에서 가장 많이 출제되는 토픽인만큼 관련 내용 지문에 대한 철저한 복습이 요구됨

기출 2024년 4월 - 사막화
2018년 9월 - 엘니뇨
2010년 6월 - 캘리포니아 북부의 수질 오염
2010년 1월 - 지구 온난화와 인간의 영향
2009년 10월 - 해양 개발

The Water of San Joaquin Valley

In most of the developed world, access to safe drinking water is taken for granted. So why is this not the case in parts of Northern California?

A In Northern California, the provision of readily available, safe water for residences and businesses requires the management of a wide variety of water quality challenges, many of which are proving difficult to overcome. These problems result from both naturally occurring processes and human actions. Many of the Q14 contaminants present in the region, Q18 such as minor traces of mercury resulting from mining, originate from past industrial activities, but some sources of pollution are more recent and increasingly problematic. In fact, new contaminants are being frequently identified in the wells of the people of Northern California.

B Q25 Water quality regulation began in the state in the 1960s and 1970s when the Porter-Cologne Water Quality Control and the Safe Drinking Water Acts were implemented by the government. These Q15 acts were designed to prevent companies from polluting local water and ensure that drinking water supplies met appropriate safe standards. Over subsequent decades, numerous laws and regulations have been introduced to control and manage other issues such as pesticide use on farms and the depositing of hazardous substances at waste sites. However, despite these efforts, a critical situation exists in Northern California, where some communities have not enjoyed clean, safe drinking water for several decades.

샌 호아킨 밸리의 물

대부분의 선진국에서, 안전 식수 이용이 당연하게 여겨지고 있다. 그럼 이는 왜 북부 캘리포니아 지역에는 해당되지 않는가?

A 북부 캘리포니아에서는, 주택 및 사업체에 즉각적으로 이용 가능한 안전한 물을 제공하는 데 있어 아주 다양한 수질 문제에 대한 관리를 필요로 하며, 이들 중 많은 것이 극복하기 어려운 것으로 드러나고 있다. 이 문제들은 자연적으로 발생되는 과정과 인간 활동 두 가지 모두에 따른 결과로 나타나고 있다. Q18 채광 산업으로 인해 생겨난 소량의 수은 흔적과 같이, 이 지역에 존재하는 많은 Q14 오염물질들은 과거의 산업 활동에서 비롯된 것이지만, 일부 오염원들은 더 최근에 생겨나 점점 큰 문제가 되고 있다. 실제로, 새로운 오염물질들이 북부 캘리포니아 사람들이 이용하는 식수원에서 자주 발견되고 있다.

B Q25 캘리포니아 주의 수질 규제는 1960년대와 1970년대에 시작되었으며, 당시에 주 정부에 의해 포터-콜론 수질 관리 및 안전 식수 관리 법령이 시행되었다. 이 Q15 법령들은 회사들이 지역의 물을 오염시키는 것을 방지하고 식수 공급이 해당 안전 기준을 충족하도록 하기 위해 고안되었다. 이후 수십 년에 걸쳐, 농장 내의 살충제 사용 및 쓰레기 처리장에서의 유해 물질 축적 등과 같은 기타 문제들을 통제하고 관리하기 위해 수많은 법과 규제들이 도입되었다. 하지만, 이러한 노력에서 불구하고, 일부 지역 사회들이 수십 년 동안 깨끗하고 안전한 식수를 즐기지 못했던 북부 캘리포니아에는 한 가지 중대한 상황이 존재한다.

ACTUAL TEST 1

C In the State of California, the highest rates of drinking water contamination can be found in the San Joaquin Valley. The most prevalent Q14 contaminants detected in wells of drinking water and the surrounding groundwater are nitrates. Contamination levels are particularly high in the Central Valley, a region that is home to more than 1.3 million people, many of whom reside in communities that are completely dependent on the contaminated groundwater. Although some contaminants result from naturally occurring processes in the groundwater, the dire circumstances seen in Central Valley are primarily a direct result of intensive Q16 agricultural and industrial practices that involved the application of fertilizers and pesticides on a massive scale for a prolonged period of time.

D Nitrate, an inorganic substance used in the manufacture of fertilizers, is by far the most prevalent and problematic contaminant in Central Valley. Q19 The hazardous levels found in the Valley have been caused by more than five decades of careless use of industrial fertilizers, as well as the improper storage and disposal of animal waste products. Nitrate concentrations gradually built up in local groundwater and eventually tainted supply wells built to serve both residences and businesses. The high levels of nitrate currently present in the Central Valley have been attributed to the death of infants and the birth of stillborn babies. Thyroid illnesses, reproductive ailments, and some cancers have also been linked to the ingestion of nitrate-rich water.

E The discovery of high levels of nitrate left many communities with no choice but to abandon their supply wells and Q22 drill further underground in search of uncontaminated water. Their efforts proved fruitless, as they discovered that deeper pockets of water were contaminated with arsenic. Arsenic naturally occurs in soil and rocks and is also a byproduct of fertilizers, pesticides, and mining activities. In the San Joaquin Valley, it was historically used in pesticides that were applied to orchards and cotton fields. Q21 Medical research has shown a connection between arsenic poisoning and reduced mental function in children, and it has also been flagged as a carcinogen and a contributor to Type 2 Diabetes. These deep pockets of groundwater were also found to contain DBCP (dibromochloropropane), a pesticide that was once commonly used on tomatoes and grapes. Q24 Although it was banned several years ago, high levels

C 캘리포니아 주에서, 샌 호아킨 밸리에서 가장 높은 식수 오염 비율을 찾아볼 수 있다. 식수원 및 인근 지하수에서 발견되는 가장 일반적인 Q14 오염물질들은 질산염이다. 오염 수준은 센트럴 밸리에서 특히 높으며, 이곳은 130만 명이 넘는 사람들이 사는 주거지로서, 이들 중 많은 사람들이 그 오염된 지하수에 전적으로 의존하는 지역 사회에 거주하고 있다. 일부 오염물질들이 지하수에서 자연적으로 발생되는 과정에 의해 생겨나고 있기는 하지만, 센트럴 밸리에서 보여지고 있는 이 대단히 심각한 상황은 주로 오랜 시간 동안 대규모로 이뤄진 비료 및 살충제 사용을 수반한 집약적 Q16 농업 및 산업 관행에 따른 직접적인 결과로 나타난 것이다.

D 질산염은 비료 제조에 사용되는 무기 물질로서, 센트럴 밸리에서 단연 가장 일반적이고 문제가 되는 오염물질이다. Q19 이 지역에서 나타나는 위험 수준은 부적절한 동물 배설물 보관 및 처리에 의해 초래된 것일 뿐만 아니라 50년이 넘는 부주의한 산업용 비료 사용 때문이기도 하다. 질산염 농축물이 지역 내 지하수에 점차적으로 축적되었고, 결국 주택 및 사업체 모두에 물을 제공하기 위해 만들어진 공급용 식수원을 오염시켰다. 현재 센트럴 밸리에 존재하는 높은 수준의 질산염은 유아 사망 및 사산아 출생이 그 원인이었다. 갑상선 질병과 생식기 질병, 그리고 몇몇 암 또한 질산염이 많은 물 섭취와도 관련되어 왔다.

E 높은 수준의 질산염 발견으로 인해 많은 지역 사회들이 공급용 식수원을 포기하고 Q22 오염되지 않은 물을 찾기 위해 지하로 더 깊이 땅을 팔 수밖에 없도록 만들었다. 이러한 노력을 헛수고로 드러났는데, 더 깊은 곳의 물은 비소로 오염되어 있었다는 사실을 발견했기 때문이다. 비소는 토양과 암석에서 자연적으로 생겨나는 것이며, 비료나 살충제, 그리고 채광 활동에 따른 부산물이기도 하다. 샌 호아킨 밸리 지역에서는, 역사적으로 과수원과 목화밭에 뿌려진 살충제에 비소가 사용되었다. Q21 의학 연구를 통해 비소 중독과 아이들의 두뇌 활동 감소 사이의 연관성이 나타났으며, 비소는 발암 물질이자 2형 당뇨병의 원인으로도 경고되어 온 물질이다. 깊은 곳에 위치한 이 지하수 지대는 또한 DBCP를 함유하고 있는 것으로 밝혀졌는데, 이는 한때 토마토와 포도에 흔히 사용되었던 살충제의 일종이다. Q24 수년 전에 금지된 것이기는 하지만, 심지어 현재도 샌 호아킨 밸리에는 높은 수준의 DBCP가 잔존해 있다.

of DBCP persist in San Joaquin Valley water sources, even in the present day.

F Q20 People who reside in low-income, underdeveloped communities are disproportionately affected by groundwater contamination in the San Joaquin Valley. Members of such communities are at a disadvantage, as their wells are typically shallower than wells in affluent areas, which leaves them more susceptible to contaminations. In addition, Q23 solutions available to ensure safe drinking water tend to be expensive, and people in these communities often do not have the means to take advantage of them. Furthermore, recent studies have shown that disadvantaged communities with nitrate-contaminated groundwater pay almost triple the recommended cost for water. So far, government-led plans for water management and effective land use have failed to adequately decontaminate sources of drinking water in underprivileged communities. One reason that the eradication of contaminants has proven difficult is that most of them do not have a distinct taste or smell, so expensive, continuous water quality testing is the only viable long-term solution.

G Currently, more than 500 rural communities in Northern California are unable to provide safe drinking water, and it is estimated that statewide solutions that would benefit these communities would require a budget increase of between $60 million and $150 million per year. At present, approximately $10 billion is spent annually on water pollution control in California, with most of it allocated for site-specific sources of pollution such as wastewater treatment. The US Environmental Protection Agency (EPA) recently committed to providing additional Q17 funding, with a goal of bringing 20 communities into compliance with safety regulations per year over the next ten years. It also Q26 plans to work directly with community leaders and provide funding for education and training to San Joaquin Valley residents in an effort to raise awareness and knowledge about preventing water pollution.

F Q20 샌 호아킨 밸리에 있는 저소득층, 저개발 지역에 거주하는 사람들은 지하수 오염에 의해 불균형적으로 영향받고 있다. 이와 같은 지역 사회의 구성원들은 불리한 입장에 처해 있는데, 그들의 식수원이 일반적으로 부유한 지역에 있는 것보다 얕기 때문이며, 이로 인해 오염 물질에 더욱 취약한 상태가 된다. 게다가, Q23 안전한 식수를 확보하는 데 이용 가능한 해결책은 비용이 많이 드는 경향이 있으며, 이 지역에 사는 사람들은 그 해결책을 활용할 만한 여유가 없다. 더욱이, 최근의 연구에 따르면 질산염으로 오염된 지하수가 있는 빈곤 지역은 물에 대해 권장되는 비용의 거의 세 배를 지불하고 있다. 지금까지, 물 관리 및 효과적인 토지 이용을 위해 정부가 주도하는 계획들은 혜택 받지 못한 지역의 식수원에서 적절히 오염 물질을 제거하지 못했다. 오염 물질 근절이 어려운 것으로 드러난 한 가지 이유는 대부분의 오염 물질이 뚜렷한 맛이나 냄새를 지니고 있지 않아서 비용이 많이 들고 지속적인 수질 테스트가 유일하게 실행 가능성 있는 장기 해결책이기 때문이다.

G 현재, 북부 캘리포니아의 500곳이 넘는 시골 지역 사회가 안전한 식수를 제공할 수 없으며, 이 지역 사회에 도움이 될 만한 주 전역에 걸친 해결책은 해마다 6천만 달러에서 1억 5천만 달러 사이에 해당되는 예산 증가를 필요로 하는 것으로 추정되고 있다. 지금은, 캘리포니아에서 연간 대략 1백억 달러가 수질 오염 관리에 소비되고 있으며, 대부분의 자금이 폐수 처리와 같은 특정 장소의 오염원을 대상으로 할당되어 있다. 미국 환경 보호국은 최근 추가 Q17 자금을 제공하는 데 전념했는데, 향후 10년 동안에 걸쳐 해마다 20곳의 지역 사회가 안전 규제를 준수하도록 만드는 것을 목표로 하고 있다. 또한 Q26 수질 오염을 방지하는 것에 대한 인식을 드높이고 지식 수준을 끌어올리기 위한 노력의 일환으로 지역 사회의 지도자들과 직접적으로 협업하고 샌 호아킨 밸리에 교육 및 훈련에 필요한 자금도 제공할 계획이다.

| Vocabulary & Expressions |

developed world 선진국 be taken for granted 당연하게 여겨지다 provision 공급, 제공 readily available 즉각적으로 이용 가능한 residence 주택 a wide variety of 아주 다양한 challenge 도전 과제, 어려운 일 result from ~의 결과로 생기다 contaminant 오염물질 trace 흔적 mercury 수은 mining 채광, 광업 originate from ~에서 비롯되다 source of pollution 오염원 well 식수원 regulation 규제, 규정 implement ~을 실시하다, 시행하다 pollute ~을 오염시키다 ensure that ~임을 확실히 하다 meet ~을 충족하다 appropriate 해당되는, 적절한 subsequent 그 다음의 pesticide 살충제 depositing 축적, 침전 hazardous substance

유해 물질 critical 중대한 rate 비율 contamination 오염 prevalent 일반적인, 널리 퍼진 detect ~을 발견하다, 감지하다 nitrate 질산염 reside in ~에 거주하다 completely 전적으로, 완전히 dependent on ~에 의존하는 dire 대단히 심각한 primarily 주로 intensive 집약적인, 집중적인 practice 관행, 관습 application 적용, 응용 fertilizer 비료 on a massive scale 대규모로 prolonged 장기간의 inorganic 무기물의 by far (최상급 수식) 단연코 careless 부주의한 improper 부적절한 disposal 처리, 처분 animal waste products 동물 배설물 concentration 농축, 농도 taint ~을 오염시키다 be attributed to A A에 기인하다 infant 유아 stillborn baby 사산아 thyroid 갑상선 reproductive 생식의 ailment 질병 ingestion 섭취 abandon ~을 포기하다, 버리다 fruitless 헛된, 결실 없는 pocket 지대, 지역 arsenic 비소 byproduct 부산물 apply ~을 적용하다 poisoning 중독 mental function 두뇌 활동 be flagged as ~로 경고되다 carcinogen 발암 물질 contributor to ~에 대한 원인 ban ~을 금지하다 persist 잔존하다 disproportionately 불균형적으로 affect ~에 영향을 미치다 at a disadvantage 불리한 입장에 있는 shallow 얕은 affluent 부유한 susceptible to ~에 취약한 have the means to do ~할 여유가 있다 take advantage of ~을 활용하다 disadvantaged 빈곤한 adequately 적절히 decontaminate 오염 물질을 제거하다 underprivileged 혜택 받지 못한 eradication 근절 distinct 뚜렷한 viable 실행 가능한 rural 시골의 it is estimated that ~하는 것으로 추정되다 benefit ~에 도움이 되다 budget 예산 with A p.p. A가 ~된 채로 allocate ~을 할당하다 site-specific 특정 장소의 commit to -ing ~하는 데 전념하다 raise awareness 인식을 드높이다

문제 14-17

다음 요약 내용을 완성하시오.
각 답변에 대해 각 답변에 대해 지문에서 **오직 1개의 단어만** 찾아 작성하시오.
답안지 14-17번 상자에 답변을 작성하시오.

The water problem in Northern California 북부 캘리포니아의 물 문제

Water sources in Northern California contain a wide variety of **14** .... , such as mercury and nitrates. Starting in the 1960s, the government established two **15** .... in an effort to regulate water quality. The majority of water pollution in Central Valley region is a result of industrial and **16** .... activities.

The US EPA has taken measures to provide additional **17** .... that will be used to educate members of rural communities and bring rural water systems into compliance with safety regulations.

북부 캘리포니아의 수원에는 수은이나 질산염 같은 아주 다양한 **14** ....를 함유하고 있다. 1960년대부터, 정부는 수질을 규제하기 위한 노력의 일환으로 두 가지 **15** ....를 확립했다. 센트럴 밸리 지역의 수질 오염 대부분은 산업 및 **16** .... 활동에 따른 결과이다.

미국 EPA는 시골 지역의 구성원들을 교육하고 시골의 수원 시스템이 안전 규제를 준수하도록 만드는 데 사용될 추가 **17**.............................을 제공하기 위한 조치를 취했다.

14. A 문단에 수은(mercury), C 문단에 질산염(nitrates)이 나오는데 이러한 것들을 오염물질들(contaminants)이라고 부르므로, 정답은 contaminants이다.

15. B 문단에 두 개의 법령들이 소개되고 이 법령들이 수질 규제를 위해 시행되었다고 하므로, 정답은 acts이다.
Paraphrasing regulate water quality(수질을 규제하다)
→ prevent companies from polluting local water and ensure that drinking water supplies met appropriate safe standards(회사들이 지역의 물을 오염시키는 것을 방지하고 식수 공급이 해당 안전 기준을 충족하도록 하다)

16. C 문단에서 센트럴 밸리 지역의 수질 오염은 농업과 산업 활동의 결과이므로, 정답은 agricultural이다.

17. 핵심어 US EPA는 G 문단에 나오는데, US EPA가 추가 자금을 제공하는 데 전념했다고 나오므로, 빈칸에 들어갈 말은 funding이다.

| Vocabulary & Expressions |

regulate 규제하다 rural 시골의 community 공동체, 사회 bring A into compliance with B A가 B를 준수하도록 만들다

문제 18-21

다음 **A-F** 중에 알맞은 것을 찾아 각 문장의 뒷부분을 완성하시오.

답안지 18-21번 상자에 **A-F** 중에 알맞은 글자를 기입하시오.

18. Mercury detected in Northern Californian water sources

북부 캘리포니아의 수원에서 발견된 수은은

북부 캘리포니아의 수원에서 발견된 수은 내용은 A 문단에 나오는데, 수은이 과거 채광 사업으로부터 기원한다고 하므로(mercury resulting from mining, originate from past industrial activities), 정답은 F이다.

19. The dangerous levels of nitrates found in Central Valley water sources

센트럴 밸리의 수원에서 발견된 위험 수준의 질산염은

D 문단을 보면, 센트럴 밸리의 수원에서 발견된 위험 수준의 질산염은 부주의한 산업 비료 사용과 적절치 못한 동물 배설물 저장 및 처리에 기인하므로(The hazardous levels found in the Valley have been caused by more than five decades of careless use of industrial fertilizer as well as the improper storage and disposal of animal waste products), 정답은 B이다.

Paraphrasing dangerous(위험한) → hazardous(위험한)
poor animal waste management(형편없는 동물 배설물 관리)
→ improper storage and disposal of animal waste products(부적절한 동물 배설물 부산물의 저장 및 처리)

20. Residents in low-income communities

저소득 지역 사회의 주민들은

저소득 지역 사회 주민들에 대한 언급은 E 문단에 있으며, 부유한 지역보다 식수원이 낮아서(shallower than wells in affluent areas) 오염물질들에 더 민감하게 남겨져 있다고 나오므로(which leaves them more susceptible to contaminations), 정답은 E이다.

Paraphrasing Residents in low-income communities(저소득 지역 사회 주민들)
→ People who reside in low-income, underdeveloped communities (저소득, 저개발 지역 사회에 거주하는 사람들)
at risk(위험한) → susceptible(민감한)

21. Arsenic in deep pockets of groundwater

땅 속 깊은 속의 지하수 지대에 있는 비소는

비소(arsenic)는 E 문단에 나오는데, 비소 중독과 아이들 두뇌 활동 감소와 연관이 있다고 하므로(a connection between arsenic poisoning and reduced mental function in children), 정답은 D이다.

A may contribute to excessive groundwater pollution.
과도한 지하수 오염의 원인일 수 있다.

B may have been caused by poor animal waste management.
좋지 못한 동물 배설물 관리로 인해 야기되었을 수도 있다.

C may not be detected by any currently-known methods.
현재 알려진 어떠한 방법으로도 발견되지 못할 수도 있다.

D may lead to mental problems in children.
아이들의 정신 문제로 이어질 수도 있다.

E may be more at risk of drinking contaminated water.
오염된 물을 마시는 위험에 처할 가능성이 더 크다.

F may have resulted from mining activities in the past.
과거의 채광 활동으로 인해 초래되었을 수도 있다.

| Vocabulary & Expressions |

contribute to ~에 기여하다 detected 발견된 excessive 과도한 groundwater 지하수 at risk 위험에 처한

문제 22-26

독해 지문 2는 **A-G**까지 일곱 개의 문단이 있다.

어느 문단이 다음 정보를 포함하고 있는가?

답안지 22-26번 상자에 **A-G** 사이에서 알맞은 글자를 기입하시오.

유의 어떤 글자든 한 번 이상 사용해도 된다.

22. a description of an attempt to locate water further beneath the ground
지하 더 깊은 곳에서 물을 찾기 위한 시도에 관한 묘사

지하 더 깊은 곳에서 물을 찾기 위한 시도에 관한 묘사는 E 문단(drill further underground in search of uncontaminated water)에 나오므로, 정답은 E이다.

Paraphrasing attempt(시도하다) → drill(땅을 파다)
locate(찾다) → in search of(찾아서)
beneath the ground(땅 밑에) → further underground(더 지하에)

23. a reason why some people cannot take advantage of safe water solutions
일부 사람들이 안전한 물 관리 해결책을 이용할 수 없는 이유

F 문단에서 저소득 주민들과 같은 일부 사람들을 위한 안전한 물 관리 해결책(solutions)은 비싸고 그렇게 할 돈도 없다는 말로 이유를 설명하기에, 정답은 F이다.

24. an example of a substance that has since been banned from use
특정 시점 이후로 사용이 금지되어 온 물질에 대한 예

사용이 금지된 물질(DBCP)이 E 문단 마지막 줄에 나오므로, 정답은 E이다.

25. an overview of laws intended to address the problem of water contamination
수질 오염 문제를 처리하기 위한 목적을 지닌 법에 대한 개요

법과 관련된 내용은 B 문단 전체적으로 나오기에, 정답은 B이다. 참고로 G 문단의 US EPA는 법이 아닌 기관이므로 G는 오답이다.

26. an outline of a plan to improve knowledge about water pollution
수질 오염에 대한 지식을 향상시키는 계획에 대한 개요

수질 오염에 대한 지식을 향상시킬 계획이 G 문단에 나오므로 (plans ~ in an effort to raise awareness and knowledge about preventing water pollution), 정답은 G이다.

Paraphrasing improve knowledge(지식을 향상시키다) → raise awareness and knowledge(인식과 지식을 끌어올리다)

| Vocabulary & Expressions |

description 묘사 locate 위치를 찾다 beneath 아래에, 밑에 take advantage of ~을 이용하다 substance 물질 ban 금하다 overview 개요, 간략 address 처리하다 outline 개요, 간략

▪ 패시지 3 [문제 27-40]

출제 포인트 | 난이도: 중상

예술 분야에서 음악과 영화 관련 지문이 자주 출제되는 편이며, 보통 예술 분야는 특정 주제의 역사나 예술과 인간 또는 예술과 사회 관계에 대한 내용이 출제됨

기출 2024년 8월 - 사진작가의 삶
2019년 7월 - 바이올린 제작
2019년 2월 - 음악과 정신 질환
2019년 1월 - 뉴질랜드 영화

THE EVOLUTION OF MOVIE TRAILERS

Movie trailers have transformed significantly over a period spanning several decades, from their very simplistic origins during Hollywood's Golden Age to the high-technology marketing tools they are today. The evolution of trailers mirrors the artistic and business-oriented transformations that have taken place within the film industry as a whole. In fact, these previews have become an industry unto themselves, with numerous Web sites and awards shows dedicated solely to celebrating the year's best trailers. These days, the announcement of a trailer for a hotly-anticipated movie garners as much attention as the release of the movie itself. However, it wasn't always this way. Q27 Early trailers were nothing more than a series of still images, crudely spliced together and attached onto the end of movies. These served their purpose of enticing some cinemagoers to return for coming features, but by today's standards, the previews were barely effective as wide-reaching marketing tools.

During the silent era of cinema, trailers did not evolve much further past the initial concept of showing a title card, a tagline, a handful of film clips, and a cast list. However, Q35 the introduction of sound in motion pictures threw open the door on the potential of trailers. The preview for the 1927 Al Jolson musical The Jazz Singer was a seven-minute trailer that partly served to announce this revolutionary change in the film industry to the public. In the promo, a man stands in front of a curtain, audibly clears his throat, and states, “Ladies and gentlemen, I am privileged to say a few words to you.” The trailer elicited intense excitement among audience members throughout the US, all of whom were amazed by the man's direct address to the audience and the voiceover narration of movie scenes.

The 1930s saw a shift in attitudes toward movie marketing, with the majority of film studios gradually moving toward

영화 예고편의 진화

영화 예고편은 할리우드의 황금기 중에 쓰였던 매우 단순한 기원에서부터 오늘날 볼 수 있는 첨단 마케팅 수단에 이르기까지 수십 년 동안 이어진 기간에 걸쳐 상당히 변화되어 왔다. 예고편의 진화는 영화 업계 내에서 전체적으로 발생되어 온 예술적이고 비즈니스 지향적인 변화를 잘 반영하는 것이다. 실제로, 이 예고편은 독자적으로 하나의 산업이 되었으며, 오직 한 해 최고의 예고편만을 기념하는 데 전념하는 수많은 웹 사이트와 시상식 행사가 있다. 현재, 뜨거운 기대를 받는 영화의 예고편 발표는 영화 자체의 개봉만큼이나 많은 관심을 받는다. 하지만, 이는 항상 그랬던 것은 아니었다. Q27 초기의 예고편은 일련의 스틸 이미지에 지나지 않았으며, 서로 조잡하게 이어져 영화마다 마지막 부분에 덧붙여졌다. 이는 일부 영화 관람객들을 끌어들여 앞으로 나올 작품을 보러 오게 만들기 위한 목적으로 쓰였지만, 오늘날의 기준으로 보면, 이 예고편은 광범위한 마케팅 수단으로써 효과는 거의 없었다.

무성 영화 시대에, 예고편은 타이틀 카드와 핵심 문구, 약간의 영상과 출연진 목록을 보여주는 초기의 개념에서 그렇게 많이 벗어날 정도로 발전하지 못했다. 하지만, Q35 영화에 음향이 도입되면서 예고편의 잠재력에 새롭게 문을 활짝 열어 주었다. 1927년 작품인 앨 졸슨의 뮤지컬 <재즈 싱어>에 대한 예고편은 일반 대중에 대한 영화 업계의 이와 같은 혁신적인 변화를 알리는 역할을 부분적으로 했던 7분 길이의 예고편이었다. 이 홍보 영상에서, 한 남성이 커튼 앞에 서서 잘 들릴 정도로 목을 가다듬은 후, “신사 숙녀 여러분, 여러분께 몇 마디 전해 드릴 수 있게 되어 영광입니다.”라고 말한다. 이 예고편은 미국 전역의 관객들 사이에서 굉장한 흥분감을 불러 일으켰으며, 그 모든 사람들이 관객들에게 직접적으로 전하는 이 남성의 말과 영화 장면에 대한 목소리 설명에 놀라워했다.

1930년대는 영화 마케팅에 대한 태도에 변화가 있었던 시기였는데, 대부분의 영화 스튜디오들이 점차적으로 예고편에 대해 더욱 세련된 방식을 향해 나아갔으며,

a more sophisticated format for trailers, and a stark difference in quality is evident when comparing the trailers for 1932's *Tarzan The Ape Man* and 1939's *Gone With The Wind*. It wasn't until the 1940s, however, that many of the characteristic flourishes we now associate with classic Hollywood trailers were introduced. Q28&38 The breathtakingly innovative trailer for John Ford's adaptation of John Steinbeck's novel *The Grapes of Wrath* was heralded as a landmark in the transition between the relatively simple trailers of the 20s and 30s and the technical prowess exhibited by those produced in the 40s. Q37 The promo begins by focusing on how Steinbeck's book has completely sold out across the country, with footage of desperate customers demanding a copy to no avail at various bookstores. Q34 The lead actor of the movie, Henry Fonda, is not introduced until approximately the two-minute mark when footage of the movie is finally unveiled at the end of the clip. This "peer pressure" approach was tremendously effective, as audience members became convinced of the popularity of the book and did not want to be the ones who missed out on seeing its big screen adaptation.

Q39 The majority of trailers produced during the 1940s and 1950s generally emphasized the fame of the lead actors and lavished praise upon the dramatic or heartfelt narratives. In the case of the psychological horror film *Psycho*, released in 1960, director Q29 Alfred Hitchcock decided to take a more indirect approach, concerned that a typical trailer would inadvertently reveal one of the film's shocking twists. Hitchcock had already become a recognizable public persona due to his prominent appearances on television, so he decided that he would insert himself into the trailer for the film. The resulting six-and-a-half-minute promo clip features Q32 Hitchcock giving viewers a personal tour of the Bates Motel, the setting of the majority of the film's scenes. The director teases viewers by alluding to horrific events that unfolded in the motel — events apparently too disturbing to describe in detail. The trailer proved extremely compelling, with those who viewed it instantly curious to find more about the events that transpired at the Bates Motel, and thus flocking to cinemas in droves.

The creators of movie trailers continued to innovate throughout the 1960s, with two trailers particularly standing out as landmarks in the evolution of the industry. In 1964, Q33 director Stanley Kubrick and Pablo Ferro, a Cuban artist, collaborated on sketch-like title cards that featured in Kubrick's film, *Dr. Strangelove*. Kubrick was so impressed with the result that he enlisted Ferro to helm

1932년의 <정글의 왕, 타잔>과 1939년의 <바람과 함께 사라지다>의 예고편을 비교해 보면 극명한 수준 차이가 분명히 나타난다. 하지만, 현재 우리가 고전 할리우드 예고편과 연관 짓는 여러 특유의 스타일들이 나타난 것은 1940년대가 되어서였다. Q28&38 존 스타인벡의 소설 <분노의 포도>를 각색한 존 포드의 작품에 쓰인 숨막힐 정도로 혁신적이었던 예고편은 20년대와 30년대의 비교적 단순했던 예고편과 40년대에 제작된 예고편에 드러난 기술력 사이의 과도기에 있어 획기적인 작품으로 불렸다. Q37 이 홍보 영상은 스타인벡의 책이 어떻게 전국적으로 완전히 품절되었는지에 초점을 맞추는 것으로 시작하며, 여러 서점에서 이 책을 요구하지만 헛수고만 했던 간절한 마음의 고객들을 담은 영상을 동반하고 있다. Q34 이 영화의 주연인 헨리 폰다는 이 예고편의 마지막 부분에 마침내 영화의 장면이 공개될 때 약 2분이 지날 때까지 소개되지 않는다. 이러한 "동료 집단의 압력" 접근 방식은 굉장히 효과적이었는데, 관객들이 이 책의 인기에 확신을 갖게 되어 영화 각색 작품을 볼 기회를 놓치는 사람이 되고 싶어하지 않았기 때문이었다.

Q39 1940년대와 1950년대에 제작된 대부분의 예고편은 일반적으로 주연 배우의 명성을 강조했으며, 극적이거나 진심 어린 이야기에 대한 칭찬을 아끼지 않았다. 1960년에 개봉한 심리 공포 영화 <사이코>의 경우에, 감독 Q29 알프레드 히치콕은 좀 더 간접적인 접근 방식을 취하기로 결정했는데, 일반적인 예고편은 그 영화의 충격적인 반전들 중 하나를 무심코 드러내 보일 수 있다는 우려에서였다. 히치콕은 텔레비전에 눈에 띄게 출연한 것으로 인해 이미 사람들이 알아볼 수 있는 대중적인 인물이 되었기 때문에, 자신을 그 영화 예고편에 집어넣기로 결정했다. 그렇게 만들어진 6분 30초 길이의 홍보 영상은 히치콕이 관객들에게 그 영화의 장면 대부분에 있어 배경이 된 베이츠 모텔에 대해 Q32 본인이 직접하는 투어를 제공하는 것을 특징으로 하고 있다. 히치콕 감독은 그 모텔에서 펼쳐진 끔찍한 사건들을 암시하는 것으로 관객들을 애타게 만드는데, 그 사건들은 자세히 묘사하기에는 분명 너무 충격적인 것이었다. 이 예고편은 대단히 강렬한 것으로 드러나서, 그것을 본 사람들이 베이츠 모텔에서 발생된 그 사건들에 관해 더 알아보고 싶을 정도로 즉시 호기심을 갖게 만들면서, 떼지어 극장에 몰려들게 되었다.

영화 예고편 제작자들은 1960년대 전반에 걸쳐 지속적으로 혁신을 일으켰는데, 해당 업계의 발전에 있어 특히 두 편의 예고편이 획기적인 작품으로 두드러진다. 1964년에, Q33 감독 스탠리 큐브릭과 쿠바인 예술가 파블로 페로가 큐브릭의 영화 <닥터 스프레인지러브>에 포함된 스케치한 것 같은 타이틀 카드 작업을 함께 했다. 큐브릭은 그 결과물에 매우 깊은 인상을 받아 자신의 영화 예고편 작업을 맡아 이끌도록 페로에게 협조 요청했다. 페로는 각각 하나의 단어만 들어 있는 단순한 흑백 타이틀 카

work on the trailer for his movie. Ferro flashed simple black-and-white title cards, each bearing a single word, at a rapid rate, only pausing occasionally to present a brief image or piece of dialogue from the movie. Q36 The trailer presents a total of 220 shots in only 97 seconds, having the effect of a camera shutter rapidly opening and closing. Although quick edits became commonplace by the 1990s, the effect was highly unique and memorable to viewers at the time of the trailer's release. In the same year, the trailer for a relatively obscure Western movie, Q30 *Gunfighters of Casa Grande*, was notable for being the first to feature a voiceover by Don LaFontaine, who coined the phrase, "In a world…," which would be used in countless trailers to come. At the time of LaFontaine's passing in 2008, it was estimated that he had lent his voice to more than five thousand movie trailers.

Q40 In the ensuing decades, movie trailers continued to become increasingly elaborate and artful, with most film studios allocating sizable budgets and production teams for the creation of each trailer. In the 1970s, Q31 trailers were frequently aired on television networks, with the trailer for Steven Spielberg's *Jaws* being shown several times per day on all major networks in the weeks leading up to the film's release. These days, as technology continues to evolve, so too does the art of trailer production and the means by which trailers are delivered, and the Internet serves as the most important marketing tool for generating public interest in both movies and the trailers that precede them.

드들을 빠른 속도로 휙 나타나게 하면서 때때로 멈춰 영화 속의 간단한 이미지나 대사 한 마디만을 보여주었다. Q36 이 예고편은 불과 97초 만에 총 220개의 장면을 보여주면서, 카메라 셔터가 빠르게 열리고 닫히는 효과를 냈다. 1990년대에 들어 빠른 편집이 아주 흔한 것이 되었지만, 그 예고편의 공개 당시에는 관객들에게 그 효과가 대단히 독특하고 기억에 남을 만한 것이었다. 같은 해에, 비교적 잘 알려지지 않은 서부 영화 Q30 <카사 그란데의 총잡이들>의 예고편은 "~하는 세계에서"와 같은 문구를 만들어낸 돈 라폰테인의 목소리가 처음 삽입된 것으로 유명해졌으며, 그 문구는 이후에 나온 수많은 예고편에 쓰이게 된다. 2008년에 라폰테인의 사망 당시, 5천 편이 넘는 영화 예고편에 자신의 목소리를 제공했던 것으로 추정되었다.

Q40 이후 수십 년 동안, 영화 예고편이 지속적으로 점점 더 정교하고 기교적으로 변하면서, 대부분의 영화 스튜디오들이 각 예고편 제작에 상당히 많은 예산과 제작팀을 할당하게 된다. 1970년대에, Q31 예고편이 자주 텔레비전 방송국에서 방송되었는데, 스티븐 스필버그의 <죠스> 예고편은 개봉 시점에 가까워지던 몇 주 동안 모든 주요 방송국에서 날마다 여러 차례 방송되었다. 오늘날, 기술이 지속적으로 발전함에 따라, 예고편 제작 기술과 예고편이 전달되는 수단도 마찬가지로 그러하며, 인터넷은 영화와 예고편이 오기에 앞서 그 둘 모두에 대한 대중의 관심을 불러일으키는 데 있어 가장 중요한 마케팅 수단의 역할을 하고 있다.

| Vocabulary & Expressions |

evolution 진화, 발전 trailer 예고편(= preview) transform 변화하다, 바뀌다 spanning ~의 기간에 걸쳐 origin 기원, 발단 mirror ~을 반영하다, 잘 보여주다 take place 발생되다, 일어나다 as a whole 전체적으로 unto oneself 독자적으로 dedicated to ~에 전념하는 hotly-anticipated 뜨거운 기대를 받는 garner ~을 얻다, 받다 release 개봉, 출시 nothing more than ~에 지나지 않는 crudely 조잡하게 splice ~을 이어 붙이다 attach ~을 첨부하다, 추가하다 entice ~을 끌어들이다 feature 특징, ~을 특징으로 하다 wide-reaching 광범위한 silent era of cinema 무성영화 시대 initial 처음의 a handful of 소수의, 약간의 clip 영상 throw open the door 새로운 문을 열다 potential 잠재력 revolutionary 혁신적인, 획기적인 promo 홍보물 audibly 잘 들릴 정도로 be privileged to do ~하게 되어 영광이다 elicit ~을 이끌어내다 direct address 직접적으로 하는 말 voiceover 목소리 녹음 shift in ~의 변화 sophisticated 세련된 stark 극명한 flourishes 미사여구, 스타일 associate 연관 짓다 breathtakingly 숨막힐 정도로 adaptation 각색 (작품) be heralded as ~로 불리다, 알려지다 landmark 획기적인 것 transition 과도기, 변천 technical prowess 기술력 exhibit ~을 드러내다 footage 영상 to no avail 헛되이, 보람 없이 unveil ~을 공개하다 peer pressure 동료 집단의 압력 tremendously 엄청나게 convinced of ~을 확신하는 miss out on ~할 기회를 놓치다 emphasize ~을 강조하다 lavish praise 칭찬을 아끼지 않다 heartfelt 진심 어린 narrative 이야기, 서사 concerned that ~임을 우려한 inadvertently 무심코 twist 반전 recognizable 쉽게 알아볼 수 있는 prominent 유명한 insert 삽입하다 allude to ~을 암시하다 unfold ~을 펼치다 disturbing 충격적인 in detail 자세히 compelling 강렬한 transpire 발생되다 flock to ~로 몰려들다 in droves 떼지어 innovate 혁신을 일으키다 stand out as ~로서 두드러지다 collaborate on ~을 공동 작업하다 enlist ~에게 협조 요청하다 helm ~을 이끌다 flash ~을 휙 나타내다 bear ~을 담고 있다 at a rapid rate 빠른 속도로 commonplace 아주 흔한 obscure 잘 알려지지 않은 be notable for ~로 유명하다 coin (단어 등) ~을 만들어내다 passing 사망 ensuing 이후의 elaborate 정교한 artful 기

교적인 allocate ~을 할당하다 sizable 상당히 많은 air ~을 방송하다 lead up to ~로 이어지다 generate interest in ~에 대한 관심을 불러일으키다 precede ~을 앞서다

문제 27 -31

A, **B**, **C** 또는 **D** 중에서 알맞은 글자를 고르시오.

답안지 27-31번 상자에 알맞은 글자를 기입하시오.

27. In the first paragraph, the writer says that the first trailers ever created
첫 번째 단락에서, 글쓴이는 역사상 처음으로 만들어진 예고편들은 ....고 말한다.

A were nominated for a wide variety of awards.
아주 다양한 상에 대한 후보로 지명되었다.

B were attached to the start of movies as previews.
영화의 예고로서 시작 부분에 추가되었다.

C were less successful as a promotion method than today's trailers.
오늘날의 예고편에 비해 홍보 수단으로서 덜 성공적이었다.

D were comprised of a series of short animated film sequences.
일련의 짧은 애니메이션 영화 장면들로 구성되었다.

초기 예고편들이 오늘날 기준으로는 마케팅 도구로써 거의 효과적이지 않았다고 하므로(by today's standards, the previews were barely effective as wide-reaching marketing tools), 정답은 C이다.

Paraphrasing the first trailers(첫 예고편들) → early trailers(초기 예고편들)
less successful(덜 성공적인) → barely effective(거의 효과가 없는)
marketing tools(마케팅 도구) → a promotion method(홍보 수단)

28. According to the third paragraph, the trailer for *The Grapes of Wrath*
세 번째 단락에 따르면, <분노의 포도> 예고편은 ....

A drew direct influence from the trailer for *Gone With The Wind*.
<바람과 함께 사라지다> 예고편으로부터 직접적인 영향을 받았다.

B included spoken excerpts from a popular novel of the era.
당시 인기 있던 한 소설의 발췌 내용을 말한 것이 포함되었다.

C was the first movie promo to incorporate sound.
소리를 포함했던 첫 번째 영화 홍보 영상이었다.

D was more technically advanced than the trailers of the 1930s.
1930년대의 예고편보다 기술적으로 더욱 발전했다.

<분노의 포도>는 상대적으로 단순한 30년대 예고편에서 기술적 솜씨를 내세운 40년대 대표작이기에(a landmark in the transition between the relatively simple trailers of the 20s and 30s and the technical prowess exhibited by those produced in the 40s), 정답은 D이다.

Paraphrasing more technically advanced(기술적으로 더 진보한) → technical prowess exhibited(드러난 기술적 솜씨)

29. What does the writer suggest about Alfred Hitchcock's strategy?
글쓴이는 알프레드 히치콕의 전략에 대해 무슨 말을 하는가?

A It showed that Hitchcock expected his film to be a box office success.
자신의 작품이 흥행에 성공할 것으로 히치콕이 예상했음을 나타냈다.

B It was an effort to prevent viewers from learning too much about the movie.
영화에 대해 관객들이 너무 많은 것을 알지 못하게 방지하기 위한 노력이었다.

C Its main aim was to introduce potential viewers to the film's main character.
주된 목적이 잠재 관객들에게 영화의 주인공을 소개해주는 것이었다.

D It was not the first time that Hitchcock had taken such an approach.
히치콕이 그와 같은 접근법을 취한 것이 처음이 아니었다.

네 번째 문단에서 히치콕은 영화의 극적반전을 예고편에서 최대한 노출하지 않으려고 하였기에(decided to take a more indirect approach, concerned that a typical trailer would inadvertently reveal one of the film's shocking twists), 정답은 B이다.

Paraphrasing reveal one of the film's shocking twists(영화의 충격적인 반전들을 보여주다)
→ learn too much about the movie(영화에 대해 너무 많은 것을 알게 되다)

30. What point is made about the trailer for *Gunfighters of Casa Grande*?
<카사 그란데의 총잡이들> 예고편에 대해 무슨 의견이 제시되었는가?

A It featured more film clips than any other trailers of the 1960s.
1960년대의 다른 어떤 예고편들보다 더 많은 영화 속 영상을 담았다.

B It helped a relatively small-scale film to find an international audience.
비교적 소규모 영화가 해외 관객들을 찾도록 도와주었다.

C It was the first trailer to be directed by Don LaFontaine.
돈 라폰테인이 감독한 첫 번째 예고편이었다.

D It marked the beginning of a narrator's successful career.
한 내레이터의 성공적인 경력에 있어 시작점이 되었다.

다섯 번째 문단에 <카사 그란데의 총잡이들>에서 성우를 맡았던 돈 라폰테인이 이후 5천개가 넘는 영화 예고편에 참여하였으므로(he had lent his voice to more than five thousand movie trailers), 정답은 D이다.

Paraphrasing narrator(나레이터) → voiceover(해설 소리)
a narrator's successful career(한 나레이터의 성공)
→ lent his voice to more than five thousand movie trailers(자신의 목소리를 5천개가 넘는 영화 예고편에 빌려줬다)

31. What was notable about the trailer for *Jaws*?
<죠스> 예고편에 대해 무엇이 주목할 만한 것이었는가?

A It was one of the first movie trailers to be screened via the Internet.
인터넷을 통해 상영된 첫 번째 영화 예고편들 중 하나였다.

B It received the largest production budget ever allocated for a trailer.
예고편에 할당된 것 중 역사상 가장 많은 제작 예산을 받았다.

C It took advantage of the medium of television to reach a potential audience.
잠재 관객들에게 다가가기 위해 텔레비전이라는 매체를 활용했다.

D It introduced several technical innovations that are still used today.
오늘날에서 여전히 이용되고 있는 여러 혁신적인 기술 요소들을 도입했다.

마지막 문단에서 <죠스> 예고편이 TV 주요 방송 채널에 하루에도 여러 번씩 방영되었다고 하므로(trailers were frequently aired on television networks, with the trailer for Steven Spielberg's *Jaws* being shown several times per day on all major networks), 정답은 C이다.

Paraphrasing took advantage of the medium of television(TV 수단을 이용했다)
→ were frequently aired on television networks(자주 TV 채널에 방영되었다)
to reach a potential audience(잠재 고객에 다가가기 위해)
→ in the weeks leading up to the film's release (개봉 시점에 다가오는 주에)

I Vocabulary & Expressions I

be nominated 후보로 지명되다 preview 예고 be comprised of ~로 구성되다 sequence 장면, 화면 draw 끌어내다, 받다 excerpt 발췌 내용 incorporate 포함하다 direct 감독하다 narrator 서술자, 나래이터 notable 주목할 만한 screen 상영하다 allocated 할당된 medium 매체 take advantage of ~을 이용하다

문제 32-37

다음 내용(문제 32-37)과 아래의 영화 예고편 목록을 보시오.

각 내용을 **A**, **B**, **C**, 또는 **D**의 알맞은 조합으로 일치시키시오.

답안지 32-37번 상자에 **A**, **B**, **C**, 또는 **D**에 해당하는 알맞은 글자를 기입하시오.

유의 어떤 글자든 한 번 이상 사용해도 된다.

32. It featured the director himself directly communicating with the viewers.
관객들과 직접적으로 의사 소통하는 감독 자신을 특징으로 했다.

네 번째 문단에서 히치콕이 직접 <사이코> 예고편에 등장하여 시청자들을 위해 직접 투어를 해주므로(Hitchcock giving viewers a personal tour), 정답은 C이다.

Paraphrasing giving viewers a personal tour(본인이 직접 시청자들에게 투어를 해줌)
→ himself directly communicating with the viewers(자신이 직접 시청자와 의사소통)

33. It was created by an artist who had previously worked with the film's director.
이전에 해당 영화의 감독과 작업한 적이 있었던 미술가에 의해 만들어졌다.

다섯 번째 문단에서 <닥터 스트레인지러브> 영화를 스탠리 큐브릭(감독)과 파블로 페로(예술가)가 작업한 이후 예고편도 함께 작업하였으므로, 정답은 D이다.

34. It introduced one of the film's performers near the end of its runtime.
상영시간 거의 끝 무렵에 영화의 배우들 중 한 명을 소개했다.

세 번째 문단에서 <분노의 포도> 예고편은 원작인 베스트 셀러에 대한 영상을 먼저 보여주고 난 후 영화 관련 영상이 나오며 그후 2분이 추가적으로 지나고 헨리 폰다가 소개된다. 따라서 정답은 B이다.

Paraphrasing near the end of its runtime(상영시간 끝 근처에)
→ approximately the two-minute mark when footage of the movie is finally unveiled at the end of the clip(예고편의 마지막 부분에 마침내 영화의 장면이 공개될 때 약 2분쯤)

35. It was notable for helping to usher in the era of sound in Hollywood movies.
할리우드의 유성 영화 시대로 안내하는 데 도움이 된 것으로 유명했다.

두 번째 문단에서 영화에 음향이 도입되면서 예고편의 잠재력에 새롭게 문을 활짝 열어 주었다고 말하면서, 이후 재즈 싱어 예고편이 소개된다. 따라서 정답은 A이다.

Paraphrasing usher in the era of sound(유성 영화 시대로 안내하다)
→ the introduction of sound in motion pictures(영화에 음성의 도입)

36. It utilized a fast-visual style that would gain widespread popularity decades later.
수십 년 후에 폭넓은 인기를 얻었던 빠른 시각적 스타일을 활용했다.

다섯 번째 문단에서 빠른 편집 기술이 1960년대 <닥터 스트레인지러브> 예고편에서부터 1990년대까지 이어졌다고 하므로, 정답은 D이다.

Paraphrasing fast-visual style(빠른 시각 스타일) → quick edits(빠른 편집)
would gain widespread popularity decades later(수십년 후에 널리 인기를 얻었다)
→ became commonplace by the 1990s(1990년대까지 흔해졌다)

37. It highlighted the popularity of the movie's original literary source.
영화의 원작인 문학 작품의 인기를 강조했다.

세 번째 문단에서 <분노의 포도> 예고편은 원작인 스타인벡의 책이 어떻게 품절되었지에 초점을 맞추었다고 하므로 정답은 B이다.

Paraphrasing highlight(~을 강조하다) → focus on(~을 강조하다)
popularity(인기) → completely sold out across the country(전국적으로 완전히 매진되었다)

List of Movie Trailers 영화 예고편 목록
A The Jazz Singer 재즈 싱어
B The Grapes of Wrath 분노의 포도
C Psycho 사이코
D Dr. Strangelove 닥터 스트레인지러브

I Vocabulary & Expressions I

runtime 상영시간 usher 안내하다 era 시대 highlight 강조하다 literary 문학의

문제 38-40

다음 내용들이 독해 지문 3에 제시된 정보와 일치하는가?

답안지 38-40번 상자에 다음 사항을 작성하시오.

참 지문의 정보와 일치하는 경우

거짓 지문의 정보와 일치하지 않는 경우

해당 없음 정보가 존재하지 않는 경우

38. John Ford was disappointed with the trailer for *The Grapes of Wrath*.

존 포드는 <분노의 포도> 예고편에 실망했다.

세 번째 문단에 존 포드의 각색(adaptation)이라는 말만 나오고 그가 실망하였다는 내용은 본문에 없으므로, 정답은 NOT GIVEN이다.

39. Trailers of the 1950s placed emphasis on the popularity of the actors.

1950년대의 예고편들은 배우들의 인기에 중점을 두었다.

네 번째 문단에서 1940, 50년대에 대다수 예고편들이 주연 배우들의 명성을 강조했다고 하므로, 정답은 TRUE이다.

Paraphrasing place emphasis on(~을 강조하다) → emphasize(~을 강조하다)
popularity(인기) → fame(명성)

40. The 1970s saw a decrease in studio demand for expensive movie trailers.

1970년대에는 많은 비용이 드는 영화 예고편에 대한 스튜디오의 수요 감소가 있었다.

마지막 문단에서는 1960년대 이후 수십년 동안, 대규모 예산을 할당하였다고 하는데, 문제에서는 오히려 감소(decrease)했다고 한다. 따라서 정답은 FALSE이다.

Paraphrasing studio demand for expensive movie trailers(비용이 드는 영화 예고편에 대한 스튜디오 수요)
→ most film studios allocating sizable budgets and production teams for the creation of each trailer(각 예고편 제작을 위해 대규모 예산과 제작팀을 할당하는 대부분 영화 스튜디오들)

I Vocabulary & Expressions I

be disappointed with ~에 실망하다 place emphasis on ~을 강조하다 demand 수요, 요구

Test 1	READING [General Training]

1. E	2. C	3. D	4. B
5. A	6. E	7. G	8. FALSE
9. FALSE	10. NOT GIVEN	11. TRUE	12. FALSE
13. NOT GIVEN	14. TRUE		
15. timeline	16. decontamination	17. soap solution	18. leak-proof containers
19. inventories	20. hazards	21. approach	22. communication
23. productivity	24. roles	25. policies	26. personalities
27. workshops			
28. vi	29. x	30. i	31. iv
32. vii	33. ii	34. xi	35. v
36. viii	37. landmark	38. voice	39. tulips
40. Projectors			

▪ 섹션 1 [문제 1-7]

출제 포인트 **난이도: 중하**

제품별로 설명이 된 광고지 또는 정보지에서 맞는 정보를 연결하는 문제(matching information)는 General Training Section 1에 빈출되기에, 이러한 문제 유형에 대한 이해 및 연습 필요

OUR RECOMMENDED RUCKSACKS

A Blacks Travel Daypack
A rucksack designed for short daytrips that's still surprisingly large enough to accommodate large loads. The innovative fabric is Q5 100 percent water resistant, so you don't need to worry should inclement weather occur.

B Kozlowski Supreme
Boasting a distinctive golden logo, this is the first rucksack to be launched by the renowned fashion designer, Mia Kozlowski. Q4 You had better start saving up if you want this bag, as the desirable Kozlowski brand comes at a price.

C Startrek Omega
From one of the most well-established brands in the market, this rucksack is perfect for those who like to be organized during a trip. Q2 With six separate zippered pockets and four side pouches, you'll always find a place to store your things.

D Bower Summit
Affordably priced, the Bower range offers a great selection

추천 배낭 제품

A 블랙스 여행용 배낭
짧은 일일 여행용으로 고안된 배낭이지만 여전히 놀라울 정도로 많은 짐을 수납하기에 충분히 큰 제품이다. 혁신적인 직물 재질이 Q5 100퍼센트 방수이므로, 악천후가 발생되어도 걱정할 필요가 없다.

B 코즐로브스키 수프림
독특한 금색 로고를 자랑하는 이 제품은 유명 패션 디자이너 미아 코즐로브스키가 선보이는 첫 번째 배낭이다. Q4 이 가방을 원하는 사람은 저축을 시작하는 편이 좋은데, 누구나 원하는 코즐로브스키 브랜드에는 그만큼 대가가 따르기 때문이다.

C 스타트렉 오메가
시중에서 가장 확고히 자리 잡은 브랜드들 중의 한 곳에서 만든, 이 배낭은 여행 중에 잘 정리된 상태를 원하는 사람들에게 완벽한 제품이다. Q2 지퍼가 달린 여섯 개의 분리된 주머니와 네 개의 옆면 주머니가 달려 있어, 언제나 물품 보관에 필요한 공간을 찾을 수 있다.

D 바우어 서밋
합리적인 가격의 바우어 제품은 잘 디자인된 아주 많은

of well-designed rucksacks. They come in a wide variety of neon colors, such as yellow, green, and pink, which means Q3 you'll definitely be visible on the mountain when wearing this bag.

배낭을 제공합니다. 노랑색과 녹색, 그리고 핑크색과 같은 매우 다양한 네온 색상으로 나오며, 이는 Q3 산에 이 가방을 메고 있을 때 분명히 눈에 잘 띄게 된다는 것을 의미한다.

E Matterhorn Pro

For those who want something reliable. With a titanium frame and double-stitched material, this bag Q6 comes with an impressive 15-year warranty covering manufacturing defects and damage through general usage. It also Q1 includes a free water bottle to help you stay hydrated.

E 매터혼 프로

신뢰할 수 있는 제품을 원하시는 분들께 권해 드립니다. 티타늄 프레임과 이중 박음질 처리된 재질로 만들어진, 이 가방은 Q6 제조상의 결함과 일반적인 사용상의 손상까지 포함하는 15년 기간의 인상적인 품질 보증 서비스가 딸려 있습니다. 또한 Q1 수분이 보충된 상태로 유지하는 데 도움을 드리는 무료 물병도 포함되어 있습니다.

F Sunrise Montero

From a relatively new manufacturer, this rucksack features innovative cushioned straps that provide optimal comfort to the wearer. At a fairly spacious 40-liters, this bag is suitable for moderate one- or two-day trips.

F 썬라이즈 몬테로

비교적 신생 제조사에서 만든, 이 배낭은 쿠션이 들어간 혁신적인 끈을 특징으로 하는 제품으로 사용자에게 최적의 편안함을 제공합니다. 꽤 넓은 40리터 부피의 용량을 지닌, 이 가방은 하루 또는 이틀 정도로 떠나는 보통 수준의 여행에 적합합니다.

G Rader Stride

This 80-liter bag is Q7 best suited to serious hikers who plan to be on the mountain for several days at a time. Available in black/grey or black/blue, this stylish rucksack is the top choice for many renowned mountaineers.

G 레이더 스트라이드

이 80리터 용량의 가방은 한 번에 Q7 며칠씩 산에 올라가 있기를 계획하는 진정한 등산객들에게 가장 적합합니다. 흑색/회색 또는 흑색/청색 조합으로 이용 가능한, 이 멋진 배낭은 여러 유명 등산가들에게 있어 최고의 선택으로 꼽히는 제품입니다.

I Vocabulary & Expressions I

rucksack 배낭 accommodate ~을 수용하다 innovative 혁신적인 fabric 직물 water resistant 방수의 should (가능성이 있는 사건을 언급할 때) ~이면, ~일 때 inclement weather 악천후 occur 발생되다 distinctive 독특한 launch ~을 출시하다 renowned 유명한 desirable (사람들이) 원하는, 매력적인 come at a price 대가가 따르다 well-established 확고히 자리 잡은 organized 잘 정리된, 체계적인 zippered 지퍼가 달린 affordably priced 합리적인 가격의 range 제품군, 제품 종류 a great selection of 아주 다양한 come in ~ 색으로 나오다 visible 눈에 잘 띄는 reliable 신뢰할 수 있는 double-stitched 이중 박음질이 된 material 재질, 재료 come with ~가 딸려 있다 warranty 품질 보증(서) defect 결함 hydrated 수분이 보충된 feature ~을 특징으로 하다, 포함하다 optimal 최적의 suitable 적합한 moderate 보통의, 중간의 best suited to ~에게 가장 적합한 mountaineer 등산가

문제 1-7

A-G 7개의 가방 이용 후기를 보시오.

다음 내용들은 어느 가방에 대해 사실인가?

답안지 1-7번 상자에 **A-G** 중에서 알맞은 글자를 기입하시오.

유의 어떤 글자든 한 번 이상 사용해도 된다.

1. This rucksack comes with a complimentary item.

이 배낭에는 무료 제품이 딸려 있다.

무료 제품을 제공하는 것은 E 상품이므로(includes a free water bottle), 정답은 E이다.

Paraphrasing come with(~딸려 오다) → include(~을 포함하다)

a complimentary item(무료 제품) → a free water bottle(무료 물병)

ACTUAL TEST 1

2. This rucksack contains several additional storage compartments.
이 배낭은 여러 추가 보관 공간을 포함하고 있다.

C 상품이 6개의 지퍼 주머니와 4개의 옆면 주머니를 갖고 있으므로(with six separate zippered pockets and four side pouches), 정답은 C이다.
Paraphrasing contain(포함하다) → with(~을 갖고 있는)
several additional storage compartments(여러 추가 보관 공간)
→ six separate zippered pockets and four side pouches(6개의 지퍼 주머니와 4개의 옆면 주머니)

3. It is easy to be seen while hiking when wearing this rucksack.
이 배낭을 메고 등산하는 중에 쉽게 눈에 보인다.

D 상품이 산에서 확실히 눈에 띄므로(definitely be visible on the mountain), 정답은 D이다.
Paraphrasing easy to be seen(쉽게 눈에 보이다) → definitely be visible(확실히 눈에 띄다)
while hiking(등산 중에) → on the mountain(산에서)

4. This rucksack is for those who are willing to purchase an expensive bag.
이 배낭은 비싼 가방을 구입할 의향이 있는 사람들을 위한 것이다.

B 상품을 구매하기 위해서는 저축이 필요하다고 하므로(You had better start saving up if you want this bag, as the desirable Kozlowski brand comes at a price), 정답은 B이다.
Paraphrasing expensive(비싼)
→ You had better start saving up if you want this bag, as the desirable Kozlowski brand comes at a price(저축을 시작하는 편이 좋은데, 누구나 원하는 코즐로브스키 브랜드에는 그만큼 대가가 따르기 때문이다)

5. Belongings carried in this rucksack will not be damaged in heavy rain conditions.
이 배낭에 넣고 다니는 소지품은 폭우가 내리는 상태에서도 손상되지 않을 것이다.

A 상품은 100% 방수이므로 악천후에도 걱정이 없으므로(100 percent water resistant, so you don't need to worry should inclement weather occur), 정답은 A이다. 참고로 should inclement weather occur에서 should는 가정법 미래 용법으로 if의 의미와 유사하다고 보면 된다.
Paraphrasing not be damaged in heavy rain conditions(폭우 속에 손상되지 않다)
→ 100 percent water resistant(100% 방수)

6. The manufacturer guarantees that this rucksack will last a long time.
제조사에서 이 배낭이 오랜 기간 지속된다는 점을 보장한다.

E 상품이 15년 품질 보증이 딸려 오므로(comes with an impressive 15-year warranty covering manufacturing defects and damage), 정답은 E이다.
Paraphrasing guarantees that this rucksack will last a long time(오랜 기간 배낭이 지속될 것을 보장하다)
→ an impressive 15-year warranty covering manufacturing defects and damage(제조상 결함이나 손상을 커버하는 인상적인 15년 기간의 보증)

7. Those who plan to go on long excursions will like this rucksack.
장기간의 여행을 떠날 계획이 있는 사람들이 이 배낭을 좋아할 것이다.

G 상품이 장기 여행을 계획하는 사람들을 위한 상품이므로(plan to be on the mountain for several days), 정답은 G이다.
Paraphrasing plan to go on long excursions(장기 여행을 떠날 계획이다)
→ plan to be on the mountain for several days(여러 날을 산에서 지낼 계획이다)

| Vocabulary & Expressions |
complimentary 무료의 storage 보관, 저장 compartment 칸, 구획 guarantee 보장하다 excursion 여행

▪ 섹션 1 [문제 8-14]

출제 포인트 난이도: 중하

코스 및 등록 관련 정보지로 General Training Section 1에 자주 출제되는 만큼 관련 내용 및 어휘 숙지 필요

Prescott Business School

Three-Day Sales Course
This is an intensive course which is Q8 designed for those who have worked in the sales industry for several years and wish to augment their current skillset with advanced, modern techniques. In order to be accepted you should have a proven record in the industry and a desire to improve yourself through hard work.
1st Day: Advanced lessons in delivering on-site sales demonstrations and establishing stong rapport with potential customers. Q9 The day ends with each participant submitting a draft sales pitch for a fictional product assigned to them by the instructor.
Q10 **2nd Day:** The day begins with each participant delivering their sales pitch in front of the other participants. Afternoon classes will focus on collaborative selling techniques and include several group activities.
3rd Day: The session focuses on methods for adding value to a product or service in order to make it more attractive. Several noted business leaders will share their insights with participants. Q11 The day concludes with a personal evaluation for each attendee.

Application Guidelines
Spaces at this popular workshop are limited, and in an effort to maintain a high standard of participants, acceptance is by interview only. Please note, however, that Q12 academic qualifications are irrelevant and do not factor into our decision-making process.

Within one week of receiving your application form and registration fee, we will schedule an interview with you and Q13 send you additional information about the workshop via e-mail. For your initial interview, you will need to tell us about your achievements in the sales industry and present some form of evidence of your accomplishments. You will also be asked to describe your current role and your thoughts on the industry in general.

Q14 For those currently based abroad who wish to apply, you will be able to participate in your first interview by using our video chat program that can be accessed through our homepage. Those who successfully pass the

프레스콧 경영대학원

3일간의 영업 과정
이는 집중 과정으로서 Q8 영업 분야에서 수년 동안 근무해 오면서 한 차원 높고 현대적인 방법을 통해 현재 지니고 계신 능력을 발전시키기를 원하시는 분들을 위해 마련된 것입니다. 수강 신청이 받아들여지기 위해서는, 업계에 입증된 근무 기록과 힘든 노력을 통해 스스로를 향상시키고자 하는 의욕이 있으셔야 합니다.
1일차: 현장 영업 관련 시연 및 잠재 고객과의 끈끈한 관계 확립에 관한 고급 강습. Q9 각 참가자가 강사에 의해 할당된 가상의 제품에 대한 구입 권고 초안을 제출하는 것으로 하루가 마무리됩니다.
Q10 **2일차:** 각 참가자가 다른 참가자들 앞에서 그 제품 구입 권고를 시연해 보이는 것으로 하루가 시작됩니다. 오후 수업은 공동 판매 방법에 초점을 맞추며, 여러 그룹 활동이 포함됩니다.
3일차: 이 시간은 더욱 매력적으로 만들기 위해 제품 또는 서비스에 가치를 부여하는 방법에 초점을 맞춥니다. 여러 유명 사업가들이 참가자들께 통찰력을 공유해 드릴 것입니다. Q11 이 마지막 날은 각 참석자에 대한 개별 평가로 마무리됩니다.

지원 가이드라인
인기 있는 이 워크숍의 자리는 제한되어 있으며, 높은 수준의 참가자를 유지하기 위한 노력의 일환으로, 수강 가능 여부는 오직 면접으로만 결정됩니다. 하지만, Q12 학력은 무관하며, 저희의 결정 과정에 영향을 미치는 요소가 아니라는 점에 유의하시기 바랍니다.

지원서와 수강료를 받은 후 일주일 이내에, 면접 일정을 정할 것이며, 이메일을 통해 Q13 워크숍에 관한 추가 정보를 보내 드립니다. 1차 면접 자리에서, 영업 분야에서 이루신 성과에 관해 저희에게 말씀해 주셔야 하며, 업적에 대한 어떤 형태의 증거물을 제시해 주셔야 합니다. 또한 현재 맡고 계신 역할과 업계에 대한 생각을 전반적으로 설명하도록 요청 받으실 것입니다.

Q14 현재 해외 지역을 기반으로 활동하시면서 지원하기를 원하시는 분들은, 저희 홈페이지를 통해 이용하실 수 있는 저희 동영상 채팅 프로그램을 활용해 1차 면접 시간에 참여하실 수 있습니다. 1차 면접 단계를 성공적으로 통과하신 분들 2차 및 최종 면접 요청을 받게 되시며, 이는 반드시 저희 캠퍼스로 직접 오셔서 참석하셔야

first interview stage will be invited to a second and final session which must be attended in person at our campus. We will provide temporary free parking permits to anyone attending the second session.	합니다. 2차 면접 시간에 참석하시는 모든 분들께 임시 무료 주차증을 제공해 드립니다.

I Vocabulary & Expressions I

sales 영업, 판매 intensive 집중적인 industry 업계 augment ~을 늘리다, 증대하다 skillset 능력 advanced 발전된, 고급의 proven 입증된 deliver a demonstration 시연하다 on-site 현장의 establish ~을 확립하다 rapport 관계 draft 초안의 sales pitch 구입 권고 fictional 허구의, 가상의 assign ~을 배정하다 collaborative 공동의 session (특정 활동을 위한) 시간 noted 유명한 insight 통찰력, 식견 conclude with ~로 마무리되다 evaluation 평가 maintain ~을 유지하다 acceptance 수용, 합격 academic qualifications 학력 irrelevant 무관한, 상관없는 factor 영향을 미치는 요소가 되다 via ~을 통해 initial 처음의 achievement 성과, 업적 in person 직접 (가서) temporary 임시의, 일시적인 parking permit 주차증

문제 8-14

다음 내용들이 지문에 주어진 정보와 일치하는가?

답안지 8-14번 상자에 다음 사항을 작성하시오.

참 지문의 정보와 일치하는 경우

거짓 지문의 정보와 일치하지 않는 경우

해당 없음 정보가 존재하지 않는 경우

8. People can sign up for the three-day course without any previous sales experience.
과거에 영업 경력이 전혀 없어도 3일간 진행되는 해당 강좌에 등록할 수 있다.

영업 분야에서 수년 동안 근무해 온 사람들을 대상으로 고안된 강좌이므로(designed for those who have worked in the sales industry for several years), 정답은 FALSE이다.

Paraphrasing previous sales experience(이전 영업 경험)
→ worked in the sales industry for several years(수년동안 영업 분양에서 일했다)

9. Participants will perform a sales pitch in front of other workshop members at the end of the first day.
참가자들은 1일차 마지막에 다른 워크숍 참가자들 앞에서 구입 권고를 시연해 보일 것이다.

1일차 마지막에는 구입 권고 시연이 아닌 초안 제출이므로(The day ends with each participant submitting a draft sales pitch), 정답은 FALSE이다.

10. Instructors will use successful companies as case studies on the second day.
강사들은 2일차에 사례 연구로 성공적인 회사들을 활용할 것이다.

2일차에 사례 연구 활용 내용이 언급되지 않기에, 그룹 활동에 사례 연구가 나오는지 알 수 없다. 따라서 정답은 NOT GIVEN이다.

11. Participants will receive feedback from instructors on the last day of the workshop.
참가자들은 워크숍 마지막 날에 강사들로부터 의견을 들을 것이다.

마지막 3일차에 참가자들의 개별 평가로 마무리되므로(The day concludes with a personal evaluation for each attendee), 정답은 TRUE이다.

Paraphrasing Participants will receive feedback(참가자들은 피드백을 받을 것이다)
→ a personal evaluation for each attendee(각 참가자를 위한 개별 평가)

12. During their first interview session, applicants will be asked about their academic qualifications.
1차 면접 시간 중에, 지원자들은 각자의 학력에 관한 질문을 받을 것이다.

인터뷰 중 학력은 관련이 없다고 하므로(academic qualifications are irrelevant), 정답은 FALSE이다.

13. Prescott Business School will send participants driving directions after scheduling an interview.
프레스콧 경영대학원은 면접 일정을 정한 후에 참가자들에게 차량 방문 안내도를 보내줄 것이다.

워크숍 관련 추가 정보를 보내준다고 하였는데(send you additional information about the workshop), 이러한 추가 정보에 차량 방문 안내도가 포함되는지 알 수 없으므로, 정답은 NOT GIVEN이다.

14. Overseas applicants can take part in the first interview session via a website.
해외 지원자들은 웹 사이트를 통해 1차 면접 시간에 참여할 수 있다.

해외 지원자들이 1차 면접에 홈페이지를 통해 참여할 수 있으므로(For those currently based abroad who wish to apply, you will be able to participate in your first interview by using our video chat program that can be accessed through our homepage), 정답은 TRUE이다.

Paraphrasing overseas applicants(해외 지원자들)
→ those currently based abroad who wish to apply(현재 해외에 있으며 신청하기 원하는 사람들)
via a website(웹사이트를 통해) → through our homepage(홈페이지를 통해)

I Vocabulary & Expressions I

previous 이전의 case study 사례 연구 driving directions 차량으로 오는 길

▪ 섹션 2 [문제 15-20]

출제 포인트 **난이도: 중**

직장 또는 업무상 안전, 위생 관련 내용 안내문은 General Training Section 2에 자주 출제되는 만큼 관련 내용 및 어휘 숙지 필요. 특히 General Training Section 2에서 출제 빈도가 높은 flowchart 유형으로 문제가 구성됨

Decontamination and clearance instructions for laboratories

This Laboratory Decontamination and Clearance Guide is designed for laboratories that plan to relocate to new premises or completely cease operations. This information will help you with your transition and ensure that you conform to all state health and safety regulations.

There are several things you must do prior to the clearance activities outlined below. First and foremost, you must notify the Environmental Safety Association (ESA) of your intent to close or transfer the laboratory. When doing so, you should send the ESA a Q15 timeline of activities regarding the movement and disposal of laboratory equipment and chemicals. Next, you must arrange a waste pickup service for all chemicals, sharp objects, and general waste, and an appropriate transportation service for any chemicals and equipment that will be moved to a new location.

Clearance activities can be performed either by in-house laboratory employees or an ESA-approved company. Begin with the Q16 decontamination of all laboratory equipment that has been used in conjunction with radioactive,

실험실 오염 제거 및 정리 작업 안내

이 '실험실 오염 제거 및 정리 가이드'는 새 부지로 이전하거나 완전히 운영을 중단할 계획인 실험실을 위해 고안된 것입니다. 이 정보는 그 변화 과정에서 도움을 드리고 반드시 국가의 모든 보건 안전 규정을 준수하도록 해 줄 것입니다.

아래에 간략히 설명된 정리 작업에 앞서 반드시 해야 하는 몇 가지 일이 있습니다. 가장 먼저, 반드시 환경 안전 협회(ESA)에 실험실 폐쇄 또는 이전 의사를 통보해야 합니다. 이렇게 하실 때, 실험 장비 및 화학 물품의 운송 및 처리와 관련된 작업 Q15 시간표를 ESA로 보내야 합니다. 다음으로, 모든 화학 물품과 날카로운 물체, 그리고 일반 쓰레기에 대한 폐기물 수거 서비스 및 새로운 곳으로 옮겨질 모든 화학 물품과 장비에 대한 적절한 운송 서비스를 반드시 마련해야 합니다.

정리 작업은 실험실 소속 직원이나 ESA 승인 업체 둘 중의 한 가지를 통해 실시될 수 있습니다. 장비가 옮겨지든 또는 자리에 남겨지든 상관없이 방사선 물질이나 화학 물질, 또는 생물학 물질과 함께 사용된 모든 실험실 장비에 대한 Q16 오염물 제거부터 시작하십시오. 실험실 이용 안내서에 상세히 설명된 Q17 비누 용액을 사용한 다음, 물로 헹구십시오. 실험실의 모든 긴 의자에서 테이프

ACTUAL TEST 1

chemical, or biological materials, regardless of whether the equipment will be moved or left in place. Use the Q17 soap solution detailed in your laboratory manual, followed by a water rinse. Remove tape and non-slip mats from all laboratory benches and wash all horizontal surfaces as well as the fronts and sides of cabinets with the same soap solution as above. Wash these surfaces starting with the highest areas in the room and proceeding to the lowest. Any surfaces that may potentially be contaminated should be treated with disinfectant. Place all chemicals and cultures in Q18 leak-proof containers and arrange them in single layers in heavy-duty cardboard boxes. Finally, notify the ESA to inform them that the clearance activities are complete.

ESA agents will arrive on-site to check chemical Q19 inventories and perform a full clearance inspection in order to ensure that the laboratory is completely free from contamination. They will also perform checks for specific environmental Q20 hazards, including faulty electrical wiring or mold. If the results from the clearance inspection fail to meet the standards set by the ESA, additional cleaning must be carried out by the laboratory staff or by an ESA-approved contractor, at the laboratory supervisor's expense.

와 미끄럼 방지 매트를 제거하고 진열장의 가로로 된 모든 표면뿐만 아니라 앞면 옆면도 위에 언급한 비누 용액으로 닦으십시오. 실험실 내의 가장 높은 쪽에 있는 부분부터 시작해 가장 낮은 쪽으로 진행하는 방식으로 이 표면들을 닦으십시오. 잠재적으로 오염되어 있을 수 있는 모든 표면은 살균제로 처리되어야 합니다. 모든 화학 물품과 배양균은 Q18 새지 않는 용기에 담아 튼튼한 판지 상자에 한 층씩 정리해 놓으십시오. 마지막으로, ESA에 통보해 정리 작업이 완료되었음을 알리십시오.

ESA 직원들이 현장에 도착해 화학 물질 Q19 재고를 확인하고 해당 실험실에 오염 물질이 완전히 제거된 상태임을 확인하기 위해 전면적인 정리 점검을 실시할 것입니다. 또한 특정한 환경적 Q20 위험 요소들에 대한 확인 작업도 실시할 것이며, 여기에는 결함이 있는 전기 배선 또는 곰팡이 문제로 포함됩니다. 정리 점검 작업의 결과 ESA에서 정한 기준을 충족하지 못할 경우, 해당 실험실 책임자가 부담하는 비용으로 소속 실험실 직원 또는 ESA 승인 계약업체에 의해 반드시 추가 정리 작업이 실시되어야 합니다.

I Vocabulary & Expressions I

decontamination 오염 제거 clearance 정리 instructions 안내, 설명, 지시 laboratory 실험실 relocate to ~로 이전하다 premises 부지, 구내 cease ~을 중단하다 operation 운영, 가동 transition 변화 과정, 변천 conform to ~을 준수하다 regulation 규정, 규제 prior to ~에 앞서 outline ~을 간략히 설명하다 notify 통보하다 intent 의도 transfer ~을 옮기다, 이송하다 disposal of ~의 처분 pickup 수거, 가져감 appropriate 적절한 transportation 운송, 교통 chemical 화학 물품 in-house (조직) 내부의 in conjunction with ~와 함께 radioactive 방사선의 biological 생물학의 material 물질, 물체 followed by 뒤이어 rinse 헹굼 horizontal 가로의 solution 용액 proceed to ~로 진행하다 potentially 잠재적으로 contaminate ~을 오염시키다 disinfectant 살균제 cultures 배양균 leak-proof 새지 않는 container 용기, 그릇 layer 층, 겹, 막 heavy-duty 튼튼한 on-site 현장에 inventory 재고 (목록) inspection 점검, 조사 free from ~가 없는 specific 특정한, 구체적인 hazard 위험 (요소) faulty 결함이 있는 mold 곰팡이 meet ~을 충족하다 carry out ~을 실시하다 contractor 계약업체 at one's expense ~의 비용으로

문제 15-20

다음 순서도를 완성하시오.

각 답변에 대해 지문에서 **2개 이하의 단어**를 고르시오.

답안지 15-20번 상자에 답변을 작성하시오.

Procedure for laboratory relocation or closure

실험실 이전 또는 폐쇄 절차

Pre-clearance activities 정리 작업 전에 할 일

Inform the Environmental Safety Association (ESA) of your intention to move or close the lab. Provide them with a **15** .... detailing activities related to the transfer of lab equipment and materials.

환경 안전 협회(ESA)에 실험실 이전 또는 폐쇄 의사를 알린다. 그곳에 실험실 장비 및 물품 이전과 관련된 작업을 상세히 설명하는 **15** ....을 제공한다.

Clearance activities 정리 작업

All laboratory equipment that has come into contact with biological or chemical substances must undergo **16** ....

생물학적 또는 화학적 물질과 접촉된 바 있는 모든 실험실 장비를 반드시 **16** ....을 거쳐야 한다.

Equipment and laboratory surfaces must be washed using a **17** .... and then rinsed.

장비 및 실험실 표면들은 반드시 **17** ....을 사용해 닦은 다음 헹궈져야 한다.

Put all chemicals in **18** .... arranged in single layers in cardboard boxes.

모든 화학 물품은 판지 상자에 한 층씩 정리된 **18** ....에 넣어야 한다.

ESA activities ESA 작업

After you inform the ESA of the completion of clearance activities, an ESA inspection team will visit the laboratory.The team will review your **19** .... of chemicals and inspect the laboratory. The team will also determine whether any other potential **20** .... are present.

정리 작업의 완료를 ESA에 알리고 나면, ESA 조사팀이 실험실을 방문할 것이다. 그 팀이 화학 물품의 **19** ....을 살펴보고 실험실을 점검할 것이다. 그 팀은 또한 다른 어떤 잠재적인 **20** ....가 존재하는지도 밝혀낼 것이다.

Follow-up activities 후속 작업

If there is a problem with the inspection, the laboratory supervisor will be told to clean the premises again, or pay to have an ESA-approved company carry out the work.

점검에 문제가 있을 경우, 실험실 책임자는 다시 한 번 해당 건물을 정리하도록 지시받거나 ESA 승인 업체에 비용을 지불해 해당 작업을 맡기도록 지시받게 될 것이다.

15. ESA에 장비와 화학물질 이동 또는 처리에 대한 시간표를 보내라고 하므로(you should send the ESA a timeline of activities regarding the movement and disposal of laboratory equipment and chemicals), 정답은 timeline이다.

Paraphrasing provide them(그들에게 제공해라) → send the ESA(ESA에 보내라)
transfer(옮기다) → movement and disposal(이동과 처리)
materials(물질들) → chemicals(화학물질들)

16. 방사선 물질이나 화학 물질, 또는 생물학 물질과 함께 사용된 모든 실험실 장비에 대한 오염물 제거(the decontamination of all laboratory equipment that has been used in conjunction with radioactive, chemical, or biological materials)가 필요하므로, 정답은 decontamination이다.

Paraphrasing come into contact with(~와 접촉되다) → used in conjunction with(~와 함께 사용된)

ACTUAL TEST 1

17. 린스 전에 비누 용액을 사용하므로(Use the soap solution detailed in your laboratory manual, followed by a water rinse), 정답은 soap solution이다.

18. 모든 화학 물품과 배양균은 새지 않는 용기에 담아 튼튼한 판지 상자에 한 층씩 정리해 놓아야 되므로(place all chemicals and cultures in leak-proof containers and arrange them in single layers in heavy-duty cardboard boxes), 정답은 leak-proof containers이다.

주의할 점은, 지문에 나온대로 leak와 proof 사이에 반드시 하이픈을 적어야 된다. 만일 하이픈이 빠지면, 세 단어가 되어 오답처리 될 수 있다.

19. ESA 직원들이 현장에 도착해 화학 물질 재고를 검토하고(check chemical inventories) 해당 실험실에 오염 물질이 완전히 제거된 상태임을 확인하기 위해 전면적인 정리 점검을 실시할 것이라고 하므로(perform a full clearance inspection), ESA 조사팀이 확인하는 것은 화학물질 재고인 inventories이다.

Paraphrasing check chemical inventories(화학 물질 재고를 확인하다)
→ review your inventories of chemicals(화학 물질에 대한 재고를 검토하다)

20. ESA 팀이 추가적으로 특정한 환경적 위험 요소들도 조사하므로(They will also perform checks for specific environmental hazards), 정답은 hazards이다.

Paraphrasing also determine whether(또한 ~인지 결정하다) → also perform checks for(또한 ~에 대해 조사하다)

| Vocabulary & Expressions |

relocation 이전 closure 폐쇄 lab 실험실 substances 물질 cardboard 판지 premises 부지, 구내

▪ 섹션 2 [문제 21-27]

출제 포인트 **난이도: 중하**

직장 내 규정 또는 직장 생활 정보는 General Training Section 2에 빈출되기에, 관련 내용 및 어휘에 대한 숙지 필요

Appendix: Settling staff disputes in the workplace

This appendix details the causes of disputes between employees and offers advice about how employers can take measures to reduce and resolve workplace conflict.

Employers should be aware that there are many different potential reasons for conflict between workers, and each reason may require a different Q21 approach. Causes of conflict can range from clashes of personality to Q22 communication breakdowns between staff and management. Almost all cases result in lower Q23 productivity in the workplace and therefore should be addressed as soon as they arise to prevent serious consequences such as project failures. The most common reasons for disputes are behaviours that coworkers find irritating, a feeling that needs are not being met and adequate resources are not being provided, differences over work methods, competition between highly-motivated workers, and unclarified workplace Q24 roles, such as cases in which a nonsupervisory worker is asked to supervise other employees.

부록: 직장 내 직원 분쟁 해결

이 부록은 직원들 사이의 분쟁 발생 원인을 상세히 설명하고 고용주가 어떻게 직장 내 갈등을 줄이고 해결하기 위한 조치를 취할 수 있는지에 관한 조언을 제공합니다.

고용주는 직원들 사이의 갈등에 대한 여러 다른 잠재적인 원인들이 존재한다는 점과 각 원인이 서로 다른 Q21 접근 방식을 필요로 할 수 있다는 점을 인식해야 합니다. 갈등의 원인은 성격 차이에서부터 직원과 경영진 사이의 Q22 의사 소통 단절 문제에까지 이를 수 있습니다. 거의 모든 경우가 직장 내 Q23 생산성 저하를 초래하므로, 프로젝트 실패와 같은 심각한 결과를 방지할 수 있도록 문제가 발생되는 대로 처리되어야 합니다. 분쟁에 대한 가장 흔한 원인은 동료 직원들이 짜증난다고 생각하는 행위들, 즉 필요 사항이 충족되지 못하고 충분한 자원이 제공되고 있지 못하다는 느낌, 업무 방식에 대한 차이, 크게 동기 부여된 직원들 사이의 경쟁, 그리고 불명확한 직장 내 Q24 역할, 관리 직책이 아닌 직원이 다른 직원들을 관리하도록 요구되는 것과 같은 경우들입니다.

Employers can mitigate the frequency and severity of workplace conflict by creating a work environment designed to preclude conflict wherever possible, and by dealing with any disputes that do arise promptly and fairly. The most important thing is to ensure that work Q25 policies are clear, and that the reasoning behind dispute mediation decisions is consistent from one case to the next. When attempting to settle a conflict, an employer should always focus on the actions of the employees, and the consequences of those actions, rather than the Q26 personalities of the individuals involved. In addition, the HR department should develop and implement conflict resolution training Q27 workshops that all managers should regularly attend. In extreme cases where conflict escalates to the point of physical violence, theft, or threatening behaviour, employers should consider notifying the police.

고용주는 가급적 갈등을 방지하기 위해 마련된 업무 환경을 만들어냄으로써, 그리고 발생되는 어떤 분쟁이든 즉각적이고 공정하게 처리하는 방법으로 직장 내 갈등의 발생 빈도와 심각성을 완화할 수 있습니다. 가장 중요한 점은 직장 내 Q25 정책들이 명확해지도록, 그리고 분쟁 조정 결정 이면에 존재하는 논리가 경우마다 일관되도록 확실히 해두는 것입니다. 갈등을 해결하려 시도할 때, 고용주는 관련된 사람들의 Q26 성격이 아니라 직원들의 행동 및 그 행동에 따른 결과에 항상 초점을 맞춰야 합니다. 추가로, 인사과는 모든 관리자들이 정기적으로 참석해야 하는 갈등 해결 교육 Q27 워크숍을 개발해 시행해야 합니다. 갈등이 물리적 폭력이나 절도, 또는 위협적인 행위가 발생되는 정도로까지 악화되는 극단적인 경우에, 고용주는 경찰에 알리는 일을 고려해야 합니다.

I Vocabulary & Expressions I

appendix 부록 settle ~을 해결하다 dispute 분쟁 detail ~을 상세히 설명하다 take measures 조치를 취하다 conflict 갈등 range 범위에 이르다 clashes of personality 성격 차이 breakdown 단절, 실패, 와해 result in ~의 결과를 낳다 address (문제 등)을 다루다 arise 발생되다 prevent ~을 막다 consequence 결과 irritating 짜증나게 하는 adequate 충분한, 적절한 resource 자원, 재원 highly-motivated 크게 동기 부여된 unclarified 불명확한 nonsupervisory 관리직이 아닌 mitigate ~을 완화하다 frequency 빈도 severity 심각성, 극심함 preclude ~을 방지하다 wherever possible 가급적 promptly 즉각적으로 fairly 공정하게 reasoning 논리, 추론 mediation 조정, 중재 consistent 일관된 attempt 시도하다 implement ~을 시행하다 extreme 극도의 escalate 고조되다 to the point of ~의 정도까지 physical violence 물리적 폭력 threatening 위협적인 notify ~에게 알리다

문제 21-27

다음 메모를 완성하시오.
각 답변에 대해 지문에서 **오직 1개의 단어만** 고르시오.
답안지 21-27번 상자에 답변을 작성하시오.

Staff disputes in the workplace 직장 내 직원 분쟁

Disputes: Causes and Effects 분쟁: 원인과 결과

- each type of conflict requires a specific **21** .... in order to reach a resolution
  각각의 갈등 유형은 해결에 도달하기 위해 특정 **21** ....을 필요로 한다
- disputes can arise when **22** .... between employees and supervisors is poor
  분쟁은 직원과 책임자 사이의 **22** ....가 좋지 못할 때 발생될 수 있다
- unresolved conflict can lead to a decrease in **23** .... and even more significant consequences
  해결되지 못한 갈등은 **23** ....의 감소로 이어질 수 있으며, 심지어 더 중요한 결과로까지 이어질 수 있다
- conflict can occur when employees' **24** .... in the workplace are not clearly defined
  직장 내에서 직원들의 **24** ....가 명확하게 규정되지 않을 때 갈등이 발생될 수 있다

Recommended Actions 추천되는 조치

- make sure that all **25** .... are clearly outlined for employees
  직원들을 위해 반드시 모든 **25** ....가 명확히 윤곽이 그려지도록 해야 한다
- refrain from focusing on the **26** .... of employees when resolving disputes
  분쟁을 해결할 때 직원들의 **26** ....에 초점을 맞추는 것은 삼가야 한다
- have the HR department establish **27** .... that will help managers with conflict resolution
  갈등 해결과 관련해 관리자들에게 도움을 줄 **27** ....을 인사과가 확립하게 해야 한다

21. 각 원인이 서로 다른 접근 방식을 필요로 할 수 있다고 하므로(each reason may require a different approach), 정답은 approach이다.
Paraphrasing specific(특정한) → different(다른)

22. 직원과 경영진 사이의 의사소통 단절 문제(communication breakdowns between staff and management)란 직원과 책임자 간 의사소통이 좋지 못할 때와 같은 의미이므로, 정답은 communication이다.
Paraphrasing between employees and supervisors(직원과 책임자 사이에)
→ between staff and management(직원과 경영진 사이에)
poor(안 좋은) → breakdown(단절, 와해)

23. 직장내 갈등이 더 낮은 생산성으로 귀결되므로(result in lower productivity in the workplace), 정답은 productivity이다.
Paraphrasing lead to a decrease in productivity(생산성에 대한 감소로 이어지다)
→ result in lower productivity(더 낮은 생산성으로 귀결되다)

24. 불명확한 직장 내 역할(unclarified workplace roles)은 직원들의 역할이 명확하게 규정되지 않음을 뜻하므로, 정답은 roles이다.
Paraphrasing unclarified(명확하지 않은) → not clearly defined(명확히 정의되지 않은)

25. 직장 내 정책들을 명확히 하라고 하므로, 빈칸에 명확히 해야할 것은 policies이다. 한 글자만 정답이 되므로 work policies는 오답처리 된다.
Paraphrasing make sure(확실히 하다) → ensure(확실히 하다)
be clearly outlined(명확히 윤곽이 그려지다) → be clear(명확하다)

26. 분쟁해결 시 사람들의 성격에 초첨을 맞추는 것이 아니므로(rather than the personalities of the individuals), 초점을 맞추지 말아야 하는 것은 personalities이다.
Paraphrasing when resolving disputes(분쟁을 해결할 때)
→ When attempting to settle a conflict(갈등을 해결하려 시도할 때)

27. HR이 모든 관리자들이 정기적으로 참석해야 할 갈등 해결 교육 워크숍을 시행해야 한다고 하므로(HR department should develop and implement conflict resolution training workshops that all managers should), 갈등 해결 관련해 인사과 관리자에게 제공해주는 것은 workshops이다. 여기서 한 글자만 정답이므로 conflict resolution training의 단어들을 정답란에 적으면 안된다.

I Vocabulary & Expressions I
resolution 해결 unresolved 해결되지 못한 outline 윤곽을 잡다 refrain 삼가다 HR department 인사과

▪ 섹션 3 [문제 28-40]

출제 포인트 | 난이도: 중

최근 제너럴 시험에 출제되었던 시드니 수산 시장 토픽을, 제너럴 시험에 자주 등장하는 기행 또는 스토리 형식의 지문으로 변형하여 출제

기출 2017년 12월 - 시드시 수산 시장

A Trip to Sydney Fish Market

A In the entire Southern Hemisphere, Q28 no other fish market comes close to the size and scale of Sydney Fish Market. Every year, the market trades almost 15,000 tonnes of seafood comprised of more than 500 different sustainable species. Around 70 employees are on-site to ensure the smooth operation of the wholesale auction and Sydney Seafood School, which is promoted as an institution of seafood excellence.

B If you hope to see the fishermen bringing in their fresh catches, you have to visit the market very early in the morning. Daily tours begin at 6.30 a.m., so my friends and I are up bright and early Q29 to meet our guide, Henry, at a restaurant just outside the market entrance. Henry starts off by briefing us on a few facts regarding the market. We are impressed to hear that not only is it the largest of its type in the Southern Hemisphere, but it is also considered the second most diverse market in the world after Tokyo's famous Tsukiji Market.

C Henry leads us onto the auction floor, where buyers are seated in rows, eyes fixated on three large monitors. We hear sounds of disappointment coming from a few of the buyers following a completed sale. Henry guesses that Q30 an inexperienced bidder possibly paid over the odds for the sale, inadvertently raising the average sale price for other sales in that category. We are all fascinated by the rapid pace and high energy on the auction floor, and urge Henry to explain it to us.

D According to Henry, Q31 the market implemented a digital auction system in 1989, marking a significant Q37 landmark in the evolution of seafood sales. Auction prices are set at least $3 above the expected market price per kilo, and rows of buyers type feverishly on keyboards, making numerous sales in quick succession. Henry points out that the system is much more efficient than the previous traditional Q38 voice auction, with barely any stock going unsold on any given day.

E Q32 The system draws direct inspiration from a 'reverse auction' system that has been used for more than a century to buy and sell Q39 tulips in flower markets in the Netherlands. In 2004, the market installed advanced digital video Q40 projectors to improve the visibility and presentation of the auction clocks. Up to 200 buyers will watch these screens each day, and

시드니 수산 시장 여행

A 남반구 전체 지역에서, Q28 다른 그 어느 수산 시장도 크기와 규모 면에서 시드니 수산 시장에 버금가는 곳은 없다. 매년, 이 수산 시장은 500가지가 넘는 다른 지속 가능한 종으로 구성된 거의 15,000톤에 달하는 해산물을 거래한다. 약 70명의 직원들이 도매 경매장 및 뛰어난 해산물 요리 학원으로 홍보되고 있는 시드니 해산물 요리 학원의 원활한 운영을 보장하기 위해 현장에서 근무한다.

B 어부들이 신선한 어획물을 들여오는 것을 보기를 희망할 경우, 아침에 아주 일찍 이 수산 시장을 방문하여야 한다. 일일 운영 시간은 오전 6시 30분에 시작되므로, 친구들과 나는 새벽 같이 일어나 Q29 이 시장 입구 바로 바깥쪽에 있는 한 레스토랑에서 우리의 가이드 헨리를 만났다. 헨리는 이 시장과 관련된 몇몇 사실을 간단히 설명해 주는 것으로 시작하였다. 우리는 이 시장이 남반구에서 동종의 시장 중 가장 크다는 사실뿐만 아니라 도쿄의 유명한 츠키지 시장 다음으로 세계에서 두 번째로 가장 다양한 시장으로 여겨진다는 말을 듣고 깊은 인상을 받았다.

C 헨리는 구매자들이 세 개의 대형 모니터에 시선을 고정한 채로 줄지어 앉아 있는 경매장으로 우리를 이끌고 갔다. 우리는 판매 완료 후에 몇몇 구매자들이 내뱉은 실망 섞인 소리를 들었다. 헨리는 Q30 한 미숙한 입찰자가 그 판매 제품에 대해 예상 외로 많은 돈을 지불했고, 이로 인해 우연히 해당 범주의 다른 판매에 비해 평균 판매가가 올랐다고 생각했다. 우리는 모두 경매장의 빠른 속도와 활기찬 에너지에 매혹되었고 헨리에게 빨리 설명해 달라고 재촉했다.

D 헨리의 말에 따르면, Q31 이 시장은 1989년에 디지털 경매 시스템을 시작했는데, 이로 인해 해산물 판매의 진화에 있어 중요한 Q37 획기적인 사건으로 특징지어지게 되었다. 경매 가격은 1킬로그램당 예상 시장 가격보다 최소 3달러 높게 정해지며, 줄지어 앉은 구매자들이 정신없이 키보드를 두드려 연달아 수많은 판매를 이뤄낸다. 헨리는 이 시스템이 경매가 열리는 어느 날이든 판매되지 않는 재고가 거의 없기 때문에 기존의 전통적인 Q38 음성 경매보다 훨씬 더 효율적이라는 점을 지적했다.

E Q32 이 시스템은 1세기 넘게 네덜란드의 꽃 시장에서 Q39 튤립을 사고파는 데 이용되어 온 '역경매' 시스템에서 직접적인 영감을 얻었다. 2004년에, 이 시장은 경매 시계의 가시성과 제시 방식을 개선하기 위해 여러 디지털 동영상 Q40 프로젝터를 설치했다. 최대 200명의 구매자들이 매일 이 화면들을 보게 되

ACTUAL TEST 1

this reverse auction system has gained a deserved reputation as the fastest and most efficient method of trading seafood.

F On the day of our visit, there are 60 tonnes of fish stacked or laid out on the auction floor, delivered in the early morning by more than 1,000 suppliers based throughout the Asia-Pacific region. Q33 As early as 2 a.m., products begin arriving and a team of quality assurance inspectors grade them based on their size, weight, and expected shelf life. Henry gives each of us a high-visibility jacket to put on before we step out onto the auction floor ourselves to get a closer look at the wide variety of fish and shellfish.

G Q34 Henry shows us a B+-grade lobster caught hours earlier, and informs us that when buying shellfish, it is crucial to check that the shells are strong as it indicates that the creature is in good health and will yield higher quality meat. As instructed by Henry, we then smell the gills of a massive fish, almost as long as a human, to test for freshness. To our surprise, he also tells us that the freshness of seafood is mainly related to the way it has been treated since being caught, and not necessarily the length of time that has passed since it was caught.

H We finish our tour with a visit to the marketplace, where we see all manner of seafood available for purchase, and then a look at the prestigious Sydney Seafood School. Q35 The school was established in 1989 and now attracts over 10,000 students per year, due in part to its impressive list of guest chefs and speakers from the culinary world. We also have a chance to check out the innovative new online-based seafood trading system that the fish market's technology team launched in 2001. Operating alongside the on-site Dutch auction, the Web-based trading facility takes fish trading to a whole new level by reaching a wider range of buyers.

I Before we leave the market, Henry tells us about some of the modifications planned for the building. He first notes that the existing market is one of the most popular tourist attractions in Sydney, with around two million people taking a tour of the premises each year. Not only does the market generate approximately $20 million annually for the local economy, but it also generates almost $70 million through tourist spending. Q36 With this in mind, the local government has

는데, 이 역경매 시스템은 해산물 거래의 가장 빠르고 효율적인 방식으로서 그만한 자격이 있는 명성을 얻었다.

F 우리가 방문한 첫째 날에, 경매장에 쌓여 있거나 펼쳐 놓은 60톤의 생선이 있었는데, 아시아 태평양 지역 전체를 걸쳐 기반으로 영업하는 1,000곳이 넘는 공급업체들에 의해 아침 일찍 배송된 것이었다. Q33 아주 이른 시간인 오전 2시에, 제품들이 도착하기 시작하며, 품질 보증 검사 담당자들로 구성된 팀이 크기와 무게, 그리고 예상 유통 기한을 바탕으로 등급을 매긴다. 헨리는 아주 다양한 생선과 갑각류를 더 가까이서 볼 수 있도록 우리가 직접 경매장 안으로 발을 들이기 전에 우리 각각에게 가시성이 높은 재킷을 주었다.

G Q34 헨리는 수 시간 전에 잡힌 B+ 등급의 바다 가재를 우리에게 보여주면서 갑각류를 구입할 때 껍질이 단단한지 확인하는 것이 중요하다고 알려 주었는데, 그것이 그 생물체가 건강한 상태이며 품질이 더 높은 살을 제공해 준다는 것을 나타내기 때문이었다. 헨리가 설명한 대로, 우리는 신선도를 확인하기 위해 거의 사람만한 길이의 엄청나게 큰 생선 한 마리의 아가미 냄새를 맡아 봤다. 놀랍게도, 헨리는 해산물의 신선도는 잡힌 이후로 다뤄진 방식과 주로 관련이 있으며, 잡힌 이후로 지나간 시간 길이와 반드시 상관 있는 것은 아니라는 점도 얘기해 주었다.

H 우리는 구매 가능한 모든 종류의 해산물을 볼 수 있는 시장 구역을 방문한 다음, 권위 있는 시드니 해산물 요리 학원을 둘러보는 것으로 견학을 마쳤다. Q35 이 학원은 1989년에 설립되었으며, 현재 해마다 10,000명이 넘는 학생들을 유치하고 있는데, 요리 업계에 속한 초청 요리사와 연사들이 포함된 인상적인 명단이 일부 이유이다. 우리는 또한 수산 시상의 기술 담당 팀이 2001년에 내놓은 혁신적인 온라인 기반 해산물 거래 시스템도 확인해 볼 기회가 있었다. 현장의 네덜란드식 경매와 함께 운영되는 이 웹 기반의 거래 설비는 훨씬 더 다양한 구매자들에게 다가감으로써 수산물 거래를 완전히 새로운 수준으로 끌어올렸다.

I 우리가 이 수산 시장을 떠나기 전에, 헨리는 그 건물에 대해 계획된 일부 개조 작업에 관해 얘기해 주었다. 먼저 매년 약 2백만 명의 사람들이 이 건물을 견학하고 있어 현재 운영되는 시장이 시드니에서 가장 인기 있는 관광 명소들 중의 하나라는 점을 언급해 주었다. 이 수산 시장이 지역 경제를 위해 연간 약 2천만 달러를 창출할 뿐만 아니라 관광객 소비를 통해

allocated $250 million to renovate the old space and create a modernized destination with a focus on retail and tourism. Henry shows us the proposed blueprint and explains how the building will integrate various attractive features while still housing a bustling auction floor and market. **One thing is for sure: we all agreed that we would love to return for another tour once modifications are complete!**

거의 7천만 달러의 수익도 발생시킨다. Q36 이러한 점을 감안해, 지역 정부가 소매 및 관광 산업에 초점을 맞춰 오래된 공간을 개조하고 현대화된 관광지를 만들기 위해 2억 5천만 달러의 비용을 배정했다. 헨리는 제안된 설계도를 우리에게 보여주면서 북적대는 경매장과 시장 구역을 여전히 수용함과 동시에 그 건물이 어떻게 여러 매력적인 특징들을 통합하게 될 것인지를 설명해 주었다. **한 가지 분명한 점은, 우리 모두 개조 공사가 완료되는 대로 또 한 번의 견학을 하러 꼭 다시 가 보고 싶다는 점에 동의했다는 사실이다!**

I Vocabulary & Expressions I

come close to ~에 버금가다 comprised of ~로 구성된 sustainable 지속 가능한 species (동식물) 종 on-site 현장에 있는 wholesale 도매의 auction 경매 be up bright and early 새벽같이 일어나다 brief 간략히 설명하다 in rows 줄지어 fixate ~을 고정시키다 following ~ 후에, 다음에 bidder 입찰자 over the odds (돈이) 예상 외로 많은 inadvertently 우연히, 무심코 fascinated 매혹된 urge 재촉하다, 촉구하다 implement ~을 시행하다 landmark 획기적인 사건 evolution 진화, 발전 feverishly 정신 없이 in quick succession 연달아 stock 재고(품) go unsold 팔리지 않게 되다 draw direct inspiration 직접적인 영감을 얻다 reverse 반대의 install ~을 설치하다 advanced 발전된, 진보한 visibility 가시성 presentation 제시 (방식) deserved 그만한 자격이 있는 reputation 명성, 평판 stack ~을 쌓다 lay out ~을 펼쳐 놓다 quality assurance 품질 보증 shelf life 유통 기한 yield ~을 산출하다 quality 양질의 gill 아가미 manner 종류 prestigious 권위 있는 due in part to ~가 일부 원인인 culinary 요리의 alongside ~와 함께 modification 개조, 변경, 수정 premises 건물, 부지 allocate ~을 할당하다 retail 소매 blueprint 설계도 integrate ~을 통합하다 feature 특징 bustling 북적대는 complete 완료된

문제 28-36

해당 지문에는 **A-I**, 9개의 문단이 있다.
아래의 제목 목록에서 각 문단에 알맞은 제목을 고르시오.
답안지 28-36번 상자에 **i-xi**까지 알맞은 숫자를 기입하시오.

List of Headings 제목 목록

i	An error on the bidding floor	경매장에서 실수(오류)
ii	The quality assurance process	품질 보증 과정
iii	Commonly traded seafood products	흔히 거래되는 해산물 제품
iv	The adoption of an electronic system	전자 시스템의 채택
v	Education and online trading	교육과 온라인 거래
vi	A market of incredible size and scope	믿을 수 없는 크기와 규모를 지닌 시장
vii	A method for trading flowers	꽃 거래 방법
viii	An investment for the future	미래를 위한 투자
ix	Overcoming financial difficulties	재정적인 어려움 극복하기
x	An introduction to our guide	가이드 소개
xi	How to check the freshness of seafood	해산물 신선도 확인 방법

28. A 문단

A 문단은 시드니 수산 시장의 엄청난 크기와 규모에 대해 설명하므로, 정답은 vi이다.

ACTUAL TEST 1

29. B 문단

B 문단은 처음 가이드 헨리를 만나고 그가 전해주는 설명이 주를 이루므로, 정답은 x이다.

30. C 문단

C 문단은 한 미숙한 입찰자의 경매 실수에 대한 내용이 나오므로, 정답은 i이다.

31. D 문단

D 문단은 디지털 경매 시스템 도입과 그 효율성이 나오므로, 정답은 iv이다.

32. E 문단

E 문단은 네덜란드 꽃 시장 거래 방법인 역경매 방식 도입에 대한 내용으로, 정답은 vii이다.

33. F 문단

F 문단은 경매장 바닥에 제품들과 이에 대한 품질 검사 과정이 주를 이루므로, 정답은 ii이다.

34. G 문단

G 문단 전체에 걸쳐, 헨리가 해산물의 신선도를 확인하는 방법을 자세하게 알려주고 있으므로, 정답은 xi이다.

35. H 문단

H 문단은 시드니 해산물 요리 학원과 온라인 기반 해산물 거래 시스템에 대한 내용이 주를 이루므로, 정답은 v이다.

36. I 문단

I 문단은 지역 정부의 투자와 그에 따른 청사진 설명이 주를 이루므로, 정답은 viii이다.

문제 37-40

다음 요약 내용을 완성하시오.

각 답변에 대해 지문에서 **오직 1개의 단어만** 고르시오.

답안지 37-40번 상자에 답변을 작성하시오.

Sydney Fish Market's auction system 시드니 수산 시장의 경매 시스템

In 1989, Sydney Fish Market introduced a new auction system that was considered a **37** .... in the development of seafood trading. The system is a significant improvement over the old **38** .... auction method. It was modelled on a system used to trade **39** .... in flower markets in the Netherlands. **40** .... were later installed on the auction floor in order to improve the visibility of the clocks.

1989년에, 시드니 수산 시장은 해산물 거래의 발전에 있어 **37** ....로 여겨진 새로운 경매 시스템을 도입했다. 이 시스템은 오래된 **38** .... 경매 시스템에 비해 상당한 개선이다. 이는 네덜란드의 꽃 시장에서 **39** ....을 거래하기 위해 사용된 시스템을 본떠 만든 것이었다. 시계의 가시성을 개선하기 위해 나중에 **40** ....가 경매장에 설치되었다.

37. D 문단에서 1989년에 디지털 경매 시스템은 획기적인 사건이었으므로(the market implemented a digital auction system in 1989, marking a significant landmark), 정답은 landmark이다.
Paraphrasing introduce(도입하다) → implement(도입하다)

38. D 문단에서 새 시스템이 이전의 전통적인 음성 경매보다 더 효율적이므로(the system is much more efficient than the previous traditional voice auction), 빈칸에 들어갈 정답은 voice이다.
Paraphrasing a significant improvement(상당한 개선) → more efficient(더 효율적인)
old(오래된) → previous traditional(이전의 전통적인)

39. E 문단에서 네덜란드 꽃 시장에서 거래된 것은 튤립이므로(tulips in flower markets in the Netherlands), 빈칸에 정답은 tulips이다. 지문에 나온대로 복수로 써야 되며, 단수로 쓰면 오답이다.

40. E 문단에 시장이 시계의 가시성을 개선하기 위해 설치한 것은 프로젝터들이므로(the market installed advanced digital video projectors to improve the visibility and presentation of the auction clocks), 정답은 Projectors이다. 대문자/소문자에 상관없이 정답 처리되지만, 단수로 쓰면 오답이다.

Test 1 LISTENING [Academic / General Training]

1. pottery	2. refreshments	3. 30/thirty	4. arranging	5. seeds
6. bus	7. Lynessa	8. dance	9. harbo(u)r	10. footwear
11. C	12. C	13. B	14. F	15. A
16. B	17. C	18. E	19. H	20. G
21. C	22. B	23. A	24. B	25. C
26. C	27. H	28. F	29. A	30. D
31. economic	32. jobs	33. technology	34. parking	35. car
36. weight	37. CO_2/CO2	38. battery	39. engine(s)	40. biofuels

▪ 파트 1 [문제 1-10]

출제 포인트 **난이도: 중하**
실제 시험에서 출제율이 높은 프로그램 또는 강좌 문의 주제로, Table Completion 문제 유형이 출제된 비교적 쉬운 문제 세트임
음원 남 - 영국 / 여 - 영국 / 스피드 - 실제 원어민 대화 스피드로 시험에서 빠르게 나올 때 속도

You will hear a telephone conversation between a woman who wants to attend Summer Festival programmes and an official at a tourist information centre. **OFFICIAL:** Thanks for calling York Tourist Information Centre. My name is Oliver. How can I help you? **WOMAN:** Hello, I heard that the city council has arranged some special programmes as part of its Summer Festival. Would you be able to tell me about them? **OFFICIAL:** Sure! There's a wide range of programmes for everyone to enjoy. I'll give you some details about a few of them. First of all, there's an interesting one taking place at Marina Art Institute.	여름 축제 프로그램에 참석하기를 원하는 한 여성과 관광객 안내 센터 관계자 사이의 전화 통화를 들어보세요. **관계자:** 요크 관광객 안내 센터에 전화 주셔서 감사합니다. 제 이름은 올리버입니다. 무엇을 도와 드릴까요? **여성:** 안녕하세요, 시의회에서 여름 축제의 일환으로 몇몇 특별 프로그램을 마련했다는 얘기를 들었어요. 그것들에 관해서 얘기해 주실 수 있으신가요? **관계자:** 그럼요! 모든 사람이 즐길 수 있는 아주 다양한 프로그램이 있습니다. 그것들 중 몇 가지에 관한 일부 상세 정보를 알려드리겠습니다. 가장 먼저, 마리나 미술관에서 열리는 흥미로운 것이 하나 있습니다.

WOMAN: OK. What's that one about?
OFFICIAL: It focuses on learning about ancient tools and weapons. There are lectures and a guided tour of exhibits. You'll also have an opportunity to make Q1 pottery that you can take home with you.
WOMAN: Hmm, that sounds interesting. Does it cost anything?
OFFICIAL: No, admission is completely free.
WOMAN: And is there somewhere to buy Q2 refreshments there?
OFFICIAL: Yes, in fact, they're complimentary from the institute's on-site cafeteria.
WOMAN: Oh, that's good to know.
OFFICIAL: Also, if you join the programme, you'll receive a one-time Q3 30 per cent discount in the gift store, so you can pick up some souvenirs.
WOMAN: Oh, great. I'm tempted, but can you tell me about some other programmes?
OFFICIAL: Another one that might interest you is at Digby Garden Centre. Group participants will learn a lot of gardening tips, and the main part of the programme focuses on planting and Q4 arranging flowers in vases and bouquets. The staff there have won awards for their expertise.
WOMAN: Actually, I do spend a lot of time in my garden at home, and I love flowers. Do members of the programme get any free gifts or anything?
OFFICIAL: Yes, at the end of the programme, you will get a wide selection of Q5 seeds that you can plant in your garden at home. You also get an attractive glass vase.
WOMAN: Wow! That sounds like something I'd like. But, the garden centre is on the edge of town and quite difficult for me to get to.
OFFICIAL: Well, you'll be happy to hear that there's a Q6 bus that runs from downtown to the garden centre every day at 9 am. And, it comes back from the centre around noon. This is totally free for all members of the programme.

OFFICIAL: Now, there's one more programme that you might like to hear about. It's taking place at the brand new Lynessa Music Hall. In case you aren't sure how that's spelled, it's Q7 L-Y-N-E-S-S-A.
WOMAN: Thanks. Go on, please.
OFFICIAL: This programme is specifically for people who want to learn how to Q8 dance. It covers several styles, including ballroom, salsa and modern hip hop.
WOMAN: Oh, that sounds fun, and I think my husband might be interested in joining that programme with me. The Lynessa Music Hall... Hmm... Is that just opposite the Q9 harbour?

여성: 좋아요. 그게 뭔가요?
관계자: 고대의 도구와 무기에 관해 배우는 데 초점을 맞춘 것입니다. 강연과 가이드 동반 전시 투어가 있습니다. 또한 집으로 가져가실 수 있는 Q1 도자기를 만들 기회도 있을 겁니다.
여성: 흠, 흥미로운 것 같네요. 거기에 드는 비용이 있나요?
관계자: 아뇨, 입장료는 완전히 무료입니다.
여성: 그리고 그곳에 Q2 간식을 구입할 수 있는 곳이 있나요?
관계자: 네, 사실, 그 미술관 건물의 구내 식당에서 무료로 이용 가능합니다.
여성: 오, 좋은 정보네요.
관계자: 그리고, 그 프로그램에 참가하시면, 선물 매장에서 1회에 한해 Q3 30퍼센트 할인을 받기에, 몇몇 기념품을 구입하실 수 있습니다.
여성: 오, 잘됐네요. 끌리기는 하지만, 다른 프로그램에 관해서도 말씀해 주시겠어요?
관계자: 관심이 있으실 수도 있는 다른 것이 디그비 원예용품점에서 진행됩니다. 단체 참가자들이 많은 원예 관련 팁을 배우게 되는데, 이 프로그램의 주요 부분이 식물 심기와 꽃병 및 부케용 Q4 꽃꽂이에 초점을 맞추고 있습니다. 그곳의 직원들은 전문 지식으로 인해 상을 받기도 했습니다.
여성: 실은, 제가 집에 있는 정원에서 정말 많은 시간을 보내고 있고, 꽃을 아주 좋아합니다. 그 프로그램 참가자들이 무료 선물 같은 것도 받나요?
관계자: 네, 프로그램 종료 시에, 집에 있는 정원에 심으실 수 있는 아주 다양한 Q5 씨앗을 받으시게 됩니다. 매력적인 유리 꽃병도 받습니다.
여성: 와우! 제가 좋아하는 것 같네요. 하지만, 그 원예용품점은 도시 가장자리에 있어서 제가 가기에 꽤 힘들 것 같아요.
관계자: 저, 매일 오전 9시에 시내에서 그 원예용품점까지 운행하는 Q6 버스가 있다는 말을 들으시면 기쁘실 겁니다. 그리고, 정오쯤에 그 용품점에서 되돌아옵니다. 이는 해당 프로그램의 모든 참가자들에게 완전히 무료입니다.

관계자: 자, 정보를 듣고 싶어하실 만한 프로그램이 한 가지 더 있습니다. 완전히 새로운 리네사 음악 홀에서 열리는 것입니다. 철자로 어떻게 표기하는지 확실치 않으실 것 같아서 말씀드리는데, Q7 L-Y-N-E-S-S-A입니다.
여성 : 감사합니다. 계속 말씀해 주세요.
관계자: 이 프로그램은 특히 Q8 춤추는 법을 배우고 싶어하시는 분들을 위한 것입니다. 여러 가지 스타일을 다루는데, 사교 댄스와 살사, 그리고 현대 힙합이 포함됩니다.
여성: 오, 재미있을 것 같아요, 그리고 제 남편이 저와 함께 그 프로그램에 참여하는 데 관심이 있을지도 몰라요.

OFFICIAL: Exactly. So you won't have any trouble finding a parking space, as there's a large parking lot there. If you're interested in registering for this programme, I recommend that you take suitable Q10 footwear. The sessions are around two hours long, so you need to make sure you are comfortable.	리네사 음악 홀이면... 흠... Q9 항구 바로 맞은편에 있는 것인가요? **관계자:** 맞습니다. 그래서 주차 공간을 찾으시는 데 아무런 문제도 없으실 텐데, 그곳에 대형 주차장이 있기 때문입니다. 이 프로그램에 등록하시는 데 관심이 있으시면, 적합한 Q10 신발을 착용하시도록 권해 드리고 싶습니다. 진행 시간이 약 2시간 길이이기 때문에, 반드시 편한 상태로 있으셔야 합니다.

| Vocabulary & Expressions |

council 의회 arrange ~을 마련하다, 조치하다 as part of ~의 일환으로 a wide range of 아주 다양한 details 상세 정보, 세부 사항 take place 개최되다, 일어나다 ancient 고대의 tool 도구 guided 가이드가 동반된 exhibit 전시(회) pottery 도자기 cost ~의 비용이 들다 admission 입장(료) completely 완전히, 전적으로(= totally) free 무료의(= complimentary) refreshments 간식, 다과 on-site 구내의, 현장의 cafeteria 구내식당 pick up ~을 구입하다, 가져가다 souvenir 기념품 tempted (마음이) 끌리는 interest ~의 관심을 끌다 participant 참가자 gardening 원예 planting 식물 심기 arrange flowers 꽃꽂이하다 expertise 전문 지식 seed 씨앗 attractive 매력적인 on the edge of ~의 가장자리에 get to ~로 가다 run (교통편 등이) 운행되다 brand new 완전히 새로운 in case (that) ~할 경우에 (대비해) cover (주제 등) ~을 다루다 including ~을 포함해 just opposite ~ 바로 맞은편에 session (특정 활동을 위한) 시간 around 약, 대략

문제 1-10

다음 표를 완성하시오.

각 답변에 대해 **1개의 단어 또는 숫자**를 작성하시오.

Summer Festival Programmes 여름 축제 프로그램

Place 장소	Main Focus 중점 사항	Additional Details 추가 세부 사항
Marina Art Institute 마리나 미술관	making **1** .... and learning about ancient tools and weapons **1** .... 만들기와 고대의 도구 및 무기에 관해 배우기	• free admission 무료 입장료 • also includes complimentary **2** .... on site 또한 현장에서 무료 **2** .... 포함된다 • participants receive a **3** .... % discount in a gift store 참가자들이 기념품 가게에서 **3** ....% 할인을 받는다
Digby Garden Centre 디그비 원예용품점	planting and **4** .... flowers 식물 심기와 꽃으로 **4** ....하기	• participants are given a selection of **5** .... and a vase 참가자들에게 다양한 **5** ....와 꽃병이 제공된다 • a **6** .... is available at 9 am and noon 오전 9시와 정오에 **6** .... 이용 가능하다

ACTUAL TEST 1

7 .... Music Hall 7 .... 음악 홀	learning how to 8 .... in a variety of styles 다양한 스타일로 8 .... 방법 배우기	• located opposite the 9 .... 9 .... 건너편에 위치 • appropriate 10 .... is recommended 적절한 10 .... 권장됨

1. 마리나 미술관에서 도자기 만들 기회가 있다고 하므로(You'll also have an opportunity to make pottery), 정답은 pottery이다.

2. 여자가 간식에 대해 묻자, 남자가 무료로 현장 카페테리아에서 무료라고 말하므로(they're complimentary from the institute's on-site cafeteria), 정답은 refreshments이다. 간식은 보통 복수형으로 쓰이며 문제 빈칸에도 문법상 복수만 정답 취급된다.

3. 기념품 가게에서 30% 할인이 되므로(30% discount in the gift store), 정답은 30이다. 문제에 per cent가 이미 있으므로 30%라고 쓰지 않도록 한다.
   Paraphrasing participants(참가자들) → if you join the programme(프로그램에 참가한다면)

4. 문제 그대로 방송에서 식물을 심고 꽃꽂이를 한다고 말하므로(planting and arranging flowers), 정답은 arranging이다.

5. 다양한 씨앗을 받을 것이다고 말하므로(you will get a wide selection of seeds), 정답은 seeds이다.
   Paraphrasing participants are given(참가자들은 받는다) → you will get(당신은 받을 것이다)

6. 9시와 정오에 이용가능한 것은 버스로(there's a bus that runs from downtown to the garden centre every day at 9 am. And, it comes back from the centre around noon), 정답은 bus이다.

7. 아이엘츠에서는 같은 철자를 두 번 말하는 대신 더블을 사용하는데, 이때 W(더블유)와 헷갈리지 말자. 정답은 LYNESSA로 대문자/소문자 상관없다.

8. 특별히 춤을 어떻게 추는지 배우길 원하는 사람들을 위한 수업이므로(specifically for people who want to learn how to dance), 정답은 dance이다.
   Paraphrasing variety of styles(다양한 스타일들) → several styles(여러 스타일들)

9. 여자가 항구 바로 맞은편이 아니냐고 묻자(Is that just opposite the harbour?) 남자가 맞다고 확인해주므로(Exactly), 정답은 harbour이다. 미국식(harbor), 영국식(harbour) 철자 모두 정답 처리된다.

10. 적합한 신발을 추천하므로(I recommend that you take suitable footwear), 정답은 footwear이다.
    Paraphrasing appropriate(적절한) → suitable(잘 맞는, 적합한)

▪ 파트 2 [문제 11-20]

출제 포인트 **난이도: 중**

실제 시험에서 빈번하게 나오는 업무 및 시설 오리엔테이션으로, 2019년에 출제된 농장 아르바이트 업무 오리엔테이션 문제를 변형함. Labelling Map의 경우, 난이도는 평이하지만, 문제 정답이 방송에서 연이어 나오기에 한번 흐름이 끊기거나 잠깐 딴 생각을 하면 틀리기 쉬움.

음원 남 - 호주 / 스피드 - 실제 원어민 독백 스피드로 시험에서 빠르게 나올 때 속도

You will hear the owner of Faraday Farm speaking to orientation participants about scheduled activities and the layout of the farm.	패러데이 농장 소유주가 오리엔테이션 참가자들에게 예정된 활동 및 농장 구획에 관해 이야기하는 것을 들어보세요.

Good morning, everyone. My name's Richard Faraday, and I'm the owner of Faraday Farm. This is your first day as temporary workers here at the farm, so I've gathered you here early this morning to give you an orientation. You'll be working here for the next four months, and this is a particularly busy period at the farm, so you have lots to learn about working safely and efficiently on the farm.

안녕하세요, 여러분. 제 이름은 리처드 패러데이이며, 패러데이 농장 소유주입니다. 오늘이 이곳 농장에서 임시 직원으로 근무하시는 첫날이므로, 오리엔테이션을 진행하기 위해 오늘 아침 일찍 이곳으로 여러분을 모이시도록 했습니다. 여러분은 앞으로 네 달 동안 이곳에서 근무하실 예정이며, 이 기간은 농장이 특히 바쁜 시기이기 때문에, 농장에서 안전하고 효율적으로 근무하는 것과 관련해 알아두셔야 할 것이 많습니다.

So, I'll start by telling you a bit about the farm itself. I first bought the land almost 20 years ago, and it has gradually evolved from a small corn farm into a large farm dealing not only in corn, but also in fruit crops, horses and livestock. Q11 Over the past few years, the farm has gained a good national reputation for the high standard of meat, dairy, fruit and grain we produce here. That is why we continue to employ only the highest standards here on the farm, and we expect all of our workers to do the same.

그럼, 농장 자체와 관련해 조금 말씀드리는 것으로 시작해 보겠습니다. 제가 거의 20년 전에 처음 이 부지를 매입했으며, 소규모 옥수수 농장에서 시작해 옥수수뿐만 아니라 과일 농작물과 말, 그리고 가축까지 취급하는 대형 농장으로 점차 발전해 왔습니다. Q11 지난 몇 년에 걸쳐, 저희 농장은 이곳에서 생산하는 질 높은 고기와 유제품, 과일, 그리고 곡물로 인해 전국적으로 좋은 명성을 얻었습니다. 이것이 바로 저희가 이곳 농장에서 계속 높은 기준을 적용하는 이유이며, 저희는 모든 직원들이 동일하게 일해 주기를 기대합니다.

We started employing temporary workers three years ago, and it has really helped us to maintain production during our busiest times of the year. Q12 In the past, some temporary staff told us they were unhappy about the lack of buses or trains between the city and our farm. So, starting this year, we will operate a free shuttle bus that will run between city hall and the farm. This should greatly benefit those of you who do not have your own mode of transportation. You'll also be pleased to know that we have raised the hourly rate for workers this year in accordance with government recommendations.

저희는 3년 전에 임시 직원들을 고용하기 시작했으며, 연중 가장 바쁜 시기에 생산량을 유지하는 데 정말로 큰 도움이 되었습니다. Q12 과거에, 일부 임시 직원들이 도시와 저희 농장 사이를 오가는 버스 또는 기차의 부족 문제가 불만스럽다고 얘기해 주셨습니다. 따라서, 올해부터, 저희는 시청과 저희 농장 사이를 오가는 무료 셔틀 버스를 운행할 것입니다. 이는 각자의 교통 수단이 마련되어 있지 않은 분들에게 크게 유용할 것입니다. 여러분은 또한 정부의 권고에 따라 올해 직원들을 위한 시급을 인상했다는 사실을 알면 기쁠 것입니다.

In a moment, I'll talk you through the schedule for today's orientation. Although you were originally told that it would finish at 5 pm, that has been changed to 3 pm Q13 The forecast calls for heavy rain and thunderstorms in the late afternoon, so we'd be wise to wrap up the proceedings as quickly as possible. But, I'll see you here bright and early at 6 am tomorrow for your first proper day of work on the farm.

잠시 후에, 오늘 오리엔테이션 일정을 말씀드리겠습니다. 애초에 오후 5시에 종료되는 것으로 들으셨겠지만, 오후 3시로 변경되었습니다. Q13 일기 예보에서 오후 늦게 폭우와 뇌우를 예상하고 있어서, 가능한 한 신속히 진행 과정을 마무리하는 것이 현명할 것입니다. 하지만, 농장에서 제대로 된 근무 첫날을 위해 내일 아침 일찍 6시에 이곳에서 뵙겠습니다.

OK, so today I'll take you around the entire farm, and you'll be taught several things by myself and some of my most experienced assistants. Now, before we set off, Q14 we're going to gather right outside the house and change into the rubber boots that we provide to each worker. As you'd expect, the ground in many parts of the farm can get very muddy.

자, 그럼 오늘은, 제가 여러분과 함께 농장 전체를 둘러볼 것이며, 저를 비롯해 일부 가장 경험 많은 보조 직원들을 통해 여러 가지를 배우게 됩니다. 이제, 출발하기에 앞서, Q14 집 건물 바로 밖에 모여 저희가 각 직원에게 제공하는 고무 장화로 갈아 신을 예정입니다. 예상하고 계시겠지만, 농장 여러 구역의 땅이 매우 질척거릴 수 있습니다.

Then, we're going to walk to the far end of the farm, past the fields, and stop at the orchard. Our apples have grown in popularity lately, and have even won some industry awards. Q15 Outside the orchard, you'll have an

그런 다음, 농장 가장 먼 곳으로 갈 예정이며, 여러 밭을 지나, 과수원에 들르겠습니다. 저희 사과가 최근에 인기를 얻고 있으며, 심지어 업계 내의 몇몇 상을 수상하기도 했습니다. Q15 과수원 바깥쪽에서, 오늘 아침 갓 따낸,

opportunity to taste some of our delicious apples, picked fresh from the trees this morning. You'll also listen to a talk on how to check the condition of the fruit.

맛있는 사과 몇 개를 시식해볼 기회를 가지겠습니다. 여러분은 또한 과일의 상태를 확인하는 방법에 관한 이야기도 듣게 됩니다.

Next, Q16 we'll go up the lane between our raspberry and strawberry fields so that you can have a look at the crops growing. Here you'll have a chance to meet some of the full-time farm workers, who will give you some useful tips. Many people think that picking berries is a simple procedure, but there's actually more to it than you'd imagine!

다음으로, Q16 자라나는 작물을 보실 수 있도록 라즈베리 밭과 딸기 밭 사이의 길로 들어설 것입니다. 이곳에서 여러분은 몇몇 유용한 팁을 드릴 농장 정규직 직원들을 만날 기회를 가지게 됩니다. 많은 분들이 베리류를 따는 것이 간단한 과정이라고 생각하지만, 실제로는 상상하는 것 이상입니다!

Q17 We'll then go across the main road and enter the corn field. We recently invested in brand new combine harvesters and other harvesting equipment, and you'll watch a demonstration on how to use these correctly and safely. It's doubtful that any of you will drive the combine harvesters yourselves, but we'll teach you the basics, just in case.

Q17 그 후에 큰 길을 가로질러 옥수수 밭으로 들어가겠습니다. 저희가 최근에 완전히 새로운 곡물 수확기계와 기타 수확용 장비에 투자했으며, 정확하고 안전하게 이 기기들을 사용하는 방법에 관한 시연을 보실 것입니다. 이 콤바인 수확기를 여러분 중 누구든 직접 운전할 것으로 보이지는 않지만, 만일을 위해 기본 사항들을 가르쳐 드리겠습니다.

By that time, you'll probably be getting hungry, so Q18 we'll stop for lunch. There's a nice spot on the lane that separates the potatoes from the cows. My wife, Mrs Faraday, will drive out to meet us there and bring some homemade soup, bread and cheese, using many ingredients actually produced here on the farm.

그때쯤, 여러분은 배가 고플 것이므로, Q18 점심을 위해 쉬겠습니다. 감자와 소를 분리해주는 길에 아주 좋은 곳이 있습니다. 제 아내가 운전하고 나와 그곳에서 우리와 만날 텐데, 이곳 농장에서 실제로 생산된 많은 재료를 활용해 집에서 만든 수프, 빵, 그리고 치즈를 가져다 줄 것입니다.

Once we feel refreshed, Q19 we'll enter the cow pasture and learn all about the importance of maintaining soil condition. The reason our livestock are so healthy is due to our nutrient-rich soil, and it's important that you follow our rules in order to keep these high standards.

일단 회복된 기분을 느끼고 나면, Q19 소를 키우는 초원으로 가서 토양 상태를 유지하는 일의 중요성에 관한 모든 것을 배우겠습니다. 저희 가축이 아주 건강한 이유는 영양이 풍부한 토양 때문이며, 이렇게 높은 수준으로 유지될 수 있도록 저희 농장의 규칙을 준수하는 것이 중요합니다.

Finally, we will briefly head back to the house, and then Q20 stop off to feed the horses outside the stable. You'll also notice the gift shop there. All staff members receive a 20 per cent discount on items for sale.

마지막으로, 집으로 잠시 되돌아온 다음, Q20 잠시 마구간에 들러 말들에게 먹이를 주겠습니다. 또한 선물 매장도 볼 것입니다. 모든 직원들은 판매 중인 제품에 대해 20퍼센트 할인을 받습니다.

Okay, now let's get ready and take a look around.

자, 이제 준비를 마치고 둘러보러 가겠습니다.

| Vocabulary & Expressions |

temporary 임시의 gather ~을 불러 모으다 particularly 특히 evolve 발전하다 deal in ~을 취급하다 livestock 가축 gain ~을 얻다 reputation 명성 employ ~을 사용하다, 쓰다 maintain ~을 유지하다 lack of ~의 부족 operate ~을 운영하다 run (교통편이) 다니다, 운행하다 benefit ~에게 유익하다, 이득이 되다 mode of transportation 교통 수단 talk A through B A에게 B를 설명하다 assistant 보조, 조수 set off 출발하다 change into ~로 갈아 신다, 갈아 입다 muddy 질척이는 far end 가장 먼 곳, 가장 끝 부분 orchard 과수원 so that (목적) ~할 수 있도록 have a look at ~을 살펴보다 procedure 과정, 절차 invest in ~에 투자하다 brand new 완전히 새로운 harvester 수확기 equipment 장비 demonstration 시연, 시범 correctly 정확히, 제대로 It's doubtful that ~할 것 같지 않다 oneself 직접 basics 기초, 기본 just in case 만일의 경우에 (대비해) by ~쯤, ~ 무렵 separate A from B A와 B를 분리하다 ingredient (음식) 재료 refreshed 회복된, 상쾌한 pasture 초원 soil 토양, 땅 nutrient-rich 영양이 풍부한 head back to ~로 되돌아가 stop off 잠시 들르다 stable 마구간 take a look around 둘러보다 cattle (집합적 개념으로) 가축용 소

문제 11-13

A, **B**, **C** 중에서 알맞은 글자를 고르시오.

Orientation Day at Faraday Farm 패러데이 농장 오리엔테이션 개최일

11. What is Faraday Farm most well-known for?
패러데이 농장은 무엇으로 가장 잘 알려져 있는가?

A The diversity of its livestock 다양한 가축
B The efficiency of its farming methods 농업 방식의 효율성
C The freshness of its produce 농산물의 신선함

농장이 높은 수준의 고기, 유제품, 과일, 곡식 재배로 명성을 얻었다고 말하므로(the farm has gained a good national reputation for the high standard of meat, dairy, fruit and grain we produce here), 이에 대한 내용이 가장 유사하게 패러프레이징 된 C(The freshness of its produce)가 정답이다. 방송에서 farm과 livestock이 들렸다고 A나 B를 선택하면 안된다.

Paraphrasing well-known for(~로 잘 알려진) → gained a good national reputation for(~로 전국적인 명성을 얻었다)
freshness(신선함) → high standard(높은 수준)
produce(농산물) → meat, dairy, fruit and grain(고기, 유제품, 과일, 곡식)

12. According to the speaker, previous temporary workers have complained about
화자의 말에 따르면, 이전의 임시 직원들은 --------------------에 대해 불평한다.

A low hourly rates. 낮은 시급
B unsafe working conditions. 안전하지 못한 근무 조건
C access to public transport. 대중 교통에 대한 접근성

예전에 임시직원들이 도시와 농지 간 버스와 기차 부족에 대해 불만족스럽다고 말했으므로(In the past, some temporary staff told us they were unhappy about the lack of buses or trains between the city and our farm), 정답은 교통 접근성인 C이다.

Paraphrasing workers(근로자들) → staff(직원들)
complained about(~에 대해 불만스럽다) → unhappy about(~에 대해 행복하지 않은)
public transport(대중교통) → buses or trains(버스나 기차)

13. The orientation will finish earlier than scheduled because
오리엔테이션이 ------------------ 때문에 예정보다 일찍 끝날 것이다.

A important tasks need to be performed. 중요한 업무가 수행되어야 한다.
B inclement weather is expected. 악천후가 예상된다.
C the speaker has an appointment. 화자가 약속이 있다.

폭우와 천둥 예보로, 가능한 빨리 끝내겠다고 하였으므로(The forecast calls for heavy rain and thunderstorms in the late afternoon, so we'd be wise to wrap up the proceedings as quickly as possible), 정답은 B(inclement weather is expected)이다.

Paraphrasing inclement weather(악천후) → heavy rain and thunderstorms(폭우와 천둥)
finish(끝내다) → wrap up(마무리하다)
be expected(예상되다) → the forecast calls for(예보하다)

문제 14-20

다음 지도에 표기하시오.

14-20번 질문 옆에 **A-I**까지 정확한 글자를 표기하시오.

Faraday Farm Layout 패러데이 농장 구획

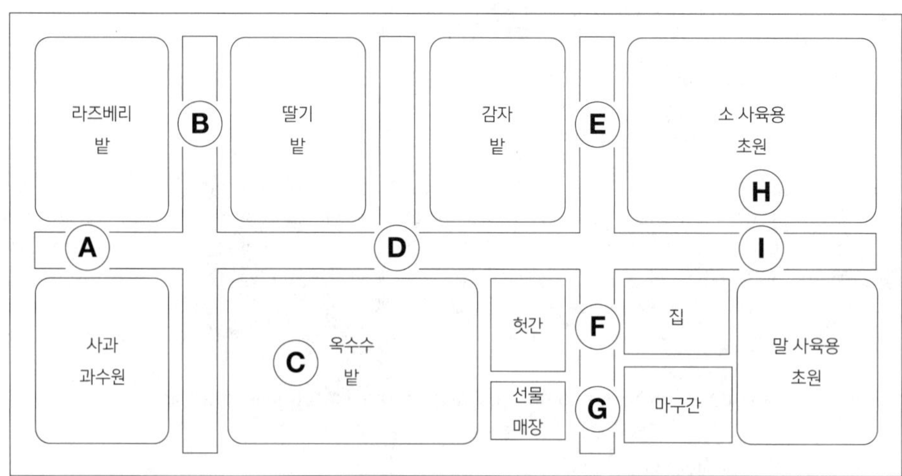

14. Changing footwear ....

신발 갈아 신기

집 앞에서 신발을 갈아 신는다고 하였으므로(we're going to gather right outside the house and change into the rubber boots), 지도에서 F가 정답이다.

참고로 Labelling map 유형에서, 먼저 시작점을 찾는 것이 중요하다. 대부분 지도에 시작점이 표시되어 있지만, 이번 문제처럼 나와 있지 않은 경우 역시 때때로 출제되므로 이러한 문제에도 익숙해지도록 한다.

Paraphrasing footwear(신발) → rubber boots(고무 장화)

15. Quality testing ....

품질 검사

과수원 밖에서 사과를 시식하고 과일 상태를 확인하는 법에 대해 들을 것이므로(Outside the orchard, you'll have an opportunity to taste some of our delicious apples, picked fresh from the trees this morning. You'll also listen to a talk on how to check the condition of the fruit.), 정답은 A이다.

Paraphrasing quality testing(품질 검사) → check the condition(상태를 확인하다)

16. Meeting coworkers ....

동료 직원 만나기

라즈베리와 딸기 밭 사이길에서 농작물이 자라는 것을 보고, 정규직 직원들을 만나서 유용한 팁들을 들을 것이므로(we'll go up the lane between our raspberry and strawberry fields so that you can have a look at the crops growing. Here you'll have a chance to meet some of the full-time farm workers, who will give you some useful tips), 정답은 B이다.

Paraphrasing coworkers(동료들) → farm workers(농장 일꾼들)

17. Machinery introduction ....

기계 소개하기

옥수수밭으로 들어가서 추수관련 기계들에 대한 사용법 시연을 할 예정이므로(We'll then go across the main road and enter the corn field. We recently invested in brand new combine harvesters and other harvesting equipment, and you'll watch a demonstration on how to use these correctly and safely), 정답은 C이다.

Paraphrasing machinery(기계) → harvester(수확용 기계), equipment(장비)
introduction(소개) → demonstration on how to use(어떻게 사용하는지에 대한 시연)

18. Lunch break ....
점심 식사 시간

점심은 감자와 소들을 분리한 장소에서 가질 예정이므로(we'll stop for lunch. There's a nice spot on the lane that separates the potatoes from the cows), 정답은 E이다.
Paraphrasing lunch break(점심 휴식) → stop for lunch(점심을 위해 멈추다)
cattle(소) → cows(소)

19. Soil maintenance talk ....
토양 유지 관리 관련 이야기

소가 있는 초원으로 들어가서 토양 상태 관리에 대해 배운다고 하므로(we'll enter the cow pasture and learn all about the importance of maintaining soil condition), 정답은 H이다.
Paraphrasing cattle(소) → cow(소)
soil maintenance(토양 관리) → maintaining soil condition(토양 상태를 관리하기)

20. Feeding animals ....
동물들에게 먹이주기

마굿간 바깥에 멈춰서 말에 먹이를 주려고 하므로(stop off to feed the horses outside the stable), 정답은 G이다.
Paraphrasing animals(동물들) → horses(말들)

▪ 파트 3 [문제 21-30]

출제 포인트 **난이도: 중상**

실제 시험 Part 3에서 출제율이 높은 두 대학생 간 마케팅 수업 과제 내용에, 가장 전형적인 문제 유형인 Multiple Choice(선다형)와 Flowchart(순서도)가 나온 전형적인 Part 3 문제임

음원 남 - 영국 / 여 - 영국 / 스피드 - 실제 원어민 대화 스피드로 시험에서 빠르게 나올 때 속도

You will hear two marketing students called Sara and Kevin discussing the market research study they are going to do together.	새라와 케빈이라는 이름의 마케팅 전공 학생들이 함께 진행할 시장 조사 연구에 관해 이야기하는 것을 들어보세요.
SARA: We need to decide on the main focus of our market research study, don't we, Kevin? Did you say you were considering looking at trends in product packaging? **KEVIN:** Yes. Specifically, I thought we could focus on the psychology behind it — how product packaging affects people's thoughts and emotions. **SARA:** Sounds interesting. Why did you choose that though? I know you've always taken an interest in consumer psychology. **KEVIN:** That's true, but the main reason is that Q21 the psychology of marketing is a core part of our course next year, so it might benefit us to learn more about it in advance. This study gives us a great opportunity to gain valuable knowledge on the topic. **SARA:** I hadn't thought of that. You're right! **KEVIN:** So, for our study, I was thinking that we should look at four of the most popular brands of snack foods. Then, we can compare how well their products sell and	**새라:** 우리 시장 조사 연구의 중점 사항에 대해 결정을 내려야 하지 않겠니, 케빈? 네가 제품 포장의 경향을 살펴보는 것을 고려하고 있었다고 말했었나? **케빈:** 응. 특히, 그 이면에 숨어 있는 심리학, 즉 제품 포장이 사람들의 생각과 감정에 영향을 미치는 방식에 초점을 맞출 수 있을 것으로 생각했어. **새라:** 흥미로운 것 같아. 그런데 왜 그것을 선택한 거야? 넌 항상 소비자 심리학에 관심을 가졌던 것으로 알고 있는데. **케빈:** 맞아, 하지만 주된 이유는 Q21 마케팅 심리학이 내년 우리 학과 과정의 핵심적인 부분이라서, 미리 그것에 대해 더 알아두면 우리에게 좋을 수도 있거든. 이 연구가 해당 주제에 대해 소중한 지식을 얻을 아주 좋은 기회를 우리에게 제공해 줄 거야. **새라:** 그 생각은 하지 못했어. 네 말이 맞아! **케빈:** 자, 우리 연구를 위해서, 네 가지 가장 인기있는 과자 제품 브랜드를 살펴봐야 한다고 생각하고 있었어. 그런 다음, 그 제품들이 얼마나 잘 판매되는지를 비교하면

ACTUAL TEST 1

determine whether the packaging is a contributing factor.
SARA: OK. We'll need to get feedback from actual consumers, in that case.
KEVIN: Yes, and that's why this topic is better than some other ones. Q22 There's nothing better than getting real feedback straight from the people that buy the products.
SARA: Yeah, let's definitely take that approach. And, we're fortunate that the university is located downtown, so we can easily speak with shoppers while we conduct our research.
KEVIN: Exactly. But, Q23 I think we should check with our course leader about the due date. March 14th doesn't really give us much time. Perhaps he would be open to pushing it back by a few days.
SARA: Yeah, some of the other students have mentioned that, too. It can't hurt to ask.
KEVIN: We can prepare by doing a bit of reading, too. I wonder if the university library has a copy of *Visual Marketing* by James Hopper. The course leader highly recommended it.
SARA: I already borrowed the Hopper book for a previous assignment. Q24 We should reserve it from the library ASAP, as I'm pretty sure they only carry a couple of copies. Even if our coursemates are choosing different topics to ours, there's still a risk that we won't be able to borrow a copy unless we reserve one now.
KEVIN: Yes, we don't want to miss out. I'm pretty sure it includes some relevant chapters on product packaging.
SARA: Yes, I believe it does.
KEVIN: I also think we could use the notes that we've taken from Professor Bush's lectures.
SARA: Oh, about the effects of different colours on purchasing habits?
KEVIN: Yes. Q25 His notes included several well-known case studies that we could reference and correlate with our own findings.
SARA: Great idea. And didn't his lecture notes include examples of unsuccessful marketing methods used by some companies?
KEVIN: Ummm, I think that was covered by a different lecturer.

SARA: Anyway, now that we know what topic we'll focus on, we need to figure out how we are going to approach the market research study.
KEVIN: Okay. Q26 First of all, we need to get images of the products whose packaging we plan to compare and investigate. We should be able to find those online.

제품 포장이 그에 대한 기여 요인인지 결정할 수 있을 거야.
새라: 좋아. 그렇다면 실제 소비자들을 통해서 의견을 얻어야 할 거야.
케빈: 응, 그리고 그게 바로 이 주제가 다른 것들보다 더 나은 이유야. Q22 제품을 구입하는 사람들로부터 직접 실제 의견을 구하는 것보다 더 나은 건 없거든.
새라: 그래, 꼭 그 접근 방식을 취하도록 하자. 그리고, 우리 대학교가 시내에 위치해 있어서 연구를 실시하는 동안 쇼핑객들과 쉽게 이야기할 수 있다는 게 다행이야.
케빈: 바로 그거야. 하지만, Q23 마감 기한에 대해서 지도 교수님에게 확인해 봐야 할 것 같아. 3월 14일은 우리에게 그렇게 많은 시간이 주어지는 게 아냐. 아마 교수님께서 며칠 뒤로 연기하는 것에 대해 받아들여 주실 거야.
새라: 응, 몇몇 다른 학생들도 그 부분을 언급한 적이 있어. 여쭤보는 정도는 괜찮을 거야.
케빈: 자료를 좀 읽는 것으로도 준비할 수 있을 거야. 우리 대학교 도서관에 제임스 하퍼의 '비주얼 마케팅' 책이 있는지 궁금해. 지도 교수님께서 그 책을 적극 추천하셨거든.
새라: 내가 이전 과제를 위해 하퍼 책을 이미 빌려봤어. Q24 가능한 한 빨리 도서관에 예약해야 하는데, 그곳에 겨우 두어 권의 책만 있는 게 아주 분명하기 때문이야. 우리 학과 친구들이 우리와 다른 주제를 선택한다 하더라도, 지금 한 권 예약하지 않으면 빌릴 수 없을 위험성이 여전히 있어.
케빈: 응, 기회를 놓치면 안되니까. 그 책에 제품 포장과 관련된 몇몇 챕터를 포함하고 있는 게 아주 분명해.
새라: 맞아, 그럴 거라고 생각해.
케빈: 우리가 부시 교수님의 강의 노트 내용도 활용할 수 있다고 생각해.
새라: 아, 서로 다른 색상이 구매 습관에 미치는 영향에 관한 것 말이지?
케빈: 응. Q25 그 강의 노트 내용에 우리가 참고해서 연구 결과물과 관련 지을 수 있는 여러 가지 잘 알려진 사례 연구 내용이 포함되어 있었어.
새라: 좋은 생각이야. 그리고 그 교수님 강의 노트에 일부 회사에 의해 활용되어 성공을 거두지 못한 마케팅 방법의 예시들이 포함되어 있지 않았어?
케빈: 음, 그 내용은 다른 교수님에 의해 다뤄졌던 것 같아.

새라: 어쨌든, 우리가 초점을 맞춰야 할 주제를 이제 알았으니까, 그 시장 조사 연구에 어떻게 접근해야 할지를 알아봐야 해.
케빈: 좋아. Q26 가장 먼저, 우리가 비교하고 조사할 계획인 제품 포장의 이미지를 구해야 해. 그건 온라인으로 찾을 수 있을 거야.

SARA: Yes, that shouldn't be too hard. Then, we need to think about what we are going to ask consumers, with regard to the packaging.
KEVIN: Right. Q27 Well, we need to think of the best questions to include in a consumer survey. I think we should try to keep it short and focused. Do you think ten questions would be enough?
SARA: I think we might need at least fifteen in order to get more accurate data.
KEVIN: Okay. Q28 And then, we need to figure out the best location to administer it. Somewhere that attracts a diverse range of consumers of all ages and demographics.
SARA: Okay, I'll give that some thought today. Q29 And, we could offer some incentives to persuade people to take part. What do you think about that?
KEVIN: That's a good idea, but it will have to be something that is free, or at least very cheap. Q30 So, once we have compiled all of our data, do you think we should present it in a table?
SARA: No. I think a graph would be better suited for this type of study.
KEVIN: You're probably right. We can easily break down our findings based on gender, age and other variables, and then present them clearly.
SARA: It sounds like we're off to a good start.
KEVIN: I agree. So...

새라: 응, 그건 그렇게 어렵지 않을 거야. 그런 다음에, 포장과 관련해 소비자들에게 무엇을 물어볼지에 관해 생각해 봐야 해.
케빈: 맞아. Q27 저기, 소비자 설문 조사에 포함할 가장 좋은 질문들을 생각해 봐야 해. 우리는 설문 조사를 짧고 집중적인 상태로 유지되도록 해야 할 것 같아. 10개의 질문이면 충분할 것 같아?
새라: 더욱 정확한 자료를 얻을 수 있도록 최소한 15개는 필요할 것 같아.
케빈: 좋아. Q28 그리고 그런 다음에, 조사를 실시할 가장 좋은 장소를 찾아봐야 해. 모든 연령대와 인구 자료를 얻을 수 있는 아주 다양한 소비자들을 끌어들이는 그런 곳으로.
새라: 좋아, 오늘 그 부분을 좀 생각해 볼게. Q29 그리고, 사람들을 설득해서 참여하게 만들기 위해 뭔가 우대 조치를 제공할 수 있을 거야. 어떻게 생각해?
케빈: 좋은 생각이기는 하지만, 무료이거나 최소한 아주 저렴한 것이어야 할 거야. Q30 그럼, 일단 모든 자료를 수집해서 정리하고 나면, 표로 제시해야 할까?
새라: 아니. 이런 종류의 연구에는 그래프가 더 적합할 것 같아.
케빈: 네 말이 맞을 것 같아. 성별과 연령, 그리고 기타 변수들을 바탕으로 우리 결과물을 쉽게 세분화한 다음, 명확하게 제시할 수 있을 거야.
새라: 우리가 순조롭게 출발하고 있는 것 같아.
케빈: 동의해. 그럼...

I Vocabulary & Expressions I

packaging 포장 psychology 심리학 behind ~ 이면에 있는 affect ~에 영향을 미치다 though (문장 끝이나 중간에서) 하지만 take an interest in ~에 관심 갖다 core 핵심의 contributing factor 기여 요소 straight from ~로부터 직접 definitely 분명히, 확실히 approach 접근 방식 conduct ~을 실시하다, 수행하다 due date 마감 기한 be open to ~에 귀 기울이다, 개방적이다 push A back A를 뒤로 미루다 by (차이) ~ 정도, ~만큼 It can't hurt to do ~하는 정도는 괜찮다 ASAP 가능한 빨리(=as soon as possible) risk 위험(성) unless ~하지 않는다면 miss out (기회를) 놓치다 relevant 관련된 effect of A on B A가 B에 미치는 영향 purchasing habit 구매 습관 case study 사례 연구 reference ~을 참고하다 correlate with ~와 관련 짓다 findings 연구 결과(물) method 방법 cover (주제 등) ~을 다루다 now that 이제 ~이므로 figure out ~을 알아내다, 찾아보다 compare ~을 비교하다 investigate ~을 조사하다 with regard to ~와 관련해 survey 설문 조사 focused 집중적인 demographics 인구 자료 incentive 우대 조치, 장려책 persuade ~을 설득하다 take part 참여하다 compile ~을 수집해 정리하다 present ~을 제시하다 table 표 be suited for ~에 적합하다 break down ~을 세분화하다, 분류하다 variable 변수 be off to a good start 출발이 좋다

문제 21-25

A, **B**, **C** 중에서 알맞은 글자를 고르시오.

21. Why is Kevin interested in investigating the psychology of marketing?
케빈은 왜 마케팅 심리학을 조사하는 데 관심이 있는가?

A He completed a module in it last year.
작년에 그 교과목 단위 하나를 이수했다.

B He thinks it will be a straightforward topic.

그것이 간단한 주제가 될 것으로 생각하고 있다.

C **He thinks it will help him with future coursework.**
향후 수업 활동에 도움이 될 것으로 생각하고 있다.

왜 심리학에 관심이 있는지 새라가 케빈에게 묻자, 케빈은 마케팅 심리학이 내년 핵심 과목이기에 미리 공부하기 원한다고 하였으므로 (the psychology of marketing is a core part of our course next year, so it might benefit us to learn more about it in advance), 정답은 C이다.

Paraphrasing future coursework(향후 교육 과정) → course next year(내년 과정)
help(돕다) → benefit(도움이 되다)

22. **Kevin and Sara agree that one benefit of their study topic is that it involves**
케빈과 새라는 ------------이 수반되는 것이 자신들의 연구 주제가 지니는 장점이라는 데 동의한다.

A **primarily Internet-based research.** 주로 인터넷을 기반으로 하는 조사
B **direct interaction with consumers.** 소비자들과의 직접적인 교류
C **collaboration with local businesses.** 지역 기업들과의 협업

케빈이 제품을 구입하는 사람들로부터 직접 실제 의견을 구하는 것보다 더 나은 건 없다며 benefit에 대해 언급하자(There's nothing better than getting real feedback straight from the people that buy the products), 이에 새라가 동조하므로 (Yeah, let's definitely take that approach), 정답은 B이다.

Paraphrasing benefit(도움이 되다) → better than some other ones(다른 것들보다 더 나은)
direct interaction(직접적인 교류) → getting real feedback straight(직접 실제 의견을 얻음)

23. **What do they decide to check with their course leader?**
화자들은 지도 교수에게 무엇을 확인해 보기로 결정하는가?

A **whether a deadline can be extended** 마감 기한이 연기될 수 있는지
B **whether a topic is acceptable** 한 가지 주제가 수용 가능한지
C **whether project allowance will be provided** 프로젝트 진행비가 제공될 것인지

케빈이 지도 교수에게 마감일 연기에 대해 확인해 보자고 하자(I think we should check with our course leader about the due date. March 14th doesn't really give us much time. Perhaps he would be open to pushing it back by a few days), 새라 역시 이에 동의하므로, 정답은 A이다.

Paraphrasing deadline(마감일) → due date(마감일)
extend(연장하다) → pushing it back(뒤로 미루다)

24. **Sara recommends reserving a copy of Hopper's book on visual marketing because**
새라가 ------------------------------ 때문에 비주얼 마케팅에 관한 하퍼의 책 한 권을 예약하도록 권한다.

A **many students have requested to borrow it.** 많은 학생들이 그것을 빌리도록 요청했기 때문에
B **there are not many copies available.** 이용 가능한 책이 많지 않기 때문에
C **it has won several industry awards.** 업계에서 주는 여러 상을 받았기 때문에

하퍼 책에 대해 새라가 책이 몇권 없어서 빨리 예약하자고 말하므로(We should reserve it from the library ASAP, as I'm pretty sure they only carry a couple of copies), 정답은 B이다.

Paraphrasing recommends(제안하다) → we should ~ (우리는 해야한다)
not many copies available(많지 않은 부수가 이용가능한)
→ only carry a couple of copies(두어권 정도만 갖고 있다)

25. **What does Kevin say about Professor Bush's lecture notes?**
케빈은 부시 교수의 강의 노트에 관해 무슨 말을 하는가?

A **They can be obtained upon request.** 요청하면 얻을 수 있다.
B **They detail failed marketing strategies.** 실패한 마케팅 전략들을 상세히 설명하고 있다.
C **They include information relevant to the study.** 해당 연구와 관련된 정보를 포함하고 있다.

케빈은 부시 교수 노트에 자신들 연구 결과와 연관되는 유명한 사례 연구들이 포함되어 있다고 하므로(His notes included several well-known case studies that we could reference and correlate with our own findings), 정답은 C이다.

Paraphrasing relevant to(~과 연관된) → correlate with(~와 관련 있다)

문제 26-30

다음 순서도를 완성하시오.

상자에서 5개의 답변을 골라 26-30번 질문 옆에 **A-H**까지의 글자 중에서 알맞은 것을 기입하시오.

A incentives 장려책	**B** payments 비용지불	**C** images 이미지	**D** graph 그래프
E database 데이터베이스	**F** location 위치	**G** stores 매장들	**H** survey 설문 조사

Main Research Steps 주요 연구 단계

Gather relevant **26** .... of specific products from the Internet
인터넷에서 특정 제품에 대한 관련 **26** .... 수집하기

⬇

Prepare a concise **27** .... for participants in the study
연구 참가자들을 위해 간결한 **27** .... 준비하기

⬇

Select a suitable **28** .... in order to interact with a diverse range of people
아주 다양한 사람들과 교류하기 위해 적합한 **28** .... 고르기

⬇

Provide **29** .... to encourage participation in the study
연구 참가를 권장하기 위해 **29** .... 제공하기

⬇

Compile all data gathered during the study
연구 중에 수집된 모든 자료 정리하기

⬇

Present findings in a **30** .... based on demographic variables
인구통계학적 변수들을 바탕으로 **30** ....로 결과물 제시하기

26. 온라인에서 제품 포장 이미지를 얻자고 하므로(we need to get images of the products whose packaging we plan to compare and investigate. We should be able to find those online), 정답은 images 기호인 C이다.

Paraphrasing gather(수집하다) → get(얻다)
Internet(인터넷) → online(온라인)

27. 케빈이 소비자 설문 조사를 포함하고 설문 조사는 짧고 집중적이어야 한다고 하므로(Well, we need to think of the best questions to include in a consumer survey. I think we should try to keep it short and focused), 정답은 survey의 H이다.

Paraphrasing concise(간략한) → keep it short and focused(짧고 집중되게 하다)
participants(참가자들) → consumers(소비자들)

28. 다양한 소비자를 불러들일 수 있는 장소를 생각해내자고 하므로(we need to figure out the best location to administer it. Somewhere that attracts a diverse range of consumers of all ages and demographics), 정답은 F이다. 보기에 G(stores)도 내용상 정답이 될 것 같지만, 방송에서 명확히 location을 말하므로 F가 정답이다.

Paraphrasing select(선택하다) → figure out(생각해내다)
suitable(적합한) → best(최고의)

29. 참석자들에게 우대 조치를 제공하자고 하므로(we could offer some incentives to persuade people to take part), 정답은 A이다.

Paraphrasing encourage(장려하다) → persuade(설득하다)
participation(참가) → take part(참가하다)

30. 데이터 정보 제시 관련해서 새라가 그래프를 제안하고(I think a graph would be better suited for this type of study) 케빈이 이에 동조하므로, 정답은 D이다.

Paraphrasing demographic variables (인구통계학적 변수들)
→ gender, age and other variables(성별, 나이 그리고 기타 변수들)

▪ 파트 4 [문제 31-40]

출제 포인트 **난이도: 중상**

실제 Part 4 시험에서 자주 등장하는 환경 관련 주제와 note completion 유형의 전형적 실전 세트로 Academic Reading 지문으로도 출제 가능성이 높은 내용임

음원 여 - 영국 / 스피드 - 실제 시험과 유사한 속도

You will hear part of an environmental science lecture about recent research and developments in sustainable transport.

Today, I'm going to talk to you about one of the most crucial aspects of sustainable development, and that is sustainable transport. As I'm sure you are all aware, transportation is a significant contributor to greenhouse gas emissions and climate change. In fact, it is estimated that almost 40 per cent of harmful emissions are a result of transportation.

In addition to the obvious environmental benefits, a wide range of social and Q31 economic benefits come from sustainable transport, and these can drive local sustainable development. The Low Emission Development Strategies Global Partnership, LEDS GP, recently issued a report which described how sustainable transport can help create Q32 jobs and improve commuter safety. It can also help to save people's time and money, and reduce government budgets, which makes investment in sustainable transport initiatives an increasingly attractive proposition.

환경 친화적 교통 수단에 대한 최근 연구 및 발전에 관한 환경 과학 강연의 일부를 들어보세요.

오늘, 저는 환경 친화적 개발의 가장 중요한 측면들 중의 하나에 관해 이야기해 드릴 것이며, 그것은 바로 친환경 교통 수단입니다. 여러분 모두 아시리라 생각하지만, 교통 수단은 온실 가스 방출과 기후 변화의 중요한 원인입니다. 실제로, 유해 배출물의 거의 40퍼센트가 교통 수단으로 인한 결과인 것으로 추정되고 있습니다.

명백한 환경적 혜택 뿐만 아니라, 아주 다양한 사회적, Q31 경제적 이득도 친환경 교통 수단을 통해 얻게 되며, 이는 국내의 환경 친화적 개발을 촉진할 수 있습니다. 저공해 개발 전략 세계 협력 기구(LEDS GP)에서 최근 친환경 교통 수단이 어떻게 Q32 일자리를 창출하고 통근자 안전을 향상시키는 데 도움이 될 수 있는지를 설명한 보고서를 내놓았습니다. 또한 시간과 돈을 절약하고 정부의 예산을 감소시키는 데도 도움이 될 수 있는데, 이는 친환경 교통 수단 계획에 대한 투자를 점점 더 매력적인 명제로 만들어 주는 것입니다.

The LEDS GP outlined three general goals in its effort to reduce the total number of motor vehicle trips, and as a result, lower greenhouse gas emission. The first goal is to improve public transit by expanding coverage areas in order to provide more accessibility, and by implementing new Q33 technology to make public transportation networks more reliable and convenient.

LEDS GP는 자동차 이동의 총 횟수를 줄여 그 결과로 온실 가스 방출을 낮추기 위한 노력의 일환으로 세 가지 일반적인 목표를 간략히 설명했습니다. 첫 번째 목표는 더 나은 접근성을 제공하기 위해 서비스 범위를 확대하고 대중 교통 시스템을 더욱 신뢰할 수 있고 편리하게 만들기 위해 새로운 Q33 기술을 시행함으로써 대중 교통을 개선하는 것입니다.

The second goal is to promote biking and walking by creating extensive pedestrian path networks, installing bike share stations throughout cities, moving parking lots further away from shopping centres and imposing harsher limits on downtown street Q34 parking.

두 번째 목표는 광범위한 보행자 도로 시스템 조성, 모든 도시 전역에 걸친 공유 자전거 대여소 설치, 쇼핑 센터에서 더 멀리 떨어진 곳으로의 주차장 이전, 그리고 시내 길거리 Q34 주차에 대한 더 엄격한 제한을 통한 자전거 이용 및 걷기를 촉진하는 것입니다.

The third goal is to increase the cost of owning a Q35 car by increasing fuel taxes, parking fees and toll costs. The aim of this is to encourage people to switch to more fuel efficient vehicles. Additionally, governments can take the extra money it receives from these price increases and allocate it for improvements to public transportation systems.

세 번째 목표는 유류세와 주차 요금, 그리고 통행료를 인상해 Q35 자동차 소유에 따른 비용을 증가시키는 것입니다. 그 목적은 사람들에게 더욱 연비가 좋은 차량으로 바꾸도록 장려하기 위한 것입니다. 추가로, 정부에서 이 비용 인상을 통해 생기는 추가 자금을 확보해 대중 교통 시스템 개선 작업에 할당할 수 있습니다.

Of course, there are also several ways we can change motor vehicles to reduce the environmental impact of transportation. Current research is focusing on reducing the Q36 weight of vehicles and the friction of tires, developing sustainable styles of driving and making continuous improvements to electric and hybrid vehicles, which are often referred to as green vehicles.

물론, 교통 수단의 환경적 영향을 줄이기 위해 자동차를 바꿀 수 있는 여러 가지 방법들도 있습니다. 요즘의 연구는 차량 Q36 무게와 타이어 마찰력 감소, 친환경적 운전 방식의 개발, 그리고 흔히 친환경 차량으로 일컫는 전기 자동차와 하이브리드 자동차의 지속적인 개선에 초점을 맞추고 있습니다.

While electric vehicle technology has the potential to reduce CO_2 emissions, this depends on the actual source of electricity. The majority of countries still derive electricity from coal, gas and oil, which means that private electric cars will probably result in similar levels of Q37 CO_2 production when compared to traditional petrol-fueled vehicles.

전기 자동차 기술이 이산화탄소 배출물을 감소시킬 수 있는 잠재력을 지니고 있지만, 이는 실제 전기 공급원에 달려 있습니다. 대부분의 국가들이 여전히 석탄과 가스, 그리고 석유에서 전기를 얻고 있는데, 이는 일반적인 석유 연료 차량들과 비교할 때 개인 전기 자동차가 아마 유사한 수준의 Q37 이산화탄소 생성물을 만들게 될 수도 있음을 의미합니다.

Recently, researchers at the Korea Advanced Institute of Science and Technology, KAIST, unveiled an electric vehicle that can charge its Q38 battery while stationary or while moving. This breakthrough completely eliminates the need to stop at a charging station, making the vehicle much more attractive to potential consumers.

최근, 한국 과학 기술원(KAIST)의 연구원들이 정차 중이거나 이동 중에 Q38 배터리를 충전할 수 있는 전기 자동차를 공개했습니다. 이 획기적인 기술은 충전소에 들를 필요성을 완전히 없애 주는 것으로서, 그 차량을 잠재 소비자들에게 훨씬 더 매력적으로 만들어줍니다.

There have also been several recent developments in hybrid vehicles, which achieve better fuel efficiency than a regular combustion engine by combining an internal combustion Q39 engine with an electric engine. Unfortunately, when it comes to sustainable transport developments, research on biofuels has been less

하이브리드 차량에도 여러 가지 최신 개발 작업이 있어 왔는데, 이는 내연 Q39 엔진을 전기 엔진과 결합해 일반적인 연소 방식의 엔진보다 더 나은 연비를 달성합니다. 안타깝게도, 친환경 교통 수단 개발과 관련해서, 생물 연료에 대한 연구는 그 전망이 덜 밝습니다. 약 10년 전에, 브라질에서 생물 연료가 교통 수단 연료의 약 17퍼센트를 차지했으며, 일부 사람들은 이를 친환경 교통 수단의 미래로 알렸습니다. 하지만, 현재 과학자들은

promising. Around ten years ago, biofuels accounted for around 17 per cent of transport fuel in Brazil, and some people heralded them as the future of green transportation. However, scientists now predict that Q40 biofuels will have little or no impact on greenhouse emissions and result in significantly higher costs over time than other green energy approaches.

Q40 생물연료가 온실 가스 배출에 거의 영향을 미치지 못하거나 전혀 영향을 미치지 못해 시간이 지날수록 다른 친환경 에너지 활용 방식보다 상당히 더 높은 비용을 초래할 것이라고 예측하고 있습니다.

So, now that we've discussed some of the sustainable transport basics, let's...

자, 이제 환경 친화적인 교통 수단의 일부 기본 사항들을 이야기했으므로, 함께...

| Vocabulary & Expressions |

crucial 중요한 aspect 측면, 양상 sustainable 친환경적, 지속 가능한 contributor to ~에 대한 원인 greenhouse gas 온실 가스 emission 배출 it is estimated that ~인 것으로 추정되다 drive ~을 촉진하다 issue ~을 내놓다, 발표하다 describe ~을 설명하다 budget 예산 investment in ~에 대한 투자 initiative (대대적인) 계획, 운동 proposition 명제, 제안 outline ~을 간략히 설명하다 in one's effort to do ~하기 위한 노력으로 motor vehicle 자동차 public transit 대중 교통 expand ~을 확대하다 coverage area 서비스 제공 구역 accessibility 접근성 implement ~을 시행하다 promote ~을 촉진하다 extensive 광범위한, 폭넓은 pedestrian 보행자 install ~을 설치하다 throughout ~ 전역에 걸쳐 further away from ~에서 더 멀리 떨어진 impose harsh limits 엄격한 제한을 가하다 toll costs 통행료 encourage 장려하다, 권하다 switch to ~로 바꾸다 allocate ~을 할당하다, 배정하다 friction 마찰(력) make improvements to ~을 개선하다 be referred to as ~로 일컬어지다 derive A from B B로부터 A를 얻다 result in ~의 결과를 낳다 compared to ~와 비교해 petrol-fueled 석유 연료의 unveil ~을 공개하다 stationary 정지 중인 breakthrough 획기적인 것 completely 완전히 eliminate ~을 없애주다 fuel efficiency 연비 combustion engine 연소 방식의 엔진 combine ~을 결합하다 internal 내부의 when it comes to ~와 관련해서는 biofuel 생물연료 promising 전망이 밝은 account for (비율 등) ~을 차지하다 herald A as B A를 B라고 알리다 predict that ~라고 예측하다 have an impact on ~에 영향을 미치다 over time 시간이 지날수록

문제 31-40

다음 필기 내용을 완성하시오.

각 답변에 대해 **오직 1개의 단어만** 작성하시오.

The Importance of Sustainable Transport

친환경 교통 수단의 중요성

Introduction

도입부

— Sustainable transport is a key component of sustainable development, and it offers three types of benefit: environmental, social and **31** ....

친환경 교통 수단은 환경 친화적 개발의 핵심 요소이며, 환경적, 사회적 그리고 **31** .... 세 가지 종류의 장점을 제공한다.

The LEDS GP Report

LEDS GP 보고서

— The Low Emission Development Strategies Global Partnership (LEDS GP) report states that sustainable transport can create more **32** .... and improve commuter safety.

저공해 개발 전략 세계 협력 기구(LEDS GP)의 보고서는 친환경 교통 수단이 더 많은 **32** ....을 만들어내고 통근자 안전을 개선할 수 있다고 명시하고 있다.

— The report lists three main goals:
해당 보고서는 세 가지 주요 목표를 제시:

- Expand public transportation coverage and utilise new **33** .... to make systems more dependable
시스템을 더욱 신뢰할 수 있도록 만들기 위해 대중 교통 서비스 범위를 확대하고 새로운 **33** .... 활용하기
- Encourage biking and walking by providing bike share stations, improving pedestrian routes and limiting **34** .... in downtown areas
공유 자전거 대여소를 제공함으로써 자전거 타기와 걷기를 권장하고, 보행자 도로를 개선하며, 시내 구역에서 **34** .... 제한하기
- Increase costs associated with **35** .... ownership and use funds collected to improve public transit
35 .... 소유와 관련된 비용을 인상하고 대중 교통을 개선하기 위해 거둬들인 자금 활용하기

New developments and future prospects 새로운 개발 사항과 향후 전망

— Much current research focuses on modifying motor vehicles and the way we drive them, including:
현재의 많은 연구가 자동차 및 그것을 우리가 운전하는 방식의 변경에 초점을 맞추고 있는데, 여기에 포함되는 것은:

- Reducing the **36** .... of vehicles
차량의 **36** .... 줄이기
- Reducing the friction of tires
타이어 마찰 줄이기
- Developing sustainable driving methods
친환경 운전 방식 개발하기

— Until new clean sources of electricity are established, production of **37** .... in electric cars will be similar to that of petrol cars.
새롭고 깨끗한 전기 공급원이 확립될 때까지, 전기 자동차의 **37** .... 생산은 석유 연료 차량의 그것과 유사할 것이다.

— Researchers in Korea unveiled new technology which allows a vehicle's **38** .... to be charged even during transit.
한국 연구원들은 신기술을 공개했는데, 이것은 이동 중에도 자동차의 **38** ....가 충전될 수 있도록 한다.

— Successful developments have also been made in hybrid vehicles, which feature a combination of two types of **39** ....
하이브리드 차량에 대해서도 성공적인 개발이 이루어졌는데, 이 차량은 두 가지 유형의 **39** ....가 결합된 것이 특징이다.

— However, **40** .... are expected to be costly in the long-term and have little impact on reducing greenhouse gas emissions.
하지만, 장기적으로 **40** ....에 많은 비용이 들어가며, 온실 가스 배출물을 줄이는 데 영향이 거의 없을 것으로 예상된다.

31. 명백한 환경적 혜택 이외에, 다양한 사회적, 경제적 이득도 친환경 교통 수단을 통해 얻게 되며, 이는 국내 환경 친화적 개발을 촉진한다고 하므로(In addition to the obvious environmental benefits, a wide range of social and economic benefits come from sustainable transport, and these can drive local sustainable development), 친환경 교통 수단의 장점으로 빈칸에 들어갈 단어는 economic이다.

32. 친환경 교통 수단이 일자리를 더 창출할 것이므로(sustainable transport can help create jobs), 정답은 jobs이다.

33. 새로운 기술을 시행함으로써 대중 교통 시스템을 더욱 신뢰할 수 있고 편리하게 만들기 위함이라고 하므로(by implementing new technology to make public transportation networks more reliable and convenient), 정답은 technology이다.
Paraphrasing utilise(이용하다) → implement(시행하다)
dependable(믿을 수 있는) → reliable(믿을 수 있는)

ACTUAL TEST 1

34. 쇼핑 센터에서 더 멀리 떨어진 곳으로의 주차장 이전, 그리고 시내 거리 주차에 대한 더 엄격한 제한을 언급하므로(moving parking lots further away from shopping centres and imposing harsher limits on downtown street parking), 정답은 parking이다. 오직 한 개의 단어만 정답처리 되므로 street parking은 오답이다.
Paraphrasing encourage(장려하다) → promote(촉진하다)
limiting(제한함) → imposing harsher limits(더 엄격한 제한을 가함)

35. 세 번째 목표는 자동차 소유에 따른 비용을 증가시키는 것이라고 말하므로(The third goal is to increase the cost of owning a car), 정답은 car이다.
Paraphrasing car ownership(차 소유) → owning a car(차를 소유하는 것)

36. 요즘의 연구는 차량 무게와 타이어 마찰력 감소, 친환경적 운전 방식의 개발에 초점을 맞추므로(Current research is focusing on reducing the weight of vehicles and the friction of tires, developing sustainable styles of driving), 정답은 weight(무게)이다.
Paraphrasing driving methods(운전 방식) → styles of driving(운전 방식)

37. 일반적인 석유 연료 차량들과 비교할 때 전기 자동차가 아마 유사한 수준의 이산화탄소 생성물을 만들 것이라고 하므로(electric cars will probably result in similar levels of CO_2 production when compared to traditional petrol-fueled vehicles), 정답은 CO_2이다.
Paraphrasing petrol cars(석유 차) → petrol-fueled vehicles(석유 연료 차량)

38. 한국 과학 기술원 연구원들이 정차 중이거나 이동 중에 배터리를 충전할 수 있는 전기 자동차를 공개했다고 하므로(researchers at the Korea Advanced Institute of Science and Technology, unveiled an electric vehicle that can charge its battery while stationary or while moving), 정답은 battery이다.
Paraphrasing during transit(이동하는 동안에) → while moving(움직이는 중에)

39. 하이브리드 차량에도 여러 가지 최신 개발 작업이 있어 왔는데, 이는 내연 엔진을 전기 엔진과 결합해 일반적인 연소 방식의 엔진보다 더 나은 연비를 달성한다고 하므로(There have also been several recent developments in hybrid vehicles, which achieve better fuel efficiency than a regular combustion engine by combining an internal combustion engine with an electric engine), 정답은 engine이다. 복수형도 정답처리 가능하다.

40. 생물연료가 온실 가스 배출에 거의 영향을 미치지 못하거나 전혀 영향을 미치지 못해 시간이 지날수록 다른 친환경 에너지 활용 방식보다 상당히 더 높은 비용을 초래할 것이라고 하므로(biofuels will have little or no impact on greenhouse emissions and result in significantly higher costs over time than other green energy approaches), 정답은 biofuels이다. 단수형은 오답이다.
Paraphrasing costly in the long-term(장기적으로 많은 비용의) → higher costs over time(시간이 지날수록 더 많은 비용)

Test 1 SPEAKING [Academic / General Training]

▪ 파트 1

[Your Life] 당신의 삶

Let's talk about what you do.
당신이 하는 것에 대해 이야기해보죠.

Q Do you work or are you a student?
당신은 일하나요 아니면 학생인가요?

A I am currently a student at Siwon University. This is the final year of my studies, so I am preparing to graduate and find a job.
저는 현재 시원 대학교 학생입니다. 이번이 제 공부 마지막해이기에, 졸업과 직장을 찾을 준비를 하고 있습니다.

[If you work] 일 한다면

Q What kind of job do you do?
어떤 일을 하나요?

A I am an accountant at a small manufacturing company. I'm responsible for writing expense reports and keeping track of our revenue streams.
저는 작은 제조 회사에 회계원입니다. 저는 경비 보고서를 작성하고 수익 흐름을 기록할 책임이 있습니다.

* expense 경비, 비용 keep track of ~을 기록하다 revenue 수익 stream 흐름

Q What do you particularly like about your job?
당신 직업에서 특별히 어떤 것이 좋나요?

A My work can be stressful, but my teammates are very supportive. We get through the workload together, and we help keep each other positive. I think it's the best team I've worked on.
제 직업은 스트레스가 많을 수 있는데, 제 팀원들이 매우 많은 힘이 됩니다. 우리는 함께 업무를 끝내고 서로가 계속 긍정적이도록 도와줍니다. 저는 이 팀이 제가 일해왔던 최고의 팀이라고 생각합니다.

* supportive 도움을 주는, 지원하는 get through ~을 끝내다 workload 업무량, 작업량

[If you are a student] 학생이라면

Q What subject are you studying?
어떤 과목을 공부하나요?

A I am studying psychology, and I'm taking several business classes, too. I'm considering doing a double major, but it depends on whether I can fit it in my schedule.
저는 심리학을 공부하고 있고, 여러 경영학 수업도 듣고 있습니다. 저는 복수 전공을 생각 중이지만, 어디까지나 제가 일정을 맞출 수 있는지에 달려 있습니다.

* psychology 심리학 double major 복수 전공

Q Why did you want to study that subject?
왜 당신은 이 과목을 공부하기를 원했나요?

A My goal is to start a career in human resources. Having a background in psychology will help me in that field. Plus, the courses are always interesting, and I enjoy the assignments.
제 목표는 인사과에서 경력을 시작하는 것입니다. 심리학 배경을 갖는 것은 그 분야에서 도움이 될 것입니다. 추가로, 그 교과정은 항상 흥미롭고, 저는 과제를 즐깁니다.

* career 경력, 직업, 직장생활 human resources 인사과

[Hometown or city] 고향 또는 도시

Let's go on to talk about your hometown or city.
당신의 고향이나 도시에 대해 이야기해보죠.

Q What is the most interesting part of your town or city? [Why?]
당신의 마을이나 도시에서 가장 흥미로운 부분은 무엇인가요? [왜죠?]

A The best feature of my city is the park, which is situated next to the river. The landscaping at the park is gorgeous and creates some beautiful scenery around the river, and there are recreational areas for sports, like football and tennis. In the summer we have community festivals at the park, and they're always fantastic.
제가 사는 도시의 최고의 특징은 공원인데, 강 옆에 위치해 있습니다. 공원 조경은 아주 멋지고 강 주변에 아름다운 경치를 만들며, 축구와 테니스 같은 스포츠를 위한 레크리에이션 장소가 있습니다. 여름에, 공원에서 주민 축제가 있는데, 축제는 언제나 환상적입니다.

* feature 특징, 특색 landscaping 조경 gorgeous 아주 멋진 scenery 경치 community festival 주민 축제

Q Has your hometown changed in any way in your lifetime? [How?]
당신의 고향이 당신이 사는 동안 어떤 식으로든 바뀌었나요? [어떻게요?]

A When I was a child, my hometown was a new residential area located outside of the city. So, over the course of my life, my hometown has attracted a lot of additional businesses and development projects. Now it's an attractive town for families, full of great facilities, restaurants and shops.

제가 아이였을 때, 제 고향은 도시 바깥에 위치한 새 주거 지역이었습니다. 그래서, 제가 사는 동안, 제 고향은 수많은 추가적인 사업체와 개발 프로젝트를 끌어들였습니다. 이제 그곳은 훌륭한 시설들, 식당들, 그리고 상점들이 가득 찬, 가족들을 위한 매혹적인 도시이죠.

* residential area 주거 지역 attract 끌어들이다 facility 시설

Q Do you think your town is a good place for young people to live? [Why/Why not?]

당신은 당신의 도시가 젊은 사람들이 살기에 좋은 곳이라고 생각합니까? [왜죠 / 왜 아니죠?]

A Since young people need to live in an area with affordable housing and plentiful job opportunities, I believe my hometown is a good place for them to live. In fact, a lot of start-up companies have appeared in my town because of the reasonable living costs, so young people can get in on the ground floor of an exciting new business.

젊은이들은 감당할 수 있는 주거와 많은 직장 기회가 있는 지역에 살 필요가 있기에, 제 고향은 그들이 살기 좋은 장소라고 생각합니다. 사실, 비싸지 않은 생활비를 이유로 많은 신규 회사들이 제가 사는 고향에 생기고 있는데, 그래서 젊은이들은 흥미진진한 새로운 사업에 처음부터 참여할 수 있습니다.

* affordable (가격이) 감당할 수 있는 housing 주거 start-up 신규, 창업 reasonable 비싸지 않은, 합리적인 living costs 생활비 get in on the ground floor of ~의 처음부터 참여하다

▪ 파트 2

Describe the first mobile phone that you had. You should say: when it was that you got your own mobile phone why you got your own phone what features the mobile phone had and explain how this phone made changes in your life.	당신이 소유했던 첫 휴대폰에 대해 말해 보세요. 당신은 다음에 대해 말해야 합니다: 언제 당신 소유의 휴대폰을 가졌는지 왜 당신은 휴대폰을 가졌는지 그 휴대폰은 어떤 특징들을 가졌는지 그리고 이 휴대폰이 당신 삶에 어떠한 변화를 주었는지 설명하세요.

[브레인스토밍]

언제: basic one, middle school – 왜: late classes, keep in touch with mom – 기능: call and text, simple game – 삶에 미친 영향: taught me how to text, vital to social life

[문법]

목적격 관계대명사 생략 mobile phone I ever had 내가 처음 가진 휴대폰

spend time 동명사 ~하는데 시간을 보내다

관계부사절 when I was ~ ~였을 때

명령문 Remember, this was ~ ~라는 것을 기억하라

접속사 및 접속부사 as, even though, however

[모범답변]

The first mobile phone I ever had was a basic one that you could slide the screen up to reveal the keys. It seems like an artefact now, but it was trendy at the time. I got it when I was in middle school.

제 첫 휴대폰은 스크린을 밀어 올리면 키패드가 나타나는 기본적인 것이었습니다. 그것은 이제 유물처럼 보이지만, 그 당시 그것은 최신 유행이었습니다. 저는 그것을 중학생 때 가졌습니다.

Like most students, I spent a lot of time studying when I was in middle school. This included a lot of late classes at academies. My mom gave me the phone so that I could keep in touch with her throughout the day. For example, if one of my classes had been cancelled, I could call her to let her know.

대부분 학생들처럼, 저는 중학생 때 공부하는데 많은 시간을 보냈습니다. 학원에서 늦게까지 많은 수업을 포함해서요. 어머니께서 그 폰을 제게 주셨는데 어머니와 하루 종일 연락할 수 있도록 말이죠. 예를 들어, 제 수업 중 하나가 취소되면, 저는 어머니께 전화해서 알릴 수 있었죠.

As I mentioned, it was a basic mobile phone. It could make calls and send text messages, but that was it. Remember, this was long before apps began appearing. However, it did have a very simple game on it called 'Snake', which I spent a lot of time playing even though it was boring.

제가 언급했듯이, 그것은 기본적인 휴대폰이었습니다. 전화를 걸고 문자를 보낼 수 있었지만, 그게 전부였죠. 앱이 나타나기 시작하기 훨씬 전임을 생각하세요. 그러나, 그것은 '스네이크'라 불리는 매우 간단한 게임을 갖고 있었는데, 비록 그 게임이 지루하긴 해도 많은 시간을 그 게임을 하며 보냈습니다.

As plain as it was, the phone was important because it taught me how to text. My mom bought it for me, but I mostly used it to chat with my friends. This got me into some trouble, especially when the teacher caught me texting in class. Anyway, that phone was vital to my social life. That is all that I can say now.

비록 정말 단순했지만, 그 폰은 제게 문자 보내는 방법을 가르쳐주었기에 중요했습니다. 어머니는 제게 그 폰을 사주셨지만 저는 대부분 친구들과 대화하는데 사용했죠. 이 일로 몇몇 어려움이 있었는데, 특히 수업시간에 선생님이 제가 문자 보내는 것을 잡았을 때죠. 어쨌든, 그 폰은 제 사회 생활에 중요했습니다. 이것이 제가 지금 말할 수 있는 전부입니다.

* mobile phone 휴대폰(미국식 cell phone) slide 미끄러지다, 미끄러뜨리다 artefact 인공품, 유물(미국식 artifact) trendy 최신 유행의 academy 학원 keep in touch with ~와 연락을 유지하다 throughout the day 온종일 cancelled 취소했다(미국식 canceled) text message 문자 메시지 as plain as it was(=even though it was plain) 비록 정말 단순했지만 text 문자 보내다

Rounding-off Question: 마무리 질문

Q In general, how often do you think people change their mobile phone?
일반적으로, 얼마나 자주 사람들이 휴대폰을 바꾼다고 당신은 생각하나요?

A I think people in my country usually change their mobile phone every three years due to the subscription contract. But some people who are really eager to use new models change their phone almost every year.
저는 우리나라 사람들은 보통 가입 약정때문에 3년마다 휴대폰을 바꿉니다. 그러나 새 폰을 사용하는 것에 정말 열심인 몇몇 사람들은 거의 매년마다 휴대폰을 바꾸죠.

* every three years 3년 마다 subscription contract 가입 약정 be eager to 부정사 ~하는 것에 의욕이 높다, 열심이다

▪ 파트 3

[Mobile phones and Smartphones] 휴대폰과 스마트폰

Q Should children have their own mobile phone?
아이들이 휴대폰을 가져야 할까요?

A I don't believe children should be given their own mobile phones because they will generally be with a caretaker, not on their own. Children spend most of their time with either a parent or an educator. Therefore, an adult will always be available to handle any communication needs. Plus, a child doesn't need that level of independence so early in life.

저는 아이들에게 휴대폰이 주어져야 된다고 생각하지 않는데, 그들은 일반적으로 혼자만 있지 않고 보호자와 함께 있기 때문입니다. 아이들은 대부분의 시간을 부모 또는 교사와 함께 보냅니다. 그러므로, 어른이 항상 어떠한 커뮤니케이션 필요를 다룰 수 있죠. 추가로, 아이는 그렇게 어린 나이에 그러한 수준의 독립성이 요구되지 않습니다.

* caretaker 보호자 available 이용가능한 handle 다루다, 취급하다 that 그 정도의, 그러한

Q What would the world be like without mobile phones?
휴대폰이 없다면 세상은 어떨까요?

A On one hand, the world existed for a long time without mobile phones, so I suppose it would survive. There is a chance that the world would become a simpler place, and maybe that would be more of a benefit than a disadvantage. Then again, mobile phones are so integral to modern life and business that our society would have a serious struggle adapting to life without them.

한편으로, 세상은 휴대폰 없이 오랜 세월동안 존재했기에, 저는 계속 살아남을 거라 생각해요. 세상이 더 단순한 곳으로 될 확률이 있고, 아마도 그것이 단점보다는 더 많은 장점이 되겠죠. 그렇지만, 휴대폰은 현대의 삶과 일에 아주 필수적이기에 우리 사회는 휴대폰 없이 사는 것에 적응하기 위해 힘든 노력을 해야할 것입니다.

* on one hand 한편 exist 존재하다 survive 살아남다 then again (앞 내용을 받아서) 그렇지만, 반대로 integral 필수적인 struggle 노력, 애씀 adapt to ~에 적응하다

Q Do you think that the way people use smartphones may change in the future?
당신은 사람들이 스마트폰을 사용하는 방식이 미래에 변하리라고 생각하나요?

A From what I've seen, the way we use smartphones has already changed since they first came out, so we should expect further changes. Smartphones used to be exciting just because they could access the internet and because they had some gimmicky apps that utilised the touch screen. Nowadays, they are fully integrated with how people live their lives, from how they manage their work to how they run their household. With further advances in wireless technology, I can barely imagine what smartphones will be capable of in the future.

제가 보기에, 스마트폰을 사용하는 방식은 그것들이 처음 나온 이래로 이미 변해왔기에, 우리는 더 많은 변화를 예상할 수 있습니다. 스마트폰은 인터넷 접속과 터치스크린을 이용한 눈길을 끄는 앱으로 인해 신나는 것이었죠. 요즘, 스마트폰은 완전히 사람들 삶의 방식과 통합되어 있죠. 일을 관리하는 방법부터 가정을 운영하는 방법까지 말이죠. 무선 기술의 추가적인 진보와 함께, 저는 미래에 스마트폰이 무엇을 할지 거의 상상조차 할 수 없습니다.

* gimmicky 눈길을 끄는, 교묘한 장치의 utilise 이용하다(미국식 utilize) be integrated with ~와 통합되다 manage 관리하다 run 운영하다 household 가정 wireless 무선 barely 거의 ~아닌 be capable of ~을 할 수 있다

[Technology and Work] 기술과 일

Q What kinds of machines are used for office work nowadays?
요즘에 어떤 종류의 기계가 사무 업무에 사용되나요?

A I think the modern office has transformed a lot because of the introduction of new devices. Of course, computers are still ubiquitous throughout an office, as are copiers and printers. However, tablet devices and even personal smartphones have changed the way people communicate for work. A simple chatroom on a mobile device has replaced the need for daily meetings and conference rooms. Furthermore, office spaces have even become less crowded as more workers take advantage of telecommuting.

저는 새로운 기기의 도입으로 현대 사무실이 많이 변했다고 생각합니다. 물론 컴퓨터는, 복사기와 프린터가 그런 것처럼, 여전히 사무실 어디에나 있죠. 그러나, 태블릿 기기들과 심지어 개인용 스마트폰들이 직장에서 사람들이 의사소통 하는 방식을 바꿨습니다. 휴대폰 상의 간단한 채팅방이 일상적인 회의와 회의실에 대한 필요를 대체했습니다. 더욱이, 더 많은 직원들이 재택근무를 이용함에 따라 사무실 공간은 덜 붐비게 되었습니다.

* transform 변하다, 바꾸다 ubiquitous 어디에나 있는 copier 복사기 printer 프린터 tablet 직사각형 판, 태블릿 chatroom 채팅방 conference room 회의실 take advantage of ~을 이용하다 telecommuting 재택근무

Q Do you think technology has brought more stress than benefits to employees? [Why/Why not?]
당신은 기술이 직원들에게 혜택보다 더 많은 스트레스를 가져왔다고 생각하나요? [왜죠 / 왜 아니죠?]

A Without a doubt, technology has made doing greater amounts of work in shorter periods of time easier, but I believe this has only caused more stress for workers. Now employees struggle to keep up with work demands, and due to constantly being connected, a late-night work request could be sent via e-mail or text message, further undoing the boundary between working hours and personal hours.
의심의 여지없이, 기술은 더 짧은 시간 동안 더 쉽게 더 많은 양의 일을 하도록 만들었습니다만, 저는 이것이 근로자들에게 더 많은 스트레스만 주었다고 생각합니다. 이제 직원들은 작업 요구를 따라잡기 위해 애쓰고, 끊임없이 연결됨으로 인해, 늦은 밤 업무 요청이 이메일이나 문자 메시지를 통해 전달되고, 더 나아가 근무 시간과 개인 시간 간의 경계를 없앱니다.

* keep up with ~을 따라잡다 work demands 작업 요구 work request 작업 요청 via ~을 통해 undo the boundary 경계를 없애다 working hours 근무 시간 personal hours 개인 시간

ACTUAL TEST 1

ACTUAL TEST 2 IELTS on computer

Test 2	LISTENING [Academic / General Training]

1. website	2. garages	3. 2009	4. 30/thirty	5. credibility
6. schools	7. utilities	8. plumbing	9. photographs	10. neighbo(u)rs
11. C	12. B	13. C	14. B	15. A
16. B	17. B	18. F	19. A	20. E
21. B	22. A	23. A	24. A	25. C
26. C	27&28. A, D	29&30. C, E		
31. fabrics	32. wool	33. clothing	34. traders	35. water
36. efficiency	37. ports	38. methods	39. fashion	40. slavery

▪ 파트 1 [문제 1-10]

출제 포인트 **난이도: 중하**

실제 시험에서 간혹 파트 1(섹션 1)에서 철자 받아쓰기 문제가 출제되지 않는데, 본 파트 1 역시 받아쓰기 문제는 빠져 있음.

음원 남 - 호주 / 여 - 영국 / 스피드 - 실제 원어민 대화 스피드로 시험에서 빠르게 나올 때 속도

You will hear a phone conversation between Edward, who lives in Glendale, and Jenny, his coworker who wants to buy a house in the area.

JENNY: Hi, Edward. This is Jenny Main from the sales team. Alyssa Boyle told me your extension. I wanted to call to ask you for some advice.
EDWARD: Oh, hi Jenny. Long time no see! What can I help you with?
JENNY: Well, I'm hoping to buy a house in the Glendale neighbourhood, and I remembered that you live there.
EDWARD: That's right. I purchased my home there in 2017. And, I'm so glad that I did. I really enjoy living there.
JENNY: Good for you! So, if you don't mind, I was hoping you could give me some tips.
EDWARD: Sure! Well, I eventually found my house through a Q1 website, but I first went to speak with a local realtor, because one of my friends said he was the best in the business.
JENNY: Oh, I'm guessing that would be Monty King. I've seen his advertisements everywhere. Was he helpful?

글렌데일에 살고 있는 에드워드와 그 지역에서 주택을 구입하고 싶어 하는 동료 직원 제니의 전화 통화를 들어 보세요.

제니: 안녕하세요, 에드워드. 저는 영업부의 제니 메인입니다. 알리사 보일이 당신 내선 번호를 알려 주었어요. 조언을 좀 요청하기 위해 전화 드렸습니다.
에드워드: 오, 안녕하세요, 제니. 오랜만이네요! 무엇을 도와 드릴까요?
제니: 저, 제가 글렌데일 지역에 주택을 한 채 구입하고 싶은데, 그곳에 살고 계신다는 게 기억 나서요.
에드워드: 맞습니다. 2017년에 그곳에 있는 집을 구입했죠. 그리고, 그렇게 해서 정말 기뻐요. 그곳에서 사는 게 정말 즐겁거든요.
제니: 잘됐네요! 그럼, 괜찮으시면, 저에게 팁을 좀 말씀해 주실 수 있었으면 해요.
에드워드: 물론이죠! 음, 저는 결국 Q1 웹사이트를 통해 제 집을 찾았지만, 처음에는 지역 부동산 중개업자와 얘기하러 갔는데, 제 친구 중의 한 명이 그 사람이 업계 최고라고 얘기해주었기 때문이었어요.
제니: 오, 몬티 킹인 것으로 생각되네요. 가는 곳마다 그 분 광고가 있는 걸 봤어요. 도움이 되었나요?

EDWARD: To be honest, I felt like he didn't listen to me at all. For instance, I wanted a place with two separate Q2 garages, but he kept trying to show me places with only one. In the end, I decided to search for a place myself.
JENNY: That's understandable. So when you started viewing houses in the area, were most of them relatively new buildings?
EDWARD: Yes. Almost all of the homes in Glendale are less than a decade old. I must have viewed around ten places, and the oldest one I saw was constructed in Q3 2009.
JENNY: OK, that's good to know. I'd prefer to buy a fairly new house. By the way, is Q4 30 years the normal term for a mortgage these days?
EDWARD: Yes, and I originally applied for that. Then, the lender persuaded me to take a 20-year one, but I wish I had taken the longer one instead.
JENNY: I see. So, you mentioned that you ended up searching for places online. Did you find that pretty easy?
EDWARD: Definitely. There are so many property websites these days. You'll be amazed by the number of houses listed online.
JENNY: Great. I just hope that I can trust all of the sellers and agents on the websites.
EDWARD: Oh, don't worry about that. If they have a certified listing online, it generally means that they have a lot more Q5 credibility.
JENNY: That's a relief to hear. I'm a little nervous about buying my first house.
EDWARD: Don't worry, that's natural. A good thing about searching online is that new technology makes it easier for people like us with hectic schedules. You can even take virtual tours of properties now.
JENNY: Wow, that will save me a lot of time. But, it won't give me a full picture of the area, will it?
EDWARD: Well, most websites provide lots of information about the area a property is in. They will tell you which Q6 schools are in close proximity to each listed house, for example. So, you can really get a good idea of the surrounding area.
JENNY: That will help a lot. And is there any information on approximate monthly costs?
EDWARD: Yes, each property has an estimate for Q7 utilities, so you can decide whether it would be within your budget.

EDWARD: Are you planning to start viewing properties ASAP?

에드워드: 솔직히, 제 얘기를 전혀 듣지 않는 것 같았어요. 예를 들면, 저는 두 개의 분리된 Q2 차고가 있는 곳을 원했는데, 그는 오직 하나만 있는 곳들을 계속 저에게 보여주려 했어요. 결국에는, 제가 직접 찾아보기로 결정을 내렸죠.
제니: 이해가 되네요. 그럼 그 지역에 있는 주택을 보기 시작하셨을 때, 대부분이 비교적 새 건물이었나요?
에드워드: 네. 글렌데일에 있는 거의 모든 집들이 10년 미만이었어요. 약 10곳을 확인해 본 게 분명한데, 제가 본 가장 오래된 곳이 Q3 2009년에 지어진 것이었어요.
제니: 알겠어요, 좋은 정보네요. 저는 꽤 새로 지어진 집을 구입하고 싶거든요. 그건 그렇고, 요즘 Q4 30년이 주택 담보 대출에 대한 일반적인 기간인가요?
에드워드: 네, 그리고 처음에는 그렇게 대출을 신청했어요. 그 후, 대출 기관에서 20년짜리로 하도록 저를 설득했는데, 그 대신 기간이 더 긴 것으로 할 걸 그랬어요.
제니: 알겠어요. 그럼, 결국 온라인으로 찾아보게 되었다고 말씀하셨는데요. 그렇게 하는 것이 아주 쉬우셨나요?
에드워드: 당연하죠. 요즘엔 부동산 웹 사이트가 아주 많아요. 온라인에 올라온 주택 숫자를 보시면 놀라실 거예요.
제니: 잘됐네요. 웹 사이트의 모든 판매자들과 대리인들을 믿을 수 있기만을 바래요.
에드워드: 오, 그건 걱정하지 마세요. 온라인으로 공인된 목록을 갖고 있다면, 일반적으로 훨씬 더 많이 Q5 신뢰할 수 있어요.
제니: 그 말을 들으니 안심이 되네요. 첫 주택을 구입하는 게 좀 긴장되거든요.
에드워드: 걱정 마세요, 자연스러운 일입니다. 온라인으로 찾는 것의 한 가지 좋은 점은 새로운 기술이 정신없이 바쁜 일정의 우리 같은 사람들에게 더 쉽다는 점이죠. 심지어 지금은 부동산 가상 투어도 할 수 있어요.
제니: 와우, 그렇게 하면 시간이 많이 절약되겠어요. 하지만, 지역 전체 사진을 보여주는 건 아니죠?
에드워드: 음, 대부분의 웹 사이트들이 부동산이 속한 지역에 관한 정보를 많이 제공해요. 예를 들면, 목록에 나온 각각의 집과 어느 Q6 학교가 아주 근접해 있는지요. 그래서, 인근 지역을 정말 잘 파악할 수 있죠.
제니: 그렇다면 크게 도움이 되겠네요. 그리고 대략적인 월 비용에 관한 정보도 있나요?
에드워드: 네, 각 부동산에 Q7 공과금에 대한 비용 견적이 있기 때문에, 예산 범위 내에 해당될지 결정하실 수 있어요.

에드워드: 가능한 한 빨리 부동산을 보기 시작할 계획인가요?

JENNY: Yes, as soon as I spot some I like, I'll go and check them out.
EDWARD: It's a great opportunity to get a proper feel for a place and check for any potential problems.
JENNY: Hmm... I'm not sure what things I should check. Do you have any pointers?
EDWARD: First of all, the Q8 plumbing. If the pipes are in poor condition, it might cost you a lot of money later on.
JENNY: Good to know. Anything else?
EDWARD: Well, people often forget about a property as soon as they finish the viewing, so make sure you use your phone to get a lot of Q9 photographs while you are there. And once the viewing is done, take some time to introduce yourself to the Q10 neighbours. They can give you some information about the area, and the property itself.
JENNY: I love that idea!
EDWARD: Great! I hope I've been able to help.
JENNY: Oh, you've been so much help. Thanks so much!

제니: 네, 제가 마음에 드는 곳을 찾는 대로, 가서 확인해 볼 거예요.
에드워드: 한 장소에 대해 제대로 된 감을 얻고 어떤 잠재적인 문제점이 있는지 확인해볼 아주 좋은 기회죠.
제니: 흠.. 어떤 것들을 확인해야 하는지 잘 모르겠어요. 조언해 주실 말이라도 있으신가요?
에드워드: 가장 먼저, Q8 배관이요. 파이프 상태가 좋지 않다면, 나중에 많은 돈을 들이셔야 할 수도 있어요.
제니: 좋은 정보네요. 그 외에 다른 것은요?
에드워드: 저, 사람들은 흔히 둘러보는 일을 완료하자마자 물건에 대해 잊어버리기 때문에, 반드시 그곳에 가 있는 동안 폰으로 Q9 사진을 많이 찍어두세요. 그리고 일단 둘러보는 일을 끝내면, Q10 이웃사람들에게 자신을 소개할 시간을 좀 가져보세요. 그 사람들이 그 지역과 물건 자체에 관한 정보를 좀 제공해 줄 수 있을 거예요.
제니: 그 아이디어가 정말 마음에 들어요!
에드워드: 잘됐네요! 제가 도움이 되었기를 바랍니다.
제니: 오, 아주 많이 도와주셨어요. 정말 고마워요!

| Vocabulary & Expressions |

extension 내선 전화 (번호) neighbourhood 지역, 인근 eventually 결국 realtor 부동산 중개업자 separate 분리된, 별개의 garage 차고 in the end 결국 view ~을 보다 relatively 상대적으로, 비교적 less than ~ 미만의 decade 10년 must have p.p. ~한 것이 분명하다 around 약, 대략 construct ~을 짓다, 건설하다 fairly 꽤, 상당히 by the way (화제 전환 시) 그건 그렇고 mortgage 주택 담보 대출 apply for ~을 신청하다 lender 대출 기관 end up -ing 결국 ~하게 되다 property 부동산, 건물 certified 인증된, 공인된 credibility 신뢰성 relief 안심, 안도 hectic 아주 바쁜 virtual 가상의 in close proximity to ~와 아주 가까운 surrounding 주변의 approximate 대략적인 estimate 견적(서) utilities (전기, 수도 등의) 공공 요금, 공과금 budget 예산 ASAP 가능한 한 빨리(= as soon as possible) spot ~을 찾다, 발견하다 proper 제대로 된, 적절한 check for (문제 등) ~이 있는지 확인하다 potential 잠재적인 pointer 조언, 충고 plumbing 배관 cost A B A에게 B의 비용을 들이게 하다 make sure (that) 반드시 ~하도록 하다 introduce 소개하다 come across (우연히) 발견하다

문제 1-10

다음 필기 내용을 완성하시오. 각 빈칸에 **1개의 단어 그리고/또는 숫자**를 작성하시오.

Edward's Property Advice 에드워드의 부동산 관련 조언

About Edward: 에드워드에 관해:

- Purchased his house in 2017.
  2017년에 자신의 집을 구입했다.
- Came across his house on a [1].
  그의 집을 [1] 에서 발견했다.
- Wanted to find a house with at least two [2].
  최소한 두 개의 [2] 가 있는 집을 찾고 싶어 했다.
- Houses viewed: oldest one was built in [3].
  확인한 주택들: 가장 오래된 것이 [3] 에 지어졌다.
- Thinks he should have taken a mortgage term of [4] years.
  [4]년의 주택 담보 대출 기간을 이용했어야 했다고 생각한다.

Benefits of searching for property online: 온라인으로 부동산을 찾는 것의 장점:

- Lots of property websites that provide extensive, diverse ranges of properties.
  광범위하고 다양한 부동산을 제공하는 많은 부동산 웹 사이트들
- Having a certified listing on a website boosts a seller's [5].
  웹 사이트에 인증된 목록이 있는 것이 판매자의 [5]을 촉진한다.
- New technology allows prospective buyers to take a virtual tour.
  새로운 기술로 인해 잠재 구매자들이 가상 투어를 할 수 있게 해준다.
- Property websites show the nearest [6] to a property.
  부동산 웹 사이트들이 부동산과 가장 가까운 [6]을 보여준다.
- Websites also estimate the cost of [7] per month.
  웹 사이트들은 또한 매달의 [7]에 대한 비용 견적을 내준다.

Advice for property viewing: 부동산을 보는 것에 대한 조언:

- Inspect [8]
  [8] 점검하기
- Take several [9]
  여러 가지 [9]하기
- Speak with [10]
  [10]와 말하기

1. 웹사이트에서 발견했다고 하므로(Well, I eventually found my house through a website), 정답은 한 글자, website이다.
Paraphrasing came across his house on a website(웹사이트에서 집을 발견했다)
→ eventually found my house through a website(결국에는 웹사이트를 통해 집을 발견했다)

2. two(두 개)와 연관된 것은 garages(차고)이므로 정답은 복수형, garages이다.
Paraphrasing house(집) → place(장소, 곳, 거처)

3. 가장 오래된 것이 2009년이므로(the oldest one I saw was constructed in 2009), 정답은 2009이다.
Paraphrasing built(지어진) → constructed(건설된)

4. 에드워드가 실제로 신청한 것이 아니고 신청했었으면 하는 것이므로 정답은 20이 아닌 30이다. years가 빈칸 뒤에 이미 나와 있으므로 years를 또 쓰면 오답이 된다.
Paraphrasing he should have taken(취했어야 했다: 실제 안 했다는 의미)
→ I wish I had taken(취했었기를 희망한다: I wish 가정법으로 실제 안 했음을 의미)

5. certified listing(공인된 목록) 관련하여 신뢰성이 더 생기므로(If they have a certified listing online, it generally means that they have a lot more credibility), 정답은 credibility(신뢰성)이다.
Paraphrasing boost(증가시키다) → have a lot more(더 많이 생긴다)

6. 웹사이트가 집과 학교와의 가까운 근접성을 보여주므로(They will tell you which schools are in close proximity to each listed house), 정답은 schools이다.
Paraphrasing nearest(가장 가까운) → close proximity(가까운 근접성)

7. cost(비용)관련하여 각 부동산마다 공과금에 대한 예측이 있다(each property has an estimate for utilities), 즉 공과금 비용을 예측한다는 의미이므로, 정답은 utilities이다.
Paraphrasing per month(매달) → monthly(월간)

8. 처음에 언급하는 조언이 배관(plumbing)이므로 정답은, plumbing이다.
Paraphrasing advice(조언) → pointer(조언)

9. 두번째로, 사진을 많이 찍어 두라고 하므로(get a lot of photographs), 정답은 photographs이다.
Paraphrasing several(여러) → a lot of(많은)

10. 이웃사람들에게 자신을 소개할 시간을 갖어라(take some time to introduce yourself to the neighbours), 즉 이웃과 말해보라는 의미이므로, 정답은 neighbours이다. 미국식 철자 neighbors도 정답이다.
Paraphrasing speak with(~와 말하다) → introduce yourself to(~에게 자신을 소개하다)

▪ 파트 2 [문제 11-20]

출제 포인트 **난이도: 중**

특정 센터, 시설, 기관 또는 관광지에서 일하는 사람이 자신이 일하는 곳에 대해 소개하는 내용으로 파트 2(섹션 2)에 전형적으로 등장하는 토픽임. 또한 파트 2에서 자주 등장하는 Multiple Choice와 Matching 유형의 문제로 컴퓨터 화면에서 문제 순서 유의!

음원 여 - 영국 / 스피드 - 실제 원어민 독백 스피드로 시험에서 빠르게 나올 때 속도

You will hear a woman called Louise who works at the Watersport Centre in the Lake District, England, welcoming a group of visitors to the centre.

스코틀랜드의 워터스포츠 센터에서 근무하는 루이즈라는 이름의 여성이 센터 단체 방문객을 환영하는 인사를 들어보세요.

Good morning, everyone, and welcome to the Watersport Centre. My name's Louise. I hope you are ready for a fun-filled, action-packed weekend of outdoor activities here. It seems like you are going to have perfect weather for it! Our centre is regarded as England's best location for kayaking and water skiing, and we offer various other watersports and land-based activities, too.

안녕하세요, 여러분, 그리고 워터스포츠 센터에 오신 것을 환영합니다. 제 이름은 루이즈입니다. 이곳에서 재미로 가득하고 흥미진진한 야외 활동과 함께 하는 주말을 보낼 준비가 되셨기를 바랍니다. 여러분은 그에 필요한 완벽한 날씨를 즐기시게 될 것으로 보입니다! 저희 센터는 카약과 수상 스키 활동에 있어 스코틀랜드 최고의 장소로 여겨지고 있으며, 기타 다양한 수상 스포츠와 육상 활동도 제공해 드리고 있습니다.

Most visitors come here for the kayaking, as it can be done by people of almost any fitness level, unlike hiking and climbing. Q11 There are recommended routes, but you are free to explore the other streams and rivers, too, as long as you don't get lost! Most people enjoy going on casual kayaking expeditions to enjoy the splendid scenery on offer.

대부분의 방문객들이 카약을 하기 위해 이곳을 찾는데, 등산이나 암벽 등반과 달리 거의 모든 운동 수준의 사람들이 할 수 있기 때문입니다. Q11 추천해 드리는 경로가 있기는 하지만, 길을 잃지만 않으시면 다른 시냇물이나 강을 얼마든지 탐험해 보셔도 좋습니다! 대부분의 사람들이 제공되는 아주 멋진 경치를 즐기기 위해 편하게 카약 탐험을 떠나는 것을 좋아합니다.

But, before you have a chance to do that, you'll be going on a short, easy hike this morning. You may have seen a selection of hiking boots in the reception area. Q12 If you want, you can borrow a pair for the hike so that you feel more comfortable, at no extra charge. However, if you want to wear your own shoes, I'm sure you'll be fine, as the terrain is pretty flat.

하지만, 그렇게 할 기회를 갖기에 앞서, 오늘 아침에는 짧고 쉬운 등산을 하러 가실 예정입니다. 안내 구역에서 다양한 등산화를 보셨을지 모르겠습니다. Q12 원하실 경우, 더욱 편안함을 느끼실 수 있도록 등산을 위해 한 켤레 빌리실 수 있으며, 추가 비용은 없습니다. 하지만, 여러분 각자의 신발을 착용하기를 원하셔도, 지형이 상당히 평평하기 때문에 문제없으실 겁니다.

Just before lunchtime, you can all take part in an archery competition in the forest behind the centre. You'll be given a lesson by our archery expert before the competition begins. Then, you'll each fire arrows at the target, and Q13 the person who receives the highest score will receive a gift certificate. All those who take part will be required to follow some specific safety precautions.

점심 시간 직전에, 여러분 모두 센터 뒤쪽의 숲에서 열리는 양궁 시합에 참가하실 수 있습니다. 이 시합이 시작되기 전에 저희 양궁 전문가가 이끄는 레슨이 제공될 것입니다. 그런 다음, 각자 표적에 화살을 쏘게 되며, Q13 가장 높은 점수를 받는 분이 상품권을 받습니다. 참가하는 모든 분께서는 특정 안전 예방 조치를 따르셔야 합니다.

After an outdoor lunch in the picnic area, you'll have a waterskiing lesson in the lake across the road from the centre. Q14 You'll be provided with a wetsuit and a life jacket, so you can all participate, regardless of swimming level. However, some of you might find the water to be too cold and prefer to stay on shore. That's entirely up to you. We'll also be arranging some games at the side of the lake for those who don't wish to try the waterskiing.

피크닉 구역에서의 야외 점심 식사 후에, 센터 길 건너편에 있는 호수에서 수상 스키 레슨을 받으실 것입니다. Q14 잠수복과 구명 조끼가 제공되므로, 수영 실력과 상관없이 모두 참가하실 수 있습니다. 하지만, 여러분 일부는 물이 너무 차갑다고 생각해 물가에 머물러 있는 것을 더 좋아하실 수도 있습니다. 이는 전적으로 여러분에게 달려 있습니다. 저희는 또한 수상 스키를 타보기를 원하지 않는 분들을 위해 호수 옆에 몇몇 게임도 마련해 드릴 예정입니다.

You'll have campfire dinner at around 6 pm, and then you'll be shown to your tents in our campground. Several convenient facilities are available on-site, most of which are free to use. There are bathrooms, shower rooms and even a games room with table tennis and billiards. Q15 However, you'll need some spare change if you wish to use the washing machine and tumble dryer. This money goes toward the general upkeep of the campground facilities.

오후 6시쯤에는 캠프파이어와 함께 저녁 식사를 하시게 되며, 그 후 저희 야영장에 있는 텐트를 보여드릴 것입니다. 여러 편의시설이 구역 내에서 이용 가능하며, 대부분은 무료로 사용하실 수 있습니다. 화장실과 샤워실, 그리고 심지어 탁구대와 당구대가 있는 게임 공간까지 있습니다. Q15 하지만, 세탁기와 회전식 건조기를 이용하고 싶으실 경우에는 여분의 잔돈이 좀 필요하실 것입니다. 이 돈은 야영장 시설의 일반적인 유지 관리에 쓰입니다.

Now, even though the weather forecast is generally looking pretty good, we might have some heavy rain during the night. Q16 If that happens, stay in your tents – the tents we provide are designed to withstand extreme weather conditions. It would be a bad idea to go outside as it will be very dark, and you could easily slip and injure yourself. You'll get a wake-up call at around 7 am and another day of adventure will begin!

자, 일기 예보가 대체로 아주 좋아 보이기는 하지만, 야간에 폭우가 있을 수도 있습니다. Q16 폭우 발생 시, 텐트 안에 머물러 계시면 되는데, 저희가 제공해 드리는 텐트는 극심한 기상 조건을 견뎌낼 수 있도록 디자인되어 있습니다. 밖으로 나오는 것이 좋지 않을 수 있는데, 매우 어두워서 쉽게 미끄러져 부상을 입으실 수 있기 때문입니다. 오전 7시쯤에 모닝콜을 들으시고 나면, 모험을 즐기실 또 다른 하루가 시작됩니다!

Now, let me give you some details about the different kayaking routes you can follow during your second day here.

자, 이곳에서 보내시는 둘째 날에 여러분께서 따라가실 수 있는 다른 카약 경로에 관한 상세 정보를 말씀드리겠습니다.

Brody River is just a short walk from the campground. Q17 This route is ideal for those with no previous kayaking experience due to the calm water, but it also serves as a nice spot for experts to practice some advanced techniques.

브로디 강이 야영장에서 아주 조금만 걸어서 가면 되는 거리에 있습니다. Q17 이 경로는 잔잔한 물살로 인해 이전에 카약을 해본 경험이 없으신 분들에게 이상적이지만, 전문가들이 몇몇 고급 기술을 연습해 보기에도 아주 좋은 곳에 해당됩니다.

Another nearby route is East River. Q18 Be warned, unless you really know what you are doing when it comes to kayaking, it might be best to avoid this one! This river flows extremely fast, and some spots have dangerous rapids that only experts will be able to pass through safely.

근처의 또 다른 경로로 이스트 강이 있습니다. Q18 주의할 점은, 카약과 관련해 정말로 무엇을 해야 하는지 알지 못하실 경우, 이 곳을 피하시는 것이 가장 좋을 수 있습니다! 이 강은 대단히 빠르게 흐르고, 몇몇 지점에 오직 전문가들만 안전하게 지나갈 수 있는 위험한 급류가 있습니다.

For anyone who has mastered the basics, and wants a moderately challenging route, White River is an excellent choice. It has a few tough sections, but nothing nearly as tricky as the rapids in East River. Q19 Also, there's a bird sanctuary area off to one side of the river, so you'll have a chance to spot several rare species.

기본 사항들을 완벽히 익히신 분들 중에 적당히 어려운 경로를 원하시는 분들에게는, 화이트 강이 아주 좋은 선택입니다. 몇몇 힘든 구간이 있기는 하지만, 거의 이스트 강의 급류만큼 까다로운 곳은 없습니다. Q19 또한, 이 강의 한쪽 면에서 조금 떨어진 곳에 조류 보호 구역이 있으므로, 여러 희귀 종을 발견할 수 있는 기회도 있을 것입니다.

And last but not least, there's Merry River. Unlike the other three rivers, this one cannot be accessed by foot, as the starting point from kayaking is about 10 miles from the centre. So, if you are interested in that route, Q20 please speak with us so that we can arrange a shuttle bus. Right, let's get ready for our first activity of the day.	그리고 마지막이지만 마찬가지로 중요한 것은, 메리 강입니다. 앞서 말씀드린 세 곳의 강과 달리, 이 강은 걸어서 접근할 수 없는데, 출발 지점이 센터에서 약 10마일 정도 떨어져 있기 때문입니다. 따라서, 이 경로에 관심이 있으시면, Q20 저희가 셔틀버스를 마련해 드릴 수 있도록 말씀해 주시기 바랍니다. 자, 오늘 첫 번째 활동에 필요한 준비를 하죠.

I Vocabulary & Expressions I

fun-filled 재미로 가득한 action-packed 흥미진진한 land-based 육상에서 하는 explore ~을 탐험하다 as long as ~하는 한, ~하기만 하면 get lost 길을 잃다 casual 편하게 하는, 격식 없는 expedition 탐험 splendid 아주 멋진 on offer 제공되는 a selection of 다양한 borrow ~을 빌리다 so that ~할 수 있도록 at no extra charge 추가 비용 없이 terrain 지형 archery 양궁 competition 시합, 경기 대회 expert 전문가 arrow 화살 gift certificate 상품권 take part 참가하다(= participate) precaution 예방 조치 be provided with ~을 제공 받다 find A to be B A가 B하다고 생각하다 on shore 물가에 entirely 전적으로, 완전히 up to ~에게 달려 있는 facility 시설(물) available 이용 가능한 on-site 부지 내에, 현장에 spare change 여분의 잔돈 go toward ~에 사용되다 upkeep 유지 관리 withstand ~을 견뎌내다 extreme 극심한 injure ~에게 부상을 입히다 details 상세 정보, 세부 사항 serve as ~의 역할을 하다 spot n. 지점, 위치 v. ~을 발견하다 practice ~을 연습하다 advanced 고급의, 진보된 unless ~하지 않는다면 when it comes to ~와 관련해 rapids 급류 pass through ~을 통과해 지나다 moderately 적당히 nearly 거의 tricky 까다로운 sanctuary area 보호 구역 off to ~에서 떨어져 있는 rare 희귀한 species (동식물의) 종 last but not least (순서상) 마지막이지만 마찬가지로 중요한

문제 11-16

알맞은 정답을 고르시오.

The Watersports Centre 워터스포츠 센터

11. Louise mentions that when kayaking, the visitors are allowed to
루이즈가 카약을 할 때 방문객들이 -------------------------이 허용된다고 언급한다.

A stop to feed local wildlife. 잠시 멈춰 지역 야생동물에게 먹이를 주는 것
B take pictures of the beautiful scenery. 아름다운 경치를 사진 촬영하는 것
C move away from the regular routes. 일반적인 경로에서 멀리 벗어나는 것

루이즈가 방문객들에게 추천 경로 말고 자유롭게 다녀도 된다고 하므로(There are recommended routes, but you are free to explore the other streams and rivers), 정답은 일반적 경로에서 벗어나도 된다는 C이다.
Paraphrasing regular routes(일반적인 경로) → recommended routes(추천 경로)
visitors are allowed to ~ (방문객들은 ~하도록 허용된다) → you are free to ~ (여러분은 ~하는 것에 자유롭다)

12. What does Louise tell the group about this morning's hiking trip?
루이즈는 오늘 아침의 등산에 대해 해당 그룹에게 무슨 말을 하는가?

A The group will stop briefly for refreshments. 간식을 먹기 위해 잠시 쉴 것이다.
B Footwear is available for those who need it. 신발을 필요로 하는 사람들이 그것을 이용할 수 있다.
C Group members can choose a different activity. 그룹 구성원들이 다른 활동을 선택할 수 있다.

아침 하이킹과 관련하여(You'll be going on a short, easy hike this morning), 안내 장소에서 하이킹 부츠를 빌릴 수 있다고 하므로(You may have seen a selection of hiking boots in the reception area. If you want, you can borrow a pair for the hike so that you feel more comfortable), 정답은 신발 이용에 대한 B이다.
Paraphrasing footwear(신발) → hiking boots(하이킹 부츠) → a pair(한 켤레)

13. What does Louise say about the archery competition?
루이즈는 양궁 시합에 대해 무슨 말을 하는가?

A No safety gear is required. 안전 장비가 필요하지 않다.
B It will be held inside the centre. 센터 내에서 열릴 것이다.
C The winner will receive a prize. 우승자가 상품을 받을 것이다.

archery competition(양궁 시합) 관련하여, 최고 점을 받은 사람이 상품권을 받으므로(the person who receives the highest score will receive a gift certificate), 우승자가 상품을 받는다는 내용의 C가 정답이다.
Paraphrasing winner(승자) → person who receives the highest score(최고점을 받은 사람)
gift certificate(상품권) → prize(상)

14. Regarding the waterskiing lesson, Louise says that
수상 스키 레슨과 관련해, 루이즈는 ------------------------------고 말한다.

A participants must be above a certain age. 참가자들이 반드시 특정 나이를 넘어야 한다
B swimming ability is not important. 수영 능력은 중요하지 않다
C an extra fee will be requested. 추가 요금이 필요하지 않을 것이다

waterskiing lesson(수상스키 레슨) 관련하여, 수영 레벨에 상관없이 모두 참가할 수 있다고 하므로(you can all participate, regardless of swimming level), 수영 실력이 중요하지 않다고 언급한 B가 정답이다.
Paraphrasing swimming ability is not important(수영 실력이 중요하지 않다)
→ regardless of swimming level(수영 레벨에 상관없이)

15. The campground facilities are free except for
무료로 이용할 수 있는 야영장 시설에서 제외되는 것은 -----------이다.

A laundry facilities. 세탁 시설
B cooking facilities. 요리 시설
C entertainment facilities. 오락 시설

campground(야영장) 관련하여, 여분의 잔돈이 세탁기와 회전식 건조기 사용에 필요하다고 하므로(you'll need some spare change if you wish to use the washing machine and tumble dryer), 세탁시설은 무료가 아니다. 따라서 정답은 A이다.
Paraphrasing free except for(~을 제외하고 무료인) → need some spare change(여분의 잔돈이 필요하다)
laundry facilities(세탁 시설) → washing machine and tumble dryer(세탁기와 회전식 건조기)

16. If there is heavy rain while the visitors are in their tents, they should
방문객들이 텐트에 있는 동안 폭우가 내릴 경우에 --------------------------------을 해야 한다.

A move to a nearby dormitory. 근처의 기숙사로 이동하기
B remain in the tent until morning. 아침까지 텐트에 머물러 있기
C contact one of the centre's employees. 센터 직원 한 명에게 연락하기

폭우가 올 때는 텐트에 머물러 있으라고 하므로(we might have some heavy rain during the night. If that happens, stay in your tents), 정답은 B이다.
Paraphrasing remain(남아 있다, 유지하다) → stay(머물다)

ACTUAL TEST 2

문제 17-20
루이즈는 각각의 다음 강 경로에 대해 무슨 정보를 제공하는가?
정답을 골라서 빈칸에 옮기시오.

Information 정보

A It passes by a wildlife zone. 야생동물 보호구역 옆을 지나간다.
B It is suitable for beginners. 초보자들에게 적합하다.
C It requires additional equipment. 추가 장비를 필요로 한다.

D It contains several rare species of fish. 여러 희귀 물고기 종이 있다.
E It requires road transportation. 도로 교통 수단을 필요로 한다.
F It has some unsafe sections. 안전하지 못한 몇몇 구역이 있다.

Brody River **17**
브로디 강

Brody River 관련하여, 이전 카약 경험이 없는 사람들에게 이상적이라고 하므로(ideal for those with no previous kayaking experience), 초보자들에게 적합하다는 의미이다. 따라서 정답은 B이다.
Paraphrasing suitable(적합한) → ideal(이상적인)
beginners(초보자들) → no previous kayaking experience(이전에 카약 경험이 없는)

East River **18**
이스트 강

East River 관련하여, 이 강은 대단히 빠르게 흐르기 때문에, 몇몇 지점에 오직 전문가들만 안전하게 지나갈 수 있는 위험한 급류가 있다고 하므로(This river flows extremely fast, and some spots have dangerous rapids that only experts will be able to pass through safely), 안전하지 못한 몇몇 구역이 있다는 의미로 F가 정답이다.
Paraphrasing unsafe sections(안전하지 못한 구역들) → spots have dangerous rapids(몇몇 지점들은 위험한 급류가 있다)

White River **19**
화이트 강

White River 관련하여, 이 강의 한쪽 면에서 조금 떨어진 곳에 조류 보호 구역이 있으므로, 여러 희귀 종을 발견할 수 있는 기회도 있다고 한다(there's a bird sanctuary area off to one side of the river, so you'll have a chance to spot several rare species). 여기서 rare species가 나왔다고 D를 선택하면 안된다. 왜냐하면 D는 새가 아닌 물고기에 대한 언급이기 때문이다. 새도 야생동물이므로 정답은 A이다.
Paraphrasing wildlife zone(야생동물 구역) → bird sanctuary area(새 보호 구역)

Merry River **20**
메리 강

Merry River 관련하여, 셔틀버스를 마련할 수 있다고 하므로(we can arrange a shuttle bus), 정답은 교통 수단 내용의 E이다.
Paraphrasing road transportation(도로 교통수단) → shuttle bus(셔틀버스)

▪ 파트 3 [문제 21-30]

출제 포인트 **난이도: 상**

최근 들어 음악 관련 연구 내용이 자주 출제되고 있기에 관련 내용과 어휘를 최대한 활용하여 본 문제를 출제함. 특히 파트 3 난이도가 예전보다 높게 실제 시험에 출제되기에 이러한 난이도를 반영함.

음원 남 - 영국 / 여 - 영국 / 스피드 - 실제 원어민 대화 스피드로 시험에서 빠르게 나올 때 속도

You will hear two students called Nick and Susan discussing how music in advertisements affects people.	닉과 수잔이라는 이름의 두 학생이 광고 음악이 사람들에게 어떻게 영향을 미치는지에 대해 이야기하는 것을 들어보세요.
NICK: I'm nowhere near finished with my research for our report on the effect of advertisement music on emotions.	**닉:** 광고 음악이 감정에 미치는 영향에 관한 리포트에 필요한 조사를 끝내려면 아직 멀었어.
SUSAN: I still have loads to do, too. What have you learned so far? Has it changed the way you think about music in advertising?	**수잔:** 나도 여전히 할 게 많아. 지금까지 알아낸 것 좀 있어? 그게 네가 광고 음악에 대해 생각하는 방식을 바꾸게 만들었어?

NICK: Well, I've always appreciated hearing a nice song by a singer or group that I like. But, in general, Q21 I've never really been concerned enough to pay attention to music in advertisements.
SUSAN: The research I've carried out so far has been quite enlightening to me. Q22 Before this project, I used to believe that music choices in advertisements were usually just arbitrary. But I now realise that a lot of my purchasing habits and fondness for certain brands are a result of clever music choices in advertising.
NICK: I know, right? Take the new advert for the Big Sub Sandwich Company, for example. The lyrics used in the music talk about healthy lifestyles and low-fat food. I just went along with it, but after giving it some thought, their products are far from healthy!
SUSAN: Q23 Exactly, that's a great example of using music to paint a false picture for potential customers. It's actually quite shocking, to be honest.
NICK: I agree. I bet the majority of people hear the song and mistakenly presume it's healthy food.
SUSAN: I'm probably guilty of that. But I'll be paying more attention from now on.
NICK: Same here! I've also been reading about how catchy jingles on TV and radio advertisements attract consumers. I remember when I was young, I'd hear more jingles than songs in advertisements. I guess they have some benefits over full songs.
SUSAN: Which do you prefer?
NICK: I always liked jingles. Q24 I'm not sure the younger generation these days would agree, but at least you could remember them easily and hum along. I think the trend these days is to get a really famous performer to endorse a brand or product.
SUSAN: Yes, we see more and more of that these days. It seems like every time I see an advertisement, it's accompanied by a really popular pop or rap song. It must really appeal to a wide consumer base.
NICK: I know. Q25 Sigma Electronics recently released an advertisement with a song that features several of the world's biggest award-winning music stars. And I can't believe they didn't even use an existing song. They managed to persuade the singers to record a brand new one specifically for the advertisement.
SUSAN: I know. I guess having a song that's solely associated with the ad makes people think of the brand whenever they hear it.
NICK: That makes sense, yeah.
SUSAN: Based on what I've read, I think we'll see some new trends emerging over the next few years. Companies seem to have really noticed how important music is in their advertising.

닉: 그게, 난 항상 내가 좋아하는 가수나 그룹이 부른 좋은 곡을 들으면서 감상했어. 하지만, 보통은, Q21 광고에 쓰인 음악에 주의를 기울일 만큼 충분히 관심을 가진 적이 한 번도 없었어.
수잔: 내가 지금까지 실시했던 조사 작업은 날 상당히 일깨워줬어. Q22 이 프로젝트 이전에는, 광고 음악 선택이 일반적으로 그저 임의적인 것이었다는 생각을 하곤 했거든. 하지만, 지금은 여러 내 구매 습관과 특정 브랜드에 대한 선호가 광고에 쓰이는 음악의 교묘한 선택에 따른 결과라는 걸 알게 됐어.
닉: 맞아, 그렇지? 빅 서브 샌드위치 회사의 새 광고를 예로 들어보자. 그 음악에 쓰인 가사는 건강한 생활 방식과 저지방 음식에 관해 얘기하고 있어. 난 단지 그것에 동조하기만 했는데, 좀 생각해보니, 그 회사 제품들이 건강함과는 거리가 멀더라고!
수잔: Q23 바로 그거야, 그게 바로 잠재 고객들에게 거짓으로 위장하기 위해 음악을 사용하는 것의 아주 좋은 예시지. 실제로 꽤 충격적이야, 솔직히 말하면.
닉: 동의해. 대부분의 사람들이 그 음악을 듣고 건강한 음식이라고 잘못 생각하는 것 같아.
수잔: 난 그것에 대해 죄책감을 느낄 것 같아. 하지만 지금부터 더욱 주의를 기울일거야.
닉: 나도 마찬가지야! 난 그리고 TV와 라디오 광고의 기억하기 쉬운 CM송이 어떻게 소비자들의 마음을 끄는지에 관한 글도 읽어 봤어. 내가 어렸을 때, 광고에서 일반 노래보다 CM송을 더 많이 들었던 게 기억나. 온전한 노래보다 그게 더 장점이 있는 것 같아.
수잔: 넌 어느 게 더 좋아?
닉: 난 CM송이 항상 좋았어. Q24 요즘 어린 세대가 동의할지는 모르겠지만, 적어도 쉽게 기억할 수 있고 똑같이 따라서 흥얼거릴 수 있잖아. 요즘 추세는 정말 유명한 음악인에게 브랜드나 제품을 광고하게 하는 것 같아.
수잔: 맞아, 요즘엔 그렇게 하는 걸 점점 더 많이 보게 돼. 내가 광고를 볼 때마다, 정말 인기 있는 팝송이나 랩 음악이 동반되는 것 같아. 그게 정말로 다양한 소비자 층의 마음을 끄는 게 분명해.
닉: 나도 알아. Q25 시그마 전자제품회사가 최근에 세계에서 가장 유명한 수상 경력이 있는 여러 음악 스타들이 나오는 노래가 있는 광고를 내놨어. 그리고 그 회사가 심지어 기존의 노래를 사용하지 않았다는 게 믿기지 않아. 그 가수들을 설득해서 특별히 그 광고만을 위한 완전히 새로운 곡을 녹음하게 했거든.
수잔: 나도 알아. 오직 광고에만 관련된 노래를 만들면 사람들이 그걸 들을 때마다 그 브랜드를 생각하게 만드는 것 같아.
닉: 응, 맞는 말이야.
수잔: 내가 읽은 바에 의하면, 앞으로 몇 년 동안에 걸쳐 몇몇 새로운 경향이 나타나는 것 보게 될 것 같아. 회사들이 광고에 쓰이는 음악이 얼마나 중요한지를 확실히 알아차린 것으로 보여.

NICK: Yes, I have the same feeling. How do you think it will change?
SUSAN: Q26 Well, it seems that some of the biggest firms are working with actual scientists to devise musical methods for influencing the emotions and moods of potential consumers. There are several sneaky ways they can do that.
NICK: Yes, that definitely seems like the way things will go.

NICK: By the way, what did you make of the Peterson study?
SUSAN: I think the Peterson study provides some key insights into the use of music to encourage people to spend money on products, and the ethics behind the practice.
NICK: But, I was shocked to find out that Q27&28 it's not been accepted by some noted experts in the field. In fact, some are quite outspoken about its perceived flaws. Why do you think that is?
SUSAN: I wouldn't be surprised if those so-called experts were working alongside some of the big companies criticised in the study.
NICK: That had crossed my mind as well. However, the findings from all the surveys and interviews certainly seem quite accurate.
SUSAN: Yes, they do. But Q27&28 what I found hard to believe is that it was administered only to people in their 20s – that's not really covering a diverse consumer base.
NICK: I did find that odd. I suppose that demographic does account for the large majority of consumer spending, but it makes the findings inconclusive.
SUSAN: Exactly.
NICK: The study does contain some interesting stuff about how different instruments elicit different emotional responses.
SUSAN: Yes, it's something I hadn't really thought about. What did it say about string instruments again?
NICK: Q29&30 Music containing short, sharp bursts of violin or cello made 87 per cent of participants feel happy or excited. That's why string music is used in many advertisements.
SUSAN: Right. But some instruments have the opposite effect. According to the study, Q29&30 brass music, including trumpets and trombones, made 78 per cent of the study participants agitated or angry.
NICK: Yes, so it's rare to hear brass music in ads.
SUSAN: And the acoustic guitar received the most positive response. Almost every participant agreed that it made them feel calm and relaxed. On the other hand, music featuring a lot of percussion instruments didn't arouse

닉: 응, 나도 비슷한 생각이야. 그게 어떻게 바뀔 것 같아?
수잔: Q26 음, 몇몇 가장 큰 회사들이 잠재 소비자들의 감정과 기분에 영향을 미치는 음악적 방법을 고안해 내기 위해 실제 과학자들과 협업하는 것 같아. 회사들이 그렇게 할 수 있는 여러 교묘한 방식들이 있지.
닉: 응, 분명 그게 일이 진행되는 방식인 것 같아.

닉: 그런데, 피터슨 연구에 대해 어떻게 생각해?
수잔: 피터슨 연구가 제품에 소비를 사람들에게 권하게 하는 음악을 사용하는 것과, 그와 같은 관행의 이면에 숨어 있는 윤리 의식에 대한 몇몇 중요한 통찰력을 제공한다고 생각해.
닉: 하지만, 난 Q27&28 그것이 해당 분야의 몇몇 유명한 전문가들에게 받아들여지지 않았다는 걸 알고 충격을 받았어. 실제로, 몇몇은 그 연구에서 인지된 결점에 대해 상당히 노골적으로 말하고 있어. 왜 그런 거라고 생각해?
수잔: 소위 전문가라는 사람들이 그 연구에서 비판한 몇몇 큰 회사들과 함께 하고 있다고 해도 놀랍지 않을 거야.
닉: 나도 그 생각이 떠올랐어. 하지만, 모든 설문 조사와 인터뷰를 통해 얻은 결과물은 분명 꽤 정확한 것 같아.
수잔: 응, 맞아. 하지만 Q27&28 내가 믿기 어렵다고 생각한 점은 오직 20대에 속한 사람들만을 대상으로 실시되었다는 건데, 정말로 다양한 소비자 층을 포함하는 게 아니거든.
닉: 나도 확실히 그게 이상했어. 난 통계 자료가 분명 대부분의 소비자 지출을 설명해 준다고 생각하지만, 그게 그 결과물을 결정적이지 못하게 만드는 것 같아.
수잔: 맞아.
닉: 그 연구는 서로 다른 악기가 어떻게 다른 감정적 반응을 이끌어내는지에 관한 흥미로운 내용을 확실히 담고 있어.
수잔: 응, 그건 내가 정말로 생각하지 못했던 거야. 현악기에 대해 뭐라고 했다고 그랬지?
닉: Q29&30 바이올린 또는 첼로의 짧고 날카롭게 터지는 소리를 담고 있는 음악이 87퍼센트의 참가자들을 기쁘거나 신나게 만들었어. 이것이 바로 많은 광고에 현악기 음악이 사용되는 이유야.
수잔: 맞아. 하지만 일부 악기들은 반대 효과를 내. 그 연구에 따르면, Q29&30 트럼펫이나 트럼본을 포함하는 금관악기가 들어간 음악에 연구 참가자의 78퍼센트가 불안해하거나 화를 냈어.
닉: 응, 그래서 광고에서 금관악기 음악을 듣는 게 흔치 않아.
수잔: 그리고 어쿠스틱 기타가 가장 긍정적인 반응을 얻었어. 거의 모든 참가자가 차분하고 편안한 느낌이 들게 해주었다는데 동의했거든. 반면에, 많은 타악기를 특징으로 하는 음악은 대부분 참가자들에게 많은 감정을 불

much emotion at all in most participants. **NICK:** Now, let's talk about the ethics behind using specific music to make people buy products...	러일으키지 못했어. **닉:** 이제, 사람들에게 제품을 구매하게 만드는 특정 음악을 사용하는 것의 이면에 숨어 있는 윤리 의식에 대해 얘기해보자...

I Vocabulary & Expressions I

nowhere near ~에 한참 못 미치는 have loads to do 할 일이 많다 so far 지금까지 advertising 광고(= advert, ad) appreciate ~을 감상하다 be concerned 관심이 있다 pay attention to ~에 주의를 기울이다 carry out ~을 실시하다 enlightening 일깨워주는 arbitrary 임의적인 fondness for ~에 대한 선호, 애호 lyrics 가사 go along with ~에 동조하다 give A some thought A를 좀 생각해보다 presume 생각하다, 추정하다 guilty of ~에 대해 죄책감을 느끼는 catchy 기억하기 쉬운 jingle CM송, 광고 음악 over (비교) ~에 비해 hum along 따라서 흥얼거리다 get A to do A에게 ~하게 하다 endorse (유명인이 나와) ~을 광고하다 be accompanied by ~을 동반하다 appeal to ~의 마음을 끌다 feature ~을 특징으로 하다, 포함하다 existing 기존의 manage to do ~해내다 brand new 완전히 새로운 be associated with ~와 관련되어 있다 emerge 나타나다, 생겨나다 notice ~을 알아차리다 devise ~을 고안하다 influence ~에 영향을 미치다 sneaky 교묘한 what did you make of ~? ~에 대해 어떻게 생각해? insight 통찰력 encourage 권하다, 장려하다 ethics 윤리 (의식) practice 관행, 관례 noted 유명한 expert 전문가 field 분야 outspoken 노골적으로 말하는 perceived 인지된 flaw 결점, 흠 so-called 소위 ~라 불리는 alongside ~와 함께 criticise ~을 비판하다 cross one's mind 생각이 떠오르다 findings 연구 결과(물) administer ~을 실시하다 demographic 통계 자료 account for ~을 설명하다 inconclusive 결정적이지 못한 stuff (명확하지 않을 때) 것, 일, 물건 instrument 악기 elicit ~을 이끌어내다 burst 터져 나옴, 파열 participant 참가자 brass 금관악기 agitated 불안해하는 rare 흔치 않은 calm 차분한 percussion 타악기 arouse ~을 불러일으키다

문제 21-26

정답을 고르시오.

Utilising Music in Advertising 광고에 음악 활용하기

21. What was Nick's attitude to music in advertisements before this project?
이 프로젝트 이전에 광고에 쓰이는 음악에 대한 닉의 태도는 어땠는가?

A He thought it was an integral factor. 필수적인 요소라고 생각했다.
B He didn't give it much consideration. 크게 고려해보지 않았다.
C He found most of it irritating. 대부분이 짜증난다고 생각했다.

이전에 닉은 광고 속 음악에 대해 관심을 갖은 적이 없으므로(I've never really been concerned enough to pay attention to music in advertisements), 정답은 B이다.

Paraphrasing didn't give it much consideration(고려를 많이 하지 않았다)
→ have never really been concerned enough(정말 관심을 갖은 적이 없다)

22. Susan says that before doing this project,
수잔은 이 프로젝트를 하기 전에 --------------------------라고 말한다.

A she was unaware of how advertisement music influenced her.
광고 음악이 자신에게 어떻게 영향을 미쳤는지 알지 못했다.

B she generally enjoyed all music in advertisements.
일반적으로 광고 속의 모든 음악을 즐겼다.

C she often purchased products endorsed by celebrities.
유명인이 광고하는 제품을 자주 구입했다.

ACTUAL TEST 2

수잔은 이 프로젝트 전에, 광고에서 음악을 선택하는 것이 그저 임의적이라고 생각했다고 말하므로(Before this project, I used to believe that music choices in advertisements were usually just arbitrary), 광고 음악의 중요성을 인지하지 못했음을, 얼마나 영향을 미치는지를 알지 못했음을 의미하므로 정답은 A이다. used to(~하곤 했었다)는 과거에는 그랬지만 지금은 그렇지 않음을 나타낼 때 사용한다.

Paraphrasing unaware of how advertisement music influenced(광고 음악이 얼마나 영향을 미치는지 모르는)
→ arbitrary(임의적인)

23. When discussing the music in a sandwich company's advertisement, Nick agrees with Susan that
샌드위치 회사의 광고에 쓰이는 음악을 이야기하면서, 닉은 수잔과 ---------------------------을 동의한다.

A it misleads consumers. 소비자들을 호도하고 있다
B it incorporates well-known melodies. 잘 알려진 멜로디들을 포함하고 있다.
C it is indicative of a new trend. 새로운 경향을 나타낸다.

샌드위치 회사 광고 음악 관련하여, 수잔이 그 음악으로 고객들에게 잘못된 이미지를 그린다고 말하자(using music to paint a false picture for potential customers), 닉이 이에 동의하면서 사람들이 건강식으로 잘못 생각하게 만든다고 한다(people hear the song and mistakenly presume it's healthy food). 따라서 사실을 감추고 소비자를 잘못 이끄는 A가 정답이다.

Paraphrasing consumers(소비자들) → customers(고객들)
misleads(호도하다) → paint a false picture(거짓된 그림을 그리다)

24. Nick prefers jingles to full-length songs in advertising because they are
닉이 광고에 온전한 길이의 일반 노래보다 CM송을 선호하는 이유는 CM송이 ---------------------이기 때문이다.

A more memorable. 더 기억하기 쉬운
B more melodic. 더 선율이 풍부한
C more relevant. 더 관련성이 있는

닉은 징글(CM송)을 좋아하는 이유로 기억하기 쉽고 따라 흥얼거릴 수 있다고 하므로(you could remember them easily and hum along), 정답은 A이다.

Paraphrasing memorable(기억에 남는, 외우기 쉬운) → remember them easily(쉽게 그것들을 기억하다)

25. What surprised both students about the advertisement made by the electronics manufacturer?
전자제품 회사가 만든 광고와 관련해 무엇이 두 학생을 놀라게 했는가?

A Its music was nominated for several industry awards.
그 음악이 업계 내의 여러 상에 대해 후보로 지명되었다.

B Its music directly referenced the products being advertised.
그 음악이 광고되는 제품을 직접적으로 언급했다.

C Its music was written exclusively for the advertisement.
그 음악이 오로지 해당 광고만을 위해 작곡되었다.

전자회사(Sigma Electronics)가 기존 곡을 안 쓰고 특별히 광고만을 위한 노래를 녹음한 사실에 놀랐다고 하므로(I can't believe they didn't even use an existing song. They managed to persuade the singers to record a brand new one specifically for the advertisement), 정답은 C이다.

방송 지문에서 awards가 나오지만 이는 작곡에 참여한 음악 스타들과 관련한 내용이지 광고음악과 연관이 있지는 않다. 따라서 A는 오답이다. 이렇듯 Multiple Choice의 보기에서는 방송에 나온 단어가 있는 보기가 오답으로 연결되는 경우가 많다. 따라서 단어만 듣고 정답을 고르면 안되고 의미를 이해하고 정답을 고르도록 한다.

또한 보기 B(음악이 광고되는 제품을 언급한다, 즉 광고 음악이 해당 광고 제품을 언급한다는 의미)의 경우도 어떻게 보면 보기 C와 의미가 비슷해서 혼동이 올 수 있는데, C가 B보다 방송 내용과 더 일치하므로 B 역시 오답이 된다. 최근 파트 3(섹션 3)에서 이렇게 혼동이 오는 보기를 주는 경우가 자주 있음에 유의하자.

Paraphrasing surprised(놀라게하다) → I can't believe(믿을 수 없다)
electronics manufacturer(전자제품 제조사) → Sigma Electronics(시그마 전자회사)
written exclusively for the ad(그 광고만을 위해 쓴)
→ record a brand new one specifically for the advertisement(특별히 그 광고를 위해 새 곡을 녹음하다)

26. In what way do the students think music in advertising will change in the future?

두 학생은 광고 음악이 미래에 어떤 방식으로 바뀔 것이라고 생각하는가?

A It will feature more well-known artists. 더 잘 알려진 예술가들을 특징으로 할 것이다.

B It will be governed by stricter regulations. 더 엄격한 규제에 의해 통제될 것이다.

C It will be more psychologically manipulative. 심리적으로 더욱 조작할 것이다.

manipulative는 '사람이나 사물을 교묘하고 부정직하게 조작하거나 조정하는'을 뜻한다. 수잔은 큰 회사들이 잠재 소비자들의 감정과 기분에 영향을 미치는 음악적 방법을 고안하고 있고 이러한 방법이 교묘하다고 하니(some of the biggest firms are working with actual scientists to devise musical methods for influencing the emotions and moods of potential consumers. There are several sneaky ways they can do that), 이는 교묘하게 사람의 심리를 조작한다는 의미이다. 닉 또한 분명 그렇게 되어간다고 하므로(Yes, that definitely seems like the way things will go), 정답은 C이다.

Paraphrasing psychologically manipulative(심리적으로 조작하는)
→ influencing the emotions and moods(감정과 기분에 영향을 미치는)

문제 27-28

두 개의 정답을 고르시오.

Which **TWO** things surprised the students about the Peterson study on music in advertising?
광고 음악에 관한 피터슨 연구와 관련해 어느 두 가지가 두 학생을 놀라게 했는가?

A the criticism it received from experts
전문가들로부터 받은 비판

B its similarity to other studies
다른 연구들과의 유사성

C the duration of the research involved
관련된 조사의 지속 기간

D the narrow age range of participants
참가자들의 좁은 연령 범위

E the wide range of musical genres it covered
그것이 다룬 아주 다양한 음악 장르들

피터슨 연구와 관련해, 닉이 몇몇 유명한 전문가들에게 받아들여지지 않은 것에 충격을 받았다고 하므로(I was shocked to find out that it's not been accepted by some noted experts in the field), 이는 전문가들로부터 비판을 받았다는 의미이므로, 먼저 A를 고를 수 있다.

그 다음 수잔이 믿기 어렵다고 생각한 점은 오직 20대에 속한 사람만을 대상으로 실시되어 다양한 소비자 층을 포함하는게 아니라고 말하므로(what I found hard to believe is that it was administered only to people in their 20s - that's not really covering a diverse consumer base), 참가자들의 좁은 연령 범위인 D가 정답이다. 이때 정답을 27번에 A, 28번에 D라고 적어도 되고, 27번에 D, 28번에 A라고 적어도 된다.

Paraphrasing surprised(놀란) → shocked(충격 받은), hard to believe(믿기 어려운)
criticism(비판) → has not been accepted(받아들여지지 않았다)
narrow age range(좁은 연령 범위) → administered only to people in their 20s(20대 사람들에게만 실시된)

문제 29-30

두 개의 정답을 고르시오.

What were **TWO** of the findings presented in the Peterson study?
피터슨 연구에 제시된 두 가지 결과물은 무엇이었는가?

A Acoustic guitars make people feel excited.
어쿠스틱 기타가 사람들을 신나게 만든다.

B Vocal music is likely to make people feel relaxed.
성악이 사람들에게 편안함을 느끼도록 만들 가능성이 있다.

C A correlation exists between string music and happiness.
현악기를 이용한 음악과 행복감 사이에 상관 관계가 존재한다.

D Percussion makes people feel motivated.
타악기는 사람들에게 동기 부여가 되는 느낌이 들도록 만든다.

E Brass instruments arouse negative emotions.
금관악기는 부정적인 감정을 불러일으킨다.

피터슨 연구에 제시된 두 가지 결과와 관련해, 닉이 바이올린과 첼로의 짧고 날카롭게 터지는 음악이 사람들을 기쁘거나 흥미롭게 하기에, 현악기가 광고에 많이 쓰인다고 하므로(Music containing short, sharp bursts of violin or cello made 87 per cent of participants feel happy or excited. That's why string music is used in many advertisements), 현악기 음악과 행복의 관계를 나타낸 C를 먼저 고를 수 있다.

그 다음 수잔이 트럼펫이나 트럼본을 포함한 금관악기가 사람들을 불안해하거나 화나게 만듦으로(brass music, including trumpets and trombones, made 78 per cent of the study participants agitated or angry), 즉 부정적 감정을 불러일으키므로 정답은 E이다. 역시 정답 순서 C, E를 바꿔서 29번과 30번에 적어도 정답 처리된다.

보기에는 acoustic guitar, string music, percussion, brass instruments 등 방송 지문에 나온 단어들이 그대로 나오므로 단어만 듣고 정답을 고르면 안되고, 단어가 들어간 문장의 의미를 파악하여 정답을 고를 수 있도록 하자.
Paraphrasing negative emotions(부정적 감정들) → agitated or angry(불안해하거나 화난)

▪ 파트 4 [문제 31-40]

출제 포인트 **난이도: 상**

파트 4에서는 한가지 사물의 역사를 설명하는 지문이 자주 나오는데, 본 문제 역시 시험에 출제되었던 목화의 역사를 설명하는 내용임. 모르는 단어가 들려도 문제를 계속해서 풀 수 있는 능력을 배양하기 위해 실제 시험보다는 조금 더 어렵게 문제를 구성함. 또다시 실제 시험에 출제될 수 있는 내용이므로 확실히 공부해 둘 것.

음원 남 - 영국 / 스피드 - 실제 시험과 유사한 속도

You will hear part of a presentation by a history student about the history of cotton.	한 역사 전공 학생이 목화의 역사에 관해 발표하는 내용 일부를 들어보세요.
During this presentation, I'm going to be talking to you about cotton, and how its use and manufacture spread throughout the world. As you probably already know, cotton is a soft fibre that grows in a boll around the seeds of cotton plants. At various points throughout history, numerous civilisations in both the Old and New World discovered or were introduced to cotton and began using it to make multi-purpose Q31 fabrics. The earliest known evidence of cotton use was uncovered at the site of Mehrgarh on the Kacchi Plain of Pakistan. Researchers discovered early cotton threads that had been preserved in copper beads and estimated that they dated back to around 5000 BCE.	이번 발표 동안, 저는 목화, 그리고 그것의 이용 방법과 제조 방식이 어떻게 전 세계로 확산되었는지 여러분에게 이야기하고자 합니다. 아마 이미 아시겠지만, 목화는 목화 나무 씨앗 주변의 꼬투리 안에서 자라는 부드러운 섬유입니다. 역사 속의 다양한 시점에, 구세계와 신세계 모두 수많은 문명 사회들이 목화를 발견하거나 도입했고, 다용도의 Q31 직물을 만들기 위해 사용하기 시작했습니다. 목화 사용에 대해 최초로 알려진 증거는 파키스탄의 카치 평원에 있는 메르가르라는 곳에서 발견되었습니다. 연구가들이 구리 구슬 속에 보존되어 있던 초기 목화실을 발견했고, 그 시기가 대략 기원전 5,000년까지 거슬러 올라간다고 추정했습니다.
Around the 5th century BCE, the Greek historian Herodotus mentions Indian cotton in his writings, likening it to higher-quality Q32 wool and praising its superior beauty and texture. When Alexander the Great's forces invaded India, the soldiers began to favour local cotton Q33 clothing over their traditional woollen garments, deeming them more comfortable for everyday wear.	기원전 5세기경에, 그리스의 역사가 헤로도토스가 자신의 글에서 인도 목화를 언급했는데, 그것을 고품질 Q32 양모에 비교하면서 그 우월한 아름다움과 질감에 찬사를 보냈습니다. 알렉산더 대왕의 군대가 인도를 침공했을 때, 병사들이 자신들의 전통 모직 의류보다 그 지역의 목화 Q33 의류를 선호하기 시작했는데, 일상 옷으로 더 편하다고 여겼기 때문입니다.

Fast forward to the Middle Ages, and cotton had become a commonly used fabric in many parts of the world. Handheld roller cotton gins had been used to process cotton in India since the 6th century, and were later introduced to other countries via interaction with Indian Q34 traders. Near the end of the 12th century, dual-roller gins began to appear throughout India and China. By the end of the 16th century, the Indian version of the dual-roller gin was prevalent in the cotton industry throughout the entire Mediterranean region. In certain locations, this mechanical device was driven by Q35 water, and it proved to be much more efficient than the earlier handheld roller cotton gins.

시간을 빠르게 건너뛰어 중세로 가면, 목화가 전 세계 많은 지역에서 흔히 사용되는 직물이 되었습니다. 6세기 이후로 인도에서는 손으로 조작하는 롤러가 있는 조면기가 목화를 가공 처리하는 데 사용되었으며, 나중에 인도 Q34 상인들과의 교류를 통해 다른 여러 국가에도 도입되었습니다. 12세기말 무렵에는, 이중 롤러가 있는 조면기가 인도와 중국 전역에 걸쳐 나타나기 시작했습니다. 16세기말쯤에는, 인도에서 제작한 이중 롤러 조면기가 지중해 지역 전체에 걸쳐 목화 산업에서 널리 이용되었습니다. 여러 특정 지역에서, 이 기계 장치가 Q35 물을 이용해 작동되었는데, 이전의 손으로 조작하는 롤러가 있던 조면기보다 훨씬 더 효율적인 것으로 드러났습니다.

Cotton manufacture was introduced to Western Europe during the Muslim conquest of the Iberian Peninsula in the 8th century. Knowledge of cotton eventually spread throughout Italy in the 12th century, when the Normans conquered the island of Sicily, and it soon spread throughout the rest of mainland Europe. When the spinning wheel was introduced to Europe in the 14th century, the cotton spinning industry boomed as a result of the increased Q36 efficiency provided by the device. Antwerp and Venice soon became bustling Q37 ports for the cotton trade, and manufacturers recognised the hugely profitable potential in the sale and transportation of cotton fabrics.

목화 생산은 8세기 이베리아 반도의 무슬림 정복 당시에 서유럽 지역에 소개되었습니다. 목화에 대한 지식은 결국 노르만족이 시칠리아 섬을 정복했던 12세기에 이탈리아 전역에 걸쳐 확산되었고, 곧 나머지 유럽 본토 전역으로 퍼져 나갔습니다. 14세기에 물레가 유럽에 소개되었을 때, 목화 방적 산업이 이 장치에 의해 제공된 Q36 효율성 증대에 따른 결과로 호황을 누렸습니다. 앤트워프와 베니스가 곧 목화 교역으로 북적대는 Q37 항구가 되었으며, 제조업자들은 목화의 판매와 운송에 엄청나게 큰 수익을 올릴 수 있는 잠재력이 있음을 인식했습니다.

During the Renaissance era, cotton became even more of a highly sought-after commodity in Europe. Vasco da Gama, a Portuguese explorer, helped to establish shipping routes in order to facilitate trade with several countries in Asia. The use of ships for trading made land-based caravans obsolete, and allowed merchants to transport greater volumes of merchandise in each shipment. Some of the most well-kept secrets of Indian cotton processing also began to move West. Indian traders and craftsmen had long concealed the Q38 methods used to create colourful patterns with cotton, but after some of them were converted to Christianity, they described their methods to a French Catholic priest named Father Coeurdoux, who passed on the information to several individuals working in the European textile industry.

르네상스 시대에, 목화는 유럽에서 엄청나게 수요가 많은 상품 이상의 것이 되었습니다. 포르투갈의 탐험가 바스코 다 가마는 아시아 여러 국가들과의 교역을 용이하게 하기 위한 수송 경로를 확립하는 데 도움을 주었습니다. 교역에 있어 배를 활용함으로써 육로 기반의 마차가 무용지물이 되었으며, 상인들이 각 수송 과정에서 더 많은 양의 상품을 운반할 수 있게 해주었습니다. 가장 엄격히 유지되던 인도 목화 가공의 몇몇 비밀들도 유럽으로 새나가기 시작했습니다. 인도의 상인들과 수공업자들은 목화로 다채로운 패턴을 만드는 데 사용했던 Q38 방법들을 오랫동안 숨겨 왔지만, 그들 중 일부가 기독교로 개종한 후에, 꼬르두 신부라는 이름의 프랑스인 가톨릭 신부에게 그들의 방법을 설명해 주었고, 이 신부가 유럽의 직물 업계에 종사하는 여러 사람에게 정보를 전파했습니다.

Several factors contributed to cotton's steady rise in worldwide importance. In Europe, members of the middle class began to place more emphasis on Q39 cleanliness and fashion, so the demand for easily washable, colourful fabric grew. The East India Company introduced cotton to Britain in the 1690s, and it immediately became the most popular fabric due to its versatility.

여러 요소들이 전 세계적으로 목화의 중요성이 꾸준히 높아지는 데 기여했습니다. 유럽에서는, 중산 계층의 사람들이 Q39 청결함과 패션을 더욱 중요시하기 시작했기 때문에, 쉽게 세탁 가능하고 다채로운 직물에 대한 수요가 늘었습니다. 동인도 회사가 1690년대에 영국에 목화를 소개했고, 용도의 다양성으로 인해 즉시 가장 인기 있는 직물이 되었습니다.

Across the Atlantic Ocean, the American cotton industry began to boom after Eli Whitney invented a new version of the cotton gin in 1793. By the middle of the 19th century, the United States had become the world's largest producer of cotton, which had an unfortunate side effect in that it led to the expansion of Q40 slavery throughout the country. In fact, in southern states known for cotton production, such as Alabama and Louisiana, approximately 50 per cent of the population were slaves. These days, the industrial production of cotton is primarily concentrated in Asian countries...	대서양을 가로질러, 아메리카 지역의 목화 산업은 엘리 휘트니가 새로운 조면기를 발명한 후에 호황을 누리기 시작했습니다. 19세기 중반 무렵, 미국은 세계에서 가장 큰 목화 생산 국가가 되었는데, 이는 불행한 부작용을 낳았는데, 미국 전역에서 Q40 노예제의 확산으로 이어졌기 때문입니다. 실제로, 목화 생산으로 잘 알려진 앨라배마와 루이지애나 같은 남부 지역의 주에서는, 약 50퍼센트의 인구가 노예였습니다. 요즘에는, 목화의 산업적 생산이 아시아 국가에 주로 집중되어 있는데...

| Vocabulary & Expressions |

cotton 목화, 면직물 spread 확산되다, 퍼지다 fibre 섬유 boll 꼬투리 civilisation 문명 (사회) fabric 직물, 섬유 thread 실 preserve ~을 보존하다 copper 구리 bead 구슬 estimate that ~라고 추정하다 date back 거슬러 올라가다 liken A to B A를 B에 비교하다 superior 우월한 texture 질감 invade ~을 침공하다 favour 더 좋아하다 garment 옷, 의류 deem 여기다 fast forward 빠르게 넘어가다 handheld 손으로 작동하는 gin 조면기(목화씨를 빼내는 기계) process ~을 가공 처리하다 via ~을 통해 interaction with ~와의 교류 prevalent 널리 퍼진 conquest 정복 conquer ~을 정복하다 spinning wheel 물레 boom 호황을 누리다 bustling 북적대는, 붐비는 sought-after 수요가 많은 commodity 상품 establish ~을 확립하다 facilitate ~을 용이하게 하다 land-based 육로 기반의 caravan 마차 obsolete 쓸모 없는 merchant 상인 merchandise 상품 conceal ~을 숨기다 convert to ~로 개종하다 priest 신부, 성직자 pass on ~을 전파하다 individual 사람, 개인 textile 직물, 섬유 contribute to ~에 기여하다 place ~을 두다 emphasis 강조, 주안점 versatility 용도의 다양함, 다재다능함 side effect 부작용 in that ~이므로 lead to ~로 이어지다 expansion 확대, 확장 slavery 노예제 concentrated in ~에 집중된

문제 31-40

다음 필기 내용을 완성하시오. 각 답변에 대해 **1개의 단어만** 작성하시오.

The History of Cotton 목화의 역사

Cotton in The Old World 구세계의 목화

- Ancient civilisations used cotton to produce [31] that had several uses.
  고대의 문명 사회는 여러 용도가 있었던 [31]을 만들어내기 위해 목화를 사용했다.
- 5th BCE: Herodotus wrote that cotton was better than [32] in terms of both its appearance and feel.
  기원전 5세기: 헤로도토스는 목화가 외양과 감촉 두 가지 모두와 관련해 [32]보다 더 났다고 썼다.
- Alexander the Great's soldiers preferred [33] manufactured from cotton.
  알렉산더 대왕의 군사들은 목화로 제조된 [33]을 선호했다.

Cotton in the Middle Ages 중세 시대의 목화

- Cotton became popular throughout many parts of the world.
  목화가 전 세계의 여러 곳에 걸쳐 인기를 얻었다.
- 6th CE: equipment used to produce cotton in India was introduced to other countries by [34] .
  6세기: 인도에서 목화를 생산하기 위해 사용한 장비가 [34]에 의해 다른 여러 국가에 소개되었다.

- 16th CE: dual-roller gins became commonplace and were sometimes powered by [35] .
16세기: 이중 롤러로 된 조면기가 아주 흔해졌으며, 때때로 [35]에 의해 작동되었다.

Cotton Spreads Throughout Europe 유럽 전역으로 널리 퍼진 목화
- Various conquests facilitated the spread of cotton production throughout Europe.
여러 정복 과정이 유럽 전역에서 목화 생산의 확산을 용이하게 했다.
- 14th CE: the spinning wheel improved the European cotton industry due to its high [36] .
14세기: 물레는 높은 [36]로 인해 유럽의 목화 산업을 향상시켰다.
- Cities such as Venice and Antwerp emerged as important [37] for cotton trading.
베니스나 앤트워프 같은 도시들이 목화 무역에 있어 중요한 [37]로 떠올랐다.
- As trade with India increased, secretive [38] of cotton processing were told to European traders.
인도와의 무역이 증가함에 따라, 목화 가공 과정의 비밀스러운 [38]이 유럽 상인들에게 전해졌다.
- The European middle class turned to cotton when people became more interested in cleanliness and [39].
유럽의 중산층은 사람들이 청결과 [39]에 더욱 관심을 가지게 되었을 때 목화로 눈길을 돌렸다.

The American Cotton Industry 미국의 목화 산업
- 19th CE: the US had become the largest producer of cotton in the world.
19세기: 미국은 세계에서 가장 큰 목화 생산 국가가 되었다.
- Consequently, increased demand for cotton led to a rise in [40], particularly in cotton-rich southern states.
결과적으로, 목화에 대한 수요 증가는 [40]의 부상으로 이어졌는데, 특히 목화가 풍부한 남부의 여러 주에서 그러했다.

31. 구세계와 신세계 모두의 수많은 문명 사회들이 목화를 발견하거나 도입했고, 다양한 목적으로 직물을 만들기 위해 사용하기 시작했다고 하므로(numerous civilisations in both the Old and New World discovered or were introduced to cotton and began using it to make multi-purpose fabrics), 정답은 fabrics(직물)이다.
Paraphrasing ancient(고대의) → old(오래된)
several uses(여러 용도) → multi-purpose(다양한 목적의)

32. 기원전 5세기, 헤로도토스가 자신의 글에서 인도 목화를 언급했는데, 그것을 고품질 양모에 비교하면서 그 우월한 아름다움과 질감에 찬사를 보냈으므로(Herodotus mentions Indian cotton in his writings, likening it to higher-quality wool and praising its superior beauty and texture), 정답인 비교대상은 wool이다.
Paraphrasing better than(보다 더 뛰어난) → praising its superior ~ (그 우월한 ~을 칭찬함)
appearance and feel(외양과 감촉) → beauty and texture(아름다움과 질감)

33. 알렉산더 대왕 병사들이 지역 목화 의류를 좋아하기 시작했다고 하므로(the soldiers began to favour local cotton clothing), 정답은 clothing이다.
Paraphrasing prefer(선호하다) → favour(선호하다)

34. 6세기 이후로 인도에서는 손으로 조작하는 롤러가 있는 조면기가 목화를 가공 처리하는 데 사용되었으며, 나중에 인도 상인들과의 교류를 통해 다른 여러 국가에도 도입되었다고 하므로(Handheld roller cotton gins had been used to process cotton in India since the 6th century, and were later introduced to other countries via interaction with Indian traders), 정답은 traders이다. 한 단어만 정답이 되므로 Indian을 쓰면 오답이다.
Paraphrasing equipment(장비) → handheld roller cotton gins(손으로 조작하는 롤러가 있는 조면기)
by(~에 의해) → via(~을 통해)

35. 16세기말쯤 인도에서 제작한 이중 롤러 조면기가 지중해 지역 전체에 걸쳐 면직물 업계에서 널리 이용되었고 이 기계 장치가 물을 이용해 작동되었다고 하므로(By the end of the 16th century, the Indian version of the dual-roller gin was prevalent in the cotton industry throughout the entire Mediterranean region. In certain locations, this mechanical device was driven by water), 정답은 water이다.
Paraphrasing commonplace(아주 흔한) → prevalent(널리 퍼진)
powered by(~에 의해 힘을 얻는) → driven by(~에 의해 작동되는)

36. 14세기 유럽에 물레가 소개되었을 때, 증가된 효율성의 결과로 목화 방적 산업이 호황을 누렸으므로(When the spinning wheel was introduced to Europe in the 14th century, the cotton spinning industry boomed as a result of the increased efficiency), 정답은 efficiency(효율성)이다.
Paraphrasing improved(향상시켰다) → boomed(번창했다)
due to its high ~(높은 ~때문에) → as a result of increased ~ (증가된 ~의 결과로)

37. 앤트워프와 베니스가 곧 면직물 교역으로 북적대는 항구가 되었다고 하므로(Antwerp and Venice soon became bustling ports for cotton trade), 정답은 ports이다.
Paraphrasing emerged as important ~ (중요한 ~로 떠올랐다) → became bustling ~ (북적이는 ~로 되었다)

38. 가장 엄격히 유지되던 인도의 면직물 가공의 몇몇 비밀들도 유럽으로 새나가기 시작했고, 인도의 상인들과 수공업자들이 그 방법을 오랫동안 숨겨 왔다고 하므로(Some of the most well-kept secrets of Indian cotton processing also began to move West. Indian traders and craftsmen had long concealed the methods), 비밀스러운 방법들, 즉 methods가 정답이다.
Paraphrasing secretive(비밀의) → secrets of(~의 비밀), concealed(숨겨왔다)

39. 유럽에서 중산층들이 청결과 패션에 더 중점을 두기 시작했으므로(In Europe, members of the middle class began to place more emphasis on cleanliness and fashion), 정답은 fashion이다.
Paraphrasing more interested in(~에 더 관심이 있는) → place more emphasis on(~에 더 중점을 두다)

40. 19세기 중반 무렵, 미국은 세계에서 가장 큰 면직물 생산 국가가 되었지만 이는 불행한 부작용을 낳았는데, 미국 전역에서 노예제의 확산으로 이어졌기 때문이라고 하고(By the middle of the 19th century, the United States had become the world's largest producer of cotton, which had an unfortunate side effect in that it led to the expansion of slavery throughout the country), 이어서 남부 지역 주들을 언급하므로(In fact, in southern states known for cotton production), 정답은 노예제인 slavery이다.
Paraphrasing rise in(~의 부상, 번영) → expansion of(~의 확장)

Test 2 READING [Academic]

1. allergies	2. dumplings	3. beverages	4. condiment	5. toxins
6. soups	7. fuel	8. FALSE	9. TRUE	10. NOT GIVEN
11. NOT GIVEN	12. TRUE	13. FALSE		
14. D	15. B	16. F	17. D	18. B
19. D	20. F	21. China	22. ridges	23. claims
24. health	25. bureau	26. cabinet		
27. D	28. E	29. A	30. F	31. B
32. glaciers	33. mosses	34. cooling	35. winds	36. climate
37. C	38. A	39. B	40. D	

▪ **파트 1** [문제 1-13]

출제 포인트 **난이도: 중**

특정 자연 자원/주제 지문이 자주 출제되는데, 이러한 지문은 내용이 어렵지 않고 전문 용어는 추가 설명이 자세히 나오기에 지문을 독해하는데 있어서 특별한 관련 지식이 필요 없음

기출 2024년 5월 - 바나나
2019년 10월 - 올리브 오일
2019년 10월- 설탕
2010년 4월 - 콩
2010년 3월 - 대나무

Bamboo

Bamboo is a fast-growing, versatile, flowering plant that is found throughout many regions of the world. With up to a thirty percent annual increase in biomass, compared to only five percent for trees, bamboo's rate of biomass generation is unmatched by any other plants. As such, it gives rise to larger yields of raw material, which is utilized extensively for a wide variety of functions. Bamboo shoots are called culms, and their strength and diversity of size historically made them ideal for use in construction. To this day, bamboo culms are laminated, cut into sheets, and laid as flooring in China and Japan. As civilizations evolved, the true versatility of bamboo was gradually uncovered, and all parts of the plant are now utilized in a growing range of industries.

In Asian medicine, particularly Chinese medicine, the leaves of the bamboo plant are commonly crushed and added as an active ingredient in medicinal teas. These teas are consumed by millions of people who wish to lose weight while cleansing their body. Bamboo leaves contain relatively high levels of protein and minerals such as riboflavin, thiamine, and iron, which are known for their health benefits. An additional advantage of medications containing crushed bamboo leaves is that they suppress Q1 allergies and promote blood circulation. Aside from their use in medicine, the leaves are also pressed flat and used to wrap steamed Q2 dumplings in several Asian cultures.

Bamboo's versatility is most evident in its myriad uses within the culinary field. The plant's sap can be extracted from the culms and then fermented to produce numerous Q3 beverages, both alcoholic and non-alcoholic. The spongy white tissue, called the pith, which lines the interior of the culms, is often pickled to create a Q4 condiment that is served alongside many dishes throughout Asia. The

대나무

대나무는 빠르게 자라며 용도가 다양한 꽃나무로서, 전 세계의 많은 지역에 걸쳐 찾아볼 수 있다. 그 생물량의 연간 증가율이 나무가 겨우 5퍼센트인 것에 비해 최대 30퍼센트에 달하는, 대나무의 생물량 발생 비율은 다른 어떤 식물도 필적할 수 없는 것이다. 따라서, 더 많은 원료 산출량이 생기며, 아주 다양한 목적으로 광범위하게 활용된다. 죽순은 마디 줄기라고 불리며, 그 강도와 크기의 다양함으로 인해 역사적으로 건축에서 이상적이 되었다. 오늘날까지, 대나무 마디 줄기는 중국과 일본에서 얇게 쪼개 여러 장으로 자른 다음에 바닥재로 깔아 사용한다. 문명이 발전함에 따라, 대나무의 진정한 용도 다양성이 점차적으로 밝혀지고 있으며, 그 식물의 모든 부분이 현재 점점 더 다양한 분야에서 활용되고 있다.

아시아의 의학 분야에서, 특히 중국 한의학에서, 대나무의 잎은 흔히 약효가 있는 차에 유효 성분으로 으깨어 추가된다. 이 차는 몸을 깨끗하게 하면서 체중을 줄이기를 원하는 수백 만 명의 사람들에 의해 소비되고 있다. 대나무 잎에는 단백질과 함께 리보플라빈과 티아민, 그리고 철분과 같은 무기질이 비교적 많이 함유되어 있으며, 이는 건강상의 이점으로 잘 알려진 것들이다. 으깬 대나무 잎이 들어 있는 약물의 또 다른 장점은 Q1 알레르기를 억제하고 혈액 순환을 촉진시켜준다는 점이다. 의학 분야에서 사용되는 것 외에도, 그 잎은 또한 여러 아시아권 문화에서 납작하게 눌러 찐 Q2 만두를 감싸는 데도 사용되고 있다.

대나무의 용도 다양성은 요리 분야의 무수한 용도에서 가장 명백히 드러난다. 이 식물의 수액은 마디 줄기에서 추출한 다음, 발효시켜 여러 가지 Q3 음료를 만들 수 있으며, 알코올과 무알코올 두 가지 모두 가능하다. 마디 줄기 안쪽에 형성되는 중과피라고 부르는 하얀 스펀지 같은 조직은 종종 절여서 Q4 양념으로 만드는데, 이는 아시아 전역의 많은 요리와 함께 제공된다. 전체 마디 줄기 자체는 이 식물에서 가장 흔히 사용되는 부분이다.

whole culms themselves are the most frequently used part of the plant. When bamboo culms are utilized in cooking, they are first placed in boiling water in order to remove any Q5 toxins and render them safe for consumption. In some cultures, the culms of larger bamboo are not only used as an ingredient, but also as a means to cook certain foods. Q6 Soups are often boiled in the hollowed bamboo culms directly over a flame. It is said that food prepared in such a manner has a subtle, unique taste. In addition to their association with cooking, bamboo culms are burned in ovens — a process called pyrolysis — to produce bamboo charcoal, a Q7 fuel that is still in common usage in China and Japan. As an alternative fuel, bamboo benefits the environment by reducing pollutant residue.

In order to reap the full benefits of strong, healthy bamboo, the plant must be cultivated and harvested under very precise conditions. Bamboo crops grow optimally in warm temperate climates. Q8&10 Since the bamboo plant has thin roots, care must be taken to protect it from strong winds, which can pull plants out of the soil in extreme circumstances. Another reason that regions of high wind are undesirable for bamboo crops is that strong gusts can damage the tips of bamboo leaves.

When it comes to soil types, bamboo can be grown and cultivated on a wide variety of soils, as long as they are free from excess rocks and roots of other plants. Q9 The optimal soil conditions for cultivating bamboo are well-drained sandy soil with a pH range of around 5.5. In order to ensure high quality and yield, animal manure and fertilizers are typically applied to bamboo crops. Bamboo plants have voracious appetites, and fertilizers prevent the soil from being washed out of nutrients too quickly. Q11 Bamboo flourishes well when fertilizers containing potassium and nitrogen are used, but it is also essential to provide other minerals and nutrients by adding manure and organic compost to the soil.

Harvesting of bamboo is carried out based on three cycles: life cycle, annual cycle, and daily cycle. Q12 Each culm of bamboo experiences a life cycle of 5 to 7 years, and they are generally allowed to reach this level of maturity before being harvested. If any of the older culms in a crop show signs of decay, they will be cut down and removed to ensure adequate light and resources for the healthy culms. The annual cycle pertains to the season in which bamboo is harvested. As bamboo predominantly grows during the wet season, disturbing the culms at this time could potentially disrupt growth and damage the crop. Likewise,

대나무 마디 줄기가 요리에 활용될 때, 모든 Q5 독소를 제거하고 소비하기에 안전한 상태로 만들기 위해 끓는 물에 먼저 넣는다. 일부 문화권에서는, 더 큰 대나무의 마디 줄기가 요리 재료로써 뿐만 아니라, 특정 음식을 요리하기 위한 수단으로써도 사용된다. Q6 수프는 종종 속을 비운 대나무 마디 줄기에 넣어 불 위에서 직접 끓인다. 이와 같은 방식으로 조리된 음식은 미묘하고 독특한 맛을 내는 것으로 알려져 있다. 요리와의 연관성뿐만 아니라, 대나무 마디 줄기는 오븐에서 태워(열분해로 불리는 과정) 대나무 숯을 만드는데, 이는 중국과 일본에서 여전히 흔히 사용되는 Q7 연료이다. 대체 연료로서, 대나무는 잔여 오염 물질을 줄여줌으로써 환경에 도움이 된다.

튼튼하고 건강한 대나무가 지닌 이점을 온전히 누리기 위해서는, 반드시 매우 엄격한 환경에서 재배하고 수확해야 한다. 대나무 작물은 난온대 기후에서 최적의 상태로 자란다. Q8&10 대나무 식물은 얇은 뿌리를 지니고 있기 때문에, 극단적인 상황에서 땅에서 그 대나무를 뽑아낼 수 있는 강한 바람으로부터 보호할 수 있도록 반드시 주의해야 한다. 대나무 작물에 있어 강한 바람이 부는 지역이 바람직하지 못한 또 다른 이유는 강한 돌풍이 대나무 잎의 끝부분을 손상시킬 수 있기 때문이다.

토양 종류와 관련해서는, 대나무는 과도한 암석이나 다른 식물의 뿌리가 존재하지 않는 한 아주 다양한 토양에서 자라고 재배될 수 있다. Q9 대나무 재배에 있어 최적의 토양 조건은 pH 범위 약 5.5 수준의 배수가 잘 되는 모래 섞인 토양이다. 높은 품질 및 수확량을 보장하기 위해, 동물 거름과 비료가 일반적으로 대나무 작물에 뿌려진다. 대나무 식물은 게걸스러운 식욕을 지니고 있으며, 비료는 흙에서 영양분이 너무 빨리 빠져나가는 것을 방지해 준다. Q11 대나무는 칼륨과 질소를 함유하고 있는 비료가 사용될 때 잘 번식하지만, 토양에 거름과 유기농 퇴비를 함께 추가함으로써 다른 무기질과 영양분을 제공해 주는 것 또한 필수적이다.

대나무 수확은 세 가지 주기를 바탕으로 실시되는데, 수명 주기와 연간 주기, 그리고 일일 주기가 그것이다. Q12 대나무의 각 마디 줄기는 5~7년 동안의 수명 주기를 겪으며, 일반적으로 수확되기 전에 이 수준의 성숙한 상태에 도달하도록 허용된다. 작물 중에 어떤 오래된 마디 줄기든지 부패의 징후를 보일 경우, 건강한 마디 줄기에 필요한 적절한 빛과 자원을 보장할 수 있도록 잘라서 제거한다. 연간 주기는 대나무가 수확되는 계절과 관련되어 있다. 대나무가 대부분 우기에 자라기 때문에, 이 시기에 마디 줄기를 방해하는 것은 잠재적으로 성장에 지장을 주고 그 작물에 피해를 입힐 수 있다. 마찬가지로, 우기 바로 직전은 최근에 솟아난 완전히 새로운 마디 줄기에 피해를 입히는 위험성이 존재한다. 결과적으로

right before the wet season presents a risk of damaging brand-new culms that have recently sprouted. As a result, the optimal time to harvest bamboo is three or four months before the wet season begins. The final consideration when harvesting bamboo is the daily cycle. Q13 Most farmers harvest bamboo crops at dawn or dusk, as this is the time of day when photosynthesis occurs at its slowest rate, resulting in lower levels of sugar in the sap.	대나무를 수확하는 최적의 시기는 우기가 시작되기 3~4개월 전이다. 대나무를 수확할 때 마지막으로 고려해야 하는 점은 일일 주기이다. Q13 대부분의 농부들은 대나무 작물을 새벽에 또는 해질녘에 수확하는데, 하루 중 이 시간대는 광합성이 가장 느린 속도로 발생되는 때이기 때문에, 수액 속에 당분 수준이 더 낮아지는 결과가 초래된다.

| Vocabulary & Expressions |

versatile 다목적의, 다용도의 biomass 생물량 generation 발생, 창출 unmatched 필적할 수 없는 give rise to ~을 생겨나게 하다 yield 산출(량), 수확(량) raw material 원료, 원자재 extensively 광범위하게 bamboo shoot 죽순 culm 마디 줄기 laminate ~을 얇은 판으로 만들다 civilization 문명 (국가) evolve 발전하다, 진화하다 a growing range of 점점 더 다양한 crush ~을 으깨다 active ingredient 유효 성분 medicinal 약효가 있는 protein 단백질 mineral 무기질 medication 약, 약물 suppress ~을 억제하다 circulation 순환 dumpling 만두 culinary 요리의 sap 수액 extract ~을 추출하다 ferment ~을 발효시키다 tissue (세포로 이뤄진) 조직 pith (과일 등의) 중과피, 속 pickle ~을 절이다 condiment 양념, 소스 toxin 독소 render 만들다 hollowed 속이 빈 subtle 미묘한 association with ~와의 연관성 pyrolysis 열분해 charcoal 숯 alternative fuel 대체 연료 pollutant 오염 물질 residue 잔여물 reap the full benefits 이점을 온전히 누리다 cultivate ~을 재배하다 harvest ~을 수확하다 optimally 최적으로 warm temperate climate 난온대 기후 soil 토양, 흙 undesirable 바람직하지 못한 crop 작물 gust 돌풍 when it comes to ~와 관련해서 free from ~가 없는 excess 과도한 well-drained 배수가 잘 되는 manure 거름 fertilizer 비료 apply 적용하다 voracious 게걸스러운 appetite 식욕 nutrient 영양분 flourish 번식하다 potassium 칼륨 nitrogen 질소 maturity 성숙한 상태, 다 자란 상태 decay 부패하다 predominantly 대부분 disturb ~을 방해하다 disrupt ~에 지장을 주다 brand-new 완전히 새로운 sprout 솟아나다 photosynthesis 광합성 result in ~의 결과를 낳다

문제 1-7

다음 도표를 완성하시오.

지문에서 오직 **1개의 단어만** 각 빈칸에 적으시오.

BAMBOO PREPARATION & USES 대나무 음식 조리 및 용도		
Part 부위	**Preparation Method** 조리 방법	**Uses** 용도
Leaves 잎	Crushed 으깨기	Used in medications to promote weight loss and inhibit [1] 체중 감량을 촉진하고 [1]을 억제하는 약물에 사용됨
	Flattened 납작하게 만들기	Used as wrappers for [2] [2]을 위한 싸개로 사용됨
Sap 수액	Fermented 발효시키기	Used to make a wide variety of [3] 아주 다양한 [3]을 만들기 위해 사용됨
Culms 마디 줄기	Pickled 절이기	The pith is pickled to produce a [4] 중과피를 절여 [4]을 만들 수 있다
	Boiled 끓이기	Culms are boiled to remove [5], before being used as ingredients 음식 재료로 사용하기에 앞서, [5]을 제거하기 위해 마디 줄기를 끓인다

ACTUAL TEST 2

Culms 마디 줄기	Hollowed 속 비우기	Empty culms are used for boiling [6] throughout Asia 빈 마디 줄기는 아시아 전역에서 [6]을 끓이기 위해 사용된다
	Burned 태우기	Undergo pyrolysis to produce charcoal used for a [7] [7]에 사용되는 숯을 만들기 위해 열분해 과정을 거친다

1. 으깬 대나무 잎이 알레르기를 억제한다고 하므로, 정답은 allergies이다.
Paraphrasing inhibit(억제하다) → suppress(억제하다)

2. 납작하게 눌러진 대나무 잎은 만두를 쌀 때도 사용되므로, 정답은 dumplings이다.
Paraphrasing flattened(납작하게 된) → pressed flat(납작하게 눌러진)

3. 수액이 발효되어 다양한 음료를 만드므로, 정답은 beverages이다.
Paraphrasing make(만들다) → produce(만들다)
a wide variety of(아주 다양한) → numerous(수많은)

4. 대나무 마디 줄기 안 중과피가 양념을 만들기 위해 절여지므로, 정답은 condiment이다.
Paraphrasing produce(만들다) → create(만들다)

5. 독소를 제거하기 위해 대나무 마디 줄기를 끓이는 것이므로, 정답은 toxins이다.

6. 수프가 속이 비어진 대나무 마디 줄기 속에서 끓여지므로, 정답은 soups이다. 대문자, 소문자 모두 정답 처리된다.

7. 대나무 마디 줄기를 태워 연료용 숯으로 사용하므로, 정답은 fuel이다.

| Vocabulary & Expressions |
inhibit 억제하다 wrapper 싸개, 싸는 것

문제 8-13

주어진 지문의 정보와 일치하는 경우 **참**, 지문의 정보와 일치하지 않는 경우 **거짓**, 정보가 존재하지 않는 경우 **해당 없음**을 선택하시오.

8. Bamboo has naturally evolved to withstand strong winds.
대나무는 강한 바람을 견딜 수 있도록 자연적으로 진화했다.

대나무는 얇은 뿌리를 갖고 있어서 강한 바람으로부터 보호할 수 있도록 반드시 주의해야 한다. 이는 강한 바람을 견딜 수 있도록 자연적으로 진화했다는 진술과 다르므로, 정답은 FALSE이다.

9. A soil pH of 5.5 is desirable for optimal growth of bamboo.
pH 수준 5.5의 토양이 최적의 대나무 성장에 바람직하다.

대나무 성장의 최적 pH는 5.5이므로, 정답은 TRUE이다.
Paraphrasing growth(성장) → cultivate(재배하다)

10. The roots of the bamboo plant are highly susceptible to damage.
대나무 식물의 뿌리는 매우 쉽게 피해를 입을 수 있다.

극단적인 상황의 강한 바람에 뿌리가 뽑힐 수 있지만, 쉽게 피해를 입는지에 대해서는 명확한 언급이 없으므로, 정답은 NOT GIVEN이다.

11. Some chemical fertilizers are more important than organic compost when growing bamboo.
대나무를 기를 때 일부 화학 비료가 유기농 퇴비보다 더 중요하다.

칼륨과 질소를 함유하고 있는 비료(chemical fertilizers)가 사용될 때 잘 번식하지만, 유기농 퇴비(organic compost)를 함께 추가하는 것 또한 필수적이다. 즉 화학 비료도 필요하고 유기농 퇴비도 필요한데, 둘 중 무엇이 더 중요한지는 지문 내용으로는 알 수 없다. 따라서 정답은 NOT GIVEN이다.

12. Most bamboo culms are harvested near the end of their life cycle.
대부분의 대나무 마디 줄기는 수명 주기 마지막이 가까워질 때 수확된다.

대나무 마디 줄기는 수확 전에 수명 주기 5-7년의 성숙기를 겪는다고 하는데, 이는 결국 성숙기 이후의 수명 주기 마지막에 재배된다는 말과 같으므로, 정답은 TRUE이다.
Paraphrasing be harvested near the end of their life cycle(수명 주기 마지막이 가까워질 때 수확된다)
→ reach this level of maturity before being harvested(수확 전에 이러한 수준의 성숙기에 도달한다)

13. Sugar levels of bamboo sap are at their highest during dawn and dusk.
대나무 수액의 당분 수준은 새벽과 해질녘 시간대에 최고조에 이른다.

새벽과 해질녘에는 수액 속 당분이 더 낮기에, 최고조 당분 수준이 아니다. 따라서 정답은 FALSE이다.

I Vocabulary & Expressions I
withstand 견디다 desirable 바람직한 susceptible 민감한

▪ 파트 2 [문제 14-26]

출제 포인트 **난이도: 중상**
신체와 관련된 지문은 아이엘츠에서 빈출되는데, 특히 인간의 오감과 뇌, 생리 현상이 자주 출제되기에 신체 관련 어휘들과 친숙해질 필요가 있음

기출 2024년 6월 - 폴 에크만의 거짓말 탐지법
2019년 7월 - 체내 시계(시차, 야간 근무 등)
2019년 1월 - 하품
2014년 11월 - 수면
2010년 3월 - 지문 감식

Fingerprint Identification

A Although ancient civilizations most likely did not fully comprehend that fingerprints could accurately identify individuals, there is historical evidence of them being used for broad identification purposes. For instance, records dating back to China's Qin Dynasty indicate that investigators sometimes took fingerprints as evidence from crime scenes, and around 300 CE, fingerprints were being presented during criminal trials in Q21 China. The Chinese historian Kia Kung-Yen even suggested in the year 650 that the comparison of fingerprints could be used as a valid method of identity verification.

지문 감식

A 비록 고대 문명 국가들이 지문을 통해 정확히 개인을 식별할 수 있다는 점을 제대로 이해했을 가능성은 거의 없지만, 폭넓은 신분 확인 목적으로 이용되었다는 것을 보여주는 역사적 증거가 있다. 예를 들어, 중국 진나라로 거슬러 올라가는 기록에 따르면 수사관들이 때때로 범죄 현장에서 증거물로 지문을 채취했으며, 서기 약 300년경에는, Q21 중국의 형사 재판 중에 지문이 제시되었던 것으로 나타난다. 중국 역사가 키아 쿵옌은 심지어 서기 650년에 지문 비교가 신원 확인의 유효한 방법으로 사용될 수 있다고 제안했다.

ACTUAL TEST 2

B It was not until the mid-17th century that scientific interest in fingerprints began to truly grow, particularly throughout Europe. In 1665, the research notes of Italian physician Marcello Malpighi described patterns of Q22 ridges that exist on the fingertips. Approximately two decades later, Malpighi's contemporary, the English botanist Q18 Nehemiah Grew, published the first scientific paper to detail the ridge structure of the skin covering the palms and fingers. However, even then, it was not known that fingerprints were unique to each individual. Q15 This hypothesis was not officially put forward until 1788 when the German anatomist Johann Christoph Andreas Mayer declared that no two people can possibly share the same fingerprint patterns.

C In 1823, the Czech scientist Jan Purkinje expanded on Mayer's work, publishing a thesis that described numerous distinct fingerprint patterns, but he did not believe the patterns could be used to credibly identify individuals. When the British politician Lord William Russell was murdered in 1840, Q19 a doctor named Robert Blake Overton recommended that the Metropolitan Police check the crime scene and victim for fingerprints. Although the police did follow Overton's advice, fingerprints did not play a role in the identification of the murderer, and fingerprint collection and analysis would not become a routine police practice for several decades.

D Several important landmarks in the evolution of fingerprint identification occurred in the second half of the 19th century. In 1863, a chemistry professor based at Val-de-Grâce military hospital in Paris made a breakthrough in the detection of fingerprints on paper and other smooth surfaces. Q17 Professor Paul-Jean Coulier discovered that the presence of iodine fumes caused fingerprints to be revealed in great detail. Later, in 1877, Sir William James Herschel Q14 instituted the use of fingerprints on contracts and property deeds that were prepared in Calcutta and the surrounding towns. This practice helped to prevent conflict and doubts over the authenticity of signatures. By registering the fingerprints of the elderly, he also prevented false financial Q23 claims from non-beneficiaries after an individual had passed away.

E With research into fingerprint detection and analysis continuing at a rapid pace, attention began to shift toward the need for a comprehensive classification and storage system. In 1880, Dr. Henry Faulds, a Scottish

B 지문에 대한 과학적 관심이, 특히 유럽 전역에 걸쳐 진정으로 커지기 시작한 것은 17세기 중반이나 되어서였다. 1665년에, 이탈리아인 의사 마르첼로 말피기의 연구 노트를 보면 손가락 끝부분에 존재하는 Q22 굴곡의 패턴이 설명되어 있다. 약 20년 후, 말피기와 동시대 사람인 영국의 식물학자 Q18 느헤미야 그루는 손바닥과 손가락을 덮고 있는 피부의 굴곡 조직을 상세히 설명하는 첫 번째 과학 논문을 발간했다. 하지만, 심지어 그때까지도, 지문이 각 개인에게 고유한 것이라는 사실은 알려지지 않았다. Q15 이 가설은 1788년에나 되어서야 공식적으로 제안되었는데, 당시에 독일의 해부학자 요한 크리스토프 안드레아스 마이어는 그 어떤 두 사람도 동일한 지문 패턴을 공유할 가능성이 없다고 공표했다.

C 1823년에, 체코 과학자 얀 푸르키네는 마이어의 연구 내용을 확장해, 수많은 특징의 지문 패턴을 설명하는 논문을 발간했지만, 그 패턴들이 믿을 수 있을 정도로 개인을 식별하는 데 사용될 수 있을 것이라고 생각하지는 않았다. 1840년에 영국인 정치가 윌리엄 러셀 경이 살해되었을 때, Q19 로버트 블레이크 오버튼이라는 이름의 의사는 범죄 현장과 피해자에게서 지문이 있는지 확인해 보도록 런던 경찰청에 권했다. 경찰 측에서 오버튼의 조언을 따르기는 했지만, 지문이 살인자 신원 파악에 있어 어떤 역할을 하지는 않았으며, 지문 수집 및 분석 작업은 수십 년 동안 경찰의 일상적인 일이 되지 못했다.

D 지문 감식의 발전에 있어 여러 중요한 획기적인 사건이 19세기 후반에 일어났다. 1863년에, 파리의 발드 그라스 군 병원을 기반으로 활동하던 한 화학 교수가 종이 및 기타 부드러운 표현에 남은 지문의 발견에 있어 돌파구를 마련했다. Q17 폴-장 쿠리어 교수는 요오드 가스의 존재로 인해 지문이 아주 상세하게 나타나게 되었다는 사실을 발견했다. 이후, 1877년에, 윌리엄 제임스 허셜 경이 Q14 캘커타와 인근 마을에서 준비된 계약서 및 부동산 증서에 지문 사용을 시작했다. 이 관행은 서명의 진위에 대한 갈등과 의구심을 방지하는 데 도움이 되었다. 노인들의 지문을 등록함으로써, 그는 또한 한 사람이 사망한 이후에 수혜자가 아닌 사람들이 거짓으로 금전적 Q23 주장을 하는 것도 방지했다.

E 지문 발견과 분석에 대한 연구가 빠른 속도로 지속되면서, 종합적인 분류 및 보관 시스템에 대한 필요성으로 관심이 옮겨가기 시작했다. 1880년에, 일본을 기

surgeon based in Japan, published a paper in the well-respected scientific journal *Nature*. In his paper, he emphasized the high accuracy of fingerprint identification and put forward a technique that could be used to record fingerprints with ink. Upon returning to the United Kingdom, Faulds met with officials from the Metropolitan Police, hoping that they would embrace and adopt his concept, but was disappointed when it was rejected at the time. Still believing in the effectiveness of his method, he described it in a letter he sent to Charles Darwin. Unfortunately, due to waning Q24 health, Darwin was unable to assist Faulds with the further improvement of the method, and instead passed on the information to his cousin, a young anthropologist named Francis Galton. Q20 Galton was immediately impressed with the concepts proposed by Faulds and worked diligently to refine them over the next ten years. The culmination of his efforts was a comprehensive statistical model of fingerprint analysis and identification that he had designed explicitly for application in the field of forensic science. Galton estimated that the likelihood of two different individuals having the same fingerprint patterns was approximately 1 in 65 billion.

F Global advancements in fingerprint identification research led to the establishment of the first official Fingerprint Bureau in Calcutta in 1897. The Council of the Governor General set up the bureau after approving a committee report recommending that fingerprints be used for the classification of criminal records. Two fingerprint experts who were employed by the Q25 bureau, Azizul Haque and Hem Chandra Bose, are recognized as the main contributors to a revolutionary fingerprint classification system. The Henry Classification System, named for their project supervisor Sir Edward Richard Henry, was later approved by the Metropolitan Police in the UK, and adopted by its own newly-established fingerprint bureau in 1901. Joseph Faurot, the Deputy Commissioner of the New York Police Department, is credited with establishing the fingerprinting of criminals as a routine practice in the United States. In 1902, Q16 the first arrest and conviction based on fingerprint evidence occurred. Henri Leon Scheffer was identified as the perpetrator of a murder after Alphonse Bertillon discovered his fingerprints on a glass display Q26 cabinet and matched them with copies of Scheffer's prints that had been taken previously. The Scheffer case received much publicity, and the effectiveness of fingerprint identification in criminal trials received worldwide recognition.

점으로 활동하던 스코틀랜드인 외과의사 헨리 폴즈 박사는 높이 평가받는 과학 저널 <네이처>에 논문 하나를 실었다. 이 논문에서, 그는 지문 감식의 높은 정확성을 강조했으며, 잉크로 지문을 기록하는 데 사용될 수 있는 기술을 제안했다. 영국으로 돌아오자마자, 폴즈 박사는 런던 경찰청의 관리들과 만났는데, 그들이 자신의 개념을 수용하고 채택하기를 바랐지만, 당시에는 거절되어 실망스러워했다. 여전히 자신의 방법이 지닌 효과를 믿고 있었던 그는 찰스 다윈에게 보낸 편지에서 그 방법을 설명했다. 안타깝게도, 쇠약해지는 Q24 건강때문에, 다윈은 그 방법의 추가 개선 작업에 대해 폴즈에게 도움을 줄 수 없었는데, 대신 그 정보를 자신의 사촌이자 젊은 인류학자였던 프랜시스 골턴이라는 이름의 학자에게 전해주었다. Q20 골턴은 폴즈가 제안한 개념에 즉시 깊은 인상을 받았고, 이후 10년에 걸쳐 그 개념들을 개선하기 위해 부지런히 작업했다. 그 노력의 정점은 명확하게 과학 수사 분야에서의 적용을 위해 그가 고안한 종합적인 지문 분석 및 감식 통계 모델이었다. 골턴은 두 명의 서로 다른 사람들이 동일한 지문 패턴을 가지고 있을 가능성이 약 650억분의 1이라고 추정했다.

F 지문 감식 연구에 있어 전 세계적인 발전은 1897년에 캘커타에서 있은 첫 공식 지문 관리국의 설립으로 이어졌다. 총독 자문 위원회는 지문이 범죄 기록 분류를 위해 사용되어야 한다고 권하는 한 위원회 보고서를 승인한 뒤로 해당 부처를 세웠다. 해당 Q25 부처에 의해 고용된 두 명의 지문 전문가인 아지줄 하케와 찬드라 보스는 혁신적인 지문 분류 시스템을 만든 주요 공로자로 인정받고 있다. 프로젝트 책임자인 에드워드 리차드 헨리의 이름을 딴 헨리 분류 시스템은 나중에 영국 런던 경찰청의 승인을 받았으며, 그 기관 내에 1901년에 새롭게 설립된 지문 관리부에 의해 채택되었다. 조셉 퍼로 뉴욕 경찰 부청장은 미국에서 범죄자들의 지문 채취를 일상적인 관행으로 확립시킨 것에 대한 공을 인정받고 있다. 1902년에, Q16 지문 단서를 근거로 한 첫 번째 체포 및 유죄 판결이 있었다. 헨리 리온 쉐퍼가 한 살인의 범인으로 확인되었는데, 알폰세 베르티옹이 유리 진열 Q26 보관장에서 쉐퍼의 지문을 발견해 과거에 채취해 두었던 그의 지문 사본과 맞춰본 뒤의 일이었다. 쉐퍼 사건은 큰 관심을 받았으며, 형사 재판에서 지문 감식의 유효성은 전 세계적인 인정을 받았다.

| Vocabulary & Expressions |

fingerprint 지문 identification 감식, 식별, 확인 comprehend 이해하다 investigator 수사관 crime scene 범죄 현장 present ~을 제시하다 comparison of ~의 비교 valid 유효한 method 방법 verification 확인, 증명 describe ~을 설명하다 ridge 굴곡 contemporary 동시대 사람 detail ~을 상세히 설명하다 hypothesis 가설 put forward (의견 등) ~을 내놓다 expand on ~을 확장하다 thesis 논문 distinct 뚜렷한, 분명한 credibly 믿을 수 있게 analysis 분석 practice 관행, 관례 landmark 획기적인 사건 evolution 발전, 진화 breakthrough 돌파구 detection 발견, 감지 smooth 부드러운 iodine 요오드 fumes 가스 cause 초래하다 institute ~을 시작하다, 도입하다 property 건물, 부동산 deeds 증서 authenticity 진짜임 beneficiary 수혜자 pass away 사망하다 shift toward ~로 바뀌다 comprehensive 종합적인, 포괄적인 classification 분류 well-respected 높이 평가 받는 emphasize ~을 강조하다 upon- ing ~하자마자 official 관리, 관료 embrace ~을 수용하다 adopt ~을 채택하다 effectiveness 유효성, 효과성 waning 쇠약해지는 diligently 부지런히 refine ~을 개선하다, 향상시키다 culmination 정점 statistical 통계의 explicitly 명백히 application 적용, 응용 forensic science 과학 수사 estimate 추정하다 likelihood 가능성 advancement 발전, 진보 lead to ~로 이어지다 establishment 설립, 확립 set up ~을 설립하다 bureau (관청의) 부, 국 contributor 공헌자, 기여자 revolutionary 혁신적인 be credited 공을 인정 받다 criminal 범죄자 arrest 체포 conviction 유죄 판결 perpetrator 가해자, 범인 receive much publicity 큰 명성을 얻다 recognition 인정

문제 14-17

지문에는 6개의 문단(A-F)이 있다. 어느 문단이 다음 정보를 포함하고 있는가?

14. reference to fingerprints to complement written verification
서면으로 된 확인을 보완하기 위한 지문에 대한 언급

D 문단에, 계약서 및 부동산 증서 같은 서류에 지문을 사용하여 서명의 진위 여부에 대한 의구심을 방지하는데 도움을 준다는 내용이 나오므로, 정답은 D이다.

Paraphrasing complement(보완하다) → help(돕다)
written(서면으로 된) → contracts and property deeds(계약서와 부동산 증서)

15. mention of the first hypothesis to state that all fingerprints are unique
모든 지문이 고유하다는 점을 말하는 첫 가설에 대한 언급

지문의 독특함에 대한 첫 가설의 언급은 B 문단 마지막에 나오므로, 정답은 B이다.

Paraphrasing first hypothesis(첫 가설)
→ hypothesis was not officially put forward until ~ (가설이 ~ 이후에 공식적으로 제기되었다)

16. mention of a trial that resulted in a successful conviction based on fingerprint evidence
지문 증거를 바탕으로 성공적인 유죄 판결이라는 결과를 낳은 재판에 대한 언급

지문을 바탕으로 유죄 판결이 난 내용은 F 문단에 나오는 1902년 사건이므로, 정답은 F이다.

참고로 A 문단 역시 중국에서 재판에 지문이 사용된 내용이 나오지만, 성공적으로 유죄 판결로 이끌었는지에 대해서는 알 수 없으므로 A는 오답이다.

17. reference to a method for detecting fingerprints using a chemical
화학 약품을 활용해 지문을 발견하는 방법에 대한 언급

D 문단에 요오드 가스로 지문이 상세하게 나타나는 것을 알았다는 내용이 나오므로, 정답은 D이다.

Paraphrasing chemical(화학 물질) → iodine(요오드)

문제 18-20

다음 연구 결과물(문제 18-20)과 아래의 연구가 명단을 보시오. 각 업적을 A에서 F까지 알맞은 연구가와 일치시키시오.

18. Published the first paper to identify ridges on the hands and fingertips
손과 손가락 끝부분의 굴곡을 확인한 첫 번째 논문을 발간함

B 문단 중간에, 느헤미야 그루가 손바닥과 손가락에 굴곡에 간한 논문을 처음으로 발행했다고 하므로, 정답은 B이다.

참고로 느헤미야 그루 앞에 마르첼로 말피기가 나오는데, 비록 이 사람이 노트에 손가락 굴곡 패턴에 대해 기술하였지만 발간(publish)을 한 것은 아니므로, A는 오답이다.

19. First person to recommend fingerprint identification to the Metropolitan Police
런던 경찰국에 지문 감식을 권한 첫 번째 사람

C 문단에서, 1840년 로버트 블레이크 오버튼이 메트로폴리탄 폴리스에 지문 감식을 권하였고, 이는 그 이후 진술되는 사람들보다 앞서므로, 정답은 D이다.

20. Devised a model of fingerprint analysis based on another researcher's concepts
다른 연구가의 개념을 바탕으로 지문 분석 모델을 고안함

E 문단에서 헨리 폴즈가 지문 감식과 분석 연구를 하였고 프랜시스 골턴이 그의 연구에 감명받아 이를 바탕으로 더 연구하여 종합적인 지문 분석 모델(model of fingerprint analysis)을 만들었으므로, F가 정답이다.

참고로 C 문단에서, 얀 푸르키네가 메이어의 연구를 확장했다는 말이 나오지만, 지문 분석(fingerprint analysis) 모델을 고안한 것은 아니므로, C는 오답이다.

List of Researchers 연구가 명단

A Marcello Malpighi 마르첼로 말피기
B Nehemiah Grew 느헤미야 그루
C Jan Purkinje 얀 푸르키네
D Robert Blake Overton 로버트 블레이크 오버튼
E Dr. Henry Faulds 헨리 폴즈 박사
F Francis Galton 프랜시스 골턴

문제 21-26

다음 요약 내용을 완성하시오. 지문에서 **오직 1개의 단어만** 각 빈칸에 적으시오.

Fingerprint Identification Research 지문 감식 연구

Fingerprints were being used for general identification purposes during criminal trials in **21** ______ around 300 CE. In the mid-17th century, European scientists studied the patterns of the **22** ______ found on the skin of the fingers and palms. Research into fingerprint identification continued over the next two centuries, and true progress occurred in the 19th century. Sir William James Herschel used fingerprints to verify official documents and prevent dishonest **23** ______ from being made with regards to the finances of the deceased. In the late-19th century, Dr. Henry Faulds took his fingerprint classification method to Charles Darwin, who was unable to help due to poor **24** ______. Two employees of the first fingerprint **25** ______ in Calcutta developed a successful fingerprint classification system that was later implemented by the Metropolitan Police in the UK. Meanwhile, in the United States, fingerprints left on a **26** ______ played a role in the conviction of a crime, proving the effectiveness of fingerprint identification.

지문은 서기 약 300년경에 [21]에서 형사 재판 중에 일반적인 확인 목적으로 사용되고 있었다. 17세기 중반에, 유럽의 과학자들은 손가락과 손바닥 피부에서 찾아볼 수 있는 [22]의 패턴을 연구했다. 지문 감식에 대한 연구는 이후 2세기 동안에 걸쳐 지속되었으며, 진정한 진보는 19세기에 나타났다. 윌리엄 제임스 허셜 경이 공식 문서를 증명하고 사망한 사람의 금전 문제와 관련해 정직하지 못한 [23]가 이뤄지는 것을 방지하기 위해 지문을 사용했다. 19세기 후반에, 헨리 폴즈 박사는 찰스 다윈에게 자신의 지문 분류 방법을 전달하려 했지만, 그는 좋지 못한 [24]로 인해 도울 수 없었다. 캘커타의 첫 번째 지문 [25]의 직원 두 명이 성공적인 지문 분류 시스템을 개발했으며, 이는 나중에 영국 런던 경찰청에 의해 시행되었다. 한편, 미국에서는, [26]에 남겨진 지문이 한 범죄의 유죄 판결에 있어 하나의 역할을 했는데, 이는 지문 감식의 유효성을 입증하는 것이었다.

21. 서기 약 300년경에 중국에서 형사 재판 중에 지문이 제시되었다고 하므로, 빈칸에 정답은 China이다.

22. 17세기 중엽 유럽에서, 손가락 끝부분에 존재하는 굴곡의 패턴이 설명되었다고 하므로, 빈칸에 정답은 ridges이다.
Paraphrasing studied(연구했다) → described(설명했다)

23. 윌리엄 제임스 허셜은 사람이 죽은 후 수혜자(상속자)가 아닌 사람들로부터 거짓된 주장을 막기 위해 지문 등록을 하였다고 하므로, 빈칸에 들어갈 정답은 claims이다.
Paraphrasing dishonest(거짓의) → false(거짓의)
with regards to the finances(금전과 관련된) → financial(금전의)
the deceased(사망자들) → an individual had passed away(사람이 죽었다)

24. 다윈이 쇠약해지는 건강으로 인해 폴즈를 돕지 못했으므로, 빈칸에 정답은 health이다.
Paraphrasing poor(안 좋은) → waning(쇠약해지는)

25. 캘커타의 직원 두 명은 첫 번째 지문 사무국(부처)에서 지문 분류 시스템에 혁신적인 기여를 하였으므로, 빈칸에 정답은 bureau이다.

26. 미국에서 유리 진열 보관장(glass display cabinet)에 남겨진 지문으로 범인을 확인했으므로, 빈칸에 정답은 cabinet이다.

참고로 빈칸에 정답은 한 글자인데, 보통 복합 명사에서 앞에 단어들은 수식을 하는 단어들이고 마지막 단어가 중심어이므로, cabinet이 정답이고 glass는 오답이 된다.

▪ 파트 3 [문제 27-40]

출제 포인트 **난이도: 중**

고생물학 및 기후변화 관련하여, 빙하기는 아이엘츠에서 리딩은 물론 리스닝 파트 4에도 나오는 주제인 만큼, 관련 내용과 어휘에 대한 숙지가 필요함

기출 2018년 12월 - 빙하기
2009년 9월 - 빙하기

Ice Age Theory

A Throughout the lifespan of the Earth, five ice ages are known to have occurred thus far. Q29 These are referred to as the Huronian, Cryogenian, Andean-Saharan, Karoo, and the Quaternary Ice Ages, the last of which is ongoing in the present day. Each ice age is characterized by alternating periods of temperate conditions and more extreme conditions. The harsher,

빙하기 이론

A 지구의 수명 전체에 걸쳐, 지금까지 다섯 번의 빙하기가 발생되었던 것으로 알려져 있다. Q29 이 기간들은 휴로니아 빙하기, 크라이오제니아 빙하기, 안데스-사하라 빙하기, 카루 빙하기, 그리고 제사빙하기로 일컬어지며, 이 중에서 마지막 빙하기는 현재에도 지속되고 있다. 각 빙하기는 온화한 환경이 지속된 기간과 더 극한의 환경이 지속된 기간이 번갈아 나타난

colder periods are referred to as glacial periods, while the relatively mild periods are called interglacial periods. The Quaternary Ice Age started about 2.5 million years ago when ice sheets in the Northern Hemisphere began to spread outwards. The Earth is presently going through an interglacial period, with the previous glacial period ending approximately 10,000 years ago.

B The geographical findings that would eventually form the foundation of ice age theory largely came about in the mid-18th century. After spending time in the valley of Chamonix in the Alps in 1742, Q31 Pierre Martel, an engineer from Geneva, published his travel journal. Q38 In it, he noted that the residents of towns within the valley explained that the oddly random dispersal of boulders was a result of the gradual extension of nearby Q32 glaciers. Several similar reports would soon come to light regarding this region in the Alps. Eventually, researchers began to note that the same explanations regarding glacier extension were also given by residents in the Val de Ferret in the Valais and the Seeland in western Switzerland, among numerous other regions throughout the world. For instance, during a trip to the Andes in Chile, the German naturalist Ernst von Bibra learned from the indigenous people that the irregular dispersal of boulders and debris could be correlated with the movement of local glaciers.

C In a paper published in 1824, the Danish-Norwegian geologist Jens Esmark proposed that erratic boulder patterns near glaciers indicated that the Earth had experienced a sequence of prolonged ice ages. Esmark believed that extreme climate change had given rise to periods of glaciation. The concepts introduced in Esmark's paper were of great interest to the scientific community, and several of his peers sought to refine his ideas further. The German geologist Albrecht Bernhardi referenced Esmark's theory in his paper published in 1832. Q39 Bernhardi hypothesized that, at certain points over millions of years, ice caps had been of such a size that they had even reached the temperate regions of the planet.

것으로 특징지어진다. 더 가혹하고 추웠던 기간은 빙하기라고 일컬어지며, 반면에 비교적 온화했던 기간은 간빙기라고 불린다. 제사빙하기가 약 250만 년 전 시작되었는데, 당시에 북반구의 대륙 빙하가 바깥으로 퍼져 나가기 시작했다. 지구는 현재 간빙기를 거치는 중이며, 이전 빙하기는 약 1만 년 전에 끝났다.

B 결과적으로 빙하기 이론의 기초를 형성하게 된 지리학적 연구 결과물은 대체로 18세기 중반에 나타났다. 1742년에 알프스 산맥의 샤모니 계곡에서 시간을 보낸, Q31 제네바 출신의 기술자 피에르 마르텔은 자신의 여행 기록을 출간했다. Q38 이 책에서, 그는 그 계곡 마을의 주민들이 기이하게 무작위로 분산되어 있던 바위들이 근처 Q32 빙하의 점진적인 확산에 따른 결과라고 설명해 준 사실에 주목했다. 알프스에 이 지역과 관련된 여러 유사한 보고서들이 곧 발표되었다. 연구가들은 빙하의 확산과 관련된 동일한 설명들이 전 세계 수많은 다른 지역들 중, 스위스 서부의 발레에 있는 발 드 페레와 씨랜드에 거주하는 주민들에 의해서도 제공되었다는 사실에 주목하기 시작했다. 예를 들어, 칠레의 안데스 산맥 여행 중에, 독일의 동식물학자 에른스트 폰 비브라는 바위 및 잔해의 불규칙한 분산이 지역 빙하의 움직임과 상관 관계가 있을 수 있다는 점을 지역 토착민들을 통해 알게 되었다.

C 1824년에 발간된 한 논문에서, 덴마크계 노르웨이 지질학자 옌스 에스마르크는 빙하 근처의 불규칙한 바위 패턴은 지구가 일련의 장기적인 빙하기들을 겪었다는 점을 나타낸다고 제안했다. 에스마르크는 극도의 기후 변화가 빙하기를 발생시켰다고 생각했다. 에스마르크의 논문에 소개된 이 개념은 과학계에서 대단히 흥미로운 것이었으며, 몇몇 동료 학자들이 그의 아이디어를 더욱 개선하려 시도했다. 독일의 지질학자 알브레히트 베른하르디는 1832년에 발간된 자신의 논문에서 에스마르크의 이론을 참조했다. Q39 베른하르디는 수백 만년 동안 여러 특정 시점에 만년설이 규모가 아주 커지면서 심지어 지구의 온화한 지역에까지 이르게 되었다는 가설을 제기했다.

D Around the same time, the German botanist Karl Schimper was carrying out research on Q33 mosses which were growing on randomly dispersed boulders not far from a glacier in Bavaria. Based on moss patterns, he concluded that the boulders must have been transported by moving ice. During the summer of 1836, Q28 Schimper took a trip to the Swiss Alps with his former university classmate Louis Agassiz. Together, they worked on a detailed theory of a sequence of global glaciations, drawing heavily from the concepts presented in Bernhardi's earlier paper, in addition to their own extensive field studies. The following year, Q27 Schimper coined the term "ice age" in reference to a period of glaciation.

E When Agassiz presented their findings to an annual meeting of leading European scientists in July 1837, Q28 the audience expressed criticism and openly cast doubts over the theory Q37 due to its disregard for established theories related to climate change. A large proportion of scientists still insisted that the planet had been gradually Q34 cooling ever since its birth. Following the rejection from the scientific community, Agassiz threw himself into intensive geological fieldwork. In 1840, he published a book titled *Study on Glaciers*. Due to a series of personal quarrels, Agassiz elected not to mention any of Schimper's research or contributions in his book, which further soured relations between the two.

F Ice age theory was not fully embraced by the international science community until the late-1870s, when the Scottish scientist James Croll published *Climate and Time, in Their Geological Relations*, in which he put forward his astronomical-based theory of climate change. Q30&40 Croll's theory took into account the effects of Earth's orbital variations on climate cycles. He effectively proved that decreases in sunlight during winter months resulted in increased accumulation of snow, and subsequently correlated this with the idea that ice caps change in size in response to solar variations. Croll also presented data that indicated that snow accumulation could alter the trade Q35 winds and warm ocean currents, eventually leading to a prolonged ice age. He suggested that when a significant orbital variation occurs in winter, the Earth will experience colder temperatures due to its distance from the Sun, resulting in an ice age approximately every 22,000 years. According to Croll's theory, multiple ice ages must have occurred throughout the Earth's history, and the last of which should have ended roughly 80,000 years ago

D 비슷한 시기에, 독일의 식물학자 칼 심퍼는 바바리아 지역에 있는 한 빙하에서 멀리 떨어져 있지 않은 곳에 무작위로 분산된 여러 바위에서 자라고 있던 Q33 이끼에 관한 연구를 실시하고 있었다. 이끼 패턴을 바탕으로 그는 그 바위들이 움직이는 얼음 덩어리에 의해 옮겨진 것이 틀림없다는 결론을 내렸다. 1836년 여름에, Q28 심퍼는 과거 대학교 동창이었던 루이스 아가시와 스위스 알프스 산으로 여행을 떠났다. 두 사람은 함께 베른하르디의 초기 논문에 제시된 개념뿐만 아니라 자신들의 폭넓은 현장 연구를 통해 얻은 많은 것들을 바탕으로 일련의 지구 빙하 작용에 대한 상세 이론 작업을 했다. 이듬 해에, Q27 심퍼는 빙하 작용 기간과 관련해 "빙하기"라는 용어를 만들어 냈다.

E 아가시가 1837년 7월에 유럽의 선구적인 과학자들이 참석하는 한 연례 회의에서 자신들의 결과물을 발표했을 때, Q37 청중은 기후 변화와 관련해 인정받던 이론에 대한 무시를 이유로 Q28 그 이론에 대해 비판을 가하고 공공연하게 의구심을 제기했다. 대다수의 과학자들은 지구가 탄생 시점 이후로 서서히 Q34 냉각되어 오고 있었다고 주장했다. 과학계의 거부 이후에, 아가시는 집중적인 지질학 현장 작업에 몰두했다. 1840년에, 그는 <빙하에 관한 연구>라는 제목의 책 한 권을 발간했다. 일련의 개인적인 시비로 인해, 아가시는 자신의 책에 대한 심퍼의 연구 내용이나 기여에 대해 전혀 언급하지 않기로 결정했는데, 이는 두 사람 사이의 관계를 더욱 틀어지게 만들었다.

F 빙하기 이론은 1870년대 말까지 세계 과학계에서 온전히 받아들여지지 않았는데, 당시 스코틀랜드 과학자 제임스 크롤이 <지질학적 관계 속의 기후와 시간>이라는 책을 펴냈고, 책에서 그는 기후 변화에 대해 천문학을 기반으로 한 이론을 제시했다. Q30&40 크롤의 이론은 기후 순환에 대한 지구 궤도 변화의 영향을 고려했다. 그는 겨울 기간 일조량 감소가 눈의 축적을 증가시킨다는 점을 효과적으로 증명했으며, 그 후에 이를 태양의 변화에 따른 반응으로 만년설의 규모가 바뀐다는 생각과 연관시켰다. 크롤은 또한 눈의 축적이 무역 Q35 풍과 따뜻한 해류를 변화시켜 결과적으로 장기적인 빙하기로 이어질 수 있음을 나타내는 데이터도 제시했다. 그는 상당한 궤도 변화가 겨울에 발생할 때, 지구가 태양과의 거리로 인해 더 낮은 기온을 겪고, 그 결과로 약 2만 2천 년마다 빙하기가 발생한다고 제안했다. 크롤의 이론에 따르면, 지구의 역사 전반에 걸쳐 여러 번 빙하기가 발생했음이 틀림없으며, 마지막은 대략 8만년 전에 끝났어야 했다.

G Concurrent with Croll's investigations, other researchers were presenting similar evidence of multiple ice ages, and several leading geologists began investigating sediments in each hemisphere to corroborate existing data. Analysis of sediments around Niagara Falls suggested that the last ice age ended between 6,000 and 35,000 years ago, and those who accepted these measurements were quick to discredit Croll's theory regarding ice age timelines. However, his general idea of orbital variations influencing Earth's Q36 climate remained undisputed and was further enhanced by the work of Milutin Milankovitch, a Serbian climatologist and mathematician. Many years later, in 1976, a modified form of Croll's theory, now known as Milankovitch Cycles, gained widespread acceptance within the scientific community.

G 크롤의 연구와 동시에, 다른 연구가들도 여러 차례의 빙하기에 대한 유사한 증거를 제시했으며, 여러 선구적인 지질학자들은 기존의 데이터를 확증하기 위해 북반구와 남반구 각각의 퇴적물을 연구하기 시작했다. 나이아가라 폭포 주변의 퇴적물 분석 내용에 따르면 마지막 빙하기는 6천 년에서 3만 5천년 전에 끝난 것으로 나타났으며, 이 측정 자료를 받아 들인 사람들은 빙하기 연대와 관련된 크롤의 이론을 금방 신뢰하지 않게 되었다. 하지만, 지구의 Q36 기후에 영향을 미치는 궤도 변화에 대한 그의 일반적인 생각은 반박의 여지가 없는 상태였으며, 세르비아의 기후학자이자 수학자인 밀루틴 밀란코비치의 연구에 의해 한층 더 향상되었다. 많은 시간이 지난 1976년에, 현재 밀란코비치 주기라고 알려진 크롤 이론의 수정안이 과학계에서 널리 인정받았다.

| Vocabulary & Expressions |

lifespan 수명 be referred to as ~라고 일컬어지다 characterize 특징짓다 alternate 번갈아 생기다 temperate 온화한 harsh 가혹한 glacial 빙하의 interglacial 간빙기의 ice sheet 빙상 geographical 지리학의 findings 결과(물) oddly 기이하게 dispersal 분산 boulder 바위 gradual 점진적인 extension 확대, 확장 come to light 밝혀지다 indigenous 토착의, 원산의 debris 잔해 correlate ~와 연관 짓다 erratic 불규칙한 a sequence of 일련의 prolonged 장기적인 give rise to ~을 일으키다 peer 동료 refine ~을 개선하다 reference ~을 참고하다 hypothesize 가설을 제기하다 ice cap 만년설 moss 이끼 transport ~을 옮기다 draw from ~에서 이끌어내다, 얻다 extensive 폭넓은, 광범위한 field study 현장 연구 coin (용어, 말 등) ~을 만들다 in reference to ~에 관하여 audience 청중, 관객 cast doubts 의구심을 제기하다 disregard 무시, 묵살 a large proportion of 대다수의 throw oneself into ~에 몰두하다 intensive 집중적인 geological 지질학의 quarrel 시비, 언쟁 elect 결정하다 contribution 기여, 공헌 sour relations 관계를 틀어지게 하다 embrace ~을 수용하다 put forward ~을 제안하다 astronomical-based 천문학 기반의 orbital 궤도의 variation 변화 result in ~의 결과를 낳다 accumulation 축적, 쌓임 subsequently 그 후로 in response to ~에 대응해 alter ~을 바꾸다 trade winds 무역풍 ocean currents 해류 concurrent with ~와 동시에 sediments 퇴적물 hemisphere 반구 corroborate ~을 확증하다 measurements 측정(치) discredit ~을 믿지 않다 undisputed 반박의 여지가 없는 modified form 수정안 gain widespread acceptance 널리 인정 받다

문제 27 -31

지문에는 7개의 문단(A–G)이 있다. 어느 문단이 다음 정보를 포함하고 있는가?

27. the first known use of the term ice age
최초로 알려진 빙하기라는 용어의 사용

D 문단 마지막에, 심퍼가 빙하 작용 기간과 관련해 "빙하기"라는 용어를 만들어 냈다고 하므로, 정답은 D이다.
Paraphrasing the first know use(첫 번째로 알려진 사용) → coin(새로 단어를 만들다)

28. the rejection of a theory developed by two former fellow students
과거 두 명의 동료 학생들에 의해 전개된 이론의 거부

심퍼와 아가시가 과거 동료 학생이었음은 D 문단에 나오지만, 두 사람의 이론이 학계에서 거부되는 내용이 E 문단에 등장하므로, 정답은 E이다.
Paraphrasing former fellow students(과거 동료 학생) → former university classmate(과거 대학교 급우)

29. a reference to the ice age that the Earth is currently experiencing

지구가 현재 겪고 있는 빙하기에 대한 언급

현재 마지막 빙하기가 지속되고 있다는 내용이 제일 앞부분에 나오므로, 정답은 A이다.
Paraphrasing be currently experiencing(현재 경험하고 있다) → be ongoing in the present day(현재 진행되고 있다)

30. a proposal for a relationship between the Earth's orbit and climate
지구의 궤도와 기후 사이의 관계에 대한 제안

F 문단에서 크롤이 발간한 이론에서 기후 순환에 대한 지구 궤도 변화의 영향을 고려했음을 제시하므로, 정답은 F이다.
Paraphrasing relationship between the Earth's orbit and climate(지구 궤도와 기후 간의 관계)
→ the effects of Earth's orbital variations on climate cycles(기후 순환에 대한 지구 궤도 변화의 영향)

31. findings taken from a traveling researcher's journal
여행하던 연구가의 기록에서 나온 결과물

B 문단에 피에르 마르텔의 여행기와 빙하의 점진적 확산에 대한 연구 결과가 제시되므로, 정답은 B이다.
Paraphrasing traveling researcher's journal(여행하던 연구가의 기록) → his travel journal(그의 여행기)

I Vocabulary & Expressions I
former 예전의 fellow 동료 experience 경험하다

문제 32-36

다음 요약 내용을 완성하시오.
지문에서 오직 **1개의 단어만** 각 빈칸에 적으시오.

Evidence for the occurrence of ice ages 빙하기 발생에 대한 증거

Pierre Martell was one of the first people to propose the extension of [32] based on irregular patterns of nearby boulders. Several researchers made similar observations, and further refined Martell's theory. Karl Schimper studied [33] growing on the boulders, and then co-developed a theory with Louis Agassiz. Many of their peers disagreed with the theory, believing that the Earth had been [34] ever since it was originally formed. James Croll later proposed that accumulation of snow could impact [35] and marine currents, giving rise to an ice age. Parts of Croll's research were later discredited, but his proposed relationship between orbital variations and [36] was later modified by Milutin Milankovitch.

피에르 마르텔은 근처 바위들의 불규칙한 패턴을 바탕으로 [32]의 확대를 제안한 첫 번째 사람들 중 한 명이었다. 여러 연구가들이 유사한 관찰을 했으며, 마르텔의 이론을 더욱 개선했다. 칼 심퍼는 그 바위에서 자라던 [33]을 연구했으며, 그 후에 루이스 아가시와 공동으로 한 이론을 발전시켰다. 많은 동료 연구가들이 그 이론에 동의하지 않았는데, 지구가 처음 형성된 이후로 줄곧 [34]했다고 믿었기 때문이었다. 제임스 크롤은 나중에 눈의 축적이 [35]와 해류에 영향을 미쳐 만년설을 발생시킬 수 있었다고 제안했다. 크롤이 연구한 내용의 일부는 이후에 믿음을 얻지 못했지만, 그가 제안한 궤도 변화와 [36] 사이의 관계는 나중에 밀루틴 밀란코비치에 의해 수정되었다.

32. B 문단에서 피에르 마르텔은 무작위로 분산되어 있던 바위들이 근처 빙하의 점진적인 확산에 따른 결과라고 하므로, 빈칸에 정답은 glaciers이다.
Paraphrasing irregular patterns of nearby boulders(불규칙한 패턴) → oddly random dispersal(기이하게 무작위 분산)

33. D 문단에서 심퍼가 바위에서 자라던 이끼를 연구하였으므로, 정답은 mosses이다.
Paraphrasing study(~을 연구하다) → carry out research on(~에 대해 연구하다)

34. E 문단에서 많은 과학자들은 지구가 계속해서 냉각되어왔다고 믿었으므로, 정답은 cooling이다.
Paraphrasing many of their peers(동료 중 많은 수) ➜ a large proportion of scientists(대다수의 과학자)
Earth(지구) ➜ planet(행성)
ever since it was originally formed(처음 형성된 이후로) ➜ ever since its birth(그 탄생 이후로)

35. F 문단에서 크롤은 눈에 축적이 무역풍과 해류를 바꿀 수 있다고 하였으므로, 빈칸에 들어갈 한 단어 정답은 winds이다.
Paraphrasing impact(영향을 주다) ➜ alter(바꾸다)
marine(해양의) ➜ ocean(대양)

36. G 문단에서 크롤의 연구 중 밀루틴 밀란코비치에 의해 더 강화된 것은 지구 기후에 영향을 미치는 궤도 변화 아이디어이므로, 정답은 climate이다.
Paraphrasing be modified(수정되다) ➜ be further enhanced(더 강화되다)

I Vocabulary & Expressions I
marine currents 해류 modify ~을 수정하다

문제 37-40

다음 내용(문제 37~40)과 아래의 연구가 명단을 보시오. 각 내용을 A, B, C 또는 D에 해당하는 알맞은 연구가와 일치시키시오.

37. Some accepted theories of climate change in the 1800s were not important.
1800년대에 받아들여진 일부 기후 변화 이론은 중요하지 않았다.

E 문단에서 아가시는 기존에 인정받는 이론을 무시했는데 이는 기존 이론에 대해 중요하지 않다고 생각한 것이므로, 정답은 C이다.
Paraphrasing accepted(받아들여진) ➜ established(인정받는)
be not important(중요하지 않다) ➜ disregard(무시하다)

38. Randomly scattered rocks are a result of glacial extension.
무작위로 흩어져 있는 바위들은 빙하 확산에 따른 결과이다.

B 문단에서 피에르 마르텔은 산재한 바위들이 빙하 확산에 따른 것이라고 하므로, 정답은 A이다.
Paraphrasing randomly scattered rocks(무작위로 흩어진 바위들)
➜ oddly random dispersal of boulders(바위들의 기이하도록 무작위의 산재)

39. Ice caps may once have stretched into warmer regions of the planet.
만년설이 한때 지구의 더 따뜻한 지역으로 뻗어 나갔을지도 모른다.

C 문단에서 베른하르디는 만년설(ice cap)이 따뜻한 지역으로 더 퍼졌다고 하므로, 정답은 B이다.
Paraphrasing stretch(뻗다) ➜ reach(도달하다)
warmer(더 따뜻한) ➜ temperate(온난한)

40. A build-up of snow is indicative of variations in the Earth's orbit.
눈의 축적은 지구 궤도의 변화를 나타낸다.

F 문단에서 크롤은 눈의 축적을 증거로 지구 궤도와 기후 변화를 설명하였으므로, 정답은 D이다.
Paraphrasing build-up(축적) ➜ accumulation(축적)

List of Researchers 연구가 명단

A Pierre Martell 피에르 마르텔
B Albrecht Bernhardi 알브레히트 베른하르디
C Louis Agassiz 루이스 아가시
D James Croll 제임스 크롤

| Vocabulary & Expressions |

scattered 산재한, 흩어져 있는 stretch 뻗다 build-up 축적 be indicative of ~을 나타내다

Test 2 READING [General Training]

1. TRUE	2. NOT GIVEN	3. NOT GIVEN	4. TRUE	5. NOT GIVEN
6. FALSE	7. TRUE	8. A	9. B	10. B
11. D	12. C	13. A	14. D	
15. disciplining	16. communications	17. hobbies	18. celebrate	19. inspiration
20. alliances	21. risk	22. Management	23. needs	24. expense
25. objectives	26. feedback	27. technology		
28. kangaroo	29. wolf	30. settlers	31. diet	32. habitat
33. C	34. A	35. D	36. B	37. C
38. C	39. D	40. B		

▪ 파트 1 [문제 1-7]

출제 포인트 **난이도: 중하**

룸메이트 또는 같이 여행할 사람을 구하는 전단지 형태의 지문이 제너럴 섹션 1(파트 1)에서 간혹 출제되는 만큼 관련 내용 및 어휘 숙지 필요

Rideshare Offer: Orlando to Chicago

We are looking for someone who wants to travel from Orlando to Chicago and would be willing to share gas and accommodation costs. The distance between the two cities is 1,154 miles, and Q1 the journey will require a driving time of approximately 18 hours. Ideally, we will drive for 9 hours per day, plus refreshment stops, and stay in a motel for one night. The plan is to set off at around 9 a.m. on Thursday, March 19th. Please note that this is a

차량 공유 제안: 올랜도에서 시카고까지

저희는 올랜도에서 시카고까지 여행하기를 원하는 분을 찾고 있으며, 연료비와 숙박비를 나눠 지불할 의향이 있습니다. 두 도시 사이의 거리는, 1,154마일이며, Q1 이 여행은 약 18시간의 차량 운전 시간을 필요로 합니다. 이상적인 방법은, 간식을 위한 휴식 시간을 더해 하루에 9시간 운전하고 하룻밤 모텔에서 머무르는 것입니다. 이는 3월 19일 목요일 오전 9시쯤에 출발하는 계획입니다. 편도로 이동하는 차량 공유 제안이라는 점에 유의하

one-way rideshare offer, Q2 as we are not certain when we will return to Orlando.	셔야 하는데, Q2 저희가 언제 올랜도로 돌아올지 확실하지 않기 때문입니다.
About us: I'm Brigitte! I'm Swedish, but I moved to Orlando with my family a few years ago. I'm 25 years old and am pursuing a career in acting. The reason for my trip is to attend an audition for a film that will be primarily shot in Chicago. Q3 A Swedish friend of mine, Agatha, will be accompanying us on the trip, just to do some sightseeing. Originally, our Mexican friend, Lola, planned to join us, but she is unable to as she will be playing a concert with her band in Orlando that particular weekend. Agatha and I are very easy-going and friendly, and we love to meet new people.	저희에 관해: 저는 브리짓입니다! 스웨덴인이지만, 몇 년 전에 가족과 함께 올랜도로 이사했습니다. 저는 25살이며, 연기 분야에서 경력을 추구하고 있습니다. 제 여행의 이유는 시카고에서 주로 촬영하게 되는 한 영화의 오디션에 참석하기 위해서입니다. Q3 제 스웨덴인 친구 아가사가 여행에 동행할 예정인데, 단순히 관광을 하기 위해서입니다. 원래, 제 멕시코인 친구 롤라가 저희와 함께 할 계획이었지만, 그렇게 할 수 없는데, 바로 그 특정 주에 올랜도에서 자신의 밴드와 콘서트를 하기 때문입니다. 아가사와 저는 성격이 매우 원만하고 친절하며, 새로운 사람들을 만나는 것을 아주 좋아합니다.
The vehicle itself is an RV (Recreational Vehicle) and comes equipped with a bathroom, Q4 a stove, pots, pans, plates, and cutlery, a microwave, and a television. Q5 It used to include a bed, but the previous owner of the vehicle removed this to enlarge the comfortable seating area.	차량 자체는 RV(레저용 차량)이며, 욕실과 Q4 가스레인지, 냄비, 팬, 접시, 그리고 식기, 전자레인지와 텔레비전이 갖춰져 있습니다. Q5 전에 침대가 포함되어 있었지만, 차량의 이전 소유주가 편안한 좌석 공간을 더 넓히기 위해 제거했습니다.
Q6 Agatha and I will handle all of the driving, so there's no need for you to have a license. Q7 All gas and accommodation costs will be split three ways and paid immediately in cash, so make sure you bring enough money along for the trip. As we are two females, we would prefer to have a third female companion, but we will still consider any men who request to join us on the trip. Please send an introductory e-mail to bsvensson@greenmail.net if you are interested.	Q6 아가사와 제가 모든 운전을 맡을 것이므로, 면허증이 없으셔도 됩니다. Q7 모든 연료비와 숙박비는 3등분해서 현금으로 즉시 지불하게 될 것이므로, 이 여행에 충분할 정도의 돈을 꼭 챙겨 오시기 바랍니다. 저희가 여자 둘이기 때문에, 여자가 한 명 더 동행하기를 원하기는 하지만, 저희와 함께 여행하기를 요청하는 남자도 여전히 고려해 볼 것입니다. 관심 있으신 분은 bsvensson@greenmail.net으로 소개 이메일을 보내 주시기 바랍니다.

| Vocabulary & Expressions |

rideshare 차량 공유 offer 제안 accommodation 숙박 시설, 숙소 approximately 약, 대략 ideally 이상적으로 refreshments 간식, 간단한 식사 set off 출발하다 pursue 추구하다 primarily 주로 shoot 촬영하다 accompany ~와 동행하다 particular 특정한 easy-going (성격이) 원만한, 편한 vehicle 차량 come equipped with ~가 갖춰져 있다 cutlery 식기 used to do ~하고는 했었다 enlarge ~을 넓히다, 확장하다 handle ~을 다루다 split 나누다 three ways 3등분 companion 동행자

문제 1-7

주어진 지문의 정보와 일치하는 경우 **참**, 지문의 정보와 일치하지 않는 경우 **거짓**, 정보가 존재하지 않는 경우 **해당 없음**을 선택하시오.

1. The travelers will arrive in Chicago on Friday.
여행자들이 금요일에 시카고에 도착할 것이다.

목요일 아침에 출발하여 9시간 운전하고 일박을 하고 다시 9시간 운전하여 시카고에 도착하므로, 결국 금요일에 도착한다. 따라서 정답은 TRUE이다.

2. Brigitte and Agatha will stay in Chicago for one week.
브리짓과 아가사가 시카고에서 일주일 동안 머물 것이다.

브리짓과 아가사가 시카고에서 일주일을 머물지, 얼마나 머물지는 지문에서 알 수 없기에, 정답은 NOT GIVEN이다.

3. Brigitte's friend Agatha is a musician.
브리짓의 친구 아가사는 음악가이다.

아가사가 음악가인지에 대해서는 지문에서 알 수가 없다. 따라서 정답은 NOT GIVEN이다. 참고로 음악가는 아가사가 아니라 또다른 친구인 롤라이다.

4. The vehicle that will be used has cooking facilities.
이용할 차량에 요리 설비가 있다.

요리 설비인 가스레인지, 냄비, 팬, 접시, 그리고 식기, 전자레인지가 딸려 있으므로, 정답은 TRUE이다.

5. The RV has had new features added since being purchased.
해당 레저용 차량은 구입된 이후로 새로운 특징들이 추가되었다.

지문에서는 구매 후 새로 추가된 물품이나 특징에 대한 언급이 없고, 다만 설치되어 있던 침대를 치웠다는 이야기만 있다. 따라서 정답은 NOT GIVEN이다.

6. Brigitte will drive the vehicle for the entire duration of the journey.
브리짓이 전체 여행 시간 동안 차량을 운전할 것이다.

브리짓이 아가사와 함께 운전할 것이라고 말하므로, 정답은 FALSE이다.

7. Gas costs will be paid equally by all three travelers.
연료비가 세 명의 여행자 모두에 의해 균등하게 지불될 것이다.

숙박비와 연료비는 현금으로 삼등분한다고 하였으므로, 정답은 TRUE이다.

I Vocabulary & Expressions I
cooking facilities 요리 설비 feature 특징 duration (지속) 기간

▪ 파트 1 [문제 8-14]

출제 포인트 **난이도: 중하**
어떠한 제품에 대한 광고지뿐만 아니라 제품 비교 평가서 또한 제너럴 섹션 1(파트 1)에서 자주 출제됨

TV Streaming Services

A Orion
Plans: For $8.99 a month, subscribers can sign up for the Orion Basic plan. For $12.99 a month, viewers have access to the Orion Plus Live TV plan, which features more than 30 live and on-demand channels and allows streaming on two screens simultaneously. Q8 Add-ons available include unlimited screens and no commercials. However, those unlimited screens come at an extra cost, with the add-on costing an additional $14.99 per month. Q13 Removal of ads costs an extra $4.99 per month. Another drawback is that the service does not allow offline viewing.

TV 재생 서비스

A 오리온
약정: 1개월에 8.99달러로, 서비스 가입자들께서 오리온 기본 약정을 신청하실 수 있습니다. 1개월에 12.99달러로, 시청자들은 오리온 플러스 라이브 TV 약정을 이용하실 수 있는데, 이는 30개 이상의 라이브 채널 및 주문형 채널을 특징으로 하며, 2개의 스크린에서 동시에 재생하는 것을 가능하게 합니다. Q8 이용 가능한 부가 서비스에는 무제한 스크린과 광고 삭제가 포함됩니다. 하지만, 이 무제한 스크린은 추가 비용이 드는데, 이 부가 서비스는 1개월에 14.99달러의 비용이 추가됩니다. Q13 광고 삭제 비용은 1개월에 4.99달러가 추가로 듭니다. 또 다른 단점으로는 이 서비스로는 오프라인 시청이 불가능하다는 점입니다.

B Streamflix

Plans: Q10 Starting at $7.99 a month for a Basic Plan, viewers can watch in standard definition on one device at a time. The $10.99 per month Premium Plan gives a high definition option and allows streaming on one more device. Not only are the base prices low, but Streamflix gains a slight edge over the competition by not charging an added fee to remove ads. It Q9 also allows you to download shows to watch offline. Potential subscribers should note, however, that there is a relatively long wait period for some TV shows to be added to the service after they originally air.

C Blast TV

Plans: The basic plan, Blast Standard, gives viewers more than 25 channels for $9.99 per month. You can get Blast Silver and an extra 20 channels for an extra $5 per month. If that's still not enough, get the Blast Gold plan, which comes with more than 60 channels for $19.99 per month. Q12 Blast TV offers a wide range of add-ons, including country- and language-specific packages. However, offline viewing is out of the question, and network sports broadcasts are pretty hard to come by with Blast TV. It's also debatable whether the price tag provides true value for money.

D Digital Prime

Plans: This service currently offers only one plan, which runs for $12.99 per month. The main perk of this relatively new service is that it allows you to Q11 watch your shows in virtual reality using the cutting-edge Digital Prime VR app. You also won't have to sit through any ads, as they are already removed by the service provider. One downside is that the service doesn't allow you to download shows to watch offline. The service also provides less content than the others, although it does Q14 have a large number of channels devoted to live concerts and sporting events.

B 스트림플릭스

약정: Q10 기본 약정에 대해 1개월에 7.99달러로 시작하며, 시청자들께서 한 번에 하나의 기기에서 일반 해상도로 시청하실 수 있습니다. 1개월에 10.99달러를 지불하는 프리미엄 약정은 고해상도 옵션을 제공하며, 추가적인 1개 기기에서 재생 가능하도록 합니다. 기본 이용 가격이 낮을 뿐만 아니라, 스트림플릭스는 광고를 삭제하기 위한 추가 요금을 부과하지 않음으로써 경쟁력에서 약간의 우위를 점하고 있기도 합니다. Q9 또한 오프라인으로 시청할 수 있는 프로그램도 다운로드할 수 있게 해 줍니다. 하지만 잠재 서비스 가입자들께서는 일부 TV 프로그램들이 처음 방송된 이후로 해당 서비스가 추가되는 데 비교적 대기 기간이 길다는 점에 유의하셔야 합니다.

C 블래스트 TV

약정: 기본 약정인 블래스트 스탠다드는 1개월에 9.99달러로 시청자들에게 25가지가 넘는 채널을 제공합니다. 1개월에 5달러를 추가하시면 블래스트 실버 약정과 추가 20개 채널을 이용하실 수 있습니다. 그래도 충분하지 않으실 경우, 1개월에 19.99달러로 60개가 넘는 채널이 포함되어 있는 블래스트 골드 약정을 이용해 보십시오. Q12 블래스트 TV는 아주 다양한 부가 서비스를 제공하며, 여기에는 특정 국가 및 언어 이용 패키지가 포함되어 있습니다. 하지만 오프라인 시청은 불가능하며, 네트워크 스포츠 방송은 블래스트 TV로 보기가 꽤 어렵습니다. 또한 이용 가격이 비용에 비해 진정한 가치를 제공하는지도 논란의 여지가 있는 부분입니다.

D 디지털 프라임

약정: 이 서비스는 현재 오직 한 가지 약정만 제공하며, 1개월에 12.99달러로 운영됩니다. 비교적 새로운 이 서비스의 주요 혜택은 Q11 첨단 디지털 프라임 VR 앱을 이용해 가상 현실로 프로그램을 시청할 수 있게 해준다는 점입니다. 또한 어떤 광고든 끝까지 앉아서 보실 필요가 없는데, 서비스 제공자에 의해 이미 삭제된 상태이기 때문입니다. 한 가지 단점은 이 서비스가 오프라인으로 시청할 수 있도록 프로그램을 다운로드할 수 있게 해 주지 않는다는 점입니다. 또한 이 서비스에 Q14 라이브 콘서트 및 스포츠 행사 전용 채널이 분명 아주 많이 있기는 하지만, 다른 서비스들보다 더 적은 콘텐츠를 제공합니다.

| Vocabulary & Expressions |

streaming (동영상 등의) 재생 subscriber 서비스 가입자, 구독자 sign up for ~에 등록하다 feature ~을 특징으로 하다 on-demand 주문형의 allow ~을 가능하게 하다 simultaneously 동시에 add-on 부가 서비스 commercial 광고 (방송) at an extra cost 추가 비용으로 drawback 단점(= downside) definition 해상도 device 기기, 장치 gain an edge over ~에 우위를 점하다 slight 약간의, 조금의 competition 경쟁(력) charge ~을 부과하다 air 방송되다 come with ~가 딸려 있다 come by ~을 얻다, 받다 debatable 논란의 여지가 있는 run 운영되다 perk 혜택 virtual reality 가상 현실 cutting-edge 첨단의 sit through 끝까지 앉아있다 devoted to ~ 전용의, ~에 전념하는

ACTUAL TEST 2

문제 8-14

A에서 D까지 TV 재생 서비스에 대한 4가지 평가를 확인하시오. 어느 서비스에 대해서 다음 내용들이 참인가?

8. This service is useful for people with more than two viewing devices.
이 서비스는 2개 이상 시청용 기기를 이용하는 사람들에게 유용하다.

A 서비스는 무제한 스크린(2개 이상 시청용 기기) 사용이 가능하므로, 정답은 A이다.
Paraphrasing more than two viewing devices(2개 이상 시청용 기기) → unlimited screens(무제한 스크린들)

9. You can download content with this service and watch it offline.
이 서비스의 콘텐츠를 다운로드해서 오프라인으로 시청할 수 있다.

B 서비스는 오프라인에서 볼 수 있도록 다운로드가 가능하므로, 정답은 B이다.

10. This service is cheaper than the other three listed services.
이 서비스는 기재된 다른 세 개의 서비스들보다 더 저렴하다.

지문의 서비스 중 최저가 상품은 $7.99이므로, 정답은 B이다.

11. You can use an innovative app in conjunction with this service.
이 서비스와 연결되는 혁신적인 앱을 이용할 수 있다.

첨단 앱을 사용하는(watch your shows in virtual reality using the cutting-edge Digital Prime VR app) 서비스는 D이다.
Paraphrasing innovative(혁신적인) → cutting-edge(첨단의)

12. This service is ideal for people who want programming from another country.
이 서비스는 다른 국가의 방송 프로를 원하는 사람들에게 이상적이다.

블라스트 TV는 특정 국가와 언어 패키지가 포함되어 있으므로, 다른 국가의 방송을 원하는 사람들에게 이상적이다. 따라서 정답은 C이다.
Paraphrasing programming from another country(다른 국가 방송 프로)
→ country and language-specific packages(특정 국가와 언어 패키지)

13. You must pay an extra fee to have adverts taken off this service.
이 서비스에서 광고를 없애는 데 반드시 추가 요금을 지불해야 한다.

광고를 없애는데 추가 요금($4.99)이 요구되는 서비스는 A이다.
Paraphrasing extra fee(추가 요금) → extra $4.99(추가 $4.99)
have adverts taken off(광고를 없애도록 하다) → removal of ads(광고 제거)

14. This service would suit someone seeking a range of sports content.
이 서비스는 다양한 스포츠 콘텐츠를 찾는 사람에게 적합할 수 있다.

디지털 프라임 서비스가 스포츠 경기 채널이 아주 많다고 하므로(have a large number of channels devoted to live concerts and sporting events), 정답은 D이다.
Paraphrasing a range of(다양한) → a large number of(아주 많은)

I Vocabulary & Expressions I

innovative 혁신적인 app 앱, 어플 in conjunction with ~와 함께 programming 방송 프로 advert 광고 take off 중단하다 suit 적합하다 a range of 다양한

▪ **파트 2** [문제 15-20]

출제 포인트 **난이도: 중**

직장 내 규정 또는 직장 생활 정보는 제너럴 섹션 2(파트 2)에 빈출되기에, 관련 내용 및 어휘에 대한 숙지 필요

Why you should encourage socializing in your workplace

Socializing at work used to be viewed as a negative thing, and managers were quick to discourage staff from gathering around the water cooler to indulge in gossip. These days, however, business owners recognize the advantages of workplace socializing, spending more time and effort encouraging productive social interaction rather than Q15 disciplining staff for having a quick chat.

One of the clear benefits of a sociable workforce is the sharing of knowledge. When a business sends several Q16 communications to staff during the workday, some employees may fail to notice one of them. While socializing with one another, employees will often discuss such communications, alerting those individuals who missed them. Social interaction also gives workers a chance to hear different perspectives on issues such as new policies or project proposals. Management can take advantage of informal environments, such as a break room, to encourage discussion about work issues and answer any questions employees may have.

When new employees come into a busy work environment, they can understandably feel overwhelmed. Encouraging the new employees to socialize helps them to settle in and feel confident. Managers should lead a new employee through all work departments and introduce them individually to all of the staff, or in larger companies, the department supervisors. While doing so, the manager should mention the new employee's Q17 hobbies and take time to introduce him or her to likeminded workers with whom the new employee has several things in common.

Socializing has clear benefits when it comes to teamwork and healthy competition. In several fields of business, particularly in sales-oriented companies, sales teams will often compete against each other to reach a monthly target and win a bonus or other incentive. Allowing these teams to Q18 celebrate their successes in the workplace, giving each other high-fives and boasting about their achievements, can have a positive effect on team spirit.

직장에서 사교 활동을 권장해야 하는 이유

직장 내 사교 활동은 한때 부정적인 것으로 여겨졌으며, 책임자들은 직원들이 냉수기 근처에 모여 잡담에 빠져드는 것을 빠르게 막았다. 하지만 요즘은, 기업 소유주들이 직장 내 사교 활동의 장점을 인식하면서, 잠깐 수다를 떠는 것에 대해 직원들에게 Q15 훈육을 하는 대신 생산적인 사교적 교류를 장려하는 데 더 많은 시간과 노력을 기울이고 있다.

사교적인 직원들의 분명한 이점 중 하나는 지식의 공유이다. 회사가 업무 일과 중에 직원들에게 여러 Q16 메시지를 발송할 때, 일부 직원들은 그 중 하나를 알아차리지 못할 수도 있다. 직원들이 서로 어울리는 동안, 흔히 그러한 메시지에 관해 이야기하면서 그것을 놓친 사람들에게 알려 주게 된다. 사교적 교류는 또한 직원들에게 새로운 정책이나 프로젝트 제안과 같은 사안에 대해 다른 관점을 들어 볼 수 있는 기회도 제공한다. 경영진은 휴게실과 같은 편안한 환경을 이용해 업무 사안에 관한 논의를 장려하고 직원들이 갖고 있을 수 있는 어떠한 질문에 대해서도 답변해 줄 수 있다.

신입 사원들이 바쁜 업무 환경에 처해 있을 때, 당연히 압도되는 느낌을 받을 수 있다. 신입 사원들에게 사람들과 어울리도록 장려하는 것은 그들이 적응하는 데 있어 그리고 자신감을 갖는 데 있어 도움이 된다. 책임자들은 신입 사원을 이끌고 모든 업무 부서를 거치면서 모든 직원들에게 또는 큰 회사의 경우에는 부서장들에게 개별적으로 소개해야 한다. 그렇게 하는 동안, 해당 책임자는 신입 사원의 Q17 취미를 언급하고 그 신입 사원과 여러 공통점이 있는 비슷한 직원들에게 소개할 시간을 가져야 한다.

사교 활동은 팀워크 및 건강한 경쟁 측면에서도 분명한 이점이 있다. 비즈니스의 여러 분야에서, 특히 영업 지향적인 회사에서, 영업팀들은 월간 목표에 도달하거나 보너스 또는 기타 성과급을 받기 위해 흔히 서로 경쟁한다. 이 팀들에게 서로 하이파이브를 하게 해주고 성과에 대해 자랑하게 하면서 직장 내에서 자신들의 성공을 Q18 축하할 수 있게 하는 것은 팀워크에 긍정적인 영향을 미

Managers can encourage teamwork by congratulating winning teams in the workplace and discussing their performance. Not only will it encourage the winners to maintain their hard work, but other teams will find Q19 inspiration in your words and double their efforts.	친다. 책임자들은 직장 내에서 이기는 팀을 축하하고 성과를 이야기함으로써 팀워크를 장려할 수 있다. 이는 이긴 사람들에게 힘든 노력을 유지하게 해줄 뿐만 아니라, 다른 팀들이 그 이야기 속에서 Q19 영감을 얻고 두 배로 노력하게 할 수 있다.
Lastly, one of the most important, yet often overlooked, advantages of socialization is that it can result in strong, unexpected Q20 alliances within your company. For instance, a member of the accounting department might forge a friendship with a member of the production department, and this alliance could result in a collaborative effort that successfully cuts the company's production costs. The same thing can arise when a customer service employee has a social relationship with a production worker.	마지막으로, 가장 중요하면서도 종종 간과하는 사교 활동의 장점 중 하나는 회사 내 끈끈하고 예기치 못한 Q20 연대감이라는 결과를 낳을 수 있다는 것이다. 예를 들어, 회계부의 직원 한 명이 생산부의 한 직원과 친분을 형성할 수 있는데, 이러한 연대 관계는 성공적으로 회사의 생산 비용을 감축하는 공동의 노력으로 이어질 수 있다. 고객 서비스 직원이 생산 담당 직원과 사교적 관계를 맺을 때도 같은 일이 발생될 수 있다.
When a customer complains about a design fault in a product, the two workers can come up with an ideal solution and response. Managers should plan inter-department social gatherings so that such alliances have a chance to be formed.	고객이 제품의 디자인 결함에 관해 불만을 제기할 때 두 직원이 이상적인 해결책과 답변을 제시할 수 있다. 책임자들은 그와 같은 연대 관계가 형성될 기회를 가질 수 있도록 부서 간의 사교적 모임을 계획해야 한다.

| Vocabulary & Expressions |

encourage 권장하다 socialize 사람들과 어울리다 be viewed as ~로 여겨지다 negative 부정적인 discourage 못하게 하다 indulge in ~에 빠져 들다 gossip 잡담, 험담, 소문 interaction 교류, 상호 작용 discipline ~을 징계하다, 훈육하다 workforce 직원들 alert ~에게 알리다 individual 사람, 개인 perspective 관점, 시각 policy 정책, 방침 take advantage of ~을 이용하다 understandably 당연히 overwhelmed 압도된 settle in 적응하다 individually 개별적으로 likeminded 비슷한 생각을 가진 in common 공통으로 when it comes to ~와 관련해서 A-oriented A 지향적인 incentive 인센티브, 성과급 celebrate ~을 축하하다, 기념하다 boast about ~에 대해 자랑하다 achievement 성과, 업적 maintain ~을 유지하다 inspiration 영감, 자극 double ~을 두 배로 하다 overlook ~을 간과하다 result in ~로 결과가 이어지다 alliance 연대, 연합 forge ~을 형성하다, 구축하다 collaborative 공동의, 협업의 arise 발생하다 come up with (아이디어 등)을 제시하다 inter-department 부서 간의 gathering 모임

문제 15-20

다음 문장들을 완성하시오. 지문에서 **오직 1개의 단어만** 각 빈칸에 작성하시오.

- Managers should encourage socializing instead of [15] staff who spend time talking.

  책임자들은 이야기하는 데 시간을 소비하는 직원들을 [15] 하는 대신에 사교 활동을 장려해야 한다.

  직원들이 잡담하는 것을 훈육 대신 장려하라고 하므로(encouraging productive social interaction rather than disciplining staff for having a quick chat), 빈칸에 정답은 disciplining이다.

  Paraphrasing managers(관리자들) → business owners(사업주들)
  socializing(친목) → social interaction(사교)
  who spend time talking(대화하는데 시간을 보내는) → having a quick chat(간단한 잡담을 하는 것)

- Socializing enables staff to find out about any [16] they have not noticed during the day.

  사교 활동은 직원들이 하루 중에 알아차리지 못했던 모든 [16].에 관해 알 수 있게 해 준다.

회사에서 하루 중 여러 업무 메시지(communications)를 보낼 때, 직원 중에 이를 놓치는 사람이 있을 수 있지만, 사교 활동을 통해 다시 이를 알 수 있으므로, 빈칸에 들어갈 정답은 communications이다. knowledge를 정답으로 고를 수도 있는데, 내용상 빈칸에 들어갈 말은 단순한 지식이 아닌 업무 메시지로, 본문에 구체적으로 언급되는 communications가 정답이다.

- Let other staff know about a new worker's [17] so that they can form a friendship.

  친분 관계를 형성할 수 있도록 신입 직원의 [17]에 관해 다른 직원에게 알려야 한다.

신입 사원의 취미를 알려서 공통점이 있는 직원들과 시간을 가질 수 있도록 장려하라고 하므로, 빈칸에 들어갈 정답은 hobbies이다.

- Allow sales teams to [18] their achievements in the workplace.

  영업팀들이 직장 내에서 성과를 [18]할 수 있게 해야 한다.

영업팀이 직장 내에서 그들의 성공을 축하할 수 있게 해야 하므로, 빈칸에 들어갈 정답은 celebrate이다.
Paraphrasing achievements(성과) → successes(성공)

- Congratulate winning teams in order to provide [19] for competing teams to do better.

  경쟁 팀들이 더 잘 할 수 있도록 [19]을 제공하기 위해 이긴 팀들을 축하해야 한다.

우승 팀을 축하하는 것은 다른 팀들에게 영감(자극)을 주려는 목적도 있으므로, 정답은 inspiration이다.
Paraphrasing competing teams(경쟁팀들) → other teams(다른 팀들)
do better(더 잘하다) → double their efforts(두배로 노력하다)

- Build [20] between staff by organizing inter-department gatherings.

  부서 간의 모임을 체계화함으로써 직원들 사이에서 [20]을 구축해야 한다.

회사 내 사교 활동을 통해 다른 부서들간 연대감을 쌓을 수 있으므로, 정답은 alliances이다. 지문에서 alliance의 복수와 단수를 모두 찾을 수 있는데, 문제 빈칸에는 문법상 복수가 들어가야 되기에 복수가 정답이다. 만일 빈칸 앞에 an이 있다면 단수가 정답이 된다.

| Vocabulary & Expressions |
enable 가능하게 하다 notice 알아차리다 organize 조직하다, 체계화하다

▪ 파트 2 [문제 21-27]

출제 포인트 **난이도: 중하**
직장 내 규정 또는 생활 정보는 제너럴 섹션 2(파트 2)에 빈출되기에, 관련 내용 및 어휘에 대한 숙지 필요

Data-gathering approaches for your project	당신의 프로젝트를 위한 자료 수집 방법들
When planning an important work project, it is often beneficial to collect information from consumers, company stakeholders, employees, or competitors. Here are four of the most effective data-gathering approaches, and an outline of their advantages and disadvantages:	중요한 업무 프로젝트를 계획할 때, 소비자와 회사 주주, 직원, 또는 경쟁 업체를 통해 정보를 수집하는 것이 종종 유익합니다. 아래에서 가장 효과적인 자료 수집 방식 네 가지와 각각의 장단점을 담은 개요를 확인해 보십시오.
Benchmarking This technique involves evaluating the leading companies within your field or industry and determining what factors have contributed to their success. By doing so, you can learn a lot from the successes of other companies, at no [Q21] risk to you or your own firm. Benchmarking allows	**벤치마킹** 이 방법은 소속 분야 또는 업계 내에서 선도적인 회사들을 평가해 그들의 성공에 어떤 요소가 기여해 왔는지를 결정하는 일을 수반합니다. 이렇게 함으로써, 여러분 또는 여러분의 회사에 대한 [Q21] 위험 부담 없이 다른 회사의 성공으로부터 많은 것을 배울 수 있습니다. 벤치마킹은 명백하게 효과적이었던 과거의 프로젝트들을 분석

ACTUAL TEST 2

you to set standards for your outcomes by analyzing those of demonstrably effective past projects. It can also be useful to help you validate your project approach in the eyes of Q22 management when the time comes to seek final approval. However, in order for it to be worthwhile, you need to find benchmarks that closely match your own project, and this is easier said than done.

함으로써 결과물에 대한 기준을 설정할 수 있게 해줍니다. 이는 또한 최종 승인을 받아야 할 시간이 다가올 때 Q22 경영진의 관점에서 여러분의 프로젝트 접근 방식을 증명하도록 도움을 주는 데 유용할 수 있습니다. 하지만, 이 방법이 가치 있는 것이 되려면, 여러분의 프로젝트와 밀접하게 일치하는 벤치마킹 대상을 찾아야 하는데, 이는 말처럼 쉬운 것이 아닙니다.

Focus Groups

You can create a focus group by assembling several people, typically between 8 and 15 per group, who broadly represent your target consumer base. This method is designed to help you understand the real, current Q23 needs of your end users, instead of simply making assumptions based on possibly outdated data. Note that it is crucial to have an experienced group leader, which can involve an extra Q24 expense. External experts will demand a sizable sum, and internal employees may require costly training beforehand.

포커스 그룹

여러 사람들, 일반적으로 그룹당 목표 소비자 층을 폭넓게 대표하는 8~15명의 사람들을 모아 포커스 그룹을 만들 수 있습니다. 이 방법은 단순히 오래 되었을 가능성이 있는 데이터를 바탕으로 추측을 하는 대신 최종 소비자들이 현재 정말로 Q23 필요로 하는 것을 이해하는 도움이 되도록 고안된 것입니다. 경험 많은 그룹 리더가 있어야 한다는 점이 중요하다는 사실에 유의해야 하는데, 이는 추가 Q24 비용이 수반될 수 있는 부분입니다. 외부의 전문가들은 상당한 액수를 요구하며, 내부 직원들에게는 비용이 많이 드는 교육이 사전에 필요할 수도 있습니다.

Surveys

Surveys have long been an effective way to gather data and ascertain the perceptions and opinions of a group of people. This method saves you time, as participants can receive the surveys by e-mail and send them back to you within a specified timeframe. This means that you do not need to attend meetings or record information first-hand. Additionally, questions can be tailored in order to fit the Q25 objectives you have set for your project. The biggest drawback of surveys is that some recipients may give the task low priority, or forget about it altogether.

설문 조사

설문 조사는 데이터를 수집하고 한 그룹의 사람들이 지닌 인식과 의견을 확인하는 데 있어 오랫동안 효과적인 방법이었습니다. 이 방법은 시간을 절약해 주는데, 참가자들이 이메일로 설문 조사지를 받은 후에 특정 기간 내에 되돌려 보내줄 수 있기 때문입니다. 이는 회의에 참석하거나 직접 정보를 기록할 필요가 없다는 것을 의미합니다. 추가로, 여러분이 프로젝트를 위해 설정해 둔 Q25 목표에 적합할 수 있도록 질문들을 조정할 수 있습니다. 설문 조사의 가장 큰 단점은 일부 답변자들이 그 일에 우선 순위를 두지 않거나, 완전히 잊을 수 있다는 점입니다.

Prototypes

A prototype is typically an early, simplified version of your proposed end product or service. Once created, this can be made available to selected consumers, who will then provide Q26 feedback that you can utilize to make improvements. Unfortunately, building prototypes can be extraordinarily expensive, and the approach is typically only suitable for companies developing and utilizing new Q27 technology, such as those in the construction or electronics industries.

시제품

일반적으로 시제품은 제안된 최종 제품 또는 서비스에 대한 초기의 단순화된 버전입니다. 일단 만들어지면, 선택된 소비자들에게 이용 가능해질 수 있으며, 그 후에 여러분이 개선하는 데 활용할 수 있는 Q26 의견을 제공해 줍니다. 안타깝게도, 시제품을 제작하는 일은 엄청나게 비용이 많이 들 수 있으며, 이 방법은 일반적으로 건설업계나 전자제품업계에 속한 회사와 같이 새로운 Q27 기술을 개발하고 활용하는 업체에만 적합할 수 있습니다.

| Vocabulary & Expressions |

stakeholder 주주 competitor 경쟁업체 outline 개요 demonstrably 명백히 validate ~을 입증하다 in the eyes of ~의 관점에서 management 경영(진) worthwhile 가치 있는 typically 일반적으로, 보통 represent ~을 대표하다, 대신하다 end user 최종 소비자 make an assumption 추정하다 outdated 오래된, 낡은 expense 비용 external 외부의 expert 전문가 sizable (금액이) 상당한 sum 액수 ascertain ~을 확인하다 perception 인식 first-hand 직접 tailor ~을 맞춤 조정하다 objective 목표 drawback 단점 recipient 받는 사람 priority 우선 순위 extraordinarily 이례적으로 suitable 적합한

문제 21-27

다음 메모를 완성하시오. 지문에서 **오직 1개의 단어만** 각 빈칸에 적으시오.

Information gathering techniques 정보 수집 방법

There are many effective ways to gather information, including:
다음을 포함해 정보를 수집하는 여러 효과적인 방법들이 존재한다.

Benchmarking 벤치마킹

- requires the analysis of successful companies in your field
  소속 분야에서 성공을 거둔 회사들에 대한 분석을 필요로 한다.
- allows you to gather data without any [21] to your company
  회사에 대한 어떠한 [21] 없이도 데이터를 수집할 수 있게 해준다.
- [22] may look to these past successes and approve your project approach
  [22]가 과거의 이러한 성공 사례를 고려해 프로젝트 방식을 승인해 줄 수 있다.
- finding projects similar to your own may be difficult
  유사한 프로젝트를 찾는 일이 어려울 수 있다.

Focus Groups 포커스 그룹

- requires a group of between 8 and 15 people
  8명에서 15명 사이의 사람으로 구성된 그룹을 필요로 한다.
- useful for identifying the genuine [23] of a consumer base
  소비자 층의 진정한 [23]을 밝혀내는 데 유용하다.
- can generate additional [24] when sourcing a suitable external or internal group leader
  외부 또는 내부의 적합한 그룹 리더를 구할 때 추가적인 [24]을 발생시킬 수 있다.

Surveys 설문 조사

- saves time by having respondents do much of the work themselves
  답변자들에게 직접 많은 일을 하게 함으로써 시간을 절약할 수 있다.
- allows you to design survey questions focused on the specific [25] of your project
  프로젝트의 특정 [25]에 초점을 맞춘 설문 조사 질문들을 고안할 수 있게 해준다.

Prototypes 시제품

- allows modifications to be made based on [26]
  [26]을 바탕으로 변경이 이뤄지는 것을 가능하게 해준다.
- normally only useful in industries where [27] is used
  일반적으로 [27]가 이용되는 업계에서만 유용하다.

21. 벤치마킹의 장점 중 하나로 회사에 대한 위험 부담 없이 다른 회사의 성공으로부터 많은 것을 배울 수 있기에, 빈칸에 들어갈 정답은 risk이다.

Paraphrasing without any(~가 전혀 없이) → at no(~없이)
your company(당신의 회사) → your own firm(당신의 회사)
gather data(자료를 모으다)
→ learn a lot from the successes of other companies(다른 회사들의 성공으로부터 많은 것을 배우다)

ACTUAL TEST 2

22. 지문에는, 최종 승인을 받아야 할 시간이 다가올 때 경영진의 관점에서 프로젝트 접근 방식을 증명하도록 도움을 주는 데 유용할 수 있다는 말이 나오는데(It can also be useful to help you validate your project approach in the eyes of management when the time comes to seek final approval), 즉 경영진이 최종 승인을 해주는데 도움이 된다는 말이므로, 빈칸에 들어갈 정답은 management이고 대/소문자에 상관없이 정답이다.
Paraphrasing in the eyes of management(경영진의 시각에서) → management may look to(경영진이 고려할 수 있다)

23. 최종 소비자들의 진정한, 현실적인 니즈를 이해하는데 돕기에, 정답은 needs이다.
Paraphrasing identify(밝히다) → understand(이해하다)
genuine(진정한) → real(진정한)
customer base(소비자 층) → end users(최종 소바자들)

24. 외부 전문가 고용이나 내부 직원 교육 모두 추가적인 비용이 발생하므로, 정답은 expense이다.
Paraphrasing generate(발생시키다) → involve(수반하다)
additional(추가적인) → extra(추가적인)

25. 자신의 프로젝트 목적(목표)에 따라 설문 질문들이 조정될 수 있으므로, 빈칸에 정답은 objectives이다.
Paraphrasing design(고안하다) → tailor(조정하다)

26. 피드백을 향상시키는데 사용할 수 있으므로(feedback that you can utilize to make improvements), 변경의 기반인 feedback이 정답이다.
Paraphrasing modification(변경) → improvements(향상)

27. 시제품은 새로운 기술이 사용되는 산업에만 적합하다고 하므로, 정답은 technology이다. 한 단어만 정답이므로 new technology는 오답이다.
Paraphrasing useful(유용한) → suitable(적합한)

I Vocabulary & Expressions I
look to 고려하다 genuine 진정한 generate 생성시키다 source 구하다 respondent 답변자 modification 변경, 수정

▪ 파트 3 [문제 28-40]

출제 포인트 **난이도: 중**
제너럴 섹션 3(파트 3)는 아카데믹 리딩과 거의 동일한 주제, 유형, 난이도로 출제되기에 아카데믹 스타일 지문에 대한 독해 대비가 요구됨

Animal Extinction in Australia

Researcher and ecologist Professor James Sutton continues to investigate the reasons behind Australia's high rate of animal extinction

I first took an interest in Australia's animal extinction problem, and the various reasons behind it, when I joined a team of paleontologists who were searching for fossilized remains of the thylacine.

More than 90% of Australia's larger terrestrial vertebrates had become extinct by around 40 thousand years ago, with the notable exceptions being the Q28 kangaroo and

호주의 동물 멸종

연구가이자 생태학자인 제임스 서튼 교수가 호주의 높은 동물 멸종율 이면에 숨어 있는 이유를 지속적으로 연구하고 있다.

제가 처음 호주의 동물 멸종 문제 및 그 이면의 다양한 이유에 관심을 가진 시점이 태즈매니아 늑대의 화석화된 유해를 찾고 있던 고생물학자들로 구성된 팀에 합류했을 당시였습니다.

호주에서 90퍼센트가 넘는 대형 육상 척추동물들은 약 4만년 전쯤에 멸종되었는데, 주목할 만한 예외가 Q28 캥거루와 태즈매니아 늑대입니다. Q33 인간이 호주 내

the thylacine. Q33 Humans are likely to be one of the major factors in the extinction of many species in Australia, but one-factor explanations are overly simplistic, as climate change and bushfires are sure to have played a part.

많은 동물 종의 멸종에 있어 주요 요인들 중의 하나일 가능성이 있지만, 요인이 한 가지뿐인 설명은 지나칠 정도로 단순한 것인데, 그 이유는 기후 변화와 산불이 분명히 하나의 역할을 했기 때문입니다.

The thylacine was once the largest known carnivorous marsupial animal. It is often referred to as the Tasmanian Tiger, due to its striped lower back, although it shared more physical characteristics with a Q29 wolf. It was native to the Australian mainland, Tasmania, and New Guinea, and is thought to have become near-extinct on the mainland around two thousand years ago, although reliable accounts of small thylacine groups place them in parts of South Australia as late as the 1830s.

태즈매니아 늑대는 한때 가장 큰 것으로 알려진 육식성 유대목 동물입니다. 이 동물은 흔히 줄무늬가 있는 등 아래 부분으로 인해 태즈매니아 호랑이로 일컬어지지만, Q29 늑대와 더 많은 신체적 특징을 공유했습니다. 호주 본토와 태즈매니아, 그리고 뉴기니가 원산지였으며, 약 2천년 전에 본토에서 거의 멸종 상태가 되었던 것으로 여겨지고 있습니다. 비록 1830년 소규모 태즈매니아 늑대 무리들이 사우스오스트레일리아의 여러 지역에 존재했다는 신뢰할 만한 이야기가 있지만요.

Some experts believe that a major contributing factor to the decline in thylacine populations was the introduction of dingoes – a type of dog – by European Q30 settlers. Proponents of this theory argue that the thylacine directly competed with the dingo for food, based on the similar appearance of the two species. This is a plausible explanation, as examinations of thylacine skulls indicate that the animal was a less effective predator than the dingo. Furthermore, the thylacine's Q31 diet was far less versatile than that of the dingo, which would consume seeds, berries, and fish in the absence of mammals. However, Q34 a counter-argument can be made that the two animals were never in direct competition for prey, as the thylacine mainly hunted at night, while the dingo hunted during the day. A broader theory is that a combination of competition for food, hunting by indigenous populations, and Q32 habitat erosion, eventually led to the absolute extinction of the thylacine.

일부 전문가들은 태즈매니아 늑대 개체수의 감소에 기여한 주요 요인이 유럽의 Q30 정착민들에 의해 도입된 딩고(일종의 개)라고 생각하고 있습니다. 이 이론의 지지자들은 두 동물 종의 유사한 외모를 바탕으로 태즈매니아 늑대들이 먹이를 두고 딩고와 직접적으로 경쟁했다고 주장하고 있습니다. 이는 그럴듯한 설명인데, 태즈매니아 늑대 두개골을 조사한 내용에 따르면 이 동물은 딩고보다 덜 유능한 포식자였던 것으로 나타나기 때문입니다. 게다가, 태즈매니아 늑대가 Q31 먹는 음식은 딩고의 것보다 훨씬 덜 다양했는데, 딩고는 씨앗과 베리 종류의 열매, 그리고 포유류가 없는 곳에서는 생선도 먹었기 때문입니다. 하지만, Q34 두 동물은 절대로 먹이를 두고 직접적인 경쟁을 한 적이 없었다는 반대의 주장도 나타날 수 있는데, 태즈매니아 늑대가 주로 밤에 사냥한 반면, 딩고는 낮 시간에 사냥했기 때문입니다. 더 확장된 이론은, 먹이에 대한 경쟁과 토착 동물들에 의한 사냥, 그리고 Q32 서식지 침해가 복합적으로 나타나 결국 태즈매니아 늑대의 완전한 멸종으로 이어졌다는 것입니다.

The introduction of invasive species, both deliberately and accidentally, has been a recurring problem in Australia's history of animal extinction, especially in the case of native birds. Q40 One incident that had a catastrophic impact on biodiversity was the grounding of the SS Makambo in June, 1918. While repairs were underway, black rats left the ship and invaded the land. The rat population thrived, and, within only six years, directly caused the extinction of several endemic ground-nesting birds such as the Lord Howe thrush. Q35 The issue was exacerbated when an ecological solution was proposed and executed: the deliberate introduction of Tasmanian masked owls. This move was designed to eradicate the rat population, but in actual fact, the introduction of the predatory owls led to the extinction of yet more bird species, including the Lord Howe boobook.

의도적으로 그리고 우연히 외래 동물 종의 도입은 호주 동물 멸종의 역사에서 재발되어 온 문제점이며, 특히 토종 새들의 경우에 그러합니다. Q40 생물 다양성에 파멸적인 영향을 미친 한 사건이 1918년 6월에 있었던 SS 마캄보 호의 좌초였습니다. 수리 작업이 진행되는 동안, 곰쥐들이 그 배를 떠나 육지로 난입했습니다. 그 쥐의 개체수는 번성했으며, 불과 6년 만에, 로드 하우 개똥지빠귀와 같이 땅에 둥지를 짓는 여러 토종 새들의 멸종을 직접적으로 초래하게 되었습니다. Q35 이 문제는 생태학적 해결책인 태즈매니아 가면 올빼미의 의도적인 도입이 제안되고 실행되었을 때 악화되었습니다. 이 조치는 그 쥐의 개체수를 근절하기 위해 고안되었지만, 실제로는, 포식자인 올빼미의 도입이 로드 하우 솔부엉이를 포함해 더욱 더 많은 새 종의 멸종으로 이어졌습니다.

ACTUAL TEST 2

While carrying out my research into Australia's extinct species, one of the most troubling and mindless examples of direct human involvement I have come across is the case of the King Island emu. This subspecies of emu was endemic to King Island, situated between mainland Australia and Tasmania, and a sizable population had long thrived on the island's abundant berries and seaweed, with barely any threat from predators.

호주의 멸종 동물 종에 관한 연구를 실시하던 중에, 우연히 접하게 된 직접적인 인간 개입의 가장 골치 아프고 무분별했던 예시 중의 하나가 킹 아일랜드 에뮤의 경우였습니다. 이 하위 에뮤 종은 호주 본토와 태즈매니아 사이에 위치한 킹 아일랜드 토종 동물이었으며, 상당한 개체수가 그 섬의 풍부한 산딸기류 열매 및 해초를 먹으며 오랫동안 번성해 왔었고, 포식자들로부터 거의 어떠한 위협도 없는 상태였습니다.

In 1802, the French naturalist Francois Peron visited the island as part of an expedition. Much of what we know about the King Island emu comes from an interview Peron conducted with seal hunters who had settled on the island. Q38 These sealers boasted that they had killed and eaten an estimated 3,600 emus during their six-month stay on the island. Fires that they had started also contributed to a decline in the emu population. Although Peron reported that the island was still swarming with emus at the time of his visit, the population had been decimated by 1805, and the species was considered extinct in 1836 when English settlers found no trace of the birds. Q36 This example of human selfishness, and the impact of indiscriminate hunting practices, is something we should keep in mind in our modern age.

1802년에, 프랑스의 동식물 연구가 프랑수아 페론이 탐험의 일환으로 그 섬을 방문했습니다. 우리가 킹 아일랜드 에뮤에 관해 알고 있는 것의 많은 부분이 그 섬에 정착했던 바다표범 사냥꾼들을 대상으로 페론이 실시했던 인터뷰에서 비롯되었습니다. Q38 이 바다표범 사냥꾼들은 그 섬에서 머무른 6개월 동안 약 3,600마리의 에뮤를 죽이고 먹었다고 자랑했습니다. 그들이 놓기 시작한 불 또한 에뮤 개체수 감소의 원인이 되었습니다. 페론이 자신의 방문 당시에 여전히 그 섬에 에뮤가 무리 지어 다니고 있었다고 보고하기는 했지만, 그 개체수는 1805년경에 떼죽음을 당했으며, 이 동물 종은 1836년에 멸종된 것으로 여겨졌고 당시 잉글랜드인 정착민들은 그 새의 흔적도 찾지 못했습니다. Q36 인간 이기심과 무분별한 사냥 관행의 영향에 대한 이 예시는 현대를 사는 우리가 마음 속에 새겨 두어야 하는 것입니다.

This brings me to my most recent research, which concerns the Bramble Cay melomys, a species of rodent that was endemic to a vegetated region at the northern tip of the Great Barrier Reef. While species such as the King Island emu were wiped out due to human action, it can be argued that human inaction played a role in the extinction of the melomys.

이 사건은 가장 최근의 제 연구를 떠오르게 하는데, 그 연구는 그레이트 배리어 리프 북단의 초목 지역 토종 설치류의 한 종인 브램블 케이 멜로미스와 관련된 것이었습니다. 킹 아일랜드 에뮤와 같은 동물 종들이 인간의 행동으로 인해 말살되기는 했지만, 그 멜로미스의 멸종에 있어 인간의 무대책이 하나의 역할을 했다고 주장할 수 있습니다.

Q39 The habitat of the melomys rises only a few meters above sea level, making it vulnerable to severe weather conditions. The root cause of the mammal's extinction was sea-level rise as a result of global warming, but this loss was entirely foreseeable and preventable. It had been known for many years that flooding of the creature's habitat was becoming more frequent and severe. My own efforts, and those of my peers, to secure government funding for conservation programs were in vain. Part of the reason is that the animal is not as iconic or charismatic as a koala or kangaroo, so Q37 it does not receive much attention from the public or the government. Unfortunately, the fate of the melomys is emblematic of the failures in Australia's management of endangered species, which has seen the country record the highest rate of mammalian extinction in the world over the last two centuries.

Q39 멜로미스의 서식지는 해수면보다 불과 몇 미터 밖에 높지 않았는데, 이로 인해 악천후에 취약한 상태였습니다. 이 포유류 멸종의 근본적인 원인은 지구 온난화의 결과로 발생된 해수면 상승이었지만, 이 동물 종의 손실은 전적으로 예측 가능하고 예방 가능한 것이었습니다. 이 생물체 서식지의 범람이 점점 더 잦아지고 심각해지고 있었다는 사실은 오랫동안 알려져 있었습니다. 보존 프로그램에 필요한 정부의 자금을 확보하기 위한 저와 제 동료들의 노력도 소용없었습니다. 일부 이유는 그 동물이 코알라나 캥거루만큼 상징적이거나 카리스마가 있는 것이 아니라서 Q37 일반 대중이나 정부의 관심을 크게 받지 못했다는 점입니다. 안타깝게도, 멜로미스의 운명은 멸종 위기에 처한 동물 종에 대한 호주의 관리 실패를 상징하는 것이며, 이로 인해 호주는 지난 2세기 동안에 걸쳐 전 세계에서 가장 높은 포유류 멸종율을 기록해 왔습니다.

I Vocabulary & Expressions I

extinction 멸종 investigate 조사하다 paleontologist 고생물학자 fossilized 화석화된 remains 유해 thylacine 태즈매니아 늑대 terrestrial 육상의 vertebrate 척추 동물 extinct 멸종된 notable 주목할 만한 overly 지나치게 play a part 하나의 역할을 하다 carnivorous 육식의 marsupial 유대목 동물 be referred to as ~로 일컬어지다 physical characteristics 신체적 특징 native to ~가 원산지인 account 이야기 place 장소를 정하다 expert 전문가 contributing 원인이 되는, 기여하는 decline in ~의 감소 population 개체수 introduction 도입, 소개 settler 정착민 proponent 지지자 plausible 그럴듯한 explanation 설명 examination 조사, 연구 skull 두개골 predator 포식자 versatile 다양한 in the absence of ~가 없을 때 counter-argument 반론 prey 먹이 indigenous 토착의 habitat 서식지 erosion 침식, 침해 invasive species 외래 종 deliberately 의도적으로 accidentally 우연히 recurring 재발하는 catastrophic 파멸적인 biodiversity 생물 다양성 grounding 좌초 underway 진행 중인 invade 침입하다 thrive 번성하다 endemic 토종의, 고유의 exacerbate ~을 악화시키다 ecological 생태계의, 생태학적인 execute 실행하다 eradicate ~을 근절하다 yet more 더욱 더, 훨씬 더 carry out 실시하다 troubling 골치 아픈 mindless 무분별한 involvement 개입, 관여 come across 우연히 마주치다 subspecies 하위 종 sizable 상당한 abundant 풍부한 threat 위협 expedition 탐험, 탐사 boast 자랑하다 swarm 무리 지어 다니다 selfishness 이기심 indiscriminate 무분별한 practice 관행, 관례 keep A in mind A를 명심하다 concern ~와 관련되다 rodent 설치류 vegetated 초목이 있는 wipe out ~을 말살시키다 inaction 무대책, 활동 부족 vulnerable to ~에 취약한 severe weather 악천후 foreseeable 예측 가능한 preventable 예방 가능한 flooding 범람, 홍수 secure ~을 확보하다 funding 자금 (제공) conservation 보존, 보호 in vain 헛수고의 emblematic of ~을 상징하는 endangered 멸종 위기에 처한 mammalian 포유류의

문제 28-32

다음 요약 내용을 완성하시오. 지문에서 **오직 1개의 단어만** 각 빈칸에 적으시오.

The fate of the thylacine 태즈매니아 늑대의 운명

The thylacine and [28] were two of the only land vertebrates in Australia that were not already extinct 40,000 years ago. Despite being dubbed the Tasmanian tiger, the thylacine more closely resembled a [29]. Some researchers have argued that [30] are to blame for the decline in thylacine population, as they introduced dingoes to their habitat. It is believed that, because the dingo was a better predator and had more variety in its [31], it was able to thrive more easily than the thylacine. However, other factors such as hunting and the degradation of [32] most likely also played a part in the extinction of the thylacine.

태즈매니아 늑대와 [28]는 호주에서 4만년 전에 이미 멸종된 유이한 육상 척추 동물 두 가지였다. 태즈매니아 호랑이로 불렸음에도 불구하고, 태즈매니아 늑대는 [29]와 더 가깝게 닮았다. 일부 연구가들은 [30]가 태즈매니아 늑대 개체수 감소의 원인이라고 주장했는데, 그들이 서식지에 딩고를 도입했기 때문이었다. 딩고가 더 뛰어난 포식자였으며, 더 다양한 [31]가 있었기 때문에, 태즈매니아 늑대보다 더 쉽게 번성할 수 있었다고 여겨지고 있다. 하지만, 사냥 및 [32]의 악화와 같은 다른 요소들도 태즈매니아 늑대의 멸종에 있어 하나의 역할을 했을 가능성이 크다.

28. 4만년 전에 이미 멸종하지 않은 두가지 호주 육상 척추 동물은 캥거루와 태즈매니아 늑대이므로, 정답은 kangaroo이다. 본문에 나온 대로 단수형으로 써야 정답처리 되며, 한 글자만 정답이 되므로 the를 쓰면 오답이다.
Paraphrasing land(육상, 땅) → terrestrial(육상의, 땅의)

29. 신체적 특징을 더 많이 늑대와 공유하므로, 정답은 wolf이다.
Paraphrasing more closely resemble(더 가깝게 닮다) → share more physical characteristics(더 신체적 특징들을 공유하다)

30. 딩고를 갖고 온 사람들은 유럽인 정착민들이기에, 정답은 settlers이다. 참고로 두 글자 European settlers나, 지문에 없는 Europeans를 답으로 쓰면 틀린다.

ACTUAL TEST 2

31. 딩고와 비교해 볼 때 태즈매니아 늑대는 덜 다양한 음식을 섭취하므로, 빈칸에 들어갈 정답은 diet이다.

32. 태즈매니아 늑대의 멸종에 부분적으로 영향을 미친 것에 서식지 침해(habitat erosion)가 있으므로, 빈칸에 들어갈 정답은 habitat 이다.
Paraphrasing degradation(악화, 저하) → erosion(침식, 침해)

| Vocabulary & Expressions |
dubbed 별명이 붙은 degradation 악화, 저하

문제 33-37

정답을 고르시오.

33. What does the writer suggest about animal extinction in Australia?
글쓴이는 호주의 동물 멸종에 관해 무엇을 암시하는가?

A It is a trend that is slowing down.
그 경향이 둔화되고 있다.

B It is less severe than in other countries.
다른 국가들보다 덜 심각하다.

C There are typically several factors involved.
일반적으로 여러 요소들이 포함되어 있다.

D There is a lack of useful information.
유용한 정보가 부족하다.

첫 문단에서 글쓴이는 인간 외에 기후 변화와 산불을 원인으로 지적하므로, 다양한 원인이 있음을 말하는 C가 정답이다. A와 B는 마지막 문단과 오히려 배치되는 설명이고, D와 관련해서는 특별한 언급이 없기에 오답이다.

34. One significant difference between the thylacine and the dingo is their
태즈매니아 늑대와 딩고 사이에서 한 가지 상당히 다른 점은 그들의 ....이다.

A preferred time for seeking food.
먹이 찾는 일을 선호하는 시간대

B physical appearance.
신체적 외형

C reproduction cycle.
번식 주기

D ideal habitat.
이상적인 서식지

네 번째 문단에서 태즈매니아 늑대는 밤에, 딩고는 낮에 사냥하므로 먹이를 찾는 시간대가 다르다. 따라서 정답은 A이다. 세 번째 문단에서 두 동물은 유사한 외모를 가지고 있다고 하므로 B는 오답이다. 두 동물 간에, C, D와 관련해서 비교하는 내용은 본문에 없다.

35. In the fifth paragraph, what does the writer suggest about the Tasmanian masked owls?
다섯 번째 문단에서, 글쓴이는 태즈매니아 가면 올빼미에 관해 무엇을 암시하는가?

A They successfully caused a decline in the rat population.
성공적으로 쥐 개체수 감소를 초래했다.

B They competed with the Lord Howe thrush for food.
로드 하우 개똥지빠귀와 먹이를 두고 경쟁했다.

C Their extinction was caused by invasive rats.
쥐들의 침입에 의해 멸종이 초래되었다.

D Their introduction caused more harm than good.
도입에 따른 득보다 실이 더 많다.

태즈매니아 가면 올빼미 도입으로 인해 오히려 문제가 더 악화되었다고 하므로, 정답은 D이다. 다섯 번째 문단에서 태즈매니아 가면 올빼미가 곰쥐를 근절하려고 도입된 것이라는 것은 언급되었지만, 개체 수 감소가 되었는지 여부는 지문에서 언급되지 않았으므로 A는 오답이다. 같은 문단에서 쥐들의 침입으로 멸종한 것은 토종 새라고 하므로 C도 오답이다. 마지막으로 B에서 언급된 로드 하우 개똥지빠귀는 태즈매니아 가면 올빼미의 도입으로 인해 멸종된 토종 새의 예시로 제시된 새로, 먹이를 두고 경쟁했다는 주장이 있었던 것은 태즈매니아 늑대와 딩고이다.
Paraphrasing more harm(더 많은 해) → be exacerbated(악화되다)

36. When describing the theory of how the King Island emu became extinct, the writer is
킹 아일랜드 에뮤가 어떻게 멸종되었는지에 대한 이론을 설명할 때, 글쓴이는 ....

A surprised that the species did not vanish sooner.
그 동물 종이 더 빨리 사라지지 않았다는 점에 놀랐다.

B disheartened by a past display of human ignorance.
과거에 보여진 인간의 무지에 낙심했다.

C confused about which predators preyed on the species.
어느 포식자가 그 동물 종을 잡아먹었는지에 대해 혼란스러웠다.

D disappointed that conservation efforts proved unsuccessful.
보존 노력이 성공적이지 못한 것으로 드러난 사실에 실망했다.

킹 아일랜드 에뮤가 언급되는 일곱 번째 문단 마지막 문장에서 글쓴이는 인간의 이기심과 무분별한 사냥 관행에 대해 비판하고 있으므로, 정답은 인간에 대해 낙심한 진술인 B이다.

37. Which of the following best summarises the writer's point in the final paragraph?
다음 중 어느 것이 마지막 문단에서 글쓴이가 말하는 요점을 가장 잘 요약하고 있는가?

A Public awareness about environmental issues is at an all-time low.
환경 문제에 대한 일반 대중의 의식이 역대 가장 낮다.

B Humans should refrain from encroaching on vulnerable habitats.
인간이 취약한 동물 서식지에 침입하는 일을 삼가야 한다.

C The government should do more to combat extinction.
정부가 멸종을 방지하기 위해 더 많은 일을 해야 한다.

D The extinction of the Bramble Cay melomys was inevitable.
브램블 케이 멜로미스의 멸종은 불가피한 것이었다.

마지막 문단에서 글쓴이는 대중과 정부의 관심과 도움이 충분하지 못해, 결국 멜로미스에 대해 막을 수 있는 멸종을 막지 못한 안타까움을 나타낸다. 이는 정부와 대중이 더 노력해야 한다는 의미를 담고 있으므로, 정답은 C이다. A처럼 일반 대중의 의식이 지금 '가장' 낮은지는 글에서 찾을 수 없는 내용이며, B 역시 인간이 멜로미스와 같은 동물들 서식지에 침입한지에 대해서는 나오지 않는다. D에서처럼 멜로미스의 멸종은 불가피한 것이 아니고, 정부의 노력으로 피할 수 있었다. 따라서 A, B, D는 오답이다.

I Vocabulary & Expressions I

reproduction cycle 번식 주기 invasive 침해의, 침략하는 vanish 사라지다 disheartened 실망한 encroach 침해하다, 잠식하다 vulnerable 취약한 combat ~와 싸우다 inevitable 피할 수 없는

문제 38-40

다음 내용(문제 38~40)과 아래의 선사 시대 동물 목록을 보시오. 각 내용을 A, B, C 또는 D에 해당하는 알맞은 동물과 일치시키시오.

38. Humans actively killed off many of this species for food.
인간이 식량을 위해 이 동물 종을 많이 죽여 없앴다.

ACTUAL TEST 2

킹 아일랜드 에뮤가 언급되는 일곱 번째 문단에 에뮤를 단기간에 많이 잡아먹었다고 나오므로, 정답은 C이다.
Paraphrasing human(인간) → sealer(바다표범 사냥꾼)
for food(식량으로) → eat(먹다)

39. This species became extinct as a result of climate change.
이 동물 종은 기후 변화에 따른 결과로 멸종되었다.

마지막 두 문단에 브램블 케이 멜로미스의 멸종 원인으로 심각한 날씨 상황과 지구 온난화가 언급되므로, 기후 변화에 따른 멸종 동물은 D이다.
Paraphrasing climate change(기후 변화) → severe weather conditions(심각한 날씨 상황), global warming(지구 온난화)

40. A sailing accident led to the extinction of this species.
항해 관련 사고가 이 동물 종의 멸종으로 이어졌다.

다섯 번째 문단에서 배의 좌초로 인해 로드 하우 개똥지빠귀의 멸종이 이어졌으므로, 정답은 B이다.
Paraphrasing sailing accident(항해 사고) → grounding of the SS Makambo(SS 마캄보 호의 좌초)

List of Extinct Species 멸종 동물 종의 목록

A Tasmanian tiger 태즈매니아 호랑이
B Lord Howe thrush 로드 하우 개똥지빠귀
C King Island emu 킹 아일랜드 에뮤
D Bramble Cay melomys 브램블 케이 멜로미스

I Vocabulary & Expressions I
actively 적극적으로 kill off ~을 대대적으로 죽이다 sailing 항해

Test 2 WRITING [Academic]

▪ 파트 1

출제 포인트 **난이도: 중**

표 문제는 보통 표 하나만 나오는 경우보다는 다른 도표와 같이 나오거나 아니면 표 두 개가 함께 나오는 경우가 일반적인데, 두 개의 데이터를 비교하여 설명할 수 있는지가 출제 포인트임

기출 2018년 11월 - 6개국의 2000년, 2050년 60세 이상 인구 표

The tables below give information about production and consumption of coffee in 2017 and 2018 in five coffee-exporting countries.
아래 표는 5개 커피 수출 국가들의 2017년과 2018년 커피 생산과 소비에 관한 정보를 준다.

커피 생산과 소비(단위: 백만 커피 포대)

생 산	2017	2018
브라질	52.7	61.7
콜롬비아	13.8	14.2
인도네시아	10.8	10.2
멕시코	4.4	4.5
베트남	30.5	29.5

소 비	2017	2018
브라질	21.2	22.0
콜롬비아	1.7	1.8
인도네시아	4.7	4.7
멕시코	2.4	2.5
베트남	2.4	2.4

* 한 포대는 60 kg이다.

The tables below indicate the amount of coffee prepared for the market and used domestically in 2017 and 2018 in five countries with major coffee exports. Overall, each country produced more coffee than it consumed, and the statistics generally remained steady between the two years, with one clear exception.

When comparing the two tables, one can readily see that the five countries produced more coffee than they consumed. This distinct contrast was most notable in two countries in particular: Columbia and Vietnam. Columbia produced 13.8 and 14.2 million bags of coffee in 2017 and 2018, respectively, but only consumed 1.7 and 1.8 million. Likewise, Vietnam produced around 30 million bags and consumed a mere 2.4 million in both years.

Between 2017 and 2018, the consumption and production numbers varied very little, with a positive or negative change of 1 million bags or fewer in most countries' production, and even less fluctuation regarding their consumption. The only exception to this trend is Brazil, whose production numbers soared from 52.7 in 2017 to 61.7 in 2018.

(174 words)

아래 표는 2017년과 2018년에 5개 주요 커피 수출국에서 시장을 위해 준비된 커피 및 국내 사용된 커피의 양을 보여준다. 전반적으로, 각 국가는 소비된 것보다 더 많은 커피를 생산했고, 통계치는 대체로 제시된 두 해 간에, 분명한 하나를 제외하고 변동이 없었다.

두 표를 비교할 때, 다섯 국가들이 소비했던 것보다 더 많은 커피를 생산했음을 쉽게 알 수 있다. 이 분명한 대비는 특히 두 국가, 콜롬비아와 베트남에서 가장 잘 알 수 있다. 콜롬비아는 1380만과 1420만 커피 포대를 2017년과 2018년에 각각 생산했지만, 단지 170만과 180만 포대를 소비했다. 마찬가지로, 베트남은 두 해 모두 약 3000만 포대를 생산하고 단지 240만 포대를 소비했다.

2017년과 2018년 간에, 소비와 생산 수치는 매우 적게 변동했는데, 대부분의 국가 생산량에 있어 플러스/마이너스 백만 포대 이내의 차이였으며, 소비에서는 더 적은 변동이 있었다. 이러한 추세의 유일한 예외는 브라질로, 생산 수치가 2017년 5270만에서 2018년 6170만으로 치솟았다.

I Vocabulary & Expressions I

domestically 국내적으로 notable 주목할 만한 fluctuation 변동 soar 급등하다, 치솟다

ACTUAL TEST 2

■ **파트 2**

출제 포인트 **난이도: 중상**

환경 관련 문제 및 원인, 그리고 그에 대한 해결책은 최근 아이엘츠 빈출 토픽임

기출 2024년 6월 - 석유, 삼림, 담수 등의 천연 자원을 함부로 사용하는 것에 대한 문제와 해결책

Natural resources, such as oil, forests and freshwater, are being consumed at an alarming rate all around the world.
전 세계적으로 석유, 삼림, 담수 등의 천연 자원이 놀라운 속도로 소비되고 있다.

What problems does this cause?
이로 인해 어떤 문제가 발생하는가?

How can we solve these problems?
이러한 문제를 어떻게 해결할 수 있을까?

Natural resources are under increasing strain, raising serious global concerns. In particular, the rapid consumption of oil, a nonrenewable resource, as well as freshwater and forests, which are renewable resources, is especially alarming. This essay discusses some key challenges and suggests potential solutions to the problems.

The strain on natural resources presents several significant challenges. Nonrenewable resources are especially limited, meaning they cannot be replenished once consumed. Once they are depleted, it could trigger an energy crisis, leading to energy shortages and increased prices for the remaining resources. This scenario could disrupt transport, industry and daily life, as oil is a primary energy source globally. Furthermore, the depletion of renewable resources often goes unnoticed because they are mistakenly viewed as expendable. Overexploitation of renewable resources, such as draining streams for water or excessive logging of forests, can quickly lead to their inability to recover.

Several solutions can address the challenges posed by the depletion of natural resources. A crucial step is to shift towards alternative energy sources. For instance, transitioning from petrol cars to electric ones can help alleviate the dependency on fossil fuels and mitigate the risk of an energy crisis. Investing in renewable energy technologies such as solar and wind power can provide sustainable alternatives that are less harmful to the environment. Additionally, it is important to manage renewable resources responsibly. Practices such as recycling water and sustainably sourcing wood can help protect water reserves and forests.

천연 자원은 점점 더 압박을 받고 있어 전 세계적으로 심각한 우려를 불러일으키고 있다. 재생 불가능한 자원인 석유는 물론 담수 및 산림의 재생 가능한 자원에 대한 빠른 소비는 특히 우려스럽다. 이 글에서는 몇 가지 주요 문제에 대해 논의하고 이 문제에 대한 잠재적인 해결책을 제시한다.

천연 자원에 대한 부담은 몇 가지 중요한 문제를 제시한다. 재생 불가능한 자원은 특히 한정되어 있어 한 번 소비되면 다시 보충할 수 없다. 일단 고갈되면, 에너지 위기가 촉발되어, 에너지 부족과 남은 자원의 가격 상승으로 이어질 수 있다. 석유는 전 세계적으로 주요 에너지원이기에, 이러한 시나리오는 교통, 산업, 일상생활에 지장을 줄 수 있다. 더욱이, 재생 가능한 자원은 소모품으로 잘못 인식되기에, 그 고갈을 간과하는 경우가 많다. 물을 얻기 위해 하천을 빼내 가거나 과도한 삼림 벌목 등 재생 가능한 자원의 과잉 개발은 자원이 회복할 수 없도록 빠르게 이끈다.

천연 자원의 고갈로 인해 제기된 문제를 해결할 수 있는 몇 가지 해결책이 있다. 가장 중요한 단계는 대체 에너지원으로 전환하는 것이다. 예를 들어, 석유 차에서 전기차로 전환하면 화석 연료에 대한 의존도를 낮추고 에너지 위기의 위험을 완화할 수 있다. 태양열 및 풍력 발전과 같은 재생 에너지 기술에 투자하면 환경에 덜 해로운 지속 가능한 대안을 제공할 수 있다. 또한, 재생 가능한 자원을 책임감 있게 관리하는 것도 중요하다. 물을 재활용하고 지속 가능한 방식으로 목재를 조달하는 등의 실천은 수자원과 산림을 보호하는 데 도움이 될 수 있다.

In conclusion, while the decreasing supply of natural resources poses numerous problems, a shift towards alternative energy sources and responsible resource management can help tackle these obstacles. By implementing these solutions, we can work towards a more sustainable future, ensuring that both current and future generations have access to the resources they need.

(292 words)

결론적으로, 천연자원의 공급 감소는 많은 문제를 야기하지만, 대체 에너지원으로의 전환과 책임 있는 자원 관리는 이러한 장애물을 해결하는 데 도움이 될 수 있다. 이러한 해결책을 시행함으로써 우리는 보다 지속 가능한 미래를 향해 노력하여, 현재와 미래 세대 모두가 필요한 자원을 이용하도록 보장할 수 있다.

| Vocabulary & Expressions |

strain 압박 concern 우려, 걱정 consumption 소비 renewable 재생 가능한 alarming 걱정스러운, 우려스러운 challenge 문제, 과제 replenish 보충하다, 다시 채우다 depleted 고갈된 shortage 부족 disrupt 지장을 주다 depletion 고갈 unnoticed 간과되는 expendable 소모용의 overexploitation (천연자원의) 과잉 개발 drain 빼내 가다, 소모시키다 excessive 과도한 logging 벌목 posed 제기된 alternative energy 대체 에너지 transition 전환하다 alleviate 완화하다 dependency 의존도 fossil fuel 화석 연료 alternatives 대안 practice 실천, 관행 reserve 보호 구역 obstacle 장애물 implement 시행하다 access 이용하다, 접근하다

Test 2 WRITING [General Training]

▪ 파트 1

출제 포인트 난이도: 중

지역 자치단체에 요청 또는 제안하는 formal letter는 빈출 문제인데, 논리적으로 자신의 의견을 각 포인트에 맞게 모두 기술해야 됨

기출 2017년 7월 - 지역 자치단체에 관광 시설 제안

Your local council has a plan to build some tourist facilities to attract more tourists to the town. The council has advertised for the residents to suggest ideas for the plan.
당신의 지역 의회는 마을에 더 많은 관광객들을 끌어들일 관광 시설을 지을 계획이다. 의회는 주민들이 계획에 대한 아이디어를 제안해달라고 광고를 하고 있다.

Write a letter to your local council. In your letter 당신의 지역 의회에 편지를 써라. 당신의 편지에는

- describe the importance of the tourism in your town
  당신 마을에 관광의 중요성을 기술한다
- explain what kind of facility you recommend
  당신이 어떤 유형의 시설을 제안하는지 설명하라
- say why you think the facility could be appropriate for the plan
  왜 당신은 그 시설이 계획에 적합하다고 생각하는지 말해라

Dear Sir or Madam, I recently learned that the town council intends to construct new tourist attractions in our town to encourage more visitors to come. Since you are taking suggestions from residents, I would like to share some of my thoughts. As you are aware, tourism is a major economic factor in our town. The tourist season brings thousands of people to our beachside town, and most businesses depend on this period to meet their annual profit goals. Therefore, whatever improves our local tourism directly affects the financial wellbeing of our town and residents. To this end, I believe demolishing the older buildings downtown and constructing small luxury hotels would attract more tourists. Currently, most visitors reserve rooms in standard hotels outside of town. Providing high-quality accommodation in town, closer to the beach, would surely be a more attractive choice. Replacing these dilapidated buildings would also complete two goals at once: it would further beautify our town, and wealthier tourists would be more likely to visit and spend money at local businesses. I hope that you will consider my proposal. Thank you. Yours faithfully, Eric Kim (187 words)	관계자분께, 저는 최근에 마을(시) 의회가 더 많은 방문객이 오도록 장려하기 위해 새로운 관광 명소를 지을 계획이라는 것을 알았습니다. 여러분이 지역민으로부터 제안을 받아들이고 있기에, 저는 제 몇몇 생각을 나누길 원합니다. 아시다시피, 관광은 우리 마을에 주요한 경제 요소입니다. 관광 시즌은 수천 명의 사람들을 우리 해변가 마을로 불러들이고, 대부분 업체들이 이 기간에 의존하여 연간 수익 목표를 맞춥니다. 그러므로 우리 지역 관광을 향상시키는 무엇이든지 우리 마을과 주민의 경제적 안녕에 직접적으로 영향을 미칩니다. 이 때문에, 저는 오래된 시내 건물들을 부수고 작은 고급 호텔들을 짓는 것이 더 많은 관광객들을 불러들일 것이라고 믿습니다. 현재, 대부분 관광객들은 마을 밖에 있는 일반 호텔 방을 예약합니다. 해변에 더 가깝게, 마을에서 고품질 숙박을 제공하는 것은 확실히 더 매력적인 선택일 것입니다. 이러한 다 허물어져가는 건물들을 대체하는 것은 또한 두가지 목적을 동시에 달성하게 합니다: 마을을 더 아름답게 하고 더 부유한 관광객들이 방문하여 지역 사업에 돈을 소비할 가능성이 더 높아질 것입니다. 저는 여러분이 제 제안을 고려하길 희망합니다. 감사합니다. 에릭 김 올림

I Vocabulary & Expressions I

encourage A to B A가 B하도록 장려하다 factor 요소 beachside 해변가 wellbeing 안녕 dilapidated 다 허물어져 가는 beautify 아름답게 하다, 꾸미다 to this end 이 목적을 위하여

▪ 파트 2

출제 포인트 **난이도: 중상**

광고가 소비에 미치는 영향은 아이엘츠에 빈출하는 토픽으로, 충분한 브레인스토밍을 통해 자신만의 의견을 논리적으로 기술하는 것이 중요함

기출 2019년 1월 - 광고의 긍정적/부정적 영향
2018년 10월 -광고의 긍정적/부정적 영향

Some people say that a product's success in the market does not reflect the real needs of consumers, but rather just the power of advertising.
어떤 사람들은 시장에서 제품의 성공이 소비자의 진정한 필요성이 아닌, 오히려 광고의 힘만 반영한다고 말한다.
What is your opinion about this?
이에 대한 당신의 의견은 무엇인가?

There is an ongoing debate about the factors that drive a product's success in the market. Some argue that consumer needs are the primary influence, while others believe that advertising plays a more significant role. Although I recognise that consumer needs contribute to the success of a product, I believe that advertising is more impactful.

Admittedly, many products succeed when they fulfil consumer needs. Specifically, everyday items tend to attract demand even without extensive advertising. For instance, basic groceries, cleaning supplies and healthcare products consistently achieve high sales as people purchase these products out of necessity. Additionally, there is a constant demand for quality products at reasonable prices. Despite minimal advertising, products that meet these requirements often report huge success in the market, driven largely by word-of-mouth recommendations.

Nevertheless, I am of the opinion that advertising has a more profound effect on a product's success by influencing consumer behaviour. One way businesses achieve this is by appealing to personal preferences through targeted advertisements. For example, websites tend to display advertisements based on an individual's online activity by showcasing products that align with their interests, often resulting in purchases. Furthermore, advertising takes advantage of people's desire to follow trends. Popular influencers on platforms such as YouTube and Instagram aggressively promote products to their followers, whether they are the latest fashion items, gadgets or mobile devices. Although these products may not be essential, they sell well due to the desire to fit in.

In conclusion, while fulfilling consumer needs is important for a product's success, advertising plays a crucial role in shaping consumer behaviour and driving sales. As a result, products can achieve remarkable revenue through effective advertising strategies.

(277 words)

시장에서 제품의 성공을 이끄는 요인에 대한 논쟁이 계속되고 있다. 어떤 사람들은 소비자의 니즈가 가장 큰 영향을 미친다고 주장하는 반면, 다른 사람들은 광고가 더 중요한 역할을 한다고 믿는다. 나는 소비자의 니즈가 제품의 성공에 기여한다는 것은 인정하지만, 광고가 더 큰 영향을 미친다고 생각한다.

인정하는 바와 같이, 많은 제품이 소비자의 니즈를 충족시킬 때 성공한다. 특히, 일상용품은 대대적인 광고 없이도 수요를 끌어들이는 경향이 있다. 예를 들어, 기본 식료품, 청소용품, 건강 관리 제품은 사람들이 필요에 의해 구매하기 때문에 꾸준히 높은 매출을 달성한다. 또한, 합리적인 가격의 고품질 제품에 대한 수요도 꾸준히 존재한다. 최소한의 광고에도 불구하고, 이러한 요건을 충족하는 제품들은 종종 시장에서 큰 성공을 알리는데, 주로 입소문을 타고 이루어진다.

그럼에도 불구하고, 나는 광고가 소비자 행동에 영향을 미침으로써 제품의 성공에 더 큰 영향을 미친다고 생각한다. 기업이 이를 달성하는 한 가지 방법은 타겟 광고를 통해 개인의 선호도에 호소하는 것이다. 예를 들어, 웹사이트는 개인의 온라인 활동을 기반으로 관심사에 맞는 제품을 보여줌으로써 광고를 표시하는 경향이 있으며, 이는 종종 구매로 이어지기도 한다. 또한, 광고는 트렌드를 따르고자 하는 사람들의 욕구를 이용한다. 유튜브나 인스타그램과 같은 플랫폼의 인기 인플루언서들은 최신 패션 아이템, 장치, 모바일 기기 등 다양한 제품을 팔로워들에게 매우 적극적으로 홍보한다. 이러한 제품은 필수품이 아닐지라도 어울리고 싶은 욕구 때문에 잘 팔린다.

결론적으로, 제품의 성공을 위해서는 소비자의 니즈를 충족시키는 것도 중요하지만, 광고는 소비자 행동을 형성하고 판매를 촉진하는 데 중요한 역할을 한다. 따라서 제품은 효과적인 광고 전략을 통해 놀라운 수익을 달성할 수 있다.

| Vocabulary & Expressions |

ongoing 계속되는 contribute to ~에 기여하다 impactful 큰 영향을 미치는, 강렬한 admittedly 인정하는 바와 같이, 확실히 extensive 대대적인, 광범위한 align with ~에 맞추어 조정하다 aggressively 공격적으로, 매우 적극적으로 gadget 장치, 도구, 기기 fit in 맞다, 어울리다 shape 형성하다 revenue 수익

Test 2 SPEAKING [Academic / General Training]

▪ 파트 1

[Weather] 날씨

Let's talk about weather.
날씨에 대해 이야기해보죠.

Q What kind of weather do you like? [Why?]
당신은 어떤 날씨를 좋아하나요? [왜죠?]

A I love cool weather like the weather in autumn, when the skies are blue and sunny, but it does not feel too warm or humid. I love to walk or jog in the fresh air without worrying about getting a sunburn. In addition, I believe the cool weather has a positive effect on my biorhythms, resulting in better moods and behaviour.

저는 가을 날씨처럼 시원한 날씨를 좋아하는데, 하늘은 파랗고 햇빛이 비치지만 너무 덥거나 습하지 않죠. 저는 햇볕에 피부가 타는 것에 대한 걱정없이 신선한 공기 속에서 걷거나 조깅하는 것을 좋아합니다. 또한, 저는 시원한 날씨가 제 생체 리듬에 좋은 영향을 주어서, 더 나은 기분과 행동으로 이어진다고 믿습니다.

* humid 습한 sunburn 햇볕에 피부가 타는 것 biorhythm 생체리듬 result in ~로 귀결되다 mood 기분 behaviour 행동 (미국식 behavior)

Q How often is the weather cold in your country?
당신 국가에서는 얼마나 자주 날씨가 춥나요?

A Winter, which is from December to February, is severely cold in my country, South Korea. But you would also feel cold in November and March, before and after the winter months. So, I would say that almost half of the year is cold in my country.

겨울은 12월부터 2월까지인데, 한국에서는 매우 춥죠. 그러나 겨울 전후인 11월과 3월에도 춥다고 느끼실 거예요. 그래서 저는 우리나라가 거의 1년에 반이 춥다고 말씀드릴 수 있네요.

[Food and Cooking] 음식과 요리

Let's go on to talk about food and cooking.
음식이나 요리에 대해 이야기해보죠.

Q What sorts of food do you like most? [Why?]
어떤 종류의 음식을 가장 좋아하나요? [왜죠?]

A I've always had a sweet tooth, so I'm a big fan of desserts, especially cakes and pastries. I try not to eat too many baked goods, but when I need to relax after a stressful day, a slice of carrot cake really hits the spot.

저는 항상 단 음식을 좋아해왔는데, 그래서 디저트, 특히 케이크와 페이스트리를 엄청 좋아합니다. 저는 빵류를 너무 많이 먹지 않으려고 하지만, 스트레스 많은 하루를 보내고 쉬려고 할 때, 한 조각의 당근 케익은 딱입니다.

* have a sweet tooth 단 음식을 좋아하다 hit the spot 딱이다

Q Do you prefer to eat out or eat at home? [Why?]

당신은 외식 또는 집밥 중에 무엇을 선호하나요? [왜죠?]

A I prefer to eat out. After working all day, I simply don't have the energy to go home and cook myself a healthy meal, so, when I do cook at home, I make something quick and easy, like ramen. That's why, most nights, I go to a local mom-and-pop restaurant where a kind old lady makes me a delicious, well-balanced meal. It has actually become a nice routine.

저는 외식을 선호합니다. 하루 종일 일한 후에, 저는 집에 가서 건강한 식사를 직접 요리할 에너지가 없기에, 제가 집에서 요리할 때는, 라면처럼 빠르고 간단한 것을 만듭니다. 그래서 제가 대부분 밤에 친절한 할머니가 맛있고 균형 잡힌 식사를 제공하는 근처 동네 식당에 갑니다. 그것은 정말 기분 좋은 일과가 되었죠.

* mom-and-pop restaurant 동네 식당 well-balanced 균형 잡힌 routine 일과

Q What kind of new food would you like to try? [Why?]

당신은 어떤 종류의 새로운 음식을 먹어보고 싶나요? [왜죠?]

A I would love to try some Indian foods such as chapati and naan. My Indian friends staying in Korea told me that they are oven-baked flatbreads and are staple foods in their country. Since I enjoy flour-based foods, I really want to try Indian-style bread. Unfortunately, however, most Indian dishes are not common in our city, so it would be difficult for me to get the chance to taste them.

저는 차파티나 난과 같은 인도 음식을 먹어보길 원합니다. 한국에 있는 제 인도 친구들이 그것들은 오븐에서 구운 평평한 빵으로 인도의 주식이라고 말해줬어요. 저는 밀가루 음식을 즐기기에, 정말 인도식 빵을 먹어보고 싶습니다. 그러나 불행하게도 대부분 인도 음식은 제가 사는 도시에서 흔하지 않기에 그것들을 맛볼 기회를 잡기가 어려울 것 같네요.

* staple food 주식 flour-based food 밀가루 음식 common 흔한

Q Do you watch cookery programmes on TV? [Why/Why not?]

당신은 TV에서 요리 프로그램을 보나요? [왜죠 / 왜 아니죠?]

A Yes, there are a few cookery programmes that I enjoy. I especially like the competitive ones where the contestants try to cook the best dish. It's fascinating to see the various ways the chefs use the same ingredients.

네, 제가 즐기는 몇몇 요리 프로그램들이 있습니다. 저는 특별히 참가자들이 최고의 음식을 요리하기 위해 경쟁하는 프로를 좋아합니다. 요리사들이 같은 재료를 갖고 다양한 방법으로 요리하는 것을 보는 것은 매혹적입니다.

* programme 프로그램(미국식 program) competitive 경쟁적인 contestant 참가자 fascinating 매혹적인 ingredient 식재료

▪ 파트 2

Describe something you bought and like. You should say: what you purchased where you bought it why you like it and explain why it is so memorable to you.	당신이 산 물건 중 좋아하는 것을 말해보세요. 당신은 다음에 대해 말해야 합니다: 무엇을 구매했는지 어디에서 그것을 샀는지 왜 그것을 좋아하는지 그리고 왜 그것이 당신 기억에 남는지 설명하세요.

[브레인스토밍]

무엇: wireless earbuds, was reluctant to buy them – 어디에서: popular shopping website, free express shipping – 왜: comfortable & easy to use, sound quality is excellent – 기억에 남는 이유: listen to music during commutes and working, enhances that part of my life

[문법]

목적격 관계대명사 accessories that I have recently purchased 최근에 구매한 액세서리

현재완료시제 I've always been fine 항상 좋았었다

After + 현재분사구문 after seeing my friends 내 친구를 본 후에

콤마 + 관계대명사 , which I wasn't expecting 그건 예상하지 못했다

접속사 while while I was running 달리기를 하는 동안

[모범답변]

My new favourite accessories that I have recently purchased are my wireless earbuds. I was reluctant to buy them because I've always been fine with regular wired earbuds. But after seeing my friends with wireless ones, I thought I'd give them a try, too.

제가 가장 좋아하는 최신 악세사리는 최근에 구매한 무선 이어폰입니다. 저는 무선 이어폰을 사는 것에 대해 꺼렸는데요, 왜냐하면 저는 항상 일반 유선 이어폰이 괜찮았거든요. 하지만 제 친구들이 무선 이어폰을 갖고 있는 것을 본 후에, 한번 시도하자고 생각했습니다.

I knew a good pair of wireless earbuds would likely be more expensive in a store, so I bought them online off a popular shopping website. I feel like I had good timing because the pair I chose were also on sale. They even came with free express shipping, so they arrived in no time.

저는 좋은 무선 이어폰은 상점에서 더 비쌀 것임을 알아서, 유명 쇼핑 웹사이트에서 샀습니다. 제가 선택했던 이어폰이 또한 할인 중이어서 좋은 타이밍이라고 생각했습니다. 이어폰은 무료 속달이 포함되었기에, 순식간에 도착했습니다.

I was hesitant to make the switch to wireless earbuds because I thought they'd be inconvenient. I was positive they would fall out of my ear and then disappear, so they'd be a waste of money. But, they're actually quite comfortable and easy to use. They fit snugly in my ear, so I don't worry about losing them. On top of that, the sound quality is excellent, which I wasn't expecting. Best of all, they've been fantastic for exercising. My earbud cord used to always get in my way while I was running, but that's no longer an issue.

저는 무선이 불편하리라 생각했기에 무선으로 바꾸는 것에 망설였습니다. 저는 귀에서 이어폰이 떨어져 나가 그것을 잃어버려 돈 낭비가 될 거라고 확신했습니다. 그러나 실은 꽤 편안하고 사용하기 쉬웠습니다. 이어폰은 제 귀에 딱 맞았기에, 이어폰을 잃어버릴 걱정이 없었습니다. 그에 더하여, 음질이 뛰어났는데, 이는 제가 예상하지 않았죠. 무엇보다도, 운동할 때 환상적입니다. 제가 달리기 하는 동안 이어폰 선이 항상 방해가 되었지만, 이제는 더 이상 문제가 아니죠.

Since I constantly listen to music during my commutes and while working, any purchase that enhances that part of my life is memorable to me. Now I take my earbuds with me anywhere I go. They've become a must-have item for me, so I always have my smartphone in one pocket and my earbuds in the other whenever I leave the house. That is all that I can say now.

제가 출근하거나 일하는 동안에 끊임없이 음악을 듣기에, 제 삶의 그러한 부분을 향상시키는 어떠한 구매도 제게는 기억에 남죠. 이제 저는 제 이어폰을 어디에 가든지 갖고 갑니다. 그것은 제게 필수 소지품이 되었기에, 저는 집을 나설 때 항상 주머니 한쪽에는 스마트폰을, 다른 한쪽에는 이어폰을 챙깁니다. 이것이 제가 지금 말할 수 있는 전부입니다.

* earbuds 이어폰 reluctant 꺼리는 fine with ~에 괜찮은 give A a try A를 한번 해보다 off ~에서(구어체) on sale 할인 판매 중인, 구매 가능한 express shipping 속달, 빠른 배송 in no time 당장, 곧, 순식간에 hesitant 망설이는 positive 확신하는 fall out of ~로부터 떨어져 나오다 disappear 사라지다 a waste of money 돈 낭비 fit snugly 딱 맞다 on top of that 그에 더하여, 뿐만 아니라 best of all 무엇보다 cord 선 used to부정사 ~하곤 했었다(과거에는 그랬지만 현재는 아님을 뜻함) get in one's way ~에게 방해가 되다 constantly 끊임없이 commute 통근 purchase 구매, 구매하다 enhance 향상시키다 must-have item 반드시 갖고 있어야 하는 물품

[Rounding-off Question] 마무리 질문

Q Is this item famous in your country or other countries?
당신 나라 또는 다른 나라에서 이 물품이 유명한가요?

A I see people using wireless earbuds everywhere I go nowadays, especially on the subway. It seems that they're quite trendy right now. They were originally developed by a popular American tech company, so I'm sure they're popular in other countries although I haven't seen for myself. Overall, I think it's another step forward in tech, and soon everyone will have them, just like smartphones.

저는 요즘 어디를 가든지, 특히 전철에서, 사람들이 무선 이어폰을 사용하는 것을 봅니다. 무선 이어폰이 이제 꽤 유행인 것처럼 보입니다. 무선 이어폰은 원래 미국에 유명한 기술 회사에 의해 개발되었기에, 비록 직접 보지는 못했지만 다른 나라에서도 인기있으리라 확신합니다. 대체로 보아, 저는 기술에 또다른 진보이고, 곧 모든 사람들이 스마트폰처럼 무선 이어폰을 갖고 있을 것입니다.

* trendy 유행하는, 최신 유행의 tech company 기술 회사 step forward 진보

▪ 파트 3

[Buy Things] 물건 사기

Q What are the advantages of internet shopping?
무엇이 인터넷 쇼핑의 장점인가요?

A The best advantages of internet shopping are convenience and affordability. You can browse through a nearly limitless selection of goods all from the comfort of your home. No matter how bizarre or obscure the item you want to purchase is, you can most likely find it on the internet. Plus, it will probably be cheaper than it would be in a store, too. Since vendors don't have to pay for overhead costs like rent and shop upkeep, they pass those savings on to the product prices. So, you save money, and your new purchase will come right to your door.

인터넷 쇼핑의 최고 장점은 편의와 적당한 가격입니다. 당신은 거의 모든 상품을 편안히 집에서 둘러볼 수 있습니다. 특이하고 잘 알려지지 않은 상품을 당신이 사고 싶든 간에, 인터넷에서 거의 다 찾을 수 있습니다. 추가로, 아마도 매장에서의 값보다 더 저렴할 것입니다. 판매자는 임대 및 가게 유지비와 같은 간접 비용을 지불할 필요가 없기에, 제품 가격에 그러한 절약된 금액을 반영합니다. 그래서 당신은 돈을 아끼고 당신의 새 구매품이 바로 당신 집까지 옵니다.

* convenience 편의 affordability 적당한 가격 browse through 둘러보다 limitless 한없는, 방대한 from the comfort of your home 당신의 집에서 편하게 no matter how 아무리 ~일지라도 bizarre 특이한, 기이한 obscure 잘 알려지지 않은 vendor 판매자 overhead costs 간접 비용 upkeep 유지비 savings 절약된 금액 purchase 구매(품), 구매하다

Q What are the differences between shopping at large department stores and small local shops?

대형 백화점과 소규모 지역 매장 간에 차이점은 무엇인가요?

A The main difference between shopping at a large department store and a local shop is customer service. At a large department store, every member of the staff is trained to provide polite and helpful customer service. But, because of corporate policies, there's only so much that an employee, even a manager, can do for a customer. On the other hand, if you have an issue at a small local shop, you'll probably speak directly with the owner. The owner can be much more flexible with your issue, and it's likely that the owner can solve your problem with a personal touch that gives you a positive impression of the business.

지역 매장과 대형 백화점 간 주요 차이는 고객 서비스입니다. 대형 백화점 매장에서, 모든 직원은 친절하고 도움이 되는 고객 서비스를 제공하도록 교육받습니다. 그러나 기업 규칙 때문에, 직원, 심지어 매니저가 고객에게 해줄 수 있는 것은 제한적입니다. 반면에, 작은 동네 매장에서 문제가 있다면, 당신은 아마도 직접 주인에게 이야기할 것입니다. 매장 주인은 문제에 대해 훨씬 더 유연하고, 사업에 좋은 인상을 주는 개인적 손길로 당신의 문제를 해결할 수 있을 것입니다.

* there's only so much 한계가 있다 personal touch 개인적 손길(방식) impression 인상

[Local Business] 지역 사업체

Q Do large shopping malls and commercial centres affect small local businesses? [How?]

대형 쇼핑몰과 상업 센터들이 소규모 지역 업체들에 영향을 주나요? [어떻게요?]

A Large shopping areas like malls and department stores have a negative impact on local businesses because a small shop cannot effectively compete against them. Commercial centres concentrate various goods – from groceries to electronics – in a single area, making it extremely convenient for shoppers to get everything they need at once. Plus, by offering such a huge selection, large commercial centres can offer lower prices. Small businesses, on the other hand, can only offer a limited range of goods, and their revenue flow is too narrow to permit the savings opportunities given by larger stores. So, these factors make it difficult for small shops to exist side-by-side with supermarkets and malls.

쇼핑몰과 백화점 같은 대형 쇼핑 장소는 지역 사업체들에 부정적 영향을 주는데 소규모 매장은 효율적으로 경쟁할 수 없기 때문입니다. 상업 센터는 한 지역에 식료품부터 전자 제품까지 다양한 물품들을 모아서, 쇼핑객들이 필요로 하는 모든 것을 한번에 구할 수 있어서 매우 편리합니다. 추가로, 엄청나게 많은 물품을 제공함으로써, 커다란 쇼핑 센터는 더 낮은 가격을 제시합니다. 소규모 사업체들은, 반면에, 제한된 범위 제품들을 제공하고 대규모 상점이 주는 할인을 허용하기에는 수익 흐름이 너무 한정됩니다. 그래서, 이러한 요인들은 소상공인들이 슈퍼마켓이나 쇼핑몰과 나란히 존재하기 어렵게 만듭니다.

* centre 센터, 중심(미국식 center) grocery 식료품 electronics 전자제품 narrow 좁은, 한정된 side-by-side 나란히

Q What types of local businesses are in your neighbourhood?

당신 동네에 어떤 종류의 지역 사업체가 있나요?

A I don't live in a busy part of the city, so there aren't any particularly special local businesses near my home. However, there are a few locally-owned restaurants. One of them is a barbecue restaurant that I really love. It has a trendy atmosphere and the meat and side dishes are very high quality. A few notable pubs have become popular in the area, too. However, other than those, my neighbourhood just has your standard variety of dry cleaners, hair salons and snack shops.

저는 시의 번화한 곳에 살지 않기에, 집 근처에 아주 특별한 지역 사업체는 없습니다. 하지만 몇몇 지역 기반 식당들이 있죠. 그 중 하나가 제가 정말로 좋아하는 바베큐 식당입니다. 최신 유행 분위기와 고기, 그리고 반찬들이 매우 고품질입니다. 몇몇 주목할 만한 술집도 지역에서 유명해졌죠. 하지만, 그 이외에, 저희 동네에는 그냥 평범한 세탁소, 미용실, 구멍가게가 있습니다.

* particularly 특별히 locally-owned 지역 기반의 atmosphere 분위기 side dish 반찬 notable 주목할 만한 pub 주점 other than ~이외에 neighbourhood 동네(미국식 neighborhood) standard 표준의, 일반적인 variety 품종, 종류

Q How important is customer service to the success of a shop?

고객 서비스는 상점의 성공에 얼마나 중요한가요?

A Customer service is crucial to the success of a store, large or small, especially because of the popularity of apps and social media these days. If someone has a bad experience at a store, they're likely to post about it online, either on their own social media page or even on a major website. So, due to the influence of internet culture, I'd say customer service is more important than ever to businesses.

고객 서비스는, 크던 작던 모든 상점의 성공에 결정적인데, 특별히 요즘 앱과 소셜 미디어의 인기 때문입니다. 만일 누군가 상점에서 안 좋은 경험이 있다면, 사람들은 그것에 대해 온라인으로 자신들의 소셜 미디어 페이지나 심지어 유명 웹사이트에도 게시할 것입니다. 그래서, 인터넷 문화의 영향으로 인해, 고객 서비스는 사업에 그 어느 때보다 더 중요하다고 생각합니다.

* crucial 결정적인 popularity 인기 app 앱, 애플리케이션 social media 소셜미디어(자신의 생각과 의견, 경험, 관점 등을 서로 공유하기 위해 사용하는 개방화된 웹페이지)

MEMO

MEMO

lab.siwonschool.com